# In Sligo Long Ago

*Aspects of the Town & County over two Centuries*

by

**JOHN C. Mc TERNAN**

Illustrated

AVENA PUBLICATIONS
1998

First published in 1998 by
## AVENA PUBLICATIONS, SLIGO
Typeset by Carrick Print 2000 Ltd.
Printed by Colour Books Ltd., Dublin.

Reprinted: 2001

ISBN 0 9520594 6 0

Cover Illustration: *Court Abbey,* Achonry c. 1790

Copyright © 1998, John C. McTernan

# Contents

VISITORS TO INISHMURRAY ..................................................... 9

BRIBERY AND CORRUPTION IN HIGH PLACES ....................... 14

A GARRISON TOWN ............................................................... 18

THE YEAR OF THE FRENCH .. ................................................. 22

LADY MORGAN : THE SLIGO CONNECTION .......................... 44

THE PUNISHMENT FITS THE CRIME ...................................... 50

THE SAVING'S BANK ............................................................. 53

RELIEF OF DISTRESS ............................................................. 60

BLOWING SANDS .................................................................. 69

BREWING AND DISTILLING ................................................... 76

LAND TENURE BEFORE & AFTER THE FAMINE ......... 88

THE 'MASS HOUSE' OR PARISH CHAPEL ..............................100

ILLICIT DISTILLATION .......................................................... 109

THE RISE AND FALL OF JOHN MARTIN ................................130

FROM STAGECOACH TO RAILWAY ......................................142

SLIGO CHURCHES ................................................................ 163

LIBERALS, RADICALS AND REFORMERS ...............................172

THE DRAINAGE OF THE OWENMORE ...................................185

THE PIONEERING FENTONS ..................................................190

SUPPLYING THE TOWN WITH GAS ......................................196

FAIRS AND MARKETS ........................................................... 215

INCREASE IN UNEMPLOYMENT ............................................270

THE GREAT FAMINE ............................................................. 276

THE SLIGO WORKHOUSE AND ITS AUXILIARIES ..................301

MEMOIRS OF A POLICEMAN ................................................319

SHORT LIVED BOBBIN FACTORY ..........................................328

BRIDGES OVER THE.GARVOGUE ..........................................332

THE LAST PUBLIC HANGING ...............................................338

MILLS AND MILLING ........................................................... 346

METRICAL COMPOSITIONS .................................................... 387

THE TURKISH BATHS ............................................................ 396

SAVED FROM THE SCAFFOLD .................................................. 404

DEMONSTRATIONS IN CHURCH ............................................. 414

BUILDING THE TOWN HALL ................................................. 424

THE ENTERPRISING SIMS ...................................................... 447

INSIDE THE MASONIC HALL ................................................. 457

THE COUNTY COURTHOUSE ................................................. 474

A MUSICAL TRADITION ........................................................ 483

A SHATTERED DREAM .......................................................... 491

REMEMBERING' 98 ............................................................... 497

STREET NAMES CHANGED .................................................... 514

TEETHING PROBLEMS OF A CO-OPERATIVE ............................ 517

INNS AND TAVERNS OF OTHER DAYS .................................... 528

ON THE HUNTING FIELDS .................................................... 539

THE CROWN SOLICITOR & THE 'CONSPIRATORS' ............... 553

THE TOWN CLERKSHIP CRUX ............................................. 562

MINING AT ABBEYTOWN ..................................................... 571

CHEESEMAKING AT CARROWGARRY ..................................... 576

THE LIGHT OF OTHER DAYS ................................................ 579

> *An Escape from Justice*
>
> *A Family Affair*
>
> *Tom Soden: an 'exemplary' Provost*
>
> *Rumours Upset a Peaceful Town*
>
> *The Last Occupants of Coolmeen*
>
> *A Process-Server on his Rounds*
>
> *Peter O'Connor's Will*
>
> *Simon takes a Bow*
>
> *Sole Fishing Rights*

DRUMLAHEEN REMEMBERED ................................................. 605

INDEX .................................................................................. 628

# ILLUSTRATIONS

| | |
|---|---|
| Cursing Stones, Inishmurray | 11 |
| The Cashel, Inishmurray | 13 |
| Hazelwood House | 17 |
| Military Barracks | 21 |
| Map of French route, 1798 | 25 |
| Plan of Battlefield of Carricknagat | 32 |
| Lady Morgan | 45 |
| Longford House | 49 |
| Killaspugbrone | 70 |
| Areas affected by 'Blowing Sands' | 74 |
| Ardtarmon Castle | 75 |
| Lough Gill Brewery | 81, 84 |
| The Distillery | 83, 86 |
| Sir Henry Gore-Booth | 94 |
| Ground Plan of Parish Chapel | 102 |
| Ports. of Bps. Browne and Gillooly | 104 |
| A poitín 'Capture' on Inishmurray | 124 |
| Cleveragh House | 130 |
| Railway Station | 155, 162 |
| A Bianconi 'Long Car' | 162 |
| Views of Calry & St. John's Churches | 167 |
| Sir James Crofton | 174 |
| Daniel Jones, Sen. | 179 |
| Templehouse & Thornhill Bridges | 186, 189 |
| Michael Fenton | 191 |
| Castletown House | 195 |
| Gas Works | 214 |
| A Fair Day in Collooney | 215 |
| Off to the Market | 230, 252 |
| Market House, Collooney | 254 |
| Butter Market | 247, 254 |
| Market House, Ballymote | 268 |
| A Soup Kitchen | 288 |
| Famine Memorial, Sligo | 293 |
| Workhouse, Dromore West | 314 |
| Sir Robert Gore-Booth & Lissadell Hs. | 323 |
| 'New Bridge' & Victoria Bridge | 336 |

Matthew Phibbs .................................................................. 343

Ballisodare Mills ...........................................................358, 359

Ballymote & Collooney Mills ........................................... 364

William Middleton & Wilbram Middleton ...................... 367

Dromore West & Bunninadden Mills ............................. 371

Collooney & Scardan Mills ............................................. 380

Skreen and Gurteen Parish Churches ............................ 421

Town Hall site .................................................................. 429

John A.Wynne & Wm. A. Woods ..................................... 432

Town Hall .......................................................................... 442

Alexander & Alexandrina Sim ......................................... 451

Masonic Hall & Harper C. Perry ..................................... 464

Members of Harlech Lodge, 1895 ................................... 467

The County Courthouse ................................................... 479

Memorials at Knockgrania & Killavil ............................... 490

Francis Barber .................................................................. 496

'98 Memorials ....................................... 499, 503, 511

Dominick Bree & Denis Moran ....................................... 505

Owen Phibbs ..................................................................... 521

Imperial Hotel .................................................................. 531

Bridge House & Gray's Inn .............................................. 534

Harp & Shamrock Hotel ................................................... 535

Charles K. O'Hara & Kieran Horan ................................. 545

Co. Sligo Hunt Group, 1964 ........................................... 549

William R. Fenton ............................................................ 558

Ald. J. Lynch & Clr. J. Keaveney ..................................... 566

Map of Abbeytown Mines ................................................ 575

O'Connor Mausoleum ...................................................... 599

Fish Pass, Ballisodare ...................................................... 605

Drumlaheen Townland ..................................................... 608

John & Helena McHugh .................................................... 611

Drumlaheen House ........................................................... 618

Martin & Mary H. McTernan ........................................... 618

St. Colum's Church ........................................................... 627

# Preface

This publication, comprising a collection of essays reflective of times past in both Town and County, is intended as a companion volume to *"OLDE SLIGOE"*. The contents, which include a wide-ranging and varied selection of subject matter, endeavours to highlight various aspects of Sligo's chequered past, while at the same time filling a discernible void in the source material available on a wide range of topics.

With each passing generation the remembrance of events and personalities that have helped to shape the present is fading fast and quietly evaporating in the sands of time. This volume seeks to redress a growing tendency to shut out the past by providing a more lively interest in the everyday happenings of times gone by.

One of the great fascinations of local history is that it relates to one's own place, to the things, the people and events of bygone days. The more we know of Sligo's past the greater is our appreciation of the things that surround us as we go about our daily chores. This series on 'Olde Sligoe' is intended to encourage this and future generations to further study and explore the rich heritage that is theirs.

# Acknowledgments

The comprehensive list of references and notes appended to each essay gives some indication of the extensive research undertaken in the preparation of this work. The value of the local newspapers in the compilation of a publication such as this cannot be over emphasised and is graciously acknowledged.

The Publishers wish to thank everybody, too numerous to list individually, who assisted in any way in the production of this volume. A special word of appreciation to County Librarian, Donal Tinney, and his staff, for the facilities provided.

# Visitors to Inishmurray

In the Summer of 1779 Gabriel Beranger, member of a Huguenot family who had been expelled from France and an artist by profession, visited Sligo as part of any extended tour of Ireland. He was accompanied on the journey by Angelo Bigari, a painter and architect from Bologna. They arrived in Sligo on June 18th, and as they approached the Town from Manorhamilton they were impressed by "the variety of charming prospects every hill afforded". They had introductions to Lewis Irwin of *Tanrego*[1] and William Ormsby of *Willowbrook*, Collector of Sligo [2], whom they subsequently described as "excellent hosts". Irwin took them on a visit to a "famous cataract" near Sligo "where in certain states of mind the water was completely carried off for some distance in spray". They also visited Carrowmore and, before returning to Sligo, ascended Knocknarea "with much fatigue, some part on horseback and part on foot".

On June 24th, accompanied by Colonel Irwin, they crossed to Inishmurray in a "revenue wherry". Beranger has left us the following description of the Island and its people: [3]

"Inishmurray is a rock of the sea, which goes sloping gently and like steps to the edge of the water on the east side towards the main shore, but on the west is high, craggy, and all precipice, with some small heads advancing on the sea, through which the fury of the waves have perforated large holes, not unlike ancient arches, where the sea roars horridly in tempestuous weather. About 130 acres are covered with a thin soil of about 5 or 6 inches deep, which produces grass to feed about 4 or 5 cows, as many horses, and 30 sheep; there is also some arable land that produces 20 barrels of corn, besides some garden stuff; the houses are five in number, and as many barns; and the inhabitants 45 or 46, including children. They are all fishermen, and sell their cargoes on the mainland. They have inhabited this Island from father to son for upwards of 600 years, and when crowded sent the supernumerary to seek their fortune on shore; they only speak Irish, except one man and an old woman; they are very hospitable to strangers, will treat and lodge them without reward; they love Col. Irwin (by who's means they have been exempted from some county

## VISITORS TO INISHMURRAY

charges), and who every year pays them a visit, by which they never lose. There is an abbey, as it is called, very rude, a church, and some other old buildings said to have been erected by Sts. Molaise and Columkill; the figure or statue in wood of the first they have there in a cell, and have daubed him all over with red paint to make him look handsome.

The inhabitants subsist on what provisions they have gathered, namely, potatoes, dry fish, milk, and now and then on mutton. They are all Roman Catholics, seem very innocent, good-natured, and devout, but at the same time very superstitious and credulous. They told us, as a most undoubted fact, that during the most horrid tempests of winter, when a case happens where a priest is required, such as to give the extreme unction to a dying person, &c., they go the seaside, launch one of their little vessels, and as soon as it touches the water a perfect calm succeeds, which continues until they have brought the priest to the Island, that after he has performed the rites of the church and carried back, the boat is returned to the Island and hauled on shore, when the tempest will again begin, and continue for weeks together. On asking them how often this miracle happened, and to which of them the care of the priest had been committed, they were veracious enough to confess, it never happened in their days, though the fact was true. There are thirteen places of devotion on the Island, called *Stations*, which the Roman Catholics visit, and where prayers are said". He then went on to describe the 'cursing altar' as follows:-

"*A kind of altar of stone about two feet high, covered with globular stones, somewhat flattened, of different sizes, very like the Dutch cheeses; the tradition is, that if any one is wronged by another, he goes to this altar, curses the one that wronged him, wishing such evil may befall him, and turns one of the stones; and if he was really wronged, the specified evil fell on his enemy; but if not, on himself, which makes them so precautionate that the altar is become useless*".
The reception accorded to the visitors is graphically described: -

"The whole lot of inhabitants came to meet Mr. Irwin, who, having bid us do as we should see him do, &c., embracing cordially all the females, we followed his example, and were conducted to one of the houses, where we dressed our fish which we had caught, viz., mullet and whitings, to which the inhabitants added some lobsters; a table was prepared in a barn, where we went to supper, &c. We had the old Irish candles, consisting of rushes dipped in tallow, which gave but a poor light.

The following morning, June 25th, got up at five; walked over the Island, following the shore and examining its curiosities and antiquities, accompanied by the only person of the inhabitants that could speak English. Drew the Abbey, the Church, etc. and plan. Came to breakfast on lobster and broiled whitings, caught before our eyes; drank wine and water. Mr. Irwin ordered our rabbits, a turkey, some fowl, and ducks, to be cut up with a leg of mutton, to which he added some greens, turnips, and carrots, and a piece of hare, which being put in a large tosspan he had also brought with him, and having seasoned it properly, put it down on a slow fire, promising us the best olio we had ever tasted. Went again to walk; was shown a whale swimming in the ocean, spouting up the water to a great height.

Saw distinctly the mountain of Croagh Patrick, in the county of Mayo, distance sixty miles. Went into every house, but could not converse with the females, as they only speak Irish; remembered the Irish phrase I formerly learned of *Togue pogue dom, a Cailin Óge*, which I repeated to every girl who immediately came to kiss me; how unfortunate it was I could ask no more! Finished our drawings; came home; adjourned all to the barn, where the olio was served up in the tosspan to have it hot; never did I taste of a better dish, nor ever did I eat so much, not withstanding, when our dessert of fine lobsters appeared, we fell to again, so that we were obliged to drink a glass extra to wash it down

After dinner, Mr. Irwin sent notice that we should embark; accordingly, all the inhabitants - men, women, and children, not one excepted - gathered round the door of our barn, and everything being ready, we walked out, followed by the people, and went to a small plain near the creek where our vessel was moored; there Mr. Irwin made them sit down in a semi-circle on the grass, and having opened a

## VISITORS TO INISHMURRAY

packet, distributed a yard of fine ribbon to every female, whom we embraced at the time; after that each male and female got a four feet long of roll tobacco, and a pair of beads each. After which he ordered one of the casks of whiskey to be broached, and be distributed round by glasses. When done, we took our leaves, embracing again the females, and walked to the vessel upon a pier of natural rock, followed by all the people. When we bended our sails, they saluted us by three cheers, which we returned; they continued looking as long as they could.

I found the scene so affecting, that it dwelt long on my mind. Our guide on the Island, the only one who could speak English told us very gravely that they had neither priest, physician, not lawyer amongst them; and that they were religious, healthy, and lived in peace without quarrel!"

\*       \*       \*       \*       \*       \*

After resting a few days, during which they inked their drawings, Messrs Beranger and Bigari set out for Boyle. On the way they stopped at Ballisodare and sketched the remains of the church and abbey. On the bridge there they were shown a stone on which a beggar used to sit constantly, who, on receiving alms, used to bestow on the giver a blessing, which became a famous toast, known as the *'Beggar's benison'*. Passing through Collooney, which was described as "an indifferent-looking town", they headed for Lough Arrow and "drew and planned" the Abbey of Ballindoon and the cairn at Heapstown. Later that day they dined with John M. Donough - "a descendant of the princes of the country". On their way to Boyle, they stopped to inspect the caves of Keash. The final entry in Beranger's diary relating to their tour of Sligo is a description of the famous caves: -

"Stopped facing Kishcorren mountain; left our chaise and horses with the servants, and walked through some fields halfway up the hill to examine the natural cave, the entrance of which is by two openings, which appeared like two huge gothic arches. Got in as far as the light would permit us; but the slippery ground and the strong smell like that of cats, and the darkness, soon brought us to the mouth again. This cavern is said to communicate with that in the county of Roscommon, twenty-four miles distances, called 'Hellmouth door of Ireland', at Rathcroghan, of which having an unruly calf could never get him home unless driving him by holding him by the tail; that one day he tried to escape and dragged the woman, against her will into the 'Hellmouth door'; that, unable to stop him, she ran after him without quitting her hold, and continued running until the next morning. She came out at Kishcorren, to her own amazement and that of the neighbouring people. We believed it rather than try it".

### *Notes and References:*

(1) Lewis Irwin (1728-1785) was the son of John Irwin of *Tanrego*, by his wife Elizabeth Harrison. His son, Colonel John Irwin was High Sheriff of Co. Sligo in 1822.

(2) William Ormsby (1718-1781), collector of Sligo Port, was the eldest son of Francis Ormsby of Willowbrook and married Hannah Wynne of Hazelwood. M.P. for Borough of Sligo 1757-1776 and High Sheriff 1757 and 1781. Died at Bruges in December, 1781.

(3) Wilde, William. *"Memoir of Gabriel Beranger . . ."* *Jn. R.S.A.I.* II pp 121-152, 1870 - '71.

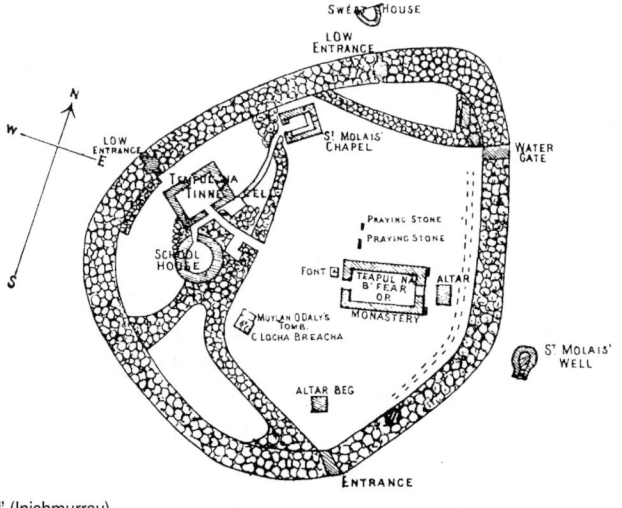

The 'Cashel' (Inishmurray)

# Bribery and Corruption in High Places

Allegations of bribery and corruption were commonplace in 18th century parliamentary elections in Sligo and elsewhere, and petitions were regularly lodged by defeated candidates seeking redress.

Between 1727 and 1776, with one or two exceptions, the Wynnes of *Hazelwood House* and their close neighbours, the Ormsbys of *Willowbrook House*, represented the Borough of Sligo in Parliament. Following the death of Francis Ormsby, who had been an M.P. from 1727 to 1751, his eldest son, William, was returned at the elections of 1757, 1761 and 1768. However, on the approach of the 1776 contest the Right Hon. Owen Wynne, who was patron of the Borough, informed Ormsby, who was his brother-in-law, that he could no longer contest the seat as it was required for another candidate of his choosing. This incensed Ormsby to such an extent that he vowed to oppose Wynne in the subsequent County election. Both gentlemen were as good as their word, and the outcome was one of the most bitter, protracted and expensive election contests on record.

In the County election of May, 1777, the aforementioned Owen Wynne and Joshua Cooper of *Markree Castle*, both outgoing, were opposed by William Ormsby and Sir Booth Gore. Ormsby came in third with 351 votes, 51 behind his rival, Wynne. Unhappy with the outcome and determined, at all cost, to unseat his brother-in-law, he lodged a petition in which he complained that Wynne and Cooper had publicly united their interest; that several of Wynne's voters were influenced by bribery and corruption; that the Sheriff, Henry Griffith, had acted all through with partiality, and that the petitioner would have had a majority, if he had rejected wrong votes and admitted right ones. He also alleged that the Sheriff had actively solicited votes against him as well as intimidating other Freeholders from voting for him.

A select Committee was appointed to investigate the complaints, and in May, 1778, they issued their findings, namely, *that Owen Wynne has not been duly elected to represent County Sligo in Parliament.* A warrant for a new election was issued later that month. The contestants were

## BRIBERY AND CORRUPTION IN HIGH PLACES

William Ormsby and Owen Wynne, the Younger. After five days of voting, and much disturbance locally, the outcome once again favoured the Hazelwood family, and once again the defiant and proud scion of the Ormsbys challenged the validity of the result. Two petitions were presented, one in July, 1778, and a second in October, 1779, to the Irish House of Commons and both in the name of William Ormsby, Esq. The text of the latter, the only one to have survived the ravages of time, reads as follows:-

*"In the last Election of a Member to serve in Parliament for County Sligo, Owen Wynne, the Younger, of Hazelwood and the Petitioner, were candidates, and Mr. Wynne was on that occasion returned by the Sheriff as duly elected; that the said Owen Wynne, after the issuing of the writ and previous to and during the poll, by himself and his friends and agents and others employed by him and by other ways and means, on behalf and on the charge of the said Owen Wynne, did give, present and allow money, meat, drink, reward, entertainment, provisions and gifts, and made promises, agreements and engagements to give and allow the same to or for the use, benefit, profit or preferment of several persons having votes in the said Election in order to procure himself to be elected for the said County in open defiance of the law; and that the said Owen Wynne did also, by himself and other persons employed by him, by money or other rewards, by way of gift, loan and other devices, and by promises, agreements and securities for such gifts and rewards for the use and benefit of certain persons or some of their family or kindred, and also by menaces and other modes of undue influence, to corrupt and procure several persons, who have a right to vote in such Election, to give their votes and several others to forbear to give their votes in that Election; and also that the said Owen Wynne was guilty of Bribery and Corruption and attempting to bribe and corrupt those who had a right to vote in that Election in order to procure himself to be returned as the person duly elected; that James Gallagher, Esq., the Sheriff and the deputy by himself appointed to take the poll, acted partially and unfairly in the execution of their respective offices as Returning Officers during the said poll, in rejecting good votes which were tendered for the Petitioner and in admitting bad ones for the said Owen Wynne; and that by the said undue means, the said Owen Wynne obtained a majority of votes on the Poll and was returned accordingly to serve in Parliament for the said County in prejudice to the Petitioner, who was duly elected and ought to have been returned."*

In a separate Petition, presented in the name of Henry Thornton

## BRIBERY AND CORRUPTION IN HIGH PLACES

and other Freeholders, the signatories alleged that several of them had tendered their votes in Ormsby's favour but these were rejected by the Sheriff. They, too, sought to have the result declared null and void and that Ormsby be permitted to sit in Parliament instead of Wynne.

All three petitions gave rise to proceedings before two separate Select Committees that lasted over eighteen months and entailed enormous expense on the respective families, the Ormsbys and the Wynnes. After many delays and postponed hearings the Committees eventually concluded their lengthy deliberations on April 25th, 1780, with a unanimous verdict, namely: *"That Owen Wynne, the Younger, was duly elected and returned as one of the Knights of the Shire to serve in this Parliament for the County of Sligo."*

From a study of all the evidence taken before the Select Committees, it is abundantly clear that the bribery and corruption complained of actually took place and was practised, very probably, by both sides to a greater or lesser degree. As to the partiality of the Sheriff, it was clearly established that the stealing of the Poll Book, of which he was the legal custodian, and throwing pages from it, containing a list of the Forty Shilling Freeholders of the County, across the battlement of Sligo bridge, could scarcely have happened without, at least, his connivance. In fairness, it must be stated that a dozen or so of the high profile backers of Owen Wynne, jun. did not approve of such action and between them guaranteed a reward of one hundred and fifty guineas for information leading to the apprehension of the perpetrator or perpetrators. They also had the following notice published in the *"Sligo Journal"* :-

### A HUNDRED AND FIFTY-FIVE GUINEAS REWARD

*"We, the under-named, taking into our most serious consideration the atrocious attack that has been lately made on the Privileges of many of the electors of the County of Sligo by some person or persons having secured or destroyed the Registry Book containing a list of the forty-shilling Freeholders of said County, and being desirous of making manifest our just abhorrence of such an infamous transaction and of doing everything in our power that may tend towards discovering the Author or Authors of such secretion or destruction, do hereby promise and engage, respectively, to pay such sum as is annexed to each of our names, to any person who is able to throw such light on the above*

## BRIBERY AND CORRUPTION IN HIGH PLACES

*abominable business, as may bring to open and public conviction the perpetrator or perpetrators of the same."*

Signed: The Hon. Owen Wynne, Joshua Cooper, Henry Hughes, Arthur Cooper, Folliott Wynne, John Martin, Robert Lyons, Phil. Burne, Robert Hillas, Hyacinth O'Rourke, Henry Griffith, Wm. Gibson and Robert Bolton.

Dated: Sligo, July 2nd, 1778

Such were the doings of the gentry and public officials in the Sligo of two centuries ago. As for the principal participants, the Wynnes continued to represent the County in Parliament until 1790, and the Borough continuously until 1802, and, thereafter, at intervals until 1860; whereas William Ormsby not only withdrew completely from public life but vacated the family seat and lived out his last years on the Continent where he died in December, 1781, in the 64th year of his age.

### Bibliography:

O'Rorke, T. *"History of Sligo"*. Vol. I. pp. 366-7.
*"Journals of the Irish House of Commons,"* 1777 - '80.

Hazelwood House, former seat of the Wynne Family

# A Garrison Town

In the mid 18th century there were four military barracks in Sligo, namely -

The *Strand Barrack* in Barrack Street;
The *Middle Barrack* in Holborn Street;
The *Horse Barrack* in Bridge Street;
The *Old Stone Fort* or *Foot Barrack* in Quay Street.

In 1758 Major James Bailie of Lord Tyrawley's Regiment of Foot, carried out a survey of the accommodation available and the general condition of the said buildings, which he referred to as the only barracks outside of Dublin in which an entire Regiment of Cavalry was quartered. His report, which was the most thorough of a series of such reports on local military establishments prepared at the behest of the Irish House of Commons, provides an insight into the nature and extent of barrack accommodation in the Sligo of two and a half centuries ago. The *Strand Barrack* accommodated seven officers and ninety-six non-commissioned personnel. Four officers' rooms and six for non-commissioned officers and men were in bad condition and wanted flooring. The walls and roof were in good condition, but the roof wanted rendering and a new cornice round the entire building. Yard wall and gate were out of repair. The stables, providing accommodation for sixty horses, were in good order.

The *Middle Barrack*, also known as the *Little Old Barrack*, or *Single Barrack*, built by Mitchelburne Knox, stood on a quarter of an acre of ground in Holborn Street and was let at £40 per annum. The whole of these buildings, except the walls, are not fit to stand, being originally too lightly built on a very improper plan. Eight of the apartments were in "an indifferent order" and Privates were quartered eight to a room and two to a bed. Most bedding and curtains were in a poor condition, while chairs and several other essential items were missing. When Lord Tyrawley's Regiment marched into the Sligo Barrack, several of the officers were obliged to take lodgings in the Town until the Foot marched out when bedding was brought for the accommodation of officers and men. The stables, which had accommodation for thirty-

A GARRISON TOWN

four horses, were also in a poor state of repair.

The *Squadron* or *Bridge Barrack*, also built by Knox c. 1750, and let at £120 per annum, could accommodate three troops. The building, which contained twenty-eight rooms, fifteen for officers and thirteen for men, was in very bad condition, apart from the officer apartments lately built but which lacked closets or other conveniences. Ceilings were bad and roofs "much out of order and wanting repairs". Floors in the privates' apartments needed repairs - "being originally laid out with slit floors". The barrack had twelve stables for one hundred and eight horses.

The *Stone Fort* or *Foot Barrack*, was described as an old one, "lying on the top of a hill leading to the Custom House near the River". It had been badly damaged in a violent storm in March, 1757. Floors and ceilings were in a bad condition in both officers and men's rooms. It was fortified by a high stone wall with four bastions, and had accommodation for two companies of foot.

Major Bailie concluded his Report by condemning both the *Middle* and *Squadron Barracks*, and recommended extensive additions and repairs to the other two, namely, the *Strand* and *Foot*, totalling £1,742.00.

---

### SLIGO BARRACKS, 1813

(1) **Permanent:**
One Cavalry Barrack, with accommodation for 8 officers and 70 rank and file.

(2) **Temporary** (leased premises):

(a) Infantry: Accommodation for 6 officers and 228 rank and file. Leased from Thos. Leydon @ £341. p.a.

(b) Infantry: Accommodation for 128 rank and file. Leased from W. O'Beirne @ £100 p.a.

(c) Infantry : Accommodation for 120 rank and file. Leased from Roger Parke @ £120 p.a.

(d) Infantry: Accommodation for 4 officers. Leased from Pat Kelly @ £40 p.a.

*(Parliamentary Papers. 1812-'13. (269) VI.)*

---

19

## A GARRISON TOWN

A century later, the *Strand Barrack*, in Barrack Street, was the only military establishment in Sligo. In the 1810's it could accommodate three Troops of Horse. Two decades later, in 1824, a new building replaced the old *Strand Barrack*. It was built of stone and comprised three large dormitories capable of accommodating seventy-two officers and men. There was also what was described as a 'cook-house' and, although there were no washing facilities, there were two water pumps close to the building. By the mid 1840's it had been enlarged to house seven officers and ninety non-commissioned officers and privates. There was also hospital accommodation for fifteen patients. In 1846 the 88th Regiment, consisting of three officers and seventy privates, were billeted there and Lieut. James O'Brien of the 6th Royal Vet. Batallion was Barrack Master. At that stage, both the *Middle Barrack* in Holborn Street and the *Squadron Barrack* in Bridge Street had disappeared without trace. In the case of the latter, the Lough Gill Brewery stood on the site. The *Foot Barrack* in Quay Street ceased to function as such shortly after Bailie's survey and was leased to Owen Wynne of Hazelwood. The Town Hall now stands on the site.*

At intervals throughout the 19th century the new Barracks housed in turn the Sligo Militia, the Sligo Rifles and the Sligo Artillery.** On the disbandment of the latter regiment in 1909, the building became vacant. Its chequered career finally came to a close in July, 1922, when it was burned to the ground by 'The Irregulars' during the Civil War. A decade later, in 1932, the Corporation built a new housing scheme, *Benbulben Terrace*, on the site.

---

\* **SEE:** McTernan *"OLDE SLIGOE"* pp.24 - 27

\*\*When the Sligo Militia arrived in Town from Longford in May, 1856, they were quartered as follows: 1st Div. in *The Charter House*, The Mall; 2nd Div. in the Barrack St. premises, and 3rd Div. in *The Linenhall*, Corkran's Mall.

# A GARRISON TOWN

A detachment of the Sligo Rifles at the Military Barracks, c. 1890.

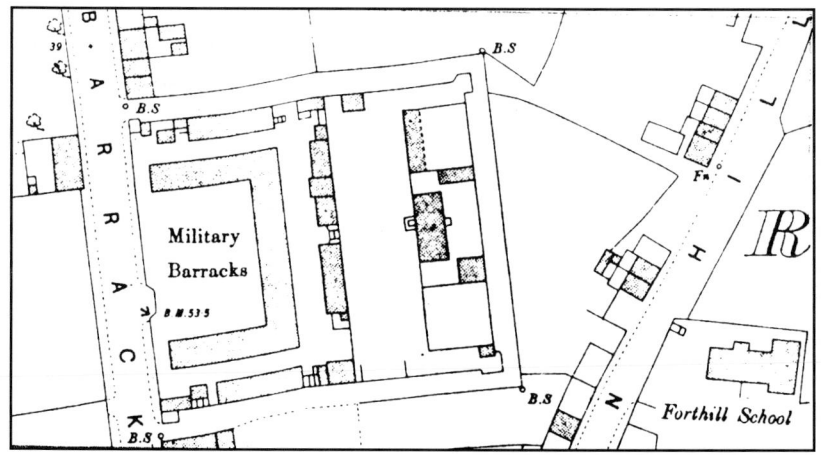

Ground Plan of former 'Strand Barrack'.

# The Year of the French

Throughout the closing decade of the 18th century County Sligo was in a very disturbed state with agrarian outrages of every description being committed on a regular basis. The execution of the laws was impeded by a system of terror - those who had sustained injury were afraid to prosecute while Magistrates were deterred from enforcing justice. The instigators of the general unrest were a secret society, popularly known as *Defenders*, whose ideology consisted of a complex mixture of agrarian agitation and revolutionary republicanism. Opposition to taxation (the county cess) and to tithes were among the objectives of this militant Catholic sect which was active north of a line from Sligo to Louth. Their methods were crude in the extreme, threatening notices, attacks on houses, administering oaths and raiding for arms. The general unrest could also be attributed to the revolutionary doctrines being propagated by the United Irishmen which had infected much of the country, no matter how remote.

In 1797 the County was proclaimed as being "in a state of disturbance", while a Captain of the yeomanry reported that the United Irishmen were active in Tireragh *"and swearing - in is undoubtedly going forward and our utmost vigilance cannot prevent or detect it."* Meanwhile, in 1796, in an effort to counter-force the threat posed by the United Irishmen at national level, it was decided to establish a network of yeomanry corps in each county. These defence associations were composed of the 'loyal and well-affected' and were almost entirely comprised of Protestants. In the closing months of 1796 the following district corps were raised : *Ballymote Infantry; Drumcliff and Carbury Cavalry; Corran-Liney-Coolavin Cavalry; Sligo Loyal Infantry; Tireragh Infantry* and the *Tirerrill Cavalry*. These corps were destined to play a not insignificant role in the suppression of the '98 Rebellion locally, as well as in other parts of the country.

The general unrest experienced throughout the County was further kindled by the arrival, in late 1797, of a large number of refugee Catholic families from Ulster, who were fleeing from religious persecution. In the circumstances, and by virtue of their expertise in the linen manufacture, they were accorded asylum. They settled, some around Coolaney, but mostly along the Tireragh coastline and into Mayo. Initially, they exhibited an industrious and peaceful demeanour but it was soon observed that they were politically active and quietly sowing the seeds of revolution. This created an unsettling influence generally, as also did rumours of an impending French invasion.

---

# ANTICIPATING A REBELLION

At a meeting of the Magistrates and Captains of Yeomanry Corps of County Sligo on the May 4th, 1797, Owen Wynne presiding, it was stated that there was good reason to believe that the 'dissatisfaction' which has been manifesting itself in the Northern parts of the Kingdom, had been lately disseminated in this and neighbouring Counties. It was decided to establish a Secret Committee, consisting of the Right Hon. Joshua Cooper, M.P., Owen Wynne, Arthur Irwin, John Martin, Thomas Soden, William Coristine, Michelburne Knox and Rev. Charles West of Ahamlish, to make enquiries and collect information. It was also resolved:-

*"That having now in this Town a considerable quantity of Ammunition and Arms detached in the hands of individuals, which, in case of a Riot or disorder, it would be practicable to seize by surprise, we highly approve of having Guards of the Yeomanry Corps mounted nightly to co-operate with such Military forces as we have at present or may hereafter have here".*

\*    \*    \*    \*    \*    \*

Reverend Charles Grove, Rector of Kilmacshalgan and a Magistrate of the County, in a letter from Sligo to Daniel W. Webber of Skreen in February, 1798, wrote:-

*"I, this day had very unpleasant news from Tiereragh. Nocturnal meetings are held in the Parish of Easkey and upwards of 300 in arms were seen yesterday there .....This day the Barony Constables came in to give up their arms lest they should be deprived of them by the rebels. Two smiths were lodged in Gaol here this day for making pikes....."*

(Extracts from *"Rebellion Papers"*, National Archives)

## THE YEAR OF THE FRENCH

Such was the situation in August, 1798, when three French frigates, carrying 1,020 troops, made their appearance off the Tireragh coast. Two days later, on August 22nd, they cast anchor in Killala Bay. That evening the troops disembarked at Kilcummin and took possession of Killala after some resistance by the local garrison. On the following day, Humbert, the leader of the expedition, marched at the head of a detachment of his men to Ballina and secured that town without a blow. On Sunday, the 26th, the French started for Castlebar, which they

General Humbert

sighted on the following morning, after a march of 24 hours by a road deemed impracticable for an army, where Humbert found British troops, 6,000 strong, drawn up in order of battle, and in a most advantageous position to receive him. His command was about 1,400 all told, 700 French and an equal number of raw Irish recruits, all greatly fatigued by the distressing march; but, without a moment's hesitation, he ordered them forward, and they not only advanced but inflicted a dishonouring defeat on the enemy. The English in confusion fled wildly through the town, pursued by such of the victors as could procure horses to carry them. They did not desist from their flight till they reached Tuam, a distance of forty miles from the scene of the encounter - thus earning for the event the name by which it is known in history: '*The Races of Castlebar*'.

The French invasion, and the success at Castlebar in particular, was the signal for a general uprising in the West.[1] A majority of Catholics looked forward to the day when they would rid themselves of British domination and now, in August, 1798, an opportunity had arrived. Bands of volunteers from Counties Mayo and Sligo hurried to join the

# THE YEAR OF THE FRENCH

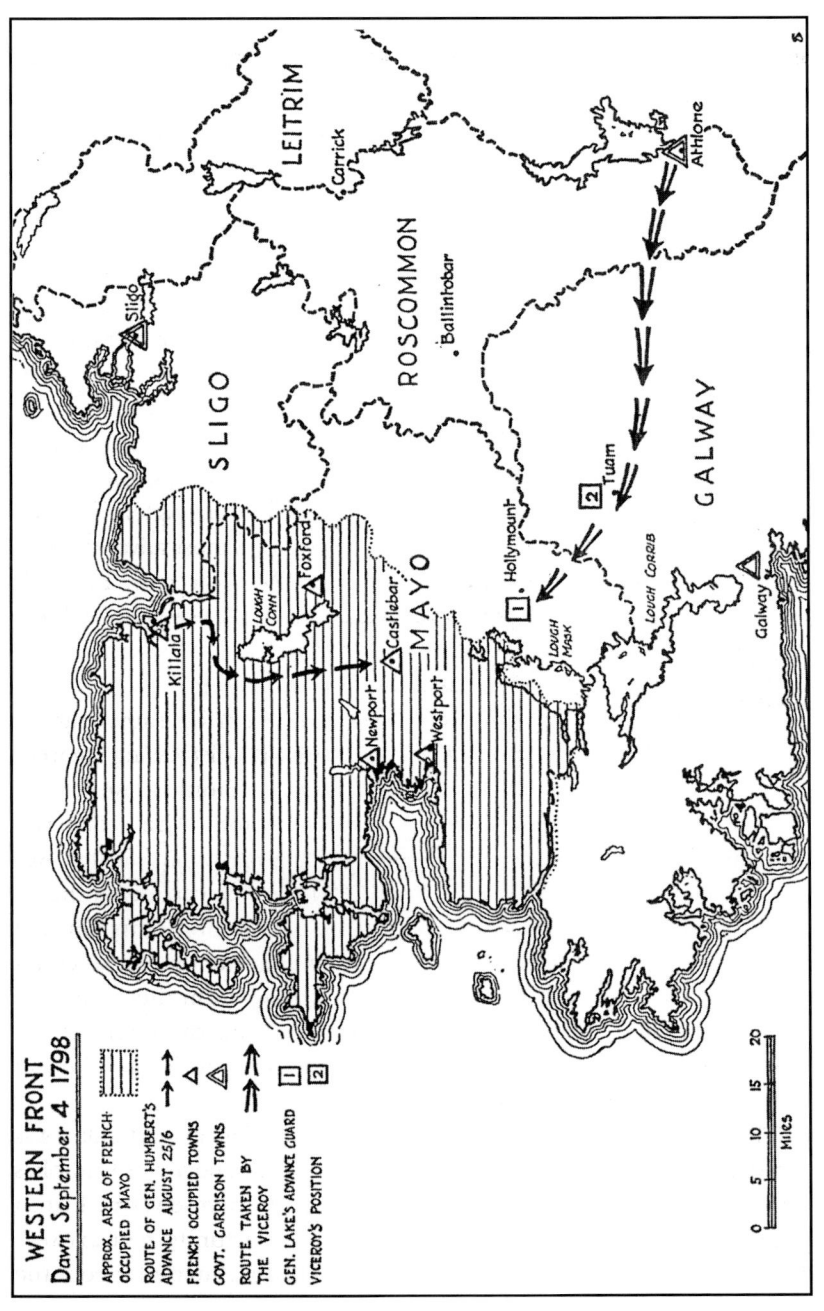

## THE YEAR OF THE FRENCH

French, amongst whom was James O'Dowd of Bonniconlon, the then head of the ancient clan, the O'Dowds of Hy-Fiachra. He resigned his commission as Captain in the Tirawley Cavalry and rode into Ballina at the head of a band of followers whose only arms were homemade pikes, and offered his services to General Humbert. He was immediately given the rank of Colonel and placed in charge of the garrison at Killala. News of the landing of the French at Killala was received with great trepidation by the Protestant population whose loyalty was beyond question. According to one commentator "the spirit of Popish dissatisfaction and fanaticism appeared nowhere so strong as in the Counties of Mayo and Sligo, and in Tireragh in particular," where the Catholic clergy, notably Father Daniel O'Donnell of Kilmacshalgan, Father Phelim MacDonnell of Easkey, Father Morgan of Dromore West and Father Owen Cowley, a native of Castleconnor but ministering in Crossmolina, amongst others, became actively involved in the Rebellion. [2] The Protestant inhabitants of Tireragh, dreading not only the approach of the French but also attack from the insurgents, and, there being no military of any kind from Ballina to Sligo, they fled to the latter for protection.

Many respectable Protestant farmers were seen on foot, driving their cattle and sheep before them, and conveying on cars their wives and children, their beds and wearing apparel. Others put to sea in small boats or fled to the Ox Mountains awaiting developments. The Protestant clergy, also, felt obliged to move on. The reverend James Neligan, Vicar of Easkey, who resided in Ballina, narrowly escaped from that place with other loyalists and, after much difficulty, arrived at *Seaview House*, the seat of Robert Hillas, J.P. When news of their arrival became known, the locals threatened to attack the house unless the visitors moved on. In the circumstances, Neligan and his party had little option but to continue on to Sligo. At the same time Nicholas Ormsby, Captain of the Tirerrill yeoman cavalry, who was quartered with his corps at Easkey, having been informed that a group had assembled in the neighbourhood and were rounding-up cattle for the use of the French, hastened to the spot, rescued the livestock and dispersed the persons involved.

As events unfolded the sudden panic exhibited by those professing loyalist sympathies was well founded. Gentleman seats, such as *Scurmore*

## THE YEAR OF THE FRENCH

(Nesbitt); *Fortland* (Browne); *Castletown* (Fenton); *Castletown Manor* (Kirkwood); *Charlesfort* (Grove) *Ardkill* (Hillas) and *Longford* (Crofton), a number of which had already been abandoned by their owners, were systematically attacked and, in some cases, also plundered by the rebels. At the later residence, Malby Crofton, described "as an aged and very resolute man", refused to abandon his home on the approach of the Insurgents. Although bedridden, he insisted on being placed on a couch at the hall door and informed his would-be assailants that if they attempted to enter it would be over his dead body.Somewhat surprised at Crofton's stubborn and defiant approach they hesitated, and on being further informed that his son James, a Captain in the Sligo Light Infantry, was not at home, the Insurgents departed, leaving the old man unmolested. Protestant churches at Kilmactigue, Easkey and Enniscrone were also attacked. At the latter , known locally as *Valentine's Church,* they tore up the flooring, broke up the pews and desecrated the tomb of the founder, the Reverend Thomas Valentine who was Vicar there from 1711 till his death in 1765. Commenting on events during the first week of the Rebellion, Reverend James Little, Vicar of Lacken, wrote as follows:

*"I never heard that any person of respectable situation or connections had encouraged the rebels to rob anything except cattle for the support of the French and recruits or to destroy the house of any loyalist. Such leaders are rather disposed to fight than to rob, to restrain than to encourage the depredations of the multitude...no loyalist house (as far as I have heard) whose inhabitants were in it, or the servants who guarded it faithful to their trust, was by violence broken into and pillaged, except under the encouragement of the French; in the instances of them breaking into churches, the hostility was not to the Protestants but to the church, the timber of the seats etc. being very useful to them. "*

The adventures of Mrs Jones, wife of Robert of Ardnaree, illustrates the disturbed state if that part of the County in August, 1798. Following upon the French landing, Mrs Jones, whose servants had left to join the Insurgents, set out with her four children and a few relatives for the long trek to Sligo. With great difficulty she made her way to *Fortland* the residence of her uncle, Robert Browne. On reaching it she found it had been attacked and was unoccupied. She then headed for *Tanrego*, the seat of her brother, Colonel John Irwin, who was then on service in Wexford with the Sligo Militia. On reaching Dromard, she

THE YEAR OF THE FRENCH

was informed that the Irwin homestead had also been attacked, that Ballisodare was in the hands of the rebels and that the bridge of Ballydrehid was no longer passable. In the circumstances, her only means of reaching Sligo was by sea. At Streamstown the little group secured the use of a boat and, after a somewhat adventurous crossing in choppy seas, they landed safely on the opposite shore in Coolera. From there they proceeded on foot to Ballydrehid where they came into contact with Captain James Wood of the Tireragh Infantry. He had them escorted on the final lap of their long journey to Sligo by way of the 'Windy Gap'.

After remaining at Castlebar for longer than he ought, Humbert set out early on the morning of September 4th at the head of his army, having sent orders to the garrisons at Ballina and Killala to join him on the march. Rain

fell in torrents as the army, complete with cannon and baggage, began its long trek towards Sligo. The first halt was at Barleyfield where the French requisitioned some provisions to be sent to Swinford, which place they entered early on the evening of the 4th. From there they proceeded to Bellaghy and, after another short halt, continued on their way to Tubbercurry.

Meanwhile, acting on the orders of Colonel Charles Vereker, who commanded the garrison at Sligo, the mounted militia of the Corran-Leyney-Coolavin yeomanry corps, under the command of Charles O'Hara, M.P. for the County, were directed to harass and impede, whenever possible, Humbert's march. On entering Tubbercurry the yeomanry met a young man named Maguire who happened to be wearing a green neckcloth. Suspecting that he was a rebel on an errand, he was shot down in cold blood by Lieutenant Knott. For three days his corpse lay on the street before it was eventually removed under the cover of darkness and buried in Ballyara close to the old monastic ruin. The yeomanry then proceeded to attack the vanguard of Humbert's army but were repelled and forced to retreat with the loss of one dead, the aforementioned Lieutenant Knott, and one wounded.

When the French army entered Tubbercurry they were greeted by the cheers and joyous acclamations not only of the townspeople but

## THE YEAR OF THE FRENCH

also by a large contingent of French and Irish, under Colonel James O'Dowd, who had marched from Ballina by way of Coolcarney and Bonniconlon and across the Ox Mountains through 'The Gap'. Along the route they left several memorials of their march, including *Frenchford*, and the *Frenchman's Grave* at Drumsheen. The latter is the final resting place of a French soldier who collapsed on the march. Beside Corr Sgeach, near the entrance to 'The Gap', there is a little lake called Loch-na-nGunnai. It was so named when another party of Insurgents, marching to join Humbert, flung their guns into its waters on hearing of the disaster at Ballinamuck.

As the Franco-Irish battalions resumed their journey towards Collooney on the morning of September 5th in atrocious weather, they presented an unusual sight. Their advance guard was headed by two figures on horseback. One was an elderly man, dressed in English military uniform and wearing a dejected air. He was astride a very old horse, unkempt and with protruding bones. A straw rope served for a bridle, and the saddle was of the same material. The rider was the yeoman officer, Harloe Knott of *Battlefield House,* whose son had been guilty of killing young Maguire in Tubbercurry. Both French and Irish were filled with such indignation on hearing of the deed that it was decided, as a punishment, to parade Knott in this burlesque fashion. Riding beside him on a splendidly groomed horse of fine proportions was a handsome French woman, carrying a sword. The two figures, as they moved at the head of the long column, attracted much attention.

At eleven o'clock in the forenoon of the 5th September the advance guard of Humbert's forces crossed the bridge of Collooney, and, considering themselves safe, halted for breakfast, while the main body stretched back for more than a mile in a straggling line along the route from Tubbercurry.[3] They had scarcely begun their meal when a cannon ball , from the direction of Carricknagat, fell in their midst and alerted them to the fact that the enemy was close at hand. Almost simultaneously a local farmer, Michael Mór Gildea of Cooney, arrived breathlessly on the scene with the news that he had seen from the Ox Mountains a body of English troops advancing from the Sligo direction

## THE YEAR OF THE FRENCH

towards Collooney. [4]

After its defeat at Tubbercurry, O'Hara's regiment of yeoman cavalry fled back to Sligo with news of Humbert's advance. Meanwhile, arrangements were already under way to strengthen the local garrison in case of attack. The Limerick City Regiment which had been stationed at Enniskillen, were ordered to Sligo. With their arrival the military establishment there totalled 856 men who had at their disposal the following artillery: two medium six-pounders; two field guns; two curricle six pounders, together with a detachment of the Royal Artillery. Initially, Colonel Vereker of the Limerick Regt. was ordered not to move out of Sligo unless he feared he could not maintain it, in which case he was to retire to Ballyshannon. Subsequently, he was directed not to await the enemy's impending attack on what was described as "an open and defendless Town", but to retreat to Ballyshannon or Enniskillen. However, when news reached him that the enemy forces were heading northwards towards Sligo, and under the impression that the main body of the French army had remained at Castlebar, the Colonel threw caution to the wind and decided to meet them on the way instead of awaiting their attack. Vereker marched from Sligo on the morning of September 5th with two field guns and detachments of the following corps:- City of Limerick Militia, 220; Essex Fencibles, 20; Loyal Sligo Infantry, 20; Ballymote Infantry, 10; Drumcliff Infantry, 16- total, 286: together with a troop of the 24th Light Dragoons and detachments from the Tirerrill, Liney and Drumcliff troops of Yeomen Cavalry. [5]

This was the force which Gildea had seen approaching. Vereker, marching through Ballisodare, arrived unobserved at Carrignagat, not far from Collooney, where a halt was made. He at once so disposed his men that their left wing was protected by the river and, to safeguard their right, he sent Captain Ormsby with a hundred of their number to occupy the slopes of the hilly ground that rose gradually on the west. Finally, he arranged the two field guns so that they would be able to command the road along which the enemy would have to advance. One was placed on a small eminence, known as *Parke's Hill* to the right, and the other to the left near the river. These arrangements he completed before the French and their allies were aware of his presence. [6] Though unprepared for the encounter, Humbert quickly

THE YEAR OF THE FRENCH

had his troops so well in hand that he was ready for advance, after a short interval, with all his force, which was 900 French and somewhat more than 1,000 Irish recruits. The action, which began at two o'clock, lasted an hour and a half and was fought with great spirit on both sides.

Humbert, aided by the advice of the local leaders who had a detailed knowledge of the locality, divided a section of his force into two columns. He ordered the first, composed mainly of Insurgents, to hurry backwards from the town, cross the river at Knockbeg and, going along the valley behind the high ground on which Ormsby lay with his detachment, attack him from the rear. The second column was ordered to advance along the low ground near the river towards the left flank of the English position. It moved with deliberate slowness, so that its full strength might be flung on the enemy at the same moment that the first column (which had to make a long detour) should attack Ormsby's column. Meanwhile, the main body of Humbert's army were under severe attack from the English musketry and from the cannon on *Parke's Hill* in particular, which was effectively worked by an English gunner named Whitters. Several French marksmen had been concentrating the fire of their muskets on him for some time, but to no avail.

Under those circumstances Humbert's aide-de-camp, Bartholomew Teeling, performed a feat unsurpassed for its daring nature and for the heroism with which it was accomplished. Little more than twenty years of age, tall and handsome, Teeling was the most conspicuous figure on the field as he dashed about on his 'gallant grey' with the orders of the General. This chivalrous soul chafed with indignation and impatience on observing the faltering of some of his comrades in arms in the presence of Whitter's cannon, and resolved to remove the cause of their anxiety or perish in the attempt. Accordingly, he struck away towards the centre of the open field, and setting spurs to horse, galloped straight to the mouth of the gun. There was a solemn pause, and all eyes were upon the horseman as he pulled up the fiery grey. He cooly raised his pistol, took steady aim, and shot the formidable Whitters dead behind the cannon. In the twinkling of an eye the intrepid youth was returning, and though hundreds of muskets were discharged, he and his horse passed through the shower of bullets unharmed back to the French, who received the hero with a shout of enthusiastic welcome.[7]

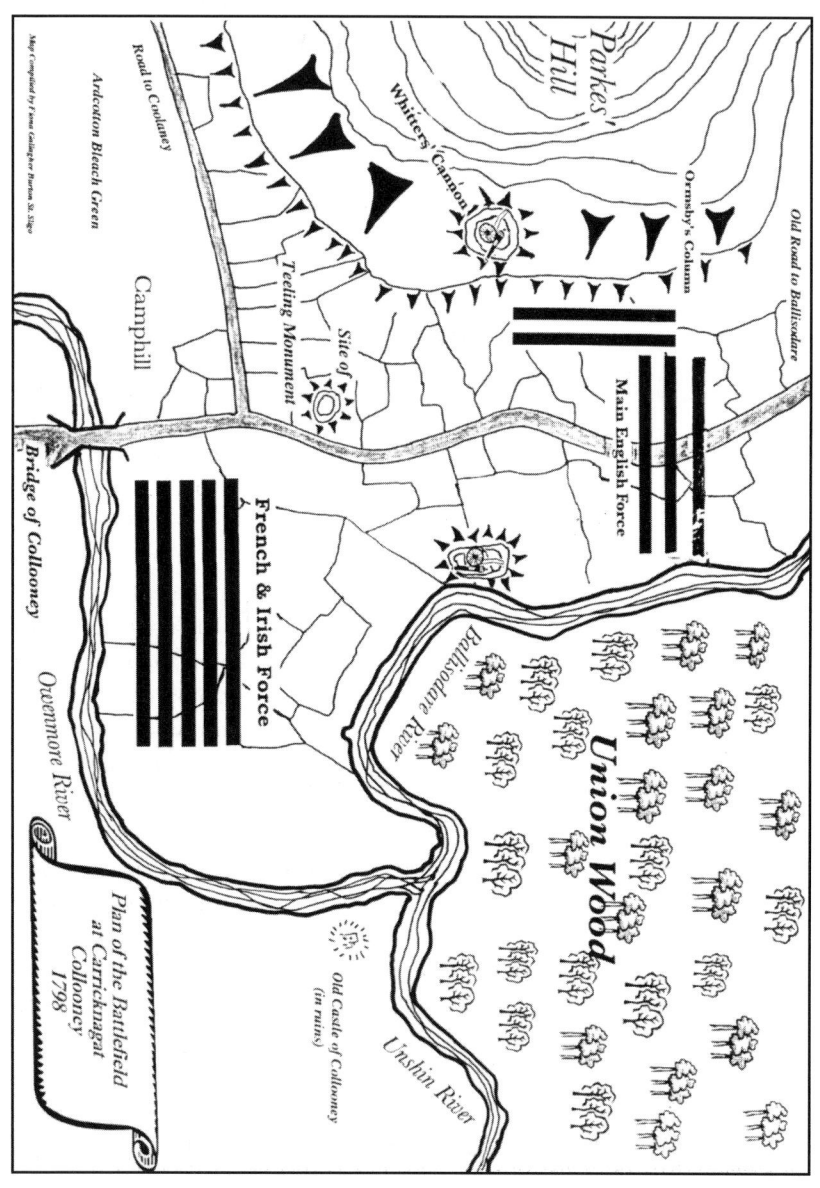

This was the turning point of the battle. The troops despatched from Knockbeg had reached *Béal Bán* and were already rushing down on the British flank, while the other column was advancing at a rapid pace from the left. There was no safety for Vereker from this double danger except in retreat; and as the Ballysadare road was no longer practicable, he ordered his men to cross the river and make for Sligo. They broke off in disorder, abandoning their cannon, and on getting out of Union Wood, scattered over the country. The French followed for some distance, but on reaching Springfield, and seeing the mountains and morasses that faced them, gave up the pursuit and hastened back to Carricknagat.

Humbert, still in doubt as to the numbers opposed, and convinced those he had defeated were only the vanguard of an army and that he would soon be attacked by the main body, rearranged his men in order of battle. They remained some time in this position, but when he learned that Colonel Vereker's troops were an independent body and that no other British force was in the neighbourhood, he gave orders for a march. Before leaving, Humbert released Knott and some other prisoners who had been placed under guard near the Protestant church while the battle was in progress. He also buried the dead, leaving under the care of a French surgeon eighteen men who were too seriously wounded to be removed. British official reports state that twenty eight were slain on the side of the French (not including Irish), and great numbers wounded, while Colonel Vereker set his own loss at seven killed and twenty two wounded, including himself and four officers. These returns hardly tell

*Bart. Teeling*

THE YEAR OF THE FRENCH

the whole truth.[8]

Shortly after 3 p.m. on September 5th, the day of the 'Battle of Collooney', news reached Sligo that Vereker's troops had been defeated and the French were advancing on the Town. On receipt of this intelligence panic seized the greater part of the inhabitants, then mostly Protestant. Momentarily expecting the arrival of the enemy, some fled for refuge to the ships in the harbour while others hurried away in the direction of Ballyshannon. However, those who were capable of bearing arms, to the number of about 300, resolved to defend the Town. They secured matchlocks and pikes and took up manned strategic positions where they were joined by a number of Protestant ministers, headed by Albert Blest, the Sligo-born evangelical dissenter, who prayed for their safe deliverance. The troops who had remained behind, when Colonel Vereker set out for Carricknagat, took up the most advantageous posts on the southern approaches to the Town and continued under arms all night. On Thursday, September 6th, Colonel Vereker who had resumed his command of the Sligo garrison, on learning that General Humbert was marching towards Manorhamilton, ordered a general retreat to Ballyshannon, leaving the Town at the mercy of the French and the Insurgents. On the following day, however, came the welcome intelligence that the danger had passed.

*"During the above anxious period"*, remarked the Editor of *"The Sligo Journal"*, *"all here was silent as the night, no business of any kind done, and nothing was seen in our streets save a few, a very few citizens, who with a holy fear kept a desultory watch. We printed not; for what had we to say? or to whom publish our tale of woe?"*

After his success at Collooney, Humbert abandoned his intention of marching on Sligo and decided instead to head for Enniskillen. Setting out from Collooney, he struck north-east, leaving the enemy still doubtful about the goal of his movements. As the long train of captured artillery encumbered his march along the rough roads, he dumped two pieces of canon over the bridge at Ballygrania and, on reaching Dromahair late at night, threw five more into the Bonet. He approached Manorhamilton in the forenoon of the 6th of September and, halting a short distance from that town, finally abandoned all intention of going into Ulster. Instead, he wheeled sharply to the south

## ADDRESS TO COLONEL VEREKER

The County Sligo Grand Jury at their meeting on October 12th, 1798,
passed the following Resolution: -

### TO COLONEL VEREKER

*By the High Sheriff and Grand Jury of the County of Sligo - The High Sheriff in the chair.*

Resolved, that our warmest thanks are justly due, and are hereby
presented to Colonel Vereker, of the Limerick regiment, for his very spirited
and judicious conduct, when undiscouraged by their superior numbers and
artillery, he marched against the enemy at Collooney, rather than wait their
attack, as also for his uncommon exertions and intrepidity during a very
severe action, by which the enemy not only received a considerable check,
but were diverted from their intended attack and pillage of the town of Sligo
and induced to direct their line of marching another way.

Resolved also, that we cannot too fully express our admiration of the
officers and privates under Colonel Vereker's command upon that occasion,
for the spirit of perseverance with which they executed all orders under such
uncommon disadvantage, and finally accomplished the object of so bold a
measure.

James Wood, High Sheriff.

C. O'Hara, Foreman.                                                 October 12, 1798.

---

and arrived at Drumkeeran on the evening of the same day. From this
sudden change of route it became evident that his object now was to
effect a junction with the Insurgents in the Midlands. He failed utterly
in this objective and was gradually encircled by the vastly superior
English forces, commanded by Lord Cornwallis. After giving battle for
half an hour at Ballinamuck on September 8th, the combined Franco-
Irish army was forced into an inglorious surrender. The long awaited
invasion not only failed, but failed utterly.

Meanwhile, a few days earlier, the combined forces of General Lake
and Colonel Crawford, who were in hot pursuit of Humbert's army,
marched from Tubbercurry and arrived at Collooney shortly after
Humbert's departure. On their way they encountered an unknown
number of stragglers and deserters from the insurgent forces and these
were summarily shot or hanged on the spot; leaving the line of march
strewn with corpses. In many instances, homes were set on fire and, in
the words of one commentator, "an indiscriminate vengeance was

wrecked on the inhabitants." The countryside from Collooney to Ballintogher was also laid waste and residents were forced to flee in terror. For months afterwards the inhabitants of this general area lived in fear while the 'Red Coats' searched for people alleged to have been 'out' with the French. Those who were known or suspected of assisting or joining them were waylaid and harassed, and such of them as fell into the hands of their pursuers were hanged or shot, and of the remainder, several escaped to America. An undated letter, signed A. Thompson, and addressed to Charles O'Hara, Esq., contains a list of some twenty suspected rebels "together with anything he could draw from the informants". Although no positive proof had so far been advanced, Thompson went on to suggest that "it might be drawn from circumstances, as for example, if Dudley Scanlon was convicted on Anderson's evidence, he might, to save his own bacon, discover his associates." The letter continues:

*"I am informed there is one Denis O'Hara, now a recruiting Sergeant in Sligo, through the interests of Mr Gore, who, after confessing his own guilt, did inform against most of them before a Magistrate of the County. Since my last I am informed there is another nest of rebels about Carrickbanagher and shall tomorrow inquire more particularly about them."* [9]

News of the disaster at Ballinamuck on September 8th reached the North-West a few days later. It was received with understandable jubilation by the loyalists but with profound disappointment by the supporters of the uprising. As fugitives arrived back with stories of the surrender and the subsequent massacre, the Insurgents, still under arms, resolved to continue the struggle. However, General Trench, the supreme commander of the British forces, had other ideas. He quickly laid plans to swiftly wipe out any pockets of resistance to be found in West Sligo and North Mayo. Commenting on the situation, the *"Sligo Journal"* wrote:-

*"We are sorry to state that for four weeks or so the Barony of Tireragh, and adjoining parts of Mayo, are in full and uncontested possession of the Rebels. Many loyalists driven from their homes and depending on the support of friends are suffering as prisoners at the hands of ruthless villians."* [10]

## RETURN OF PERSONS SUSPECTED OF HAVING BEEN ENGAGED IN THE LATE REBELLION.

**Name** | **Observations**

Dudley Scanlon: With others swore United Irishmen in Ballymote on 3rd of September last and endeavoured to persuade John Anderson, Sub-Constable, to swear also in preservation of his life.

Michael Scanlon: Severley wounded in French service in Rebellion.

Martin Rogers, Michael Rogers, Thos. Scanlon, Patt. Kearns: Martin Rogers was taken before Mr. Bridgeham for an attempt to swear Mich. Hughes and was severely wounded in the arm in the rebellion.

John and Bryan: Whoody (Doody ?): Absent during the rebellion.

Mathew Doyle: Represented to be a fellow of infamous character. A swearer-in of United Men and Captain of Rebels.

Tim Killoran: Confessed to Mr. Perceval that he had marched with the French to Ballinamuck and there deserted them.

Bryan Scanlon: A ruffian of infamous character. Said to be the person who divided the leather stolen from Mr. McKim among the rebels at Ballymote.

Patrick and Michael Davey: Taken in arms on return from Ballinamuck.

Thos. amd Jas. Davey: Absent while the French were at Killala Bridge; At Dromahair a Constable met Jas. and one Killalea returning from Ballinamuck.

John Finan, son of Lawrence: A bayonet and pike found in his house. I think I could produce two boys who knew him to have brought home those things from Ballinamuck.

"Old Lawson of Ballinaboll knows more of the rebels than most having been employed at Collooney to kill sheep for them."

## THE YEAR OF THE FRENCH

On Friday, September 21st, 1798, Lord Portarlington set out from Sligo for Ballina at the head of 800 men, consisting of his own and the Queen's County Regiment; a detachment of the 24th Dragoons; the Tireragh Yeomen Infantry, commanded by Captain James Wood, and the Tireragh Yeomen Cavalry under Captain Ormsby, together with two pieces of cannon. They halted that evening at *Arkill Lodge* in the Parish of Templeboy, where they proposed to bivouac for the night. No sooner had they done so then they were attacked by a small insurgent force who discharged several volleys into the camp. The fire was returned after which the Insurgents drew up in a regular line for an engagement but, "when the enemy field guns opened fire", they quickly retreated, having suffered a number of casualties.

Early on Saturday Portarlington's march was resumed. At the bridge of Easkey he was subjected to another attack but again the rebels were obliged to retreat with some losses. Towards evening the village of Scurmore was reached and it was decided to camp there for the night. Some hours before, a battalion of pikemen under Captain Truc, Colonel Patrick Barrett and Captain Henry O'Kane had left Ballina and marched north by the coast, intending to challenge the enemy advance from Sligo. Ahead of them they saw a long trail of smoke, indicating the approach of Portarlington's troops. The rival forces met near Scurmore where, for nearly an hour, an obstinate engagement continued and resulted in the pikemens' retreat before a heavy artillery fire. As the enemy cavalry were preparing to pursue, the skill and stratagem of an Insurgent frustrated their design. Local tradition recalls how Seamas 'Dubh' Horkan rallied the few cavalry of the Irish force and covered the retreat of its infantry so that they were able to reach Ballina in safety. During the conflict a curious incident occurred which has been related as follows by Musgrave:-

*"Not far from the scene of action lies the village of Carrowcardin, where a few Protestant families lived, who, from their peaceable demeanour and good conduct, possessed the regard even of the rebels; so that, partly by giving them entertainment and money as long as they were able, and partly by hiding themselves in the bogs and corn-fields, they had hitherto avoided the captivity which their brethren suffered. On this day, a rebel party commanded by John McDonough, otherwise Pitcher, on their march to attack the King's troops, were ordered to enter the village and force every man who was able to carry arms to*

*join their party. They there met with a number of poor Protestants, some of them reaping their corn, others concealed in their houses, all of whom they forced along with them at the peril of their lives, even without arms to defend themselves, and placed them in the front of the line. When the rebel army gave way, these unfortunate men fled among the crowd towards their own homes; but, having been overtaken by the cavalry, they fell in the indiscriminate slaughter of the rebels. It was in vain that they endeavoured to explain the cause of their being there, or to justify their conduct as the troops, elate with victory, and inflamed with revenge, took no time to examine the circumstances of their situation.*

*The rebel leader, McDonough, by whose order these innocent people had been driven to their death, was subsequently captured and hanged. It had been authoritively stated that 300 were killed in what is sometimes referred to as 'The Battle of Enniscrone'.* [11]

In the course of their march through Tireragh, Portarlington's command plundered and burned houses in which pikes or property plundered from loyalist subjects were found, while all the while, a cutter of 14 guns patrolled the coastline to prevent possible escape by sea. The flaming homesteads in their line of march were clearly visible to the Insurgents at Killala as they prepared for a final stand. In their midst was Father MacDonnell of Easkey who was compelled to flee from his residence on the arrival of Portarlington's army and take refuge with the rebels across the Bay. The last thing he witnessed before leaving was the blazing homes of his flock. Commenting on the conduct of the army, Bishop Stock had this to say:- "Their rapacity differed in no respect from that of the rebels, except that they seized upon things with somewhat less of ceremony or excuse, and that his Majesty's soldiers were incomparably superior to the Irish traitors in dexterity at stealing."

The insurgent forces, numbering 800 and under joint French and Irish command, made their last stand at Killala on September 23rd, where they were encircled and overpowered by a combined English army who numbered in excess of 3,000. No mercy was shown by the victors and the rebels suffered wholesale slaughter, totalling in the region of 400. Most of

THE YEAR OF THE FRENCH

those who survived were taken prisoners and met their death on the scaffold or were forcibly exiled. Repression followed on defeat but, thankfully, the hand of the law appears to have fallen less heavily in Sligo than in neighbouring Mayo.

A year or so after Carricknagat magistrates were appointed by royal warrant to investigate the claims for compensation preferred by those who alleged that they suffered in the Uprising, and, who got, in consequence, the name of *Suffering Loyalists.* The Magistrates appointed for County Sligo were:-

William Harloe Phibbs of Bloomfield, High Sheriff,1814;
Arthur Irwin of Streamstown and Willowbrook, H.S. 1795;
Rev. Charles West, Vicar of Ahamlish, J.P. and Land Agent;
Rev. Carncross Cullen of Skreeny, Manorhamilton;
Rev. William Duke of Branchfield and subsequently of Collooney.

They held their first meeting on the 30th September, 1799. The routine was to read the claim, to examine the claimant or his witness on oath, and to admit, reject, or modify the application as they judged fit. If they admitted the claim, either in whole or in part, they gave a certificate for the amount and if they rejected it they gave their reason for doing so, such as, that the claimant was not a loyalist, that they did not believe he had suffered for his loyalty, or that he was not furnished with a certificate of good conduct from the 'resident clergyman' or parson. In all, 218 claims were submitted, with amounts ranging from £I.I0s to £1,947. 10.4d., and totalling £15,717.12.9d. Claims, for the most part, related to damages to and loss of such items as houses, furniture, crops, farm animals, firearms etc. Many claimants exaggerated their losses to such an extent that the compensation actually paid out came to only one quarter of what had been sought, and the number of claims were reduced from 218 to 197. The names of the claimants, and details of their claims, published in both O'Rorke's and Wood-Martin's histories, throw considerable light on the state of the County two centuries ago.

## Notes & References

(1)  *A night or two after the landing at Killalla, about three hundred young fellows of the parishes of Ballysadare and Kilvarnet, assembled at Killasser, near*

## THE YEAR OF THE FRENCH

*Annaghmore, and entered into an engagement to proceed in a few days to the French camp but, after they took the advice of their priests and thought better of the matter, the three hundred dwindled down to three individuals, who, of all were assembled at Killasser, were the only persons to carry out the engagement.*

(O'Rorke *Ballysadare & Kilvarnet*)

(2)  Father Owen Cowley was educated on the Continent and acted as interpreter to the French on their arrival. After the Rebellion he had to go "on the run" and a reward of £300 was offered for his capture. He fled for safety to Muingwore, in the parish of Castleconnor, and took refuge in an underground cavern where he died in 1799. He is buried in an unmarked grave in Killanly.

(3)  On their way the pikemen are said to have plundered *Templehouse*, the seat of Rev. Phillip Perceval, who had been active against the United Irishmen.

(4)  *"Several inhabitants of Collooney and the neighbourhood quitted their houses on the approach of the French, taking themselves to the Ox - Mountains and Union Wood, and bringing with them such household goods as they could conveniently carry. They drove before them their horses, and hundreds of these animals were kept for weeks roaming through the wood, in order that they might be beyond the reach of military requisitionists"*

(O'Rorke *"Ballysadare & Kilvarnet"*)

(5)  *"Sligo Journal"*                              14-9-1798

(6)  "The battle field presented a different appearance then from what it offers at present. The land which is now all in pasture, was then in tillage and the fences were so low as to be little obstacle in the way either of cavalry or infantry. The present road was not then in existence and the old one, which was about twenty or thirty yards nearer to the river, ran in a straight line to the bridge of Collooney".

(O'Rorke *"Ballysadare & Kiltvarnet"*)

(7)  Bartholomew Teeling, a native of Lisburn, enlisted in the French service as a young man. He acted as aide-de-camp to General Humbert during the Irish campaign. After the defeat at Ballinamuck he was taken prisoner, court-martialled and executed at Arbour Hill on September 24th, 1798.

(8)  The action at Collooney was one of the most celebrated of the whole Rebellion. Honours of all kinds were showered on Colonel Vereker. Parliament voted him its thanks, Dublin confirmed on him the freedom of the city, while the Corporation of his native Limerick struck a medal bearing the legend *To the Heroes of Collooney* and also named a street, *Collooney Street*, in his honour.

# THE YEAR OF THE FRENCH

(9) O'Hara (of Annaghmore) Mss. (National Library of Ireland).

(10) *"Sligo Journal"* 21-9.1978.

According to depositions sworn before Rober Hillas of *"Seaview"*, William Stenson of Ballygilcash, Kilmacshalgan; John Armstrong of Ballymeeny and Robert Atkinson of Ballykeg, both in the Parish of Easkey, were taken prisoners by a group of armed rebels on September 7th-8th. They were then imprisoned in a house in Ballina and threatened with death.

(11) According to local tradition the Scurmore massacre took place in a field known locally as *Chapelfield*. Amongst those killed wre Jim Sheridan of Gurtahorra; Mick Philbin of Carrownrod and - McLoughlin of Cooga.

**BIBLIOGRAPHY**

Anon. *"Impartial Relation of the Military Operations in Ireland, 1978"* Dublin . 1799

Gordon, Rev. James *"History of the rebellion in Ireland, 1998"*. Dublin. 1801

Gribayedoff, Valerian. *"The French Invasion of Ireland in 1798"* New York. 1890.

Hayes, Richard. *"The last Invasion of Ireland. "* Dublin. 1937.

Jones, John. *"Engagements during the Rebellion 1798"*. London. 1805.

Musgrave, Richard. *"Memoirs of Different Rebellions in Ireland"* Dublin. 1801.

O'Rorke, Terence. *"Ballysodare and Kilvarnet"*. Dublin. Dublin. 1878

Pakenham, Frank. *"The year of Liberty"*. London. 1969

Stock, Bp. *"A Narrative of what Passed at Killala ... 1798"* London. 1800

Wood-Martin, W.G., *"History of Sligo"*. Vol. 3 Dublin. 1892. Reprinted 1990

Col. Charles Vereker

# 'BATTLE OF COLLOONEY' Recalled

"The 5th of the present month was the seventy-ninth anniversary of the Battle of Collooney Bridge. Only one man in the village recollects that day. The Protestant inhabitants mostly went to the hamlet of Union. The discharge of cannon and small arms startled the boys from their play, and their mothers soon got them in and closed the doors. The action lasted some hours, and the Protestant volunteers fought bravely. The last of them, Robert Clark, died twenty years ago. Edward Ferguson of Drumcliffe and Andrew Williamson of Ballymote were killed. The Limerick Militia proved that "they who fight and run away, may have to fight another day". The French showed their accustomed bravery and Teeling and some of his Irish friends proved that the penal laws only deprived the English Crown of some of its bravest soldiers. The French marched next day to Dromahair, and the absent inhabitants came back here to empty houses. The feather beds were emptied in the yards, and the ticks filled with every thing valuable that could be carried away. The French did not plunder, and were indignant with their Irish followers for doing so. The stragglers would have been severely dealt with by martial law, but humanity prompted to save life by pulling down a large turf rick and getting the strangers there as labourers, and thus saved their lives. The weather was particularly fine and the take of herring enormous. The news of 'The French are coming' spoiled the broiling of them, and prevented many from taking a hearty breakfast of fish and potatoes. The French encamped at 'Carricknagat', and part of the townland is called *Camphill* since then. Two Frenchmen died here of their wounds soon after, an officer and his orderly, and they were buried near the female schoolhouse. Lieutenant Rumley, of the Limerick Militia, came here wounded, and died after he was removed to Sligo. Colonel Vereker got a Peerage for the part he took in the action. He told the loyal Volunteers to put a rag-weed on their breasts to distinguish them from the Insurgents".

*Sligo Independent 15.09.1877*

# Lady Morgan:
# The Sligo Connection

Theatre in Sligo dates back to the mid 18th century, and possibly earlier. It has been suggested that the first playhouse was close to the Quays, [1] but subsequently moved to Water Lane and later still to *The Linenhall*, on Corkran's Mall, now incorporated in *The Embassy* complex. Touring companies, notably Dublin's Theatre Royal, visited Sligo on a regulare basis and usually performed a series of plays over a three week period.

In the late 18th century Robert Owenson, a native of Collooney and the father of the celebrated Lady Morgan, was a frequent and popular performer before Sligo audiences. He came of Catholic stock but subsequently converted to Protestantism and anglicised his surname, changing it from Mac Owen, or Mac Eóin, to Owenson. It is said that his father, a tenant farmer, had eloped with the young daughter of a local baronet whose family disowned her. As a young boy he was taken in as a domestic by the family of 'Commodore' Irwin of Oakfield with whom he resided for a number of years.[2] He subsequently moved to Dublin where he got involved in the theatre.

Biographers of his daughter claim that Owenson, in his youthful years, showed some symptoms of the genius that he afterwards displayed in his characterisations on the stage of Crow Street theatre.[3] His personification of the Irish character won him acclaim far and wide. Invariably, he completed his tour of the provinces in Sligo and availed of the opportunity to visit his mother's cousins, the Croftons of Longford House, who, for the sake of his accomplishments and entertainment, are said to have "conquered their old prejudices."[4] Thought the local gentry did not support his theatre, they condescended to invite him to dinner, where he sang for his supper. "Give him a bottle of claret and a jug of poteen and Owenson forgot his care," commented a contemporary Sligo resident.

In Owenson's day the Sligo theatre was located in Water Lane and was only fitted with pit and gallery. Fitzpatrick, his daughter's biographer, [4] was the correspondent of a number of Sligo residents who remembered Miss Owenson and her father. Their reminiscences contain some delightful pen-pictures of the actor manager and his little daughters both within and outside the theatre. In one instance, we see them leaving their lodgings with Mrs. Brown in Market Street, and pausing, on their way to the Theatre, at Doctor Henry's Apothecary's Hall in High Street, where the little coquette, Sidney, had one of her earliest conquests busily transcribing into presentable scripts her first literary efforts. In others, we see her growing up into attractive womanhood, returning each season with her father and his Company to Sligo, engaging in mild flirtations with a succession of eligible and ardent suitors, including Harloe Phibbs, 'Commodore' Irwin, Richard Everard and a host of others; or as a pensive young authoress musing in the cloisters of Sligo Abbey or in ecstatic raptures over the beauty of Glencar, Aughris or the Knocknarea countryside.

Lady Morgan

We can also picture her, and hear her, as the centrepiece of an attractive gathering in Feeney's seated at her harp or accompanying her father in his favourite Italian and Irish ballads. Penury also came her way, when in 1798 Owenson and his Company were marooned in Sligo, its members behind barricaded windows and doors, and the Theatre's improvident landlord impounding their props and almost all their personal belongings. But another Sligoman come to the rescue and *'The Wild Irish Girl'* went on to become a national figure .

The accident of a remote Connacht cousinship opened the door for Owenson's attractive and talented daughter, Sydney, who stayed at the hospitable home of the Croftons for long periods in the opening years of the 19th century, partly as governess and, in her own words, "partly as a poor relation, in consideration of the credit she had become to the distinction of being the grand-daughter of the House of Crofton". Her sojourns at *Longford* gave her the opportunity of meeting with the old Connacht gentry and experiencing, at first hand, life in the ' Big House'.

It was here, at the ancient Crofton seat, in the picturesque countryside between mountain and sea, an area rich in historical associations, that the genius of Lady Morgan first come to light. According to her, Sligo was "a wondrously gay place" in the opening years of the last century, and in later life she frequently acknowledged her indebtedness to the place and its people as the source of her inspiration. In her earliest work - *"The Wild Irish Girl"*, most of which was written at *Longford House*, the heroine, *'Gloriana'* , who was endowed with all the characteristic Irish virtues and accomplishments, was inspired by Elizabeth Crofton, the future wife of Col. Northcote of Sligo.

It was at *Longford*, too, that the future Lady Morgan wrote her *"Patriotic Sketches"* . Throughout the work she displays a thorough sympathy with the people and places she describes, and the *"Sketches"* contain some graphic accounts of the manners and customs prevailing in this area almost two centuries ago. At the Crofton seat, which is described as "a real old Irish country-house", she witnessed a great deal of the somewhat primitive manners of the old country gentry and the stately grandeur of a remote 'ancestral hall' experiencing a mixture of sordid discomfort. In one of the *"Sketches"* she writes of her affection for the Crofton family and displays an intimate knowledge of the historical associations of the area :-

*"My heart had long owed a pilgrimage to this remote and little known Barony - for it was the residence of a dear and respected friend for whom the heart had long throbbed with an insatiable pulse of gratitude, tenderness and affection . .*

*Longford House, the ancient family-seat of Sir Malby Crofton, Baronet, was the goal of my little journey, and I reached its venerable avenue at a season of the day peculiarly favourable to the soft chiaro-oscurs of picturesque beauty: with the old gloomy avenue of an ancient mansion-seat,there is, I think, invariably connected a certain sentiment which bears the heart back to 'other times,' and awakens it to an emotion of tender reverence, and melancholy pleasure. For* myself, I have never walked beneath its interwoven branches uninfluenced by a certain feeling, in which memory's pensive spell mingled with the speculations of awakened fancy.

Of the old castle of Longford nothing now remains but a few fragments that mark its site, and are strewed amidst the vegetation which covers a cave, the probable asylum of many an unhappy fugitive in days of civil horror, or religious persecution. Near the spot where the castle once stood, moulders the ruin of a small  building, whose dilapidated portal still bears a Spanish inscription, intimating that it was the 'retreat of a priest and his yellow-haired companion.' It was in fact erected, as tradition  asserts, by one of the lords of the castle, for his youngest son, who had in the Elizabethan days forfeited the revenues of an abbey of which he was superior; but whether the forfeiture arose from his attachment to popery, or to the yellow-haired companion, oral history has preserved no record.

Near this retreat stands a small oratory or cell, furnished with a ruined altar, and some curiously carved heads of saints; while several fragments of rude sculpture and entablatures, with mottoes in Latin or Spanish, lie scattered around it."

In another well known work, *"Lays of an Ancient Irish Harp"*, published in 1807, she penned highly wrought metrical lines inspired by the antiquities in the vicinity of the Crofton seat :-

> *"The castle lies low, where towers frowned so high,*
> *And its landscape is awfully bold;*
> *The mountains around lift their heads to the sky.*
> *And the woods many ages have told,*
> *And many a pilgrim has pillowed his head*
> *In the cell that moulders away;*
> *And many a brave chief and warrior had bled*
> *Near those walls that now fall and decay".*[6]

Elsewhere she paints a vivid picture of life in the 'Big House' in the opening years of the last century :-

> '. . . *Then came the dinner, the horse-shoe table, the side board, side-tables and window stools, with a plate on the knee and a bit in the corner at last provided for all . . . Rounds of beef, which none resisted, haunches of venison and legs of mutton were entrees that required no substitute. A creel of potatoes and a bowl of fresh butter left no wish for more brilliant or less substantial fare, while a vacant place was left for the soup which was always served last. Jorums*

## LADY MORGAN: THE SLIGO CONNECTION

*of punch were stationed round the capacious hearth while port and sherry were ranged along the tables with the door opening into the wide drawing room disclosing to view the cask of claret. . . '*

Dublin may claim Lady Morgan, and Ireland honour her, as a precursor of the Anglo-Irish novel, but Sligo must not be denied - as the works which made her famous are Sligo through and through, both in background and characters. It seems most probable that her Irish chieftain is a composite picture of The Mac Dermot, *Prince of Coolavin*; and the Sligo merchant, who redeemed her fathers' property in 1798, was none other than Ignatius Everard; while 'Father John' was the Parish priest of Sligo, the burly but courtly John Flynn, who later became Lord Bishop of Achonry. Even Thady Connellan, the celebrated Irish scholar from Tireragh, had his measure taken and his character delineated in the years when he was a hedge schoolmaster by day and the leader of the *'Threshers'* by night.

In her own way, Lady Morgan not only immortalised the Croftons and the surrounding countryside, but also has the distinction of being the earliest of the modern writers to introduce Sligo to a national audience.

### *References :*

(1)  Wood-Martin, W. G. *"History of Sligo"*. Vol. 3.

(2)  Gibbon, Skeffington. *Recollections, 1796 - 1829.* Dublin. 1829.

(3)  Campbell, Mary. *"Lady Margan"*. Essex. 1988.

(4)  Fitzpatrick, W.J. *"Memoirs of Lady Morgan"*, London. 1860.

(5)  Letter dated March, 1856.

(6)  Writing in 1910, the then head of the Crofton family, Sir Malby, noted that the castle was entirely destroyed and trees were now growing on the site. "The little chapel is very small and is embedded in trees".

*Longford House*: the former Crofton residence

# The Punishment Fits the Crime

The sentences handed down by Judge Jebb at the Spring Assizes in March, 1822, were consistent with the sentencing policy of that era. Before the court were James Boland, who was convicted of the crime of rape, and Patrick Corcoran, found guilty under the Whiteboy Act. In passing a sentence of death by hanging on both, the Judge addressed them individually as follows:-

*"Patrick Corcoran, you have been indicted for that you, on the 7th of February, did forcibly break into the house of Myles Higgins, also assaulting and injuring his dwelling-house. You are also indicted for breaking into the house of John Feeny, and assaulting his habitation - and on both of those charges you have been found guilty. James Boland and Patrick Corcoran, both of the crimes on which you have been convicted, was upon the clearest evidence; you have had, each of you, a patient trial by a gracious Jury, and a Jury of great respectability, who have paid every attention to you cases, and on a full and a patient examination of all the circumstances, have pronounced you guilty of the crimes with which you have been charged - and these crimes are of such a nature, that it is quite impossible for me to hold out the least hope of pardon.*

*James Boland, you and another ruffian attacked a decent, married woman, who was going peaceably along the high-way, in company with her brother; you seized her and took her into a silent place, almost in the presence of her brother, and within the hearing of her husband, and though she told you she was a married woman and the mother of four children, you have violated her person, and each of you committed a rape on her body, and manifested a brutality of disposition, a savage indecency of conduct, a disrespect of human nature, that raises such disgust in the human mind as it is impossible to express in adequate terms; it is extraordinary to what degree of depravity you must have been brought, when you could, in the shameless and abominable manner, each in the presence of the other, commit this crime on a married woman; it is of the deepest injury that can possibly be inflicted on her family, on her husband, and on herself; it is therefore quite necessary, for the sake of example, as well as to make reparation to the persons thus wounded and injured, beyond the power of healing, that your life shall fall a forfeit to the law. I call on you, therefore, as*

## THE PUNISHMENT FITS THE CRIME

*you have no hope of mercy in this world, to atone for this crime and other sins you have committed because no one could have committed such a crime as yours at the first.*

*You, Patrick Corcoran, have been convicted of a crime totally of a different nature, but one as mischievous in its effects - one that is destructive of the peace and good order of society, and at this time so mischievous in many parts of Ireland, that it is quite necessary also that your death shall, if possible, be the dreadful example that shall affright and deter others from pursuing such dreadful crimes, and restore this country to a state of peace. The daring banditti of which you were a member, in confederacies of a similar kind throughout the country, have for their object the destruction of all law; they wish to prevent, by the terror of their midnight attacks, and by the destruction of the habitations and property of the peaceful inhabitants of this country, and by the savage acts which are resorted to when these are not sufficient to deter - by murders, by burnings, and every ferocious deed that can distinguish and characterise a savage people - they endeavour to terrify landlords from enforcing the payment of their rents, and all other persons from enforcing their legal rights.*

*I trust the dreadful example of your execution will put a stop to this cruel banditti in this country; and I hope that this, the first execution that has taken place in the County of Sligo for this crime, will be a sufficient example. You have no hope of pardon in this world, therefore, endeavour to atone for the mischief you have done, by repentance and by making a full confession of this and the other crimes that you have been concerned in, and endeavour, as far as you can, by your advice to your unprincipled associates, to deter them from pursuing their dreadful designs.*

*The time that each of you have to live is but short - apply to your clergy and receive from them the consolations of religion - pray to God, through your Redeemer, for the remission of your sins. It now remains for me to pass on each of you the dreadful sentence of the law - that you, James Boland, and you, Patrick Corcoran, be each of you taken from the place you now stand to the Gaol, and from thence to the place of public execution, the gallows, and there you and each of you, will be hanged by the neck until you are dead - and the Lord have mercy on your souls". \**

Boland seemed much more affected at the passing of this sentence than Corcoran, who seemed very hardened. Corcoran was ordered for execution on Thursday, 4th of April, at Carrownabinna, in the Parish

\* *"Sligo Journal"* 23-3-1822

of Easkey; and Boland on Saturday, 6th of April, at Sligo. The *"Journal"* of April 10th carried the following brief report on Boland's execution:-

*"On Saturday last, the 6th inst. James Boland, the unfortunate person convicted at our last Assizes of a rape, was executed in front of the New Prison. He acknowledged his guilt and died penitently".*

At the same court Thomas Murray was sentenced to transportation for life for breaking into the Ballinacarrow Bleach-mill and carrying off some linen. He belonged to a party who were administering unlawful oaths and conspiring to burn Colonel Perceval's dwelling house. He was immediately sent, under escort by a party of Dragoons, to Cork, to be put on board a convict ship for transportation to Australia.

A Convict Ship in full sail.

# The Savings' Bank

The first Savings' Bank established on self-supporting principles was at Ruthwell, in the County of Drumfries, in 1810, by a Presbyterian Minister named Duncan, News of his enterprise quickly spread and by 1816 upwards of seventy similar institutions had been established in England and Wales. The movement attracted the attention of politicians and Bills were introduced in Parliament to co-ordinate procedures for their management and, also, the regulation of interest rates.

In 1817 an Act sought to encourage the establishment of Savings Banks in Ireland. Under its provisions, Trustees and Managers were required to formulate rules and regulations for approval at the Quarter Sessions. Depositors were restricted to an investment of not more than £50 per annum and the rate of interest was usually at or around 4%. The number of Savings Banks increased steadily in the following years, and by 1828 there were 487 such institutions operating in England, Wales and Ireland, with deposits totalling 15 million pounds.

The Sligo Savings Bank was established in 1820 and continued in existence with variant degrees of prosperity for half a century.[1] In June, 1823, the Bank closed for a short period due to difficulties in funding the wages of the clerk but re-opened in a few weeks, as the following advertisement in the *"Sligo Journal "* indicates :-

*"The Trustees, Directors, and Managers of the Sligo Savings Bank are requested to meet at the Court House on Monday next, the 4th August, at 3 o'clock to elect a Treasurer for the ensuing year and to transact other business, By order, S, M"Creery, Sec.*

*" N.B.   The Bank will in future be held  in a room adjoining the Excise Office, and will be open as usual from 10 till 12 o'clock on Mondays.*

*Sligo, July 28th, 1823. "*

At a meeting of the Trustees in February, 1828,  Owen Wynne presiding, the following Resolutions were agreed on :

That after a minute and careful examination into the accounts of the  Sligo Savings' Bank, as audited by the Rev William Armstrong and  Andrew Walsh,  Esq.,

## THE SAVINGS' BANK

we find that the money deposited and due to the Public is at this date    .    .    .

.                                                                    £5, 830. 15. 6d.

To pay which there is at the credit of the Sligo Savings' Bank with the Government, as per receipts from the Cashier of the Bank of Ireland , Dublin  . . .

£5, 830. 15. 4d.

Cash in Treasurer's hands .   .   .                          £   37.  6. 7d.

Leaving a surplus since last settlement in favour of Savings' Bank to meet the current expenses thereof of                £37.  6.  3d.

An accompanying Notice in the *"Journal "* informed the public that deposits were received by Vernon Davy's, Actuary to the Bank, every Monday between the hours of 10 a.m and 12 noon at the office of James Cochran, Esq., Wine St.[2]

In June, 1829, apparently in response to rumours circulating locally that the Bank was in some difficulty, a special meeting of the Trustees and Managers was convened. Present were Colonel William Parke, George Dodwell, Robert Barklie, John Ormsby, William Faussett (Provost), James Cochran and Martin Madden. The meeting, which was chaired by Col. Parke, passed the following Resolutions:-

1. That the Trustees of this Bank are the following Gentlemen, who were originally appointed in 1820, and at subsequent periods, namely:
   *Presidents:*  E.S. Cooper, Esq., M.P. and Owen Wynne, Esq., M.P.
   *Trustees:*    Col. John Irwin; Col. Alexander Perceval; Col. Wm. Parke; Major Charles K. O'Hara; John Armstrong; Dr. Patrick Burke, Bishop of Elphin; Rev. William Armstrong; Rev. William Grove; John Ormsby; William Faussett; Martin Madden and James Cochran.

2. That is is not the desire, or intention of this Board to discontinue the Saving's Bank, but that, on the contrary, they desire to encourage it by every means in their power.

3. That after an accurate investigation of the affairs of the Bank by Messrs William Faussett and Martin Madden, in the presence of other Trustees, we are satisfied that the sums due by the Bank to Depositors amount to £8,954.15.11d, of which sum £2,460.8s 3d was deposited at various dates by the Board of Trustees for the encouragement of industry in the County of Sligo, in order to increase their funds by the interest allowed in the Saving's Bank.

## THE SAVINGS' BANK

4.  That the affairs of the Bank have been conducted with great regularity and propriety, and that it is at present in a sound and prosperous state.
5.  That the Trustees feel themselves called on to express their conviction that Mr. Vernon Davy's, their Actuary, is entitled to their confidence and that of the public, and that he is hereby requested to continue his valuable services in that same capacity.

An analysis of the half yearly returns, April, 1829, gives an insight into the level of savings per depositor:

| Depositors :93 under | £ 20 | each | ...... | £ | 692. | 17. | 4d. |
| 74 | £ 50 | " | ...... | £ | 2,238. | 12. | 11d. |
| 42 | £ 100 | " | ...... | £ | 2,552. | 19. | 10d. |
| 3 | £ 150 | " | ...... | £ | 359. | 8. | 7d. |
| 1 above | £ 200 | " | ...... | £ | 206. | 13. | 4d. |
| | | | | | | | |
| 213 | Deposits amounted to | | | £ | 6,050 . | 12. | 0d. |
| In addition, one Charitable Society had on deposit. | | | | £ | 2,643. | 2. | 7d. |

The Annual Report for 1835, as published in the *"Sligo Journal"*, listed the names of Presidents, Trustees and Managers of the Bank- all men of standing in Town and County :

## *SLIGO SAVINGS' BANK*

### PRESIDENTS:

Owen Wynne, Esq. (Chairman)
Edward J. Cooper, Esq. M.P.

## THE SAVINGS' BANK

### TRUSTEES:

Colonel Perceval, M.P.
C. K. O'Hara, Esq.
Col. Irwin
Sir R. G. Booth, Bart.
John Wynne
John Armstrong, Esq
Col. Parke
John Martin, Esq.,

Rev. C. Hamilton
Wm. Faussett, Esq.
John Ormsby, Esq.
Rev. Wm.Armstrong
Herbert Clifford, Esq.
Rev. Dr. Burke
James Cochran, Esq.
Martin Madden, Esq.

### MANAGERS :

Johm Scott
Wm. Christian
Abraham Reed
Thomas Mostyn
William Patrickson
James Beatty

James O'Donnell
Thomas Read
Andrew Welsh
Lawrence Vernon
John Neary
James Henry

By November, 1846, there were 1,043 depositors and savings amounted to £35,088, which was the largest amount at the credit of the

---

### RETURNS FOR HALF-YEAR ENDING NOVEMBER, 1842

| Depositors : | 217 under | £ 20. | £ 1,698. 7. 3d. |
|---|---|---|---|
| | 318 between | £20 - £50 | £ 9,853.18. 8d. |
| | 71 " | £50 - £100 | £ 4,954. 0. 0d. |
| | 36 " | £100 - £150 | £ 4,442. 6. 7d. |
| | 3 " | £150 - £200. | £ 495. 0. 0d. |
| | 645 Deposits totalled : | | £ 21, 443.12. 6d. |

---

Bank at any stage during its existence. In the Famine years the Bank went into sharp decline, as many investors withdrew their savings to sustain them in a time of great want or, in some instances, to finance a passage to America. Between May, 1848, and November, 1851, a total of £19, 500 was withdrawn, leaving only £12, 859 to the credit of the Bank. Its very survival during that period was due, in great measure, to the efforts of Vernon Davys, Accountant and Actuary, [3] and of

## THE SAVINGS' BANK

Captain William Faussett, a long-standing Trustee of the Bank.

The tide began to turn in the latter half of 1851 when the number of depositors rose to 486, with a corresponding increase in investment capital. Between 1852 and 1856 deposits rose from £13,290 to £20,382. A break down of the 1856 returns reveal the following level of savings:-

| | | | |
|---|---|---|---|
| 31 | Depositors saved less than | | £ 1 each |
| 78 | Saved | between | £ 1 - £5. |
| 78 | " | " | £ 5 - £10 |
| 85 | " | " | £10 - £15 |
| 49 | " | " | £15 - £20 |
| 106 | " | " | £20 - £30 |
| 121 | " | " | £30 - £40 |
| 41 | " | " | £40 - £50 |
| 68 | " | " | £50 - £75 |
| 27 | " | " | £75 - £100 |
| 14 | " | " | £100 - £125 |
| 5 | " | " | £125 - £150 |
| 6 | " | " | £150 - £200 |
| 1 | Charitable Institution ..... £190 . | | |

In accordance with legislation then enacted, deposits could be made in amounts of 1/- and upwards but could not exceed £30 in a given year. Savings in excess of 20 /- qualified for an interest rate of £2.18.6d. per annum. All deposits were paid into the Bank of Ireland who allowed a rate of £3. 5s per annum. The difference between the two rates was used to meet the operating expenses of the Savings' Bank.

In 1855 the Bank was open three days a week for a total of fifteen hours. Operational costs including the salaries of Vernon Davys, Actuary, and Roger D. Robinson, Auditor, came to £100 per annum. Seven years later, in 1862, the Bank opened only one day a week on Mondays, for seven hours, despite a substantial growth in business, depositors having increased by 30% from 623 to 904, and deposits by 50%, from £16, 845 to £25,921. For reasons not now clear, the Bank's business showed a sharp decline in the late 1860's, both in number of depositors and in volume of savings.

## THE SAVINGS' BANK

The Sligo Savings' Bank continued to operate until December, 1873, when the following Notice, publised in the local newspapers, announced its closure :

---

SLIGO SAVINGS'S BANK
Certified under the Act of 1863.
Notice is Hereby Given

That at the Annual meeting of the Trustees
And Managers of the Sligo Savings' Bank
Held this day, it was Resolved to Dissolve the said Bank
And a consent for such dissolution was therefore
signed by  Three-fourths in number of said Trustees
and Managers.

Signed  : Vernon Davys,
Actuary of the said Savings Bank .

Sligo. 8th, 1873.

---

Record of Depositors and Deposits, 1830 - 1870.

| YEAR | NO. OF DEPOSITORS | AMOUNT DEPOSITED |
|------|-------------------|------------------|
| 1830: | 243 | £  8,091. 17.   6d |
| 1833: | 353 | £12,141. 11.   8d |
| 1835: | 394 | £15.466. 17.   7d |
| 1838: | 450 | £17.626. 10.   8d |
| 1840: | 598 | £24 825. 10.   0d |
| | | |
| 1846: | 1,043 | £35,088.  0.   0d. |
| 1850: | 553 | £15,453. 15.   6d. |
| 1852: | 526 | £13,859.  0.  10d. |
| 1853: | 601 | £15,181. 13.   0d. |
| 1854: | 486 | £13,290.  0.   0d. |

## The Savings' Bank

| | | | | |
|---|---|---|---|---|
| 1855: | 646 | £18,341. | 6. | 10d. |
| 1856: | 710 | £20,382. | 10. | 0d. |
| 1857: | 710 | £21,392. | 9. | 0d. |
| 1862: | 904 | £25,921 | 10 | 6d. |
| 1864: | 708 | £19,892. | 0. | 10d. |
| 1869: | 251 | £ 5, 362. | 10. | 0. |
| 1870: | 269 | £6, 125. | 10. | 6. |
| 1873: | 658 | £22,853. | 18. | 0d. |

### Notes And References

(1) *"Sligo Independent "*                12-6-1858

(2) *"Sligo Journal"*                21-3-1828

(3) Vernon Davys of *Rosehill House,* and subsequently of Stephen Street, brewer and merchant, Manager of the Savings Bank; Agent for the Gore-Booth estate for a time, died in Wales in 1879 aged 70. His son, Josiah Cochran Davys, was Solicitor to both the Poor Law Guardians and the Grand Jury, and later Clerk of the Crown and Peace for County Sligo.

(4) William Fausset J.P. of *Willsboro House,* was Provost of Sligo for many years and Deputy Sheriff, 1834. He was a member of the Reformed Corporation in 1842 and, at the time of his death in 1847, was the oldest resident Magistrate in the County.

# Relief of Distress and a Mismanaged Fund

The first recorded failure of the potato crop in County Sligo occurred in 1739. There were also partial failures on at least ten occasions between then and the severe food shortage of 1822. Famine and pestilence usually went hand -in hand. In a letter, dated Sligo, May 1822, it was stated :- "Fever stalks upon the heels of famine . . . It would be impossible for you to conceive or me to describe the state of the poor among us - the most appalling description would fall far short of the reality . . ." The severe distress being experienced arose from the almost total failure of the humble potato - the staple diet of the people - as result of heavy rains that had lasted for months and left the fields untilled.

In an effort to alleviate the hardship and sufferings being experienced on a wide scale, a public meeting took place in Sligo Courthouse on May 14th, 1822, to inquire into the state of the Poor and devise ways and means of relieving them. Four sub-committees were set up, representing different areas of the Town, and these reported back a week later. The report of Messrs Alexander Cochran and Martin Madden, in respect of District no 4 - namely, that part of the Town and precincts lying to the north-east of the River, read as follows :-

"We have been earnestly employed accordingly since Sunday morning last till this day, and now annex a statement in different classes of those in a distressed situation within the said district :-

| | | |
|---|---|---|
| 170 Labourers,, whose families amount to 807 persons. | | |
| 96 Widows, | 303 | " |
| 24 Weavers, | 111 | " |
| 22 Brogue or Show-Makers, | 125 | " |
| 9 Coopers, | 38 | " |
| 7 Masons, | 36 | " |
| 3 Blacksmiths | 23 | " |
| 4 Carpenters, | 18 | " |
| 2 Sawyer's, | 16 | " |

## RELIEF OF DISTRESS AND A MISMANAGED FUND

| | |
|---|---|
| 5 Nailers, | 30 persons |
| 18 Extra families, of different classes, | 85 " |

Total: 360 families. Total in number:      1,592 persons

The distress of mostly all the above number is truly great; and in many instances, particularly where bad health (which we are sorry to say is very frequent) is combined with poverty, hardly supposeable.

We were very particular in going into every house and minutely examining into their general conduct, state of health, and means of support, attended and assisted by two respectable men living in the same district, and well acquainted with its inhabitants; that during such examination we witnessed several instances of distress not to be described, many of them, particularly on last Sunday (a dreadfully wet day,) being without turf, and destitute of either meal or a potato.

Want of labour for the labourer, and want of means to carry on their trades by the mechanics appear to us to be the cause of the present distress, which we strongly recommend to the early attention of the General Committee; and we would also suggest that some relief might be afforded to the widows and females of the above number, by instituting a manufacture or spinning of flax and wool, and, with those three classes being provided for, there would remain but one class, namely, those who from inability by sickness, or old age, cannot do any manner of work, and for whom we see no manner of providing, but by donation. We beg to observe the above list of distressed persons live in the town and suburbs of Sligo, without reference to any who live beyond them in our district, within the Union of St. John's.

The Committee, having empowered us to give immediate relief-money, meal, or potatoes- in cases of very urgent distress, we yesterday visited nearly 210 families, whose circumstances demanded instantaneous assistance, among whom we distributed 40 pecks of potatoes and £10 in money or meal. There are yet several families in our district whom, for want of time, we have not been able to see and administer to them their necessary portion.

Sligo, May 22, 1822.<br>
(Signed) ALEX. COCHRAN.<br>
M. MADDEN.

*P.S.* Your Committee beg leave to add that from the poverty of the lower class they have in very many instances been obliged to give up their houses and go into lodgings with other families, and the consequence is that in many small houses there

RELIEF OF DISTRESS AND A MISMANAGED FUND

are 3, 4, or 5 families, which, should a fever break out in the summer, there is no knowing what will be the end."

(Signed)    A.C.
    M M.

The gravity of the situation was highlighted in July of that year when it was noticed that some people, in desperation for food, had already commenced digging that season's crop before it was fit to do so. In an effort to counteract this the local Relief Committee published the following Notice in the *"Sligo Journal"* on July 27th, 1822 :-

---

# NOTICE

*"The Committee for the Relief of the Poor in the Town of Sligo and Union of St. John's, lament to find, that some Persons have commenced Digging their Potatoes, not giving them sufficient time to yield their produce. In order to prevent a proceeding so destructive to the Crop, the Committee have resolved, that if any Persons, now on the lists for Relief, by Labour or otherwise, are found Digging their Potatoes before the 20th of August, they shall be forthwith deprived of benefit from the Funds of the Committee. If the practice be persisted in, it will tend to deprive the Poor themselves of subsistence hereafter."*

---

The *Journal* added the following footnote :-

*"We trust the Committee will not think of relaxing their exertions before the end of the present month, as we are persuaded if the Poor are thrown on the produce of the season earlier, the consequence will be most injurious".*

\*    \*    \*    \*    \*    \*

The distress was by no means confined to Sligo Town, but was widespread throughout the County. The extent and nature of the problem is best illustrated by the following extracts from letters addressed to the London-based *"Committee for the Relief of the Distressed Districts in Ireland"* :- [1]

## RELIEF OF DISTRESS AND A MISMANAGED FUND

*From The Rev. James Neligan, Kilmactigue,*
*dated 24th of May, 1822*

"This parish, which contains above seven thousand souls, consists almost entirely of the poorest class of tenantry, who hold their lands as joint tenants in common, at a very high rate, much indeed above the value. At the best of times, they were unable to pay their rents, and support their families with any degree of comfort; but, at the present time, their distress is very great indeed. Their crops in the last harvest proved very deficient, both in quantity and quality, particularly the *potatoes*, which did not produce above one half of the usual return. It is well known that their support through the year depends almost exclusively on potatoes (their corn being applied to the payment of their rents), and these have been almost exhausted the last month, so that many of the poor people have not had seed to plant, which will be attended with a fresh calamity next year. Fodder has been so scarce that many of the cattle have died for want of food, and more are so wretchedly poor, that they will not yield any price, and even such as they are, the owners are killing them to supply the place of other food. Groups of starving beggars, consisting often of seven in a family, are crowding the roads and houses, and those who at other seasons are able to assist them are now rendered entirely incapable. Some hundred families have already abandoned their dwellings and gone out to beg through the country at large, at least the women and children have done so, whilst the men have gone to England or elsewhere, to try to obtain work."

*From the Rev. William Urwick, Sligo,*
*1st June, 1822.*

"Though the following representations are gloomy, we believe multitudes of objects remain yet undiscovered, and we fear that in another month, notwithstanding our utmost efforts, the aspect will be even worse than it is now. Before their distress was published, all the little furniture of their cabins had been sold, even to their only pot for boiling their provisions, and some within the last day or two have been discovered stealing for food the sea weed which had been carried out to the fields as manure for potatoes.

## RELIEF OF DISTRESS AND A MISMANAGED FUND

The degree of wretchedness existing among the lower classes, almost exceeds belief. In every direction whole plots of ground remain unoccupied for want of potatoes,wherewith to plant them. Several families have subsisted for days upon boiled water-cresses, without tasting oatmeal or a potato. In part of one district, 360 resident families,containing 1592 individuals, have been discovered, whose circumstances demand assistance. Some persons, it is believed, have died from absolute want. Already the number of patients in our Fever Hospital is nearly doubled; and disease, the invariable attendant of extreme poverty, is daily spreading. In the suburbs of the Town alone, between 3000 and 4000 objects crave relief, who are alike destitute of the necessaries of life and the means of procuring them."

*From Col. Perceval, Temple House,*
*dated 6th June,* 1822.

"No later than yesterday, I heard of one unfortunate family that had not had any provisions for the last fortnight or three weeks and principally subsisted on herbs. The family consisted of the father, mother, seven young daughters, (and the mother daily expecting to be confined again), and a niece. They were respectable Protestants and had been ashamed to make their distress known. I gave them a barrel (80 stone) of potatoes, and a hundred weight of oaten meal. The father, who came to take home the provisions, was ordered his dinner in my house, and upon getting food he fainted three times. He said some of his children were in convulsions for want of food, and the whole family upon being relieved of hunger were seized with illness, and are now keeping their bed (if a bed it can be called.) Many, many instances of similar distress exist."

*From Owen Wynne, Esq M. P. and Chairman of the Committee*
*for the Town of Sligo,*
*1st July, 1822.*

"Notwithstanding our exertions, want and wretchedness continue to increase around us. Members of the Committee as they pass along the streets are followed by crowds of hungry creatures, whose appearance attests the urgency of their distress, but to whom we are unable to give

## RELIEF OF DISTRESS AND A MISMANAGED FUND

assistance. To-day a young woman fainted through hunger. Members of the local Committee feared deception, and as is always done, they entered into a strict investigation of the circumstances. It appeared that she was the eldest of ten children, all dependent on the exertions of their once comfortable, but now destitute parents. The mother had obtained a ticket for purchasing provisions at reduced prices, in order to do which, having disposed of every article of furniture, and parted with the shoes from off her feet, she had taken the ring from her finger, which she had worn for twenty-two years as the sign of marriage union and fidelity, and sold it for tenpence! We regret to state, that the number of patients in our Fever Hospital is doubled, while dysentery and cholera morbus are prevailing to an alarming extent among the poor, which the Dispensary and Fever Hospital physicians attribute to the destitute condition of our population."

*From Charles King O"Hara, Esq. Nymphsfield,*
*17th June, 1822*

"The many cases of deepest distress are only discovered by visiting their houses, where families, heretofore in affluence, have been found sinking in silence to the grave, anxious to conceal their wants even from their nearest neighbours. I am happy to observe, that not a single instance has occurred of riot, theft, or even complaint. The poor people are most grateful for the exertions made in their behalf, and we must ever acknowledge the unparalleled benevolence of the sister kingdom with the deepest sense of gratitude."

\*      \*      \*      \*      \*      \*

Arising from the great distress experienced in Ireland, and Connacht in particular, in 1822, a London-based Committee, known as the *"Committee for the Relief of the Distressed Districts in Ireland"* was formed at a meeting in the *City of London Tavern* on May 7th of that year. A large sum of money was subscribed by the benevolent citizens of the Metropolis and elsewhere in England, and also by the nobility and gentry of Ireland, towards the relief of the numerous poor. County Sligo benefited to the tune of £16,000 and this was expended as follows:

## RELIEF OF DISTRESS AND A MISMANAGED FUND

| | | |
|---|---|---|
| Remittances | . . . . . . . . . . . . . . . . . . . . . | £9, 055 |
| Provisions | . . . . . . . . . . . . . . . . . . . . . | 4, 056 |

Grants for encouragement of:

| | | |
|---|---|---|
| Local industries | . . . . . . . . . . . . . . . . . . . . . | £3, 200 |
| Seed potatoes | . . . . . . . . . . . . . . . . . . . . . | 590 |

In addition, a sum of £2,095 was raised locally. The distress continued to the end of summer, when an abundant harvest followed. As the charitable relief was no longer necessary, the London-based Committee closed their accounts, leaving a large credit surplus on their hands. After some deliberation it was decided that the balance should be divided and lent to the localities in the west of Ireland requiring it most, at a low interest. A sum of £3,870 was sent to Sligo, with instructions that it was to be lent out under the directions of a paid secretary, acting under a local Committee and Trustees specially appointed to supervise the faithful discharge of the Fund.

A Loan Office, located in Stephen Street, was successfully operated throughout the 1820's and 1830's under the supervision of Henry Brett and James Noble, in turn. However, by 1845 it was discovered that all was not well - the accounts were in a state of confusion. There were allegations of funds having been misappropriated. It appears that monies from the Fund were lent,at excessively high rates of interest, to unauthorised borrowers and often without adequate security. On becoming aware of the situation, the Trustees called in an accountant from the Provincial Bank to examine the records and report accordingly. In the course of the inspection many inaccuracies were discovered, but worse still, a sum in excess of £500 could not be accounted for. On receipt of this information two of the Trustees, William Faussett[2] and Sir William Parke,[3] took the matter up with Edmund Homan[4] the then Secretary and Supervisor at the Loan Office, and demanded an explanation.

Failing to get a satisfactory response, an emergency meeting of the Trustees was convened at which Parke moved the following Resolution: *"That Mr. Homan's salary be stopped until the deficit was made good."* A majority approved and it was acted upon without delay. A few months later in October 1845, the Secretary of the London Committee arrived in Sligo to investigate the accounts of the Loan Fund and ascertain

## RELIEF OF DISTRESS AND A MISMANAGED FUND

how far the intentions of his Committee were carried out in providing relief for the industrious poor of Sligo. During his sojourn here, he attended a meeting of the local Trustees at which Parke moved a Resolution dismissing Homan from his post. Surprisingly, he failed to get a seconder. There the matter was allowed to rest for the time being, leaving the local Trustees to sort the matter out to their own satisfaction.

Some weeks later at the Ballymote Quarter Sessions, Edmund Homan was one of two candidates seeking the post of Barony Constable of Carbury. When nominations were being considered William Parke successfully opposed Homan's appointment on the grounds that he had proved himself incompetent in the performance of the duties attached to the Loan Office. Homan took offence at the charge levelled against him in public, and was so enraged that he followed Parke into the public street and abused him "in a most violent manner."[5] He also threatened him with assault. But the brave Sir William did not take too kindly to such intimidation and sought to redress the situation by swearing informations against his antagonist. Homan retaliated by bringing an action for slander and sought £1,000 in damages.

The case, which came before the Sligo Assizes in February, 1846, aroused widespread interest locally. Several witnesses were examined in support of the plaintiff but such was the weight of evidence against Homan regarding his mismanagement of the Loan Fund that the Jury took very little time in reaching a verdict, namely, that Sir William Parke, as Trustee, did not act under the influence of vindictive feelings towards, or speak maliciously of, Mr Homan in protecting the interests of the Charitable Loan Fund. The presiding Judge, Baron Richards, awarded costs to the Defendant.[6]

Mindful of the successful outcome of the legal confrontation, Parke remained firm in his opposition to Homan's appointment to public office. Two years later, in April, 1849, at a meeting of the Magistrates of the County, Sir William, described as "a plain, open spoken, honest man ", resisted the appointment of Edmund Homan as High Constable of Carbury for a second time. He repeated the grounds for his objection, adding that Homan had made no effort to make good the deficit, as he had promised. [7]

## RELIEF OF DISTRESS AND A MISMANAGED FUND

The Sligo Reproductive Fund was terminated in March, 1847, by order of the London based Committee for the Relief of the Distressed Districts, and the balance of the funds transmitted to the Bank of Messrs La Touche & Co, to finance the purchase of seed oats for struggling farmers in times of scarcity, Thus ended, on an inglorious note, the transactions of the Sligo Loan Fund "presenting  a rather sombre appearance - confusion and mismanagement within and certainly neither plaudits nor approbation from without. "[8]


### *Notes & References* :

(1) *"Report of the Committee for the Relief of Distressed Districts"*.  London.  1823.

(2) William Fausett of *Willsboro House*, Provost of Sligo for most years between 1819 and 1842;  Deputy Sheriff of  the County, 1834 and Member of the Reformed Corporation, 1842.  At the time of his death in July, 1847, he was the oldest resident Magistrate in the County.

(3) Sir William Parke (1779 - 1851), the eldest son of Roger Parke of *Dunally House*, had a distinguished career in the Army, before he retired in 1819 with the rank of Lieutenant-Colonel.  High Sheriff of County Sligo 1820 and 1838;  Grand Juror and Magistrate.  A prominent member of the

Liberal Party, he was knighted by Earl Mulgrave, the Lord Lieutenant, in August, 1836.  He died in September, 1851 and is buried in Drumcliffe churchyard.

(4) Edmund Homan of Colga was at times a Tithe Commissioner and Collector of Co. Cess. Despite the blemish to his character arising from the mismanagement of the Loan Fund and the objections of William Parke, he eventually succeeded in being appointed Barony Constable of Upper Carbury in 1851.  He died in November, 1882, aged 80 years.

| | | |
|---|---|---|
| (5) | *"Sligo Champion"* | 28 - 3 - 1846 |
| (6) | ibid. | Opus cit. |
| (7) | ibid. | 28 - 4 - 1849 |
| (8) | ibid. | 3 - 4 - 1847 |

# Blowing Sands

In the closing years of the 18th century and the opening decades of the 19th, the sand was in motion along the entire coastline from the entrance to Ballisodare Bay northwards to the county boundary at Bunduff. As early as 1793 there was an instance of a tenant on the Palmerston estate at Mullaghmore being allowed a rebate of £20 on his rent for what was described as "encroachment made by the blowing sands"[1] However, it was not until twenty years later that the inundation became a major problem over the said coastal area, affecting the Nicholson and Walker estates in the Parish of Killaspugbrone, and the Gore-Booth, Gethin, Bishop of Elphin and Palmerston properties in the parishes of Drumcliffe and Ahamlish. As the situation worsened, the unfortunate tenants had few options: either retreat before the advancing sands, or cling on, where at all possible, to their wretched cabins as long as the roofs withstood the added weight-load.

In the 1830's, some 500 acres were inundated to a depth of up to ten feet. By 1844, 700 acres of the Ecclesiastical Commission's property and 500 acres belonging to other proprietors, were covered. The residents of the townland of Ballintemple were particularly badly hit. Formerly, they had paid county cess on 105 acres but by 1836 only 5 acres were taxable. Their plight was matched by the situation faced by a group of forty families in the townland of Ballymuldorry who, although their cottages were almost covered in sand, were unwilling to move to the more exposed inland areas. Across Sligo Bay, at Strandhill, a different approach was adopted. The inhabitants of the townlands of Larass, Killaspugbrone and Carrowbunnaun retreated to higher ground towards the foot of Knocknarea and well clear of the encroaching sand. By the mid 1830's the ruins of Killaspugbrone Church were almost buried while 400 acres in the immediate neighbourhood were covered by sand. [2]

The strange phenomenon of blowing or drifting sand, though by no means peculiar to County Sligo, [3] attracted widespread attention. In Lewis's *"Topographical Dictionary"* we read that the blowing sands extended northwards from the village of Knocklane and covered an area of about four square miles. "They have already covered a great tract of good land and about one hundred and fifty cabins and are constantly in motion, giving a dreary and desolate appearance to the countryside. The ruins of Ardtarmon Castle are deeply buried in the sands.....".[4] A year later, in 1836, the Reverend Charles Clarke described the scene thus: *"The drifting sands are making dreadful inroads on the cultivated lands of the Board of Guardians. To the north of Lissadell the townlands of Ballineden and Ballintemple, belonging to the bishopric of Elphin, and those of Ballymuldorry and part of Ardtarmon, the property of Sir Robert Gore-Booth, within the last few years have been entirely covered to a depth varying from one to ten feet.... A more desolate scene cannot well be imagined."* He then went on to state that there were 64 families at Ballintemple and their only source of livelihood was fishing, as little or no land was available to them for tillage. [5]

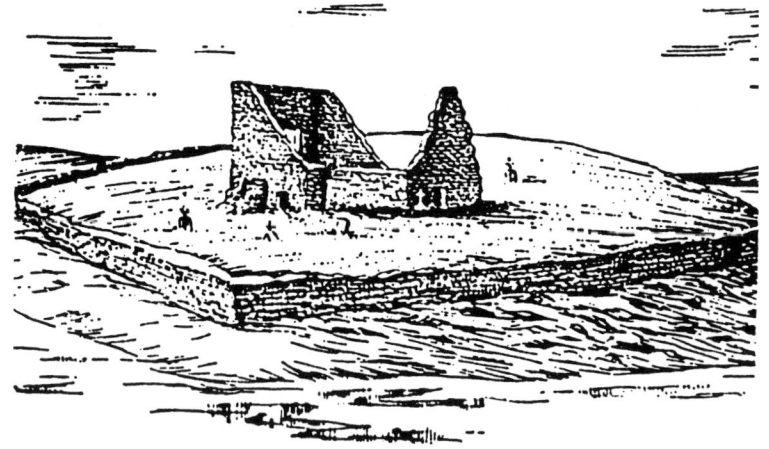

Ruins of Killaspugbrone Church which were almost buried by the sands.

Five years later in 1841, a *"Sligo Champion"* correspondent visited the area and reported as follows:-

*"There is a part of the Lissadell estate, now called the 'sand' - and very properly so-called, as 800 acres of it is nothing more than a sandbank; yet, a few years ago, this area was one of the most flourishing in the County and the soil could not be surpassed for richness and fertility. That situation has now been changed to one of utter desolation in consequence of the Western winds which have drifted the sands over a large extent of this countryside. In former*

BLOWING SANDS

*times it was studded with comfortable farm houses, inhabited by a respectable tenantry; the houses are still there, still inhabited but under far different circumstances. The sand has gradually increased to such a height that most of the miserable occupiers can only enter their cheerless dwellings by the chimnies. This may appear incredible, but, nevertheless, it is a fact......"* [6]

In 1843, James Fraser, a seasoned traveller, described the situation in the vicinity of Raughly thus:-

*"Adjoining Raughly the devastating effects of the drifting sea sand along the flat shore is seen to a fearful extent. There are few more desolate scenes in our island than that which the once fertile plains now present. It requires no stretch of the imagination to describe what may have been the appearance of this place; the remains of many houses can still be traced and, till lately, at least a hundred inhabited huts, nearly overwhelmed, presented more the appearance of the dens of wild animals than the habitation of human beings. The fragments of the ancient church, with the taller of the rude tombs, are still seen peeping over the accumulating sand; the ruins of Ardtarmon Castle, the former seat of the ancestors of Sir Robert Gore-Booth, Bart., the present possessor, still preside over the desolate scene."* [7]

Another visitor, Thomas C. Foster, the *"Times"* Special Correspondent, also reported on the scene that same year:

*"On the coast of Sligo, near the bay, large districts of country and some of the finest lands of the County have been destroyed by the drifting sea-sand. The sand blows with the north-west wind from Raughly Point and from Knocklane Hill to the neighbourhood of Ballymuldorry. Upwards of 1,000 acres of arable land have in this manner been covered with sand. About 100 acres of land have thus been destroyed by the sand from Knocklane Hill during the last two years. The cottages of the small farmers are often covered up with sand, and they are obliged to shovel it away to creep down to the doorways. They are frequently obliged to shovel the sand from the thatch of their house, to prevent its weight breaking through the roof....."* [8]

An even more graphic description was penned by an anonymous scribe:

*"In 1845, being requested by a Constable to take the depositions of a man (supposed to be dying) who had been badly beaten, we almost waded through this wilderness, saw no house, and were wondering how much farther we had to go, when suddenly the Constable stopped opposite to what appeared to be a thatched potato-pit, nearly covered in sand. 'This is the house' said he, 'the ladder is on*

## BLOWING SANDS

*the other side'. We went round, saw an opening in the thatch, and the end of a ladder protruding; by this means we descended, and dimly descried the poor man and his family, by means of light given by the hole in the roof, and by the chimney. His recovery was slow, and when, able to be moved, he was at once carried off to his neighbours in the adjoining townland, as by that time the sand had completely covered the roof of his former dwelling."* [9]

The sandhills from Streedagh to Mullaghmore were also in motion and the devastation was nearly as great. Lord Palmerston's estate at Mullaghmore included the most northerly extent of the sand blow and it was here the drift was at last checked. In 1822 Palmerston planted some 200 acres under sand with bent (*'arundo arenaria'*) at a cost of approximately £5 an acre. It was very much a trial and error exercise. At first, the bent was planted in rows but this proved ineffective as the wind blowing in one direction, cleared the sand from the spaces between the plants. To overcome this defect the bent was subsequently planted in staggered rows so that gaps in one row were covered by plants in the next row. This approach appears to have provided sufficient cover whilst at the same time trapping the sand effectively. In all, he planted in the region of 1,000 acres with bent in line with the sea-shore, and this, in time, finally arrested the blowing movement of the sand. Fine grass gradually grew under the bent and developed into good pasture. In some instances, Palmerston planted unprepared ground, with *'Pinus Martima'* and this resulted in the formation of a shelter belt, on the leeward side, of 300 trees an acre.

The Commissioners for Waste Lands visited the area in the mid 1840's to inspect the situation for themselves and were highly impressed by the success that had crowned the judicious management of the experiment:-

*"The surface, exposed to all the fury of the western gales, has been rendered firm on the low sandhills, which are gradually becoming covered with clover and trefoil, while the seedling 'pinus martima', springing up in the sand among the bent, afford a fair promise that they may serve the same good purpose as in the sandy plains near Bordeaux...... It might have been expected that this success would have induced all others in the neighbourhood to adopt a similar course; but, though we did not visit the scene of desolation described by Mr. Clarke, we saw enough from the mail-coach road to convince us that much of that district was still abandoned to the sand though apparently less exposed*

## BLOWING SANDS

*than the wild headland of Mullaghmore.....*"

Over the following years the example set by Palmerston was followed by other landed proprietors in the parish of Drumcliffe and in the Coolera peninsula.[10] The surface was gradually coated over and, in due course, the sand covered wastes became valuable grazing land for sheep and young stock and also for the rearing of rabbits. The experiment was carried out with equal success at Bowmore and the 'Greenlands' at Rosses Point by Messrs Barber and Yeats, and in the townland of Killaspugbrone by the Walkers of *Rathcarrick House,* and at Carrowdough by Samuel Barrett of Culleenamore.

Close on forty years later, in 1881, Thomas C. Foster, the *"Times"* correspondent, paid a return visit and described the changes effected on the Gethin estate:-

*"We drove across the flats and swamps of Johnsport towards Knocklane, which I last saw in 1843. Then, there was scarcely a bit of grass on the 600 acres, the houses being buried several feet in the sands. A lake of some 20 acres was also covered. But how things have changed! There are now no sands to be seen but the richest grass, with herds of cattle and sheep grazing. During the painstaking reclamation works, the lake was drained and a quantity of bent was planted and grass seeds sown which have not only checked but completely reversed the progress of the sands...."* [11]

Another instance of the efficacy of planting bent was cited by Wood-Martin:-

*"In the neighbourhood of Raughly (on the south-west shore), about a mile of shingle, which formed a barrier against the mighty Atlantic waves, was gradually, but irresistibly, driven back at the regular rate of a foot each year. One very stormy night a breach was effected by the ocean and the tide ran inland amongst the sandhills for a considerable distance, scattering the shingle rampart right and left. The remedy tried was planting along the beach, bent, which was carefully attended to, and renewed when necessary. Thus the sandhills were bound together and increase in solidity year by year. They now form an effectual rampart against the breakers".* [12]

The enterprising efforts of Lord Palmerston and the other landlords well over a century ago not only succeeded in halting the mass movement of sand, which was attributed to over the cultivation of areas close to the seashore, but also stabilised the effected area to such an extent that there has been no re-occurrence of the problem.[13]

# BLOWING SANDS

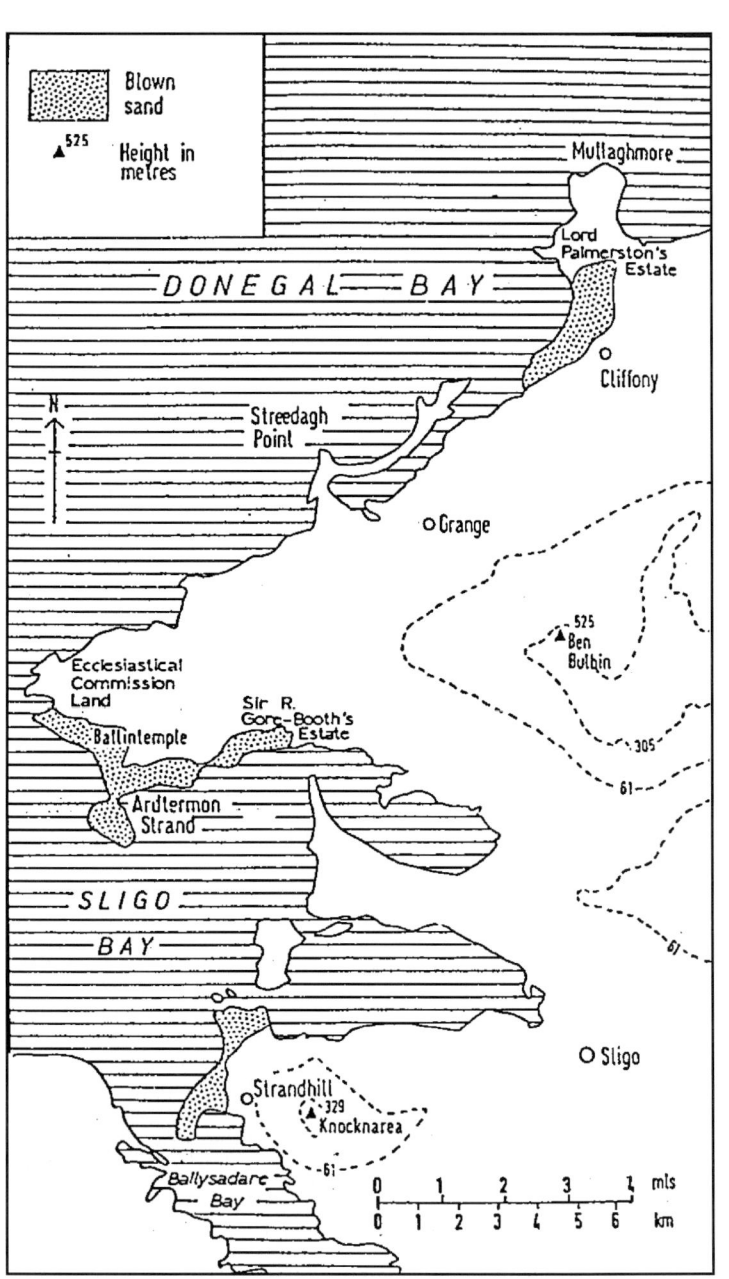

# BLOWING SANDS

## Notes & References:

(1) Palmerston Rentals, 1788 - '96.

(2) Lewis, S. *"Topographical Dictionary of Ireland"*. London, 1837.

(3) The Belmullet area of Mayo and the district of Rosapenna in Donegal were similarly affected.

(4) Lewis , S. *opus cit.*

In his evidence before the Devon Commission (1844-45) Francis Barber of Rahelly stated that up to 2,000 acres in the vicinity of Knocklane were covered by drifting sand, 700 of which were covered in his lifetime.

(5) Poor Law Inquiry, 1836. Appendix F.

(6) *"Sligo Champion"*                    20 -1 -1841

(7) Fraser, James *"Handbook for Travellers in Ireland"*. London, 1844.

(8) Foster, Thomas C. *"Letters on the Conditions of the People of Ireland"*. London, 1846.

(9) Wood-Martin, W.G. *"History of Sligo"* .   Vol.3 p. 282

(10) By 1854 some 300 acres had been planted on the Gore-Booth estate.

(11) *"Times"* March, 1881.

(12) Wood-Martin, W.G. *"History of Sligo"* Vol. 3. pp. 282-3

(13) For further details on tree and bent planting on the former Palmerston estate in the Parish of Ahamlish -
**SEE:** McGowan, J. *"In the Shadow of Benbulben"*. Sligo. 1993. pp. 168 - 9.

Ardtarmon Castle

# Brewing and Distilling

For over a century brewing in Sligo afforded an ample scope for enterprise. As far back as 1770 Thomas Holmes was conducting a brewery at Farmhill in the townland of Rathedmond. He was subsequently joined in the business by the brothers, John and Charles Anderson. In March, 1823, the local *"Journal"* carried an advertisement informing the public that the Brewery was producing "a plain wholesome ale" and invited the friends and customers of the late Proprietor [1] to continue supporting their product. By the mid 1820's the Andersons had terminated their association with Farmhill and established their own brewery in Ratcliffe Street. Meanwhile, the old establishment had been taken over by Richard Anderson, jun., who, in April, 1829, announced that he was brewing an ale "of superior quality" and had employed an experienced London brewer. A week later Messrs. Anderson & Co. stated that they had no connection with the brewery at Farmhill, although it would appear that they (the Andersons) were all members of the same extended family. A decade later Richard Anderson had also vacated Farmhill and transferred his business to 14 Knox's Street. The old brewery at Farmhill, which had fallen into a dilapidated state, collapsed in a heap of rubble on the night of the *'Big Wind'* in January, 1839.

Brewing in early 19th century Sligo was not confined to the western suburbs. One Dunbar Jameson operated a small brewery at Buckley's Ford, convenient to the entrance-gate to Doorly Park at the Riverside. In 1822, following Jameson's death, the concern was taken over by John Smyth, Grocer and Wine Merchant of Market Street, where he commenced the production of ales, beer and porter "free from adulteration of any sort".

Throughout the 1820's and into the following decade, there were five breweries operating in Sligo, namely, Smyth's of Buckley's Ford; Anderson & Co., Ratcliffe Street; Richard Anderson of Farmhill and subsequently of Knox's Street; Martin Madden & Co., Ratcliffe Street, and Cochran and Davys in Bridge Street. Anderson & Co., after a short period in Ratcliffe Street, moved to larger premises at Water Lane, where Moses Baird had operated a brewery for a short time prior to

## BREWING AND DISTILLING

### Porter, Ale and Beer
# BREWERY
## JOHN SMYTH

RESPECTFULLY informs his friends and the Public, that having taken the Brewery at Buckleysford (lately held by Mr. Dunbar Jameson) he has commenced the Manufacture of PORTER, ALE and BEER, which he engages to be produced from the very best Materials, and free from adulteration of any sort. He therefore presumes to hope that upon fair trial his Brewery may be found worthy of a portion of public favour.

*Sligo. April 2nd, 1822*

### FARMHILL BREWERY.
### 1829

RICHARD ANDERSON, jun. begs leave to now acquaint the Public and his Friends, that he is Brewing ALE of a very superior sort, and respectfully solicits a trial, that proof may be made of the quality; having engaged a very experienced Brewer who conducted one of the most respectable Establishments in London, he will be enabled to sell as cheap, and trusts he will give as much satisfaction as any other persons in the trade, to those who honor him with their custom.

*Sligo. April 23, 1829.*

Advertisements in *"Sligo Journal"*

## BREWING AND DISTILLING

1822. At their new location the Andersons traded successfully for a decade and a half before finally transferring the business to Bridge Street. Close-by, in what was subsequently known as Blackwood's Yard, Martin Madden, described as *'Corn ,Wine and Spirit Merchant, Brewer and Tabacco Manufacturer of 5, Ratcliffe Street'*, operated a brewery for four decades or so before ceasing operations in the early 1850's.

In 1828 James Cochran, a local merchant, leased a number of plots off Bridge Street, the largest of which had been held by the Commissioners of Barracks in Ireland and housed the *Horse Barracks*, embracing an area in excess of one acre and extending from The Mall to the *Meat Shambles* at the New Bridge. Three years later, in 1831, John Cochran, eldest son of the aforementioned James, formed a partnership with Vernon Davys of *Rosehill House* and built a brewery and malt stores in the form of a large quadrangle on the site at a cost of £3,000. The concern, known as the *Lough Gill Brewery* was operated by Davys, a brewer by profession, for a decade but closed in 1842 when he was declared a bankrupt.

After being vacant for a number of years the complex was acquired by Messrs. Anderson & Company, who moved from their Water Lane premises. The principal of the firm, John Anderson, spared no expense in enlarging and modernising the Bridge Street brewery. Lofty buildings of solid limestone, containing an extensive kiln, a malting store and basement cellars quickly made their appearance, rendering it one of the most complete establishments of its kind to be found in any provincial centre. In order to ensure the purity of the product and avoid any contamination with sewerage, fresh waters from the lake were piped directly to an extensive storage tank or cistern at the brewery. The waters of Lough Gill, it was asserted, produced a blend of ale and porter that could not be surpassed! Experienced brewers were employed to supervise the operation and their sparkling ales quickly commanded a big trade, outdistancing the local rivals, Messrs. Madden and Richard Anderson, and eventually hastening their collapse.

*"From the banks of Lough Erne to the Plains of Boyle, and from the sea to the lordly Shannon as it flows from its source, no other ale was drank but Anderson's ale, made in the Lough Gill Brewery. Not only were the licensed houses supplied with it, but accounts were opened with the proprietors of all the*

BREWING AND DISTILLING

*lordly mansions scattered throughout Sligo, Mayo, Roscommon and Leitrim. Of the time we speak of, ale on draught was the article principally consumed throughout Connacht, and the population found in the ale manufactured in the Lough Gill Brewery a wholesome pleasant liquor which quenched the thirst and proved an excellent aid to digestion. Indeed, Englishmen who came to Ireland for business or pleasure, were heard to say that the ales turned out by the Brewery were fully equal to that produced in the land of their birth".* [2]

---

## NOTICE.

WE beg leave to return our sincere thanks to the Gentlemen and our numerous friends in town and country, who have always favored us with their custom ; and intimate that we have taken those extensive Concerns known as the LOUGH GILL BREW-ERY, which we are at present fitting up, and are now removing all the Coppers, Brewing Utensils, &c., from the Premises in Water Lane. We are confident we will furnish excellent drink, and therefore hope for a continuance of that patronage we have so long enjoyed.

### ANDERSON & CO.,
BREWERS.

Sligo, 9th February, 1849.

---

In the third quarter of the last century public taste with regard to malted drinks became somewhat changed. Creamy porter, both draught and bottled, came into favour alongside the established ales. Charles Anderson, who headed the firm at that period, was both a far-seeing businessman and an eminent brewer. He realised that if the products of the Brewery were to retain their honoured place under the changed circumstances of the time, he had little option but avail of new technology. Eminent contractors, brought over from England, introduced new and improved methods of producing malt and hops and converting it into porter and ale of superior quality. *Lough Gill* ales and porter became the preferred choice of the drinking public over a wide area and outsold rival Dublin brands in many outlets. Porter and ale from the Sligo brewery was also exported in large quantities. [3] In March, 1883, Messrs. Anderson & Co. published details of an analysis

BREWING AND DISTILLING

of a sample of their porter, made by Dr. C.A. Cameron, Professor of Chemistry in the Royal College of Surgeons, which indicated that this particular product of the Sligo brewery was of first class quality [4]

When Charles Anderson retired from business in 1883, he had laid the foundation of a greatly expanding business in ale and porter. However, his successors in title were inexperienced in the brewing business and failed to capitalise on their inheritance. In the circumstances, the Bank of Ireland, who was owed £2,500, took legal proceedings and forced the sale of the entire Bridge Street property, including the *Lough Gill Brewery* and the *Bridge House.* It was purchased in October, 1893, from Robert Anderson, nephew of the previous owner, by Edward Foley, a local Wine and Spirit merchant.

The new owner set to work with energy and enthusiasm and in a short space of time the products of the *Lough Gill Brewery* were back in

---

*Royal College of Surgeons.*
*Dublin.*
*March 21st. 1883.*

*I have examined a specimen of Porter submitted to me for that purpose by Messrs. Anderson & Co., Sligo, and the following are the results at which I have arrived :-*

*100 parts contain:*

| | |
|---|---|
| *Water* ........................................... | *85.41* |
| *Alcohol* ........................................... | *6.46* |
| *Sugar, Dextrase Compound & Glycerine...........* | *0.92* |
| *Albuminoids* ........................................... | *0.40* |
| *Acetic Acids* ........................................... | *0.19* |
| *Oily, Resinous & Bitter Principles* ................... | *0.40* |
| *Mineral Matter (Ash)* .................................... | *0.22* |
| | *100.00* |

*This is an exceedingly good specimen of Porter; it is, indeed, above the average quality for that article, containing 8% of Extract and 6% aromstic and sufficiently bitter and sweet, and, without being acid, it has not that disagreeable liquoric flavour so common in porter.*

*Charles A. Cameron*

# BREWING AND DISTILLING

Contemporary sketch of the Lough Gill Brewery

favour with the public. Phoenix-like the turn-out was doubled and the scene was a hive of industry providing much needed employment. Additional buildings were erected and new machinery installed. Vincent Nightingale, a brewer of considerable qualifications, was employed to direct and supervise the operation. When fully operational the brewery could boast of an extensive coopering shop where all the casks used in the Brewery were made and repaired; well -horsed drays and capable draymen were employed to make deliveries of porter and ale to customers near and far, and an extensive bottling department added. The mineral water trade was also housed here and bottles of soda water, lemonade, etc. embossed with the firm's name, were a common sight on shelves in outlets over a wide area. At the close of the 19th century the brewery and malting premises were the most extensive outside of Dublin and Cork, covering close on two acres and producing upwards of 60 barrels a day.

Foley's *Double Crown Stout* enjoyed a growing reputation into the present century.[5] However, in the post World War 1 era, the *Lough Gill Brewery* faced growing competition from outside, notably from the products of Messrs. Arthur Guinness, and was eventually forced out of business. Thereafter, until the premises closed in the mid 1960's, Messrs. Foley continued with the manufacture of minerals and the retailing of bottled ales and beers.[6]

81

BREWING AND DISTILLING

*Notes & References:*

(1)  Thomas Holmes, who was also Linen Inspector for Sligo, died at *Farmhill* in June, 1818.

(2)  *"Sligo Champion"*                    20-9-1899

(3)  ibid                                           opus cit

(4)  *"Sligo Independent"*              31-3-1883

(5)  *Kilgannon's Almanac, 1909.*

(6)  The Rehabilitation Institute now occupies the former Brewery premises.


# Martin's Distillery:

The earliest reference to a distillery in Sligo dates from 1739. In that year John De Butts was credited with producing great quantities of *'uisce beatha'* in what was described as "one of the largest and best conveniences in Ireland" [1] A decade later, in 1749, there were two in production, De Butts' concern and another operated by Thomas Lindsay.[2] A firm, trading as Alexander Stewart & Co, announced in January, 1805, that their Sligo Distillery had commenced operating in Castle Street. Indications are that this undertaking had a short existence, most likely because of the competition it faced from the proliferation of 'illicit' distillers in the County at that time.

The fourth and most recent distillery of which we have knowledge was that established by Abraham Martin, an enterprising merchant of early 19th century Sligo. In or about the year 1815 he built a distillery at the Riverside on a site described in contemporary records as the 'Island in the River'. In evidence before a Select Committee in 1816 it was stated that the Sligo Distillery was "a very considerable undertaking, providing a considerable quantity of the spirits consumed locally". [3] Over the following two decades *Martin's Distillery,* also known as the *Sligo Distillery,* enjoyed much success and its product achieved a notoriety all its own. This was particularly so after the visit of George 1V. to Ireland in 1821. On that occasion samples of Martin's brew were presented to the King and his *entourage,* and his Majesty, who was an experienced and first-rate judge of strong drinks, commended

82

## BREWING AND DISTILLING

the beverage so warmly, that his lieges made it a point of loyalty to take to deep potations - the result being that the Sligo distillery was hardly able to supply the demand which arose in Dublin - though the high-road between Sligo and the capital was constantly traversed with drays laden with Martin's Whiskey. In 1825 a Spirit and Wine Warehouse, under the management of Francis Allingham, was opened in Knox's Street for the sale of Martin's malt spirits, "pure and unadulterated", as received from the Distillery. [4]

The Distillery, Riverside c. 1870

Four years later, in 1829 distillation by steam was introduced, a process capable of distilling 10,000 gallons of low wine in twenty-four hours. News of this advancement in technology made headlines in the local Press who published the following Declaration, signed by Martin:-

*"I do hereby certify that I have in operation in my Distillery in this Town a Low Wine Still, the invention of Mr. William Morrissey, which is now in full work to my entire satisfaction. This Still is on the principle of continued distillation, and is capable of distilling 10,000 gallons of Low Wine in 24 hours, consuming not more than three tons of coals, and as the distillation is performed by means of steam, the Whiskey produced is remarkably fine flavoured. By this process no separation of Low Wines is necessary - the strong and the weak being mixed, and expeditiously converted into spirits of any required strength in one operation, the feints remaining not exceeding, in general, the quantity equal to 25 or 30 gallons of proof Spirits. Given under my hand at Sligo, this 11th day of December, 1829."*

*Abraham Martin.*

# BREWING AND DISTILLING

The Lough Gill Brewery c. 1870 (above) and
(below) Anderson's Old Brewery, Water Lane, recently demolished.

BREWING AND DISTILLING

In 1834 Abraham Martin leased, for a term of three lives, "the buildings, offices and stores, known as *The Sligo Distillery*, together with the stills and other machinery used for the purpose of distillation", to his son, Gregory Cuffe Martin, who had formed a partnership with Martin Madden, the aforementioned Radcliffe Street brewer. The annual rent was £400 and the lessors were bound by a number of clauses, namely -

* Not to interfere with or alter the watercourse;
* Not to interfere with the bed of the River which would in any way harm the fishery;
* Adjacent buildings could not be converted into Mills for the manufacturer of wheaten flour. [5]

The Distillery continued to operate successfully under the new management, employing a workforce of fifty or so, and producing 120,000 gallons of whiskey per annum.[6] In 1838 informations were filed by the Inspector of Excise against Messrs. Martin & Madden & Co. in relation to certain irregularities in the fermenting process and discrepancies in returns as to the quantities of spirits on hands on given dates in December, 1838. This resulted in a fine of £200 being imposed by the Court of Exchequer. Not long afterwards, in 1841, the partnership between Martin and Madden was dissolved and the concern closed. Following the accidental death of Gregory Cuffe Martin in August, 1844, the Distillery "capable of producing 7,000 gallons of spirits per period" was advertised for letting, together with an adjoining Corn Mill, Malt House and Stores. Messrs. J.& T. O'Donovan leased it for a period but following the death of Abraham Martin in November, 1853, the Distillery, described as "an extensive concern, with an abundant supply of water and containing five large brewing coppers, a steam boiler and a cast iron mash tun", was offered for sale "or letting for a long lease".

The former Distillery and adjoining premises remained vacant until leased in 1857 by the Collooney miller, Alexander Sim, jun. In 1871 the entire property consisting of five roods, was offered for sale in the Landed Estates Court and acquired by Messrs Middleton & Pollexfen, subsequently Messrs W. & T.G. Pollexfen & Co. Ltd., and

# BREWING AND DISTILLING

The Distillery and Mills, Riverside, 1996.

BREWING AND DISTILLING

already in their possession on a week to week tenure. In 1943 the property passed to Alfred Carroll's *North West Trading and Cold Storage Co. Ltd.* After a succession of owners the distillery and adjoining properties were acquired in 1997 by Millbrook Construction Ltd., who are currently in the process of building an extensive apartment block and hotel on the site.

***Notes & References:***

(1)  Henry, Wm. *"Hints Towards a Natural and Topographical History of Sligo.....1739"* (unpublished).

(2)  *Elphin Diocesan Census, 1749* (Unpublished).

(3)  *Parliamentary Papers*, 1816-9-436.

(4)  O'Rorke, T. *"History of Sligo"* Vol.2. p. 526.

(5)  Registry of Deeds 1834 Bk 19. No. 15.

(6)  Lewis, S. *"Topographical Dictionary of Ireland"*, 1837.

---

# THE SLIGO BREWERY

The Proprietors spare neither expense nor trouble in producing

## DOUBLE AND SINGLE STOUTS

EQUAL TO ANY STOUT BREWED ELSEWHERE.

## Ask for FOLEY'S Double Stout,

MADE ON UP-TO-DATE PRINCIPLES with the BEST MATERIALS

---

# LAND TENURE before and after the Famine

## 1. Pre Famine:

The Devon Commission, whose function was to investigate land tenure and ascertain the causes of discontent in Ireland, was set up in November, 1843. By the time it had made its Report in April, 1845, it had recorded the testimony of over one thousand witnesses from all parts of the country, in addition to numerous written submissions. The Commissioners sat in Sligo on the 12th and 13th of July, 1844, and noted the evidence of the following witnesses:–

**George Beatty**, Farmer, Finnod, Dromore West; **John Brett**, Land Agent, Tubbercurry; **Andrew Baker**, Grazier and Farmer, Redhill, Gurteen; **Revd. Lewis Potter**, Rector of Dromard; **Lt. Col. Sir Wm. Parke**, Magistrate, D.L. Landed Proprietor, Dunally; **Francis Barber**, Farmer, Rahelly, Drumcliffe; **Martin Garrity**, Land Surveyor, Sligo; **Thomas Phibbs**, Grazier, Cloonamahon; **John Armstrong**, Landed Proprietor and Magistrate, Chaffpool; **William Clarke**, Land Surveyor, Calry; **Michael Gethin**, Attorney, Sligo; **Wm. Christian**, Miller and Farmer, Rathbraghan; **Edward Howard Verdon**, Newspaper Proprietor, Sligo; **James Simpson**, Farmer, Mt. Edward, Grange; **Sir Robert Gore-Booth,** Landed Proprietor, Lissadell and **John Moffett**, Solicitor and Landed Proprietor, Merville.

Charles King O'Hara , J.P., of *Annaghmore*, Landed Proprietor and Chairman of the Board of Guardians, was also interviewed at some length, and in the course of his evidence gave the following details concerning the state of agriculture, size of farms, level of rents and duration of leases:-

*"I am well acquainted with the lower half of the Barony of Leyney, comprising the Parishes of Killoran and Kilvarnet and the half-parish of Ballisodare, together with six townlands in the adjoining Parish of Achonry, also the townland of Cloonacurra in the adjoining Barony of Tirerill, containing in all 35,000 statute acres, of which 11,000 may be mountain, bog*

## LAND TENURE BEFORE AND AFTER THE FAMINE

*and water. The population is about 11,500, according to the 1831 census and I know it has not increased much since. There has been a great deal of emigration, and we have been diminishing our numbers. The district affords opportunities for extensive and renumerative improvements.*

*Of late, the state of agriculture has improved, particularly where leases have expired, by draining, fencing, planting, levelling, making farm roads, a better system of ploughing and general management, and the introduction of green crops in the last few years. There has been a good deal of turnip seed sown this year. General drainage has been effected by the landlords, who are now introducing furrow-draining. The rotation of crops is still principally potatoes and oats; in some cases the four-shift system has been introduced, though not perfectly established, it being very difficult to effect the proper application of the clover crop. The manures most used are stable dung, bog-mud, sea-weed, limestone gravel, and burning, where not prevented: lime and sea sand are occasionally used.*

*There are no large tillage farms in this district; there are a few of about 100 acres, held exclusively in grazing, in fattening cows and sheep, and in rearing young stock in general. Farms of all sizes are of a mixed character, partly grazing and part tillage; many of the larger holders break up yearly a portion of the farm in con-acre; potatoes and oats, three or four or five crops, according to the quality of the ground; and sometimes two crops of oats, and three of potatoes; that is , five successive years of tillage. They then lay down the land with grass seed, often without leaving it wasted, to recover a coat of natural grass or weeds, and pastured by light stock, until in some measure renovated, when it is again con-acred. With regard to size, there are in the district about fifteen farms of 100 acres; twenty exceeding 50; fifty exceeding 25; two hundred exceeding 10, and about 180 under ten – mostly labourers hold the latter class.*

*The rents are fixed by private contract, by proposal and by valuation, made sometimes by the landlord, his agent, sub-agent, or driver; sometimes by intelligent land-surveyors, or farmers; and it is generally an acreable sum, from £1.5s per statute acre. I have no land, except village gardens, set above 18s. per statute acre, which is nearly 30s. the Irish acre; when sublet, the rent is often much higher in this district. The letting valuation is on a par with the poor law valuation, but it may be right to explain that this was one of the first districts valued, and it was checked by myself, being the Chairman of the Board. I have myself set no land above the poor law valuation.*

*Tenants generally hold immediately under the proprietor; in old leases,*

## LAND TENURE BEFORE AND AFTER THE FAMINE

*sometimes under middlemen, rarely under the courts. The immediate tenants are in the best condition, and some under a fair middleman are very comfortable. These under the courts, I should say, are decidedly the worst; they are unsettled, uncertain in their tenure and often much harassed by receivers. The usual way is for some person to attend at the court and become the tenant for five years. There is generally a casual landlord who sets the land as dear as he can. The late settings in this district are mostly at will - the old ones are by lease, sometimes for three lives, or one life or thirty-one years, or one life and twenty-one years. In this district long leases have proved injurious to the conditions of the tenants and improvement to the land. The tenant having secured a long term, procrastinates, gets into lazy habits, neglects his business, alienates portions of his farm to meet his rent or engagements, or provide for his family; goes on con-acring and impoverishing until his land is exhausted and himself a pauper, or his land is covered with paupers - himself the greatest.*

*On the death of parents, children are sometimes apprenticed out; sometimes the ground is subdivided amongst them; sometimes the eldest son gets the ground; the others, the personal property; and often they are left alien on the farm of the eldest son, who is overloaded by incumbrance until the expiration of the lease. Labourers are often the sons of small farmers, sometimes occupiers of a house and garden only, and sometimes a cow's grass, held at will, and paid for by labour and shifting - meaning the industry of a wife weaving a little web of cloth. Sometimes they are suffered to erect a hut on a bog or waste, or reclaim it by potatoes, and then they are, sometimes, charged rent and sometimes removed; but these are cases of under-tenants and practiced against the wish of the landlord.*

*Con-acre prevails generally, and is most anxiously sought for by the lower orders, who urge much the setting of land for potato ground. The acreable rent varies from £10 to £5 the Irish acre, or, £6. 10s to £3. 10s the statute acre. Oat ground from £7 to £4 Irish, or, £3. 15s to £2. 10s a statute acre; and where the tenant finds manure, from £2, the Irish acre, or £1. 5s, the statute, to no charge. This is paid for by cash, the sale of part of the crop, by labour, or promissory notes, and recovered by process at the Quarter Sessions.*

*Employment is spring or harvest is easily procured, at from 1s to 8d. a day; at other times, much employment is afforded by the landlord's improvements. I do not begin my work on the farm till the 1st day of July, when the potatoes are covered, and from that to the 1st of October I may give 300 day's employment; that is the time they are most in want of work. Their turf is cut, and the potatoes*

LAND TENURE BEFORE AND AFTER THE FAMINE

*a second time are covered, and all things are growing, and they are idle. There are very few agrarian outrages in this district, and those arising mostly from ribbon and other combinations, and not from animosity to the landlord. The people are naturally peaceable and well disposed, anxious to cultivate the goodwill of their landlord and be advised by him."*

John Armstrong of *Chaffpool House,* in the course of his evidence stated:-

*"People on holdings of three or four acres support themselves by tilling the land; by labour or going to England. Many of them are glad to get a day's labour with the gentlemen of the County, or from some of the bigger farmers. At times during the year labour is scarce, and numbers go from this district to England to labour. Those who go to England are the smallest class of farmers, or their sons, and they continue to go to the same farmer, if they are men of good character. There is generally an undertaker who takes as many men as are wanted; he forms his party in Ireland, and takes a certain number over. Others go on speculation, but those who get employment upon some estates here do not go to England to work to the same extent. I can speak of my own experience, for I employ as many as I can, particularly those in arrear. I usually at the end of the half-year, when I find people not able to pay, make out some work and clear off arrears. Others do the same.*

*Those obliged to go to England bring home amounts varying from £3 to £5, with £3. the average. Some who go earlier in the season, for the hay harvest, bring home £5; those who go for the corn harvest will bring £3 or £4. Some may bring home a great deal more, but those persons attend both the hay harvest and the corn harvest. I can state that generally the persons going to England improve their condition much by it. Some few, who go and remain for years in that country, come back with a great deal of money . . ."*

LAND TENURE BEFORE AND AFTER THE FAMINE

# 2. Post Famine:

Shortly after the Land League came into being in the Autumn of 1879, the *"Times"* of London sent a Special Correspondent to Ireland to report on the state of the country, and especially on the Land Question. In the Spring of 1881 he visited Sligo and, in the course of the following weeks, wrote a number of articles on conditions in different parts of the County and on the Lissadell estate in particular:-

"Estates in Sligo present a proportion of absentees, who withdraw large rentals from the country, who spend little in developing their inheritance, and relegate their authority to agents more or less competent, sometimes non-resident. Hitherto, there has been small excuse for continuous absenteeism. The landlord, now with some reason, complains that the attractions of his estate are diminished; that he has no political power; and that his right of sport is interfered with, hunting is sometimes interdicted, his game is shot by a few refractory tenants and by poaching intruders, and shooting on moor and bog, formerly productive, is reduced in value. The tenantry, moreover, are less trustful, friendly, and pleasant to meet even if they are not positively evil-disposed. This disruption between landlord and tenant has, unfortunately, extended to the estates even of kindly resident proprietors, In the best districts of Sligo the farms range from 30 to 50 acres. There is much more pasture than tillage. The subsoil is generally limestone and gravel. Even where drained, unless this primary improvement is followed up by tillage, the land is prone to grow rushes, and the grass becomes rough and coarse.

Rents average about 20s. an acre, but lands are generally let according to the  head of cattle they will carry , and range from less than Griffith's valuation to 100 per cent, over it. Although not excessive and seldom raised except in the case of estates that have changed hands, they are probably as much as can be afforded under the prevailing non-recuperative style of farming. Changes of tenancy are not common. They only occur among the smaller improvident holders,  There are few evictions; tenant-right is not generally recognised; landlords have usually objected to it, on the plea that it swallows up the incomer's capital and costs the landlord a fancy figure

92

## LAND TENURE BEFORE AND AFTER THE FAMINE

if he desires to double up several holdings or take farms into his own hands.

Landlords lay out nothing in improvements; the buildings erected by tenants are of a limited, pristine description, rough, not always very durable, frequently placed in the wrong spot, and their imperfections sometimes conveniently concealed by a liberal dressing of limewash. Leases are decreasing, and are seldom asked for or given, except to the larger tenant ; but a few granted even since 1870 recognise a limited tenant-right. The Land Act of 1870 here as elsewhere, has certainly checked landlords' outlay, and has not proportionally increased tenants' improvements. It has not, as has sometimes been asserted, increased litigation, comparatively few appeals against exorbitant rents are brought under the cognizance of the County Court Judge.

Throughout Sligo there is a good deal of waste land, by some still estimated at 100,000 acres, but this includes the moors and bogs of the Ox Mountains, where a considerable elevation interferes with successful cultivation. The improvements on the mountain, undertaken upwards of 30 years ago by the Irish Waste Land Company, on the west of Lough Easky, I am told, have not generally proved remunerative. Reclamation, unless followed up by proper tillage, as already stated, rarely answers; the coarse grasses assert supremacy, and soft, boggy soils unless fertilised with phosphates and mineral salts, and firmed by clay, sand, or cultivation, shortly produce only poor, innutritive herbage. In Sligo,as in so many other counties, by draining, by more liberal cultivation, by more careful collection and husbanding of manure, greatly better returns may be obtained from the cleared bogs already reclaimed and from pastures now wet, sour, and neglected.

Sir Henry Gore-Booth, of Lissadell, on the sudden death of his father's agent, undertook the charge of the estates which he now owns, and managed them most successfully for ten years, inaugurating a very thorough system of accounts and book-keeping, which are sadly deficient on some Irish estates. Since his accession the the property in 1876, he has continued to direct the general management. Few owners or agents have such intimate knowledge of their tenantry, their holdings,or their necessities, The people have been wont to come to Sir Henry as their adviser and friend, as their arbiter in family feuds,

## LAND TENURE BEFORE AND AFTER THE FAMINE

Sir Henry Gore-Booth

and as their depository for wills and marriage settlements. He has a curious, carefully kept record of the troubles, disputes, and condition of his poor neighbours. In settling difficulties, his intervention has prevented much litigation, a pugnacious pastime in which even the poorer class of Irish are too fond of indulging. The estate at Lissadell, on the coast, six miles north-west of Sligo. and at Ballymote, 14 miles south of the Town, together measure 31,774 acres. Griffith's valuation is £16,774. the actual rental is £15,000, putting a reasonable valuation on the house and demesne, where the planting and arrangements made 40 years ago testify to the taste and judgment of the late Sir Robert Gore-Booth. His neighbours and tenants declare him to have been a model country gentleman, kindly-hearted and liberal, ever ready to aid and improve his people, most zealous and helpful during the famine years of 1846-8, when it is said he spent £40,000 in food and other assistance.

The present Baronet does not think that the Land Act of 1870 has been altogether a success. With the increased security conferred on the tenant, it enabled him to get more credit than was good for him; commodities not always needed or fitting were pressed on both man and wife; the necessity of payment seemed far deferred; and when bad times come other creditors were often more exacting than the landlord. The pauper tenant received handsome remuneration for being cleared out of his wretched hovel, his hopelessly small holding, his debts and difficulties. The better man, with a farm valued at more

## LAND TENURE BEFORE AND AFTER THE FAMINE

than £50 of annual rent, and who has probably expended thereon much more labour and capital, deserves recognition and some protection against disturbance. In some parts of the country the Act of 1870 has provoked disputes and litigation, sometimes increased by a certain class of lawyers; but no such annoyances have occurred in this part of Sligo. Frequent revaluations, or even the prospect of them, unsettle tenants, and check the little enterprise they might otherwise exert.

On the Lissadell estate there are 522 tenants. of which 110 pay less than £4 of annual rent, 352 range from £4 to £20, while 60 are at £20 and over. On the Ballymote estate there are 454 tenants, 112 renting at less than £4; half of these, however, are town tenants; 264 pay between £4 and £20 and 80 have a rental of £20 or over, The tenants virtually have fixity of tenure. An occasional experiment has been made of allowing tenant-right, but it has been limited to £10 an acre. The system would, however, be of little advantage on these estates, in as much as few changes of tenancy occur. Payments are allowed for any substantial improvements made by the tenants. Rents are generally under the Government valuation, and have not been advanced for 40 years. On two townlands where the valuation was admittedly low, a 15 per cent. allowance was offered last year, but now 25 per cent. is demanded. There have been only six evictions in ten years of idlers who would neither work nor pay. A few of the larger holdings are let on lease; the smaller have no memorandum of agreement, and the Land Act now diminishes the need of any covenants. There is no notable difference as to the paying capabilities or prosperity of the small as compared with the larger tenants. On whatever sized holdings, the active and thrifty seem to thrive. Poor rates are 2s in the pound; county cess about 2s 4d.

A great deal has been done, both by the late and present owners, to improve their property. Assistance has always been given in draining; for building, and lime and slates are furnished. As the old leases of middlemen fell in, townlands have been squared. That of Cloonagh has an area of 300 statue acres; its valuation is £159 15s. ; its rental, £134. Six years ago, when the lease expired, it was in 560 separate divisions or fields, many acres were unnecessarily occupied in fences, paths, and roads ; the 43 occupiers, with a few cottagers living in small mud cabins, were crowded in hamlets; one man had his farm scattered in 15 different places; another had his seven acres in 29 divisions.

The people themselves were alive to the need of a more economical distribution. A surveyor laid out roads and squared the plots, letting them according to the number of holders, arranging, as far as possible, that a fair proportion of good and bad land went together. With Sir Henry's own assistance, a fair valuation, which has always given satisfaction, was put on the new farm. From 560 divisions the number was reduced to 43, conveniently grouped around new houses, for the building of which help was given. Assistance was also accorded for the removal of old fences, the making of new ones, and the cutting of main drains. Upwards of a mile of road was constructed, usefully employing the labour of the tenantry and of their available horse and donkey carts; this and all the other works were personally superintended by Sir Henry. Doonfore townland, at a cost of £500, has more recently been similarly treated. It has an area of 470 acres, a valuation of £355 10s.; the rental is £370.; the holdings range from four to six acres, charged at 12s. to 15s. an acre. Several good houses have been built by tenants receiving money from friends in America. The handy seaweed proves useful manure. Turf is brought from the bogs seven miles distant. But for the employment Sir Henry gives in gardens, woods, and on his home farm, the population would be decidedly redundant. The townland of Carrigeens, containing 289 acres of useful, improvable land, with a valuation of £224 15s. and a rental of £212 3s. 7d., two years ago was also squared, help being given to the holders in the making of roads, fences and houses; eight to ten acres is the average of the farms, but one man pays £25 a year ; another with 44 Irish acres, rented at £33, with a good house and buildings, bought out the previous tenant for £850, obtained as a legacy from America. The pity is that half the population of these townlands could not be deported and their holdings doubled in size. Without fishing, or work independently of their farms, the families, even on the best land, have not scope for reasonable subsistence and progressive improvement.

The following interesting statistics gathered by Sir Henry Gore-Booth in December, 1872, will give some idea of the resources of his tenantry :-

## LAND TENURE BEFORE AND AFTER THE FAMINE

|  |  | Lissadell | Ballymote |
|---|---|---|---|
| Statute acres ... ... ... ... |  | 12,000 ... | 12,815 |
| Griffith's valuation, including |  |  |  |
| Ballymote town ... ... ... .... |  | £6,307 ... | £8,796 |
| Rental ... ... ... ... ... ... ... |  | £5,342 ... | £7,490 |
| Males ... ... ... ... ... ... ... |  | 1,439 ... | 1,376 |
| Females ... ... ... ... ... ... |  | 1,388 ... | 1,409 |
| Males emigrating during |  |  |  |
| previous ten years ... ... ... | | 227 ... | 212 |
| Females " " " |  | 166 ... | 172 |
| Horses, valued at | £17. 0 .0. | 219 ... | 172 |
| Mules " " | 4. 0. 0. | 15 ... | 11 |
| Asses " " | 1 2. 0. | 186 ... | 268 |
| Cows " " | 14. 0. 0. | 1,453 | 1,206 |
| Cattle, two-year old " | 14. 10. 0. | 748 ... | 550 |
| Do., one year old " | 9. 10. 0. | 761 ... | 518 |
| Calves " " | 4. 0. 0. | 998 ... | 828 |
| Sheep " " | 3. 0. 0. | 1, 775 ... | 652 |
| Lambs " " | 2. 0. 0. | 899 ... | 586 |
| Pigs " " | 3. 0. 0. | 791... | 563 |
| Goats " " | 0. 7. 6. | 13 ... | 116 |
| Dogs " " | — | 238.... | 350 |
| Estimated value of livestock ... |  | £43,470 | £41,215 |

The coast villages are generally miserable and poor; the resource of land and sea seldom conduces to prosperity. With the alternative modes of livelihood neither seems to be made the best of. Cottagers often squat upon the small farms, and when the fishing or the potatoes fail it adds seriously to the destitution. These evils are exemplified at Ballyconnell, four miles from Lissadell and nine miles south of the pleasant watering-place of Grange. Ballyconnell belongs to Mr Gethin and Mrs Huddleston, both absentees, not known even by sight to their tenants. The valuation is £419 8s. There are 102 tenants and about ten cottagers. The population is said to have doubled within 30 years. About the Famine-time the townland was enclosed and squared. The families appear large, averaging at least five or six in each one-room house, built of mud or rough stone, usually low and dark, innocent of

## LAND TENURE BEFORE AND AFTER THE FAMINE

lath and plaster; the thatch, liable to ripped off by the wild Atlantic winds, is only held on by straw ropes placed at nine-inch intervals over the roof. The furniture is of the sparest and rudest description, consisting of one, occasionally of two, beds, a rough table, and a few benches; the donkey and any cattle, pigs, or poultry, of course, are housed with their master. Many of the older people, especially the women, cannot speak English. The people evidently are of mixed descent, but a few families partake of the distinctive Celtic type. The children, seldom shod, are not very regular winter attendants at school, but the last three months' average shows 46 boys and 59 girls, the latter usually attending longest. Children able to pay are charged 1d per week, but many are defaulters, and the non-payers increase.

Three or four acres appear to be the average extent of the holdings; of this area about one-half is cultivated, the remainder is a sandhill bearing beuty grass, or bog, which towards the shore is frequently under water. Sometimes the tillage land is ploughed; more generally it is cultivated by the spade. Almost invariably under potatoes, the crop is poor and uncertain; oats ripen badly and are knocked about by the high winds. A little guano is sometimes bought for manure. Not half the families have a cow; more have the easily kept patient ass. Many of the holders have the use of the common, but declare it is poor, generally overstocked and always bare. The hay they have generally to buy in winter, on credit, costs 5s per cwt. Those able to keep a cow do fairly well; the milk greatly helps the potatoes and Indian meal, which are the staple diet. Home-grown potatoes and a little oatmeal are fairly plentiful from harvest until about March, when Indian meal has generally to be got, usually on credit, and is paid for in summer either by an extra take of fish, by the produce of the cow, or by the crop of oats. I am told that some of the land is charged at 40s an Irish acre; the general complaint is that rents have been repeatedly raised, especially on those farming fairly. Another grievance is the 4s 2d per £1 imposed 16 years ago for the privilege of cutting or gathering seaweed, and charged indiscriminately to all tenants, whether they use it or not. Little is now made out of kelp or other seaweed. The charge for the weed has, however, been remitted from the rent of 1879, and the tenants resolutely declare that they will never pay it again.

One old woman, reputed the patriarch of the village, has about four

## LAND TENURE BEFORE AND AFTER THE FAMINE

acres, pays £7 13s. of rent for these and her one-roomed cottage, grows three-quarters of an acre of potatoes and a little piece of oats, and is mistress of a cow and a donkey. Thomas Carway has four Irish acres for which he pays £2 10s. This seems moderate, but his father built the house, and drained, reclaimed, sanded, and clayed the poor bog, which could not previously feed a rabbit; 10s. a year was put on three years ago for making a watercourse, which, having since fallen in, leaves matters worse than formerly - half the holding, indeed, is under water.

Mike Herity has a cottage and an acre of cut-away bog; he used to earn £10 to £15 by fishing, but asserts that he now does not make one-third of this. The boats are old; they do for weed cutting, but not for following the fish thirty to forty miles out, where they now often go. To succeed as fishermen new boats appear needful; new nets, costing £9 to £15; new lines, costing 40s. Daniel Micken has five Irish acres; pays £8 2s 10d, including rack money; grows an acre each of oats and potatoes; has a cow and his pigs comfortably quartered on the premises.

Michael Conway is better off than some of his fellows; his father and uncle were noted makers of poteen, and the profits therefrom are expended on a better house, which cost fully £20, and a few extra buildings. His rent is £12 10s 4d. He has about two acres of potatoes, which produce £6 to £7 an acre, and are mostly used for household consumption. About the same area is under oats, yielding six to seven sacks an acre. The produce of two cows, he estimates, should pay the rent, while the pair of calves sold in autumn will fetch £6. The cattle, whether grazing in his own piece or on the common, must be herded, tied, or shackled, for the turf fences are low and full of gaps. Michael Conway, jun. has six and a half Irish acres; his valuation he believes to be £9 5s.; his rent, £13 2s. 4 ; his rates reach £1 4s. 8d ; he generally boards out his cow and ass, which hence do not yield him as large profits as if they were kept at home.

Although it is easy to recognise the life-long struggle for a bare subsistence and the untoward surroundings which steep the small holders in perennial poverty, it is most difficult to carry out feasible plans which will effectually amend their condition and protect them from being occasionally subjected to absolute destitution."

# The 'MASS HOUSE' or Parish Chapel

The earliest reference to a Catholic place of worship in Sligo, other than 'The Abbey,' is contained in the Depositions taken before a Court of Inquiry into the activities of non-jurying Popish priests which took place in October, 1712. A number of witnesses, amongst whom was Thomas Corkran, merchant, confessed on oath that they had heard Mass two weeks earlier at "the Chappel or Mass-House in Sligo". The precise location of this place of worship was not stated, although the celebrant was named as Peter Feighney, a registered priest for the Parish of Killadoon.

The rigours of the Penal Laws had abated somewhat by the second half of the 18th century, allowing Catholics to worship with greater freedom, this despite the infamous 'Discovery' clause of the Queen Anne Act *"To prevent the further growth of Popery"*. An extant document in the Registry of Deeds [1] records that in February, 1776, William Burton of Burton Hall, Carlow, leased to Thomas Corkran of Sligo, Esq. "the Mass-house situated, lying and being in the Abbey Quarter and Parish of St. Johns, with the small enclosure thereto belonging", to hold for a term of thirty-one years at an annual rent of £1.10s. This Deed was witnessed by William Burton, the lessor, and by Martin Hoban, surety for Corkran, and Bernard Murphy, Gents, both of the City of Dublin. Corkran, the lessee, a descendant of the Thomas Corkran who figured in the Depositions of 1712, was none other than *Tomás Gallda*, the reputed despoiler of the Abbey and the builder of two thoroughfares, namely, Corkran's Mall (now J.F. Kennedy Parade) and Thomas Street. Unfortunately, the said Deed contains no details as to the precise location or a description of this place of worship. In all probability, it was little more than a small stone-built slated structure situated in a quiet *cul-de-sac* on the outskirts of the Town, subsequently known as Mass Lane.

Father John O' Flynn, who had been educated on the Continent, was appointed Parish Priest of Sligo c.1775 and immediately set about

## THE MASS HOUSE OR PARISH CHAPEL

the building of a larger church to accommodate a growing population, a process which was finally completed by his successor. Tradition has it that the new edifice was built around an earlier one, most likely the 'Mass-house' mentioned in the 1776 Deed, indicating not only a more commodious church, complete with galleries, but also that divine worship continued uninterrupted on the site from at least the mid 18th century, and probably much earlier. The location of the new Parish Chapel, which was dedicated to St. John, and described by a contemporary as "one of the best in the Kingdom", was S.E. of the junction formed by Chapel Lane, now Chapel Street, and Chapel Hill, where the *Cheshire Home* now stands. The Select Vestry of St. John's Church of Ireland made a contribution towards the building fund. The French consul, Coquebert de Montbret, visited the Parish Chapel on the occasion of his tour in 1791, and wrote as follows :

*"Not far from The Abbey is a catholic church. Service in the church is conducted in Irish, and judging by the loud manner in which they express their devotion, certain passages in the service rouse the emotions of those present ...... The Irish language is said to be spoken best in Sligo...." [2]*

Half a century later, in 1836, Samuel Lewis described the Chapel as "a structure of spacious dimensions".

In 1809 John O'Flynn was elevated to the See of Achonry and in November of that year was consecrated bishop in the Parish Church he had built. He was succeeded by Rev. Patrick Burke, subsequently Bishop of Elphin.[3] In addition to his pastoral duties, the new Parish Priest and Administrator involved himself in the politics of the day, notably, Emancipation and Repeal of the Union. On the occasion of the Borough election of June, 1826, he used the pulpit to exhort those of his parishioners who had a vote to use it in support of the candidate most sympathetic to Catholic grievances. The *"Sligo Journal"*, a Conservative organ, took umbrage at what it regarded as clerical interference in the election process and accused the reverend Administrator of 'haranguing his flock after a religious ceremony on subjects neither found in Bible or Missal."

His successor, as Administrator, was Rev. James Donlevy ,[4] the most outspoken cleric in the Sligo of that era, a man who used his remarkable oratorical powers to great effect whether in the pulpit or on the political platform, and one who played a significant role in having candidates of avowed Liberal principles returned as M.P.'s for

## THE MASS HOUSE OR PARISH CHAPEL

the Borough in 1832 and 1837. He spoke at the hustings on both occasions and stoutly defended his right of "electioneering from the pulpit" in order to secure the return of a representative who would be sympathetic to Catholic claims in Parliament. His support of John P. Somers in preference to the outgoing John Martin in the 1837 election drew down upon him the wrath of the local *"Journal"*, who referred to him in such uncomplimentary terms as "General Agitating Donlevy" and "that bigoted domineering clerical agitator". [5]

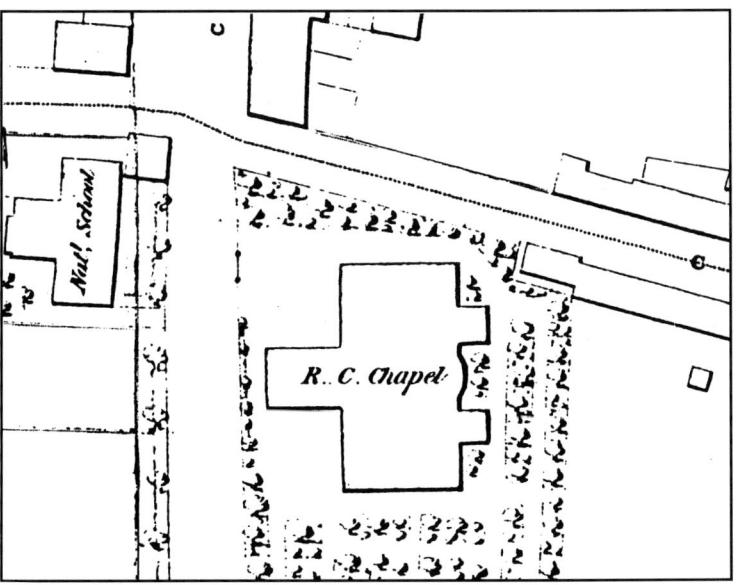

Donlevy's immediate successors as Administrators of the Parish, notably Rev. Owen Feeney and Dr. Thomas Phillips, followed in his footsteps. The latter figured prominently in the 1852 Borough election in which Somers (outgoing) was opposed by an English Catholic nobleman, Charles Towneley of Lancashire, who contested the seat at the invitation of Bishop George Browne and the local Liberals. In the course of the canvass Towneley was accompanied by either the Bishop or his Administrator, and sometimes by both, and on one occasion they jointly addressed Liberal supporters from the window of Towneley's hotel. Passions were running so high during the campaign that on the Sunday before the election Dr. Phillips ascended the pulpit after Mass

## The Mass House or Parish Chapel

had ended and roundly denounced the outgoing M.P. who happened to be seated in the gallery. Pointing towards Somers, he branded him as a traitor to his religion and country, and boldly proclaimed that anyone who supported him "voted for hell and the devil", while those who cast their vote for Towneley would place themselves "safely in the arms of God and the light of Heaven". [6] On the occasion of the election of Town Commissioners in January, 1852, Dr. Phillips admitted, when challenged, to using his influence with Catholic householders in order to secure a particular outcome .[7]

Clerical interference in political affairs, especially in parliamentary contests, continued into the following decade. On the Sunday before the 1868 Borough Election, in which the candidates were Captain Woulfe Flanagan (Liberal) and Major Knox (Conservative), Bishop Laurence Gillooly, who had succeeded Dr. Browne in 1858, addressed the congregation in the Parish Chapel and warned that Catholics who voted for the Tory candidate would be considered 'rotten branches' and should be 'lopped - off'. They could also be required to make reparation "before they could be reconciled with God".[8] On the following Sunday, before commencing his sermon, the Bishop directed that those in the congregation who had voted for Knox, the successful candidate, should remove themselves from the body of the church to the porch. It is not recorded how many worshippers responded, apart from one Martin Boyle, who held the rank of Sergeant in the Sligo Militia. He later told a Committee of Inquiry that as a result of what had taken place he stopped attending Mass there and went to the Friary instead.[9] It was also stated in evidence that on the following Christmas morning two worshippers, who had abstained from voting, were not allowed onto the gallery but were directed by the Administrator, Rev. John Morris, to hear Mass in the porch. [10]

In both pre and post Emancipation times the Parish Chapel was the nerve centre of Catholic activity in the greater Sligo area. Prior to the building of the new Friary in High Street, it was the principal place of Catholic worship for the down-trodden inhabitants and a small group of the fairly well-to-do middle class, successful merchants such as the Henrys, Kellys, Maddens, O'Beirnes, O'Connors and Tuckers. Successive generations of Sligonians worshiped within its walls in dark and difficult days, during the distressful 1820's and the cholera of 1832.

## THE MASS HOUSE OR PARISH CHAPEL

George Browne (above) and Laurence Gillooly (below),
19th century Bishops of Elphin.

## THE MASS HOUSE OR PARISH CHAPEL

Throughout the dreadful Famine years it acted as a temporary refuge from the realities of a cruel existence as well as a place of worship for countless numbers from different parts of the County, and further afield, who were either awaiting admission to the Workhouse or, most likely, seeking a berth on an emigrant ship at the Quays. Daniel O'Connell worshiped at its altar on the occasion of Repeal rallies in both 1837 and 1843, and Father Mathew, the Apostle of Temperance, preached from its pulpit to an overflow congregation in September, 1840.

On occasions throughout the 1830's the Parish Chapel was used as a meeting place for the local Liberal Party whose objectives were the improvement of the material welfare of their fellow citizens as well as fairer representation in Parliament. Membership was not exclusively Catholic and was open to broad-minded Protestants who favoured Reform. It was at one such meeting in January, 1836, that a discussion took place on the possibility of establishing a newspaper which would reflect their political views, a move that resulted in the founding of *"The Champion or Sligo News"* five months later. In 1852 both Dr. MacHale, Archbishop of Tuam, and Rev. Daniel Jones, S.J. formerly of *Banada Abbey*, preached to overflow congregations in aid of local charities. In March of the following year, Bishop Browne of Elphin presided at the inaugural meeting of the County Club, an umbrella for the Liberal Party.

On Sunday, February 13th 1852, considerable alarm was caused by an unusual incident during last Mass. As the Rev. Andrew Quinn, C.C. was preaching his sermon, a section of an archway gave way and fell to the ground. Immediate panic seized portion of the congregation and, fearing that the gallery was about to collapse, a number of them made a mad rush to the door while several others forced themselves out of the windows which were on a level with the ground floor. Although Fr. Quinn tried to assure them there was no danger and to remain in their seats, it took some time to allay their fears. Eventually, with the assistance of other clergy, order was restored. Fortunately, nobody was injured, though the church was densely crowded. [11]

In June, 1845, Dr. George Browne, the then Bishop of Elphin, convened a meeting of the clergy and parishioners in St. John's Chapel to discuss the possibility of building a Cathedral. It was well attended

## THE MASS HOUSE OR PARISH CHAPEL

and, after some discussion, a decision was reached to proceed with the erection of an edifice "suitable to the wants of the area and worthy of the Diocese". The following Resolution, proposed by James Tucker, M.D., and seconded by John Neary, was unanimously adopted:-

*"That our revered Prelate, the Right Rev. Dr. Browne, and the Clergy assembled at Visitation yesterday, deserve our warmest gratitude for their munificent donations of £365 towards the erection of a Cathedral for our populous Town and extensive Diocese; and that we, his Lordship's Parishioners, do cheerfully co-operate in carrying out so laudable an undertaking by subscribing the sums fixed to our respective names."*

It was decided to form a Management Committee composed of Subscribers of £20 and upwards and also a Finance Committee to receive subscriptions. Merchants and Traders of Sligo were requested to give Letters of Introduction to the Rev. Gentlemen appointed to collect in other towns in Ireland, England and Scotland. Membership of the various committees were, for the most part,          composed of the leading Catholic merchants of the Town - Peter O'Connor, Michael Gallagher (Mayor), Martin Madden, Edward Kelly, John Neary, Jeremiah O'Donovan, John Delany and James Madden. Upwards of £1,100 was either subscribed on the spot or guaranteed, the Bishop and several gentelmen contributing £100 each. Others, with equal liberality, gave £50. "Its with feelings of unmixed pleasure and unfeigned delight that we announce that a decision has been made by the clergy and laity of the Diocese to erect a magnificent Catholic Cathedral in Sligo", commented the *"Sligo Champion"* [12] It was loud in its praise of "the energy and zeal" displayed by Dr. Browne in what was a bold undertaking and went on to suggest that the proposed edifice would be on a scale to render it equal to any other ecclesiastical building in Ireland and worthy of Sligo.

Within a few weeks three of the diocesan clergy, carrying letters of introduction from local merchants and traders, both Catholic and Protestant, were dispatched to England and Scotland to collect funds. By August subscriptions, both at home and from abroad, had exceeded the most sanguine hopes of the Committee. As the various fund-raising activities were swinging into action in the Autumn of 1845, the first indications of the impending failure of the potato crop, with the resulting Famine, began to appear. As the situation considerably

## THE MASS HOUSE OR PARISH CHAPEL

worsened in the following year, the project was abandoned for the time being.

In the immediate aftermath of the Famine the Parish Chapel was extended at a considerable cost. In February, 1855, the Rev. Henry Marshall, D.D., a distinguished convert to Catholicism, preached a Charity Sermon to raise funds to liquidate the debt already incurred in making it a place of worship large enough to accommodate a growing congregation and an ecclesiastical building worthy of the Town. Four years later, in 1859, the Renovation Fund was still £500 in the red and local merchants were invited to subscribe amounts ranging from £5 to £20.

The plans for a Cathedral, left in abeyance in the wake of the Famine, were revived on the appointment of Dr. Laurence Gillooly as successor to Dr. Browne. in 1858. In August 1859, he secured a renewable lease from Sir Gilbert King of two adjacent properties close to The Lungy, described as Edward Stephen's plot and Eubule Ormsby's large garden, known as 'The Bowling Green'. This was the site chosen for the Cathedral of the Immaculate Conception which was commenced in 1867 and consecrated in 1874.

The former Parish Chapel in Abbeyquarter was then converted into an Industrial School for girls, known as St. Laurence's Orphanage, under the care of the Sisters of Mercy. What remained of the former Chapel complex was demolished in the mid 1980's to make way for a *Cheshire Home*.

### Notes and References:

(1) Registry of Deeds. Bk. 312. p. 105.

(2) De Montbret, Coquebert. *"Tour in Connaught, 1791"*.
In *"Galway Arch. Soc. Jr."* Vol. 36, 1977 - '78.

(3) Patrick Burke (1779 -1843) was the first Bishop of Elphin to make Sligo his place of residence, living for a time at *"Seaville"*, a thatched cottage at Finisklin. In 1840 he decided to move to a more central location in the Diocese, and when this became known a deputation of leading citizens, consisting of both Catholics and Protestants, petitioned him to remain but to no avail. He died at Ballymoe three years later.

## THE MASS HOUSE OR PARISH CHAPEL

His successor, George Browne, D.D. who had previously been Bishop of Galway, ruled the Diocese from 1844 till his death in 1858. He resided for a few years at *Marino House*, Finisklin, before taking up residence at Summerhill, Athlone.

(4) **See:**  McTernan : *Worthies of Sligo* p. 371-375.

(5)  *"Sligo Journal"* July, 1837

(6)  Minutes of Evidence taken before the Select Committee on the Sligo Borough Election Petition, 1853.

(7)  *"Sligo Champion"*  2 - 2-1852

Rev. Thomas Phillips., D.D. who was Administrator in Sligo from 1849-1854, was appointed Parish Priest in Roscommon in 1854. He was succeeded by the Rev. Patrick Boyle and later by Rev. John Morris.

*(8)  "Report of Committee appointed to Inquire into corrupt practices at the last Election for Sligo Borough, together with Minutes of Evidence".* Dublin .  1870.

At the Inquiry, Dr. Gillooly denied he used the actual words attributed to him by Sergeant Boyle - although admitting that what he had said more or less meant the same. He further explained that those in the congregation who had voted for Knox were moved to the porch as he feared trouble from the supporters of Flanagan.

In its Report to Parliament the Committee concluded that "some of the acts of Dr. Gillooly and certain of his clergy amounted to undue influence".

(9)  ibid  opus cit.

(10)  ibid  opus cit.

(11)  *"Sligo Champion"*  19-2-1853

(12)  ibid  21-6-1845

# Illicit Distillation

Songs and stories abound concerning the exploits of the poteen men down through the ages. The illicit distiller has been the subject of many travellers' tales, often giving him a romantic halo and a glowing description of his operations coloured, perhaps, by the distiller's hospitality. In the distant past he had very little to fear from the law; there were no organised police forces, magistrates were unlikely to be active against him and no excise officer could safely pursue him without the protection of a military escort. The illicit distiller was a common enough figure in Ireland, particularly on the western seaboard where grain was cheap, turf and water plentiful and poverty endemic. This situation made light of the risks of the trade and heightened the appeal of its product.

At the beginning of the 18th century there were three types of legal distillers. There were the privileged persons who could distil spirits for use in their households; there were keepers of inns and taverns who distilled spirits for sale to their clients; and there also emerged specialist distillers making spirits for sale generally. As the century progressed illicit distillation increased in this and neighbouring counties. The revenue officers did what they could, with military protection, to combat it, but their numbers were not adequate to deal effectively with the problem. The work was dangerous and they were often attacked when 'still' hunting. In 1742 the Surveyor of Excise reported that the Barony of Tireragh was "well inhabited with a great number of private brewers who could be suppressed". As a result, it was decided to place the area under the immediate attention of one officer, namely, John Foreside, gauger and coast officer, at a salary of £40 per annum. He was instructed to pay particular attention to the many creeks and good landing places along that coastline.

By 1761 distillers were required by law to register in an effort to bring all distilling within closer excise control. When the pressure of the new regulations became too much domestic distilling generally ceased, but some operators continued in the business by retreating to quieter spots in the surrounding countryside beyond the prying eyes of the revenue officers. Two years later, in 1763, Daniel Looney,

## ILLICIT DISTILLATION

Surveyor-General of Excise, with a Company of Horse from the Sligo garrison, is reported to have caused "great havoc" among the private distillers of the County, destroying hundreds of barrels of oats and wash, particularly in the Ballyfarnon direction". [1]

In 1783 the Government introduced new methods in the fight against illicit distilling by imposing on the county, or town, a fine of £20 for any "still, alembic or blackpot found", and the fine was raised by a Grand Jury presentment, or in modern terms, by an addition to the rates. The Revenue Commissioners determined each case and they were empowered to swear-in collectors of excise as sub-commissioners to undertake this task for them. Thus, the officers of the Excise judged the case and determined the county or town liable. The inhabitants, who would have to pay the fine, were not cited as defendants and had no opportunity of rebutting liability. To fine a whole county or town was manifestly unjust and, after pressure in Parliament, the area to be fined was reduced in 1785 to the parish or townland and the Grand Jury presentment was to be confirmed by the judge at the next assize. The judge, however, could not determine a case or hear an appeal, he merely had to be satisfied that the process of levying the fine was in order.

In 1791 the fine was reduced to £10 in country districts but, as the penalty applied to each discovery, a barony in an illicit distilling area could well run up a large bill in fines. Far from enlisting the inhabitants as unpaid excise men this law banded them together to prevent the discovery of stills. Nor did the law have much effect on landlords whose first interest was their rents. Illicit distilling to the landlord sometimes meant getting a good rent for poor land. The Act of 1791 did, however, try to remedy one serious injustice, it made provision for objections to be raised to the imposition of a fine. Despite all these enactments, 'moonshining' continued unabated. In some districts the 'mountain dew' was sold as openly as if the dealer had a formal licence for the sale. The consequences of all this was that the country was inundated with the beverage to such an extent that if a traveller, going the road, called to a way-side house for a drink of water, he was pretty sure to receive it strongly fortified with home-made brew!

In 1788 several armed parties were privately raised under the authority of the Lord Lieutenant, each of a dozen men under two officers. They operated in areas in the Counties of Sligo, Leitrim and Fermanagh. It is said that these parties succeeded in suppressing illicit distilling in the areas in which they operated, but only because these distillers moved to adjoining districts. Twenty years later, c.1813-15, excise officers stationed at Carney, Easkey and Tubbercurry were each assigned a sergeant and twenty foot soldiers to assist and protect them in tracking down the poitín makers.[2] Before a Select Committee in June 1813, William Gregory, a Revenue Officer, offered some observations on efforts to curb private distillation:-

*"At Sligo I found much activity had been exerted by the Officers, but they have many disadvantages to encounter in their operations against the distillers. Usually, they must march a considerable distance before arriving at the place of attack, and are so closely watched by persons employed for that purpose that, upon the first movement of the troops, the whole countryside through which they direct their course is immediately alarmed........ Arising from the frequent visits of the Revenue Officers, accompanied by the military, into these places most noted for private distillation and the seizures which have been lately made, the trade is much reduced and the price of illicit spirits considerably raised and difficult to procure..... The stills here are of large dimensions, but mostly of tin; those of copper are of a small size......"* [3]

He further stated that corn mills in the Sligo area were being used to a greater extent than elsewhere, to his knowledge, for grinding illegal malt.

---

# ILLICIT DISTILLATION

Spring Assizes, 1813. Co. of Sligo.

| | | |
|---|---|---|
| Found Guilty: | .............................. | 31 |
| Acquitted: | .............................. | 9 |
| Bench Warrants Issued: | .............................. | 64 |
| No. of persons Indicted: | .............................. | 106 |

*(Parliamentary Papers, 1812-13 (269) VI.)*

---

Further efforts to curb the activities of the 'moonshiners' resulted in the formation, in 1818, of the Revenue Police, armed and equipped, living in barracks and employed almost wholly against the illicit distiller. It was not until 1854 that the Royal Irish Constabulary were,

## ILLICIT DISTILLATION

for the first time, employed, in addition to the Revenue Police, in the suppression of illicit distillation. Daniel Webb-Webber of Leekfield, Skreen, an Assistant Barrister for the County, gave evidence before a Select Committee on Illicit Distillation in 1816. [4] In his estimation the making of poitín was on the increase. What had originally been confined to mountainous districts had, in latter years, become much more general, principally as a result of a change in policy, namely, imposing fines on townlands rather than on individuals. This change made it more profitable for the illegal distillers and he was aware of instances of some collusion between them and the Revenue Police. He also had personally witnessed much individual suffering as a result of individual fines "resulting in the substance of an entire family being sold off to pay the fine of a delinquent." The number of illegal stills in operation in the County had greatly increased since the fining of townlands was introduced and, unfortunately, there was a view abroad that 'private' whiskey was both "wholesome and palatable" whereas 'Parliament' whiskey was "unwholesome and to a degree deterrious". According to Webber none of the illicit distillers in the area were men of 'substance' and, in his opinion, nothing short of transportation would put a stop to the practice. However, Beresford Lovett, Inspector-General of Excise, who had been employed as an Inspector in Sligo and adjacent counties in 1808, did not altogether share Webber's viewpoint. Lovett held that the imposition of penalties on individual townlands tended to suppress the illicit trade. As proof of this, he cited the case of Messrs. Stewart's Distillery in Sligo whose output had been drastically reduced between 1810 and 1814 during which period the townland fines had been suspended. This he interpreted as conclusive evidence that such penalties were quite effective.

The extent of illicit distillation in County Sligo in the opening years of the 19th century may be gauged from extant records of the period. It was rated the sixth highest poitín-making area in the country and over a seven and a half year period, between 1806 and 1816, when the revelant Act was in operation, informations were received in respect of 1,268 cases resulting in 780 convictions and yielding a staggering £25,000 in fines. [5] At the Summer Assizes, 1816, 54 fines @ £25 each were levied on 41 townlands in 21 Parishes. Kincuillew, in the Parish of Kilmactigue, had the distinction of heading the list with four

ILLICIT DISTILLATION

## FINES ON TOWNLANDS 1806 - 1816

| Year Total of Fines | Informations Received: | Number of Convictions | |
|---|---|---|---|
| 1806 (½ year) | 10 | 8 | £400 |
| 1807 | 69 | 45 | £2,250 |
| 1808 | 139 | 69 | £3,450 |
| 1809 | 153 | 25 | £1,250 |
| 1810 (½ year) | 87 | 71 | £3,350 |
| 1810 (July) - 1813 (Dec.) Act Suspended | | | |
| 1814 | 489 | 304 | £7,810 |
| 1815 | 199 | 173 | £4,325 |
| 1816 | 122 | 85 | £2,174 |

convictions. At both the Spring and Summer Assizes the following year, 1817, a total of 50 fines were levied on 36 townlands, with Knockbrack and Barnaribbon heading the list. The geographical spread was much the same as at the previous assize, with the parishes of Ahamlish, Castleconnor, Drumcliffe, Kilfree, Kilmacshalgan and Kilmactigue having the most convictions.

## SUMMER ASSIZES, 1816
### Fines Imposed on Townlands

| PARISH | TOWNLAND | NO. OF CONVICTIONS |
|---|---|---|
| Drumcliffe | Barnaribbon | 2 |
| Kilturra | Doobeg | 2 |
| Kilfree | Moygara | 2 |
| Toomour | Knockbrack | 3 |
| **SPRING ASSIZES, 1817** | | |
| Ahamlish | Gortnaleck | 2 |
| Castleconnor | Killanly | 3 |
| Drumcliffe | Aughagad | 2 |
| " | Barnaderrig | 2 |
| " | Barnaribbon | 2 |
| Kilmactranny | Ballinashee | 2 |

# TOWNLANDS FINED FOR ILLICIT DISTILLATION

## Spring Assizes, 1816

| Parish | Townland |
|---|---|
| Ahamlish: | Ardnaglass |
| Ballinakill: | Tunnagh |
| Ballisodare: | Collooney, Knockbeg and Lugnamackan |
| Castleconnor: | Muckduff |
| Cloonacool: | Cloonacool |
| Dromard: | Carrowrad[2]*, Cloonagh, Carrowconnor and Lavagh |
| Drumcolumb: | Bricklieve |
| Drumrat: | Rooskybeg |
| Emlaghfad: | Emlaghgissan |
| Killadoon: | Carrickglass, Killadoon and Mount Town |
| Killaspugbrone: | Strandhill |
| Kilfree: | Cloonsillagh,[2] Cuilmore, Doon[2] and Moygara |
| Kilglass: | Culleens,[2] Leacan [2] and Leaffony [2] |
| Killery: | Correagh |
| Kilmacallan: | Cartronroe and Cleavry [2] |
| Kilmacshalgan: | Belville and Doonbeakin |
| Kilmactigue: | Kincuillew [4] ,Knockbrack [2] and Stonepark [2] |
| Kilmactranny: | Ballyculleen and Drimronan |
| Kilross: | Ballygawley |
| Shancough: | Cabragh and Carrowmore |
| Templeboy: | Ballygreighan, Doonmadden [2] and Lugdoon |

\* Numerals indicate the number of fines [6]

## ILLICIT DISTILLATION

Private stills were not uncommon in the early years of the last century. They were set up in places where they would least be expected, such as in the kitchens of the nobility and the stables of clergymen. Dr. O'Rorke, the county historian, refers to the patronage the 'still' received from a 'man of the cloth' in the Collooney area. The Reverend William Duke prided himself on the strength, flavour and age of his poitín. After getting a supply from the usual source the parson had it always re-distilled in order to increase the strength of the spirit. On one occassion, while employees were running the whiskey through the still in an outhouse at Camphill, the place took fire. Luckily, the blaze was noticed by neighbours coming from Mass in the parish chapel and their combined efforts succeeded in bringing the outbreak under control. Needless to say, no action was taken against the Reverend Duke![7] A few years later the occupant of *Willbrook House*, who had it leased from the Ormsbys, installed a private still in the basement and took to the manufacture of poitín. It is not known how long he was engaged in the contraband business when a spark ignited the surrounding woodwork, and soon the whole house, fixtures, floors and roof were ablaze - leaving nothing standing but the darkened walls of the once imposing mansion-seat which had been built to the specifications of the German architect, Richard Castels. [8]

The hazards and risks endured by the Revenue Police in their efforts to seize illegally distilled spirits and bring the culprits to justice have been noted from time to time in the local press. Accounts of 'disturbances', one at Doonecoy and the other at Heapstown, both in the 1820's, illustrate the problems encountered and the remedies adopted:-

*The Revenue Police*

*"From the great extent to which this*

## ILLICIT DISTILLATION

*trade is carried on in Doonecoy and its immediate neighbourhood, a Requisition had been issued by Charles T. Henry, accompanied by Mathew Ormsby, Esq., Preventative Surveyors of Excise; when on the 5th inst. a party of His Majesty's 25th Regiment proceeded thither, under the command of Lieutenant Gilbert, who, whilst on their route, made an extensive seizure, which having secured under escort, and arriving at Doonecoy Mill, made a seizure of 30 barrels of malt, and took seven prisoners; while endeavouring to secure same, many hundreds of persons assembled around the Mill, armed with sea-scythes, forks, bludgeons and fire-arms; and, in consequence of the fewness of the number with the Revenue Officers, it was deemed prudent to retire upon the seizure already made, and await a reinforcement which Mr. Henry had reason to expect from his local knowledge of the country, and were promptly and most effectually afforded by Captain Wood of Seafort House. The whole proceeded at an early hour the next day, notwithstanding a hail and snow storm, and took a large quantity of the property. Several of the ringleaders were taken prisoner and brought before Captain Moore, the next Resident Magistrate, and gave ample security to take their trials at the ensuing Assizes.*

*Every praise is due to Mr. Gilbert, and the detachment under his command, for their uncommon forbearance under the circumstances of great provocation; nor can too much praise be given to those vigilant and meritorious Officers who evinced no small share of adroitness and address to save themselves and their party from as formidable and illegal a mob as at this moment disgraces any part of this Kingdom".*[9]

Three years later, in February, 1825, the scene moved to the Geevagh area:-

*"An occurrence, marked by a daring spirit of turbulence and, we fear, tragic results, took place at Geevagh last week. A party of Revenue Police proceeded to that neighbourhood and after destroying a quantity of pot-ale, made their way to Heapstown where they had reason to suppose they would find a large concealment of malt, etc. They had not proceeded far when they perceived a mob of several hundred persons approaching in different directions, sounding horns, etc. and armed with pitch forks, loys and stones. All efforts to induce them to disperse quietly having failed and with the situation every minute becoming more perilous, the fatal signal was given and a volley discharged which resulted in their immediate retreat.... It is stated that one man was killed and two wounded."* [10]

Throughout the 1830's there were further reports of successful raids

ILLICIT DISTILLATION

and subsequent convictions. At the Sooey Petty Sessions in November, 1834, Thomas Gunning and Thomas Coleman were each convicted of having "harboured, kept and concealed" certain quantities of illicit spirits. Each was fined £6, but Coleman was subsequently sent to gaol for three months in default of payment. A year later, in November, 1835, Lieutenant James St. Laurence of the Revenue Police carried out a number of successful raids in the Tubbercurry area, uncovering fifteen private distillations, thirty gallons of spirits and eight hundred and forty bushels of illicit malt. Eight men were arrested and lodged in Sligo Gaol. In December, 1848, the Revenue Police raided an old dwelling house at Kilross where they found an illicit still at full work. Nine 'moonshiners' were arrested and an extensive range of apparatus seized.

In the mid 19th century illicit distillation was fairly widespread in Sligo, and this gave the Judges on the Connacht Circuit no little trouble, hardly an assize passing without numerous convictions. Poitín was made, now and then, in all parts of the County but the manufacture was so common and so constant in Drumcliffe and Ahamlish, that nine-tenths of the 'Still Cases' as they were called, came from those areas. The penalty, in ordinary cases, such as 'having a still', 'using a still', 'making pot ale', 'having singlings', 'malting grain', etc. was imprisonment for a week, with a fine of £10. Failure to pay resulted in six months in gaol.

According to evidence given in 1853 by George Knox, a resident Magistrate of the County, before a Parliamentary Committee, illicit distillation was widely

### NUMBERS CONFINED IN SLIGO GAOL FOR ILLICIT DISTILLATION OFFENCES IN APRIL OF EACH OF THE FOLLOWING YEARS, 1835-55. [11]

| Year | Number |
|------|--------|
| 1835 | 42 |
| 1836 | 19 |
| 1837 | 24 |
| 1838 | 30 |
| 1839 | 6 |
| 1840 | 3 |
| 1841 | 1 |
| 1842 | 9 |
| 1843 | 17 |
| 1844 | 12 |
| 1845 | 10 |
| 1846 | 6 |
| 1847 | 6 |
| 1848 | 49 |
| 1849 | 37 |
| 1850 | 33 |
| 1851 | 24 |
| 1852 | 23 |
| 1853 | 12 |
| 1854 | 30 |
| 1855 | 30 |

# SEIZURES OF ILLICIT SPIRITS

"Early this week a party of eight Revenue Police raided an island in Lough Arrow where they seized a considerable amount of illicit matter, including thirty barrels of malt. Five men and a woman where taken into custody. As the convoy of four boats made their way to the mainland at Ballyrush Bridge, a heavy swell and a stiff breeze developed and one of the boats capsized with the loss of three policemen, named Stacey, Sherritt and Whittaker".

*"Sligo Journal" 19 - II - 1830*

"On Wednesday night last, at about half-past eleven o'clock, Constable John Simons and Sub-Constables Young and Phillips, were on patrol on *Victoria Line* when their attention was drawn to a boat rowing up and down the River. Having some suspicion in their minds, they concealed themselves behind the wall, and in a few minutes saw the boat coming near the shore. Later they perceived men bringing kegs under their arms and laying them down on the beach. When all the kegs were taken out of the boat, the police rushed and seized them, and also arrested three men, whose names are Michael and John Heraughty and John Waters, all of Innishmurray Island. The prisoners were brought before T.H. Williams, Esq., Mayor, and Dr. Wood, J.P., who committed them for trial at the Petty Sessions. The five kegs of poteen and the boat are in the Police Barrack."

*"Sligo Journal"  14-2-1862*

## ILLICIT DISTILLATION

practiced in the baronies of Leyney and Coolavin, and on the increase.[11] At an earlier period Tireragh was to the fore and this necessitated the stationing of extra police there in an effort to quell the practice. It was also suspected that a large number of mills and kilns, especially those no longer functioning as such, were associated in some way with the high prevalence of illegal distillation. The combined efforts of the Constabulary and the Revenue Police does not appear to have improved the situation, judging by the following comment in the *"Sligo Chronicle"* in March, 1864 :-

*"During this Winter the making of poitín has rapidly increased in this part of the country. At every Petty Sessions held throughout the County charges either of distilling the liquor or having it in possession are regularly dealt with by the Magistrates..... It would appear that this branch of native manufacture has lately crept into this Town as some components of the trade and some of the forbidden stuff were recently found in a premises next door to a Magistrate.... Recently, at Aughamore, eighteen individuals were caught in the act when the police raided a house.... It is difficult to understand the risk when Scotch whisky is almost as cheap."* [12]

| SEIZURES MADE BY THE REVENUE POLICE IN CO.SLIGO, 1850 - 51 | |
|---|---|
| Stills: | 85 |
| Worms: | 83 |
| Other Utensils: | 1,080 |
| Gallons of Spirits: | 225 |

A week earlier the same newspaper had reported a big seizure of illicitly distilled spirits on Dernish Island, including five kegs of whiskey and fifty gallons of wash. The estimated value of the seizure was £50. The daylight raid surprised a number of men who scattered in all directions. In 1896 a number of cases came before the Petty Sessions at Tubbercurry, while six men were arrested in the Dromore West area after a large quantity of wash, a still and some utensils were found in the mountains nearby. [13]

The price of 'Mountain Dew' varied from time to time, depending on the price of barley and oats. If there was a good harvest and prices were low the illicit distiller prospered. If, on the other hand, corn was

## ILLICIT DISTILLATION

A Still (as depicted in Hall's *"Ireland"*, 1841 - 43)

scarce and prices high he might have to suspend operations as farmers usually preferred to send their grain to the market rather than direct sales to the illicit distiller. In the early 19th century, at the end of the Napoleonic Wars, poitín sold at from 7/- to 8/- a gallon in Sligo, compared to 6/- to 8/- in Donegal. At that time a 24-stone barrel of oats sold for 14/- and if well managed could produce eight gallons of 'common whiskey', thus yielding the distiller a handsome profit. Prices fell sharply in the early 1840's but recovered somewhat after the Famine. In the 1850's a poitín maker could earn "a clear average profit" of 3/- a gallon. Thirty years later it sold at 10/- to 12/- a gallon but during World War 1 prices shot up to 8/- a bottle or in the region of £3 a gallon.

As the 19th century drew to a close it was extremely difficult to distil spirit from oats and barley owing to the increased vigilance of the police, and was replaced by molasses. Those engaged in illicit distillation complained at the new and improved telescopes used by the police which enabled them to perceive smoke curling up in suspicious localities. For the surreptitious distillers it was a case of a house divided against itself. The seizures effected by the police were

ILLICIT DISTILLATION

generally made from information given by neighbours, or rivals in the business.

*     *     *     *

Inishmurray Island, lying a few miles off the Ahamlish coastline, and widely celebrated for the richness of its monastic remains, was for a long time famous for the making of 'mountain dew' or, 'whiskey' as the inhabitants preferred to call it. The relative isolation of the Island facilitated the distillation of the 'pure native' and greatly favoured the traffic upon which the Islanders lived. Connoisseurs of such beverages asserted that Inishmurray 'whiskey' was "of the purest and most delectable quality". As soon as the officers of the excise became aware of the extent of the illegal trafficing they set about applying a remedy. At first, a steamer paid occasional visits to the Island but rough seas frequently prevented a safe berthing. Now and again, a successful landing was achieved, as for example, on January 9th, 1836. Under the cover of darkness a party of Revenue Police from Sligo, led the Lieutenant St. Laurence, succeeded in making a landing from the coast-guard tender, *Racer*. The *"Journal"* reported on the event as follows:

*"As soon as the 'Racer' was got as near to the Island as practicable or safe, Mr. St. Laurence, who is an excellent swimmer, prepared to land in defiance of every obstacle. He got the boat made ready, which he had brought from Sligo, towed after the vessel, into which himself and party, with two or three sailors, immediately got, and pushed off for the Island, at the imminent risk of their lives and contrary to the advice of experienced mariners. However, they succeeded in landing without any accident and seized a still, head and worm, which they took with them, together with twelve sacks of barley malt. They arrested two men who were duly convicted and sent to prison, and destroyed several vessels with large quantities of spent wash together with a great deal of barley and malt which they could not remove in consequence of a severe worsening of the weather......"[14]*

The risks taken and the hazards endured by the Revenue Police on such expeditions, and the understandable re-action of the Islanders was also commented upon:-

*"Too much praise cannot be given to Mr. St. Lawrence for his intrepidity and boldness in performing this exploit. He had been out all the day, until late on the evening of the 8th and had taken but little or no refreshment, or repose, after a very fatiguing and harassing day's march, when he proceeded to the Island.*

121

ILLICIT DISTILLATION

*He would have taken a great many prisoners, as all the dwelling houses had malt in them, but for a person who saw the cutter and gave the alarm. The Islanders had suffered severely from a former visit of the Revenue, and the sight of St. Lawrence's boat pulling towards the shore caused great panic, and all the inhabitants left their beds and, in the fright of being taken, rushed into the street - in puris naturalibus - or stark naked.*

*An old woman beholding the havoc which St. Lawrence made among the stills, malt and vessels, in the anguish of her heart fell upon her knees, and called aloud in Irish on Father Molaise to curse the cruel intruders.* " [15]

It is said that on one occasion a party of Revenue Police, who went there on a still-hunting expedition, were forcibly detained by the severity of the weather for close on three weeks. Although they had destroyed over a ton of barley malt and seized a large quantity of spirits, the Islanders treated them with hospitality and great consideration.

| Revenue Police Stations, Co. Sligo: 1853 | | |
|---|---|---|
| Bellaghy: | 10 | personnel |
| Ballymote: | 48 | " |
| Grange: | 46 | " |
| Skreen: | 47 | " |
| Tubbercurry: | 63 | " |
| Sligo: | 26 | " |

At length, the authorities hit upon a plan that proved very effective. A police station was opened on the Island in the late 1850's or early 1860's. While numbers varied from time to time, the personnel usually consisted of a Sergeant and two Constables. This proved to be a master stroke - the making of illegal 'whiskey' was no more. In one fell swoop the principle economic activity of the Islanders had ceased to function, and the inhabitants had to fall back upon the wretched subsistence which they could obtain from tilling such a rocky and desolate spot. As a result, the population went into sharp decline and those that remained could barely subsist. While relationships between Islanders and the Royal Irish Constabulary were initially quite cordial, they became somewhat strained as the years progressed and the inhabitants struggled to survive. Eventually, the police were subjected to a boycott.

ILLICIT DISTILLATION

Their supplies and communications were cut-off, and with no prospect of a resolution to the problem, the station was eventually closed down.[16]

The enforced withdrawal of the Royal Irish from the Island in January, 1890, was the signal for the resumption of illicit distillation, using treacle, brown and white sugar and barley as the principle raw materials. A few months later the local *"Independent"* carried an article entitled *"Inishmurray - A Land Flowing with Poteen Whiskey"*, from which is culled the following extract :-

*"Martin Heraughty, the so-called 'King', now finding himself in the full plentitude of autocratic power, charged all his male subjects to form a joint-stock company for the purpose of manufacturing spirits. In the adoption of this policy his 'Majesty' saw the best bond of unity, and the best shield against the temptation of disloyalty for lucre. As a directorate over the company he appointed Johnny Mannion, Jimmy Heraghty, Michael Waters and 'Micky Ruagh'. At present the 'Kingdom' may be described as a huge distillery, in which immense quantities of molasses are converted into a species of intoxicating drink. This liquor the 'King' and his subjects manage to import surreptitiously into Sligo, Leitrim and Donegal, and which, being sold for about 12s per gallon, is quickly bought up by fourth-class publicans and rural votaries of Bacchus. The prosperity of the company may be inferred when it is mentioned that applications from Cloonagh, Ballyconnell and Grange have been received for shares in the concern, and that many young men who emigrated from Streedagh and Maugherow to the lately established kingdom are, according to recent advices, doing well.. "* [17]

In December, 1897, a party of police made a successful landing and seized and destroyed almost two hundred gallons of wash.

What is reputed to have been the largest quantity of illegal spirits ever captured in the County was discovered on Inishmurray in May, 1924, when a party of Gardai, accompanied by military personnel, made a lightening raid. "A small distillery" was the terminology used to describe the find. The Islanders were taken completely by surprise and a still was discovered in actual working order. Gardai captured eight kegs of poitín; over a thousand gallons of wash; three stills and several barrels of treacle and a quantity of dry grain. Three Islanders, namely, Michael Waters ('King'), Dan and Michael Heraughty, were taken before a special sitting of the District Court. Waters was sentenced to

## ILLICIT DISTILLATION

three months hard labour and fined £50, while the two Heraughtys also got three months each and fined £25.[18] In passing sentence the District Justice, D. J. Flattery, stated that poteen traffic would have to be rooted out. "Any idea that the inhabitants of Inishmurray Island had a right to carry on this illicit trade has got to vanish".

Six years later in 1930, the self-styled 'King', Michael Waters, found himself in conflict with the law once again. He and Patrick Brady were found in possession of sixteen gallons of poitín and were brought before Grange Court. Waters was fined £200, mitigated to £25, and Brady a similar fine reduced to £15.[19] Another raid on the Island in June, 1932, led to the capture of a large quantity of illicit spirit, plant and materials to an estimated value of £470. The haul consisted of fifty gallons of poitín, together with wash, malt, three still heads and a copper worm. Ten still-houses, all of which showed traces of recent usage, were also located and destroyed.[20] The illegal whiskey trade on Inishmurray declined only on the outbreak of World War 2 and the introduction of sugar rationing. This led to a significant drop in the income of the inhabitants and was a major factor in the final abandonment of the Island in 1948.[21]

A 'Capture' on Inishmurray c. 1940

In the present century the story of illicit distilling has generally been devoid of much except to the romantic and the tourist.

124

ILLICIT DISTILLATION

The 'moonshiner' is most likely a farmer with a small holding whose spirit trade is entirely local and quite small. The penalties in relation to his financial standing are most prohibitive - having been increased from £50 to £1,000. for the first offence.[22] This penalty also applies to anyone in possession of materials for the making of illicit spirits. Poitín made from malt and grain would be a rarity nowadays, treacle being the base most in use. The few stills found in recent times, mostly in areas adjacent to the Ox-Mountains, have been small and inefficient. Despite a considerable increase in spirit duties, convictions, which totalled seventy-four for the entire country in 1950, had dropped to less than half that figure a decade later.[23] In 1995 it was estimated that in or about two hundred illegal stills were still operating in the Republic and yielding something in the region of sixty thousand gallons of illicit 'whiskey'.

Illicit distilling is likely to persist as long as there is a duty on spirits. It is poor stuff compared with the legal article, but it is cheap and will always have its advocates who will praise it with the zeal of eccentrics.

## Notes and References

| | | |
|---|---|---|
| (1) | MacDonagh Mss. No.VII. | |
| (2) | Parliamentary Papers | 1816 (436) IX |
| (3) | " " | 1812-13 (269) VI |
| (4) | " " | 1816 (436) IX |
| (5) | " " | 1816 (490) IX |
| (6) | Grand Jury Presentment, | 1816 |
| (7) | O'Rorke, T. *"Ballisodare and Kilvarnet"*. | Dublin. 1878. |
| (8) | " *"History of Sligo"*. | Vol. 1.p.455 |
| (9) | *"Sligo Journal"* | 9-3-1822 |
| (10) | ibid | 5-3-1825 |
| (11) | Parliamentary Papers | 1854 (53) X |
| (12) | *"Sligo Chronicle"* | 12-3-1864 |
| (13) | *"Sligo Independent"* | 15-4-1896 |
| (14) | *"Sligo Journal"* | 15-1-1836 |
| (15) | ibid | opus cit. |

## ILLICIT DISTILLATION

In April, John Wynne of *Hazelwood House,* who held the Island under lease from Lord Palmerston, wrote as follows: "The great evil of the inhabitants is their habit of illicit distillation which they carry on more for the purpose of providing their cattle with food in winter than even for the profit of the whiskey..... The practice is very demoralising......"

(16)  *"Sligo Independent"*   25-1-1890

(17)   ibid    29-3-1890

(18)   ibid     7-6-1924

(19)   ibid   15-2- 1930

(20)  *"Sligo Independent"*   25-6-1932

(21)  Heraughty, P. *"Inishmurray"* Dublin 1982. (Reprinted 1996.)

(22)  "Customs & Excise (Misc. Provisions) Act, 1988." Sect. 14.

(23)  In the first six months of 1954 four cases of illicit distillation came before the District Court and related to the Aclare, Coolaney, Culleens and Curry areas. The last case to come before a Co. Sligo court was in 1988, when a resident of Tullycusheenbeg was convicted and fined £1,000, mitigated to £500, at Tubbercurry court.

Other works consulted:

*"Journals of the Irish House of Commons",* 1750 - 1800.

Connell, K.H.  *"Illicit Distillation : An Irish Peasant Industry".*
      [ "Historical Studies", 3, 1961]

McGuire, E.B.  *"Irish Whiskey: A History of Distilling in Ireland. Dublin.* 1973.

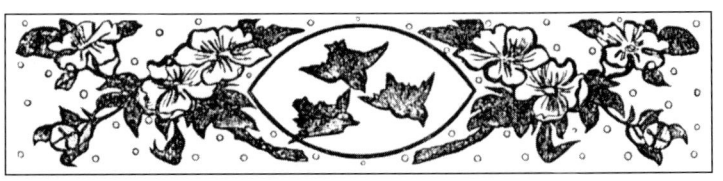

# Private Distillation in Kilmactigue

"Private distillation is the only feasible means the poor people here have of paying their rents, and supporting their families; and this they carried on more briskly than ever last year, when there was no penalty on the townlands; and many of them have said, that if it were made a felony, they would not desist, as they might as well hang as starve. They will only get 14s. per barrel, of 24 stone, for their oats, after carrying it 12 or 14 miles to market; for which, last year, they would have got nearly three times that price. A barrel of good oats, well managed, will produce eight gallons of common whiskey, which will sell for seven or eight shillings per gallon. They use various stratagems to elude the searches of the revenue officers, who frequently visit the neighbourhood. Sometimes they have their material concealed in caves, or the stacks of corn; at other times they remove them to the bogs and mountains, where they distill their liquor. While they are at work, they generally have a couple of videts on the roads by which the searching party is likely to approach; who, on perceiving them, convey the intelligence with great speed so that every thing is removed before the approach of the military. But their surest safeguard is to keep the Constable, or confidential guide, employed by the revenue officer, in constant pay, as he can either keep back the information; or should he find his employer intent on paying an unsuspected visit, when his friends are at work, he can dispatch a faithful messenger to warn them of the danger. This man, or one of his family, pays regular visits to the distiller in the parish, and gets from a crown to ten shillings from each of them, in proportion to what they have on hands. At one meeting, he received upwards of £5 for protection, which he assured them of having.

It happened lately, that some of them refused to contribute as liberally as he wished, and in revenge for their neglect or refusal, he brought the revenue officer and a party of the army by surprise among them, who made three seizures of whiskey, potale, and malt. Fortunately for the townland a party of the soldiers having separated from the revenue officer, made three other seizures, but were prevailed on by the owners, to take money from them in compensation, and to withdraw without making any discovery; by which collusion, the townlands were saved from being heavily fined, and the property of the individuals preserved, which was applied, partly to regale themselves and their friends, and partly to assist in paying their rents. However, when the danger was removed, the persons who were happy at having so fortunate an escape, and grateful to the soldiers for their good nature in sparing them, now became the assailants in turn; made application to the military officer commanding the party; complained of the extortion committed on them, and had their money restored.

Notwithstanding their many escapes, through stratagem, bribery, and want of exertion in the officers, still the people who follow this precarious and dangerous occupation, often suffer severe losses, and sometimes are reduced to beggary by the practice; yet they will persevere in it to the last. There are very few townlands in this parish, in which one family at least is not constantly employed in distilling, and often many at the same time, according as they can get their corn prepared for it. About two sacks is the quantity malted and distilled at each turn, which is easily concealed, and quickly put through the process. As there is no barley grown here, some of the people tend to buy it in the neighbouring parishes, which, when made into malt, they mix with oaten malt: which process produces the greatest quantity of spirits; but in general it is made from oats alone. Barley is now bought for 8d. per stone, which last year cost 1s. 8d. and it is supposed it will be still cheaper. There are no regular distillers here, but every man understands the trade, and carries it on as opportunity may serve. Some of them buy small stills, with the necessary apparatus, not altogether for their own use, but to hire out to others, who pay them from three to five shillings for each turn, according to the quantity they have to run. This is a great evil in the country, as the innocent and unoffending are obliged to pay for the faults of those who carry on this clandestine traffic, in many instances, wholly without the knowledge of those who live in the same townland with them, by observing the greatest secrecy, and generally doing the work by night.

Government has not as yet devised any method to put a complete stop to the evil: for the laws in force whilst they enrich the revenue officer, and those employed in the execution of them, are reducing the country to a state of distress and beggary, without producing the intended effects; yet observations and long experience might suggest a plan, which would effectuate the purpose without oppressing the individuals, who neither join in the practice, nor partake of the profits. The time to stop the evil is in its infancy, that is in the

# ILLICIT DISTILLATION

preparation of the malt which it must pass through the process of grinding. The mills in any parish or district are but few, and it would be much easier to guard or attend to these, than to a district containing 1000 families. In this parish, (which may serve as a standard for many others) there are five small mills, which are almost constantly employed in grinding malt, as the quantity of meal is very small. They scarcely earn forty shillings in the year by the toll on corn made into meal; one such mill would be perfectly sufficient for the use of the inhabitants for that purpose. Here then is the stage at which the mischief might be arrested with success; which might be done by destroying four out of five of these petty mills, and paying them in compensation as much money as they could show they earned by their lawful grist. As to the other mill, which might be allowed to remain, the proprietor of that, as well as the miller, and his assistants, should be bound in a heavy penal bond, that no malt, except such as paid duty, and was regularly permitted, should be ground therein. One or more of the Barony Constables, by having an additional salary allowed him, along with that which the County pays, might be stationed in the neighbourhood, with the powers to inspect, search for and seize any illicit malt which might be found therein; and further entitled to a certain proportion of the penalty, in the case of his convicting the party of committing an offence against the act. The miller, whose emolument is very small on grinding malt, (being only tenpence for a sack) would not be likely, for so small gains, to run the risk of a heavy penalty. Thus the attention of all parties interested would be directed to one place only in a large district, instead of being distracted by endeavouring to attend to a great number of places scattered over the country. If even the penalty had been laid on the malt, as well as on the potale and spirits, and that the revenue officer was to be entitled to his proportion of such a penalty, much more benefit would arise from that measure than from the manner in which it is now conducted. At present the officers are careless about the malt, as they have nothing to gain by seizing or destroying it; and many of them do not wish to meet with it in that state, thinking that at the more advanced stages it would produce something profitable to them if detected. Even a great part of what has been seized by them, and scattered about, has been afterwards gathered and, when cleaned by the owners, applied to the purpose of distillation."

Extracted from *"PARISH OF KILMACTIGUE"* by James Neligan, Rector and Vicar, written c. 1810, and published in Mason's *"Parochial Survey of Ireland"*. Dublin.1816.

# The Rise and Fall of John Martin

The Martins, believed to be of Scotch origin, settled in Sligo in the 17th century. Subsequent generations of the family progressed in wealth and influence. In 1738 Arthur Martin was admitted a Freeman of the Borough; his grandson, Charles, became Ballast Master in 1759; his great-grandson, Abraham, purchased the Cleveragh estate, and great-great-grandson John, was appointed High Sheriff in 1782. John's eldest son, Abraham Martin (1772-1853) was the most prominent and wealthiest merchant of his day. He owned a distillery, a fishery, flour mills and a bakery, in addition to landed possessions in the County.

Cleveragh House: suburban seat of the Martin Family

Property begot ambition and he longed for the day when a Martin would be returned as Member of Parliament for the Borough. The resolution of this dream was placed on the shoulders of his eldest son, John. Antipathy towards the Wynnes of Hazelwood, whose family, or their nominees, held the Parliamentary representation for over a century, had probably as much to do with the resolution as mere ambition. There was also an on-going dispute between Abraham

## THE RISE AND FALL OF JOHN MARTIN

Martin and the Wynnes regarding the collection of tolls and customs at the markets and fairs which eventually led to an action for trespass at the Assizes, litigation that gained Martin much popularity locally. It was no ordinary enterprise to wrest Sligo from the Wynnes, but fortune favours the brave! The circumstances of the time, namely, the formation of the Liberal and Independent Club in 1828; the enactment of Catholic Emancipation the following year, and the opening-up of the Borough to popular representation, greatly enhanced and facilitated his chances of success. Abraham's *protégé* carried a high profile - he was both amiable and popular, Vice-Chairman of the Board of Guardians, a member of the Grand Jury, a Magistrate and Deputy-Lieutenant of the County.

In late 1828, or early the following year, John Martin, who openly professed similar principles, was nominated by the Liberals to contest the Borough seat against the sitting member, John Wynne. It is said that Daniel O'Connell, on the occasion of a visit to Sligo, expressed some doubts as to Martin's political convictions, although, as an individual, the 'Liberator' held him in high esteem. However, thanks mainly to the promptings of the indomitable Dean Donlevy, the local Catholic Administrator, Martin's nomination was eventually endorsed.

In advance of the dissolution of Parliament in October, 1832, Martin published his Election Manifesto:

### *TO THE INDEPENDENT ELECTORS*
### *OF THE BOROUGH OF SLIGO*

*Gentlemen,*

*An opportunity of asserting the Independence of the Borough being at last presented, I offer myself as a Candidate to Represent you in the ensuing Parliament. My principles are well known to my fellow townsmen, and a desire to secure their Independence, whoever might be their Representative, has at all times characterised my conduct in connexion with our local politics.*

*In offering myself to your consideration, I need hardly express my determination, to give my attention to local interests, and industriously to press upon the Legislature whatever may tend to serve the commercial concerns of our Town. In all questions of national importance, I trust I shall be found on the side of Equity and Liberty, of economy in Finance, cheapness and*

131

*expedition in Law, the impartial administration of Justice, the abolition of*
*sinecures and unmerited pensions, and the fair representation of the People on*
*the great principle of Parliamentary Reform which you have obtained.*

*As an individual, I thank you for your support and your exertions to*
*secure my election; brought up among you, you have known my principles, you*
*have perceived my interests to be bound up with your own, and you are willing*
*to confide to me the important trust of sustaining our liberties and interests in*
*Parliament. Permit me to express my thanks for your confidence so far, and to*
*assure you that it shall never be misplaced.*

> *I have the honour to remain,*
>> *Gentlemen,*
>>> *Your most obedient*
>>>> *Humble servant,*
>>>> *JOHN MARTIN.*

Sligo, Nov. 19, 1832.

---

In contrast, Wynne's Address was short and devoid of any detail:-

## TO THE ELECTORS of the BOROUGH OF SLIGO

*Gentlemen,*

*As a constant resident in your neighbourhood, and naturally devoted to*
*the interest of Sligo, I take the earliest opportunity of offering myself as a*
*Candidate for the Representation of the Borough. I shall lose no time in*
*waiting on each of the Electors to solicit their support.*

> *I have the honour to be,*
>> *Gentlemen,*
>>> *Your obedient humble servant,*
>>>> *JOHN WYNNE*

The election, which was marked by street violence between
supporters of the opposing candidates and wholesale intimidation at
the hustings, opened in the Courthouse on Monday, December 17th,
1832. After the writ had been read by the Returning Officer, the
proceedings opened with the candidates being formally proposed and
seconded. Major G. Bromhead of *Cairnsfoot House* proposed John

Wynne as a fit and proper person to represent the Borough. Andrew Walsh of Union St., merchant, seconded the nomination. Captain Wm. Vernon of *Marino Cottage*, Finisklin, said he had the honour of proposing his friend and relation, John Martin, whom he described as "a friend of the poor and needy and whose many acts of kindness could not be overlooked". "Gentlemen, you have got your freedom, and I hope by coming forward manfully to give your votes, you will prove you deserved it". The nomination was seconded by William Patrickson of the firm of Scott and Patrickson, merchants. Both candidates were then afforded an opportunity of addressing the assembled voters. Wynne spoke of his family's long association with the Town and County and defended the principles that had characterised his parliamentary career since he succeeded his father, Owen Wynne, two years earlier. On presenting himself, John Martin was loudly cheered and it was some time before his voice could be heard above the commotion:-

*"Electors of Sligo, the day has at last arrived when you have the power of choosing your own representative ... I am happy to see so many of the respectable inhabitants of the Town crowding around me and by their presence showing their anxiety in this struggle. I feel proud and highly honoured in being the man in whose person your Independence is to be asserted, and I come forward, not to gratify a personal ambition, but to see the Town of Sligo made free ... I feel proud in throwing myself into the breach to fight for your freedom ... Should you do me the honour to return me, I trust I shall in Parliament have an opportunity to promote the good of my native country and, in particular, the welfare and interests of the Town. The same power which now puts me in, will hurl me from that high station should I at any time neglect my duty or the prosperity of the merchants and inhabitants of Sligo."* [1]

The question for a show of hands was then put by the Provost and was decided to be in favour of Martin. A poll was then demanded by Wynne. The voting continued over five days and, at the end of each, both sides claimed a majority. On the morning of the final day two additional candidates, namely, Gregory Cuffe Martin, brother of John, and Robert Jones of *Fortland House* (Conservative) entered the contest, presumably to take votes that might otherwise be lost to one or other of the principal contenders.

The contest was finally brought to a close at 5 p.m. on Friday, December 21st when the state of the poll was declared as follows:-

## THE RISE AND FALL OF JOHN MARTIN

| | | |
|---|---|---|
| John Martin | ............................ | 213 |
| John Wynne | ............................ | 159 |
| Cuffe Martin | ............................ | 20 |
| Robert Jones | ............................ | 5 |

The result was greeted with loud cheers and unprecedented expressions of joy. Cries of 'MARTIN FOREVER' echoed and re-echoed through the lofty building. When the noise had finally abated, Martin came forward and congratulated the voters on the "triumph of Independence", notwithstanding the widespread and menacing attitude adopted by the Wynne supporters. "I now go into Parliament as your free and unpledged representative - you have confided and placed in my hands a great and important trust, and I assure you that your confidence in me shall never be misplaced".

John Wynne, who was visibly disappointed with the outcome, did not see his opponent's success as the triumph of Independence - "when no honest man dare come forward to my support without subjecting his property to attack or even endangering his life, and when the Electors of the Town were hurried and herded to the poll by the threats of the Priest, Donlevy", whom, he alleged "had desecrated the temple of God by converting it into an arena for political discussion". This statement was greeted by tremendous groans and yells and the remainder of his speech was barely audible above the uproar. As Wynne withdrew from the scene Dean Donlevy stepped forward and, amid another outburst of clapping and cheering, he demanded the right of reply to the accusations that had been hurled at him by the scion of the House of Hazelwood:-

*"Gentlemen, I assure you I did not intend to raise my voice in this assembly to-night, but retire satisfied that victory has been achieved - the victory of Independence over intolerance... I have opposed Mr. Wynne as an unfit person to represent a Catholic people. I have opposed Mr. Wynne because he opposed the dearest interests of the religion of which I am a Minister, including a grant to Maynooth College and Catholic Emancipation, and I am charged with acting irreligiously in giving expression to those feelings. I plead quietly and say that it is my determination never to be deterred from a repetition of the same line whenever it may be necessary".* [2]

## THE RISE AND FALL OF JOHN MARTIN

The customary Chairing of the successful candidate was reported upon as follows by the *"Sligo Journal"*:-

*The Chairing of John Martin, Esq., M.P. took place on Monday last. At an early hour the streets were much crowded and among the numerous spectators were various groups of country people who had come to town to witness the spectacle.*

*The Chair, which was tastefully and handsomely ornamented with blue and white silk, on which were appropriate mottoes and devices, was placed on a large platform that had been brought from Martin's Distillery at the Riverside to his son's Committee Rooms, where the newly elected Member mounted the triumphal car amidst cheers of applause and congratulations, and was surrounded by his personal friends. The platform, which was drawn by relays of supporters and headed by a band, proceeded up Old Market Street, into High Street and Market Street before touring the Town and finally stopping at his father's Town House in Knox's Street. Personal friends and admirers of Mr. Martin displayed banners and buntings from their houses. All passed off with much good humour and tranquillity."* [3]

In the week after his election the following Address to the Independent Electors of the Borough of Sligo was published in the *"Journal"*:-

*Gentlemen,*

*Accept my sincere thanks for the honour you have conferred on me in returning me as your Representative for the ensuing Parliament. The triumphant majority by which the freedom of our Town has been secured must be a source of gratification to every independent mind. Believe me it shall ever be my sincere endeavour, by my future conduct, to merit the confidence placed in me by the independent inhabitants of Sligo.*

*I have the honour to be,*

> *Gentlemen,*
>> *Your obliged, and*
>>> *Faithful humble Servant,*
>>>> JOHN MARTIN.

Dec. 27, 1832.

Martin's success was marked by a Banquet in his honour, and that of his father, Abraham, which took place in the *Hibernian Hotel* on January 7th, 1833. It was given by the Independent Electors of the

## THE RISE AND FALL OF JOHN MARTIN

Borough and attended by a representative gathering of Liberals, Radicals and Reformers. The room was elegantly decorated with appropriate devices and mottoes, such as *"THE FIRST REPRESENTATIVE OF THE PEOPLE"* and *"THE FIRST FRUITS OF LIBERTY"*. Numerous toasts were proposed and drunk to in the course of the night. In response to *"ABRAHAM MARTIN AND THE TRADE OF SLIGO"*, the doyen of Sligo merchants said he was "delighted to be found amongst the foremost of his fellow businessmen in asserting their Independence". [4]

There was no contest at the next Parliamentary election in January, 1835. John Martin was returned unopposed for a further term but not before he pledged himself anew to support Corporate Reform and an equitable adjustment of the Tithe question. This he did on the occasion of a meeting with a number of prominent Liberals in Bishop Burke's residence in Finisklin. It was subsequently alleged that a number of those who had backed him in 1832 did not entirely approve of his conduct in Parliament but had sacrificed their feelings rather than create a division among themselves. [5] In an advertisement in the local press Martin assured his constituents that his principles remained unchanged:- [6]

*I return my most sincere thanks for the high honour you have conferred upon me by having for the second time chosen me as your Representative in Parliament.*

*I have already declared to you the principles by which I shall be guided, and which I should hope are such as to commend themselves to your approbation; and I trust, that my Parliamentary conduct shall ever be found in such strict accordance with my professions, that I may be enabled to retain, that which is to me of the most inestimable value, namely, the confidence of the Independent Constituency of Sligo.*

*I have the honour to be,*

    *Gentlemen,*

        *Your most attached servant,*

        JOHN MARTIN

John Martin's professed loyalty to the Liberal principles that had won him popular support in both 1832 and 1835 appears to have waned somewhat with the passage of time and, particularly, after he had united his fortune with that of the petulant Lord Stanley, formerly

## THE RISE AND FALL OF JOHN MARTIN

Chief Secretary for Ireland, who had seceded from the Whigs in 1834 and subsequently joined the Conservatives. There were accusations of his abandonment of his old friends; of allying himself with those whom he had formerly bitterly opposed and of reneging on the principles he once advocated.

The first evidence of mounting dissatisfaction with Martin's Parliamentary performance surfaced in editorials in the *"Sligo Champion"* in mid 1836 when he was taken to task for his handling of the Irish Tithe Bill. Contrary to assurances, he voted against the ministerial measure aimed at removing the infamous tithe system. It accused him of following the Tory line, of acting as the dupe of Stanley and "of sacrificing the good wishes of his friends without winning new ones". "In 1832 he was the professed friend of liberal measures; he opposed John Wynne, who was a rank Tory, and by the interests and votes of the Radicals of Sligo, he was successful. He continued loyal to his promises until the breaking-up of the Cabinet and after that he almost invariably joined the enemies of his country - he abandoned his old friends and threw himself on the arms of the very men who were formerly his enemies..." [7] In response to these accusations, an anonymous scribe in the *"Sligo Journal"* came to Martin's defence, claiming that his support of the Government was based on what he considered most conclusive to the welfare of the country, and the only criticism that could be levelled against him was that he did not go the full length of his constituent's "unreasonable and unfeeling demands". [8]

With the approach of the Election of August, 1837, it was clear that John Martin no longer had the support and backing of a majority of the Borough voters. The Liberal Club, which had been dormant for a time, was re-vitalised and diligently set about finding an alternative candidate. Eventually, after much soul-searching, and acting on the promptings of Dean Donlevy, and with the approbation of Daniel O'Connell and Bishop Patrick Burke, John Patrick Somers, once referred to by 'The Liberator' himself as "my young friend", was chosen as the standard-bearer of the Liberal voters of the Borough. Somers, who was the son of Pat Somers of Chaffpool and his wife, Mary Taaffe, was educated at Harrow where he became friendly with Lord Palmerston who had inherited large estates in this County. He also numbered Daniel O'Connell amongst his list of acquaintances.

137

## THE RISE AND FALL OF JOHN MARTIN

Somers received a great reception from the Liberals and their supporters on his arrival in Sligo in mid July, 1837. A week later they met in the 'Long Room' of Boyle's *Hibernian Hotel* before parading the streets of the Town. This was followed by a rally in Market Street which was addressed by a number of prominent Liberals. Later in the evening Bishop Burke visited the Tally Rooms and was accorded a big welcome. In the course of a short address to the assembled voters he was at pains to make it clear that had John Martin acted under the influence of his promises, both implied and expressed, in 1835, there would be no need for an election, as he would be returned unopposed. In his address to the Independent Electors of the Borough, Somers undertook to support Municipal Reform, the abolition of Tithes, etc., issues upon which Martin had reneged. The watchword for the campaign was: "SOMERS AND INDEPENDENCE".

John Martin contested the election with the backing of the Tories and a handful of what was described as 'moderate Liberals'. His Address to the Electors was shorter than usual and contained no specific promises. [9]

*Gentlemen,*

*I respectfully offer myself as a Candidate for the distinguished honour of again representing my native Town.*

*Sincerely anxious to remove every abuse which can be found in the institutions of our country, I am at the same time not less solicitous to preserve that which is sound.*

*With such sentiments I now solicit your suffrages, and confidently anticipate that I shall be placed, by your kindness, in the high station of your Representative in the ensuing Parliament.*

*Your most obedient humble servant,*
    JOHN MARTIN.

Although his campaign lacked much of the bustle and activity of the 1832 contest, it was, nevertheless, backed by all his father's wealth and influence and sustained by the House of Hazelwood. The Protestant voters of the Borough, with a few exceptions, also rallied to his support.

The Borough election opened in the Courthouse on August 2nd,

## THE RISE AND FALL OF JOHN MARTIN

1837. In proposing the nomination of John Martin, Major Charles Parke recommended him to the assembled voters as "a fit and proper person to represent Sligo in Parliament". "We all know him as a perfect gentleman, most amiable in his disposition, and best of all, a man of strict integrity; he was uncompromising in his principles and incapable of yielding to the factious domination of any party, having no other object in view but what he regarded as the welfare and prosperity of his country. His conduct in the late Parliament is duly appreciated by the respectable portion of his constituents who fully acquit him of any charge of inconsistency or impropriety". The nomination was seconded by Captain James Reed who assured all and sundry that his nominee could count on the support of "all the respectable voters of the Borough". Somers was nominated by Martin Madden and seconded by Andrew Walker, both of whom had been ardent supporters of Martin in the two previous contests. The candidates then addressed the assembled electorate in turn. In his speech John Martin castigated his former political allies and friends for the abuse and criticism that had been levelled against him before proceeding to defend his Parliamentary record:-

*"Electors of the Borough of Sligo: At the outset I wish to appeal to your sense of justice and fairplay for a patient hearing. You are all well aware how grossly I have been abused; my character has been aspersed in private and openly impinged in a newspaper recently established in this Town... While I have no personal ambition to be returned to Parliament, I nevertheless feel myself bound by a sense of duty to do so in order to rescue the representation of this Borough out of the hands of a self-constituted junta - a set of gentlemen calling themselves Liberals. Gentlemen, if they were liberal they would not have treated me in the manner they have done. Now, I would ask the electors of Sligo why a body of men of that description - superior neither in rank, property or respectability - should arrogate to themselves the right of returning a Member of Parliament for this Borough, and dictate to the rest of the constituency. It has been said that my conduct in the last Parliament has been inconsistent with my conduct in the prior one. I deny that. I also deny that I have violated my pledges in any way..."*[10]

Somers' Address was short. He assured the voters that the liberality of his principles were well known and, if elected, he "wouldn't deceive the people of Sligo."

## The Rise and Fall of John Martin

After four days of voting, the poll closed on Saturday, August 5th, when the following result was then declared:

| | | |
|---|---|---|
| Somers | ........................ | 262 |
| Martin | ........................ | 208 |

The outcome was received with great acclamation. The successful candidate thanked all who had supported him, and renewed his promise that he would work for the interest of all parties and of Sligo. Martin, in a rather emotional address, reflected on what he saw as the reasons for his defeat:-

*"Gentlemen, I presume it is scarcely necessary for me to entreat your indulgence on the present occasion, as I am now taking my leave of public life and may never again present myself to your notice; but I feel it due to myself and my friends to offer a few remarks before I retire from the hustings . . . Notwithstanding what my honourable opponent said yesterday, I attribute my defeat to intimidation, and to intimidation alone. If the electors were left to act on their own feelings and without undue influence, I should, instead of being in a minority of 54, have a majority amounting to that number.*

*Gentlemen, I assure you I undertook this contest on no light grounds. I had as good grounds for expecting success as ever a candidate had, and if those who promised me their votes, or even half of those who broke their pledges, had come forward in my favour, I should have been in a majority. Many of my father's tenants were compelled to act contrary to their own wishes, some were carried off by force and imprisoned in a hotel in this Town, then brought up to the hustings and compelled to vote against me ... "* [11]

He then proceeded to stoutly defend his Parliamentary record and explain his reasons for voting as he did on a number of issues.

Some of Martin's comments provoked an immediate response from Dean Donlevy who remarked that the Liberals had taken the former M.P. at his own word, namely, that whenever he gave dissatisfaction to his constituents he would loose their support. According to the Dean the only reason why Martin lost the popular vote was his reneging on the principles upon which he was returned in the first instance; he had allowed himself to be misled insidiously and proved himself "no longer fit to represent our feelings in Parliament". He concluded by stating that John Martin would continue to be held in the highest respect as a private citizen.

## THE RISE AND FALL OF JOHN MARTIN

After his defeat John Martin retired from public life, although he unsuccessfully contested a vacancy on the Town and Harbour Commissioners in both 1838 and 1842. His health, which was reported as giving grounds for concern in the closing months of his Parliamentary career, continued to decline. In April, 1844 he was reported as being seriously ill. He subsequently went to England for treatment where he died in February, 1846, aged 38. In death, the old antagonisms were quickly forgotten and all creeds and classes joined in mourning the premature passing of a "most amiable and gentlemanly character, a man of intelligence and rare business acumen".

The rise and fall of John Martin epitomises the volatile nature of the political scene in the Sligo of a century and a half ago, at a time when elections were fiercely contested and the secrecy of the ballot had not yet arrived. In retrospect, it could be argued that the scion of the House of Cleveragh was rather harshly treated by the Liberals and their kindred, but such was the principled approach to the issues of the time that a public representative, of whatever persuasion, who reneged on promises, solemnly given, could hardly expect the continued support of a majority of the electorate. John Martin was not the only M.P. to be treated in this manner. His successor, John P. Somers, suffered a similar fate a decade later.

### *References:*

| | | |
|---|---|---|
| (1) | *"Sligo Journal"* | 21-12-1832 |
| (2) | ibid | 28-12-1832 |
| (3) | opus cit. | ibid |
| (4) | ibid | 18-1-1833 |
| (5) | *"Sligo Champion"* | 1-7-1837 |
| (6) | *"Sligo Journal"* | 16-1-1835 |
| (7) | *"Sligo Champion"* | 11-6-1836; 1-7-1837 & 8-7-1837 |
| (8) | *"Sligo Journal"* | 17-6-1836 |
| (9) | ibid | 21-7-1837 |
| (10) | *"Sligo Champion"* 5-8-1837 & | *"Sligo Journal"* 4-8-1837 |
| (11) | *"Sligo Journal"* 11-8-1837 & | *"Sligo Champion"* 12-8-1837 |

# From Stagecoach to Railway

Travel in Ireland in the 18th century was, as it had been for generations untold, either on foot or on horseback. However, the improved condition of Irish roads in the latter years of the century made for ease of movement and greater communication between Dublin and provincial cities and towns. Between 1780 and 1850 horse drawn transport enjoyed a golden age and the stagecoach held pride of place on the roads, followed closely by the mail car. Travel in the coaching age was both slow and expensive and was not immune from hazards and discomforts. Robbery by highway men constituted a real danger and the mail coaches, in particular, were obliged to carry guards armed with blunderbusses and loaded pistols. The earlier mail coaches carried only five passengers, four inside and one outside, but as the vehicles got larger up to twenty could be accommodated. In 1790 a Stage Coach service was inaugurated between Dublin and Sligo which took twenty one hours, or thereabouts, to complete the journey. It was not until half a century later that the distance had been reduced to fifteen hours' duration, and this only in perfect weather conditions.

Before the construction of the mail coach road between Sligo and Boyle, the Dublin mail was carried via Enniskillen. An advertisement in the *"Sligo Journal"* of June, 1805, announced that the Sligo, Enniskillen and Dublin Royal Mail was accompanied by a 'well-armed guard'; that the time taken for the journey was 26 hours and the fare was £2.12s. The first Mail Coach from Sligo to Dublin, via Boyle and Longford, was commenced in 1808 and was operated by Richard Bourne. The Royal Canal Company opposed the venture vigorously and lowered its own rates to discourage travellers from going by the coach. However, the people of Sligo stood by Bourne and his new conveyance, and at a public meeting in September, 1809, presided over by Abraham Martin, bound themselves by resolution to support it. The Mail Coach was drawn by four horses and carried a maximum of ten passengers, six inside and four outside. It departed from the *Nelson Hotel*, Linenhall Street, at 9.30 a.m. and travelled at an average speed of eight miles per hour as far as Kinnegad where it connected with the Galway Mail to Dublin. It returned to Sligo in the afternoon. There were two stages

FROM STAGECOACH TO RAILWAY

between Sligo and Boyle, one at Lackagh and another at Ballinafad. At some of the stages coaching inns were established to cater for the weary travellers. In 1811 communication between Sligo and Dublin was cut off for nine days owing to a heavy snowfall in the Midlands. A somewhat similar situation arose in March, 1855, when severe weather conditions resulted in the Mail Car not reaching Sligo for three days.

By the 1830's 4-horse Mail Coaches were plying to Dublin, Derry and Ballina, each with accommodation for eight passengers, four inside and four outside, at an average fare of 3d a mile. At the same time a Car travelled to Boyle from *Ross's Hotel*, Jail Street, four mornings a week, and on Saturdays another Car departed from the *Spinning Wheel* in High Street for Ballina. John Algeo ran a car to Manorhamilton three days a week at a return fare of 2/6d, while the *Enterprise Light Coach* was advertised as operating on the Sligo-Enniskillen route.

A new Day Coach between Sligo - Ballina - Castlebar was introduced in 1828, and five years later, in May, 1833, a Sligo-Derry Car was inaugurated. A daily service between Ballyshannon and Sligo was introduced in February, 1837. The return fare was 3/- for the four-hour journey and the local depot was *Mason's Hotel* on The Mall. The following year an enlarged coach, capable of carrying sixteen passengers, four inside and twelve outside, commenced operations on the Dublin route. It travelled up on Mondays, Wednesdays and Fridays and returned the following days. The journey took sixteen and one quarter hours, departing Sligo at 4.45 a.m. and Dublin at 5.45 p.m. By 1851 a 2-horse Mail Car covered the distance in what was then a record thirteen hours.

In September, 1838, Charles Bianconi, the 'King of the Irish Roads',

143

introduced a 3-wheeled Car between Sligo and Longford, which connected with Dublin by a newly inaugurated boat service on the Royal Canal. The Car departed Sligo at 6 a.m. and reached Longford eight hours later. However, passengers did not arrive in Dublin until 8.30 p.m., fourteen and a half hours after boarding the Car in Sligo. The single fare to Dublin was 6/6d for the Car and 5/6d for the boat. Those who wished to travel first-class on the boat paid an additional 2/6d. Following upon the opening of the Dublin-Mullingar rail link in 1848, both the Sligo-Dublin Mail Car and the Sligo-Dublin Day Coach operated to and from the latter terminus.

At a public meeting in the Courthouse in 1840 it was suggested that a Mail Car service should be introduced to traverse the Geevagh-Ballyfarnon road to Drumsna where it would connect with the Sligo-Dublin coach, thus saving almost two hours on a trip to Dublin, the route being several miles shorter. The Grand Juries of Sligo and Leitrim were requested to carry out major improvements to sections of the aforementioned route.

---

## COACHING SERVICES ex SLIGO, 1839

| | |
|---|---|
| **To Boyle:** | a 2-horse Car from the *Nelson Hotel* at 4.15 p.m. daily. |
| **To Enniskillen:** | Mail Car from *Nelson Hotel* at 12.05p.m. daily. |
| **To Longford:** | Bianconi 4-horse Car from O'Neill's. High Street, at 5.45.p.m. daily. |
| **To Manorhamilton:** | Car from the *North Hotel*, The Mall, on Tuesdays, Fridays and Saturdays. |

---

In June, 1846, Lewis G. Jones of Ardnaree and Dromore West, introduced a Day Car service on the Ballina to Sligo route. Three years later the Post Office entered into a contract with him to carry the mail between the said towns. A few years later, in 1854, Bianconi commenced running a Car on the route and a decade later both operators entered into a partnership whereby Jones reverted to operating the Day Car service and Bianconi took over the Mail Car, dividing whatever profits accrued. This arrangement continued in

FROM STAGECOACH TO RAILWAY

# SLIGO & DERRY COACH

THE Proprietors of the SLIGO and DERRY MAIL CARS respectfully inform the Public that on

## Monday, 6th of May

They will commence running coaches between

## Sligo and Derry,

Through in one day, carrying

### Four Inside, and Five Outside Passengers;

And trust that moderate Fares, good Horses, and careful Drivers, with strict attention to the comfort of Passengers, will afford general satisfaction.

The Coach will start from the Nelson Hotel, Sligo, at Five o'Clock, morning and arrive at Derry at Six o'Clock, evening in time for the Belfast Coach; and will leave the commercial Hotel, Derry, at Six o'clock, morning and arrive at Sligo, at Seven o'Clock, evening.

Fare -       Sligo to Derry, Inside, 15s. Outside, 10s.
             Sligo to Strabane, Inside 12s. Outside, 8s.

**25th April, 1833.**

---

## Dublin and Sligo
## DAY - COACH

*Carrying 4 Inside and 12 Outside passengers.*

THE Public are respectfully informed that the Sligo Day-Coach continues as usual, leaving this Office on the Mornings of Monday, Wednesday and Friday, a quarter before Six o'clock; stops twenty minutes for Breakfast at Enfield, and reaches Sligo at Ten o'clock p.m. Will return thence (during the Summer months) a quarter before Five o'clock, on the Mornings of Tuesday, Thursday, Saturday, stop twenty minutes at Boyle for Breakfast, and reach Dublin at Nine in the Evening.

The above arrangement will commence on and after Monday next, the 9th Inst.
Royal Mail Coach Office, 48, Dawson-street,
3rd April, 1838.

145

FROM STAGECOACH TO RAILWAY

place until March, 1867, when Bianconi's operations were taken over by John Walsh, his former agent in the Sligo area. Throughout the following two decades Walsh and Jones were in competition on the route, the former operating the Mail Car and Jones a Day Car.

The stage or mail coach rarely made news, but there were exceptions. In September, 1858, the *"Chronicle"*carried the heading : ROBBERY OF THE SLIGO MAIL. Its report of the incident ran as follows:-

*"On Monday, the 6th inst., the Coach which carries the mail from Sligo to Mullingar left the Post-office here at the usual hour, with the sack containing the mail for Dublin safely deposited in a well under the guard's seat. The well was covered with a lid secured by a lock, the key of which was in the guard's custody, so that access to the mail could not be had without his consent, except by open violence, or in consequences of his culpable neglect. When the Coach arrived in Boyle the mail from that town was put into the well with the Sligo bags, and the Coach continued its journey, but when it arrived at its destination, and the lid was raised, neither of the bags was to be found. They had both disappeared."* [1]

As far as can be ascertained it was never established whether the mail, which contained bank parcels and private correspondence with valuable enclosures, was lost or stolen, even though the Post Office authorities offered a reward of £25 for information.

Accidents to passengers were not very common but they did occur from time to time. In most instances they arose from the poor condition of the roads, as for example in 1860, when Charles O' Hara, the Crown Solicitor for Sligo, was thrown from a Bianconi car as it jolted along from one pothole to another on the road between Collooney and Drumfin. It appears that the wheel of the Mail Car got into one of the many 'ruts' that abounded on that stretch of roadway and he was pitched off and had one of his knees seriously injured in the fall. This incident prompted a concerned ratepayer to complain on the condition of the mail coach road:-

*"I was going to Boyle a short time ago by Bianconi's Express Coach, and near Collooney there was a hole worn in the middle of the road so deep, that had the wheel go into it, we were almost certain to have a break-down or an upset. So dangerous was it that one of our County Magistrates, who happened to be in the coach, thought it necessary, for the public safety, to send a message to the*

146

FROM STAGECOACH TO RAILWAY

*police, ordering them to take charge of this dangerous place until it would be filled in. Let anyone go from Sligo to Ballymote and ask himself if he ever saw any public road in such a disgraceful state....*" [2]

On another occasion, in August, 1861, Martin W. Phillips, a Sligo merchant, who was an outside passenger on the Dublin Mail Coach, was thrown heavily to the ground outside Drumsna after the axle of the front wheel broke and the vehicle turned over on its side. As a result he suffered a fractured shoulder and subsequently took an unsuccessful action at the Sligo Assizes against Bianconi and his local agent, John Walsh.

In February, 1836, as the Sligo Mail Coach approached Carrick from Dublin, it overturned on a heavily flooded stretch of roadway after the horses bolted. One of the outside passengers, a

young man named Corcoran from Ballinacarrow, the only son of a respectable widow, was thrown face downwards into the water and drowned before he could be rescued. His brother-in-law, who was sitting beside him, was also thrown to the ground but  fortunately escaped an untimely end. Another passenger, Peter Phibbs of Sligo, escaped a similar fate by clinging on to the iron rails of the coach. Four female passengers travelling inside escaped injury. [3]

What might well have been an accident, resulting in a number of fatalities, occurred in 1862. The Sligo-Enniskillen Day Coach was returning to Sligo via Fivemilebourne on September 18th. As it descended Morerah Hill the horses, which had been proceeding at a gentle trot, suddenly broke into a gallop and, with the driver unable to restrain them, were unable to take a bend in the road. The vehicle mounted a loose stone fence and came to rest half in and the half out of the adjacent field. The outside passengers, six in all, including the

147

FROM STAGECOACH TO RAILWAY

driver, were tossed into the field while a number of female passengers inside were badly shaken. Miraculously, there were no serious injuries apart from bruising and lacerations sustained by Messrs Kidd and Balfour, prominent Sligo merchants, who were amongst the outside passengers. The coach was badly damaged but the horses escaped with minor scratches. The relieved passengers were taken to their destination by two local Cars.

In July, 1856, a rather unusual case came before the Sligo Assizes. David Cullen of Castlecar brought an action against Charles Bianconi for £19.10s in respect of loss and injuries sustained while travelling on the Mail-Coach between Boyle and Sligo in December, 1855. The facts of the case had already been outlined in a letter written by Cullen and published in the *"Sligo Chronicle"* four months earlier.[4] It was addressed to Charles Bianconi, Longfield, Clonmel :-

> *Castlecar,*
> *Manorhamilton.*
> *10-3-1856*

*Sir,*

*On Thursday, December 6th last, my daughter and myself, having been in the County of Galway, took our seats on your Car at Williamstown, paying a fare of 16s to Sligo. We stopped at Monson's Hotel in Boyle and were forwarded by him on the Mail Coach of Friday morning between 4 and 5 o'clock.*

*Sat outside between the coachman, whose name was Kelly, a man who never drove me before. At about eight miles from Sligo a gale of wind got under my hat and blew it back on the roof of the coach. I shouted to the coachman and told him what had happened but he made no exertion to pull up until I shouted a second time and a third time. By then the hat had fallen off the roof of the coach onto the roadway. The guard stood up and was in the act of getting down to take it up when the coachman said he would not allow him and drove off, leaving me at the risk of my life, with my grey head bare - which is now entering its 70th year - exposed to the inclemency of a frosty morning.*

*I remonstrated with him but to no purpose. My daughter said I should go inside the coach, to which he replied that the coach was full, though there was not one in it - she and I having been all the passengers from Boyle to Sligo. In about ten minutes afterwards we arrived at the first stage from Sligo, and while*

148

*changing horses, I asked him to direct the helper to go and search for my hat. This he refused to do. His conduct was inhuman.*

*I trust you will afford me redress by ordering my hat to be paid for - it cost 11s.6d. and was very little worn. If my health suffers, I shall let you know; and as to any chastisement you may inflict on the perpetrator of such strange conduct, I leave to your own judgement. I have been travelling coaches forty-five years and such an occurrence I never witnessed before.*

*Sincerely,*
*David Cullen ".*

When the case came before the Assizes, David Cullen, the plaintiff; John Kelly and John Darcy, coachman and guard, on the Mail-Coach, and Hughes, Bianconi's local agent, gave evidence and were cross-examined at some length. Edward Pollock, solicitor for the defence, pleaded that Her Majesty's Mail Coach could not be delayed "whether Cullen's head was too big or his hat too small as to fly off his head...... No coachman could be expected to pull up on a windy morning with restive horses, thus endangering the lives of other passengers....."[5] After listening to both sides, the Judge directed the Jury that should they find their verdict against Bianconi, there should be proof of negligence on the part of the coachman; however, if the coachman or guard acted uncourteously or uncivil, Bianconi was not accountable. The Jury, having deliberated for some time, reached a verdict, dismissing Cullen's claim but adding that he had been treated "very inhumanly".

The following description of a locally operated Mail Car of that era was far from complimentary and most likely unrepresentative of the service generally:- *"In the year 1838 the only public conveyance between the towns of Sligo and Enniskillen for the carriage of either Her Majesty's mail or liege subjects was a one-horse jingle, a real old Irish jaunting car. The passengers seldom exceeded two and the average length of time wasted was twelve hours; but when - a rare event - the full compliment of four passengers was obtained, then what with stopping to repair the fractures of the harness, walking half the way to ease the horse and other incidents, the pilgrimage was not accomplished inside fifteen hours. The first change of horse from Enniskillen was at Blacklion and the second at Manorhamilton......"*[6] By 1858 the

FROM STAGECOACH TO RAILWAY

situation on this route had improved considerably. A well-appointed coach plied daily between Sligo and Lisbellaw railway station, the station nearest to Sligo at that time. In addition, a Mail Car, capable of carrying fourteen passengers, plied daily between the towns.

In 1841 a Stage Coach, operated by local hotelier, William Hudson, plied between Sligo and Ballina thrice weekly, departing at 6.a.m. It had accommodation for thirteen passengers who breakfasted at Easkey and arrived at their destination at 11.45. An improved daily service was introduced in 1846. A 2 -horse Car named *Independent Fair Trader* was introduced on the Ballymote-Sligo route in August, 1842, by H.B. Irwin, the proprietor of *Irwin's Hotel* in that town. It operated on Tuesdays, Thursdays and Saturdays, departing from Ballymote at 8.a.m. and returning from Sligo at 6.p.m.

---

## Mail and Stage Coaches ex Sligo in 1849:

1. Day Coach to Mullingar, connecting with Dublin train;
2. Day Car to Mullingar, connecting with Dublin train;
3. Sligo-Ballina-Castlebar Mail Coach;
4. Sligo-Ballina Day Coach;
5. Sligo-Derry Mail Coach;
6. Sligo-Enniskillen Mail Coach;
7. Sligo-Dublin Mail Coach.

---

In 1853, in addition to Bianconi's Mail Car and Jones's Car, both operating between Sligo and Enniskillen, a new stage-coach service linking Sligo and Omagh was introduced. It ran three days a week and gave connections to Derry by means of a newly inaugurated train service. By mid 1850's Bianconi was operating the following services ex Sligo - the Dublin Mail; Dublin Day Coach, and Cars to Enniskillen, Strabane and Westport. He also ran a Car service linking Ballina and Tubbercurry via The Gap. In 1863 this service was extended to Ballymote to connect with the newly extended rail connection linking Dublin with Sligo. One of the prize horses used by Bianconi in his local coaches was named *John Sadlier* in memory of John Sadlier, deceased, the Tipperary-born banker who had been M.P. for the Borough of Sligo between 1853 and 1856.

In 1855 the local press carried an advertisement stating that Cannon's 2-horse Car has commenced plying between Ballymote and Sligo on Tuesdays and Saturdays and served Ballisodare and Collooney. The same operator also ran a 1-horse Mail Car between Drumfin and Tubbercurry via Ballymote and Bunninadden, which gave a connection with the Dublin Mail.

---

## DAY & MAIL COACH TIME-TABLE, 1851

**Dublin-Sligo Day Coach:**

Dublin (dep.)  . . . . . . . . . . . . . . . . . . . . . . . . . . . . . 7.30 a.m.

Sligo (arr.)  . . . . . . . . . . . . . . . . . . . . . . . . . . . . . .8.00 p.m.

**Sligo-Dublin Mail Coach:**

Sligo (dep.)  . . . . . . . . . . . . . . . . . . . . . . . . . . . . .4.00 p.m.

Dublin (arr.)  . . . . . . . . . . . . . . . . . . . . . . . . . . . . .3.15 a.m.

Dublin (dep.)  . . . . . . . . . . . . . . . . . . . . . . . . . . . . .7.10 p.m.

Sligo (arr.)  . . . . . . . . . . . . . . . . . . . . . . . . . . . . .8.25 a.m.

**Sligo-Ballina-Castlebar Mail Car:**

Sligo (dep.)  . . . . . . . . . . . . . . . . . . . . . . . . . . . . .7.00 a.m.

Castlebar (arr.) . . . . . . . . . . . . . . . . . . . . . . . . . . . .2.55 p.m.

---

The coming of the railways heralded the death-knell of the stage coach. However, the coaching era did not come to an abrupt end. The spread of the railways was a slow process and the horse drawn coaches and cars continued to operate, feeding the railway system as well as providing a transport service in the more remote areas. After the retirement of Charles Bianconi in 1866, John Walsh, his local agent, took over the services and operated them from the old Bianconi offices a few doors from the *Imperial Hotel* in Linenhall Street.[7] Regular services were introduced to Rosses Point, Strandhill and Bundoran. In the summer season a 14 - seater 'Long Car' did regular trips daily to the Point. He also retained and operated the contract for the transportation of mails to Ballina and Bundoran.

As the century progressed competition became very keen on the local routes, as for example in 1875, when the Jones Company placed Cars on the Bundoran and Enniskillen routes in opposition to Walsh.

Throughout the 'Eighties and 'Nineties the distinctive 'Long Cars' and 2-Horse vehicles, operated by Walsh, and newcomers, Collery and McGoldrick, were a common sight on the roads of Sligo and the North-West generally, transporting passengers to seaside resorts and sporting fixtures, in addition to regular scheduled services.

The arrival of the motorcar and omnibus in the opening decade of this century led, eventually, to the demise of the coaching era.

---

## Time Table of Conveyances from Sligo - 1857

**Sligo Mail**       (Two-horse Car):
Arrives at Ballina 11.25 a.m.; leaves 12.45 p.m. and reaches Sligo 5.54 p.m.

**Sligo Day Cars:**   A two horse Car (Jones): Leaves Ballina 6.45.a.m.; reaches Sligo 11.45.a.m. and arrives in Ballina 8.00 p.m. A two-horse car (Bianconi) also leaves Ballina 10.30 a.m., passing through Dromore West for Sligo. Arrives in Ballina in time for the Car to Castlebar.

**Dublin Mail** (Bianconi):
Leaves Sligo 4.30 p.m. reaching Mullingar in time for the Mail train. Arrives Sligo 7.45 a.m.

**Sligo Day Coach** (Bianconi):
Leaves Sligo 10 a.m. and arrives in Longford in time for the up train. Leaves Longford 11 a.m. and arrives in Sligo at 6.30 p.m.

**Strabane Car** (Bianconi):
Leaves Sligo 8.45 a.m. and arrives in Strabane in time for the train to Derry. Leaves Strabane 6.00 a.m. and arrives in Sligo 3.40 p.m. in time for the Dublin Mail.

**Enniskillen Car:**  Leaves Sligo 11.00 a.m. and arrives at Sligo at 7.30 p.m.

**Westport Car**    (Bianconi):
Leaves Sligo 9.00 a.m. passes through Dromore West, Ballina, Castlebar and arrives in Westport 6.50 p.m. Leaves Westport 5.30 a.m. and arrives in Sligo 3.40 p.m.

## THE SLIGO MAIL

"A perfectly new equipage, in the shape of a Mail Coach, was driven into Town on Thursday last, Patrick's Day. The horses were very superior, and the coach-man, Pat Featherston, had their heads most tastefully decorated with evergreens. The whole turn out looked exceedingly well, and was very much admired".

*"Sligo Champion"* 21-3-1853

# The Coming of the Railway

By the 1830's the railway era had already arrived in Great Britain and schemes for railways had spread to Ireland, resulting in the construction of the Dublin and Kingstown and Dublin and Drogheda railways. By 1836, when the Royal Commission on Irish Railways was appointed to enquire into the best means of promoting the construction of a general system of railways in Ireland, a Dublin-Sligo railway had been planned and surveyed by private interests, the route chosen being that actually built later, i.e. via Mullingar, Longford, Carrick-on-Shannon and Boyle.

Nothing came of this scheme but in 1837 the Royal Commission recommended the building, with Government assistance, of trunk railways from Dublin. One arm of the Northern trunk was to go to Enniskillen via Navan and Cavan; and if this had been built at the time, no doubt Sligo would have been served soon afterwards by a branch from Enniskillen. However, no general Government assistance in building railways in Ireland was forthcoming and little further happened until the phenomenon known as the 'Railway Mania' reached Ireland in 1844/46.

In December, 1844, a meeting of the Gentry, Merchants and Traders of the Town and County was convened for the Courthouse to press for a railway connection for Sligo. The meeting was presided over by the Mayor, Michael Gallagher, and a Resolution, proposed by Henry Lyons and seconded by James Caldwell, was adopted, namely, *"That a*

*Committee of the following gentlemen draw up a memorial to the Board of Trade soliciting their support to the proposed Dublin-Mullingar line, and to the proposed Newry and Enniskillen Railway, as being most calculated to serve the interests of Sligo as well as the country at large."*

The Committee appointed consisted of the Mayor, Wm. Kernaghan, Peter O'Connor, John Scott, R. Robinson and John Delaney. [1]

In February, 1845, the prospectus of the proposed Enniskillen to Sligo railway, providing a link with Belfast, was published.[2] The Provisional Committee consisted of prominent residents of Counties Sligo and Leitrim, headed by John Wynne of Hazelwood and the proposed route was via Manorhamilton through Glencar, Drumcliffe South, Springfield, Rathbraughan, Ballytivnan and Rathquarter to a terminus at the rear of the tenements in Barrack Street.

A number of schemes to serve Sligo from various parts of the country were registered provisionally but the only one to obtain Parliamentary approval was the Sligo-Shannon Junction Railway which, in conjunction with the proposed Sligo Ship Canal, was intended to connect Sligo with the Arigna valley mining area. Both projects were authorised in 1846 but never progressed any further. At a public meeting in Sligo in May, 1852, presided over by the Mayor, Edward H. Verdon, the following Resolution was adopted:-

*"That as Sligo is the first port in commerce, yielding more revenue than any other, in the Province of Connaught, this meeting is of opinion that its onward progress is much retarded for want of Railway communication with the metropolis; and that, as the Dundalk and Enniskillen Railway, is about to be completed, the desired connection can be formed by extending it to Sligo, which will give to the line of Enniskillen, and the Counties of Cavan, Fermanagh and Leitrim, the advantages that a fine shipping port such as Sligo affords for the exportation of their produce, advantages that cannot fail to secure the zealous co-operation of the several landed proprietors through whose estates the proposed line would run".*

It was also resolved that the following gentlemen form a Committee to take such steps as they may deem advisable for the formation of a company to construct a Railway connecting Sligo and Enniskillen, so as to complete the line of communication to Dublin, namely, the Mayor, Roger Walker, Patrick Bucan, William Phibbs, Wm.C. Tute, Alderman Williams and Moses Monds. [3]

A train about to depart from the Sligo terminus c. 1875
*(Somerville Coll. S.C.L.)*

FROM STAGECOACH TO RAILWAY

Meanwhile, the building of railways from Dundalk and Derry to Enniskillen had been authorised, as also was a line from Dublin to Longford via Mullingar. In 1846 a number of local railway protagonists reached an agreement whereby the Midland Great Western (M.G.W.) Railway would seek Parliamentary approval for an extension of the Dublin-Longford line to Sligo. Unfortunately, the necessary application to Parliament had to be abandoned as the M.G.W. found it necessary to concentrate its efforts in obtaining authorisation for an extension from Mullingar to Galway in order to block a rival concern. With the onslaught of the Famine, not only was the proposed Longford-Sligo extension abandoned but the building of the already authorised Mullingar-Longford branch was also deferred indefinitely.

By 1852 there had been considerable improvement in national confidence and activity, and in that year the Corporation passed a resolution expressing "their most anxious wish to have Sligo connected with the capital by means of a railway, and that both as a body and individually they would give their best support and assistance to any public company formed for such object".[4] The M.G.W. again interested itself in the matter of a branch running north from Mullingar, and in the same year obtained an Act of Parliament reviving powers to extend the railway to Longford. The Act also authorised a further branch from this line to Cavan but the matter of extending as far as Sligo was still left in abeyance. In November, 1852, the *"Champion"* reported that the afore-mentioned Company had been "roused into action" and "that steps are about to be taken to extend the Mullingar line to Sligo".[5] The Longford branch, built by that famous railway contractor, William Dargan, was opened to traffic in November, 1855.

Growing concern with the delay in linking Sligo with one or other of the existing railway systems prompted Sir Malby Crofton, the High Sheriff, to convene a meeting of the Landed Proprietors, Merchants and Traders in the Courthouse in November, 1855. Opinions were divided as to whether the Dublin line should be extended via Carrick and Boyle or by way of Strokestown and Boyle, while others had an expressed preference for an extension from Enniskillen. Eventually, the following Resolution, proposed by Col. Knox Gore and seconded by Bryan Owen Cogan, was passed unanimously :-

*"That it is the opinion of this meeting that the time has arrived when the*

## FROM STAGECOACH TO RAILWAY

*County of Sligo may justly consider itself entitled to the very great advantages of a Railway, having its terminus in the Town of Sligo".*

*"That it appears to this meeting that the natural line for this Railway, and also the most desirable for the interests of the Town and County, is the line from Longford via Strokestown and Boyle, to Sligo."*

*"That we recommend to the Grand Jury of the County to give to any Company who will undertake to carry out and construct this line within a limited period, such reasonable guarantee on the rates of the County and on a certain expenditure per mile as shall appear sufficient to secure such Company from loss.*[6]

Commenting on the outcome of the meeting, the *"Chronicle"* expressed the hope that after the long wait their patience would shortly be rewarded, and agreed that a line from Sligo to Longford would be "the most advantageous to this Town and County". [7]

As other schemes for North Connacht were being brought forward, Parliament waited until 1857 before deciding what railway it would sanction. Finally, it authorised the M.G.W. to build the long awaited Longford-Sligo extension via Strokestown and Boyle. However, this was subsequently changed to run via Carrick and Boyle, the route originally proposed in the 1840's. In August, 1858, the Directors of the M.G.W. advertised for contractors to build the line. The contract was awarded to Messrs. Smyth and Knight, a well established English firm of railway contractors, and work commenced before the end of the year. The length of the extension line from Longford to Sligo was given as $57\frac{1}{2}$ miles, 24 of which was within this County, with two branches - one at Ballisodare to the mills at Knockmuldowney and the second from the Sligo terminus to the Ballast Quay, all of which was to be constructed on a gauge of 5 feet 3 inches.[8] The *"Champion"* was elated with the news:-

*"The long expected commencement of operations on the Boyle to Sligo railway has at length taken place and measures are on foot for the speedy and efficient execution of the contract to ensure the opening of the line to public traffic within the next eighteen months or two years. This is cheering news and we augur the best results to all classes of our community."* [9]

By early 1859 the contractors were hard at work on the Boyle-Sligo section, and at Ballymote alone a large number of workmen were employed and considerable progress had already been made in laying the permanent way.[10] However, in the neighbourhood of Sligo, work had come to a standstill at the end of January in consequence of labourers refusing to work for nine shillings a week. The stoppage lasted for over a month and was finally resolved when the contractor gave an increase on the wages previously paid.[11]

The work of building the railway continued throughout 1859, 1860 and 1861. At the half yearly meeting of the Railway Company in June, 1861, the following information was given in respect of the progress of the works between Longford and Sligo:-

## 1. Longford - Boyle:

*The fencing and earthworks of this section are in active progress. One-half of the distance has been fenced off, and faces have been opened in more of the cuttings. In masonry considerable progress has been made. The large bridge over the River Boyle is all but complete, and several road and other bridges are in an advanced state. Drains have been opened through the entire length of the bogs where ever these occur; but the wetness of the autumn has somewhat retarded this portion of the work.*

## 2. Boyle - Sligo:

*The earthworks of this section are in an advanced stage, and may easily be completed within six months. The heavy cuttings, however, close to Sligo, are not so forward as the remainder, and will require nine months for completion. I have requested all contractors to use their exertions at this point. All the principal bridges are completed, a few only of minor importance remaining on hand, sixteen miles of line - seven of which are continuous - have been constructed and two and a half miles of permanent way have been laid down. All the rails and fastenings, and seven-eights of the sleepers for this contract, have been delivered and a considerable portion of them are already distributed.* [12]

By November, 1861, the Boyle-Sligo section had been completed, apart from the station buildings, and the first excursion train, carrying engineers and overseers, ran from Rathedmond to the North Roscommon town on the 5th inst., completing the outward journey in one hour and seven minutes. [13]

The official opening of the extension, Longford - Sligo, which had taken three years to complete at a cost of £450,000, had been planned for September 1st, 1862, but, by the time the entire works had been completed and the line inspected and approved by the Board of Trade Inspector, the opening date was deferred to December 3rd, 1862. On that date the first train to run left Sligo for Dublin at 7.15a.m. However, the official ceremonies were reserved for the incoming train from Dublin and this left Broadstone terminus at 8.30a.m. with a party aboard which included the directors and chief officers of the company. The train consisted of a steam engine of the period, a brake van, another van, a first class carriage and the now famous vehicle known as the 'Dargan Saloon'. The inaugural train made a rather triumphal journey to Sligo, being greeted with cheers at the stations on the new extension by the local inhabitants, many of whom had never seen a train before. As it entered Sligo station at 1.30p.m. the party aboard were greeted by the exploding of fog signals on the rails and the cheers

---

### MIDLAND GREAT WESTERN RAILWAY

### OPENING OF THE EXTENSION TO SLIGO

NOTICE IS HEREBY given, that the Line from Longford to Sligo will be opened for Passenger Traffic, on WEDNESDAY, 3rd December, 1862. The following Trains will run between Dublin and Sligo:-

| | **DOWN** | |
|---|---|---|
| Dublin Departure, | 8.30 a.m. | 4.00 p.m. |
| Mullingar, do., | 10.20 " | 5.55 p.m. |
| Sligo arrival, | 1.45 p.m. | 9.15 " |
| | **UP** | |
| Sligo Departure, | 6.45 a.m. | 3.40 p.m. |
| Mullingar, do., | 10.10 " | 7.05 p.m. |
| Dublin Arrival, | 12.00 Noon, | 9.30 p.m. |

For times of Departure from intermediate Stations, see Company's Time Tables.

W. FORBES, Manager.

Broadstone, Dublin, 25th November, 1862.

FROM STAGECOACH TO RAILWAY

of a great crowd assembled on and around the platforms. A salute of welcome was fired by the local Constabulary and an official reception committee was present, consisting of members of the Corporation and the Town and Harbour Commissioners headed by the Mayor, Thomas H. Williams. The day was treated as a holiday in Sligo and in the evening a banquet was held in the Grand Jury room of the Courthouse. The proceedings were under the chairmanship of the Mayor, who in the course of his address remarked that "the spell which bound Sligo had been broken...... It will now be possible in the one day to breakfast in Sligo, dine and do business in Dublin and be home for tea - a great improvement on the old coaching days."[14]

---

**Awards to Landowners/Occupiers, in the Union of Sligo, whose property was interfered with by the Dublin line and Terminus Building, September, 1858.**

| | |
|---|---|
| Thomas Phibbs, Ballinaboll, owner and occupier; | £441.7s. |
| Pat Quinn, Ballinaboll, lessee and occupier; | 5. 0. |
| William Flaherty, Ballinaboll, occupier; | 5. 0. |
| Thomas Flaherty, Ballinaboll, occupier; | 5. 0. |
| Michael Kelly and Mathew Kelly, Ballinaboll, occupiers; | 4. 0. |
| Ecclesiastical Commissioners, Ardcotton, owners; | 15. 0. |
| Rev. William C. Townsend, Ardcotton, occupier; | 5. 0. |
| Martin J. Madden, Bleachgreen, owner and occupier; | 800. 0. |
| Ecclesiastical Commissioners, Bleachgreen, owners; | 0.1. |
| William Phibbs, Bleachgreen, lessee; | 0.1. |
| Edward Nicholson and Mrs. Blair,Kilmacowen, owners; | 5. 0. |
| Henry Lyons, Carrowkeel, owner; | 50. 0. |
| Alexander Sim, Knappaghbeg, owner and occupier; | 324. 11. |
| Abraham Dobbin, Knappaghbeg, occupier; | 0.5. |
| Hume and Ramsey, Rathedmond, owners; | 340. 0. |
| Ramsey and Ramsey and others, Rathedmond, lessees for ever; | 100. 0. |
| Fenton and Gilmore, Rathedmond, owners; | 133. 0. |
| William C. Tute, Rathedmond, lessee and owner; | 147. 4. |
| Henry Lyons, Rathedmond, lessee and occupier; | 100. 0. |
| Peter O'Connor, Rathedmond, lessee and occupier; | 800. 0. |
| The Harbour Commissioners of the Port of Sligo, Rathedmond, owners and occupiers ; | 500. 0. |

## FROM STAGECOACH TO RAILWAY

### Notes and References (Coaching):

| | | |
|---|---|---|
| (1) | *"Sligo Chronicle"* | 11-9-1858 |
| (2) | ibid | 8-3-1862 |
| (3) | ibid | 5-2-1836 |
| (4) | *"Sligo Chronicle"* | 15-3-1856 |
| (5) | *"Sligo Champion"* | 28-6-1856 |
| (6) | *"Sligo Chronicle"* | 11-9-1858 |

(7) John Walsh, subsequently of *Edenhill*, died in March, 1894. He was Mayor in 1880. His son, Martin, a veterinary surgeon by profession, subsequently carried on the business for a decade or so.

### Notes and References (Railways):

| | | |
|---|---|---|
| (1) | *"Sligo Champion"* | 4-1-1845 |
| (2) | *"Sligo Journal"* | 28-2-1845 |
| (3) | ibid | 7-5-1852 |
| | & *"Sligo Champion"* | 10-5-1852 |
| (4) | Wood-Martin, W.G. | *"History of Sligo"* Vol. 3. p.212 |
| (5) | *"Sligo Champion"* | 22-11-1852 |
| (6) | ibid | 8-12-1855 |
| (7) | *"Sligo Chronicle"* | 1-12-1855 |

(8) The Kilfree to Ballaghaderreen branch line did not proceed until the passing into law of the Act of 1866.

| | | |
|---|---|---|
| (9) | *"Sligo Champion"* | 22-1-1859 |
| (10) | *"Sligo Chronicle"* | 12-3-1859 |
| (11) | *"Sligo Champion"* | 26-3-1859 |
| (12) | ibid | 23-6-1861 |
| (13) | *"Sligo Chronicle"* | 7-11-1861 |
| (14) | *"Sligo Champion"* | 5-12-1862 |

Between 1863 and 1923 various proposals were put forward, or revived, for linking Sligo by rail with other networks such as : Sligo - Enniskillen; Sligo-Bundoran, Sligo-Claremorris and Sligo-Ballina. Consideration was also given to a tramway between Sligo and Bundoran, with a link to Rosses Point, and for a light railway joining the Port of Sligo with the mining area at Arigna via Collooney, Riverstown and Geevagh. However, they all fell through with the exception of Sligo-Enniskillen, which was opened in 1882, and Sligo-Claremorris, which line was completed in 1895.

# FROM STAGECOACH TO RAILWAY

Sligo Railway Station c. 1900 and
(below) a Bianconi 'Long Car' about to leave the depot, Corkran's Mall.

# Sligo Churches:

## Divided Opinions On Crosses, Pews and Vaults

### The Calry Vaults:

In March, 1817, a suggestion was made at a meeting of the Vestry of the Union of St. John's for the building of a Chapel-of-ease to cater for an increasing Protestant population in Sligo and its surroundings. After much debate, and the lapse of a few years, the idea was ultimately adopted and the Board of First Fruits gave a grant of £900 towards the cost of the church and a Glebe House. The site on The Mall was well chosen, being prettily situated on a height overlooking the Garvogue River. All the stones for the structure were quarried on the spot and this, to some extent, explains the relatively small cost of the building, a figure in the region of £3,000.[1] Calry Church, a plain Gothic building with a tower and graceful spire, built by local contractor, John Lynn, was consecrated in June, 1824. The first appointment to the "perpetual Curacy or Chapelry of Calry" was the Rev. William Armstrong, who ministered on The Mall until his death in March 1840, aged 46.

When plans for the church were being considered in February, 1821, a Resolution was passed which approved of the vaults beneath the building being applied for the benefit of the Union, with the exception of two on the eastern side which were to be reserved for the Calry curate. Abraham Martin of Cleveragh, a leading merchant of that era, offered to build the vaults at his own expense, provided he was permitted to use them for the storage of wine and spirits. Not everybody was happy with this suggestion, a majority considering it more prudent to have the work undertaken at the expense of the parish. Accordingly, a loan was raised for the purpose, the intention being that three of the vaults would be sold as crypts. For reasons unclear at this remove, that plan never materialised and no income accrued to the Union. It was also the intention to build a Sexton's House at the west end of the church which would also act as a Gate

SLIGO CHURCHES

Lodge for the Glebe House to the rear, but this too was not proceeded with and the Sexton had to content himself with an abode in the vault area.

At a meeting of St. John's Vestry in April, 1831, the possibility of securing an income from the vaults was raised by John Black, merchant and Town and Harbour Commissioner. At that stage two of the vaults were occupied by the Curate, two by the Sexton while the fifth accommodated the flues and coals for heating the church. Black was highly critical of this arrangement and in particular the retention of two of the vaults by the Reverend Armstrong "for his own use". Black's suggestion that these should be leased did not meet with general approval, principally on the grounds that the avenue leading to the vaults was the Reverend Armstrong's property and lettings to the public would encroach on his privacy.

John Black was unhappy with the decision of the Vestry and the controversy soon found its way into the letter columns of the *"Sligo Journal"*, with the Curate stoutly defending a continuation of the *'status quo'* and Black advocating the adoption of the original proposals, namely, that the vaults be Let as wine or spirit stores, yielding an income of £15. per annum which would not only help to pay off the debt outstanding on the Church but secure a reversionary income forever to the Union.[2] Having brought the issue into the public arena, Black then threatened to resist the payment of church cess:-

*"The attempt made at the last Vestry to deprive the Union of its rights and the benefit of so valuable a property , was unjustifiable, but I trust that the parishioners will effectually resist this effort to convert this public property into the particular property of the Curate,"* he wrote. *"It cannot be possible, that the Rector or Curate of Calry can be serious in advocating such a breach of public faith for any personal advantage they could derive from the use of these vaults. If they are a necessary convenience to the Calry Glebe, let them have a preference of them, but surely, they are as well able to pay the parish the rent of them as thousands of the poor parishioners are to pay the Church Cess...... I am determined to resist the payment of this cess as far as I can legally, until I see the legitimate resources of the Union applied as they ought to be ......... "*

As far as can be ascertained, there the controversy was allowed to rest. Whatever intentions John Black had of pursuing the matter ended abruptly with his death from cholera in August, 1832.

SLIGO CHURCHES

*Notes and References:*

(1) The *"Parliamentary Gazeteer"* (1844-45) states that the church cost
£5,246.15s., of which £823.00 was raised by subscription and the sale
of pews.

(2) *"Sligo Journal"*            8-4-1831
         *ibid*             15-4-1831
         *ibid*             22-4-1831
         *ibid*             29-4-1831

# A Cross or a 'Pot Stick'?

The Independent, or Congregational community in Sligo was
established by one Andrew Maiben, a Scotch Presbyterian who was
engaged in the linen trade. Finding himself in some disagreement with
the doctrines preached by the local ministers, he commenced his own
prayer meetings in the crumbling ruins of Sligo Castle in or about the
year 1750. One of his earliest and perhaps most note-worthy converts
was Albert Blest, who subsequently became his son-in-law and Irish
agent for the London Hibernian Society. [1]

To cope with an increasing number of followers a small Union
Chapel was built in Waste Garden Lane in 1791. Half a century later
this proved inadequate and plans were afoot to build a more
substantial edifice. The person credited with the successful completion
of what was a most ambitious undertaking was a Corkman, the
Reverend Noble Shepperd, who was appointed a minister in Sligo in
1835. Unhappy with the wretched accommodation in the existing
Chapel, he immediately set about collecting funds, mostly in England,
for the projected undertaking. His efforts in this direction were quite
successful but the project had to be abandoned with the arrival of the
Great Famine.

In 1849 it was decided to proceed with the building of a church and
school. A site in Stephen Street, adjacent to the Primitive Weslyan
Methodist Chapel, was leased from John Wynne of Hazelwood, at an
annual rent of £19.4s. The architects of the new edifice were Messrs.
Blacknett & James of London. An advertisement in the local press of
June 8th, 1849, sought tenders from "reputable builders" for the

165

## SLIGO CHURCHES

erection of the "New Independent Chapel". Plans and specifications were available for inspection in the offices of Alderman Anderson in the *Lough Gill Brewery*. John Lynn, Union Street, one of the foremost builders in the North West, was entrusted with the contract.

By the Autumn of 1850 the building was well progressed, roofed and a cross placed on top of the bell turret. Some months later this symbol of Christianity was unceremoniously removed from its perch. On learning of this development the then editor of the "*Sligo Champion*", the outspoken Edward Howard Verdon, questioned the motive behind the removal of the cross and replacing it with something resembling a 'beetle' or a 'pot stick', and suggested that it resulted from the anti-Papal agitation then in vogue in England. Accusing the Reverend Shepperd of permitting his better judgement, "to be outweighed by the bigotry and fanaticism of some of his followers", the Editor took the opportunity of crediting the architect "with some good taste" in adopting a cross in conformity with the old English style. [2]

These comments spurred the spirited Minister into an explanation as to why the change was necessary :-

"*Sir,*

*Will you permit me to inform you and all others who may have the slightest interest in the subject, that the 'finale' on the top of the belfry of the new Independent Chapel, to which you refer in your last, was put up by mere mistake......*" [3]

The forthright Editor, unconvinced of the accuracy of the Reverend Shepperd's statement, as it did not tally with the facts as generally known, returned to the subject with renewed vigour a week later:-

"*The Rev. Mr. Shepperd alleges that the cross was erected by 'mere mistake'. This statement is an extraordinary one. He had daily an opportunity of seeing the plans and specifications of the building, which were in the possession of the clerk of works. He did see them. Upon these plans, we have been informed, the cross was placed. Can this be denied? Is it possible? - will anyone believe that Mr. Shepperd never looked at the plans - never inspected them, or gave his tacit consent to the erection of the cross? But whether the cross was in the plans or not, it is an indisputable fact that it was erected, and we think the reasons assigned for its removal are most lame and impotent*"....[4]

## SLIGO CHURCHES

Calry Church, with the Rectory in the foreground.

St. Johns 1776

SLIGO CHURCHES

The Reverend Shepperd promptly replied in a further effort to explain his action. According to him, the architect's drawings had five different enrichments for the top of the bell turret - a cross and four others. When he and his friends examined them they unanimously rejected the cross as an appropriate symbol. That was in July, 1850, and the subject did not call for further consideration until the cross was observed in position six months later.

*'I had no notion of its existence until I saw it in its position - that I directed its immediate removal without consultation with anyone - and, you will, perhaps, take my assurance that I should have done so, (that is) I should have corrected the mistake, irrespective of events in England.....'*

The Reverend Shepperd concluded his remarks by stating that he had no quarrel with his Roman Catholic fellow townsmen "and I wish to have none." [5]

There the controversy was allowed to rest. The church, which also incorporated a school, was opened for service in August, 1851. The adjoining Manse was built in 1862 and served as the residence of the Reverend Shepperd until his death in August, 1875, aged 71 years.[6]

***Notes and References:***

(1) **SEE:** McTernan. *"Worthies of Sligo".* pp 324 - 327

(2) *"Sligo Champion"*  25-1-1851

(3)    *ibid*    1-2-1851

(4)    *ibid*    8-2-1851

(5)    *ibid*    22-2-1851

(6) As the years progressed the Congregational or Independent congregation in Sligo declined and, as a result, the church ceased to function as a place of worship half a century ago. In 1952 the property was acquired by the County Council and converted into a Public Library and Museum.

# Pew Owners Unhappy

At the meeting of the Easter Vestry for the Parish of St. John's in April, 1855, with the Rev.Edward Day, Rector, presiding, the following Resolution was adopted:

*"That in consequence of the increased applications for sittings, the pews of the Church be re-modelled to afford the required accommodation; and that plans and an estimate be laid before the adjourned Vestry as soon as possible, the sanction of the Ecclesiastical Commissioners having been obtained for the purpose".* [1]

Commenting on this proposal, the *"Chronicle"* considered any infringement of the rights of the owners of pews as "a most unwise and illegal innovation" which showed little or no consideration towards old members of the congregation "whose families had sat in these pews for a great many years". It went on to suggest that pew-owners should enter a formal protest at the intended 'remodelling', and inform the churchwardens that they would be held responsible for any interference with vested rights. It also warned that should the proposal for new pews be accepted, all new sittings would be at " the uncontrolled disposal of the churchwardens." [2]

The adjourned Vestry, called to consider replacing old-fashioned square pews with narrow seats or 'slips', took place in the Vestry Room on April 24th, with the Rev. Edward Day in the chair. There was a good attendance of both pew owners and parishioners, and the ensuing discussion revealed conflicting views on the issue before the meeting. At the outset, the Rector stated that existing pews accommodated 262 worshippers, but under the new plan this would be increased by 170 to 432 seats. The cost of the alterations was estimated at £80. He then read a letter from the Bishop who expressed himself in favour of the removal of existing pews "which were highly objectionable", and their replacement with seats facing the pulpit which, in his opinion, "were more suitable to the decencies of public worship".

In a protracted and sometimes 'heated' discussion, Henry Griffith, J.P. of *Castleneynoe* was foremost in the denunciation of the proposed change which, he stated, was "totally against the general feeling of the parish". He also contended that there was ample accommodation in the church for all parties. He was supported in his views by Bartholomew Carter, M.D., of Wine Street, who claimed he had been a regular worshipper in the church for over half a century:

*"The stalls which I see laid down on that chart will not increase the area of the church,"* he said. *"It will be found difficult to accommodate nine people in each pew; public devotion will also be greatly interrupted by persons passing*

*through these narrow stalls, and unless it can be shown that the area will be enlarged by cutting up the pews, the project should be abandoned. And now let me ask why should these pews be cut up and thus disfigure one of the finest and most beautiful churches in Britain or Ireland?....."*

Roger C. Parke, Richard Gethin, William Ormsby and Edward Pollock, Solicitor, were all critical of any interference with private sittings. John Wynne of Hazelwood took an opposing stance, maintaining that the proposal did not interfere with vested rights, as the change would merely give a sitting in another shape. He complimented the Rector on bringing forward a proposal which sought to increase the accommodation for public worship by their parishioners. Captain Fawcett supported this viewpoint. After a long debate, a Resolution declaring that the further consideration of the question be postponed for a year, having been carried, the meeting adjourned.

The re-modelling of the pews was alluded to again by the Rector at the Easter Vestry in March, 1856. [3] He availed of the opportunity of informing the meeting of the Bishop's great surprise "that an enlightened congregation such as St. John's would be in favour of retaining the old pews". Seeking to avoid a fresh confrontation on the matter, the Rector hastened to add that, as his views on the matter had been opposed the previous year, he did not wish to seek a re-opening of the debate. The matter was then dropped.

*References:*

(1)  *"Sligo Chronicle"*      14 - 4 - 1855
(2)        *ibid*         21 - 4 - 1855
(3)        *ibid*         29 - 3 - 1856

# A Nocturnal Outrage

In the spring of 1883 Joseph Clarence of Ballisodare, building contractor, was engaged in carrying out certain alterations to St. John's Church of Ireland, John Street, in accordance with plans prepared by a celebrated ecclesiastical architect. The chancel was extended and a new East window of Gothic design, complete with a handsome stained

## SLIGO CHURCHES

glass, was placed in position. A new Vestry Room and an organ chamber were also provided. A Celtic cross of Ballisodare limestone was placed on the apex of the gable of the chancel. The parishioners responded most liberally and a Bazaar realised a profit of £600.

These improvements gave offence to some church-goers, more especially those of Low Church proclivities who were of the opinion that the alterations had too 'High' a tendency and were approaching too closely the ritualistic standard of which the cross, the emblem of Christianity throughout the civilised world, formed the culminating point.

On Monday, June 11th, 1883, it was discovered that the cross had been pulled down the previous night. This was achieved by the perpetrators mounting the scaffolding, which was still in place, placing a rope round the base of the cross and pulling it from its upright position. Fortunately, it did not fall to the ground but came to rest, undamaged, on the wooden scaffold beneath. Within hours the cross had been quietly re-positioned by the workmen.

As might be expected, this nocturnal "sacrilegious outrage" created a great deal of excitement and was loudly condemned by a majority of church-goers who favoured the changes that had taken place. A printed notice, signed by the Churchwardens, Messrs. Wm. Pollexfen and J.C. Davys, was published within days, offering a reward of £20 for information as to the identity of the perpetrators. At this remove there is no evidence to suggest that anyone was ever apprehended for what was a most unusual outrage.

### Reference:

*"Sligo Independent"*                     16 - 6 - 1883

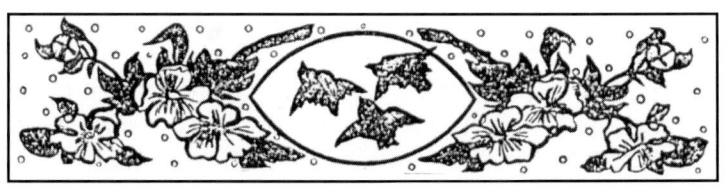

# Liberals, Radicals and Reformers

Liberal Clubs began to make their appearance throughout the country in the mid 1820's as localised urban political organisations of the Catholic Association in its struggle for Emancipation. They were once described as places "where men of all religions met to unite their efforts for the promotion of political freedom and universal benevolence". Membership was not exclusively Catholic, the middle-class orientation of the Clubs included Liberal Protestants who were sympathetic to Reform. Their significance lay in the manner in which the Clubs represented local opinion to the central organisation. After the emancipation victory of 1829 they became somewhat more Radical and were sometimes referred to as 'Independent Clubs' whose political energies were directed into the movement for the Repeal of the Union.

The Sligo Liberal and Independent Club was formed in October, 1828.[1] Its stated purpose was - "to watch over and protect the Forty-Shilling Freeholders of the County should they suffer persecution on account of the conscientious discharge of their duty towards their Religion and Country". The maintenance of the principle of civil and religious liberty was uppermost in the minds of that somewhat select grouping who assembled in the Catholic Schoolhouse in Chapel Lane* that Autumn day one hundred and seventy years ago. Amongst the attendance were the leading Catholic gentlemen, six of whom were Magistrates of the County. Officers elected were - Charles MacDermot, *Prince of Coolavin* (President); Joseph 'Mór' McDonnell, Doocastle, (Vice-President); Martin Madden, merchant (Treasurer) and John Tucker of Springfield (Secretary). The Committee consisted of Bishops Burke (Elphin), MacHale (Killala) and McNicholas (Achonry); The O'Conor Don; Daniel Jones (Benada); Andrew Kelly (Camphill); Michael Keogh (Geevagh); Patrick and Charles O'Connor (Sligo); Thomas Phillips (Cloonmore); Francis O'Beirne (Sligo and Jamestown) and Rev. James Donlevy, Administrator, Sligo. In addition, Committees were formed in each Barony who were delegated to report

* Now Chapel Street

## LIBRALS, RADICALS AND REFORMERS

regularly to the Central Committee on the activities, numbers, etc of Protestant Freeholders, popularly known as *'Brunswickers'*. They were also expected to form a register of Independent Freeholders and to submit reports on the state of the Registry, the equivalent of today's Register of Electors, throughout the County. Those who subscribed to the original Declaration paid an annual subscription of 10/-

In January, 1836, a public meeting to prepare an Address to Earl Mulgrave, the Lord Lieutenant, on his anticipated visit, was convened for the Parish Chapel. The out-going High Sheriff, Thomas Jones, having refused to get involved or make the Courthouse available, a capacity crowd, estimated to have exceeded two thousand in number, and consisting mostly of Catholics, together with a few Liberal Protestants, crowded the sacred edifice. According to a report in the *"Dublin Evening Post"*, "a great many of them were the frieze-coated men of the County, substantial farmers and freeholders as well as many mercantile inhabitants and shopkeepers of the Town." The chair was taken by Sir James Crofton of *Longford House* amidst great acclaim. He was seated alongside Bishop Patrick Burke and other dignitaries on a specially constructed rostrum in front of the High Altar. The significance of the occasion was commented upon by Richard Everard, Barrister-at-Law, when proposing the first Resolution:-

*"At the outset, I wish to congratulate myself and you that we have seated in the chair, at this great and influential meeting, a gentleman of our County - one of the ancient and distinguished lineage of your land - one whose ancestors have been for centuries, as far back as the distinguished name of Crofton can be traced by the local historian, identified uniformly with the welfare and incessantly devoted to the interests of your County .*

*We are assembled here today for a constitutional and most praiseworthy purpose, in the temple of that God whom we all worship in common; and I congratulate you in the most heartfelt manner at having such a man and of such a race placed at the head of this assembly. To have such a chairman is valuable in the extreme, if it were only that it prevents the possibility of our being, under any circumstances, exposed to the necessity of calling, to preside at this meeting, upon any of those new and unfledged converts to Liberal opinions.*

*It affords me a source of sublime emotion, which is not unmingled with heartfelt gratification, that in this place, where I first raised my voice in prayer to the Almighty, I should now be destined to raise it on behalf of the liberties of my fellow-men; and should be the medium of proposing a tribute of respect and gratitude from the Town and County with which I have been identified from my earliest years...."*

Martin Dillon Manning, J.P., Heapstown, seconded the Resolution. Edward Howard Verdon of Ballina, subsequently a founder member and first editor of the *"Sligo Champion"*, in an eloquent address, congratulated the 'Independent' men of Sligo on their triumph over "bigoted ignorance and unexampled intolerance". "The Borough of Sligo", he said, "had at last asserted its independence and had wiped off the stigma of Toryism". [2]

This meeting could be regarded as a watershed in local politics. It was the first public gathering of the Catholic Freeholders of Town and County, joined by a few Protestant sympathisers, since Emancipation. Those who espoused the 'popular cause' a century and a half ago were generally despised and ridiculed. Many of them, notably the Protestant members, have been described as "men of fearless independence, though aristocrats by birth". The local Protestant and Conservative organ, the *"Sligo Journal"*, kept a close eye on the proceedings, and its comments and reports on the historic gathering were laced with sarcasm:-

Sir James Crofton

*"Apart from half a dozen of wealthy mercantile inhabitants, it was impossible to discover by the garb or lineaments of the entire array of one individual with the slightest pretensions as a gentleman... Sir James Crofton, whose beaming countenance shed a ray of light around our frigid Tory clay,*

## LIBRALS, RADICALS AND REFORMERS

*ascended the altar and took the chair with that dignified deportment so characteristic of great men. Not being 'au fait' in his elevated berth, he was instructed as a novice and sat 'in cathedra', like the Pope himself. ... Mr. Everard spoke with much animation in praise of liberty ... "*[3]

A meeting of Liberals, chaired by Dean Donlevy, took place in the Parish Chapel in April, 1836. Upwards of thirty members attended, including Martin and James Madden, merchants, and their three nephews, Andrew, Thomas and William Kelly of Sligo and Camphill; Andrew Walker, merchant, Henry O'Connor, merchant and Laurence McTernan, solicitor. At the meeting it was decided to establish a newspaper advocating the views and politics of the Liberals/Radicals of Sligo - an historic event with far reaching consequences. What was then little more than an ideal became a reality a few months later with the publication of the first number of the *"Sligo Champion"*.

The Liberals and Radicals of Sligo, who had already achieved a notable victory by the return of the popular candidate, John Martin, in preference to the out-going member, John Wynne of Hazelwood, in the Borough election of 1832, were gradually exerting themselves to progress the advent of municipal reform and get rid of the old Tory Corporation - an ambition that was finally achieved in 1842. These successes prompted the *"Champion"* to boldly proclaim: "There is no County outside of Galway that can boast of so numerous an aristocracy as Sligo ... All the representatives of ancient respectability are Liberals..." [4]

The long awaited visit of Earl Mulgrave took place in August, 1836. His Excellency was accorded a warm reception by the Liberals, while the Protestant gentry and yeomanry boycotted the proceedings. He was presented with an Address of Welcome and paraded through the streets, which were specially illuminated for the occasion, with great pomp and ceremony. After the High Sheriff, James Knott of Battlefield, a Tory, had refused to make the Courthouse available, William Parke of Dunally, manfully came to the rescue and opened the building. In return, he was conferred with a knighthood by the Lord Lieutenant, the only Sligonian on record to be thus honoured on his native heath.

In November, 1836, acting in consort with the Registration Club in Dublin, a local branch, known as the Reform Registry Association of

County Sligo, or Registration Club for short, was formed at a meeting in the Linenhall, presided over by Sir James Crofton. The attendance included Daniel Jones, Sir William Parke, Major Bromhead, Dr. Patrick Burke, D.D., John Patrick Somers and numerous Catholic clergy from all parts of the County. It was decided to press for 'Independent' and popular representation in Parliament.

In April, 1837, in advance of the Parliamentary elections, a meeting representative of Liberals, Radicals and Reformers met in the Courthouse, under the chairmanship of Daniel Jones, sen., High Sheriff. The event was widely noticed in the local press, and a week later the *"Sligo Journal"* carried some doggerel verse, signed "Devil's Print", which not only made a mockery of the meeting but wrote disparagingly of the participants and the chairman in particular. [5]

# *The Banada Bear*

### Scene - The Interior of the Club-room.

"The evening arrived and the Club-room was cram'd
With Priest-ridden serfs who could *never* be d-d,
If they'd only attend to the Pastoral *charge,*
Which the *Gen'ral* had meant for the people at large.
His Deanship announced with a smile of delight
That the *Banada Bear* would be with them that night;
He said that the Tories, without more delay,
Should be kick'd out of office the *very next day.*

This *sentence* was halted with a rapturous shout,
Which was echoed again by the rabble without;
When the noise had subsided, the General said -
'That the monthly subscriptions that night should be paid;'
So he begged them to lay down the *requisite* then,
And show themselves patriots, christians and men;
He assur'd them that men should be shun'd as a *grub,*
Who'd refuse to subscribe to the Liberal Club.

The *dust* was laid down, and the guests sat around,
And a *something* seem'd sitting in silence profound

On the phiz of each publican, butcher and nailor,
And *Volunteer robber*, and tinker, and tailor.
Poor Sir James, Major B. or bluff Col. Sir B-y,
Had never before look'd so shy or so silly;
I marvelled to think that those *gents* would sit down,
With the scrub, the refuse, and the plagues of our Town.

If the *levelling* system must now be the go
With the Knight and the Baronet, let it be so;
But no wonder the gentry should feel some alarm,
When the Knight and the tinker go arm in arm.
But what reeks it now, let the *pair* jog along,
Tis mine to proceed with my tale or my song:
Those *gentlemen* sat like inanimate logs,
Save when silence was broke by '*Reform*, ye dogs!'

Some gemmen were emptying and filling their glasses,
And toasting the health of the lads and the lasses;
While others were reeling like ships in a storm,
And quaffing the health of Sir Bill and Reform -
When who should arrive but the Banada Bear,
With a gaping wide mouth and a horrible stare;
His arrival was hailed with a lenghten'd huzza,
Till *Bruin* called silence by raising his *paw.*

'Now let us to business without more delay.'
And he grin'd like a tiger when watching his prey:
'Now, *gentlemen*, first we'll begin with the jail,
For such are the orders of Dan and his *tail.*
We'll root out the Governor, Deputy, and all
Who have ever responded to Perceval's call;
And e'en for a *twelvemonth* we'll banish the crew,
Who've been hugging the banner of orange and blue.'

Now, *gentlemen*, mind what I often have told,
That I'm sickly, and gouty, and feeble, and old;
So tell me just what ye would have me to do,
And I'm at your service to banish *that* crew.'

# LIBRALS, RADICALS AND REFORMERS

'The Bridewells,' cried one, 'you must certainly know,
That the keepers are Tories, and out they must go.'
'Ballymote,' quoth the General, 'there's an orangeman there.'
'Then out he must go,' says the Banada Bear.

Twas agreed that the Club should proceed in array,
To banish the Tories from office next day;
So they muzzled poor *Bruin* and led him along,
'Mid the shouts and the yells of a ruffianly throng;
With the aid of a pole he first limped to the gaol,
And ordered the officers out *head* and *tail;*
Next he visited Bridewells and Court-houses, too,
And dismissed every keeper without more ado.

So now *Mr. Bruin,* may loll in his *chair,*
And reflect on the song of the Banada Bear.
Down with old Bruin, and down with his *cub.*
And down with the dog-kennel, slaughter-house Club;
And down with the rebels who'd dare to invade
The *Province* which William a *Kingdom* had made.

Huzza for our King, our Religion and Laws,
And huzza for the glorious Conservative cause;
Huzza for the banner of Orange and Blue,
And for Cooper, and Martin, and Perceval, too."

In Decemeber, 1837, the outgoing Sheriff, Daniel Jones, convened a meeting of the Freeholders of the County for the purpose of drawing up an Address to forward to Queen Victoria on her accession to the throne. It was chaired by Sir James Crofton and was fairly well attended, although largely boycotted by the Tory element. The following is the text of the Address agreed upon:

### May it Please your Majesty

*"We, your Majesty's loyal and dutiful subjects, the Freeholders of the County of Sligo, in county meeting assembled, humbly approach your Majesty with the assurances of our sincere and fervent attachment to your Majesty's person, and*

# LIBRALS, RADICALS AND REFORMERS

*of steadfast loyalty to the Throne.*

*We beg to tender to your Majesty our most grateful acknowledgements for your Majesty's declaration to extend to all classes the benefits of the Constitution and to assure your Majesty of our unbounded gratitude for the policy pursued by your present advisers in their government of Ireland."*[6]

The Liberal cause received a major boost with the appointment of Sir William Parke, as High Sheriff of County in 1837, in succession to Daniel Jones. He made his presence felt by empanelling a Jury composed of eleven Catholics, all members of the Liberal Club, and only one Protestant, to adjudicate on cases on appeal and mostly on matters relating to the franchise. His action, described by the *"Journal"* as "an extraordinary manoeuvre", caused a "big sensation" locally; it was deemed by the Assize Judge to be contrary to statute, and he was fined £10. [7]

After the formation of the Liberal-Independent Club in 1828, at a time when Reform was very much a live issue, John Martin, the son of Abraham Martin, the foremost Sligo merchant of his day, was nominated to contest the Borough seat in Parliament in opposition to

Daniel Jones, sen.

John Wynne (Conservative), the sitting member. At the close of a vigorously fought contest in December, 1832, Martin, the 'popular' candidate, had scored a notable success over the scion of the powerful Hazelwood family, winning by 213 votes to 158. Martin was returned unopposed at the next election in January, 1835. However, at the subsequent election two years later, the Catholic-Liberal support was no longer forthcoming for Martin as, in the estimation of a majority of voters, he had reneged on the principles upon which he had been supported in the first instance and twice returned to Parliament. In his place, thanks mainly to the promptings of Dean Donlevy and with the

## LIBRALS, RADICALS AND REFORMERS

'blessing' of the *'Liberator'* himself, the mantle was placed on the shoulders of John Patrick Somers, the son of Patrick Somers of Achonry. On polling day his nomination was proposed and seconded by two highly respected merchants and prominent Liberals, namely, Martin Madden and Andrew Walker. When the ballot was declared the 'popular' candidate had scored a decisive win over the outgoing member, John Martin. A Liberal majority of a hundred or so on the Registry made the outcome a foregone conclusion. [8]

In 1837 the Liberals and their kin presented a firm and united front to the common foe, the Tories. According to a commentator in the *"Champion"*, a Sligo Radical of that period avoided fraternising with the 'enemy'. Both parties kept very much aloof "and eyed each other with a cautious and jealous eye".[9] Following the passing of the Municipal Act of 1842, the subsequent elections resulted in a Liberal majority on the Corporation and the election of Martin Madden, a leading member of the Liberal Club, as Mayor in 1843, the first Catholic to fill the position since the Reformation. The Liberals retained the mayoralship over the following years: Michael Gallagher (1844 - 45), Henry O'Connor (1846) and Andrew Walker (1847). They were followed by Edward Howard Verdon (1850 - 54), Daniel McGill (1855), John McGowan (1856 - 58) and John McCarthy (1859). In 1867 it was unanimously resolved that the office of Mayor would in future be elected alternatively from those holding Conservative and Liberal opinions. This arrangement continued in operation until 1889.

At the County election of 1837 the hostility of the Liberals and their bedfellows was directed at both outgoing members, namely, Edward Joshua Cooper and Colonel Alexander Perceval (Conservative), and the latter in particular, who was noted for his intolerance. Daniel Jones, jun. of Benada, described as "a gentleman of high rank", was put forward as the Liberal standard-bearer. The planned strategy was that Cooper, who had many friends amongst the Liberals, should not coalesce with Perceval but stand alone, and this would ensure the return of both Cooper and Jones. However, this arrangement did not work as planned due to a notorious breach of faith on the part of a section of the Protestant gentry who reneged on promises made at the hustings. The youthful Jones failed by a narrow margin to oust Perceval in an election in which passions ran high, and was marked by

## LIBRALS, RADICALS AND REFORMERS

widespread intimidation, kidnapping and even death.[10] The election of 1837 was not only a milestone in the struggle for popular representation in Parliament, it being the first occasion that the Tory monopoly in the County was challenged; but is also marked the emergence of the Catholic clergy openly canvassing at the hustings in the Liberal interest.

What were known as the *'Forty-Shilling-Freeholders'*, namely, those who held a lease for life of a house or land in which the lessee had an interest worth 40/, were granted the vote in 1793. This placed Catholics and Protestants on equal terms as far as the franchise was concerned, and the more Freeholders a landlord had as tenants the greater his influence at elections. However, with the passing of the Emancipation Act 1829, the qualification for the franchise was raised from 40/- to £10.[11] This move led to a huge reduction in the number of electors in the County, dropping from 5,036 in 1829 to 610 a year later. According to one commentator "political gratitude was never so unpleasantly exemplified as in the fact that candidates who were returned by the votes of their tenants acquiesced in the proposal to deprive them i.e. the tenants, of their franchise".

The advent of the Liberal Party dramatically altered the voting patterns of the Catholic Freeholders and a minority of Protestants. Instead of steadfastly voting for their landlord, as hithertofore, they switched their allegiance to the Liberal nominee, as evidenced by the increased support for General King in the 1830 County Election. Success for the Liberals could only be achieved by securing a majority on the Registry, and this gave rise to a rush of applicants for registration in the Liberal/Radical interest, and to a lesser extent by Conservatives, at the various Quarter Sessions throughout the 1830's. In December, 1836, eighteen Radicals and seven Conservatives were registered at Ballymote and seventeen and nine, respectively, at Sligo.[12] In the following October twenty four Radicals were admitted to the franchise in the Borough as against four for the Tories, giving the former a majority of seventeen on the register.[13] Three years later there were in excess of two hundred and thirty applications in the Liberal interest alone for adjudication by the Court, less than half of whom were approved. In 1842 the Liberals were in control of two of the three Wards in the Borough, holding 16 of the 24 seats. The registrations, which were a slow process owing to the tedious and

LIBRALS, RADICALS AND REFORMERS

## List of Applicants for Registration in the Liberal interest, October, 1840.

| NAME: | ADDRESS: |
|---|---|
| Bree, Daniel | Collooney |
| Burns, James | Altanelvick |
| Carty, Patrick | Castledargan |
| Carty, Michael | Culleens |
| Clarke, Thomas | Carrowmorris |
| Conmee, Martin | Aderavoher |
| Connor, Henry | Breeogue |
| Crofton, Sir. James | Longford House |
| Cullenan, Owen | Grange Ormsby |
| Cunningham, Bryan | Loughanalteen |
| Cunningham, Michael | Drinaghan |
| Fallon, Terence | Cartronhugh |
| Feeney, Francis G. | Ballinamona |
| Flanelly, Thomas | Corkaghmore |
| Foley, Francis | Drumnasoohey |
| Gilgan, John | Loughanalteen |
| Healy, Bryan, | Derrylihan |
| Horan, Denis | Curscagh |
| Kelly, William | Doonflin |
| Kelly, Roger | Tubberanania |
| Kelly, Thady | Drumconora |
| Lavelle, Rev. Edward | Kilglass |
| McHugh, Manus | Carrownaguilta |
| O'Connor, John | Tunnagh |
| O'Hara, Michael | Carrowgubbadagh |
| O'Hara, James | Carrowmore |
| Philbin, John | Ballybeg |
| Parke, Sir William | Dunally |
| Quinn, James | Sligo Town |
| Sweeney, James | Culleens |
| Walsh, Mathew | Breeogue |

## LIBRALS, RADICALS AND REFORMERS

scrutinising investigation into the holdings, etc. of each candidate for
the franchise, usually gave rise to much excitement in the vicinity of
the Courthouse and party feelings ran high. This was particularly the
case in January, 1837. Barristers engaged in the Registry Court,
supervising the enrolling of voters on their respective sides, carried
their vindictive feeling beyond the precincts of the building. On
January 7th Counsellors Matthew Baker (Conservative) and James
Casserly (Liberal) were about to fight a duel when they were
interrupted by the police. On the following morning they met again at
Fivemilebourne where shots were exchanged. The meeting, however,
was broken-up for a second time by the police, and Baker was stoned
by the mob as he effected his escape on horseback.[14] A week later,
Counsellors Walker and Ramsay, both of whom were engaged in court
on opposite sides, held a meeting on Bowmore racecourse, where they
exchanged three shots each. The cause of the dispute was the same,
disagreement at the registry.[15]

In March, 1853, a County Club, to look after the interests of the
Liberal Party, was formed at a meeting in the Catholic Schoolhouse,
presided over by Dr. George Browne, Bishop of Elphin. Also in
attendance were Dr. Patrick Durcan, Bishop-Elect of Achonry, clergy
from three dioceses and a number of Catholic gentlemen. The new
association was to be known as the *Sligo Independent Club* whose aim was
to secure "a pure and independent representation of the County in
Parliament". Martin Madden of *Camphill House* was appointed
Treasurer and Patrick McNiffe (Sligo) Hon. Secretary. Through their
combined efforts John Sadleir, the Liberal nominee, was returned as
Member for the Borough later that year. A Reading Room was also
established in Old Market Street for the benefit of members and
continued to function for a decade or more.

Between 1837 and 1869, at which later date the Borough was
disfranchised, the seat was held alternatively by the Liberals and the
Conservatives. Somers in 1841, 1847 and 1857; Charles Towneley in
1848 and 1852; John Sadlier in 1853 and Richard Armstrong in 1865
successfully contested the representation of the Borough under the
banner of the Liberal Party.

Despite the best endeavours of a vocal and growing opposition,
representation of the County in Parliament remained in Tory control

## LIBRALS, RADICALS AND REFORMERS

until the mid century, but in 1852 Richard Swift, and in 1868 and 1874, Denis O'Connor, took one of the seats in the Liberal interest. Sir Robert Gore-Booth was the last Tory to be returned for the County. On his death in 1877 he was replaced by Robert Edward King-Harman, who stood as a Home-Ruler. Between the 1880's and 1918 both County seats at Westminister were held by Home-Rulers and Nationalists, to be followed in 1918 by Sinn Féiners.

### References:

| (1) | *"Sligo Observer"* | 6 - 11 - 1828 |
|------|------|------|
| (2) | *"Dublin Evening Post"* | 21 - 1 - 1836 |
| (3) | *"Sligo Journal"* | 22 - 1 - 1836 |
| (4) | *"Sligo Champion"* | 3 - 9 - 1836 |
| (5) | *"Sligo Journal"* | 5 - 5 - 1837 |
| (6) | *"Sligo Champion"* | 6 - 1 - 1838 |
| (7) | *"Sligo Journal"* | 16 - 3 - 1837 |
| (8) | *"Sligo Champion"* | 12 - 8 - 1837 |
| (9) | ibid | 18 - 4 - 1844 |
| (10) | McTernan, J.C. *"Olde Sligoe"*, pp. 289-292 | |
| (11) | *"Sligo Observer"* | 9 - 4 - 1829 |
| (12) | *"Sligo Journal"* | 6 - 1 - 1837 |
| (13) | *"Sligo Champion"* | 4 - 11 - 1837 |
| (14) | Wood - Martin, W.G. *" History of Sligo."* Vol.3.p.321 | |
| (15) | *"Sligo Champion"* | 14 - 1 - 1837 |

# DRAINAGE of the Owenmore

The drainage of the Owenmore and Arrow rivers has been an emotive issue for generations untold. Over the past century and a half successive governments have been petitioned, without success, to fund the extensive works necessary to relieve the seasonal flooding of thousands of acres in the catchment area.[1] As far back as 1840 the Sligo Board of Guardians were concerned by the losses being sustained annually by landlords and their tenants in the affected areas. In an effort to ameliorate the situation they commissioned Messrs. Robinson and Gregory, Civil Engineers, to undertake a survey of the Owenmore and its tributaries and recommend ways and means of relieving the recurring flooding.

The resultant survey established that upwards of 1,300 acres were liable to annual inundation which, in the Surveyors' opinion, did "great injury to the adjoining lands, destroyed crops and carried away great quantities of hay". They estimated that should "an efficient drainage" be undertaken, in addition to the afore-mentioned acreage, a further 2,000 would be "considerably improved". In their view this could be achieved if the proprietors, whose lands were subject to flooding, would co-operate under the provisions of the various Drainage Acts and have all the natural and artificial obstructions in the bed of the River, which they had identified, removed. The following is the text of the Report. [2]

*September 7th, 1841.*

*Sirs,*

*In conformity with your instructions we have carefully examined the river Owenmore and its tributaries and from Information received, when heavy rain falls, the small streams flowing into the river contribute more than with the present obstacles existing are capable of discharging in a given time; its surface therefore continues to rise while the influx exceeds the efflux and in time overflowing its banks, the redundant waters diffuse themselves over the land which continue for a long time submerged.*

DRAINAGE OF THE OWENMORE

*We propose that the following obstructions should be removed which, if carried into affect, would allow the overplus of water to flow on through its natural channel.*

*Commencing at Ballinacarrow bridge, we find on proceeding up there is a rise according to Ordnance Survey of two feet, the ford here should be removed, the river is deep on each side, the bed of which is composed of detached limestone rocks and gravel.*

*The next obstruction to the free passage of the water is an eel weir, commonly called the rampart, crossing the river in a transvex direction between the townlands of Ballinacarrow North and Carrownree, which, from enquiry, is the principal cause of flooding the lands up to Templehouse Lake. We would suggest that this should be entirely removed, which if done, would be a material injury to the bleach mill, as this rampart was thrown across to keep a sufficient supply of water for its purpose, but when the benefit which would accrue to the country is taken into consideration, there will be found a large balance in favour of its removal.*

Templehouse Bridge

*Proceeding further up we find between the townlands of Cloonamanagh and Ballinacarrow South, another ford with large stepping stones; the river here should be deepened and the stepping stones removed, but we cannot make an accurate estimate as to the depth the different fords should be sunk without making actual sections, but as near as we can judge, we should say about four feet, the river is deep on each side and its bed composed of detached rocks, gravel*

## DRAINAGE OF THE OWENMORE

and sand; there is also another ford here nearly seven perches in lenght through which a cut should be made, its bed being composed of gravel principally, and loose stones.

Between the townlands of Rathbane and Clooneen, is a long ford of nearly thirteen perches in length, the depth of the river varying at present from two to four feet deep. We would recommend a deep cut to be made through this; probable bed of river (from enquiry) consists of detached rocks, gravel and sand.

There is another ford similar to the last between the townlands of Rathbane and Cluid, (near the island) which must offer great obstruction, it is nearly twenty perches in length and choked with weeds. We propose that this ford should be cleared and a deep cut made through it; bed similar to the last but a greater accumulation of mud.

There are no impediments worthy of notice from this to Templehouse, except that the river should be cleared in several places. There is a rise of five feet from Ballinacarrow bridge to Templehouse Lake.

Having passed the lake and proceeded as far as Carrowkeel, a second weir presents itself which principally is the cause of flooding the land up to Oldrock bridge, as it is a perfect level for that distance. This weir should be taken down and the bed of the river sunk, being formed of hard gravel and loose stones for about fifteen perches below and seven above.

In time of flood the water rises from five to seven feet at Oldrock bridge. There is evidently a considerable rise in the bed of the river here, which impedes the progress of the water and should be sunk several feet; the bridge would most likely be undermined and should be rebuilt.

Between the townlands of Cloonakeevy and Oldrock is a ford about twelve perches in length, through which a cut should be made; the bed of the river principally gravel, easily worked.

The next impediment is a ford between Ardconnell and Ballinaglogh, composed of extremely hard gravel and rocks, and a little further up is a third weir, which we find from inquiry to be the chief cause of the land being inundated to Carrickrathmullen bridge. Should those impediments be taken away and the bed of the river deepened considerably, it would be necessary to have a small bridge thrown across at Ballinaglogh eel weir, as this always has been a great thoroughfare.

At Aughris is a tributary which floods a considerable portion of land for nearly half a mile; and we are of opinion if the weir at Ballinaglogh was removed and the foregoing improvements effected, the river would be sufficiently

## DRAINAGE OF THE OWENMORE

*lowered to carry off the influx of water, which would be otherwise spread over the adjoining lands.*

*The river from Aughris to Carrickrathmullen bridge, will require to be straightened and cleared in several places, as the greater portion of it between these two points is serpentine and very much choked with weeds, which, of course impedes the water to a considerable extent.*

*Near Carrickrathmullen bridge a tributary empties itself into the river from the new cut lately made, and this stream, being small and very crooked, is not capable of discharging the body of water which comes down in time of flood, besides being impeded in its course by the small bridge on the road from Ballymote to Ballaghaderreen. We recommend this stream to be straightened and made wider, also the bridge removed and a large one built. The remainder of the river from this bridge to Coagh, where the Battlefield river joins, should be cleaned and straightened in several places, as it is almost impossible for the water to force its way through, owing to the quantity of weeds and mud which have been accumulating from year to year. If these improvements were carried into effect, there would be sufficient fall for the Battlefield river to discharge its waters in time of flood without being forced back on the land.*

*The remainder of this river from Coagh is in similar state to that which has last been described, being if anything worse, with regard to weeds, it would require to be cleared the greater portion of the way and straightened in several places, also two small fords removed.*

*After the proposed alterations being effected, upwards of 1,309 acres would be improved, and a general increase in value of one third.*

*We have the honour to be Sir,*

> *Your obedient servants,*
> > *ROBINSON and GREGORY,*
> > *Civil Engineers*

The Surveyors predicted that in return for a relatively small outlay, the bed of the Owenmore could be lowered, its course straightened and its banks raised where necessary. "This work is altogether highly important", they concluded. "The landlord and the occupier would be mutually benefitted, the redundant labour of the Barony of Corran would be usefully employed and much land brought into profitable cultivation". [3]

DRAINAGE OF THE OWENMORE

## Notes and References:

(1) The catchment area of the Owenmore River, which consists of the Owenmore, the Arrow and Owenboy rivers, totals in the region of 160,000 acres. The Owenmore consists of three sections: the rising section with steep gradients; the middle section with poor gradients, backfalls, ill-defined banks and a build-up of silt; and the third, or discharge section, where the river flows over rock rapids into the sea at Ballisodare.

(2) *"Sligo Journal"*                7.3.1845.

(3) In recent times the Arrow-Owenmore Drainage Committee renewed their efforts to secure funding for the relief of the flooding. The following is the phased approach submitted to the Minister of State at the Department of Finance:

Phase One:    Removal of obstacles causing flooding between Templehouse Bridge and Ballisodare;

Phase Two:    Removal of obstacles causing flooding on the Arrow River from its source to the junction with the Owenmore at Collooney;

Phase Three: Removal of obstacles causing flooding on the Owenmore River from its source to Templehouse Bridge.

In November, 1996 it was announced that a Grant of £200,000 had been sanctioned for flood relief on the Owenmore.

Remains of Old Bridge spanning the Owenmore at Thornhill, Ballinacarrow.

# The Pioneering Fentons

Emigration from Ireland during the late 18th and early 19th centuries was chiefly to America and Canada. It was not until the 1830's that an increasing number of emigrants choose Australia as their destination. This, doubtless, arose from the introduction in 1829 of government assisted migration which resulted in very few having to pay their own passage - the cost of which ranged from £10 to £15. In October of that year the *"Sligo Journal"* carried an advertisement giving details of a sailing from Dublin to Van Dieman's Land (Tasmania) in December of that year. Messrs. Black and Mostyn were listed as the local agents.

In 1828 Captain Michael Fenton, son of Capt. Michael Fenton, J.P. of *Castletown House,* Easkey, who had been on service in India, sold out of the army under favourable emigration terms and, with his wife Bessi, sailed for New South Wales where Fenton had been promised a grant of almost two thousand acres. He subsequently sold this holding and purchased another in New Norfolk, Tasmania. His wife, widow of Captain Campbell and formerly Mrs. Knox from Derry, kept a day to day account of their early years in the new Colony. This was subsequently published under the title of *"The Diary of Mrs. Fenton".*

Once settled in his new home Michael Fenton, in a letter home to Castletown, painted such a favourable picture of life in Tasmania that it immediately aroused the interest of others within the family circle. Michael's cousin, Captain Thomas M. Fenton of *Dromore House,* had also joined the army and had served at Martinique and at the siege of Plattsburg in the USA before returning to England in 1820. While cousin Michael soldiered on, Thomas retired from the army rather than serve in India. In 1820 he married Leonara Anderson, described as "a rich lady from Bath". For a man with a wife, eight children and a large establishment, a decision on whether or not to sell his share of the family estate and transport bag and baggage, together with workmen and servants, on such a long and hazardous voyage to far off Australia was no easy task, and it required months of consideration before a final decision could be made.

By the late Autumn of 1830, Thomas Fenton had finally made up his

THE PIONEERING FENTONS

mind to join his cousin but he allowed himself almost a year to perfect his plans and make the necessary financial arrangements. He crossed to Liverpool, where he purchased an American built trading vessel named *Lindsays*. It was a 270-ton three masted ship, ninety-four feet long by twenty-eight feet broad. There, he had it fitted-out before sailing it back to Sligo where final arrangements were made for the daunting voyage. In the midst of all his preparations Captain Fenton took time off to attend a function in his honour in the Courthouse on which occasion he was the recipient of an Address from the Magistrates of County.

Weather conditions are said to have been very favourable as the Fentons and their passengers bade adieu to their friends and relatives on the quays and the *Lindsays* sailed down the estuary on the first leg of the long voyage ahead. The date was November 26th, 1831, and on board were Thomas Fenton, his wife, Leonara, and their eight children, whose ages ranged from one to eight years. Sharing accommodation with the family were Catherine

Michael Fenton, Speaker of the Tasmanian House of Assembly, 1856

Fenton (sister); Dr. Fowler and three other cabin passengers as well as seventy-six indentured servants and their families from Dromore and Easkey, all steerage passengers, who were required to work Fenton's

## THE PIONEERING FENTONS

estate and that of his cousin in Tasmania. Fenton was entitled to claim a bounty of twenty pounds per family from the Immigration Commissioners in respect of his passengers.

The *Lindsays* was scheduled to call at Liverpool on its way but after only a few days at sea it ran into very rough weather and sprung a leak. They put into Greenock in Scotland where part of the cargo was discharged before essential repairs could be undertaken on its coppered bottom. After a few weeks by Clydeside the *Lindsays* set sail again on January 17th and followed the classic route for sailing ships down to Rio de Janeiro. Two months later the *"Sligo Journal"* reported the safe arrival in Rio of Capt. Thomas Fenton and family. "His party are all well on arrival in Spanish America except one man named McCrann who ran away from the vessel in Scotland", noted the *"Journal"*. The last stage of the adventurous voyage took about three months to complete, and it was not until June 22nd, 1832, that the *Lindsays* docked at Hobart Town in Tasmania, thus marking the successful end to an undertaking of remarkable courage and endurance which had taken seven months to complete. A few weeks had elapsed before the *"Sligo Journal"* was in a position to inform its readers that "Thomas Fenton and Family had arrived safely at their destination".

On arrival, Fenton settled on a large estate of nine thousand acres which was not far distant from that of his cousin, Michael. There, he was subsequently joined by his brother, John Fenton. All three Fentons quickly settled down in their new surroundings and gained a reputation amongst their fellow colonists as fearless and hard working Irishmen in a region that was subsequently called *Fenton's Forest*. Michael Fenton from Castletown became a successful politician and had the distinction of being the first Speaker of the Tasmanian House of Assembly in 1856. Descendants of the Fentons of Castletown and Dromore are still flourishing on the Australian continent, far away from the Tireragh of their ancestors.

\*     \*     \*     \*     \*

Half a century after the *Lindsays* had sailed for Australia, another member of the Fenton family took off for Patagonia in South America, namely, Thomas Fenton, eldest son of Michael and Jane (nee

THE PIONEERING FENTONS

McCloughry) of *Castletown House.* Born in 1850 he studied medicine in Dublin and qualified as a doctor. In 1880, or thereabouts, he and his wife, Mary, and young son, Gerald, set sail for South America where he took up the post of medical practitioner at Sandy Point, Magallanes. He found it difficult to subsist, and rear an increasing family, on a monthly income of $300 a month, and in a letter home to his mother at Castletown, dated July 3rd 1885, he mentioned this fact more than once, and went on to detail his successful venture into sheep farming on a large scale as a means of increasing his income. His extensive holding became widely known as *Fenton Station.* *

Magallanes
July 3rd, 1885

My dear Mother,

I have wished to write to you for a long time, but owing to the unsettled state of things in this place I kept waiting until I could send you a favourable account as to what 'Dame Fortune' has been doing with me during the last few years.

To commence, I must let you know that my sheep farming speculation has been the most fortunate step, and perhaps the most important of my life; in fact were it not for my 'Hacienda' I could never live with my increasing family on my profession in this country: as it is, thank God, I am doing nicely; with my next year's increase at lambing time I expect to have upwards of 5,000 sheep and have in the last few days concluded a contract with a friend of mine here who has the necessary capital to import after February next the number of 6,000 more from the Falkland Islands. Our contract is for seven years, at the end of which time we shall dissolve the partnership, dividing everything between us. By this transaction I gain 1,000 sheep and have half my rent paid. With ordinary good luck, under this agreement, I consider my fortune made! Next year I shall commence with 11,000 sheep (ewes) and shall shear about 22,000 sheep, which after paying all expenses, will leave a profit of something over £100 per 1,000 sheep; and, as you can understand, I can not possibly do badly under any circumstances. As regards land, I have at last succeeded in obtaining 86,000 hectarias, or an extension of fourteen miles by twenty-five, more or less, which in English measurement equals two and a quarter acres, so that my estate will be more or less the size of the County Sligo.

---

* Letter published courtesy of Miss C. Campbell, 'Coillte Luighne', Beltra, a grand-daughter of the late W. R. Fenton, *Ardaghowen House.*

## THE PIONEERING FENTONS

I am trying to negotiate a third section of land, 20,000 hectarias next to mine, and if you think you are not too old yet to move to a new country, I can always make room for you, and believe me, My dear Mother, you might do worse than follow my fool's advice, as I feel perfectly confident that after living a few years in this Country you would wonder why you ever lived so long in Ireland; why my very servants in this country live better than you ever did in Castletown.

I have with the practice of years become a famous obstetrician, and as the pampas are becoming every day more populated, I can always pick up a few gold 'crumbs' which would always come in handy. There is one thing, however, I very much require and in fact must have; that is a few good servants for my house in the pampas, the most necessary for the present being a washer-woman, who can be handy at every thing; besides if you could find me a man and his wife, it would suit me admirably, a young married couple for example, no matter if they have one or two children. I have bread enough for all; I would pay them £40 per year or even a little more if they could not be had at that. You can get them as cheap as you can, but they must sign a contract with me for at least 7 years; later on I shall require many out-door hands for shepherds, but for this year the man and his wife will do, as I have been lately under very heavy expenses on the farm, building little houses etc. and consequently for this reason cannot spare much money".[2]

By 1885 Dr. Fenton had a family of six, three boys and three girls, the youngest of whom was but a few months old. Having described them in some detail, including their individual characteristics, etc. in the letter to his mother, he concluded by expressing understandable concern as to their future education:

"Taking them all in all they are not a bad looking crowd but what is better, Thank God, they are all healthy and well shaped without either fault or blemish. My great nightmare is, how I am to educate them? if I could get some good woman to teach them I would willingly pay a reasonable sum, so that at least they might be educated for a few years, until they were strong enough to go to a good school. Perhaps you may be able to recommend a suitable party who would undertake the work. [3] Mary continues fresh and healthy and a good mother and wife; My own health has not been too good of late; I suffered from dysentery and rheumatism, not to speak of a few grey hairs above the ears, otherwise I am, Thank God, pretty well.

With love to all, I remain ever yours affectionately,     *Thomas Fenton ".*

Dr. Thomas Fenton died in his adopted country c. 1908. His descendants continue to prosper in the South American continent.

# THE PIONEERING FENTONS

## Notes:

(1) Elder brother of William Russell Fenton of *Ardaghowen House.*

(2) A number of 'volunteers' from Easkey responded to Fenton's request and went to South America to assist him in the running of his extensive estate.

(3) Gerald, eldest son of Thomas and Mary Fenton was sent back to Ireland and educated by his uncle, W.R. Fenton. He subsequently qualified as an eye specialist.

Castletown House, Easkey c. 1890

# Supplying the Town with GAS

In 1834 a number of Sligo residents, led by one Andrew Drysdale, petitioned Andrew Liddell of Glasgow, an expert in the field, to submit a report on lighting the Town with gas. The resulting survey was considered by an *ad hoc* Committee, consisting of Abraham Martin, Martin Madden and George Dodwell in December of that year. It recommended the establishment of a gas company with a capital of £5,000 in £10 shares, and that the shares, as far as possible, should be taken up by consumers of gas. The necessary buildings, including a gasometer, a 100-foot high chimney, the laying of 1,500 yards of mains and 540 yards of branch pipes etc., in addition to the building of a Manager's house, was estimated to cost £4,500. Annual outlays, including salaries and wages (£190), coal (£225), ground rent (£15), was calculated to amount to £610. Revenue was estimated as follows:

* Lighting of street lamps ........................................ £225
* Lighting of public houses (60 of the 90) ............... £115
* Lighting of shops, offices, churches ...................... £480
* Lighting of private houses (100 of the 400) ........... £330

making a total of £1,150, and leaving a credit balance of £500 to be divided between the shareholders.

The prospectus, which was published in January, 1836, met with "the most cordial approbation" and a number of the 'respectable' inhabitants of the Town, including the Provost and members of the Town and Harbour Commissioners, subscribed as prospective shareholders. [1]

A few weeks later a meeting of the inhabitants was convened in the Courthouse to adopt measures for carrying into effect the much desired plan of lighting the Town with gas.[2] The meeting, which was presided over by the Provost, William Fausset, adopted the following resolutions:-

* That a joint Stock Co. be formed with a share capital of £5,000;
* No individual to be allowed to subscribe more than ten shares @ £10 each;

## SUPPLYING THE TOWN WITH GAS

* A committee of 24 shareholders to be named who would meet weekly to carry the project forward.

Despite the enthusiasm displayed at this meeting, the *"Journal"* subsequently noted that there was evidence of an increasing apathy towards the project. [3] In June, 1836, the aforementioned Committee met to re-consider the plan in the light of new information, namely, that the undertaking as already envisaged would require more capital than was at first supposed. After some discussion it was decided to call a public meeting on June 15th to decide on a course of action. The gathering attracted only a handful of people, and the Provost, who presided, suggested that the proposal be abandoned as impracticable. While no final decision was made on that occasion, three months later the *"Champion"* announced the abandonment of the project. [4]

---

### GAS LIGHT COMPANY

A General Meeting of the Shareholders and Inhabitants of the town of SLIGO, will take place on

WEDNESDAY NEXT, the 15th of June.
AT THE COURTHOUSE
The chair will be taken at TWO o'clock.

S. Doyle, Secretary

June 9th, 1836

---

The idea of lighting the Town by gas was revived early in 1839 with the arrival in Sligo of James Colquhoun, a civil engineer from Sheffield.[5] He took a lease of a house, yard and garden on the south side of Wine Street, formerly occupied by William Middleton, at an annual rent of £45.[6] Over the following months the necessary buildings and fittings were put in place for the production of gas. In May, Colquhoun signed an agreement with the Town and Harbour Commissioners for replacing the street oil lamps with gas, the terms of which were as follows:

* Eighty lamps to be erected at a distance of from 45 to 50 yards apart;

## SUPPLYING THE TOWN WITH GAS

* Lamps to be supplied with good and pure gas for seven years commencing 15th September, 1839, @ £3.15s per annum for each light, payable on 15th April and 31st December;
* Each burner to consume from 4 to 4.5 cubic feet per hour and the lights to be of equal brilliancy to street lamps in Londonderry and Dublin;
* Lamps to be erected, lit and kept in repair by James Colquhoun at his own expense;
* Each light not to be liable to burn for a longer period than 2,000 hours each year;
* The lamps to be lighted at sunset and to continue lit until half an hour before sunrise.

Early the following year, 1840, there were indications that Colquhoun's undertaking was in danger of collapse for want of capital. A public meeting was called at which it was announced that he was desirous of forming a Gas Company and providing local entrepreneurs an opportunity of investing in what he considered would be a profitable undertaking. He proposed a share capital of £6,000, of which he would retain £3,500 and guarantee a premium of 6% to the shareholders who held the remaining £2,500 for a term of seven years, after which time Colquhoun would either sell his shares or retain an interest in the concern, depending on what the other shareholders decided. His proposal was considered highly satisfactory by those present and a large number of shares were taken up there and then.[7] A group of local businessmen, including Martin Madden, Abraham Read, Thomas Hudson, Thomas Little, Peter O'Connor, Richard Anderson, William Patrickson and Edward Kelly, became shareholders. In a Deed of Assignment, between Colquhoun and the Sligo Gaslight and Coke Company, dated May 29th, 1840, the former agreed to supervise the completion of the Gas Works and to manage the affairs of the Company for the agreed term.[8]

Over the following years the workings of the Company gave much dissatisfaction and grounds for complaint. In November, 1843, at a meeting of the gas consumers in the *Nelson Hotel,* it was decided to appoint a delegation, consisting of Gregory Cuffe Martin, Moses Monds, Richard Smith, Robert McBride and Henry Lyons, to meet

## SUPPLYING THE TOWN WITH GAS

Colquhoun and seek a reduction from 13s.4d per 1,000 cubic feet of gas to 10s.6d, as well as an improvement in the quality of the product. In the course of the discussion Abraham Martin expressed the opinion that the low pressure frequently being experienced by consumers was due to the inadequacy of the plant to meet the needs of a town the size of Sligo. The meeting with Colquhoun resolved little or nothing, he maintaining that the price could only be reduced by an increase in consumption. The *"Journal"* expressed disappointment at the outcome and voiced the opinion that if the Town and Harbour Commissioners operated the Gas Works, which they could have done under existing legislation, not only would prices be lower but the profits would be such as to pay the entire Town expenses .[9] The said Commissioners,

---

# NOTICE
# TO GAS CONTRACTORS

The Commissioners of the Town and Harbour of Sligo, hereby give Notice that they will receive Sealed Tenders on or before MONDAY, the first of JUNE next for Lighting the Town of Sligo with GAS, for a period of one, three or seven years.

Application to be made to the Secretary, Union St., Sligo, who will furnish all information which may be required as to the number of lamps to be lighted, the hours of lighting etc. etc.

SAMUEL DAVIDSON, Secretary

Dated 6th May, 1846

---

who were the Company's biggest customer, were also unhappy and sought a reduction in the contract rates as well as improvements in street lighting, this despite the fact that the Company more than once found it necessary to cut-off the street lighting because of the Commissioners' default in payment, as contracted. Eventually, due to mounting pressure from both the Commissioners and private consumers, the price of gas was reduced from 13s.4d. to 12s.6d per 1,000 cubic feet in January, 1844.

Despite this reduction and an improvement in the supply to consumers, the editorials and letter columns of both the *"Journal"* and

## SUPPLYING THE TOWN WITH GAS

| | | | |
|---|---|---|---|
| No. of Shareholders residing in Sligo: | 19 | - | holding collectively £4,530 worth of stock. |
| No. of Shareholders residing elsewhere: | 5 | - | who held £470 worth of stock. |

| | | |
|---|---|---|
| Dividends paid in 1841 | @ | 5% |
| Dividends paid in 1843 | @ | 6% |
| Dividends paid in 1845 | @ | 7% |

No. Dividends paid in 1846 - 1850:

| | | |
|---|---|---|
| Dividends paid in 1851 | @ | 3% |
| Dividends paid in 1852 | @ | 5% |
| Dividends paid in 1854 | @ | 6% |

### PRICE OF GAS

| | | |
|---|---|---|
| October, 1847 to Dec. 31st 1851 | @ | 10s.6d. per 1000 ft; |
| January, 1852 to Dec. 31st. 1853 | @ | 8s.6d. per 1000 ft; |

January, 1854, price increased to 10s. 10d.
in consequence of high price of coal.

*"Sligo Champion"* 16 - 12 - 1854

the *"Champion"* continued to heap criticism on the Company, and on the management in particular. Much of the fault-finding was directed towards the "hideous monopoly" enjoyed by the Company who paid a handsome dividend and whose Directors were in receipt of salaries of between £30 to £40 per annum "for making a dozen calls to the Gas Works during the year where they enjoyed a glass of wine and cake with

Mr. Colquhoun's presentment for Gas supplied to the Courthouse, was adopted after a great deal of discussion, during which the Grand Jury intimated that, owing to the quality of the gas, and its going frequently out, they would probably be compelled to discontinue it, and resort to candles, though the fixtures required for it had cost nearly £100.

*"Sligo Journal"* March, 1845

## SUPPLYING THE TOWN WITH GAS

the Management at the public expense".[10] This culminated in another public meeting of consumers in November, 1845, at which the quality of the gas and irregularity of supply was discussed at length. Colquhoun, who was present, readily admitted that there was cause for complaint but regretted that a number of leading citizens, who had assured him of support, had not fulfilled their promises. Nevertheless, he promised to investigate the laying of new mains and pipes in streets in low-lying parts of the Town as well as immediate attendance to genuine complaints regarding quality and supply. He announced a reduction in the region of 2s. 6d. as from January, 1846.

Although Colquhoun's announcement was welcomed by those present, the *"Journal"* entered the fray once again. Commenting on the afore-mentioned meeting of gas consumers, it wrote:-

*"The inhabitants of Sligo are at last forced to bestir themselves. The gas nuisance is intolerable. It is too bad to be paying 11 or 12s per 1,000 feet for foul gas, of which every night a large quantity passes through the pipes. The management of the Gas Works have been unequivocally condemned. The last Grand Jury expressed their determination to give it up. The Town Commissioners have in like manner expressed their dissatisfaction, and the public generally are loud in their complaints. The price, compared with other towns, is high, but that is not the chief complaint - the quality of the gas, the lateness of the light and its frequent going out are felt to be still greater grievances..."* [11]

It then went on to state that the Committee of Management, consisting of James Madden, Peter O'Connor, John Hegarty, Wm. Kernaghan and Edward Kelly, could not escape blame for the situation that had developed.

As already noticed, James Colquhoun, the largest shareholder, held a lease of the Gas Works for seven years. When his term ended in April, 1847, it appears that he was reluctant to surrender possession of the Works and the Management Committee were required to take proceedings against him in Chancery. When the Company eventually got control in October of that year, they set about re-organising the Works. New pipes, as promised by Colquhoun some months earlier, were laid down; new machinery installed, and the price of gas fixed at 10s. 6d per 1,000 feet. However, there was no significant injectment of additional capital and, in the words of a *"Champion"* editorial, "the

201

Directors continued cobbling as best they could". Renewed efforts were undertaken to recover outstanding debts "while liabilities were kept afloat by bills endorsed by individual shareholders". In the years 1846 to 1850 no dividends were paid. Matters had improved by 1853, following upon the appointment of Thomas Gilcriest as Secretary to the Company, and an announcement that it was in a position to guarantee sufficiency of supply and a reduction in price to 8s.6d - "as cheap as anywhere in Ireland". The tender for lighting the Town for 1854 -55 was £3.5s. for each lamp, fifty of which were to be extinguished at midnight. On the other hand, Harbour lights were charged at the higher rate of £4 each.

In November, 1854, the Company announced that it was about to make an application to Parliament for an Act of Incorporation, and published the following Notice in the local Press:-[12]

---

### NOTICE
# THE GAS LIGHT COMPANY OF SLIGO

Notice is hereby given that application will be made in the ensuing session of Parliament for an Act for Incorporating certain persons established as a Joint Stock Company, called the SLIGO GAS LIGHT AND COKE COMPANY, and for altering, amending, and enlarging the powers given to the said Company, under and by virtue of a certain Deed of Settlement, or Trust Deed, dated the 29th day of May, 1840; and for conferring upon the said Company powers to sue and be sued by its Officers; and for more effectually lighting with Gas the Borough and Suburbs of Sligo; and for enabling the said Company to raise, levy, and receive rates, tolls and rents, for the use of gas and lights to be supplied by the said Company; and to purchase and hold land and to open the several streets, roads, lanes, thoroughfares and places, situated within said Borough of Sligo, and the Municipal Boundaries thereof, and within the Parish of St. John, Barony of Carbury and County of Sligo, and all other, the Suburbs of Sligo; and to lay down, erect and maintain along and throughout the same pipes, posts, works and all proper convenience for the supply of Gas and Light.

And Notice is hereby further given, that all such powers will be taken in the said Act as may be found necessary and requisite to enable the said Company to carry the purposes of the said intended Act fully and effectually into execution.

**Dated this 8th day of November, 1854.**
**Charles Sedley, Solicitor of said Company and for said Bill.**

---

SUPPLYING THE TOWN WITH GAS

In December, 1854, a public meeting was called for the purpose of ascertaining the views of the inhabitants of the Town on the proposed incorporation. The following Resolution, proposed by Daniel McGill, and seconded by Captain Pyne, was passed unanimously :-

*"Resolved - That we, the inhabitants and ratepayers of the Borough of Sligo, at a public meeting assembled in the County Court-house, do hereby dissent from the proposed bill of incorporation sought by the Sligo Gas Company, inasmuch as we conceive that same is wholly unnecessary, and may hereafter lead to an injurious monopoly, on the part of the said company, to the serious detriment of the gas consumers of this town".*

In addition, the following gentlemen were appointed to act as a Committee to take such steps as they might consider advisable to oppose the passing of the Bill in Parliament : Hugh Conlon, Maurice Conry, Alderman Tighe, Michael Hunt and John Coyne.[13] The Corporation also called a special meeting to consider the matter and a majority of members were opposed to the move, as was the *"Sligo Champion"* :- [14]

*"The shareholders of the Sligo Gas Company have taken a bold step. They have resolved to make application in the ensuing Parliament for an Act incorporating certain persons (private individuals) established as a joint stock company. The powers they seek are of no light nature. Heretofore, they have had a monopoly in gas in Sligo, and, consequently, the price of that article is exceedingly high, probably higher than in any other Borough in Ireland. They are now about to strengthen and make permanent that monopoly by an Act of Parliament".*

Despite strong local objections, the Bill for incorporating the Sligo Gas Company received the Royal accent in July, 1855. The preamble to the Act reads as follows:-

# The Sligo Gas Company's Act, 1855

WHEREAS by a Deed of Settlement bearing Date on the Twenty-ninth Day of May, 1840, certain Persons formed themselves into a Company, under the Name of the *"Gaslight and Coke Company of Sligo"*, for the Purpose of supplying the Town of Sligo and the Inhabitants thereof with Gaslight, both for the public Purpose of lighting the Streets of the said Town, and also for the Purpose of supplying Gaslight to such of the

203

## SUPPLYING THE TOWN WITH GAS

Inhabitants of the said Town and its Vicinity as might choose to contract for the same with the said Company: And whereas it was by the said Deed of Settlement provided that the Capital of the Company should be Six thousand Pounds, divided into Six hundred Shares of Ten Pounds each, and the whole of the said original Share Capital has been subscribed for, and Five thousand six hundred Pounds, being the Amount of Five hundred and sixty Shares in the said Company, have been paid up but no Payment in respect of the remaining Forty Shares has as yet been made: And whereas, in accordance with the Provision hereinafter contained, the Capital of the said Company has been increased to Nine thousand Pounds by the Creation of Six hundred additional shares of Five Pounds each : And whereas the whole of the said additional Shares have been subscribed for, but no Payment in respect thereof hath hitherto been made or required: And whereas the said Company have constructed their Works in the said Town of Sligo, and have long since laid down Pipes, and have since 1842 supplied and are now supplying with Gas the greater Part of the said Town of Sligo, and intend to extend the said Supply as the same may be required by or on behalf of the Inhabitants of the said Town of Sligo: And whereas the said Company would be better able to carry on their Undertaking if they were incorporated, and if certain Powers were conferred upon them by Parliament; but these Objects cannot be accomplished without the Authority of Parliament: May it therefore please Your Majesty that it may be enacted; and be it enacted by the Queen's most Excellent Majesty, by and with the Advice and Consent of the Lords Spiritual and Temporal, and Commons, in this present Parliament assembled, and by the Authority of the same.

The purpose for which the Act was inacted and the names of the Committee of Management on date of incorporation were also stated:

The Company shall be continued and maintained for the Purpose of manufacturing Gas, and for providing Gasometers, and all Apparatus, Machinery, and Buildings necessary for that Purpose, and for lighting with gas the several streets, roads, lanes and public Passages, and Churches, Chapels, Public Buildings, Shops, Taverns, private Houses, Warehouses, and other Buildings and Places, within the Limits of this Act, and also for selling and disposing of Coke, Tar, Ammoniacal Liquor, and every Produce, Refuse or Residuum arising or to be obtained from the Materials used in or necessary for the Manufacture of Gas, in such Manner as the said Company may think proper.

## SUPPLYING THE TOWN WITH GAS

The several Persons who immediately before the passing of this Act constituted the Committee of Management of the *"Gaslight and Coke Company of Sligo"*, that is to say, *Richard Hand Wood*, of *Sligo*, Surgeon; *George Leech*, of *Sligo*, Merchant; *Moses Monds*, of *Sligo*, Merchant; *James Harper*, of *Sligo*, Steam Packet Agent; and *Henry Lyons*, of *Sligo*, Merchant and Alderman; shall be the First Directors of the Company hereby incorporated, and they shall continue in Office until the First Ordinary Meeting of the Company to be held in the Year One thousand eight hundred and fifty-six.

In practical terms the 1855 Act empowered the Company to manufacture and supply gas within the Parliamentary boundary; its authorised Share Capital was increased by £3,400 to £9,000, and the maximum charge for gas could not exceed 10s.6d per 1,000 cubic feet.

In 1859 the Gas Co. unsuccessfully appealed against a revised valuation of £200 on their Wine Street premises. Under cross-examination at the hearing hitherto unpublished details relative to the workings of the Company came to light:-

* Works occupied half an acre;
* Original buildings and fittings cost £2,550;
* Invested capital, £9,000. Paid -up £5,600;
* Returns for 1858 showed receipts at £2,568 and outgoings at £2,031;
* Directors received £30 each per annum and Thomas Gilcriest, Secretary, was in receipt of a salary of £100.

At the A.G.M. in March, 1864, the following Shareholders were in attendance : - Messrs. Richard H. Wood (Chairman), Peter O'Connor, Moses Monds, James Tighe, Henry Lyons, Alexander Lyons, John Lyons, Thomas Little, William Middleton, James Sedley, George Pollexfen, William Monds, George Leech, James Harper, William Clarke, Thomas Gilcriest, William A. Woods and Thomas R. Wilson. The statement of accounts for year ending 31 December, 1863, listed the principal items of income as follows : Town Lighting £330; Harbour Board Contract £329; Private Consumers £1,412 and sale of coke and tar £255. Extensions to works and mains totalled £880, leaving a credit balance of £1,785. On the proposal of Charles Sedley,

## SUPPLYING THE TOWN WITH GAS

seconded by Peter O'Connor, it was decided, on a vote, that in future the Press would be admitted to the annual gathering.

In 1868 the price of gas was reduced to 5s.10d per 1,000 cubic feet and, in 1872, was further reduced to 5s.6d, which compared favourably with Waterford (5s.6d) and Galway (7s.0d). The accounts for 1869 recorded a 25% increase in sales to private consumers over a six-year period, and a credit balance of £1,477.4s.6d. which, after paying a dividend of £720, left a surplus of £757.4s.6d. Despite a marked improvement in the Company's performance, there were still complaints concerning the "flickering dullness of the street lamps" as well as the poor quality of the light. A meeting of gas consumers was convened in January, 1879, to consider the price of gas with a view to a further reduction. Numerous speakers demanded that a fairer proportion of the Company's profits be diverted to the advantage of users, instead of going into the pockets of the shareholders. Edward Gayer, Proprietor of the *"Sligo Champion"*, proposed the following Resolution, which was carried unanimously :-

*"That we, the gas consumers of this Town, in public meeting assembled, deprecate the course pursued by the Sligo Gas Company, and we are forcibly impressed with the conviction that the rate which we are at present asked to pay for gas is excessive, and by no means warranted by the current prices of labour, coal and iron, which are the principal items chargeable for its manufacture and supply"* [15]

A deputation, consisting of Messrs. Harper Campbell, Bernard Collery, Richard McDonagh and Joseph Golden, was appointed to wait upon the Gas Co. However, before the deputation had an opportunity of meeting with the Directors, the following statement was issued on behalf of the Company:-

*"Having examined the accounts, the Directors have decided to reduce the price of gas by five pence as from April next. A further reduction of a similar nature will be considered from January, 1880."* [16]

Simon Cullen presided at the A.G.M. in March, 1889. Also present were E. Crawford, Alex. Lyons, W.A. Woods, E.J. Tighe, Peter O'Connor, Henry Lyons and A.I. Middleton, together with newly appointed Manager, C.B. Tully. Despite a serious deterioration in its financial affairs, as a result of writing-off bad debts that had accumulated over a period, and a loan of £2,000 still unpaid,

## SUPPLYING THE TOWN WITH GAS

shareholders were assured that the Company was solvent. In the circumstances, the Directors agreed to a reduced renumeration of £20 per annum. On the positive side, plant and works were valued at £11,995; sales of gas had increased by £273.7s; a new sulphate of ammonia plant was in production, while improvements to works and mains, costing £3,000 over the previous four years, had resulted in the provision of constant pressure for domestic cookers for the first time. An editorial in the *"Sligo Chronicle"* a week later expressed an understanding of the problems being experienced by the Company while, at the same time, being critical of the Directors:- [17]

*"Considering that the Gas Company is a comparatively small one, it has had a career of considerable vicissitude and is only now emerging from the effects of bad management into something like a sound financial state. The Company was unfortunate in its late Secretary who absconded with a cash deficiency, and also in the directorate who were content to let matters slide so long as a dividend was disclosed at the end of each financial year, although the dividend was being paid out of capital..... It seems odd that a Company with a capital of only £9,000 should pay its Directors and Auditors £170 in salaries...."*

In comparison with the previous half century, the 1890's were a period of steady growth for the Sligo Gas Company. Additional plots adjacent to the Works, one in Wine Street and the other in Adelaide Street, were acquired by lease while renewal of mains and improvements to plant became a priority. Domestic consumption of gas increased, prices continued in a downward trend and profits showed a marked improvement.[18] The Director's Report for the year ending 1893 was the most positive and forward-looking in the history of the Company:-

"Gentlemen - Your directors have the pleasure to report that the business of the Company and their financial position has greatly improved during the past year.

A nett profit has been made amounting to £681.5.8d after writing off £300 for depreciation of works and plant, out of which we recommend a dividend at the rate of £6 per cent per annum, free of income tax, to be paid on the 14th of April next, which will absorb £540, leaving a balance of £141.5s.8d. to be carried forward to the current year.

Your works have been greatly improved by the addition of a range of

IMPORTANT

# REDUCTION IN GAS

From and after 1st APRIL next

THE PRICE OF GAS IN SLIGO WILL BE

# FURTHER REDUCED

From **5**s. to **4**s. **2**d.

PER 1,000 CUBIC FEET FOR PRIVATE LIGHTING, AND

From **3**s. **4**d. to **2**s. **9**d.

FOR COOKING, HEATING AND GAS ENGINES

Gas Works, Sligo.
5th March, 1895.

## SLIGO GAS WORKS

|  | 1890 | 1896 |
|---|---|---|
| No. of Public Lamps: | 170 | 176 |
| No. of Consumers: | 465 | 613 |
| Length of Gas Mains: | 7 miles | 7½ miles |
| Cubic feet of Gas Made: | 16,220,000 | 23,714,000 |
| Tons of Coal Carbonised: | 1,800 | 2,963 |
| Receipts: | £3,864 | £4,694 |
| Expenditure: | £3,415 | £3,862 |
| Gross price to Consumers per 1,00 cubic feet: | 5s. 5d. | 4s. 2d. |

substantial workshops, comprising smithy, machine shop, carpenter's shop, and gas fitter's shop. The distributing plant has also been considerably extended by a new main and lamps for lighting the Deep Water Berths; 42 new consumers have been supplied, and many of the mains throughout the Town relaid with larger pipes, at a total cost of £460 1s. 2d. which has been charged to capital.

Your directors are pleased to state that they have obtained the Provisional Order to increase the capital of the company by £6,000, and they propose asking the sanction of the shareholders to raise the necessary amount required to extend the works, and to pay off the mortgage to the Bank."

---

# INCOME AND EXPENDITURE ACCOUNTS

### Year ending December 31st. 1900

**Income:**

| | |
|---|---|
| Sales of Gas by Meter: .......................... | £4,116. 6. 8d |
| Sales of Gas by Contract : ........................... | 560.13. 2 |
| Meter rents: .......................... | 136. 1. 7 |
| Sales of Coke, Tar, etc.: .......................... | 1,283.16. 5 |
| Cleaning of Lamps: .......................... | 238. 9.11 |
| | £6,335. 7. 9 |

**Expenditure:**

| | |
|---|---|
| Manufacture of Gas (Purchase of Coal, Wages etc.) ..................... | £3,625. 7.5d |
| Repairs to mains, meters, cookers, public lamps, plant etc. ................... | 1,131. 4. 6. |
| Rents and Rates: .......................... | 265. 1.10. |

**Management:**

| | |
|---|---|
| Directors Fees, Salaries etc. ......................... | 591. 6.4. |
| Miscellaneous: | 50.15.4 |
| | £5,663.15.5. |

## SUPPLYING THE TOWN WITH GAS

The improved performance was attributed, to a large extent, to the enterprise and business acumen of the newly appointed Manager, Cornelius B. Tully, who had been previously in the employment of the London Gas Light Co. Commenting on his achievement, the *"Independent"* paid him this tribute : "When he took over the management in the late 1880's the affairs of the Company were in a bad state - its shares were practically unsaleable, its gas defective, its rates excessive and things were approaching collapse. Within a few years of taking control he has succeeded in bringing the affairs of the Company to a creditable state...." [19]

In January, 1897, the Gas Co., responding to a discussion at a Corporation meeting, as to the possibility of lighting the Town by electricity, issued a circular which stated that electric lighting would be eight times more expensive than "incondensent gas light". There the matter was allowed to rest until 1924. In that year the Gas Co. promoted the Sligo Lighting and Electric Power Bill which sought legislative authority to light the Town with electricity. A number of clauses in the Bill were vigorously opposed by the Corporation who feared the creation of a monopoly [20]. However, after these were modified to the satisfaction of the 'City Fathers', the Bill was passed into law in July of that year. It has the distinction of being the first Private Bill to have been passed by both Houses of the Oireachtas. [21]. Thereafter, the Sligo Gaslight Company became the *Sligo Lighting and Electric Power Company,* although it never exercised its functions with regard to street lighting, namely, changing from gas to electricity.

In the opening decades of the present century profits averaged out at between £600 and £700 per annum. The A.G.M. in March 1915, was presided over by Robert Gorman. Directors present were Arthur Jackson, Henry Lyons, John Connolly and Dr. Thomas Gilcriest, while apologies for inability to attend were received from Col.James Campbell and Edward Tighe. Profits for the year ending December 31st. 1914, amounted to £620.10s. In the course of his annual report the Secretary, Richard Browne, stated that a new retort house and an upgraded distribution system had greatly improved both the quality and pressure of the gas supply throughout the Town. Paid-up capital stood at £13,000 and it was decided to pay shareholders a dividend of 5%. [22]

## SUPPLYING THE TOWN WITH GAS

W.B. Allen was Manager of the Company from 1904 to 1912 and was succeeded by Frank Browne. The latter held the position until 1923 when an unprecedented development forced his resignation. In October of that year the Company's outdoor staff, members of the Transport Worker's Union, went on strike in support of those advocating the release of political prisoners. In an effort to maintain a supply of gas to consumers the Directors called in the Army to operate the works but Browne, who disapproved of the move, refused to co-operate and resigned his post. As a result, the temporary operators, inexperienced as they were in such matters, were unable to maintain sufficient pressure to meet demands and for three nights the Town was left in complete darkness. [23] John Douris acted as temporary Manager until the appointment, the following year, of another Englishman, J. Albert Pemberton, to the post. During his stint with the Company the distribution pipes were upgraded, a network of new connections put in place and the price of gas reduced by 10d per 1000 cubic feet, to 8s.4d. He was succeeded by Louis Casewell from Belfast; and after his unexpected demise in 1959, the affairs of the Company in its final years were managed by Wm. Stuart MacGregor.

From the Thirties onwards competition from the Electricity Supply Board led to a substantial drop in income both from street lighting and domestic consumption. A shortage of fuel during the 'Emergency' led to a further reduction in the manufacture of gas and it became increasingly difficult to maintain the works and the distribution system to the required standards. In the post-war years revenue went into a sharp decline while operating costs were on the increase. At the A.G.M. in July,1960, the accounts for the year ending December 31st. 1959, revealed an operating loss of £976.19s. Present were Alfred McHugh (Chairman); John C. Cole; John C. Cole (jun.); John W. Lyons and Alexander C. Lyons (Directors) and Michael O'Brien, Secretary. [24]

Throughout the Fifties production was being gradually scaled down and in 1962 the Company was placed on the market as a going concern. It was purchased by local businessman, J.J. Higgins who, in September of that year, announced that, as the plant was beyond economic repair, the supply of gas to consumers would be discontinued as soon as existing domestic cookers had been converted to operate on bottled gas. [25] The Gas Works, a distinctive landmark in

SUPPLYING THE TOWN WITH GAS

## THE SLIGO LIGHTING & ELECTRIC POWER COMPANY

# REPORT OF DIRECTORS

- AND -

# STATEMENT OF ACCOUNTS

## FOR THE

### Year ended 31st December, 1959

NOTICE is Hereby Given that the Annual General Meeting of the Shareholders of the above Company will be held at the Company's Offices, Wine Street, Sligo, on Friday, the 8th day of July, 1960, at 12 o'clock (noon) for the following purposes:-

To receive and consider the Statement of Accounts
and Balance Sheet, together with the Directors'
and Auditors' Reports for the Year ended the 31st
December, 1959.

To clear two Directors.
To Appoint Auditors.
To transact any other business that may be brought
before an Annual General Meeting.

*By Order of the Board.*

M. O'BRIEN,
Secretary.

Wine Street, Sligo.
15th June, 1960.

## SUPPLYING THE TOWN WITH GAS

the Wine Street area, were finally closed down in 1964 and subsequently dismantled. In 1968 *Best's Supermarket,* which was later acquired and operated as *Dunne's Stores,* opened on the site.

Thus ended the Sligo Gaslight Company after a chequered existence of a century and a quarter. The Sligo Steamship Company apart, it had the distinction of being the only locally owned and operated company of that era.

### Notes and References

| | | |
|---|---|---|
| (1) | *"Sligo Journal"* | 15-1-1836 |
| (2) | ibid | 29-1-1836 |
| (3) | ibid | 10-6-1836 |
| (4) | *"Sligo Champion"* | 24-9-1836 |
| (5) | Colquhoun was also involved in the supply of gas in Limerick, Wexford, Carlow and New Ross in the 1840's. | |
| (6) | Registry of Deeds | 1839. Bk. 17 No. 173 |
| (7) | *"Sligo Champion"* | 18-4-1840 |
| (8) | Registry of Deeds | 1840.Bk. 12 No. 179 |
| (9) | *"Sligo Journal"* | 15-12-1843 |
| (10) | *"Sligo Chronicle"* | 13-9-1862 |
| (11) | *"Sligo Journal"* | 7-11-1845 |
| (12) | *"Sligo Chronicle"* | 11-11-1854 |
| (13) | *"Sligo Champion"* | 23-12-1854 |
| (14) | ibid | 18-11-1854 |

The Borough Improvement Act of 1869 empowered the Corporation to purchase, by agreement, the undertaking of the Sligo Gas Company. However, despite the criticisms levelled at the Company over many years, these powers were never invoked.

| | | |
|---|---|---|
| (15) | *"Sligo Champion"* | 4-1-1879 |
| (16) | ibid | 11-1-1879 |
| (17) | *"Sligo Chronicle"* | 6-4-1889 |

(18) In 1884 there were 4 miles of mains and 310 private consumers. By 1890 the mains were 7 miles in length and the number of consumers had increased to 405.

| | | |
|---|---|---|
| (19) | *"Sligo Independent"* | 5-3-1896 |

## SUPPLYING THE TOWN WITH GAS

(20)      ibid                    5-4-1924 and 7-6-1924
Street lighting by gas cost the Corporation in the region of £1,000 in 1924.

(21)      ibid.                          5-7-1924

(22)      ibid                          27 -3-1915

(23)      ibid.                          3-11-1923

(24) Director's Report & Statement of Accounts, 1959. The workforce in its
final years included Mary McGauran (Secretary); Paddy Ryan
(Foreman); Michael Ryan (Collector / Fitter); Christy House;
Paddy Verdon; Michael Sweeney; Ted Campbell; Pat Gilgan;
Paddy Hamilton; Thomas McNiffe; Michael and Joseph Burns,
Roger Brennan and James Conboy.

(25) *"Sligo Champion"*                          29-9-1962

The Sligo Gas Works

# Fairs & Markets

## 1. FAIRS

The practice of holding fairs for the purpose of exhibiting, selling and buying goods dates back to ancient times. In Ireland the *Aonach* was the commonest form of public assembly and its main object was the celebration of games, sports and pastimes. With the passage of time, especially in the post Norman period, fairs, or temporary markets, where buyers and sellers gathered to transact business, began to develop. These were usually held at regular intervals, generally at the same location and time of year. Historically, fairs were created to solve the early problem of distribution and the primary function was the promotion of trade.

In modern parlance the word 'Fair' was applied to a gathering where the principal business was concerned with the buying and selling of livestock. Many modern fairs were a continuation of old time gatherings that continued uninterrupted from age to age but gradually changed their purpose to meet the requirements of succeeding generations. Old fairs often lasted two or more days and were organised in a recognised sequence of goods and livestock, often

## FAIRS AND MARKETS

terminating in sports and horse-racing, and not infrequently in bloodshed.

Over the centuries the Fair Day was an important event in rural Ireland. Apart altogether from its economic function, socially it had an added significance, it was a meeting place for the farming community over a wide area. Although most fairs were held on the streets of villages and towns, there were usually designated areas for the sale of different types of livestock - cattle, sheep and pigs - and farmers usually set out at an early hour in order to 'stand' their produce at a prime location. The process of buying and selling was often a rather delicate and prolonged affair as both buyers and sellers held out for the best possible bargain before a deal was clinched. Sometimes this was achieved without undue delay but very often it was necessary for a third party to become involved before a deal was brokered. This was

| LOCATION | GRANTEE | DATE | DETAILS OF GRANT |
|---|---|---|---|
| Ardnaglass: | Rory McSweeney | 1618 | Tuesday market & 2 Fairs: June 11th & September 14th |
| Ballisodare: | Edward Crofton | 1617 | 1 Fair: July 22nd/23rd |
| Ballymote: | Sir James Fullerton | 1604 | Monday market and 2 fairs: May 1st & August 24th |
| " | Robert Dillon | 1633 | 2 additional Fairs: July 30th / 31st and October 2nd/3rd |
| Belclare: | Sir Arthur Gore | 1685 | 2 Fairs: August 15th /16th & December 1st / 2nd |
| Bricklieve: | Robert Dillon | 1633 | 2 Fairs: May 31st/June 1st and November 1st/2nd |
| Cullaghmore: | Dr. John Leslie | 1677 | 3 Fairs: May 15/16th, October 10th/11th; December 22nd/23rd |

## FAIRS AND MARKETS

| LOCATION | GRANTEE | DATE | DETAILS OF GRANT |
|---|---|---|---|
| Collooney: | Bryan McDonagh | 1616 | Wednesday market and 1 Fair: July 25th/26th |
| " | Bryan McDonagh | 1622 | Tuesday market and 2 additional fairs: April 24th & November 11th |
| Coolaney: | Teige O'Hara | 1613 | 1 Fair: August 15th/16th |
| Grange: | Thomas Soden | 1684 | 4 Fairs: April 20th; Aug. 16th; Oct. 18th & Nov. 29th, with an additional day for each |
| Roslea: | Lionel Guest | 1603 | Saturday Market and a Fair of three days i.e. eve, day and morrow of St.Michael the Archangel. |
| " | Godfrey Brereton | 1782 | Re grant |
| Sligo: | Sir James Fullerton | 1604 | Saturday Market & 2 Fairs: June 24th and Sept.29th |
| " | Sir James Craig | 1627 | Additional market on Tuesdays and 2 extra Fairs: March 17th/18th and August 1st/2nd. |
| " | Earl of Strafford & Thomas Radcliffe | 1674 | Re Grant. |
| Templehouse: | Wm. Crofton | 1611 | A Wednesday Market & 1 Fair: July 20th/21st |
| " | Wm. Crofton | 1618 | An additional Fair: October 28th/19th |

217

## FAIRS AND MARKETS

| LOCATION | GRANTEE | DATE | DETAILS OF GRANT |
|---|---|---|---|
| Tubberscanavan: | Arthur Cooper | 1686 | 2 Fairs: Trinity Monday & September 4th and the day following "with the usual tolls and customs" |
| " | Joshua Cooper | 1760 | Grant of two additional Fairs: May 17th and October 31st |
| Tullaghnaglogg: | Charles Delahyde | 1617 | Saturday Market and 1 Fair: August 15th/16th |

**Over the following two centuries additional Patents were issued as follows:**

| | | | |
|---|---|---|---|
| Aclare: | Wm. Ormsby - Gore | 1848 | A Saturday Market and 4 Fairs: June 24th; August 11th, October 2nd and Nov. 13th |
| Ballinacarrow: | John Perceval | 1731 | Tuesday Market and 4 Fairs: May 3rd; June 3rd; October 3rd & December 3rd, with an additional day after each. In 1757 Richard Fleming, who had a lease of the tolls and customs, sublet same to his son, Archibald. |
| Bellaghy: | Annelsey Knox | 1819 | Wednesday Market |
| Bunninadden: | Benjamin Burton | 1758 | Wednesday Market and 4 Fairs: May 28th; August 6th; October 9th; Nov. 27th. |

## FAIRS AND MARKETS

| LOCATION | GRANTEE | DATE | DETAILS OF GRANT |
|---|---|---|---|
| Castlebaldwin: | Dr. Henry Nicholson | 1712 | Wednesday Market and 4 Fairs: May 23th; July 16th, August 26th, and Oct.20th, with an additional day after each. |
| Cliffoney: | Viscount Palmerston | 1781 | A Wednesday Market |
| Tubbercurry: | James Napper | 1750 | Monday Market and 2 Fairs: May 11th and Nov. 18th. In 1802 Richard Phibbs Irwin leased customs /tolls of Fairs to Alexander Irwin for £20. 19s a half year. |

known as 'splitting the difference'. The presence of a variety of 'characters', such as wandering musicians, fortune-tellers and vendors of all types of household goods added greatly to the atmosphere of the time-honoured event.

Following the great upheaval in 17th century land ownership, many of the grants to English settlers included patents for the holding of fairs and markets. While some of the sites specified were places of assembly of long standing, new fairs were established to suit the needs of the time. The earliest list of Fairs in the County of which we have knowledge dates from the 17th century when *Letters Patent* - an official document conferring an exclusive right - were granted to individual landlords, mostly new settlers or 'adventurers', authorising the holding of Fairs at specified locations and on given dates. Between 1603 and 1685 a total of fourteen such Patents were granted.

The proprietors of fairs established under Patent were entitled to levy customs or tolls on those who made use of the venue for the sale or purchase of livestock. An Act of Parliament (77th of Geo. III.) quantified the levy as follows:-

| | |
|---|---|
| Every Bull, Bullock or Cow .............................. | 1d |
| Every Calf, Hog or Pig ................................. | ½d |
| Every Suckling Pig, Sheep or Lamb .................. | 1d |

FAIRS AND MARKETS

It was also enacted that a printed board be displayed in a conspicuous place at the entrance to the Fair Green, specifying in legible characters, the custom or toll being claimed. As time progressed various irregularities crept in - such as tolls being taken up by people with no legal entitlement to such; no toll boards in use or, if so, charges were in excess of that permitted by law. In the late 1820's efforts were made to enforce the regulations in this respect and summonses were issued against the collectors of tolls at Bunninadden, Tubbercurry and Sligo.

## TOLLS AT FAIRS   1823 - 1843

| VENUE: | TOLLS PAYABLE TO: | COMMENTS: |
|---|---|---|
| Ballintogher: | Benjamin Stradford. Collected by Laurence Clancy. | A small board upon which the tolls are printed is usually put up on the Fair Day. |
| Ballisodare: | E.J. Cooper. | Toll collector, Mrs. Gildea; has a toll board but does not put it up on Fair Days. |
| Ballymote: | Viscount Kirkwall. Collected by Philip Gormely. | Tolls collected at Fairs only. Toll board put up sometimes but none on Market Days. |
| Bellaghy: | Claimed by Annesley Knox of Rappa Castle, Co. Mayo. | |
| Beltra: | John Irwin. | |
| Bunninadden: | Mrs. Thompson of Mt. Irwin. Collected by James Ruane and Thady Gannon. | |
| Castlebaldwin: | | Ditto - as Ballintogher |
| Collooney: | Joshua Edward Cooper. Collected by J. Alexander. | No toll board |

220

## FAIRS AND MARKETS

| VENUE: | TOLLS PAYABLE TO: | COMMENTS: |
|---|---|---|
| Coolaney: | Charles O'Hara. | |
| Easkey: | Colonel Brereton. | No tolls collected |
| Enniscrone: | Robert Orme, leased to Henry King. Collected by Robert Leech and John Caffrey. | |
| Grange: | Capt. James Soden. | No toll board |
| Riverstown: | Arthur B. Cooper. | Tolls collected |
| Sligo: | Owen Wynne. Collected by William Christian. | |
| Templehouse: | Alexander Perceval. | No boards displayed |
| Tubbercurry: | Claimed by Richard P. Irwin of Muckelty. Collected by Patrick Davey and Patrick Feehily on behalf of Jones Irwin. | |
| Tubberscanavan: | Joshua Edward Cooper. Collected by J. Alexander. | No toll board |

A century ago it was estimated that nine-tenths of fairs were held on the public roads, with no accommodation being provided by the proprietor who collected the tolls at such fairs. In some cases the village street or roadway was so crowded that the mail-coach was obliged to "go in a walk" through the fair. The system of collecting tolls as livestock were being driven from the fair often led to a near riot as both buyers and sellers tried to force their way out and avoid payment, if possible. In many cases, the owners of the toll did everything to maximise the returns. It is said that Edward Synge Cooper regularly supervised the collection at Tubberscanavan Fair, and on one occasion galloped his horse in pursuit of a poor man's pig that had wandered off without the custom having been paid.

The Repeal of the Corn Laws in 1846, and the resulting reduction in cereal cultivation, not only led to a big increase in livestock numbers

FAIRS AND MARKETS

but also in the number of fairs. The coming of the railway, and the facility provided for the easy transportation of animals, gave a great impetus to fairs in towns and villages served by rail. In County Sligo the fairs at Ballintogher, Ballisodare, Ballymote, Collooney, Coolaney, Curry, Tubbercurry and Sligo, in particular, attracted increased livestock numbers as well as buyers from long distances.

A number of fairs in the County had their respective characteristics:- Carney was famous for its sheep; Tubberscanavan for springers; Ballymote, Ballintogher and Castlebaldwin for general stock and Carricknagat for horses. However, the staple attraction at several of the county's fairs at the close of the 18th and the beginning of the 19th centuries were the faction fights. The story is told that in the 1820's 'Collector' Owen Wynne of Sligo, witnessing one of these fights in progress at Carricknagat, rode in among the combatants with the object of separating them but, both sides resenting his interference, turned on him and beat him most savagely. This resulted in twenty of them being arrested and lodged in Sligo Gaol and subsequently sentenced to terms of imprisonment, with hard labour, for periods ranging from one to two years.

## Faction Fights:

Reports of faction fights at Ardnaglass, Ballintogher, Beltra, Carricknagat and Tubberscanavan were chronicled in some detail in the local press and are reprinted here to illustrate the vicious nature of such encounters.

## Beltra Fair, 1782

"On Tuesday last was committed to the County Gaol, by Lewis Francis Irwin, Esq., Michael Kenny, Owen Kenny, Maurice Marley, and Francis M'Cowen, taken in a riot the 20th instant at the fair of Beltra, in this county. They were part of a gang lately formed and, it was said, often met in the baronies of Leyny and Tireragh; were in number not less than two hundred, who call themselves 'the regiment of cudgelers,' and said they were commanded by one Meaghan. At the fair and place above mentioned, about a hundred of them assembled

FAIRS AND MARKETS

with oak boughs, and armed with cudgels and other weapons, offending and striking several people as they passed along. A party of *The Independent Tyreril Volunteers,* engaged in recruiting for the navy, was attacked by this daring banditti, who pelted them so severely with stones as to oblige them to take shelter for some time in the *Strand-house;* but Mr. Irwin, hearing of the affair, went immediately to their assistance."

*"Sligo Journal"* August, 1782

# Balllintogher Fair, 1825

"A faction fight on the evening of the Fair lasted a considerable time. Each clan came armed with shillelaghs which flew around and made lasting impressions upon divers heads and shoulders, which tended to repress some of the martial rage by the copious bleedings which ensued...The riot was eventually suppressed by the police"

*"Sligo Journal"* 11-6-1825

# Ardnaglass Fair, 1828

"Some days ago, at the Fair of Ardnaglass in this County, a riot took place. A few of the Constabulary having been on the spot, they very properly used every exertion in the suppression of the tumult. Having apprehended two persons, they were leading them out of the Fair, when a number of men amounting, as we are informed, to three hundred, attempted a rescue of those in custody, in the course of which, so close was the collision of the parties, that a carbine was wrestled from a Constable and broken to pieces.

The violence of the mob was such that the Constables, in self defence, were compelled to fire upon them - the consequence was that two men were wounded and the small Constabulary force of five in number, succeeded in carrying off the persons originally apprehended, and lodged them in the County Gaol. Informations have been duly sworn against them and they now lie under the commitment of a Magistrate of the County."

*"Sligo Journal"* 24-6-1828

FAIRS AND MARKETS

# Tubberscanavan Fair, 1830

"At the Fair of Tubberscanavan, which was held on Monday last, a desperate affray took place between two parties, near relatives, which lasted a considerable length of time. One man, whom we believe interfered for the purpose of quieting the contestants, received a severe stab in the side from a bayonet and is not expected to survive. A poor woman was also wounded by a pistol ball, but not dangerously. We have not heard the particulars which led to the quarrel."

*"Sligo Journal"* 21-5-1830

# Sligo May Fair, 1837

"The peasantry on the evening of Saturday were very riotous; we have seldom seen the termination of a fair pass in such bustle and uproar. The Constabulary were called to the scene of the riot early in the evening where, by timely interposition and exertions, comparative order was restored and the peaceably disposed had an opportunity of returning home unmolested..."

*"Sligo Journal"* 12-5-1837

\*　　　\*　　　\*　　　\*

A number of years ago the following rather apt inscription was copied from a weathered tombstone in the old cemetery in Collooney. It recalls the memory of one William Wix who died in a faction fight in 1766:

> *"Here lies the body of William Wix*
> *Who died in the year Sixty-six;*
> *By the bludgeon's blow he was laid low -*
> *At the Fair of Tubberscanavan".*

Almost a century later a young man named John Mitchell was murdered on his way home from the Fair of Tanrego (*alias* Beltra). Two years later, on June 18th, 1849, a quarrel broke out at Ballymote fair during which one James Gallagher was fatally stabbed. The last recorded faction fight in the County took place in February, 1877, and was reported on as follows in the local *"Chronicle"*:-

"A serious faction fight occurred last Monday in the townland of

224

Rathribbon, near the gate of *Markree Castle*, between some number of persons who were returning from the fair of Carricknagat. The following are the names of the respective parties, as far as can be at present ascertained:-Peter Costello of Roughan; Michael Costello, Annaghcarty; Bartly Doogan, Roughan; Thomas Flynn, Carrowkeel; Bartly Mulvany, Mullaghmore, on one side, while on the opposite side were Andrew Meehan, John McGowan and James McGowan. The fight lasted for some time, and dangerous wounds were inflicted upon some of the parties. Peter Costello, Michael Costello and Bartly Mulvany were seriously stabbed and otherwise injured. They were immediately attended by Dr. Ayres Moore, Medical Officer of Collooney district. Constable McDowen of the Colloney station, with some of his men,

## VALUATION OF FAIRS 1855-1856

| Fair | Proprietor | Leased To | Valuation |
|------|-----------|-----------|-----------|
| Aclare: | Walter Henry | John Burns | £10 |
| Ardnaglass: | Wm. D. Webber | Wm. Graham | £3 |
| Ballinacarrow: | R. W. Hall-Dare | in fee | £5 |
| Ballintogher: | James Fleming | Wm. Lougheed | £15 |
| Ballisodare: | Edward J. Cooper | in fee | £15 |
| Ballymote: | Sir R. Gore-Booth | John Morrison | £40 |
| Bellaghy: (Market & Fairs) | Rev. St. George Knox | James Johnston | £20 |
| Beltra: (alias Tanrego) | Capt. R. Olpherts | in fee | £4 |
| Benada: | Rev. Wm. Jones | Roger Jones | - |
| Bunninadden: | Alex Perceval | John Ruane | £9 |
| Carney: | Sir. R. Gore-Booth | in fee | £10 |
| Carricknagat: | Wm. Phibbs | in fee | £5 |
| Castlebaldwin: | James Simpson | Hugh McKeon | £13 |
| Collooney: | Edward J. Cooper | in fee | £15 |
| Coolaney: | Charles O'Hara | James Smith | £6 |
| Curry: | Richard Phibbs | Barth. Naughton | £6 |
| Easkey: | Godfrey Brereton | John McNama | £8 |
| Farniharpy: | W.D. Webber | Barth. Kavanagh | £4 |
| Roslea: | Richard Brinkley | in fee | £4 |
| Sligo: | John Wynne | in fee | £5 |
| Templehouse: | R.W. Hall-Dare | in fee | £5 |
| Tubbercurry: (Markets & Fairs) | Reps. of R.P. Irwin | John Brett | £60 |
| Tubberscanavan: | Edward J. Cooper | in fee | £4 |

were attending the fair while the fight was going on; but on his return in the evening, from information received, he proceeded to Dr. Moore's residence and found the three injured men. He next proceeded to the scene of the conflict, where he perceived lying on the road McGowan, seriously injured and bleeding very much. McGowan having been brought to the barrack, identified the two Costellos. He states that he was attacked and beaten by twelve or thirteen men. The injured men are at present lying in hospital. Six of the party have been arrested and lodged in Sligo Gaol."

*"Sligo Chronicle"* 10-2-1877

# NOTABLE FAIRS

## Ardnaglass:

A patent to hold two fairs at Ardnaglass, in the parish of Skreen, on June 11th and September 14th, was granted to Rory McSweeney in 1618. The Fair Green was within the shadow of the ruins of the old castle of the same name which figured prominently in the 1641 Rebellion and subsequently in the Williamite Wars.

After the McSweeneys were dispossessed the customs of the fair passed to the Jones family. In 1819 Loftus Jones of Tubberpatrick leased part of the lands of Ardnaglass, the lands of Ardabrone, together with the customs of the Fair and a paddock thereon to Catherine Leech for a rent of £22.12s. a half year.*

By the 1830's the rights to the fair had been acquired by the Webbers of Leekfield, at which time there were four annually, namely, June 1st; August 13th; September 23rd and November 12th. The value of the tolls and customs in the mid 19th century, then on lease to William Graham, was given as a mere £3., but three decades later were estimated at from £30. to £40. There were five fairs in the 1840's; three in 1889; four in 1905 and six in the 1950's. In its latter years it was mostly a sheep fair and the tolls - 2d for sheep and 1d. for lambs - were collected by the owners of the Green, the Clarke family of Ardnaglass.

* Registry of Deeds. Bk. 738 p.33

## FAIRS AND MARKETS

# Ballymote:

A patent for the holding of fairs at Ballymote on May 1st and August 24th was granted to Sir James Fullerton in 1604. Three decades later , in 1633, two additional fairs were sanctioned, one on July 30th and the other on October 2nd, together with the following day in each case. A century later ownership of the tolls passed to the Fitzmaurices, the new proprietors of Ballymote, and in 1833 to Sir Robert Gore-Booth.

There were six fairs in the 1830's and by mid century the number had increased to seven. There was an enclosed Fair Green of two acres, or thereabouts, for the sale of cattle. Sheep were sold on the streets and pigs on a vacant site in front of the Courthouse. Tolls, which were estimated at £40 per annum, were collected from buyers leaving the market. This resulted in cattle receiving "bad treatment" at the four exists which were usually manned by fifteen to twenty men. In evidence before the Fairs and Markets Commission, 1852, the methods of clearing cattle were explained as follows by Patrick Curran, a Sligo exporter:-

*"They have some sort of paper on a stick and the people themselves put hands on it as they pass and say whether they have bought or sold. If any doubt exists as to whether the truth is being told, they oblige you to touch this paper, but if you get clear, no matter whether you sold or not, they do not seek to recover".*

In 1863 a correspondent in the *"Sligo Journal"* reported as follows on the January fair:-

*"I am happy to inform you that the fair held on Monday last clearly proved the vast benefit which the opening of the railway from Longford has conferred upon this locality. English, Scotch, Meath and Westmeath buyers, availing themselves of the facility of travelling now first opened to them, attended and sales were brisk at improved prices for every description of stock. The prices in the victualling department ranged as follows: Beef, first class, 52s to 56s per cwt; second class, 44s to 50s; mutton, 5d to 6d per lb; pork 35s to 38s per cwt. There were some fine springers and milch cows on offer, but inferior classes seemed more in favour. For the latter, prices stood at about £8 to £12 10s per head; strippers and dry cows, £6 to £9 10s; store heifers and bullocks, £4 10s to £11 10s each; store sheep were worth from 28s to 40s each; store pigs, 35s to 50s; slips, 26s to 38s per pair.*

*There was a very large number of horses on show, and the better sort*

FAIRS AND MARKETS

*commanded a ready sale, English dealers buying freely at prices ranging from £28 to £75. A good many farming and hack horses changed hands at from £8 to £23. I am inclined to believe that when the facilities for reaching Ballymote become more generally known in the sister kingdoms, the fair will become one of the first in this part of the province. The townspeople are greatly encouraged by the result of this fair, the first held since the opening of the railway, and the steamers trading between Sligo, England and Scotland, will largely benefit by the ready means now afforded to dealers for the conveyance of stock for shipment across the channel".*

The scale of tolls in operation in the 1880's were as follows: Cattle 3d to 6d; Pigs 3d; Horses 6d and Sheep 2d, and these were estimated to yield in the region of £300 per annum. In 1886 a monthly fair was established for cattle. It was held on the first Wednesday of each month, with a pig fair on the previous day. This situation remained unchanged until 1958 when the Fair Green was acquired by the North Western Regional Co-Operative Society for use as a mart. A new era had dawned.

# Bunninadden:

Original patent was granted to Benjamin Burton in 1758. In addition to a Wednesday market, there were four fairs May 28th;

---

### BUNNINADDEN GREAT FAIR: Nov. 1893.

This celebrated Fair will be held on MONDAY next, the 27th instant. It is notorious that Stock of all kinds sold at this Fair brings prices that cannot be excelled at other Fairs. The undernamed, who has taken over Toll Rights from Trustees of the Estate, has erected a Weigh-bridge for the accommodation of Buyers and Sellers; and himself and his assistants will be prepared to give every facility to all persons attending this as well as the other Fairs held.

*Roger McDermott*

---

August 6th ; October 9th and November 27th. In the early 19th century ownership of the Fair and tolls were vested in Col. Alexander

---

\* *"Sligo Journal"* 30-1-1863

FAIRS AND MARKETS

Perceval of Templehouse. In October, 1829, a number of men were convicted at the Tubbercurry Petty Sessions of collecting illegal tolls at the Fair of Bunninadden, and were fined 40s. for each offence.

By the 1880's there were six fairs, the largest of which were that of November 27th and January 14th and the tolls were collected by a local man named Morrison. The Fair Green was not enclosed and sheep and pigs were sold on the roadside. A monthly fair was introduced at a later date and continued until the advent of the Ballymote Mart.

# Carricknagat:

Tradition has it that this celebrated Horse Fair had its origins in a 'patron' formerly held on February 1st at Toberbrida, or Tubberbride, where young men amused themselves by running and jumping horses while their elder folk performed the 'stations'. On occasions horses were bartered or sold and in time Toberbrida became a place of business as well as a devotional site. Eventually, when the owners or occupiers of the land objected to the trespassing, the miniature fair was transferred to Carricknagat on the other side of Collooney.

From small beginings the Fair of Carricknagat and its equestrian competions gained a widespread notoriety and attracted buyers and sellers from near and far. As time progressed general livestock was also offered for sale at the February fair. In 1830 the "Sligo Journal" noted that a "totally good show of stock of every description was on view. It was once considered the best horse-fair in the County but on this occasion there was a noticeable falling-off" [1] However, six years later matters had improved. "Horses of a superior kind were anxiously looked for and several were sold advantageously; one from this Town realised £40, and a few others went to near the same amount; draught horses fetched from £15 upwards..." [2] In 1855 the price of good horses was 'so exorbitant' that few exchanged hands. Horses that two years earlier sold for £20, fetched £45.

In 1858 the "Chronicle" regretted "a great fall-off" in the once famous Horse Fair when compared with what it had been twenty years earlier. "The show of strong horses was good but few well bred colts were exhibited. Northern buyers appeared as usual but in consequence of the poor show of horses, few exchanged hands" [3] Three years later

## FAIRS AND MARKETS

Off to the Market

the same source noted that this "celebrated Horse Fair" was well attended and the supply of young horses was good.

This "great Western fair" appears to have enjoyed reasonable success in the 1860's, a good supply of horses and a good attendance of buyers or dealers from the North of Ireland, Manchester, Lancashire and Yorkshire, a developement which was attributed to the opening of the rail connection between Dublin and Sligo. However, in 1880, the *"Champion"* reported a noticeable decline :- "The once celebrated fair was held on Monday last and we are sorry to find that year after year it looses in importance. On Monday we noticed a marked decline in both quantity and quality of all kinds of animals; but notably in horses which is very much to be regretted, this being the leading fair in the Province some years ago. This falling-off has been gradually but steadily going on for a long time and judging by Monday last the time is not far distant when it will be a thing of the past" [4] The highest price, that of £80, was paid by Captain Browne of the 20th Regiment to James Nelson of Sligo for a superior hunter. The fair concluded with the usual jumping contests organised by members of the County Sligo Hunt Club. The revival of an old established custom, which had its origins at the 'patron' days at Toberbrida, aroused much interest amongst the fairgoers. Contrary to these gloomy predictions the time honoured

FAIRS AND MARKETS

Horse Fair continued in existence. In February, 1943, the Fair was switched to nearby Ballisodare and attracted a good supply of quality horses together with general livestock. Good working horses sold for £70 while 5 - 6 year olds made from £25 to £65.

Despite the decline in the horse population in the World War 2 years, this annual event of much antiquity continued to be held at its new venue with varying degrees of success until the general demise of fairs in the early 1970's.

### References

| (1) "Sligo Journal" | 5 - 2 - 1830 |
|---|---|
| (2)      ibid | 5 - 2 - 1836 |
| (3) "Sligo Chronicle" | 6 - 2 - 1858 |
| (4) "Sligo Champion" | 7 - 2 - 1880 |

# Carney:

In 1677 Dr. John Leslie obtained a patent to hold three fairs on a 3-acre site in the townland of Cullaghmore, and incorporating the Manor of Ardtarmon, on the following dates : May 15th/16th; October 10th/11th and December 22nd/23rd. The proprietorship of the tolls and customs passed from Leslie to the Gores of Ardtarmon and subsequently to the Gore-Booths of Lissadell. The following report on the Carney Fair was published in the "Sligo Journal" on May 1st, 1829 :-

*"The May, or 'Great Fair', of Carney was held on Tuesday last. The show of stock exhibited was, on the whole, very good and business went off briskly in the early part of the day. There was a large supply of sheep, which were in excellent demand; some lots went off as low as 16s; others realised from 30s. to £2. There was a brisk demand for springers and heifers and prices ranged from £5 to £7. Milch cows were in bad supply and the prices offered were discouraging in the extreme."*

In the 1830's there were two fairs annually, on May 28th and June 24th, mostly for cattle and sheep. The May Fair of 1833 was well attended and stocked "with every description of black cattle, most of which realised high prices" From 6 a.m. buying and selling was brisk and prices were well above the average. However, the evening of the fair was marred by "the proverbial skirmishing and flowing of blood.*

\* "Sligo Journal" 31-5-1833

## FAIRS AND MARKETS

Carney had a reputation for bloody contests between rival gangs, and it is said that one of the last faction fights in the County took place here in the latter half of the last century.

In 1846, as the Famine was beginning to bite, there was "a good show of horned cattle, milch cows and springers on view." Average prices ranged from £9 to £13, but one prime cow sold for £19. Fat sheep were uncommonly dear at from 35/- to 50/-. No references can be traced to this Fair between 1847 and 1860, at which date it was revived for a short period. The May Fair in 1862 was "unusually brisk" and well attended by buyers and sellers. There was what was described as "an excellent" supply of one-year old calves "but sheep were scarce and prices dull". The famous fair was revived for a second time at the turn of the century and continued to be held on May 26th and June 24th as hithertofore. In 1918 four new fairs - 13th of March, April, October and November - were announced, in addition to the two long established dates. After a further lapse, the Fair was revived in April, 1950, by the Drumcliffe Young Farmer's Club.

# Collooney:

In 1616 Bryan McDonagh was granted a patent for the holding of a two-day fair on July 25th/26th in Collooney. A further grant of two additional fairs, on April 24th and November 11th, was made in 1622. After the Cromwellian connfiscations of the late 17th century these rights passed to Richard Coote and finally, by purchase in 1727, to Joshua Cooper of Markree.

During the opening decades of the 19th century there were annual fairs in Collooney and this number had increased to seven by 1880. At that stage the fair was described as the "best in the County", a circumstance that was greatly assisted by the convergence of three seperate railway lines on the town. The tolls were collected by Barth. Coghlan of Ballymote who, on occasions, employed fifteen men, "armed with stout blackthorn sticks" to assist him in the gathering of same as buyers and sellers emerged from the fair.

The Fair-Green was 4 acres in area and enclosed by a stone wall, six feet high. It was restricted for the sale of cattle while other livestock, including horses, were sold on the streets. The income from tolls were

FAIRS AND MARKETS

estimated at between £300 and £400 per annum in 1888.

Collooney Fair, by virtue of its central location and the availabilty of rail transport, continued to prosper in the first half of this century when the number of annual fairs rose to thirteen.

# Dromore West:

Under a lease, dated October, 1766, Robert Browne of Fortland let the lands of Dromore, with the fees, poundage, customs and duties imposed at the pound and at all fairs which thereafter would be held on the lands of Dromore, to Thomas Fenton. In 1826 his grandson, Captain John Fenton of *Dromore House*, on coming into possession, reduced the custom by one quarter and appropriated two and a half acres of ground for use as a Fair Green. This was subsequently enclosed by a wall. By virtue of its central location it is reputed to have been one of the best fairs in the Barony of Tireragh and in the mid 19th century was yielding annual tolls in the region of £50.

Prior to the 1830's the fairs were held on variable dates, dictated by feast-days, etc., but Captain Fenton altered this custom and arranged fairs on fixed dates, namely, first Thursday in January; June 6th and December 29th.

In 1852 the fair of Dromore was boycotted after Fenton refused the use of the Green for an election rally in support of Richard Swift, the Liberal candidate in the County election of that year.*

Following Captain Fenton's death in 1858, the Dromore property, including the tolls of five fairs, passed by purchase to Dr. Alexander Henry of Croydon, and in 1870 to a new proprietor, William B. Lougheed. By the end of the century the number of fairs had increased to twelve and thus it remained over the following decades.

# Sligo:

By Letters Patent, dated 1604, Sir James Fullerton was granted permission to hold two fairs in Sligo on June 24th and September 29th, with rights to tolls and customs. This grant was confirmed eight years later by the King James Charter of 1612 in which Fullerton and

* See: McTernan *"Olde Sligoe"* pp. 317-320

## FAIRS AND MARKETS

his heirs were given the right to hold two fairs in the "Abbey Town of Sligo", one on the festival of St. John the Baptist and the other on the feastday of St. Michael. In 1627 permissiom was granted for the holding of two additional fairs, on March I7th/I8th and August Ist/2nd.

The proprietorship of the Sligo fairs passed by re-grant, in 1674, to William, Earl of Strafford and Thomas Radcliffe. In 1722 the rights passed to Owen Wynne as purchaser of a portion of the former estates of Wentworth and Radcliffe. In 1739 these were leased by the latter to John Knox. Subsequent to Wynne's acquisition the venue for the fair was transferred from O'Crean's Cross to a 1.75 acre site at Ballytivnan on the old Bundoran Road, on or convenient to where St. Joseph's church now stands. According to McParlan [1] there were only two fairs in Sligo in 1800, one on March 29th and the other on July 5th. However, by 1840 the number had doubled.

At the March fair, 1848, the livestock on offer were described as being "of poor quality", prices were so low that farmers preferred to take their stock home rather than sell at inferior prices. The business of the fair was disrupted for a time by an unusual event - a cow giving birth to a 3-legged calf. Two years later the same fair was described as "one of the worst ever remembered" and the show of cattle was far beyond the supply required. The tolls on that occasion only amounted to 35s. [2]

In 1852 there were five fairs annually and tolls were paid on all cattle sold, a system which led to much fraud, illegal oaths and perjury both here and elsewhere. [3] The Sligo May Fair of 1857 merited the following notice in the *"Sligo Champion"*:-

*"The May Fair of this Town was held on Saturday last. There was a very full Green of young and dry stock, which were, however, mostly of an inferior kind, and generally in very low (almost starved) condition, owing to the great and generally scarcity of fodder. Some dry cows, of large frame, brought as high as from £13 to £14 5s.; heifers of good stamp sold pretty well. Springers, of which there was a fair supply, were in brisk demand - many changed hands, at what we considered good prices. Thomas Robertson refused 15 guineas for a handsome springer. The extreme prices asked for the very few fat cattle offered for sale, and the butchers not being in immediate want, prevented any sales being effected. A fine fat bull, a beautiful animal, of about seven cwt. weight, belonging to the Right Hon. John Wynne, Hazlewood, could have been sold at*

FAIRS AND MARKETS

*20 guineas, equal to 3 guineas per cwt., sinking the offal. There was but a small supply of sheep and lambs - any 'fit for the knife' went off quickly at from 7 to 8d. per lb. There was a poor show of horses, and the English horsedealers at this fair felt a good deal disappointed. One four year old untrained draft mare of Mr. Wynne's was the only animal worth noticing; she was held at 30 guineas, 28 being refused. ".*

In March, 1864, the venue for the Sligo Fair was transferred from Ballytivnan to a 2-acre enclosed field adjoining the Pig Market in Temple Street and opposite the main entrance to the Market Yard[5]. The change was instigated by John Wynne of Hazlewood, the proprietor of the tolls and customs of both the Fairs and the Markets, who favoured a more central location convenient to both the Railway Terminus and the Port. Over the succeeding decades the number of fairs increased, from five to monthly, in addition to the quarterly fairs, known as the 'Patent Fairs', an arrangement that remained in place into the 1960's.

The rights to the fairs (and markets) of Sligo were acquired by Sligo Corporation in 1885. Thereafter, tolls were charged on all cattle exposed for sale and collected on leaving the fair. The schedule of tolls in operation were also raised and were as follows :- Bulls, cows or heifers over 2 years - 3d; ditto under 2 years - 2d; mules or asses - sheep, lambs, goats - 1d, and hogs and pigs - 1d. The income from tolls a century ago was estimated at £300 per annum. In May, 1890, a Horse Fair was established in addition to existing cattle fairs.

### References:

(1)  McParlan, J. *"Statistical Survey of Co. Sligo"*. Dublin, 1801.

(2)  *"Sligo Journal"*                   29 - 3 - 1850

(3)  Fairs & Markets Commission, 1852.

(4)  *"Sligo Champion"*                8 - 5 - 1857

(5)  ibid                                        2 - 4 - 1864

# Templehouse:

The original patent was granted in 1611 to William Crofton of Templehouse for the holding of a fair on July 20th /21st in the townland of Carrowntawy. In 1618 permission was granted for an

FAIRS AND MARKETS

additional fair on October 28th/29th. Following the marriage of Mary Crofton, daughter and heiress of the aforesaid William, to George Perceval in 1665, the rights to the tolls passed to the latter family.

By the beginning of the 18th century Templehouse fair was a well established event and attracted livestock "from the farthest parts of County Mayo and elsewhere."* By the 1830's there were three annual fairs, namely, May 24th, July 30th and November 7th, catering for cattle, horses and wool. On or very convenient to the Fair Green were two public houses and a Police Barracks.

In 1904 the venue for the fair was described as "an open common", and a proposal by Henry L'Estrange, the Perceval agent, to have it walled-in was objected to by local residents on the grounds that it would interfere with an old right-of-way. The thrice annual fair continued in existence into the 1950's.

# Tubberscanavan:

The original patent "to hold two yearly fairs on the lands of Tubberscanavan, one on Trinity Monday and the other on the 4th of September, and on the following day after each, with the usual tolls and customs", was granted to Arthur Cooper of Markree in 1686. In 1760 his successor, Joshua Cooper, was granted two additional fairs to be held at the village, a mile S.E. of Collooney, on May 17th and October 31st..

In September, 1847, at the height of the Famine, the *"Journal"* reported that the fair was well attended and "numerously supplied with every description of cattle". Several English and Northern buyers attended and purchased freely at rather advanced prices, particularly stock for slaughter. Milch cows ranged from £10 to £16; sheep fetched from £1.15s. to £2.10s; and pigs, of which there were but few for sale, maintained high rates. It was estimated that from 750 to 1,000 head of stock were disposed of.

At the November fair in 1852 the same source reported that the there was "an immense number of black cattle and, in spite of numbers, prices were fully on par with the late high quotations." Despite its favourable report on the fair, the *"Journal"* was highly critical of the accommodation which it described as "quite

FAIRS AND MARKETS

inadequate", with most of the livestock standing on the public road, and went on to urge the owner of the tolls, Edward J Cooper of *Markree Castle*, to "afford the public with the accommodation of a good field, with adequate room."[2]

The coming of the railway led to the demise of this long established fair. In May, 1865, it was transferred to Collooney on the instructions of Col. Cooper.

*References:*

(1)  *"Sligo Journal"*                                24 - 9 - 1847
(2)  ibid.                                                5 - 11 - 1852

# Tubbercurry:

In 1750 a patent was granted to James Napper for the holding of two fairs, May 11th and November 18th. Forty years later, in 1793, the tolls and customs of the fair were sub-let by Mathew Meredith of Ogham to Alexander Irwin of Muckelty. By the turn of the century the Irwins appear to have acquired ownership of the fair (and market). In 1802 Richard Phibbs of Streamstown, then residing in Dublin, had sub-let the tolls and customs of the seven annual fairs to his kinsman, Alexander Irwin of Muckelty, for £20. 19s a half year. In the 1820s these were collected by two local men, Patrick Davey and Pat Feehily. By the mid century the revenue accrued to John Brett.

In 1829 Jones Irwin, a brother to Richard P. Irwin, was charged with collecting illegal tolls and for not having a toll-board on display at the Fair of Tubbercurry on October 5th. When the case came before the local Petty Sessions he admitted liability on both counts and was fined 40s.

An anonymous visitor arrived in Tubbercurry on a Fair-Day in 1859 and penned his impressions as follows:*

*"I arrived in Tubbercurry by Bianconi's car at 5.30 on Tuesday, just in time previous to the break up of the Fair, and was thus afforded an opportunity of seeing a goodly gathering of my countrymen in this portion of the Island ... It was no easy matter, I can assure you, for the car to pass through the dense throng of people from the entrance of the town to the Hotel. However, I am not annoyed, 'but the reverse', at the slow motion of the vehicle as I thereby obtained*

* *"Sligo Champion"* 8-10-1859

FAIRS AND MARKETS

*a good view of the people and had time for scrutiny which I could not otherwise have obtained. Imagine Donnybrook Fair at its 'full' and you have something approaching to, but not exceeding the number that met my view as I sat on the high, but low-backed car. Here the parallel ends, in so much as I could not with truth describe the people as bearing any close resemblance to those who are or were wont on a visit 'The Brook'. There was nothing of the showy, flaunting frippery displayed upon the persons of the female at Tubbercurry, but instead they were arrayed in sensible, serviceable, and I may add, very becoming attire, and this was the rule, the exceptions being very few. The male portion were also well dressed, and, thank God, such an appearance of real comfort pervaded the mass, that it was hard to realise to one's mind that these were people who suffered so severely - almost to death - during the Famine years.*

*As to the Fair; it was what is termed 'slow'. Of cattle there was a large supply, but with the exception of milch cows, for which there was a brisk demand at prices varying from £6 to £8, there were not many sales. Of sheep very few changed hands at 45s, but good lambs were in request at from £1 to £1.5s. There were no prime pigs in the Fair, and the few sales effected were at prices ranging from 40s to 45s. per cwt. Up to 10 o'clock p.m. a great number of people remained about in the town, but not the slightest tendency to disturbances was manifested, everything was as peaceable as could be desired; a walk through the crowds as late as nine o'clock convinced me of this - which is another hopeful sign of the times, and therefore worthy of honourable mention".*

By the 1880's there were twelve fairs in Tubbercurry but no Fair Green. The tolls were collected by Nicholas Devine. With the dawn of the new century this fair enhanced its long standing reputation as the principal mart for livestock in South Sligo.

# STATE OF OTHER FAIRS, 1888 *

BALLINTOGHER: Landlord: William Lougheed of Ballinakill who also acts as collector. There is a Fair Green for cattle only and sheep are sold on the street. There are five fairs: February, June, July, October and December. Tolls, which are valued at £90 per annum, are collected from buyers.

* Extracts from *"Commission into Working and Management of Markets and Fairs"* 1888.

## FAIRS AND MARKETS

**BALLISODARE:** Landlord: Colonel Edward H. Cooper of *Markree Castle.* Tolls collected by Barth. Coghlan of Ballymote. Two fairs held annually on November 9th and December 15th. A 2 -acre Fair Green is fenced by a stone wall, four and a half feet high but accommodation is poor with cattle, sheep and pigs "all thrown together and stock are much abused." The tolls, (similar to those in operation at Collooney) and estimated at £10 to £15 a year, are paid on leaving the market.

**BANADA:** A 3-acre Fair Green but not enclosed. The two principal fairs are November 27th and January 4th. Tolls : Pigs 4d. Sheep 2d and cattle 3d to 4d.

**BELTRA:** Landlord: Richard J. Verschoyle. He employs men to lift the toll but does not let the fairs. No Fair Green and the public road is made impassable. Annual returns not worth much.

**COOLANEY:** Landlord: Charles W. O'Hara, Annaghmore. Collector of tolls, : Thomas Harte. Five fairs annually in May, July August September and December. Estimated value of tolls, £80. A Fair Green for cattle is surrounded by a stone wall fence. Sheep and pigs sold in the street.

**FARNIHARPY:** Landlord: Charles P. Webber. Collector John Cameron. There is a public road running through the land for which custom is charged. Three in the year. Tolls :- Cattle 3d to 6d, Sheep 2d and Pigs 3d.

In 1801 there were 70 fairs at 22 locations throughout the County. By the mid century the number of fairs had grown to 108 at 27 venues. Fifty years later these had further increased to 167 in 23 villages and towns. In post World War 2, c. 1950, the number of fairs peaked at a record 223 at 27 venues. However, the advent of Cattle Marts in the

FAIRS AND MARKETS

early 1970's, coupled with newly introduced regulations governing the
movement of livestock, contributed to a sharp decline in attendances
at fairs and eventually led, in the closing years of that decade, to the
total disappearance of a time honoured institution.

---

## THE DECLINE OF THE FAIR

Fair Venues - 1970:
Aclare - Ballintogher - Ballisodare - Ballymote - Coolaney - Collooney
- Culleens - Dromore West - Easkey - Farniharpy - Grange - Gurteen
- Riverstown - Sligo - Tubbercurry.

Fair Venues - 1975:
Ballisodare - Coolaney - Collooney - Culleens - Dromore West - Easkey
- Riverstown - Tubbercurry.

Fair Venues - 1980:
Coolaney - Collooney - Dromore West - Easkey - Tubbercurry.

---

# LIST OF FAIRS 1800 - 1950

**1800:**

Ardnaglass (4); Ballinacarrow (4); Ballintogher (4); Ballisodare (2); Ballymote
(3); Bellaghy (3); Beltra (2); Benada (2); Bunninadden (4); Castlebaldwin (4);
Cliffoney (4); Collooney (6); Dromore West (2); Easkey (2); Enniscrone (2);
Farniharpy (4); Roslea (1); St. James Well (1); Sligo (2); Templehouse (3);
Tubbercurry (7) and Tubberscanavan (4).

**1840:**

Ardnaglass (5); Ballisodare (7); Ballinacarrow (4); Ballintogher (4); Ballymote
(5); Benada (7); Bellaghy (4); Beltra (2); Bunninadden (6); Carney (2);
Carricknagat (1); Castlebaldwin (4) Cliffoney (5); Collooney (6); Coolaney (5)
; Curry (4); Dromore West (5); Easkey (2); Enniscrone (2); Farniharpy (4); St.
James' Well (1); Quigaboy (4); Roslea (5); Sligo (4); Templehouse (3);
Tubbercurry (7) and Tubberscanavan (4).

**1950:**

Aclare (12); Ardnaglass (6); Ballinacarrow (5); Ballintogher (8); Ballymote
(12) ; Ballisodare (6); Beltra (3); Bunninadden (12); Carney (2);
Carricknagat (I); Castlebaldwin (2); Collooney (13); Coolaney (12); Culleens
(12); Curry (2); Dromore West (12); Easkey (5); Enniscrone (6); Farniharpy
(12); Grange (13); Gurteen (12); Larkhill (12); Roslea (3); Riverstown (12);
Sligo (13); Templehouse (3) and Tubbercurry (12).

FAIRS AND MARKETS

# LIST OF FAIRS - 1900

Aclare: Last Wednesday of each month.

Ardnaglass: June 21; Aug. 17; Sept. 23; Oct. 23.

Ballinacarrow: May 14; June 14; July 14; Oct.14; Dec.14.

Ballintogher: Jan. 22; Febr. 28; April 24; June 8; July 28; Aug. 31; Oct. 17; Dec.8.

Ballymote: First Wednesday of each month.

Ballisodare: Nov. 9; Dec. 15.

Banada: Jan.6; Whit Monday; June 29; July 25; Aug. 28; Oct 18.

Bellaghy: Feb. 14; Mar. 14; Easter Monday; June 9; July 9; Aug. 14; Sept. 18; Nov. 14; Dec. 21.

Beltra: Day before Shrove Tuesday; May 21; Aug. 20.

Bunninadden: Jan. 14; May 20; June 22; Aug. 6; Sept. 10; Oct.9; Nov. 27.

Carricknagat: Feb. 1st.

Castlebaldwin: June 4; Nov. 3.

Collooney: March 23; May 3 & 17; June 30; Sept. 18; Oct. 31; Nov. 21.

Coolaney: May 29; July II; Aug. 29; Sept. 29; Dec. 5.

Curry: Ascension Thursday ; Corpus Christi.

Dromore West: Jan. 6; Febr. 6; Mar. 6; April 6; May 6; June 6; July 14; Aug. 14; Sept. 14; Oct. I5; Nov. 15; Dec. 22.

Easkey: Mar. 17; May 1; June 1; Nov. 18; Dec. 14.

Enniscrone: First Monday after Whit Monday; Sept. 18; Dec.14.

Farniharpy: Mar. 30; 27th of every other month.

Grange: Jan. 20; Febr. 20; Mar. 20; April 20; May 20; June 2 & 29; July 25; Aug. 25; Sept. 29; Oct.28;Nov. 29; Dec.10

Roslea: May 19; July 9; Oct. 28.

Riverstown: 14 of March, April, May, Sept., Oct., Nov., Dec.

Sligo: First Tuesday in Jan. Febr. April, June, Sept, Nov. Dec.; March 27th; first Saturday in May; July 4; Aug. 11; Oct. 9.

Templehouse: May 24; July 30; Nov. 7.

Tubbercurry: Second Wednesday of each month.

FAIRS AND MARKETS

# TOLLS & CUSTOMS AT FAIRS, 1888

### Ballisodare - Collooney:

| | |
|---|---|
| A milch cow | 6d. |
| A dry cow | 5d. |
| A heifer or bullock over 2 years | 4d. |
| A fat bullock | 5d. |
| A yearling bullock or heifer | 6d. |
| A yearling calf or sheep | 2d. |
| A pig | 3d. |
| A horse | 6d. |
| A lamb | 1d. |
| A tent or booth | 1.0d. |

### Ballymote:

| | |
|---|---|
| Each milch cow | 6d. |
| Each dry cow, bullock, heifer | 5d. |
| Each 2 year old bullock or heifer | 4d. |
| Each 1 year old bullock or heifer | 3d. |
| Each horse, filly or colt | 6d. |
| Each foal, ass or mule | 3d. |
| Each sheep | 2d. |
| Each lamb | 1d. |
| Each pig | 3d. |
| Each load of young pigs | 6d. |
| Each tent, booth or pedlar's stand | 1.0d. |
| Each meat stand | 6d. |
| Each hucksters, nailers or leather cutter's stand | 4d. |
| Each bag of meal, hide or skin | 3d. |

### Sligo:

| | |
|---|---|
| Every bull, cow, heifer; over 2 years old | 4d. |
| Every bull, cow, heifer; under 2 years old | 3d. |
| Every horse, mare or gelding | 6d. |
| Every mule and ass | 3d. |
| Every sheep, lamb and goat | 1d. |
| Every hog or pig | 1d. |
| Use of pen for sheep or pigs; per animal | ½ d. |
| Every cart, wagon or dray used for sale of goods | 1.0d. |
| Every carriage, gig and car exposed for sale | 1.0d. |
| Every hawker, pedlar offering goods for sale | 3d. |

242

FAIRS AND MARKETS

## LARKHILL, BALLISODARE, COUNTY SLIGO: FAIRS 1936

A new Monthly Fair will be held at Larkhill on 7th of EVERY MONTH FOR CATTLE, SHEEP AND PIGS. If Fair falls on Sunday it will be held on Monday following. Tea Rooms, and other accommodation available for buyers. The above is a very important Fair, and Tireragh is noted for its great supply of healthy, and thriving stock.

Your co-operation and attendance respectfully invited.

DANIEL O'CONNOR,
Larkhill.

## CARNEY (SLIGO) NEW FAIRS, 1918
### for Cattle, Sheep, Pigs, and Horses.

| March | - | - | 13 | October | - | - | 13 |
| April | - | - | 13 | November | - | - | 13 |

The old Fairs held as usual, viz., May 26th, June 24th. Fairs falling on Saturday or Sunday will be held on Monday.

## CULLEENS (Co. Sligo) FAIRS, 1972
### (Cattle, Sheep and Pigs)

| January | Friday 21st | July | Friday, 21st |
| February | Tuesday, 22nd | August | Tuesday, 22nd |
| March | Wednesday, 22nd | September | Friday, 22nd |
| April | Friday, 21st | October | Monday, 23rd |
| May | Monday, 22nd | November, | Wednesday, 22nd |
| June | Thursday, 22nd | December | Friday, 22nd |

**Ulster Bank Sub-Office on All Fair-Days - 12.30 to 2 p.m.**

FAIRS AND MARKETS

# 2. MARKETS

Unlike fairs, markets are entirely the product of economic need. The difference between a market and a fair is suggested by the words themselves. Every fair is a market but every market is not a fair. Over the centuries markets have been held on a regular basis, usually weekly, but bi-weekly in the larger towns, as the items for sale are mostly perishable commodities; whereas fairs were held a few times a year or monthly at most.

Originally, markets were held on the streets, but as time progressed and the volume of commodities for sale increased, the narrow thoroughfares became very congested. In an effort to ease the situation, and more particularly to facilitate the collection of tolls, the proprietors of the markets usually assigned specific areas, or enclosed yards, for the sale of commodities such as butter and corn. In Sligo, for instance, the Wynnes, the local patentees, established a Corn Market for the sale of all types of grain, in addition to other items, and also a Butter Market, where lump butter could be weighed, graded and sold. Certain areas of the Town were assigned for the sale of pigs, fish, seaweed and turf, and stiff penalties were enforced for breaches of these regulations.

Over the centuries individual chieftains or lords of the manor were granted charters for the holding of weekly or bi-weekly markets, as distinct from fairs, in the following villages and towns :- Aclare - Ardnaglass- Ballinacarrow - Ballymote - Bellaghy - Bunninadden- Castlebaldwin- Cliffoney - Collooney - Roslea - Sligo- Templehouse - Tullaghnaglug- Tubbercurry. The right to custom or toll was not identical to a market, it had to be specially mentioned in the charter. By 1852 more than half of the aforementioned markets had lapsed, leaving six still operating, namely, Aclare - Bellaghy- Ballymote - Tubbercurry - Sligo.

## The Butter Market:

Butter was Ireland's most important agricultural export in the late 18th and throughout the 19th century. In many cases the rural economy was orientated towards its production, with much of the land

## FAIRS AND MARKETS

under grass or fodder crops to sustain the dairy herd. Over a long period, but especially throughout the last century, the production of butter was one of the staple industries of this and neighbouring counties. In most cases, but especially in the baronies of Corran and Leyny, the revenue generated from the production of butter was the principal means of paying the landlord's rent.

The Sligo market was the leading mart in the north-west for the sale of butter. The earliest reference to it is to be found in the Corporation records of 1787. In September of that year James Soden was appointed Public Weightmaster of Butter. [1] Extant records suggest that the market place for this commodity was then located close to *'The Shambles'* at the north end of Knox's Street, on or close to where the Post Office now stands.

Two centuries ago there were numerous dairies in the Sligo area and the export of butter became very considerable.[2] The increase in production resulted from improvements in the presentation of the product. The time honoured practice of packing it into crocks was replaced by the use of well coopered casks which had the effect of greatly improving the quality.[3] In 1819 Owen Wynne, 'Weighmaster and Butter Taster', erected a purpose-built Butter Market off Lower Quay Street and south of the Custom House Yard, on a site leased from Lord Palmerston.It was rectangular in shape but somewhat irregular in both depth and breath, being 209 to 241 ft. long by 71 to 115 ft. wide. It had extensive storage sheds on both sides, a caretaker's house to the right of the main entrance-gate and the yard was paved in cobbled stones. Wynne is reputed to have spent upwards of £3,000 on the project, a development that gave a great impetus to the trade, with the volume of butter passing through on each market day rising from 1,500 to 2,000 casks. The standing of Sligo butter on the Liverpool and other markets also increased considerably.

Over the following three score and ten years, or so, it was the most important mart in Sligo and a centre of commerce unrivalled in the North West. The economy of the Town, and more particularly that of the farming community in this and neighbouring counties,depended upon it to varying degrees. On market days between May and October, and especially on Saturdays, the market was crowded to overflowing and rows of carts, loaded with casks or firkins of butter, stretched

## FAIRS AND MARKETS

backwards in a line along the Old Quay as their owners waited patiently for their turn to have their produce inspected, weighed and graded for sale to merchants and shippers. In its heyday upwards of 1,800 to 2,000 firkins were sold on a single market day and Sligo butter enjoyed a high reputation on both the London and Glasgow markets. The prices paid to producers matched, and at times, surpassed, that of other Irish marts. "Sligo butter is in great repute in Liverpool", commented the *"Journal"* in April, 1825. "Its widely recognised for its inflexible integrity regarding inspection and management". [4]

Some insight into the problems small farmers had to contend with to get their produce to the market were outlined by Francis Barber of Rahelly in 1836. [5] According to his evidence the butter was packed after successive churnings - sometimes it took half the summer to fill a firkin - and was conveyed to the market on carts and not infrequently on the backs of horses. He attributed the inferiority of the butter from the North Sligo area to a want of cleanliness, the small herd of cows which made repeated churnings necessary to fill the firkin and to the custom of churning both the milk and the cream, thus obtaining a large quantity but inferior quality. When it arrived at the market the butter was weighed and tasted by the nominee of the official weightmaster, who divided it into six different qualities and branded the firkins accordingly. The merchants and shippers then purchased it on the basis of these gradings but made a difference in the prices paid according to the following ratio: - 6/- a cwt between 'Firsts' and 'Seconds'; 8/- between 'Seconds' and 'Thirds'; 10/- between 'Thirds'and 'Fourths' and between 'Fourths' and 'Fifths'. Butter sold on the Sligo market in the opening decades of the 19th century was subject to the following charges:- Id. for branding an empty cask; 1d for tasting and marking the quality of the butter; - 3d for a ticket stating the weight of a cask before it could be sold to a merchant. In addition, there was a 2d charge for custom, all of which was paid by the seller.[6] By the mid century these charges had been reduced somewhat: weighing 2d; inspection 1d; cooperage 1d a firkin and toll 2d.

The Irish Butter Act of 1812 introduced new controls for the regulation of the markets, including quality and price. In 1825 the Merchants and Traders of Sligo petitioned Parliament against proposed changes in the legislation. In their submission it was stated

246

FAIRS AND MARKETS

that since the passing of the 1812 Act the butter trade of the Port had more than doubled in quantity and the product had obtained a "very high character" in the markets to which it had been exported. They did, however, suggest the introduction of new regulations which would prevent certain frauds being practiced by both sellers and unprincipled exporters.[7] The protection of the butter trade from frauds was further considered at a meeting of the merchants and other interested parties in November, 1831, chaired by Edward J. Cooper, M.P. The evils that allegedly had crept into the trade and which gave most concern, were the placing of false tares on casks by sellers and alterations in official gradings by exporters. In an effort to have the trade purged of these frauds, a number of country gentlemen and merchants volunteered to form a committee and petition Parliament on the matter and adopt whatever measures they considered necessary for the improvement of the trade locally.[8]

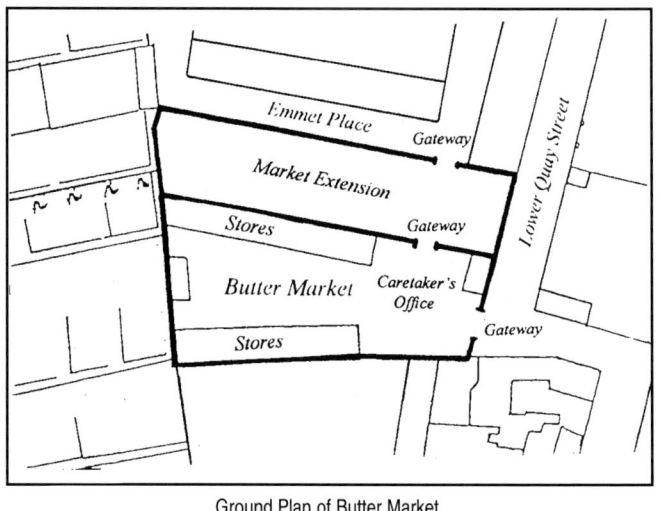

Ground Plan of Butter Market

Throughout the 1830's and 1840's the butter trade in Sligo experienced a period of uncertainty, due to the aforementioned illegal practices. The dilemma facing producers was highlighted by Thomas Foster, the *"Times"* correspondent, who wrote as follows:-

*"The country-people complain a good deal about the way in which the butter sales are conducted. A weighing-master and inspector are appointed to weigh*

247

the butter, and brand its quality, as 1st, 2d, 3d, &c and the butter was formerly sold according to the brand of these officers. The brand is still retained, but under an Act of Parliament passed in 1830 the trade is thrown open, and it is optional to individuals to adopt the regulations of the market or not. Under this system, the weighing-master's brand is regularly altered and inferior butter is sold as first quality butter. This, it is said, tends to injure the character of the market, and to promote the production of an inferior article. The brand of the officer has ceased to be of any value, and each cask has to be examined and tested by the purchaser. In this manner the farmers are often imposed upon; they cannot sell their butter by the market price of the brand; the dealers test it with their augers, and bid what they choose for it less than the branded value. The farmers are generally dissatisfied with this price, and hawk their butter about from one dealer to another, till it gets so bored into as to become deteriorated in value, and they are then compelled to sell it for less than its worth. It would seem advisable either to resort strictly to the old law, and make the officers' brand the test of the quality of the butter, protected by penalties, or to do away with the brands altogether, as they are now merely deceptive.[9]

---

## SLIGO BUTTER MARKET

| | | | |
|---|---|---|---|
| No. of firkins sold, | 1832: | . . . . . . | 53,450 |
| "          " | 1833: | . . . . . . | 48,523 |
| Average Exports, | 1820-23: | . . . . . . | 25,670 firkins |
| "          " | 1840's: | . . . . . . | 48,000 firkins |

---

A few years later, in 1852, Moses Monds,[10] in his evidence before the Fairs and Markets Commission, also referred to this problem:-

*"The frauds on the part of the purchasers are so numerous that nearly all honourable traders are driven out of the market. Butter made seconds and thirds by the Inspector are frequently changed into firsts and seconds by the trader; and I have frequently known a quantity of butter, sold to the trader by farmers living ten or fourteen miles distant from Sligo, being returned to the farmer late in the day, when the market was over because the trader did not like the inspection. Such occurrences take place every day and the farmer has no legal remedy but to sue the trader for his breach of contract"* [11]

He then went on to highlight the "irregularities" being practiced by the sellers"-

## FAIRS AND MARKETS

*"The frauds in the butter market are great on the part of the sellers. The tare of the firkin is often more than that branded upon it, and the quality is not the same throughout. Sometimes but very rarely, it is adulterated, too, with other substances, and very often coloured".*

A typical example of the 'trickery' being exercised by "the dexterity of a few crafty hirelings towards the guileless rustic sellers" came before the courts in February 1848, when a poor widow from Roughan, Ballintogher, summoned an adroit customer named Sharkey for defrauding her of 5/- on the sale of a half cwt. cask of butter after the price had been agreed at £2. [12]

In an effort to improve the image of the market and rid it of fraudulent activities, John Molony was appointed Butter Inspector in 1849. His arrival heralded a new era in the chequered history of the Sligo Butter Market; confidence was quickly restored and the supplies of butter offered for sale increased dramatically. On the week ending October 26th, 1849, there was a record 2,400 firkins on sale. A year later the *"Journal"* announced that the sale of butter "exceeded anything before witnessed." "Vast quantities are being shipped weekly by the cross-channel steamers . . . Sligo has now become the market for the surrounding counties". [13] In 1852 there was an increase of 15,000 firkins, butter fetched 100/- a cwt, and upwards of £30,000 was shipped in one month.[14] The market had now regained its exalted position and was rated 2nd or 3rd best market in Ireland. Much of the credit for this improvement was attributed to Malony, an efficient Inspector.

The continued improvements in the fortunes of the trade was commented on by the *"Champion"*:-

*"Of late years we have noticed a considerable increase in the transactions of the Sligo Butter Market. From inquiries made in the proper quarter we have been able to ascertain that the receipts of the market for 1852 exceeded those of the preceeding year by the large number of 12,000 firkins. This indicates that this branch of trade, which for a considerable time was declining, is again rapidly improving and enlarging...".[15]*

This trend continued in the years that followed. In April, 1857, the average number of firkins on sale on market days was 1,300 and business was described as "brisk and prices firm", ranging from 103/- for 'firsts' to 90/- for 'fourths'. In March, 1860, the local butter merchants issued a circular addressed to farmers and coopers,

## FAIRS AND MARKETS

pointing out that the firkins in use were too large and not uniform in size.[16] They were also too light and incapable of holding the pickle necessary for the preservation of butter. Instead, they recommended firkins of a uniform size, that would hold 70 - 75 lbs. of butter, and the use of American oak for heading and siding, essential for exporting to foreign markets.[17]

---

# ADVICE TO MAKERS OF BUTTER

*The Butter Season for the present year being now close at hand, I deem it my duty to advise farmers to be more particular than hithertofore in the selection of empty firkins. I have frequently given this advice before; but in some districts the farmers are so careless as to persist in using those large and badly made firkins, which bring discredit on the Butter Market, and serious loss to the owner. A good Firkin enhances the value of the Butter - a bad Firkin depreciates its value.*

*Where the interest of the farmer is involved, I should expect that he would be glad to get advice, and act upon it promptly and willingly.*

*I know full well that the Coopers, by getting timely notice, are prepared to make the Firkins at whatever standard may be required. I therefore place before farmers and coopers the dimensions requisite for a Firkin to contain 70lbs, payable five stone:-*

| | |
|---|---|
| *Length of Staves:* | *17 inches.* |
| *Diameter of Head and Bottom:* | *12½ inches.* |

*Farmers who may be desirous to bring their Butter to market in a creditable manner have now an opportunity to give the Coopers directions about the size of Firkins; and should the Farmers act on the advice I here give them, it will cause much benefit to themselves, and lead to considerable improvement in the Butter.*

*Cleanliness, good casks and bringing the butter fresh to market, are three essential points, which, if observed, will place the farmers of this part of the country in as good a condition as those of any other part in Ireland.*

*The advice contained herein is principally intended for the Butter Makers of Sligo, Leitrim and Roscommon.*

*John Malony, Butter Inspector.*
*Sligo Butter Market, April 1855.*

FAIRS AND MARKETS

The quality and grading of Sligo butter was the subject of an article in a Scottish newspaper in 1877: [18]

*"If Sligo 'firsts' are such, there is not better butter in Ireland. But should 'seconds' be made 'firsts' and 'thirds' made 'seconds' , the character of Sligo butter is thereby injured . . . The retailers of Sligo butter naturally expert 'firsts' to be 'firsts', 'seconds' to be 'seconds' and 'thirds' to be 'thirds'........ "*

This would indicate that the unlawful practice of some merchants and shippers in altering the gradings of the Butter Inspector had re-surfaced, or perhaps it had never been fully eradicated. In any event, it resulted in a number of Scottish agents making it known that Sligo `brands' were no longer of any value on the Glasgow market. [19]

## The Weighmaster:

With their purchase of the Strafford-Radcliffe estate in 1722, the Wynne family acquired the right to hold markets in Sligo and to levy tolls on goods sold. Their involvement in the Butter Market can be traced back to the 1780's, or thereabouts, when Thomas Soden was appointed Public Weighmaster of butter. The Irish Butter Act of 1812 vested in the Corporation the patronage of the appointment to the joint offices of Weighmaster and Taster of Butter. Owen Wynne of Hazelwood, who had inherited the ownership of the local markets and tolls, was, as patron of the Borough, the first appointee to this post. He and his son, John A. Wynne, who was appointed in 1842, performed the duties of the office by appointing a paid deputy who was responsible for inspecting, weighing and grading the butter as it came into the Market. The fees payable under the Act for this service were retained by the Wynnes.

The new Borough Council elected under the Municipal Act of 1840 was not happy with the Wynne monopoly of the markets, and that of the Butter Market in particular. In initial contacts John Wynne was reluctant to admit the right of the Corporation to even discuss the matter. However, in January, 1850, he did agree to meet a committee of the Corporation at which it was mutually agreed that the matter be referred to the courts and the points at issue decided "by an amicable suit". [20] A few months later, and "soley for the purpose of having the matter tried", the Corporation appointed Thomas Kelly, Mayor, to be

251

## FAIRS AND MARKETS

Weighmaster and Taster of Butter. The case of the Corporation v. Wynne concerning the right of appointment of a Weighmaster of Butter was tried in the court of Queen's Bench. The verdict was adverse to the Corporation and Wynne's appointment was not disturbed. However, the court avoided giving judgement on the central point at issue, namely, whether or not the Corporation had the right of appointment. [21]

Following the death of John A.Wynne in 1865, his successor, Owen Wynne, decided to dispute the right claimed by the Corporation regarding the appointment of the Weighmaster. [22] The latter's response was the appointment, in December, 1867, of Mayor-elect James Tighe, as Weighmaster and Taster of Butter for the Borough of Sligo. Meanwhile, the Butter Market , run by Wynne's nominees, continued to operate and Tighe instituted proceedings against William Clarke, an employee of Wynne , for "an alleged disturbance of his right to the office of Weighmaster of Butter in the markets of Sligo and for depriving him of the fees derivable from same". Clarke's defence was a denial of the plaintiff's right to the office. The case was heard in Galway in 1869, and a verdict was recorded in favour of the plainfiff, James Tighe. [23]

Butter and Eggs for the Sligo Market

## FAIRS AND MARKETS

In June, 1869, the *"Sligo Journal"* reported that "a most amicable arrangement" had been arrived at with regard to the transfer of the Butter Market from Owen Wynne to the Corporation. James Tighe, representing the latter body, took formal possession of the market on the morning of June 5th at a rent agreed upon "and he is now installed as Weighmaster and Butter Taster of this most important market'.[24] The Sligo Borough Act of 1869 conferred on the Corporation the power to establish markets, fairs and slaughter houses within the Borough and to purchase the existing market rights, together with bonds and buildings used in the market, from Owen Wynne.

Following the death of Alderman James Tighe in 1880 the post of Weighmaster and its emoluments - the tolls alone were valued at £140 in 1855 - became the property of the Corporation.[25] The Mayor for the time being was appointed temporary Weighmaster. New brands were introduced for casks bearing the words *Sligo Corporation* in a circle and displaying the specific qualification 'first', 'second', 'third', etc in the centre. In 1883 negotiations commenced for the purchase of the Sligo markets, including the Butter Market, together with all market rights and buildings thereon, from the Wynne family. These were finally completed in February, 1885, [26] and a new Butter Inspector, Patrick McAviney, was appointed to supervise and run the Market with the assistance of eight other employees.

A lack of uniformity in the classification of butter had long been a problem on the Sligo market. On the occasion of the Taxation Inquiry Commissioners sitting in Sligo in 1877, the local butter merchants presented them with a Memorial complaining of "a deficient and faulty classification of the different classes of butter," and prayed for suggestions as to the ways and means by which this could be eliminated.[27] The matter was raised again in November, 1885, when the Sligo Butter Trade Association petitioned the Corporation, the new owners of the Market, to investigate alleged irregularities in the management of the Butter Market, most of which centred around the inspection method in operation, namely, the "over marking" of qualities by Inspector McAviney.[28] The Corporation responded by appointing a sub-committee to inquire into the matter and report back. A Public Inquiry, which was attended by farmers and merchants, as well as McAviney, was held in the Town Hall in February, 1886. [29] In

# FAIRS AND MARKETS

The MARKET HOUSE, Collooney c. 1900 (above) and
Stores in the SLIGO BUTTER MARKET (below).

## FAIRS AND MARKETS

its subsequent Report to the Corporation the committee stated that the allegations of the merchants "had not been fully sustained"; that re-augering i.e. reducing quality deductions and market quotations of merchants, did more injury to the market than a slight error of judgement - if such occurred - by the Inspector. They recommended changes in the regulations, namely, that an official market quotation, under the supervision of the Mayor, be issued every Saturday, of actual average prices paid for the different grades; that during the winter months a kit or small firkin be used instead of the large one, observing that the sooner butter can be sold, the better the quality will be. The committee also recommended the abolition of the custom of deducting 1.lb from the weight of every firkin of butter. [30]

The re-arrangement of the Butter Market was undertaken by the Corporation in the mid 1880's. Physically, it was no longer in a position to cope with the volume of butter passing through, an average of 1,000 firkins every Saturday. The overcrowding and general congestion was such that it was almost impossible for the Inspector and his officials to perform their duties. Eventually, portion of the adjacent *Cadger's Field* was acquired from the Ashley estate, the market area was extended and an additional entrance and exit provided. Thereafter, the weighing,tasting and branding of firkins was advantageously performed in an enclosed area, out of reach of both sellers and buyers. In September, 1885, the *"Independent"* reported that 1,177 firkins were sold in the market the previous Saturday and fetched 104/- for 'firsts' and 92/- for 'seconds' - prices higher than those quoted on the Cork market on the same day. This state of affairs attracted farmers not only from Fermanagh and Leitrim but also from Longford, Roscommon, Mayo and Donegal and, in the opinion of the *"Independent"*, this was attributed to the "impartial judgement" of Patrick McAviney, Butter Inspector and the "correct weighing" of Patrick Feeney and Robert Boyd. [31] By September, 1888, the number of firkins had risen to 1,500 and by October, 1890, had reached a record 1,696.

The continued improvement in the affairs of the Butter Market were reflected in the following report in the *"Daily Express"* in August, 1889: -

*"...Saturday's butter market in Sligo has fully verified the prophesy that the market of this Town would become one of the finest emporiums for the butter*

255

*trade in Ireland. Mr McAviney, the efficient Butter Inspector, had to inspect upwards of 1,000 firkins and the advice and good counsel he has been giving to farmers and their wives is beginning to tell. The butter brought into the market is very superior to what was presented some years ago and it realises a high price on the Glasgow market ........ The friction which for some time existed between the butter merchants and the Corporation and the Inspector has nearly altogether ceased..."*

---

## A Visit To The Butter Market

"I took a stroll on Saturday last through the Butter Market and a pleasing and interesting sight met my view. Congregated in this busy mart were farmers and their wives and daughters in unusually large numbers, and a casual glance made it apparent to me that a greatly increased trade was being carried on in this centre of commerce.

I ascertained that there had been brought into the market upwards of 1,200 firkins of butter which had been carefully prepared, and neatly packed. The appearance of the butter controverted, at least so far as this market is concerned, the complaint which has not infrequently been made across the water of the untidiness of Irish butter as sent into the markets. There was, no doubt, at one time, some ground for this complaint which enabled foreigners successfully to compete with Irish producers in the London market. But this, of course, does not apply to the Sligo market. A ready sale was effected on Saturday, the prices realised being generally as follows: - superfine, 114s; firsts, 110s; seconds 105s; thirds, 96s. The inconveniences occasioned owing to the very limited dimensions of the market were very apparent. It is estimated that there were some 1,600 persons in the market at one period of the day, and the Inspector frequently found himself almost hopelessly wedged in among the people. The Corporation should see to it that this state of things is obviated as speedily as possible. The blank wall from the entrance to the stores might with considerable advantage be removed and the field leading to the Artisans' Dwellings opened out for the purposes of the market. The farmers have a right to expect this at the hands of the Corporation".

*"Sligo Chronicle"* 1.10.1887

FAIRS AND MARKETS

At a time when the Sligo Butter Market seemed poised for further expansion, more modern methods of making and marketing butter were introduced. The arrival of Horace Plunkett's Co-Operative Movement and the establishment of creameries in such traditional butter making areas as Achonry, Ballymote, Drumcliffe, Ballintrillick, Sooey and Riverstown in the mid or late 1890's had a detrimental effect on the long established Butter Market. The competition from the creameries led to a serious decline in the volume of butter being offered for sale at the weekly market. Between 1890 and 1894 the number of firkins dropped by 4,640 per annum, and two years later there was a further drop of 2,000. By 1905 it was less than one-third of what it had been a decade earlier.[32] Writing to Horace Plunkett in June, 1908, Dr. Clancy, Bishop of Elphin, reminisced on bygone days:-
*"Within my own recollection the Sligo Butter Market, a spacious quadrangle, used to be packed with firkins from end to end on at least three days a week. Now, it is practically derelict. With its decline shipments from the Port, cartage on the Quays and the cooperage in a hundred busy workshops has dwindled to an infinitesimal part of what they were..."* [33]

In July, 1909, Peter Tighe succeeded McAviney as Butter Inspector at 15/- a day and on his death in 1913 was replaced by John Bray. The number of firkins coming into the market in 1916 was only 1,700 and at year's end there was a deficit of £30 in its operation. Business continued to decline and by October, 1919, only 40 firkins, on average, were being offered for sale at the weekly market. After a long debate the Corporation finally decided, though not unanimously, in late 1919, to move the Butter Market to the Corn Market, or Market Yard, in an effort to reduce operational losses. The move to the new location did nothing to reverse the decline - it rather hastened its demise. An advertisement in the local press in July, 1924, informed producers that the market had re-opened for the season. By October, 1925, it was reported that the supply of butter had shrunk to a trickle, although prices remained high. The long established and once thriving market peetered out without a murmur a year later.

After the Butter Market Yard had ceased to function as such in 1919, it experienced a rather chequered existence. Portion of it, known as the Inspector's Shed, in what was originally the *Cadger's Field*, was leased by the Corporation to Messrs J. & T. Mahon who conducted

FAIRS AND MARKETS

a saw mill on the site for close on forty years. It was subsequently occupied by Shamrock Fertilisers Ltd. and more recently by Messrs Noyek & Son, timber merchants. The remainder of the Yard was used as an abbatoir by local butchers and also for the stabling of horses. In the mid 1960's the Corporation re-possessed the old section of the Market and utilised it as a Municipal Yard. In 1997 the entire property was sold to Messrs Swangale for commercial development.

The Butter Market, a well known landmark and the centre of commerce and trade for more than a century, is the latest of the 'institutions' of 'Olde Sligo' to be demolished in a frenzy of late 20th century developments.

---

## LIST OF MARKET TOWNS IN COUNTY SLIGO
### - 1852 -

| Name: | Date of Patent: | Grantee: | Market Day: |
|---|---|---|---|
| Aclare : | 1848 | Wm. Ormsby-Gore. | Saturday |
| Bellaghy : | 1819 | A. Knox-Gore | Wednesday |
| Ballymote: | 1605 | Sir James Fullerton | Thursday |
| Easkey: | 1782 | Godfrey Sill | Wednesday |
| Sligo: | 1604 | Earl of Strafford | Saturday |
| | 1621 | Sir James Craig | Tuesday |
| Tubbercurry: | 1706 | James Napper | Monday |

Patents had also been granted for the holding of Markets at the following locations but these were not functioning in 1852:-

Ardnaglass (Tuesday); Ballinacarrow (Tuesday);
Bunninadden (Wednesday); Castlebaldwin (Wednesday),
Cliffoney (Thursday); Collooney (Wednesday); Enniscrone (Friday);
Roslea (Saturday); Templehouse (Wednesday);
Tullaghnaglug (Saturday).

FAIRS AND MARKETS

## *Notes & References:* [Butter Market]

(1) Wood-Martin, W.G. *"History of Sligo"*.      Vol.3. p.237

(2) McParlan, J. *"Statistical Survey of Sligo"*.      Dublin. 1801

(3) O'Rorke, T. *"History of Sligo"*.      Vol.1.. p.357

(4) *"Sligo Journal"*      23 - 4 - 1825

(5) Parliamentary Papers (Poor Law Series). Vol.33,1836.

(6) *"Minutes of Evidence before Select Committee on the Butter Trade in Ireland"*,      1826. V. 406

(7) *"Sligo Journal"*      23 - 4 - 1825

(8) ibid      25 - 11 - 1831

(9) Foster, T. *"Letters on the Conditions of the People of Ireland*. London. 1846.

(10) Moses Monds, the builder of *Baymount House,* Ballincar, was a successful Sligo merchant. He was a member of the Reformed Corporation and Mayor in 1849; Editor of the *"Sligo Journal"* for a period; Chairman of the Town and Harbour Commissioners and subsequently Secretary. He died in December 1889.

(11) *Minutes of Evidence before Markets and Fairs Commission, 1852.*

(12) *"Sligo Journal"*      25 - 2 - 1848

(13) ibid      25 - 10 - 1850

(14) Markets & Fairs Commission. opus cit.

(15) *"Sligo Champion"*      12 - 9 - 1853

(16) The merchants included; Miller & Hall; Abraham Dobbin; Harper Campbell; Wm. Clarke; H & J Gorman; Middleton & Pollexfen; Michael Foley and Michael Milmoe.

(17) *"Sligo Champion"*      24 - 3 - 1860

(18) *"Paisley Gazette"*      24 - 3 - I877

(19) *"Sligo Chronicle"*      22 - 5 1886

(20) O'Higgins, A. *"The Sligo Borough Act, 1869 - a Milestone in the Decay of Ascendancy"*. (Unpublished)

(21) *"Sligo Champion"*      18 - II - 1854

(22) O'Higgins, A. opus cit.

(23) *"Sligo Independent"*      29 - 5 - 1869

(24) ibid.      5 - 6 -1869

(25) *"Sligo Chronicle"*      19 - 6 - 1880

## FAIRS AND MARKETS

(26) *"Sligo Champion"*                    14 - 2 - 1885

(27) *"Sligo Chronicle"*                   19 - 6 - 1880

(28) The list of Signatories included J. Sinclair; Robert Pettigrew;
     Robert B.McNeily; Ml. Milmoe & Son; James Robertson; James Kidd;
     R. Graham and W. & J Pettigrew.

(29) *"Sligo Independent"*                 20 - 2 - 1886

(30) ibid.                                 29 - 5 - 1886

(31) ibid                                  12 - 9 - 1885

(32) ibid                                  11 - 3 - 1908

(33) *"Irish Homestead"*                   13 - 6 - 1908

---

## SLIGO MARKET PRICES, 1828

| | | |
|---|---:|---:|
| Wheat, per barrel | 16s. | 0d |
| Oatmeal, per cwt. | 10. | 0. |
| Oats (24 stone) | 16. | 0. |
| Potatoes, per stone | 0. | 2. |
| Barley, per stone | 9. | 0. |
| Kelp, per cwt. | 1. | 6. |
| Hides, per lb. | 0. | 3. |
| Calf skins, per lb. | 0. | 2. |
| First Flour, per stone | 2. | 3. |
| Second Flour  "  " | 1. | 7. |
| Third Flour   "   " | 0. | 9. |
| Tallow, per stone | 5. | 4. |
| Mould Candles, per lb | 0. | 8. |
| Dipped Candles | 0. | 5. |
| Best Soap per 1b | 0. | 5. |
| Brown Soap per 1b | 0. | 4. |
| Pork, per 1b. | 0. | 3. |
| Beef, per 1b. | 0. | 4. |
| Mutton, per 1b. | 0. | 3. |
| Butter, First, per cwt | 79. | 6. |
| Butter, Second, per cwt | 73. | 6. |
| Butter, Third, per cwt | 65. | 6. |

*"Sligo Journal"*     22 - 1 - 1828

FAIRS AND MARKETS

# Number of Firkins offered for Sale on the Sligo Market, 1888 - 1899

| 1888 | ............................................. | 30,440 |
|------|-----|--------|
| 1890 | ............................................. | 28,640 |
| 1891 | ............................................. | 25,501 |
| 1892 | ............................................. | 24,758 |
| 1893 | ............................................. | 27,400 |
| 1894 | ............................................. | 24,000 |
| 1895 | ............................................. | 20,490 |
| 1896 | ............................................. | 18,390 |
| 1897 | ............................................. | 18,103 |
| 1899 | ............................................. | 10,139 |

# RETURNS FROM CO-OPERATIVE CREAMERIES, 1901

| Creamery: Sales: | Membership: Supplied | Paid up / | Butter Share Capital: | Gals. of Milk |
|------|------|------|------|------|
| Achonry: | 665 | £ 963 | £ 8,290 | 456,177 |
| Ballinfull: | 330 | 443 | 4,237 | 223,956 |
| Ballintrillick: | 304 | 536 | 5,184 | 280,340 |
| Ballymote: | 656 | 1,051 | 11,618 | 633,501 |
| Collooney: | 1,304 | 2,315 | 13,202 | 668,299 |
| Drumcliffe: | 330 | 798 | 7,718 | 379,837 |
| Gurteen: | 396 | 713 | 4,233 | 236,452 |
| Kilmactranny: | 385 | 890 | 5,970 | 308,261 |
| Riverstown: | 415 | 702 | 6,372 | 374,264 |
| Sooey: | 496 | 1,021 | 9,562 | 524,928 |

FAIRS AND MARKETS

# The Corn Market:

By letters patent of King James 1., dated June 25th, 1604, in the 5th year of his reign, licence was given to Sir James Fullerton to hold 'in the Abbey-town of Sligo", a weekly market on every Saturday with the customs, issues and emoluments of the market but without specifying the amount of the toll. In 1627 Charles 1. granted a patent to Sir James C. Craig, Knight, authorising the holding of a Tuesday market "at Bishop O'Crean's Cross, *alias* Laghtenaspicke". Almost half a century later, in 1674, a re-grant of the said two markets was made to William, Earl of Strafford and Thomas Radcliffe. In 1673 the market of Sligo "was resorted to from far and near by many people to buy cattle, sheep and horses, being one of the famousest marts for that purpose of any in that part of that Kingdom".[1] Some years later, in 1689, there are references to the Protestant settlers in Tireragh bringing their meal, cattle and other commodities to the Sligo market. [2]

Initially, the market was held on the streets, principally on or adjacent to the thoroughfare now known as Old Market Street. After the Wynne family acquired the tolls and customs of the markets in 1722, the market place was moved to the site of the present Market Yard, described in contemporary documents as being "south of St. John's church and alongside the newly created High Street" [3], which constituted part of the Burton estate and upon which Owen Wynne built a new Market House. In 1739 he leased the tolls and customs of the Fair and Markets to one John Knox, together with the said building, with the exception of the upper rooms which he reserved for his own use. [4]

Following the appointment of Owen Wynne, the 'Patron' of the Borough, to the office of Weighmaster, he proceeded to wall-in or otherwise enclose the aforementioned market-place which extended over an area of 125,000 square yards. Initially, there was only one gateway, that leading from High Street, and this resulted in great confusion and much congestion, on market days, especially on Saturdays, but by the mid 19th century two additional gateways had been provided, one leading directly to Knox's Street by way of Harmony Hill and the other into Temple Street. The Town Office, the equivalent of to-day's Town Hall, which had been built at the patron's

FAIRS AND MARKETS

---

# NOTICE

The public are hereby cautioned against buying or selling in the streets or other places within the precincts of the Town of Sligo (except the Public Market, the property of Owen Wynne, Esq) any grain or other article on which toll is payable in said markets.

Notice is hereby given that legal proceedings will be forthwith taken against any person or persons buying or selling same on the streets.

Signed: Wm. Christian.
Toll Collector for Owen Wynne.
Dated: June 21st 1832.

---

expense and where the Provost sat for the execution of his official duties, was situated close to the High Street entrance. It also functioned as the Wynne estate Rent Office. Other buildings included a large weighbridge, a store in the centre of the yard and a caretaker's house. The new market-place, now known as the *Market Yard*, was originally called the *Corn Market*. In evidence before the Fairs and Markets Commission in 1852 it was described thus: *"The Corn Market has ample accommodation, possesses a sufficient number of beams, weights and scales and is well enclosed. Standard weights are used in the market, and are regularly inspected by the Inspector of weights and measures appointed by the Grand Jury. No weight less than seven pounds is used in weighting a sack of oats in the market, and fourteen pounds are usually deducted for the tare of the sack."* The market was supervised by a Weighmaster, who also acted as an Inspector for the checking of all grain offered for sale. This procedure was deemed necessary in an effort to eliminate an old established custom of placing inferior grain in the centre of a sack and better quality at either end! It was also customary to publish weekly market prices in the local newspapers. As far back as 1711 the regulation of the markets occupied the attention of the Corporation when stringent rules were laid down as to the size of loads of fuel, straw and hay. In 1781 attempts were made to regulate the meat market. Under the local Act of 1803 it was permissible "to set or place any goods, wares or merchandise in streets or lanes" provided that this arrangement did not interfere with the Patron's rights to tolls and customs.

FAIRS AND MARKETS

After the opening of the new market-place, Wynne, not wishing to deprive stall-holders of their livelihood, allowed 'standings' or stalls on the public streets, notably in Market Street and High Street, on Tuesdays and Saturdays, provided that the requisite tolls were paid. No 'standings' were allowed on the streets on other days and all stall-holders were obliged under penalty to recourse to the Market Yard where they were charged the going rates. However, in 1832, the position was changed. Grain and other commodities, upon which toll was payable, were no longer permitted on the public street. In accordance with the terms of the Sligo Improvement Act of 1869, the Corporation were empowered to prohibit "any unauthorised or abolished market or fair, and the hawking, display or sale of animals, provisions and merchandise in the streets or public places other than in the authorised market places".

---

# CORPORATION OF SLIGO

## *Fairs and Markets*

The Corporation of Sligo having purchased, acquired, and taken possession from Mr. Owen Wynne, and all other person's interest therein, his and their interests, rights and title in the tolls, rents, stallages, fees and charges leviable or levied within the Borough of Sligo, for markets and fairs, and the several fair greens and market places, where the markets and fairs are held, and all rights, privileges and franchises relating thereto. Notice is hereby given that all tolls, rents, stallages, fees and charges are now payable to said Corporation who have appointed persons to collect same respectively. And for the further and better regulation of said Markets and Fairs, bye-laws will be made and published of which due notice will be given to the public, as is required by the several Statutes in that behalf made and provided.

Dated this 20th day of February, 1885.

James Nelson, Mayor.

### TO ALL WHOM IT MAY CONCERN

---

Sligo was widely known as a grain producing county as far back as the 18th century. In 1807 upwards of 37,000 barrels of oats and oatmeal were exported through the port. In 1830 one merchant alone shipped

FAIRS AND MARKETS

8,000 tons and in the following three years exports averaged between 136,000 and 154,000 quarters.[5] Grain came to the Sligo market from a radius of upwards of sixty miles and five counties. It was a common occurrence to see horse-drawn waggons arriving in the early morning and patiently waiting for the gates to open. Large amounts also came by hired carmen who, in the absence of the owners, sometimes went directly to the grain merchant's yard where false weights were often used to the detriment of the seller and a loss of toll revenue to the

---

## SLIGO MARKETS - 1888

**Corn Market, High Street.** - For the sale of wheat, oats, potatoes, barley, rye, flax-seed, turnips, fruit and all other kinds of vegetables, cabbage, garden plants, and nursery produce; fish, game, turkeys, geese, ducks, cocks, hens, chickens, all kinds of poultry, wild fowl, rabbits and hares; eggs and pork, wool, frieze, dillisk, cranagh; coopers', carpenters' and wood-turners' ware; carrigeen moss; farming implements, earthenware, basket rods, and tin ware; old and new furniture, wearing apparel and marine stores.

| | |
|---|---|
| **Temple Street:** - | For the sale of hay, straw and clover; horses, colts, ponies, mules, and asses. |
| **Butter Market:-** | For the sale of butter in firkins, butts, or crocks, print and lump butter. |
| **Jail Road, Armstrong's Row and Abbey Street:-** | For the sale of seaweed, turf, and bog wood. |
| **Pig Market, Temple Street:-** | For the sale of live pigs on foot, crell or cart pigs, sheep, lambs and veal calves. |
| **Cattle Market, Temple Street:** - | For the holding of monthly and other fairs for the sale of cows, heifers, bullocks and all other kinds of cattle not assigned to other markets or places. |

## FAIRS AND MARKETS

Patron. In an effort to eliminate this type of fraud, which was quite prevalent in the opening decades of the last century, and also to discourage a long standing practice of selling corn on the street, constables, in the employment of the Town and Harbour Commissioners, were stationed on market days at various street junctions in an effort to divert all grain carrying carts and waggons towards and into the Market Yard where the toll was collected and the corn weighed on the official scales. In the Corn Market there was a charge of 3d for each sack of grain - the equivalent of 24 stones - made up as follows : 1d custom; 1d for ticket and 1d for assistance in respect of each sack. Farmers generally brought their grain to the market in lots of three or four sacks.

*     *     *     *     *

The Corn Market, or Market Yard, was the scene of some notable events in the history of the Borough. In May, 1758, John Wesley, the founder of Methodism, preached in the Market House to "a numerous congregation". He also addressed a congregation there in 1762. On June 28th 1765, he noted in his diary : "I took my usual stand in the Market House at Sligo". In October, 1840, Father Mathew, the 'Apostle of Temperance', preached there and over three days administered the pledge to an estimated 18,000 from all over the north-west. In September, 1842, the Sligo Union Agricultural Society held its first Cattle Show there, and in August, 1847, on the occasion of a Parliamentary Election, a spacious platform was erected in the centre of the YARD from which the only nominee, John Patrick Somers (outgoing), was proposed, seconded and declared duly elected by Andrew Walker, Mayor, to the thunderous cheers of a large gathering of supporters. [6]

The first of a number of mass demonstrations to be held there was a Tenant Right meeting in October, 1869, which attracted an attendance in excess of 1,500, many of whom wore green ribbons as hat bands or rosettes. The meeting was chaired by Denis O'Connor, M.P. and also on the platform were Bishop Laurence Gillooly, Peter O'Connor J.P,. Richard Vereschoyle, J.P, Henry Lyons, J.P., Terence O'Rorke, P.P. and Hugh McTernan, J.P., who acted as one of the organisers. [7] Six years later in August, 1875, it was the scene of a large

FAIRS AND MARKETS

rally marking the centenary of the birth of Daniel O'Connell, the 'Liberator'. [8] On the occasion of laying the foundation stone of the 1798 Memorial at the Market Cross in September, 1898, a monster rally, chaired by P.A. McHugh, took place in the Market Yard. Other speakers included William O'Brien, ex M.P., Bernard Collery, M.P. and John O'Dowd.[9]

Following the purchase of the markets from the Wynne family in 1885, the Corporation drew up a list of Bye-Laws regulating all aspects of the control and management of the markets under their control, including the Corn Market. Arrangements were made to have it open at 6 a.m. (February - October) and 7 a.m. for the remainder of the year for the reception of corn and other commodities. However, the business of the market did not commence until 9.a.m. As the Corporation continued to collect customs and tolls, they furnished the requisite standings, stalls, tables and benches necessary for the public display of goods.

In 1965 the old Market House in the centre of the Yard, together with a Storehouse at the Temple Street end, were demolished and the entrance gates removed. Thereafter, the Market Yard became a relatively open area for the first time in over a century and a half. Despite recent develpments, it is still, and likely to remain so for the forseeable future, the Market Place of Sligo.

---

## Corn Market: Income & Expenditure 1885-87

| Income: | Rents - average over 3 years: | £70. 7s.8d. |
| | Tolls: | 343. 18s.4d. |
| | | £414. 6s.0d. |
| Expenditure: | Head rent/taxes - average over 3 years: | £201. 12s.0d. |
| | Wages: | £106. 0s.0d. |
| | Repairs, etc. | 52. 15s.0d. |
| | | £360. 7s.0d. |

FAIRS AND MARKETS

## BALLYMOTE MARKET TOLLS, 1888.

Each firkin of butter sold on the market ................ 2d.

Each firkin, if weighed and coopered ................ 4d.

Each bag of corn sold on market ................ 1d.

Each creel, bag or load of agricultural produce ................ 1d.

Each bag or sack upwards of 30 stones ................ 2d.

Each parcel of roll butter, 14 lbs. or upwards ................ 2d.

Each draught of wool per hundred ................ 6d.

The former MARKET HOUSE, Ballymote

FAIRS AND MARKETS

*References:* [Corn Market]

(1) *"The Present State of Ireland"* London. 1673.

(2) O'Dowd, Mary *"Power, Politics and Land in early Modern Sligo".* Belfast. 1991.

(3) ibid.

(4) Registry of Deeds            Bk. 93. p.463

(5) McTernan John C. *"Memory Harbour"* Sligo, 1992. Appendix 3

(6) *"Sligo Journal"*                 6 - 8 - 1847

(7) *"Sligo Chronicle"*             30 - 10 - 1869

(8)      ibid                    7 - 8 - 1875

(9) *"Sligo Champion"*            17 - 9 - 1898

*Bibliography:* [Markets & Fairs]

"An account of all Schedules of Customs, Tolls and Duties delivered to the Clerks of the Peace in the several Counties and Towns in Ireland". 1823. XVI.149

"Returns of places where Customs and Tolls and Duties are Levied". 1824 XXI. 703.

"Minutes of Evidence before Select Committee on Butter Trade in Ireland". 1826. V. 406.

"Minutes of Evidence before Select Committee on Tolls and Customs in Ireland". 1830. XXVI. 437.

"Reports of Select Committee into Tolls and Customs at Fairs and Markets (Ireland)". 1834. XVII. 229.

"Report of Commissioners appointed to Inquire into State of Fairs and Markets (Ireland)1852". 1854-55. XIX.

"Minutes of Evidence before Select Committee on Working and Management of Fairs and Markets, 1888".

"Fairs Exempted from Provisions of Weighing Cattle......" 1894. LXXVII. 634.

*"Thom's Directory".*                 1850 - 1975

*"Old Moore's Almanac".*           1950 - 1980

# Increase in Unemployment Causes Concern

Although the Irish Famine of the 1840s was primarily a rural catastrophe, the failure of the potato crop in 1845 had severe consequences for the urban working class. This was particularly so in Sligo where trade and industry were bound closely to the agricultural economy of the surrounding countryside. Sligo at that time was a Town of 10.000 inhabitants. It had almost no manufacturing industries apart from a distillery, a number of small breweries and a few flour mills in and around the Town. The chief source of its prosperity was its maritime trade. Sligo had developed in the previous decades into the largest and busiest port in Connacht and the only port of importance between Derry and Galway. The bulk of its trade was the export of corn, meal, flour, butter and provisions. It was also the chief market town of the North-West, its hinterland encompassing Co. Sligo and much of the neighbouring counties of Donegal, Mayo, Leitrim and Roscommon. Improved communications and the introduction of steamships to the export trade extended the inter-independence between the port town and its growing economic hinterland.

The following Report, drawn up by members of the Town and Harbour Commissioners in December, 1845, illustrates how vulnerable an economy such as Sligo's was to market fluctuations. The disruption of the harvest had a twofold effect on the working class population of the Town. Firstly, because of the partial failure, and anticipated total failure, of the potato crop, the harvest in other crops being retained for subsistence rather than sold or exported. The effect on the provisioning trade was devastating. Exports of grain and oats ceased almost completely and by December 1845 the numbers employed were half what they had been in the corresponding months of the two preceding years. Secondly, the distress caused by unemployment was deepened by food shortages and consequent price increases. Although less than half the potato crop of 1845 in the Sligo area was lost, the price of a stone of potatoes, which in the Spring had stood at less than 2d, was 6d or more by the Winter.

### Increase In Umemployment Causes Concern

The report was sent to John Wynne of Hazelwood who, in his capacity as a Magistrate and Chairman of the Town and Harbour Commissioners, had been requested to communicate with the Government's Relief Commission, detailing the extent of the potato blight and local distress and suggesting means for its alleviation. After an introductory statement of the facts, the Report continued:-

*"We, therefore, most earnestly entreat you to represent to your friends, who may have most influence with the Government, this awful state, and approaching distress; and that unless some immediate relief be obtained the disaffection which exists on the borders of this County will extend amongst us, making property, liberty and life insecure. We have deemed it prudent to keep this state of distress as private as possible, recommending employers to divide their employment, by giving alternately, 3 days work to one, and 3 to another, which some have been doing, and others have made advances in the rates of wages to enable them in a small degree to meet the exorbitant prices charged for the necessaries of life, which affect all classes, even those who have hitherto been comfortable and independent. The failure of the potato crop has caused the farmers to hold back their grain crops, and the decrease in the provision curing trade has deprived the inhabitants of the large supply of offal which had hitherto been obtained. This decrease is caused by the demand for live stock in England and the steam communication between this port and Glasgow, and Liverpool ; this added to the loss of cattle by disease in summer, and the consequent high prices have prevented the merchants engaged in that trade being able to make up but a very small portion of the usual supply.*

*We know you have not been unobservant of these facts, but we have deemed it our duty to state them as the causes of the distress which is now felt to such an alarming extent in our Town. Our County is blessed with peace, and our Town if compared with any of its extent of population in the United Kingdom will, we feel confident, show as little, if not less, crime or outrage. This moral feeling may be justly attributed to the good disposition and feeling existing between the employers and the employed. The gentry and landed proprietors, as also the merchants of the Town, have subscribed a sum about £1,500 for the purpose of deepening the Port and Harbour. You, as one of the principal subscribers, know how we have been disappointed by the Board of Works in not giving us the assistance which they had promised if we made up a like sum by local subscriptions. Within the last 30 years we have not got a pound from the Government by way of grant or loan. We have endeavoured to get on by our*

# INCREASE IN UMEMPLOYMENT CAUSES CONCERN

*own resources which have been applauded by Captain Washington, the Tidal Commissioner. And we now confidently expect we shall get what our patience deserves, and our necessities require. We have now stated plain facts for your representation to the Government, and we earnestly hope they will not pause in doing something to give immediate relief. Our Port and Harbour require improvement. Four or five thousand pounds judiciously expended would give the required relief, and be of great utility to the trade of the Port. We have already paid the government engineer (Mr. Gibbons) who had been sent down by the Board of Works to make a survey and report on the requisite improvements, to which reference can be made without incurring delay. We will feel most happy to find this our Report meets the attention which the cause of humanity, the safety of the Town and County demand, tendering our zealous co-operation to any measure which may tend to that object."*

The Report, dated 22nd December, 1845, signed by M. Gallagher (Mayor), M. Kernaghan, Wm. Patrickson, Peter O'Connor and Henry O'Connor (Mayor elect), continued:

*"Agreeable to the resolutions passed at the meeting of the Town and Harbour Commissioners on the 15th inst., at which you presided, for the purpose of enquiring into the distress amongst the labouring population of this Town for want of employment, we beg to wait on you with the Report of the particulars of our inquiry, relative to the number of persons employed in the several stores and yards within the Town during the months of November and December 1843, 1844, and the present year.*

*We have taken much pains to ascertain the facts which we regret to find far exceed the extent we had supposed ; our enquiry has been conducted quietly, so as to create no excitement, or give cause to any false returns: this you will please accept as our apology for not sending you our Report sooner.*

*You will see that our Town requires immediate attention, when we find more than the seventh part of the population in want of employment, or the means of procuring the necessaries of life; their patience and good disposition will, we very much fear, be broken, unless some immediate relief is given by some public employment. The disposition of the poor here is different to that in other parts of the country : they are not prone to drinking, indolent or lazy, but are most willing to do anything rather than seek relief in a Poorhouse; of this you have had sufficient experience in your constant attention at that establishment. We find the state of trade as follows:*

# Increase In Umemployment Causes Concern

50 corn & provision stores & yards
2 breweries
1 distillery
1 flour-mill
1 coach-factory.

*There were employed in 1843 and 1844 averaging both years, (the greater number in 1844):-*

| Quay-porters | Coach makers | | Coopers | Labourers | Carters |
|---|---|---|---|---|---|
| In 1843 & 44 :- | 12 | 107 | 684 | 45 | 50 |
| In 1845 :- | 8 | 42 | 357 | 33 | 20 |
| Leaving unemployed | 4 | 65 | 327 | 12 | 30 |

*Besides several others in various trades, there are 438 men, who have, on an average, a family of five, including a wife, children or aged and destitute parents; thereby making more than 2,560 souls. You will be pleased to take further note that there are several of those on the employed lists who are kept on pay by their former employers through sympathy for their conditions and in the hope that something, ere this time, would have been done by Public Works. The awful visitation of the failure of the potato crop, the increase of which you have taken such lively and praiseworthy exertions to prevent, has baffled all prescribed remedies, and each succeeding day brings further information of failures, where safety was expected".*

## COMPARITIVE ACCOUNT OF THE NUMBER OF LABOURERS, COOPERS & CARRIERS EMPLOYED IN SLIGO 1843 - 1845

| Street & Store | Owners or Occupiers | 1843 Labourers | 1844 Coopers | 1845 Labourers | 1845 Coopers | Trade or Business |
|---|---|---|---|---|---|---|
| New Market Lane | James Gallaher | 12 | - | 12 partially | - | Corn Trade |
| Corn Market | Wm. Christian | 7 | - | 7 | - | Custom, Weigh Master |
| Pound St. | Widow of Killelea | 12 | - | 6 | - | Butter and Salt |
| Pound St. | Hugh Rooney | 12 | 4 | 16 | 8 | Provision, Beef & Pork |
| Pound St. | Dominick Henry | 8 | - | 8 | - | Tobacco & General |
| Old Market St. | Peter O'Connor | 24 | - | 12 | - | Corn & General |
| Old Market St. | Robert Sherlock | 12 | - | 12 partially | - | Grain & Rectify Distillers |
| Old Market St. | John Hart | 10 | - | 6 partially | - | Grain & Salt |
| High St. | M. Giblin & Co. | 14 | - | 6 partially | - | Grain |
| High St. | Andrew Walker | 14 | - | 14 | - | Tobacco, Chandling, Gen. |
| High St. | Wm. Kernaghan | 26 | - | 6 | - | Grain, Brewery, etc. |
| Radcliffe St. | M. Madden & Co. | 20 | 1 | 15 | 1 | Grain & General Trade |
| Water Lane | W.A. Woods | 4 | - | 1 | - | Tan Yard |
| Water Lane | John Anderson | 11 | 1 | 11 | 1 | Brewery |
| Castle St. | Dr. Conolan | 12 | - | 2 | - | Corn Store |
| Castle St. | Moses Monds | 8 | - | 6 | - | General Trade |
| Linen Hall St. | John Read | 12 | - | 8 | - | Coach Builder |
| Riverside | G.C. Martin & Co. | 40 | 2 | - | 2 | Distillery |
| Riverside | J & F. O'Donovan | - | - | 20 | - | Distillery |
| New Bridge St. | James Waddle | 24 | 4 | - | - | Corn & Provision Store |
| New Bridge St. | Dr. Conolan | - | - | 12 | 4 | Corn & Provision Store |
| Stephen St. | Edward Kelly | 8 | - | 4 | - | Grain Store |
| Holborn St. | H. Kelly & Cleary | 6 | 2 | - | - | Beef & Pork |
| Old Bridge St. & Old Quay St. | Abraham Martin | 30 | - | 24 | - | Flour Mills & Grain Store |
| Knox St. | John Beaty | 10 | - | 4 | - | Corn Store |
| Knox St. | Robert Miller | 2 | - | - | - | Herring Store |
| Knox St. | Robert Ramsay | 30 | - | 24 | - | Corn Store & Chandler |

INCREASE IN UNEMPLOYMENT CAUSES CONCERN

INCREASE IN UNEMPLOYMENT CAUSES CONCERN

| | | | | | | |
|---|---|---|---|---|---|---|
| Old Quay St. | Jn. O'Connor | 4 | - | 6 | - | Grain etc. |
| John St. | Isaac Cordukes | 6 | 1 | - | - | Provision & Hams |
| John St. | Richard Smith | 2 | - | 12 partially | - | Corn Stores |
| John St. | James Hudson | 8 | - | 4 partially | - | Corn Stores |
| John St. | Henry O'Connor | 8 | - | - | - | Pork & Provision |
| Wine St. | Robert Culberston | 12 | - | 5 | - | Grain & Provision |
| Wine St. | Henry Gorman | 8 | 4 | 10 | 4 | Grain & Meal |
| Wine St. | Henry O'Connor | 50 | 20 | 8 | 3 | Butter & Provision |
| Union St. | H. Campbell | 20 | 2 | 10 | 2 | Provision, Butter, Corn |
| Union St. | A. Welsh | 20 | 3 | 6 | 2 | Provision & Hams |
| Lynn's Place | I. Cordukes | 16 | - | 6 | 1 | Provision & Grain |
| Lynn's Place | Jas. Harper | 6 | 2 | 4 | 1 | Provision & Hams |
| Knox St. | Edward Kelly | 70 | 50 | 10 | 10 | Butter & General |
| Knox St. | Andrew Derrig | 6 | 2 | 4 | 1 | Provision & Grain |
| Knox St. | Michael Giblin | - | 6 | - | 1 | Provision |
| Finisklin Road | John Delaney | 11 | - | 5 | - | Cooperage |
| Finisklin Road | Cooper & Co. | 10 | 1 | 6 | 1 | Grain |
| Old Quay | Hugh Leighton | 24 | 2 | 4 | - | Provision |
| Old Quay | Dr. Conolan | 10 | - | 4 | - | Grain & Provision |
| Old Quay | Michael Connolly | 10 | - | 6 | - | Grain |
| Old Quay | Geo Tate | 6 | - | - | - | Grain |
| Old Quay St. | Jas. Campbell | 10 | - | 6 | - | Grain |
| Old Quay St. | R.B. Wynne | 3 | - | 1 | - | Sugar & Wine |
| Old Quay St. | F. Hudson & Co. | 4 | - | 4 | - | Coal |
| Old Quay St. | Middleton & Co. | 4 | - | 4 | - | Coal |
| Old Quay St. | O'Rorke & Co. | 2 | - | 2 | - | Coal |
| Old Quay St. | Jas. Cochran | 2 | - | 2 | - | Import |
| **Total Unemployed** | | **696** | **107** | **355** | **42** | |
| | | **355** | **42** | | | |
| **Total of Unemployed Grain & Provision Store** | | **341** | **65** | | | |

# The GREAT FAMINE

The Great Famine, which devasted Ireland between 1845 and 1850, was the most tragic and horrific event this country has ever known. It changed the course of Irish history and its effects locally were such as to reduce the population of the County from 180,000 to 128,000 in the space of five years or so. By 1851 roughly one-third of the people had gone - they had died of fever or hunger, or had emigrated.

In the opening decades of the 19th century the rural population had a cheap and plentiful source of food. The potato, introduced to Ireland about 1590, could grow in the poorest conditions with very little labour. There is no doubt that this easily grown, vitamin packed food, assisted the enormous growth of population which rose from three million people in 1800 to about eight million in 1845. The potato was the staple food of most of the population, and when it failed completely, there was nothing to fall back on. Conditions of life in Ireland in the decade before the Great Famine were bad and in some parts of the country they were worse than others. Within County Sligo these varied from one estate to another. In some instances landlords had taken an interest in the management of their estates, but others had allowed their lands to be let to middlemen who further sub-let to farmers who in turn sub-let in smaller quantities. Sub-division had gone on to such an extent that by 1841 almost two thirds of the farms in the County were less than five acres in extent. The population, too, was large, and there was little alternative employment apart from agriculture, so the competition for farms was keen, so keen that the rents paid were quite uneconomic. The result was that the population lived, even in normal times, on the verge of starvation.

In 1843 newspapers carried news from America of a disease which had attacked the potato. In June, 1845, reports began to come from Europe that a new blight had been noticed in Belgium and other European countries. In August there were reports of the appearance of the mysterious disease in parts of England, and eminent botanists there were unable to identify either the cause of the rot or a remedy for it. The disease had no name but was variously referred to as 'blight', 'distemper', 'the rot' or 'the blackness'. In September sightings of the

## THE GREAT FAMINE

disease were reported in Ireland but the extent to which the Irish crop had been affected by the blight was not obvious until the general digging of the potatoes in the month of October.

The earliest reference to the failure of the crop in County Sligo appeared in the *"Sligo Journal"* of October 10, 1845. Two weeks later the *"Champion"* confirmed that the blight had indeed made its appearance, and it called upon the landlords to act with forbearance and liberality. In mid November, 1845, the Poor Law Guardians, representing the various electoral divisions, met to ascertain the condition of the potato crop throughout the County. All reports confirmed that the disease was widespread; that one-half of the crop was lost, and, with the disease daily progressing, potatoes which were perfectly sound three weeks earlier had become useless. In the light soils one-sixth to one-tenth was affected, while in heavy wet soils between a half to three quarters were destroyed. The *"Champion"* considered the prevailing conditions "most gloomy and disheartening," and concluded that the various remedies for checking the progress of the disease were ineffectual. "The rot in the potato resembles cholera - and like it, it will not be arrested until it has destroyed a certain portion of the crop."[1]

The worst fears expressed in the fore-going editorial were confirmed by a letter published in its columns in October 1845. The contributor was John Coghlan, C.C., Gurteen, who wrote as follows:-

*"It is utterly impossible to convey to you a true picture of the alarming state of despondency into which the people of this Parish have been thrown by the extensive rot in the potato crop. There are eleven hundred families in it and there is scarcely one that has not suffered, many have all their potatoes totally lost..."*

*"It is quite common that a potato field tried today may be good and sound, and in three days after in a state of melancholy putrefaction. My heart bleeds to contemplate the dark future that appears before the suffering people. They have neither oats, nor money, nor potatoes nor the hope of relief from a kind and indulgent landlord."* [2]

Another letter from Father James Henry of Kilshalvey presented an even more despairing picture of the reality of the situation on the ground: -

*"The potato distemper made its appearance in this neighbourhood about three*

*weeks ago. In ten or twelve days there was not a field in the Parish but was in some degree infected with this terrible scourge ... All hands, at its first appearance, were at once set to dig. Thinking that if the potatoes could be got sound out of the earth, they would remain so, some were not then much alarmed, for although they would tell you all was lost in one field, they were not so badly off in the next ; but a few days more proved that not a basketful could be found without a few, either less or more infected. They gave up digging altogether, hoping that things would mend but, alas, they hoped in vain".* [3]

A month later a correspondent from the Achonry area reported that in a Parish comprising some eight hundred families everyone's crop was affected to a greater or lesser degree. On average, one-quarter of the crop was unsound, and he instanced the case of a tenant giving up an acre of land in exchange for one barrel of sound potatoes. Also in November, Patrick Flannelly, P.P., Easkey, stated that up to one-third of the crop in his area was not fit for human consumption and famine was unavoidable.

When the blight appeared in the Autumn of 1845, it was seen as a threat to the subsistence of the poor. The Government took steps to meet the situation by buying in from America £100,000 worth of Indian corn or maize. However, this was not the most efficient substitute for potatoes - it was hard to mill, it was difficult to digest and people who were accustomed to the bulk of the potato in the stomach were left unsatisfied by Indian corn. It became known as *'Peel's brimstone'*, partly because of its bright sulphur yellow colour, and partly because of its effects on the digestive system. Depots were established throughout the country for the storage and distribution of the Indian corn. Sligo was the principal depot for the North-West and sub-depots were established at Ballymote and Tubbercurry, while the coastguard stations at Enniscrone and Raughly performed a similar service. By March, 1846, a good portion of the population were without food or the means to procure it. They were living on the bounty of their neighbours and what little they could get from Relief Committees. In the Barony of Leyny, for example, there was, in the words of Jemmet Duke of *Newpark,* "an abudance of distress - the wasted forms, the sunken eyes and the palid cheeks of the wretched peasantry tell a tale , a fearful tale of misery and famine". All the while there was a plentiful supply of potatoes on the weekly Sligo market. On Saturday,

# THE GREAT FAMINE

May 2nd, 1846, there were 140 tons for sale, with little evidence of disease and at prices varying from 1/- to 1/5d a peck, but the starving poor, for the most part, had not the means to purchase even the smallest quantity. Sheep and pigs were sold in droves at reduced rates at local fairs for export and slaughter in Britain.

On the occasion of a meeting of the Sligo Board of Guardians in the Workhouse on April 20th, 1846, a group of one hundred or so able-bodied workmen assembled near the Old Bridge in Stephen Street. Two sixpenny loaves were purchased and placed on polls after which they proceeded in an orderly fashion to the Workhouse where they positioned themselves in full view of the assembled Guardians. After some initial contacts, a six man deputation was admitted and their spokesman urged that employment be provided for the relief of their destitute condition and that of their families. Complaints were also raised concerning the prices of commodities in the local shops. Before departing the group were assured by Chairman, John Wynne, that everything possible would be done to give them some relief. [4]

## Relief Committees

At a meeting of the Magistrates and Poor Law Guardians in May, 1846, convened to ascertain the extent of the distress in Town and County, it was decided to form Relief Committees in the different baronies. These came into existence within a few weeks and were composed, for the most part, of the local gentry, Government officials and clergymen of all persuasions. Their duties were threefold: solicit subscriptions from local landlords, initiate public works and distribute Indian corn. These committees were answerable to the Relief Commission in Dublin who gave grants in direct proportion to the amount of money raised locally. Over the following year the activities of the various Relief Committees received some publicity in both the *"Champion"* and the *"Journal"*, such as appeals for funds, reports of meetings and the listing of subscriptions received. The principal subscribers to the individual committees were listed as follows:-

COOLAVIN RELIEF COMMITTEE

| | |
|---|---|
| Dublin Relief Committee | £40 |
| Calcutta Relief Committee | £30 |
| Viscount Lorton (Absentee) | £20 |

279

## THE GREAT FAMINE

| | |
|---|---|
| Lord De Freyne (Absentee) | £10 |
| Joseph A. Holmes (Monasteraden) | £20 |
| Rev. Edward Powell (Kilfree) | £10 |
| Rev. Peter Brennan (Kilfree) | £10 |
| Andrew Baker (Redhill) | £5 |

### CORRAN RELIEF COMMITTEE

| | |
|---|---|
| Sir Robert Gore-Booth (Lissadell) | £100 |
| Rev. John Garrett, jun.(Yorkshire) | £10 |
| Robert Duke (Newpark) | £3 |
| Dr. Lougheed (Ballymote) | £3 |
| Abraham Motherwell (Ballymote) | £2 |
| Robert Morris | £1 |

### SLIGO TOWN RELIEF COMMITTTEE

| | |
|---|---|
| Peter O'Connor (Cairnsfoot House) | £100 |
| Edward Kelly (Merchant) | £100 |
| Dr. Conolan | £50 |
| Edward J. Cooper (Markree Castle) | £30 |
| Henry Lyons (Merchant) | £25 |
| John Wynne (Hazelwood House) | £20 |
| William Phibbs (Seafield) | £10 |
| Major Charles K. O'Hara (Annaghmore) | £10 |

### TIRERAGH RELIEF COMMITTEE

| | |
|---|---|
| Messrs Howley (Belleek & Cooga) | £35 |
| Col. A. K. Gore (Belleek Castle) | £30 |
| Col. E. Wingfield (Scurmore) | £20 |
| William Phibbs (Seafield) | £20 |
| Capt. John W. King (Tanrego) | £20 |
| Robert & Lewis Jones (Fortland) | £10 |
| Rev. Patrick Flannelly, P.P., Easkey | £10 |

### TIRERRILL RELIEF COMMITTEE

| | |
|---|---|
| Edward J. Cooper (Markree Castle) | £50 |
| William Ormsby-Gore (Absentee Landlord) | £10 |
| William Weir (Lakeview) | £10 |
| John Ormsby (Casltedargan) | £10 |
| Michael Keogh (Geevagh Lodge) | £10 |

### TUBBERCURRY RELIEF COMMITTEE

| | |
|---|---|
| Mrs. Jones (Benada) | £30 |
| John Armstrong (Chaffpool) | £30 |
| James A. Knox (Absentee Landlord) | £25 |
| William Phibbs (Seafield) | £20 |
| William Ormsby-Gore ( Absentee Landlord) | £10 |
| Henry Irwin (Streamstown) | £10 |
| Rev. Daniel Mullarkey P.P.(Tourlestrane) | £3 |

## THE GREAT FAMINE

Much of the secretarial and organisational work of the Relief Committees was usually left to the local clergy, both Catholic and Protestant. Malachi Brennan, P.P., Ahamlish; Dominic Noone, C.C., Grange; Patrick Flannelly, P.P., Easkey; James Henry, P.P., Kilshalvey; Peter Brennan, P.P., Kilfree, John Coghlan, C.C., Gurteen and Owen Feeney P.P., St. Johns, took every opportunity of drawing the attention of the authorities, both by private correspondence and letters to the Press, to the failure of the crop in the first instance and then to the famine and destitution, fever and death widespread in their respective areas. A number of Protestant clergymen were equally untiring in their efforts to assist their parishioners, irrespective of creed or class. In the parish of Achonry, Dean Edward Hoare and his curate, John Hamilton, worked day and night alongside the Catholic curates, John Gallagher and John McHugh, feeding over 4,000 in the Spring of 1847. Hoare was also Chairman of the Upper Leyny Relief Committee and took every opportunity of goading the local landed proprietors into funding soup kitchens and relief works. As an incentive he offered to contribute 2s-6d in the £. on his ecclesiastical property in each of the four electoral divisions in his area, and to employ seven labourers between July and November, provided that the landlords gave employment proportionally.

In neighbouring Kilmactigue, the Rector, William Tyndall, manned soup kitchens daily for long hours until he contracted fever and died in July, 1847. He was assisted locally in the relief work by the Catholic curate, Thomas Judge. Across the Ox Mountains in Tireragh, James Burrows, the elderly Rector of Castleconnor, fed four hundred families weekly at Killanly Glebe in the Spring of 1847 until he collapsed from exhaustion and fever. In Sligo town, Edward Day, Rector of St, Johns, and Noble Shepperd of the Congregational or Independent Church, worked unceasingly for the poor and hungry. The most zealous worker in the area of local relief was undoubtedly John Garrett , Rector of Emlaghfad, who served on no fewer than six committees. He attained national prominence by virtue of his numerous applications seeking Quaker relief; of his outspoken criticisms of the Relief Commission, and of his many letters to the press concerning the widespread distress being experienced in the Barony of Corran. He personally supervised boilers at venues as far apart as Ballymote, Bunninadden and Drumfin,

281

THE GREAT FAMINE

and also took turns at distributing food at the Rectory daily. [5]

# Public Works

In March, 1846, legislation was passed enabling Grand Juries to approve of road works and generally to initiate schemes for the employment of the able-bodied poor. While the types of work undertaken varied from barony to barony, they consisted, for the most part, of making new lines of roads, building bridges and repairing or improving existing routes. There were many delays in organising the new works - they had to be assessed locally and then approved by the Board of Works before proceeding - and all the while labourers were in the greatest distress and many in a state of a starvation. "Employment to a considerable extent, believed to be in the region of 1,500, is daily afforded on the public works in different parts of the County", wrote the *"Sligo Journal"*.[6] "There are 400 men at work in the Barony of Corran and Sir Robert Gore-Booth has every tenant on his extensive property, in the region of 150, profitably occupied other than on the public works".

At a special Presentments Session in Coolaney in April, 1846, works totalling £12,000 were approved, including a new line from Kilcummin to Ballyglass, known locally as *'Stirabout Road'.* In July a public meeting, chaired by John Armstrong of Chaffpool, took place in Ballymote to discuss and approve of Relief Works in the Barony of Corran. Among the projects approved were a new line of road from Knockaglass to Quarryfield; ditto from Emlagh to Clooncunny; ditto from Knockaconnor to mearing of Roscommon, being part of a new line from Ballymote to Boyle, and 550 perches of road between Oldrock and Templehouse Bridge, in addition to numerous minor works such as cutting down hills and filling hollows on existing roads. At a meeting of the Carbury Relief Committee in August, Malachi Brennan, P.P., Ahamlish, complained about the large workforce employed in the Drumcliffe area as compared to his parish where the people experienced even greater distress. He stated that he could get up to 1,000 men who would be glad to take meal instead of money from work. [7]

An extraordinary Presentments Session for the Barony of Carbury

282

## THE GREAT FAMINE

took place in Sligo Courthouse on September 20th, presided over by John Wynne. The meeting attracted an overflow of interests - members of the public who were anxious for news of what public works were being approved with a view to securing much needed employment. Among the presentments adopted were the following - new lines of roads linking Rathbraughan and Willsboro; Cregg and the Lower Rosses; Siberia to Scardan; Finisklin to Gibraltar; Albert Road to junction of Mail Coach Road; Victoria Bridge to Ballytivnan and Wine Street to the Pig Market. Other works included deepening the River between Buckley's Ford and the Distillery; laying a main sewer from Pound Street through Market Street and Radcliffe Street; enclosing the cemeteries at both the Fever Hospital and Ahamlish Church and embanking the Ballast Quay.

By February, 1847, a total of 22,000 workers, who were paid an average of 8d. a day, were employed on the public works in County Sligo. In addition, there were was an inspecting Officer paid 30/- a day; an Assistant Officer £1. a day, exclusive of travelling; an Inspector of payment's I5/- ; eight Assistant Engineers, eighteen Pay Clerks; seventy-five Check Clerks and five hundred and forty-six Overseers. The *"Champion"* was infuriated at this widespread jobbery. In an editorial headed "Management of the Public Works", it made a scathing attack on the whole system:

*"We cannot in conscience refrain any longer from denouncing the gross and infamous system of jobbing going on in the County, with reference to the manner in which the Public Works have been conducted and managed. In the midst of the calamity which has fallen upon us, we find the landlords trading upon the miseries of the people. The Board of Works is humbugged, the Government*

*cheated, and the Poor defrauded. A gigantic swindle is now carried on in the County. The poor are not relieved by the vast grants of money given by a liberal ministry, but the sons of the Magistrates, of Grand Jurors, of Parsons and rich farmers - all these are quartered upon the public. We saw, for instance, two men overseeing seven labourers; we have Inspectors, Paymasters, Overseers - officials of all ranks and grades in every locality not selected for their ability but because they have interest - because they can command the voices of the landlords of the County . . ."* [8]

William Bennett, a Quaker, who visited County Sligo in March, 1847, has left us his impression of the Public Works : -

*"We first encountered the Public Works, so called, outside Tubbercurry. These consisted in making new roads and altering old ones, in many cases worst than useless, and obviously undertaken without judgement, for the mere sake of employment. Independent of the moral effects of useless labour, it was melancholy and degrading in the extreme to see women and girls withdrawn from all that is decent and proper and labouring in mixed gangs on the public roads; not only in digging with the spade and pick, but in carrying loads of earth on their backs and wheeling barrows like men and breaking stones, while poor neglected children were crowded in groups around bits of lighted turves in various sheltered corners along the road . . . They pay 6d and 7d per day to women and girls and 8d to men - the lowest paid anywhere . . "* [9]

Not withstanding the criticisms, the huge numbers flooding to the works, scrambling for a chance to earn a little money, an average of 6/- a week, made for an administrative nightmare. Often people most in need failed to get work because places were taken by those in no such need but knew someone on the local Committee. In fairness to the Board of Works, they daily faced a dilemma - many of those applying for work were so weakened by want that they could scarcely lift a shovel. Nobody, it seems, had the heart to turn them away. The total Presentments for relief works in the County, 1846-'48, came to £217,802. It is estimated that 306 miles of new roads were made and several additional miles of existing routes improved or repaired.

At a meeting of the Sligo Union in September, 1846, Father Malachi Brennan painted a gloomy picture of conditions in his neighbourhood. He instanced the case of a man who dug forty yards of a ridge, out of which he got but one meal for his family. Despite the employment afforded by Lord Palmerston in the vicinity of

## THE GREAT FAMINE

Mullaghmore, there were 1,200 destitute families in that parish. Conditions were somewhat better in Drumcliffe. Sir Robert Gore-Booth had 280 men at work and there were some 300 on the public works, nevertheless, 200 families were in extreme distress and the supply of Indian meal had been exhausted.[10] The distress was not confined to rural areas alone. In Sligo Town a number of workmen, numbering in the region of one hundred, assembled at the Mail Coach Road and marched into town in an effort to highlight their plight and that of their starving families. A few of them protested outside the premises of a number of merchants whom they alleged had combined to maintain prices of flour and meal at an unacceptable high level. At the same time the police were busily engaged escorting vans delivering bread to local institutions in case of robbery, while large numbers queued outside the flour and meal stores hourly waiting in shivering poverty for a miserable pittance". [11]

In December the *"Journal"* carried news of an increasing death rate. "The people are dying fast for want of food", it wrote, while at the same time noting that the Workhouse was full and could afford no further relief, leaving hundreds with no place of refuge. Equally depressing was the report of Captain Gilbert to the Central Relief Commission:

*"The whole system is failing, you find starvation all over the place. The distress is increasing weekly. In the upper half of the Barony of Leyny 20,000 of a population of 27,000 are destitute . . . It is absolutely necessary that 2,000 men, now out of employment, be relieved to keep them from starvation. In the parishes of Curry and Kilmactigue several deaths have occurred from want. It is estimated that 700 passed towards Sligo from Mayo on their way to Amerca this week. One lot consisted of ten carts and 109 souls. In the immediate neighbourhood of Sligo Town there are at least 200 more destitute men seeking employment and no work in progress where they can be employed. Deaths have increased this week due to the severity of the weather and labourers have great difficulty in remaining on the works".*

At the same time groups of destitute people were daily flocking into Sligo in search of food. According to the *"Champion"*, the Town was "inundated with strange beggars - we never saw anything like it before", and it urged the authorities to do something for these homeless strangers , "poor penniless wanderers", as it called them.

The Winter of 1846-'47 was an appalling one of famine , fever and

285

## THE GREAT FAMINE

death. A prominent agent in Sligo wrote as follows to the Secretary of the Treasury in London in February, 1847: -

*"A heavy fall of snow and a hard frost, since the 7th instant, has interrupted the public works and filled our highways and streets with paupers and starving people of all descriptions who, during the suspension, are left without any resources of their own for the subsistence of themselves and their families. Groups of women and children are swarming about our streets from the rural districts: they beg all day and pay 3d a week for passing the night on straw in some of the houses in the outskirts of the town. A few days since an inmate of one of these houses of refuge died in the night and was thrown into the street."*

---

# VICTIMS OF THE FAMINE

"Yesterday evening I observed on the much frequented bye-path, known as the 'Double Ditch', leading from Temple-street to the Circular Road, what at first appeared to be a mound of rubbish, with a little newly cut grass strewn over it; being obliged to leave the path to pass, I was horrified at discovering that a human being lay beneath it. On inquiry, I found that it was a poor boy in fever, that he had lain there since Tuesday week, (having failed to get admittance to the hospital) exposed day and night to the inclemency of the weather. I, at once, waited on a member of the Board of Health, who immediately gave orders to the carter belonging to that body for his removal to the hospital; but on visiting the place again this morning, the miserable being was there, and still alive.

There are also at this moment, while it pours rain, seven persons in fever lying on straw under the wall enclosing the new Fever Hospital where they have lain all night, perhaps longer, exposed to the weather without the smallest shelter or convenience, except their own wretched garments. Is there no remedy for such a state of things? Disease, in any form, fever particularly, is a dreadful thing in itself, even if the patient is surrounded with comforts, but what must those creatures endure, when it is accompanied with the miseries I have detailed; and is it possible, in a Christian country, that there are no means to prevent a recurrence of it?

A Correspondent in *"Sligo Journal"*
*24.06.1847*

## THE GREAT FAMINE

In the Summer of 1846 expectations were high that the new potato crop would bring relief, but such hopes were rudely dashed in July when the *"Champion"* carried the following grim news : "The Potato rot has again been discovered to exist to a considerable extent in this neighbourhood". The position was calamitous. The whole crop was wiped out and a new Government, led by Lord John Russell, took office in the midst of the crisis. There was an immediate change in policy - relief thenceforward was to be by public works only. The Government would not interfere with the course of trade. Food depots were to be maintained at Sligo and other centres but they would not offer goods for sale while local merchants had any stocks, and then only at the prevailing market price. In an effort to alleviate the hardships resulting from the change in policy, a number of landlords, notably John Wynne and Sir Robert Gore-Booth,opened food depots on their estates. Conditions generally were steadily deteriorating, as instanced by the following statements. Writing from Sligo on October 28th, Isabella Soden, of Moneygold, observed: -

*"Prices here are exhorbitant...potatoes 3/6d a sack...Indian meal not to be had. The people who have conacre from me...say they will not pay...They think the Magistrates are rather too conciliatory. God Almighty alone can avert all the ills that threaten this devoted land. The tenants intend eating all our cattle but say they will commence with Lord Palmerston's, then take Mr. Brennan's and thirdly mine!*[12]

Destitution in North Sligo was so extreme that even James Walker, Palmerston's Agent, opened his eyes. Early in October he reported to Palmerston as follows: -

*I am sorry to say that the Ahamlish Estate is in great want by the total failure of the Potato Crop and very little corn produced on it, so much so, that unless a supply of Indian Meal or other breadstuff is immediately supplied for the wants of the tenantry, the consequences may be very dangerous. Yesterday, which is the weekly market day of Sligo, all the flour & meal was disposed of to the prior applicants. Your (Ahamlish) tenants are so far from Sligo that I would recommend your Lordship to allow me to constitute a Depot at Mullaghmore or Cliffony, and thro' some of the Sligo merchants to get in a small cargo of Indian Corn, Rice or Rye, and have it retailed there for ready money, as there will be employment for the people, under the Labour Act, if carried out."*
[13]

THE GREAT FAMINE

# Soup Kitchens

In February, 1847, the Government finally gave up on the Relief Works and brought in the "Act for the Temporary Relief of Destitute Persons in Ireland", better known as the *Soup Kitchen Act*, the main aim of which was to establish temporary feeding facilities instead of relief works. The new system, which became operational in May of that year, proposed to give the destitute a gratuitous supply of food - one meal a day at an estimated cost of 3d. A family of eight would thus get 2/- worth of food for their daily support. The Soup Kitchens were opened in various localities and were principally supported by private subscriptions. In Upper Leyny alone nine soup kitchens were kept in operation at a weekly expenditure of £75. In the district of Achonry, containing 20,000 souls, one half were receiving rations in June, 1847. That Summer there were 53,000, or almost half of the population of

THE GREAT FAMINE

| RETURNS FROM TEMPORARY FEVER HOSPITALS | | | |
|---|---|---|---|
| | | 12.10.47 | 04.02.48 |
| Carney: | (James Barber, Steward) | 56 | 38 |
| Collooney: | (Wm. Armstrong, Steward) | 118 | 84 |
| Coolaney: | (Thomas Church, Steward) | 62 | 52 |
| Skreen: | (George Wayne, Steward) | 22 | 41 |

the Sligo Union , receiving rations daily. In the Lissadell district 87 out of every 100 were in receipt of such rations. John Delaney, a Sligo merchant, who operated a bakery close to the Quays, opened a Soup Kitchen fitted with two boilers. Up to three hundred destitute people were daily in receipt of one quart of 'nourishing' soup, thanks to Delaney's generosity. Between November, 1847 and April, 1848, the British Relief Association contributed £3,500 in feeding school children in the Sligo Union. The soup kitchen scheme, as such, ended in September, 1847. At its peak the scheme fed three million a day countrywide and reached most areas of need.

# Fever

Previous famines in Ireland had been accompanied by fever and the Great Famine was no exception. Reports of fever began to come into the Relief Commissioners in early 1847; people were dying quickly, in frightful numbers, and typhus was spreading like wildfire. The Workhouse hospitals were far too small to deal with the numbers pouring in. Almost every inmate was suffering with some form of illness, but there was no space to keep the sick away from those free of fever. At the height of the epidemic scores of unfortunate fever-ridden men and women might be seen lying on wads of straw along the road from the Calry Church to Ballinode, waiting their turn to be received into one of the roofed structures. In an effort to cope with the worsening situation, temporary wooden fever wards, called 'fever sheds' , were erected in the grounds of the Workhouse at Ballytivnan. When this measure failed to cope with the worsening emergency, temporary Fever Hospitals were opened in Carney, Collooney, Coolaney, Gurteen, Skreen and Tubbercurry, which together catered

THE GREAT FAMINE

for from four to five hundred inmates.

In March, 1847, the *"Champion"* reported as follows: "The rapid increase of infectious distempers throughout this Town and County is truly alarming . . . In the Town this deadly disease is hourly increasing. Nor is this to be wondered at; one day last week a hundred pauper families flocked into Sligo in a state of the most appalling destitution and took shelter in those wretched hovels in the suburbs . . . With the approach of warmer weather and the pauper population becomes more dense, contagious diseases will also increase". [14] A month later it was reported that there were more than 1,000 fever patients within the Borough, and the Town was infected by droves of strange beggars from neighbouring counties. In June the *"Journal"* stated that the terrible malady had in no way abated - a number of new cases were reported weekly, hospitals were overflowing and no further patients could be admitted. In addition, groups of wandering mendicants could be seen daily lying in public places. [15] In an effort to prevent the further spread of fever, Humphrey Gillmor, a Board of Health official, was given the task of inspecting the dwellings of the poor throughout the Town with a view to having them cleaned and whitewashed. He was also empowered to round up wandering mendicants and have them imprisoned or ran out of town. The *"Champion"* went so far as to suggest that all fever cases should be removed to temporary huts erected at a remote location. [16] The numbers who died of fever, probably ten times more than those who died of hunger, will never be known. Thousands simply disappeared, never reaching hospitals or workhouses. Where bodies were buried at all, it was rarely in churchyards but in unmarked hillside graves.

## Black '47

In January, 1847, the Mayor, Andrew Walker, convened a meeting in the Courthouse for the purpose of raising subscriptions for the relief of the poor. Several substantial donations were received from local merchants, headed by Peter O'Connor and Edward Kelly, £100 each, and the said Andrew Walker, £30. Later that month the *"Champion"* published a letter from Dominick Noone, C.C., Grange, in which it was stated that in the western part of Ahamlish there were 425 families,

## THE GREAT FAMINE

numbering 2,278 souls, almost all of whom were in absolute want and had no employment under the Relief Works, save 187, and the indications were that this number would shortly be reduced to 110. Continuing with his account, Noone wrote: -

*"No language can give a description of the awful state of the people, many of whom have not eaten one regular meal for the last three weeks, they are plucking up the stumps of cabbages and carrying them away, and many of them are known to search for the wild herbs of the fields. The people are dying in scores in this district and there is no plan in place to relieve their wants - save the efforts of Ormsby Jones of Streedagh, who supplies his neighbours with Indian meal..."* [17]

In February, the *"Champion"* reported five deaths from starvation in the Drumcliffe area in the course of a week. One of the victims was a Mary Conway whose family had been in a starving state for over three weeks. The day before her death she set out on foot for Sligo to purchase a little food. On the following morning she was found dead on the roadside with a half-stone bag of meal grasped firmly in her hands. The Coroner's verdict : "Died from exposure to cold and previous want of the necessities of life". In a subsequent issue the paper carried a report that there were upwards of thirty corpses in cruedly made coffins on the roadside at Dunfore, in the same parish, awaiting the arrival of the Coroner. On February 26th the *"Champion"* editoralised as follows on the worsening situation: " The sufferings of our unhappy people are beyond description. Every hour the calamity is increasing." As time progressed coroner's inquests no longer afforded anything like a true account of the misery that prevailed as hundreds of unfortunate creatures died of starvation or fever upon whom inquests were no longer held. In the words of the *"Champion"* "they were hurried to the grave coffinless and shroudless, and so great is the mortality that ancient customs are forgotten and we now see no such thing as a well attended funeral. Everything about us would lend one to suppose we are in the midst of a dread plague..."

By mid March, 1847, the County was reduced to a condition almost too deplorable to be adequately described. [18] In Ahamlish deaths from starvation  averaged seven a day. Conditions elsewhere were equally apalling - contagion and famine were claiming hundreds by the week. "Kilfree is now a plague spot and were it not for the immense aid which the zealous and indefatigable Parish Priest, Peter Brennan, was able to

291

## THE GREAT FAMINE

afford from charitable donations, mostly from England, the distress would be multiplied tenfold - there being no grain and the people living upon cabbages and turnips".[19] In October it was estimated that there were 1,000 starving and unemployed paupers in Cloonoghill, 825 in Kilturra and 781 in Kilshalvey.[20] Details of deaths from starvation were weekly reported upon in the local newspapers. During the Spring of 1847 the *"Sligo Champion"* published what it called "Our Catalogue of Horror", names and addresses of the victims of starvation and fever where inquests had been conducted by either Alexander Burrows or Meredith Thompson, the County Coroners.

Conditions in Kilturra and Kilshalvey in South Sligo were highlighted by the Reverend John Garrett, Vicar of Emlaghfad, in a letter to the Relief Commission in Dublin, dated August 1847, in which he vigorously protested at the proposed reduction of rations from 1,000 to 134 in one fell swoop. "Fever and dysentery have carried off the heads of families in great numbers and the strongest, who were the chief support of their families, emigrated to escape the contagion", he wrote, "leaving behind feeble children and elderly parents unable to labour and totally depending on rations. It is a sad and most painful duty that we all have to discharge - to cast into starvation thousands of poor feeble families just recovering from fever and without a morsel of food until the new Poor Law is in operation." In the adjacent parish of Kilfree fever and dysentery were carrying off the population by the dozen, while absentee landlords, De Freyne and Cadell in particular, were serving processes of ejectment and had lately levelled several houses. [21]

In February, 1847, Captain O'Brien of the Board of Works paid a visit to the Knocklane area of North Sligo, in the company of Sir Robert Gore-Booth, and subsequently penned the following graphic account of what he had witnessed: -

*"The first place I visited was a wretched hamlet of three cottages with out-houses containing three families numbering in all 32 persons which belonged to three brothers. The whole having lived on 12 acres which they had inherited from the father who when a young man had obtained a lease for a period of lives. They lived on the potatoes. They drew fuel from a neighbouring bog for which they paid little or nothing and they paid for the rent by raising a little corn and by the sale of a pig. Last year they thought themselves so well off that they refused*

The SLIGO FAMINE MEMORIAL, depicting an Emigrant Family, unveiled at Lr. Quay Street, July 1997.

## THE GREAT FAMINE

*to take £60 to give up their lease -now they are starving.*

*One of the brothers and three others of the family had died during the previous weeks. The widow was lying on the ground in fever and unable to move. The children were bloated in their faces and belllies and their limbs were withered to bones and sinues, with rags on them which scarcely preserved decency and assuredly afforded no protection from the weather. They had been found that day gnawing the flesh and bones of a pig that had died in an out-house.*

*Sir Robert then took me to a place covered by sand and containing sixty cabins or huts and housing, on average, a family of five. It was impossible to enter without crawling on hands and knees I went into a number of these cabins indiscriminantly just as they were in our path.*

*In the first into which I crawled with difficulty lay a coffin holding the owner's wife, who had died three days before of want. The owner stood near to the door having come from the public works where he had been earning 8p a day, to see to burying his wife, and he told me he was about to depart to dig a hole to put her in and try and get a couple of men from the works to help him carry her there. A skeleton of a living child was in a craddle in a corner near the turf. A woman, a neighbour, was sitting by it and rocking the craddle and said it would be dead by morning, and added, 'truly, it would be better if we were all dead'. The child's craddle and a broken table, these were the entire furniture. The door of the second cabin we came to was shut. We called and knocked. A voice answered from within. The door gradually opened and out of the hole appeared the head of a man. By degrees we saw his body as he crawled into the light and knelt down in the doorway his head touching the upper framing, that is the eves of the roof. His face and lips were colourless, his entire clothing consisted of a dirty coarse shirt in shreds. When he saw us he called out 'send for the priest, I'll be gone before morning, I am dying of starvation'.*

*In answer to our question, he said he could do nothing, he could not go to the works. His belly was all swelled, he had bad pains down his back. Sir Robert asked him if he had anyone to send to the meal depot two miles away. He called a little girl to the hut and while awaiting directions as to where to obtain half a stone of meal, the man cried out, 'Can you give me any bread?, I'll be dead before the meal comes'... This was no isolated case."*

Contrary to general belief, the potato crop of 1847 was not affected by blight, because weather conditions were too dry, but the crop itself, though sound, was far too small to make any difference to the ongoing

## THE GREAT FAMINE

tragedy. In February, 1848, Captain Gilbert, Inspector to the Poor Law Commissioners, commented as follows on the prospects for the new crop in County Sligo ;-

*"In travelling through the country I regret to see so little preparation by the farmers for the ensuing crops; scarcely anything is doing except by large landed proprietors. There are still extensive haggards of corn perceptible in every electoral division; the small tenants complain that they have not the means of preparing their ground nor corn to sow ... The potatoes are now getting scarce in the markets; but I believe that those who have them can live without disposing of them, or making use of them, are hoarding them for planting in the spring, and that the markets are merely supplied by small farmers who are obliged to sell for subsistence, and not having manure nor any means of preparing manure necessary for planting them. I find that the potatoes planted in the autumn and those that are now in the pits, are tolerably free from the late disease".* [22]

Later that month the *"Champion"* painted a gloomy picture of the prevailing distress:-

*"The misery which the people are now enduring beggars all description. From all quarters we hear the most lamentable accounts. Persons who were last year enjoying comparative wealth - who had, at least, the means of keeping the wolf from the door, are now reduced to the lowest ebb of want and destitution. The Guardians of the Sligo Union are, to do them justice, endeavouring , to the best of their ability, to supply the wants of the destitute . . . However, those under the control of the Boyle and Ballina Unions are not so fortunate. In Kilturra and Kilshalvey, for example, no out-door relief is afforded and a great majority of the inhabitants are, at this instant, living solely upon turnips and the supply of this watery, unsubstantial food will soon be exhausted. Last week three people died for want of food".* [23]

In all areas dysentery prevailed to a considerable extent, especially where famine was rampant. Despite their sufferings the poorer classes exhibited a great repugnance to entering the Workhouse, preferring the alternative of subsisting daily on a chance meal of shellfish or garbage of the most pernicious kind.

In August, 1848, the *"Champion"* carried the dreaded news: "LOSS OF THE POTATO CROP". "A tremendous calamity has just fallen upon us. The Potato crop is gone; of this there can be no doubt. It is with sorrow we announce that the disease has set in with the greatest virulence. Fields which were perfectly sound on Sunday were, on our

## THE GREAT FAMINE

revisiting them, in the short space of three days quite withered and black. The blight has arrived; the crop is destroyed and the awful fact bursts upon us that we are on the eve of another year of famine".[24]

---

Deaths from Starvation, week-ending January 9th, 1847 as per Inquests conducted by Alexander Burrows, Coroner, in the Barony of Tirerril:

**Mary Cunningham**    **of Carrickbanagher:** "died for want of sufficient food".

**James M'Garry**    **of Ardcurly:** "died of insufficiency of food and clothing to support life".

**Patrick Ward**    **of Tawnagh:** "deceased came to his death by starvation".

**Michael Kilmartin**    **of Ummeryroe:** "deceased came by his death by starvation".

**Bridget McDermott**    **of Doonsheheen:** "died of want of food".

**Patrick Dyer**    **of Ardagh:** "died of starvation and want of proper clothing".

**Edward Tighe, John Tighe, Ann Tighe of Aghanagh:** brothers and sister, "died of starvation and want of proper clothing".

**Thomas McManus**    **of Kilmactranny:** "deceased came to his death by hunger and cold".

*Sligo Champion 16.1.'47*

---

# The Landlords

There has been much debate and not a little disagreemant on the role of landlords in Famine times. The situation varied greatly throughout the country. As regards County Sligo, it can be stated that most resident proprietors assisted their tenants to a greater or lesser degree by providing employment on their estates, subscribing generously to Relief Committees, importing food to feed hungry tenants and, in a few instances, providing financial assistance to those wishing to emigrate. Fortunately, a majority of the larger landlords

# THE GREAT FAMINE

were residing in the County, notable exceptions being Lord Palmerston and William Ormsby-Gore. These apart, the estates of the absentee landlords were located, for the most part, in the south of the County and in the Barony of Coolavin in particular. Landlords such as De Freyne and Cadell, and their agents, acted very inhumanely towards their tenantry, in some cases even evicting in the midst of famine and pestilence.

## SIR ROBERT GORE-BOOTH , Lissadell:

On the outbreak of the Famine he employed 200 men at 1/- a day, and as the situation worsened every able-bodied tenant on his extensive properties in North Sligo and Ballymote was profitably occupied. He spent in the region £9,000 on the purchase of food and paid the passage of 1,122  emigrants on chartered vessels to New Brunswick, at a cost of £6,000.

## MAJOR CHARLES O'HARA, Annaghmore:

He gave employment to 350 men as well as supplying needy tenants with a liberal provision of oatmeal. In October, 1846, and January, 1847, he imported cargoes of Indian corn and wheaten flour for local distribution. At Christmas, 1848, he supplied one hundred families with bread and meat as well as a gallon of beer each, together with a supply of blankets to the more needy. Between 1841 and 1846 he filled the onerous position of Chairman of the Poor Law Guardians, Sligo Union.

## JANE PERCEVAL, Templehouse:

The wife of Colonel Alexander Perceval, M.P. worked diligently with her daughters in bringing succour and relief to needy tenants. She employed fifty women at needlework and fed twenty families daily. She died in January, 1847, from typhus caught on visits to the homes of the poor.

## JOHN WYNNE, Hazelwood:

One of the most extensive landlords in the County, who was Chairman of both the Sligo Union and the local Relief Committee, was most

THE GREAT FAMINE

sympathetic to the plight of the poor not only in his own area but throughout the Union. In the words of the *"Champion"* he "evinced a desire to stand by the people in the emergency".[25] He was a prominent contributor to the funds of the various Relief Committtees, and regularly purchased potatoes and other foodstuffs at the Sligo market for distribution to those most in need. He expended £1,000 under the Land Improvement Act in the electoral divisions of Drumcliffe and Calry; paid out £1,000 a year to labourers on his estate and, in certain instances, gave assistance to emigrant families.

By and large the landlord class responded positively to the plight of their tenantry and strove to alleviate their general distress. As the calamity worsened and the income from rentals fell rapidly, the financial standing of some landed proprietors became rather precarious. Their economy was ruined and a number of estates ended up in the bankruptcy court in the post Famine years.

# Emigration

Sligo was one of the principal emigration ports on the western seaboard. Between 1750 and 1850 it was the focal point for emigrants from the North-West and served as an outlet for the neighbouring counties, in both Connacht and Ulster. In 1846, the year after the 'blight' appeared, there was a marked increase in the numbers emigrating through the Port. By June 3,800 had sailed to Canada alone and between October and December upwards of 3,000 more had followed. These unfortunates were the first of the panic-stricken thousands who fled the country after it became apparent that the potato crop had failed completely.

The Winter of 1846-47 dragged on, snow fell, the Public Works failed and food became unprocurable. For the first time ever emigration continued throughout the winter months. There were upwards of fourteen vessels in the Port in the first week of April. They were arriving daily with Indian corn and taking out emigrants on the return voyage, with an average of five or six sailings weekly for the United States and Canada. By the end of June, 1847, a total of 9,990 had left, an increase of 6,190 on the previous year. In October the

## THE GREAT FAMINE

*"Champion"* estimated that not less than 13,000 had emigrated in the preceeding months. [26]

A not insignificant element in the mass exodus of 1847 was Landlord Assisted Emigration. In addition to Sir Robert Gore-Booth who sent out three vessels, Lord Palmerston also transported up to 2,000 of his tenantry from North Sligo to Canada in nine vessels between March and October, 1847. One of the ships, *Carrick of Whitehaven*, foundered off Cape-de-Rosiers drowning 87 of the 135 emigrants on board. Between them, both Palmerston and Gore-Booth assisted in the clearance of over 3,000 souls from adjoining estates in the Parishes of Ahamlish and Drumcliffe in 'Black '47'.

Between 1841 and 1851 an estimated 34,190 emigrants sailed from Sligo. Accurate statistcs are available for the period 1847-1851, and these reveal that 24,557 passengers sailed on 162 vessels as follows:

| Year | No. of Vessels | Passenger Numbers |
|------|---------------|-------------------|
| 1847 | 64 | 13050 |
| 1848 | 24 | 3078 |
| 1849 | 38 | 3978 |
| 1850 | 19 | 2404 |
| 1851 | 17 | 2047 |

A break-down of the fore-going totals for the years 1847-1850 suggest that in:

| | | |
|------|------|------|
| 1847: | 11,904 | went to Canada; |
| | 1,146 | went to the U.S.A. |
| 1848: | 2,331 | went to Canada; |
| | 747 | went to the U.S.A. |
| 1849: | 2,313 | went to Canada; |
| | 1,665 | went to the U.S.A. |
| 1850: | 1,395 | went to Canada; |
| | 1,009 | went to the U.S.A. |

The late Martin Kelleher of Doocastle, a note historian and folklorist, stated that one of the sad effects of the Famine was the large number of imbeciles it left in its wake. "I often heard my father say that one could not go a mile of the road without meeting some 'softie'.

## THE GREAT FAMINE

Neighbours would be heard to comment: *"God help him - his brains went soft with the hunger"*. This was but one of the awful legacies of the Great Famine of a century and a half ago.

### Notes and References:

(1)  *"Sligo Champion"*          29-11-1845

(2)      *ibid*          25-10-1845

(3)      *ibid*          3-11-1845

(4)  *"Sligo Journal"*          24-4-1846

(5)  The following relief was received from the Society of Friends (Quakers) in 1847 : Two cargoes of Indian corn, valued at £1,850: one Boiler; £702 in cash and 7,806 lbs of seed. They also contributed £20 to each of the local Relief Committees.

(6)  *"Sligo Journal"*          21-8-1846

(7)      *ibid*          *opus cit.*

(8)  *"Sligo Champion"*          20-2-1847

(9)  Bennett, Wm. *"Six weeks in Ireland"*. London. 1847.

(10) *"Sligo Journal"*          4-9-1846

(11)     *ibid*          2-10-1846

(12) Messrs Stewart & Kincaid (Unpublished Papers)

(13)     *ibid*

(14) *"Sligo Champion"*          20-3-1847

(15) *"Sligo Journal"*          4-6-1847

(16) *"Sligo Champion"*          8-5-1847

(17)     *ibid*          30-1-1847

(18)     *ibid*          13-3-1847

(19)     *ibid*          19-6-1847

(20) *"Sligo Journal"*          23-10-1847

(21) **SEE** *"The Destitution Survey"* (Roscommon, 1997) for returns of Catholic clergy of the Diocese of Elphin concerning conditions in individual parishes, October, 1847.

(22) Parliamentary Papers 1847-1848. Vol. 54

(23) *"Sligo Champion"*          12-2-1848

(24)     *ibid*          19-8-1848

(25)     *ibid*          23-5-1846

(26) **SEE:** McTernan *"Memory Harbour"* (Sligo, 1992) for details on emigration from the Port of Sligo.

# The Sligo Workhouse and its 'Auxialaries'

The Irish Poor Law Act of 1838 divided the country into 130 Unions in each of which was built a Workhouse for the relief of the distressed. The Workhouses were administered by a Board of Guardians, consisting of representative ratepayers of the Union. Each Union was rated for the number of poor it sent to the Workhouse - half of which was to be paid by the tenants and half by the landlords. When the burden of paying the rate became too heavy for the tenants, an amendment exempted those rated at £4 or less. In order to qualify for relief under the Poor Law, those who held more than a quarter of an acre of land had to surrender it. Initially, indoor relief only was to be administered and no relief was granted to anyone who remained outside the Workhouse.

With the exception of those areas (a) in the Barony of Tireragh adjacent to Ballina, (b) in the Barony of Leyny close to Swinford and (3) in the baronies of Tirerill, Corran and Coolavin within a 10-mile radius or so of Boyle, the remainder of the County formed the Poor Law Union of Sligo.[1] The first election of Poor Law Guardians, who were charged with the administration of the Union, took place in August, 1839. The following were the successful candidates and the areas they represented:-[2]

| Electoral Division: | Elected: |
| --- | --- |
| Borough of Sligo: | OwenWynne, John Anderson. James Boyle, Knox Barrett. Henry O'Connor and James O Donnell. |
| Calry: | Richard B. Wynne. |
| Drumcliffe: | Follis Clarke and Richard Gethin. |
| Carney: | James Barber. |
| Lissadell: | Sir Robert Gore-Booth and John Gallagher. |
| Rossinver: | Patrick Lunny. |

301

## THE SLIGO WORKHOUSE AND ITS 'AUXILIARIES'

| | |
|---|---|
| Cliffoney: | P atrick McIntyre and William Gallagher. |
| Knocknarea: | John Delaney. |
| Kilmacowen: | William Phibbs. |
| Ballisodare: | James Simpson and William Phibbs. |
| Coolaney: | Thomas Smith and Henry Burrows. |
| Collooney: | Cooper Wm. Armstrong and Thomas Phibbs. |
| Ballintogher: | Thomas Mulrooney. |
| Ballinakill: | Abraham Martin. |
| Riverstown: | Arthur B. Cooper (jun.). |
| Drumfin: | Alexander Duke and Samuel Gilmor. |
| Ballymote: | George Dodwell and Philip Gormley. |
| Cloonoghill: | John Taaffe. |
| Cloonacool: | John Gray. |
| Tubbercurry: | John Brett, Walter Henry and Thomas Cooke. |
| Dromard: | Charles Beatty. |
| Skreen: | William Graham and John McMunn. |
| Templeboy: | Martin Burns. |

The newly elected Board of Guardians, numbering thirty-nine in all and predominantly Conservative in outlook, had their first meeting in the Grand Jury Room of the Courthouse in August, 1839 at which Charles Kean O'Hara was elected Chairman and John Martin, Vice-Chairman. Charles O'Connor was appointed Clerk of the Union at a salary of £60 per annum. Initially, the Guardians met once a month but during the Famine years weekly meetings became the norm.[3]

At their meeting in January, 1840, the Guardians decided to proceed with the building of a Workhouse to accommodate 1,200 inmates. The estimated cost was £11,000, all but £2,000 of which was to be borne by the Union. The contract was awarded to Messrs Kethside, and Robert O'Hara was appointed Clerk of Works. The site chosen was at Ballytivnan, between the Old Fair Green and Ash Lane, and was leased from Owen Wynne at £50 per annum. The *"Champion"* was very critical of the choice, claiming that it was "little more than a marsh". The building, quadrangular in shape, was designed by George

## THE SLIGO WORKHOUSE AND ITS 'AUXILIARIES'

Wilkinson and faced onto Ash Lane rather than the main Bundoran Road.[4] On its completion in November, 1841, the cost of building and furnishings came to £12,842., or 18% more than had been budgeted for. This gave rise to an inspection by the Commissioners appointed to investigate the execution of such contracts. In their subsequent Report they made the following observations:-

*"The site, though sloping, was not irregular, but had more consideration and circumspection been used in the first instance and the House been made to front the high road and been placed near it, the extra costs might have been altogether avoided and the drainage rendered more effective. The flagging was done at the particular request of the Guardians and the House has been considerably benefitted thereby . It has been so well built that it is classed at above average .."* [5]

In mid 1841 advertisements were published in the local press seeking applicants for the posts of Physician (salary £50 per annum); Master of the House (salary £50); Matron (£30); Porter (£15); Schoolmaster (£20) and Schoolmistress (£15). The first inmates, sixteen in number, were admitted on December 18th, 1841. Thereafter, there was a slow but steady influx of able-bodied but destitute people. As conditions quickly worsened in the Autumn of 1846, there was an unprecedented rush and by December the House was full and hundreds were turned away weekly for want of room.

### No. of Paupers in Sligo Workhouse, 1844 - '47

| Date: | | Able-Bodied: | Hospitalised: | Others: | Total: |
|-------|------|------|------|------|------|
| Nov. | 1844: | 97 | 45 | 261 | 403 |
| Nov. | 1845: | 106 | 48 | 262 | 416 |
| Nov. | 1846: | 230 | 157 | 700 | 1,087 |
| May | 1847: | 229 | 249 | 445 | 923 |
| March | 1848: | – | – | – | 1,707 |

Although the Famine had not yet reached its height, the Workhouse system was beginning to collapse under the demands being made upon it. Standards of care, already low, collapsed complely. Nevertheless, the slightest hope of food of any kind and shelter was enough to bring crowds to the gates,begging for admission. In the

# THE SLIGO WORKHOUSE AND ITS 'AUXILIARIES'

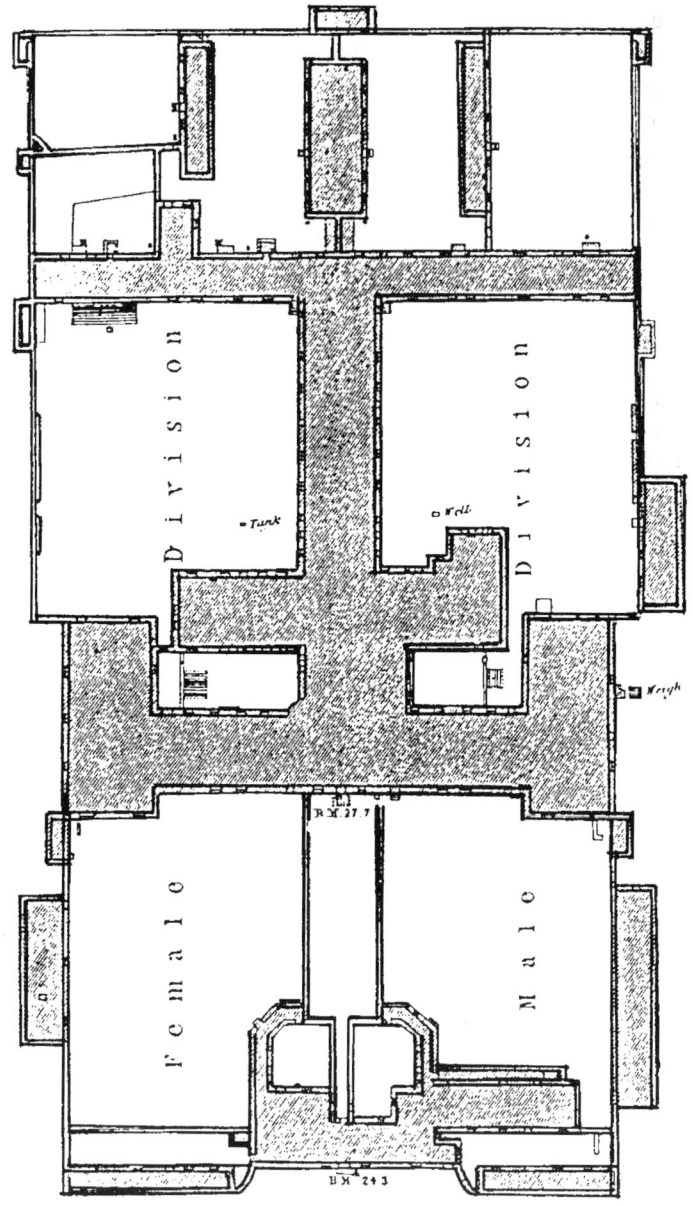

Ground Floor plan of the Workhouse

## THE SLIGO WORKHOUSE AND ITS 'AUXILIARIES'

Spring of 1847 fever and dysentery was sweeping the countryside and the inmates of the Workhouse did not escape. "The asylum for the poor in Sligo is nothing better than a pesthouse", commented the *"Sligo Champion"* in February, "and those who entered it have to brave both pestilence and death". A month later the situation had worsened and there were 500 ill with fever. "The conditions in the Poorhouse are becoming hourly more lamentable... Mrs. Charlton, the Matron, Mr. Evans, the Master and Mr. O'Connor, the Clerk of the Union, have all been carried off within the last few days by malignant typhus fever. The paid nurses are ill and the House is now one scene of confusion and pestilence..." [6] In addition, the principal entrances to the Town were crowded with people dying of fever and starvation. Captain Gilbert, following his appointment as temporary Inspector to the Poor Law Commissioners for the Union, submitted weekly reports on the the state of the Workhouse. The following extracts from his correspondence for the period November, 1847 to February, 1848, provide an inside view of the prevailing conditions as well as some of the remedies adopted to cope with conditions in what was an unprecedented situation and one that was worsening by the day. [7]

*Sligo. November 3, 1847.*

*In conformity with your instructions, I have inspected the workhouse of this Union, and attended yesterday the meeting of the Board of Guardians, having previously given orders to the collectors and relieving officers to attend also.*

*The poor-house I found extremely clean and well regulated, but containing more people than it was originally intended to hold. Several paupers went out, and a considerable number were admitted. There are now about 50 paupers more than the complement. Orders were given to send out 13 infirm old men and 130 widows and children to receive out-door relief, in order to make room for able-bodied men who have made applications to be admitted. There is a large building, an old Charter House, which has for some months been occupied as a temporary fever hospital. It was proposed yesterday that the patients, being now few in number, should be removed to the County Hospital, and the house made available for as many orphan children as it would contain. There are at present 360 in the poor-house, and the charter-house will hold about one-half. It is about half a mile from the poor-house, surrounded by a good wall; and if sheds*

## THE SLIGO WORKHOUSE AND ITS 'AUXILIARIES'

*were erected in the yard, or an addition made to the house, the whole of the orphans could be removed to make room for able-bodied paupers.*

*There are between 400 and 500 children, besides the orphans, in the poor-house; and I strongly recommend that some temporary buildings or sheds should be erected within the walls of the poor-house to contain the whole of the children.*

*The present heavy debt, being nearly £10,000, almost precludes the possibility of erecting any new buildings without the co-operation and entire assistance of the Commisioners.*

*Sligo. November 10, 1847.*

*I attended yesterday the meeting of the Board of Guardians at the poor-house From the number of applicants to be admitted into the poor-house, distress must be rapidly increasing; nearly 100 paupers were refused admittance for want of room. I have strongly urged on the Guardians the absolute necessity of erecting temporary sheds immediately for the male and female children by day; also sheds as temporary day-rooms for the men and women; by which means these four apartments might be converted into dormitories; a nursery is also very much required, and must, if possible, be erected.*

*Sligo.November 24, 1847.*

*"I beg leave to report for the information of the Commissioners, that I attended the meeting of the Guardians at the poor house yesterday. The day previous, 130 old and infirm people, with their children, were sent out of the house and placed on out-door relief, to make room for the able-bodied, of which class 250 were admitted; the poor-house is at this moment containing upwards of 200 more than it ought, or can conveniently accommodate. The house was surrounded by several hundreds anxious for relief; of the able-bodied some were admitted, and the remainder were ordered out-door relief until Friday, when an adjourned meeting of the Guardians will be held. Contracts are entered into for the erection of sheds for the boys' and girls' schools, and the present school-rooms will be converted into dormitories for the able-bodied paupers, as soon as the sheds are completed which will be in about a fortnight. The Charter House, which I have mentioned in my former reports, is at last in possession of the Guardians, and is undergoing cleansing and repairs for the accommodation of about 350 orphan children, and which will be also ready in a fortnight."*

## THE SLIGO WORKHOUSE AND ITS 'AUXILIARIES'

```
┌─────────────────────────────────────────────────────────────┐
│                                                               │
│        SLIGO UNION STATISTICS, 1841 - 1850                    │
│                                                               │
│   Persons admitted to Workhouse: ........................  31,021  │
│                                                               │
│   Number Discharged:          ........................  25,321  │
│                                                               │
│   Number Died:                ........................   2,530  │
│                                                               │
│   Highest No. in Workhouse & Auxiliaries:                     │
│        (July 3rd, 1849)       ........................   4,075  │
│                                                               │
│   Highest No. on Out-door Relief:                             │
│        (July 21st, 1849)      ........................   9,866  │
│                                                               │
│   Total of rates levied on Union:  ...................  £71,425  │
│                                                               │
│   Amount due for Buildings:   ........................  £15,910  │
│                                                               │
│                        "Sligo Champion" 1-6-1850              │
└─────────────────────────────────────────────────────────────┘
```

*Sligo . December 22, 1847.*

*"I attended the meeting of the Board of Guardians for this Union yesterday. The poor-house was as usual, surrounded by paupers, mostly able-bodied, who were exceedingly clamorous for relief; 542 were admitted, who entirely filled the new sheds and other accommodation afforded by the removal of the orphan children to the house provided for them.*

*From the crowded state of the house, fever and dysentery are on the increase; and two additional fever sheds are to be erected immediately to meet this advance of disease.*

*It has been found very difficult to carry out the system of the New Poor Law from the laxity of the Guardians, a few of whom only can be made attend.*

*Mr. Wynne, the Chairman, Mr. Wood, and some few more gentlemen, deserve the highest credit for their assiduity and labour, meeting at 11.00 o'clock in the morning, and from that hour until 7 o'clock and late in the evening, perseveringly endeavouring to perform the very onerous duties imposed on them, and meeting frequently more than twice the same week, with the most indefatigable spirit".*

## The Sligo Workhouse And Its 'Auxiliaries'

*Sligo. February 9, 1848.*

*"I regret I cannot report favourable on the state of this Poorhouse. I attended the meeting of the Guardians yesterday, and the medical report laid before the Board was very unsatisfactory. There were 29 new cases of fever, all of which were removed into the County Fever Hospital and 57 new cases of dysentery.*

*During the month of January I am sorry to say there were 109 deaths in the house; and whilst the Guardians were assembled yesterday, the assistant matron was taken to the Fever Hospital in a very precarious state".*

*Sligo. February 23, 1848.*

*In forwarding to you the proceedings at the meeting of the Board of Guardians yesterday, I beg leave to state for the information of the Commissioners that there are now upwards of 1,800 in the house, and about 7,300 getting out-door relief.*

*I regret still to report unfavourably of the sickness in the house; there were 35 deaths last week; out of that number 31 were children, who died from measles and dysentery, and the four adults from dropsy and old age. There were 25 new cases of fever which were removed to the County Fever Hospital, and 46 cases of dysentery; this latter disease appears to be increasing.*

*The Charter House, the property of Mr. Wynne of Hazelwood and now occupied by the orphan children, is free of rent, and will be so for the next two years. There is a large shed attached to the premises, which for £30 or £40 will make excellent school-rooms, and a dining hall, and they will be commenced immediately.*

*There are two fields in the rear of the house, also the property of Mr. Wynne, which the Guardians have taken at a moderate rent; and the boys will be taught gardening and field operations. This will not only be advantageous to the boys themselves, but by selling the produce will considerable more that pay the rent.*

\*　　\*　　\*　　\*　　\*　　\*

At the best of times, the Workhouse was a grim institution. Families were torn apart, as men and women lived in different sections and children were seperated from their parents. The food, consisting of two meals a day of oatmeal, potatoes and buttermilk, was often poorly cooked and stale. The conditions for entry were so strict that most people only went there as a last resort. It was reported that many of the small farmers in the Ballymote and Tubbercurry areas would rather starve than give up their holdings and go to the Workhouse. However, for a great majority of the starving and destitute people it was the only place of refuge.

The operation of the Poor Laws in the Sligo Union were described in some detail by John Wynne, Chairman of the Union 1846 - 1850, before a Select Committee in May, 1849. In the course of his evidence he stated:-

*"The able-bodied within the Union did try on several occasions to fill the Workhouse with a view to obtaining out-door relief. On two successive days I myself signed admissions for 1,150. Of those only 350 accepted relief in the Workhouse. We gave out-door relief to all the infirm and sick who applied for it. We cleared all the infirm wards and left none in the House.*

*According as distress increased in the Union we found it necessary to increase in-door relief, and as it increased we then put out widows with one or more children; the only exception we made were the orphans; we did not place them on out-door relief, instead we hired an additional house for them . . We never gave out-door relief to the able-bodied.*

*In July, 1848, 10,053 were in receipt of out-door relief, and 1,882 on in-door, but these decreased rapidly until the end of the year when the former dropped to 994 by December 2nd. The numbers have increased again this season, but we did not find it necessary to give out-door relief to the able-bodied.*

*There are a vast number of women, deserted by their husbands, on our list. We have at present 124 deserted women with 278 children, which is, we think, one of the most grievous parts of the whole system - that the husband either runs away to Scotland or England, and earns 10s or 12s. a week and leaves his whole family to be supported in the Workhouse. There is a decidedly growing evil that women professing to have been deserted seek relief. We see more and more of it everyday. The more determined we are to admit everybody to the Workhouse the more the able-bodied abscond and leave us their wives and families to support".[8]*

# AUXILIARY WORKHOUSES

As already mentioned, the Workhouse at Ballytivnan was unable to cope with the numbers seeking admission at the height of the Famine.

## THE SLIGO WORKHOUSE AND ITS 'AUXILIARIES'

In an effort to meet this demand, and at the same alleviate the problem of chronic overcrowding, the Poor Law Guardians leased a number of large buildings, mostly empty Corn Stores, which they had adapted to house children and orphans. In May, 1850, a correspondent from the *"Sligo Champion"* visited the different Auxiliaries and reported as follows:

# Charter House, The Mall: *

"In this place you see the use of a Poor Law. It is the refuge for children of both sexes under twelve years of age, who have been either deserted by their parents or are orphans. Captain Gilbert's gymnastic folly is in force in this establishment as well as in the main house. There are two schools; the female school appears to be well conducted. We had not an opportunity of hearing any of the classes in the boys' school examined, owing to the absence of the master, who had to attend the Workhouse on duty. He also acts as school master, though we think the two offices incompatible. The Guardians are in possession of a considerable piece of land behind the house, where there is, at present, the finest and the largest field of flax we have ever seen. Potatoes and various vegetables are also planted, but it appears that the young thieves, with which Sligo is infested, sometimes pay the place a visit.

The Charter House is beautifully situated, and nothing can be more delightful than the scenery to be witnessed from both the front and rear of it. Indeed, the young children could not be sent to a more healthy place; we may observe that the house is kept with great neatness, but this remark applies to all the poorhouses."

# Quay Street Auxiliary:

"This house, (formerly a corn store), is situated at the Old Quay quite close to the river. It has now upwards of 600 inmates but is capable of accommodating 1,000. The paupers in this auxiliary are all female adults. When you enter, you observe groups of strong women sitting here and there doing nothing but waiting for their dinner. What is to be done with them? Are they to remain there during their life-time? Is there no plan by which their condition could be bettered and the Union saved the cost of their maintenance? Every woman in it is able to earn her bread if she were placed in a way to do it.

* Built c. 1752 as an Erasmus Smith School, it operated as such until 1833.
It now forms part of the Grammar School.

Sooner or later some scheme must be laid down to better their own condition in life and at the same time, relieve the ratepayers.

Some of the women were engaged in spinning and knitting but not the one sixth, there being little or nothing to do, as sufficient frieze has not been manufactured to last all the houses for twelve months to come.

This house is kept in excellent order, and it is remarkable that not a single case of cholera occurred in it. We attribute this, under God, to the admirable state of the sewers and the excellent supply of the very purest and best water. When the tide is in, the sea flushes the sewers, and, twice in the twenty four hours, carries away all impurities."

## John Street Auxiliary:

"In this establishment there are three hundred and forty two boys, beyond fifteen years, doing nothing. They are herded together like so many cattle. There is no school; no employment, idleness is the predominant feature of the place - its besetting sin. From the rising sun in the east to its sinking in the western ocean - during a long, long June day, they spend their time in profitless, demoralising indolence. The master, (who is a kind,well-meaning, good hearted man,) assured us that the boys were most willing to work - most willing to do anything they were put to, and that nothing weighed so heavily upon them as the tedious hours of their unoccupied time. They are quiet, docile and obedient, yet, at the period of life when their minds are as wax to receive an impression and as steel to retain, they are neglected, abandoned, and forgotten. They do not work, neither can they want. Yet they are willing to labour; to give a hard day's toil in return for the scanty bit they receive. Why not seek out some mode of employment for them? Why leave them together like so many beasts of the field; untaught, unoccupied; at liberty to follow the bent of their own inclinations and run riot? - Can no effort be made to save them? Are those children of sorrow doomed? Will they never know the exquisite luxury of carving their own bread? Shall their youth - the prime of their existence, be wasted away, in demoralising idleness within the gloomy walls of an Auxiliary Work-house?"

## Wine Street Auxiliary:

"In this house we find a number of children of both sexes; they are well cared and well attended to. A schoolmaster of considerable ability instructs them. He is a pauper; though well informed he could not earn enough outside of the house to support him. So much for the profession of letters! We think he has a claim upon the

Guardians and that his honest and useful labour should be rewarded by increased rations and a small salary.

The house is inferior to none in the manner in which it is kept. But it is useless to praise any of them for their cleanliness, regularity, and order; they are in this respect perfect."

## Ballincar Lunatic Auxiliary:

"This is the refuge for the incurable lunatics. Poor, harmless creatures! Some of them sit from the time they are brought out in the morning until they retire to bed at night, basking in the sunshine. You cannot say they live, they only vegetate; they possess a horrible existence between life and death; their senses paralysed; their minds gone, everything lost in the wreck of intellect; they are terrible memorials of human infirmity and human weakness.

Thank God, that those, his afflicted, helpless creatures, are not utterly abandoned. What charity could do for them has been done. In the quiet, comfortable well-regulated asylum provided for them they can end their days in peace."

\* \* \* \* \* \*

In February, 1849, there were 3,140 inmates receiving in-door relief - 1,920 adults in the Workhouse and Fever Hospitals[9] and 1,220 in the Auxiliary Workhouses, mostly children and orphans. The following year the numbers on in-door relief were substantially reduced. However, it took four or five years more before the numbers in the Workhouse had been reduced to pre-Famine levels of between 400 and 500 inmates. It was not until the mid 1850's that the awful effects of the 'Great Hunger' and the people's dependence on the Poor Laws for shelter and sustenance had been significantly reduced.

# SLIGO UNION

The following are the number of persons who received relief in the Sligo Union, during the week ended Saturday the 27th January, 1849:

| No. | Electoral Divisions | Indoor | |
|-----|---------------------|--------|---------|
| | **Outdoor** | | |
| 1. | Sligo | 482 | 718 |
| 2. | Ballisodare | 122 | 437 |
| 3. | Ballintogher | 142 | 228 |
| 4. | Ballinakill | 150 | 298 |
| 5. | Ballymote | 176 | 451 |
| 6. | Calry | 19 | 97 |
| 7. | Carney | 40 | 68 |
| 8. | Cliffoney | 19 | 34 |
| 9. | Coolaney | 178 | 401 |
| 10. | Collooney | 179 | 296 |
| 11. | Cloonoghil | 92 | 408 |
| 12. | Cloonacool | 98 | 182 |
| 13. | Drumcliff | 40 | 106 |
| 14. | Drumfin | 150 | 395 |
| 15. | Dromard | 80 | 206 |
| 16. | Knocknarea | 34 | 77 |
| 17. | Kilmacowen | 68 | 151 |
| 18. | Lissadell | 74 | 312 |
| 19. | Rossinver | 15 | 25 |
| 20. | Riverstown | 140 | 294 |
| 21. | Skreen | 107 | 285 |
| 22. | Tubbercurry | 203 | 447 |
| 23. | Templeboy | 84 | 200 |
| | Union at Large | 303 | 420 |
| | **Total** | **3055** | **6669** |

The Union Workhouse, Dromore West, as it stands to-day. The Workhouses at Sligo and Tubbercurry have been demolished.

THE SLIGO WORKHOUSE AND ITS 'AUXILIARIES'

## WORKHOUSES - COUNTY SLIGO

| Dromore West: | Building Costs: | £4,650 |
|---|---|---|
| | Fittings, etc.: | 815 |
| | Site Acreage: | 7.2 |
| | Accommodation: | 800 |
| | | |
| Sligo: | Building Costs: | £10,875 |
| | Fittings: | £1,910 |
| | Site Acreage: | 9 |
| | Accommodation: | 1,200 |
| | | |
| Tubbercurry: | Building Costs: | £4,650 |
| | Fittings, etc.: | £1,220 |
| | Site Acreage: | 12 |
| | Accommodation: | 500 |


## AUXILIARY WORKHOUSES

1. Charter School: The Mall (now Grammar School):
   Accommodation - 350 orphans.

2. Old Quay: formerly a Grain Store:
   Accommodation - 600-900 females.

3. John Street: Grain Store leased from Andrew Black:
   Accommodation - 340 boys.

4. Wine Street: Henry O'Connor's Store:
   Accommodation - 200-300

5. Temple Street: James Henry's Store at rear of the Market Yard:
   Accommodation - 500.

6. Ballincar: An asylum for mentally affected paupers:
   Accommodation - 50.

# An Irish Workhouse *

"The workhouses in Ireland being of immense size, appear to have been designed with a view to render them picturesque, and to diminish the appearance of their real magnitude; the rooms are placed in double width, to insure effective superintendence. The style of most of the buildings is that of the domestic Gothic, being best suited for the materials available in their construction, the walls being built with rubble masonry, which would have required more dressing and cut stonework had the Italian or common domestic style of buildings been adopted. The use of the dirty and perishable 'rough-casting' or 'dashing', so common in Ireland, appears to have been avoided as much as possible. The buildings, by their arrangement, are capable of being extended in various ways; and the houses, as constructed, are considered only as portions of buildings, planned to a larger scale, according to drawings which were deposited with the clerk of the Union.

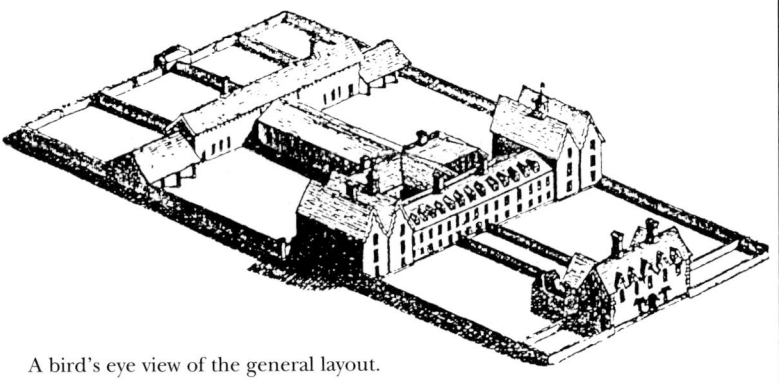

A bird's eye view of the general layout.

The workhouse may be considered to consist of four separate structures, containing as follows:- The entrance building, which contains the waiting hall for paupers applying for admission, and the porter; - the board room on the upper floor in which the Guardians meet and determine the admission of applicants for relief; - the

## THE SLIGO WORKHOUSE AND ITS 'AUXILIARIES'

probationary wards, with four separate yards for containing those paupers when admitted; and who are here examined by the medical officer, and washed in a bath supplied with hot and cold water.

Paupers affected by any disease are retained in these wards until in a fit state to go into the body of the house. Previously, however, they are deprived of their old clothes, which are fumigated, and deposited for return (if required), and they are then dressed in a comfortable suit of the workhouse clothing. The main building contains, in the centre, the master's and matron's apartments, around which are the store-rooms, the kitchen and workhouse, the school-rooms for boys and girls separate, and the several wards, to which they command immediate access.

The third division contains the dining-hall and kitchen and washhouse; buildings which are all arranged in connection with the yards of the paupers employed or having access thereto, so as to avoid passages and other separations which interfere with proper classification.

The infirmary is a distinct building, and conveniently placed for access; on each side is a building reserved for male and female idiots - a class of inmates unprovided for in buildings of the kind in England, and whose location here greatly relieves the lunatic institutions of the country.

The upper floor of the buildings contains dormitories, from which the paupers are excluded in the daytime. The arrangement for sleeping is entirely novel, and for such large buildings infinitely beyond the arrangement of bedsteads, - the advantages of which are detailed in the architect's report to the Poor Law Commission, as contained in the annual report for 1841, in which the bedsteads that are used are also described, and are of a kind different from those used in any other buildings, and very conducive to order and cleanliness."

Extract form Hall's *"Ireland: its Scenery and Character"*. London. 1841-43.

## THE SLIGO WORKHOUSE AND ITS 'AUXILIARIES'

### *Notes and References:-*

(1)  In 1847 the number of Poor Law Unions nationwide were increased from 130 to 162. In accordance with the terms of the Act two additional Unions were formed in County Sligo, namely, Tubbercurry and Dromore West. Small to medium sized Workhouses were built at both locations in 1850 - 1851, at which time the worst of the Famine had passed.

(2)  At the next election in March, 1841, not all the divisions were contested and the only changes in representation were as follows :

| | |
|---|---|
| KNOCKNARE A: | Mathew Walsh. |
| COLLOONEY: | Bryan O. Cogan. |
| BALLINTOGHER: | Edward L. Neynoe. |
| DRUMFIN: | Henry Milmoe. |
| BALLYMOTE: | Francis Mc Donagh. |
| CLOONOGHILL: | Charles O'Connor. |
| TUBBERCURRY: | John Armstrong and Jones Irwin. |

(3)  Between 1839 and 1842 the press was excluded from meetings. As a result, and the loss of official records for the period 1839 - 1848, all that is known of the proceedings is whatever was released to the *"Champion"* and the *"Journal"*.

(4)  The Workhouse stood on the site of the present St. John's Hospital and was demolished in the 1960's. In 1855-'56 a new entrance, together with a Gate Lodge, was opened onto the Bundoran Road and a boundary wall built around the 9 - acre site.

(5)  *"Parliamentary Papers".*                    Vol. 30. 1844.

(6)  *"Sligo Champion"*                             20-3-1847

(7)  *"British Parlliament Papers - Famine (Ireland)",* Vols. 2 - 3. Shannon. 1970.

(8)  *"Select Committee on Poor Laws (Ireland),"* 1849.

(9)  There were small fever hospitals operating at Carney, Collooney, Coolaney, Skreen and Tubbercurry.

# Memoirs of a Policeman*

Samuel A. Waters, the son of an R.I.C. Constable, and grandson of William E. Waters, one of the first Chief Constables appointed in 1836 when Sir Richard Peel reorganised the Irish Police Force, was born in Dublin in 1846. He spent most of his youthful days in Carrick-on-Shannon where his father was stationed. At the age of fifteen he was apprenticed to a firm of German shipbrokers in London, and subsequently rose to the post of chief shipping clerk. In 1836 he returned to Ireland and, following in the footsteps of his immediate ancestors, joined the Royal Irish Constabulary. His first assignment was to Grange where he remained for five years, 1864-1870.

When he retired many years later, he wrote a memoir of his experiences as a police officer. The following extracts, taken from an unpublished typescript in the Lissadell archives, relate to his stint in North Sligo:-

"My first station was Grange, a village half way between Sligo and Bundoran. I got lodgings with the post-mistress on very reasonable terms. My father sent me a young untrained horse, which with the help of my mounted orderly, I broke into saddle and harness in a very short time. This was in the year 1866 when the Fenian conspiracy was beginning to spread through the country. The mountain district round Grange was full of young Fenian enthusiasts. They assembled at night for drills etc. and it was a great part of the duty of the Police to trace and disperse these gatherings. Fortunately, they had no arms of any account and they never dreamed of facing a well equipped body of police. Their scouts gave the word if we approached near their meeting places and they forthwith broke up and dispersed.

I always loved outdoor sports and in Grange I devoted every spare hour, and I had plenty of time for shooting, fishing and hunting. The great man of the district, Sir Robert Gore-Booth of *Lissadell House*, kept a pack of Harriers and a fine house always open to his friends in unbounded hospitality. He was always most kind to me. I had a room at my service whenever I wished to go there in the winter months and a horse from his stable to ride to the hounds. The family spent the summer at his London residence. I almost invariably formed one of the party at his covert shoots and in walking the mountains after grouse. For fishing I kept a small boat on Lough Melvin, near Bundoran, and many a happy hour I put in after salmon there. Kinlough, where I stabled my horse when fishing the lake, was some twenty miles away. I used to leave home at 3 a.m., drive to Kinlough, getting there about 7 a.m., fish all day till dark and get back to Grange late at night. There was some fishing on the River Bundoran which runs from Lough Melvin to the sea, and I took many a good salmon out of it.

I was a keen cricketer in those days having been initiated in a small club when in London, and I am fond of the game to the present hour. I started cricket wherever I went, if it was at all possible. I admit I never was any real good at the game. I was smart and active in the field, but never excelled with either bat or ball. At Grange, I set some of the young Constables to work in a rough field. After a while a few civilians joined us, and I managed to get up a scratch eleven. We got so pleased with our progress at the game that I challenged a team from a Regiment in Sligo to come out and play a match against us. A crowd of country folk assembled and we started the game, but, alas, the soldiers were too much for us and we got badly beaten. Of course, cricket had never before been seen in or near Grange, and the crowd had no idea of how the game was going. Towards the end, however, I noticed a lot of stalwart young fellows collecting together at one end of the field. They were Fenians, every man of them, and I was rather uneasy. Suddenly one, who appeared to be a leader, came up and called me aside :-

*"They tell us, Sir, the soldiers are beating you"?*

*"It is too true I fear"*, I replied.

*"Be gorrah, we wont's stand that"* said he. *"There's a crowd of us here ready to back you, and, if you say the word, we'll beat the Divil out of them"*.
I had great trouble in persuading him that it was only a friendly match and no ill feeling, but he went away very dissatisfied.

We all went for sea bathing in the summer to Rosses Point. The men's bathing place was on the sheltered side of the mouth of the river which ran up to Sligo. When there was an ebb tide a strong current was noticeable in the immediate area. I was bathing all alone as usual, and I struck out to sea boldly and swam on until I thought I heard a distant shout. I looked back to see the shore apparently flying away from me, and I realised I was being carried away by the tide. I turned about but

I could make no headway. Fortunately two priests, who were bathing a short way off, saw what had happened. They threw on some clothes and rushed back to the village where, with some difficulty, they got a boat and rowed to me. I was picked up unconscious, just faintly paddling in the last extremity after over two hours of swimming. The local newspapers reported the rescue, and declared it was the prayers of the good priests alone that enabled me to hold out so long!

The winter of 1868 was a very hard one. Snow fell heavily, and travelling by road was difficult and dangerous. We daily expected a rising of the Fenians. I slept always with a pistol under my pillow, and the men in the barracks next door with loaded carbines by their beds. We had arranged, in the case of an outbreak, to retire to *Lissadell House* which had been placed in a state of defence by Sir Robert. All windows were sandbagged and loopholed, guns mounted on the roof, and trees cut down round the house. Mounted patrols went out every night and co-operated with the police. These patrols were carried out by the groom and stable attendants, and also by the male members of the family and by guests. A great friend of mine, Capt. Charles Wynne, son-in-law of Sir Robert, always took his turn, accompanied by a guest, usually one Capt. Martin. The patrol of these two scouts invariably led to Grange about midnight. They put their horses up in my stable and spent a night with me over a game of cards, with occasional refreshers of whiskey punch.

I often laughed to myself when I heard the ladies at Lissadell sympathising with them on the hardships they endured - out all night on horseback in such weather. Many a sly wink passed between Charley Wynne and me when this happened. He was a most cheery companion who had gone through the Crimean War from first to last and then to the Indian Mutiny. His tales of adventure were many and wonderful; and the marvel was that, in all his battles and skirmishes, he never got a wound. He had been in and out of the Redan, had led the forlorn hope at Delhi, and had been in hundreds of scraps without ever getting a scratch.

He was a perpetual Grand Master of the *'Pig and Whistle Club'* at Lissadell, an institution which arose in this way. Sir Robert Gore-Booth had a strong prejudice against smoking in the house. He would not allow it even in the Billiard Room, and there was no smoking room.

When reasoned with about this he would say that smoking was only fit for servants and grooms; and if gentlemen chose to indulge in it at Lissadell they might go to the kitchen, where they would find congenial company. Charley Wynne took him at his word and he instituted the *Pig and Whistle Club,* the members of which were any gentleman residing in the house who wished to smoke before going to bed. The place of assembly was the large kitchen in the hours after the ladies had retired for the night. There was a great white wood table in the centre of the room; and when a new arrival turned up, he had to be initiated with the solemn rites as a Member of the Club, and was required to carve with his penknife on the table, a large tombstone, on which was recorded his name and the date of his initiation. The table in my time was pretty well covered with these carvings, amongst which were names of many distinguished men. *Lissadell House* was infested with rats, and a common amusement in the *'Pig and Whistle Club'* was to destroy some of them in this fashion. Next to the kitchen range was a large hot plate, in which there was a hole near the floor. Late at night rats used to continually pop in and out of this hole. The smokers used to make a pool by putting in a coin a-piece. Then each in turn took a large kitchen knife and stood beside the hole, holding the knife just over it. As a rat put its head out, down came the knife; and with luck, the rat lost its head. The game was that each subscriber got five minutes with the knife and the one who killed the most rats took the pool!

The outbreak of the Fenian Conspiracy took place in the Spring of 1867. I have already referred to the drilling and preparations made by the young men in the Sligo mountains. So serious had this become that, at one time, the American Fenians had arranged to open a campaign in the district; and, with this object a vessel was chartered at New York, laden with arms, and manned by a number of Irish American officers who had served in the Civil War between North and South, which had ended not very long before this period. This vessel, named the *Jacknell,* sailed for the Sligo coast with the intention of landing the arms and officers there; and they fully believed that a well organised army was waiting to receive them. A certain Colonel Burke was despatched to Sligo some weeks before the ship was expected, to make all arrangements for her reception. This man arrived disguised

# MEMOIRS OF A POLICEMAN

Sir Robert Gore-Booth

Lissadell House

as an English touring artist. He stopped at a hotel in Sligo, and there made acquaintance with the Constabulary officer and the Resident Magistrate, with whom he fraternised and became quite intimate. He soon discovered that there was no army available, and that the prospect of a successful rising in Sligo was quite hopeless. He, therefore, decided to meet the *Jacknell* at sea and warn the officers on board that the game was up. He hired a small sailing vessel on the excuse that he was sketching coast scenery; and, in this boat, he spent his time sailing in the Bay, waiting for the arrival of the American ship. He appeared in my district at Mullaghmore, a small village on the coast near Cliffony; and, for a time, made this his headquarters with his boat. I interviewed him there; but, as he had letters of introduction from the Sub- Inspector at Sligo and from the Resident Magistrate, I did not interfere with him.

In due course the *Jacknell* turned up. He boarded her off the coast and turned her back. Some of the crew objected to going to sea again as provisions were running short, and there was a fight on board in which two of the American Fenian officers were wounded. These men were taken on shore at night and left lying on the beach, where they were discovered next morning by the Coastguards who at once sent for me, and I arrested them and had them conveyed to a hospital in Sligo. These were the first of the crew of the *Jacknell* who were made prisoners. The ship eventually sailed around the coast; and as provisions failed, the rest of the American Officers were landed at Wexford, and were all made prisoners, tried and convicted.

The Island of Inishmurray, which lies about six miles out in Sligo Bay, was the great headquarters of the poteen makers. During the winter months the Islanders were mainly employed in distilling poteen from grain supplied by the farmers on the mainland. The coast of Inishmurray is rock bound, and there was but one little inlet in which it was possible to beach or launch a boat without the help of the island people. A landing could only be effected in perfectly calm weather; and it was the duty of the Coastguards to watch for a spell of frost, likely to keep the sea calm for a day or two, and then call upon me to furnish a force of police, which they conveyed to the Island in one of their boats. We always left at the early hour of the morning and landed just at daybreak, when we searched the Island thoroughly and invariably

MEMOIRS OF A POLICEMAN

made considerable seizure of stills, still heads, worms, wash, poteen and all the paraphernalia of the smugglers.

Once only we were caught by a sudden change of weather and had to spent ten days on the Island. We had landed a couple of days before Christmas, and were thus compelled to spent the festive season as best we could among the Islanders. We took possession of the school house; we commandeered a small rick of turf and kept up a good fire, over which we cooked such meals as we could secure. The Islanders had for generations a *'Royal Family'* of their own, to whom they paid a certain amount of respect. At the time I am writing about, they were governed by a *'Queen'*, a very kindly old woman, who lent us a kettle, a frying pan and a saucepan; and, with these utensils, we did all our cooking. There were plenty of geese, ducks, and chickens to be had, and we chopped these up and fried them on the pan with potatoes. There were five Coastguards and four Policemen besides myself. We all slept on the floor, and we had not our clothes off all the time. Of course, there was no chance of shaving; and, when the weather moderated sufficiently to launch the boat, we were a very bedraggled party as may be imagined.

The *'Queen'* had been very civil to us; and, in spite of law and order, I left her quietly most of the illicit material which we had seized. She was so grateful that she asked me to taste a drop of a special brew of poteen which she reserved for herself and family. When I consented, she produced a quart bottle from a secret hiding place and also an empty egg shell into which she poured a liberal tot of the spirit for my consumption. I asked her had she nothing but an egg shell to drink out of, and she told me the boys had a dance in her house before Christmas; and, having too much to drink, they fell out amongst themselves, had a free fight, and smashed every article of glass or crockery ware in the place!

The Gore-Booths were keen sailors. Sir Robert kept a yacht at Cowes and Charley Wynne had a small schooner at Rosses Point, and a smart little cutter on Lough Gill. The schooner was named *The Waif* and many a cruise I made in her in the Bay. The cutter on the lake, however, was our most constant resource in the summer months, and I learned all I ever knew of yachtsman's lore on board of her.

Every year there was a regatta on the lake, mostly for small sailing and towing boats. Charley Wynne's brother, who resided on the lake

325

shore, owned another cutter, and there was a continual rivalry between the two as to which was the better boat. At one regatta, a special race was arranged for yachts of the tonnage of these vessels, but it was a *sine qua non* that three boats should start or there could be no race. The only other boat on the lake, qualified to start, was a freak craft which had been built by a timber merchant in Sligo, on a plan of his own, designed for great speed. It certainly had the speed but was hopelessly unstable without any wind on the beam. It has twice already been capsized and been retrieved from the bottom of the lake.

O'Connor, the owner of this weird craft, had entered her to make up the race; but, as the day turned out very squally, he cried off at the last moment, and refused to sail her. I was in Charley Wynne's yacht, and I volunteered to man the boat, if O'Connor would consent. With some hesitation he agreed, and I prevailed upon a young bank clerk, whom I knew in Sligo, to come with me. We got up sail in good time, and started with the other two boats. We knew quite well what we had to expect, so we took off all our clothes, save shirt and trousers, and away we went with a strong breeze behind us down the lake. We simply ran away from the other two boats until we came to a buoy, round which we had to jib, and beat back home. Our craft came round gaily and laid over on the first tack. Suddenly, a squall struck us, and over she went, filled and went down. My friend and I jumped into the water and swam about till we were picked up, none the worse, but I believe the yacht lies at the bottom of the lake to this day. This was my first and last experience of a race at a regatta, though we had plenty of friendly tussles on the lake between the river boats.

Charley Wynne supervised the building of a 30 ton cutter at Lissadell which was to beat everything of its class at Cowes. I am sorry to say it was a melancholic failure. Like O'Connor's boat, it was hopelessly crank. The day it was launched, it turned turtle the moment it reached deep water. It was re-floated, ballasted with lead and started for the Isle of Wight, but never got there. After many adventures, it got as far as Poole, where it stuck in the mud, and in the mud it was left, and we heard no more of the *'Zerana'*!

Shall I ever get away from Grange I wonder? So many reminiscences of these early days keep cropping up. I will tell of some spiritualistic experience I had at Lissadell. When in London for the season, the

## Memoirs of a Policeman

Gore- Booths had come across a wonderful medium called Holmes, who was, at this time, mystifying London with remarkable demonstrations of his power in calling up the spirits of the dead, and inducing them to give remarkable manifestations. They returned to Lissadell full of these experiences, and proceeded to hold seances in the hope of getting some exciting results. I joined in the proceedings, at first, I admit in a very incredulous frame of mind; but certainly things occurred which were very difficult to explain. We used to sit round a table in the dark with the fingers touching and forming a circle. Presently, the table began to move up and down, and slight noises, resembling taps, were heard. One of us asked if a spirit was there, and a tilt of the table was the reply in the affirmative. Then questions were asked, and replies received by calling out the alphabet, a tilt of the table, or a rap at a particular letter, eventually forming words and sentences. I may at once record the fact that never did we get from the spirits, if spirits they were, the smallest atom of information of the slightest use of any human being. Some of the replies were indeed ridiculous, and some absolutely false. As an illustration of this, I may mention one case in which Sir Robert was greatly interested. I attended a contested election in Sligo, at which serious riots occurred. During one of these riots, a certain Captain King, a cousin of Sir Robert's, was shot dead, and Sir Robert was very anxious to know who fired the fatal shot. It was generally believed, and I thought with reason, that the shot was accidentally fired by a companion of King's who was holding his arm while the mob pressed upon him, and who held a revolver in his other hand. Capt. King's friend, however, refused to accept this theory, and maintained that it was deliberate murder. At our seances at *Lissadell House*, Sir Robert always asked the spooks to help him to trace the murderer. The replies were invariably absurd. I suppose in the course of half a dozen sittings, the spirits spelled out a dozen names of persons, not one of whom was near the scene when the tragedy occurred.

Of adventures in poteen hunting and in arresting Fenians, quelling riots etc., in the Grange district, I could fill pages......".

*\* Reprinted from typescript in the Lissadell archives,*
*and published courtesy of Sir Josslyn Gore-Booth*

# Short Lived Bobbin Factory

In the late 1860's Malcolm McNeill, an industrious Scotsman, established a Bobbin Factory or, Pirn Mill, on a site adjacent to the Ballast Quay and Lynn's Dock. The factory, which went into production in 1870, made bobbins, or pirns, for the textile trade at home and abroad, as well as handles for a wide variety of household and farm implements from home-grown timber. By degrees the operation was extended on ground leased from the Harbour Board, new buildings erected and the latest machinery installed. The former residence of Robert Lynn, then deceased, was leased at a rental of £60 per annum and converted into offices. Within a few years the factory and adjoining timber yards covered an area extending from Lynn's Place to the Custom House Quay. The success of the venture, trading as Messrs. Malcolm McNeill & Son, provided increased employment, mostly experienced workmen and trainee boys, rising from a few dozen in the initial stages to two hundred within a decade.

A description of the operations carried out in the Bobbin Factory has been recorded by Wood-Martin:-

*"Within a comparatively recent period a steam mill was established in Sligo for the production of a variety of common articles of wood of which the chief output was spools or pirns. Immense circular saws cut the trunks of trees into portable logs, whilst others slice them into sections of thickness corresponding to the height of the required spool, and long lines of workmen perform with bewildering rapidity their various duties, tending towards the production of the perfected article. Everything is done by steam, with skilled hands, assisted by intricate and delicate machinery, and as the Messrs. MacNeill supply the leading thread manufacturers with these pirns, the majority of the spools handled by the deft fingers of the 'fair ladies' of Sligo are the product of this factory"* [1]

In 1889 Messrs. McNeill, who were also extensive shippers of timber, became involved in a strike at the Port. A handful of their employees, who worked on the unloading of imported timbers, sought a wage increase of 4/- a week in line with the demands of other dockers. Eventually, the dispute was resolved to the advantage of the Port workers, including the McNeill employees. As a result, a section of the

## SHORT LIVED BOBBIN FACTORY

workforce in the Bobbin Factory became restless and by means of threats and intimidation sought to emulate the actions of their fellow workers on the Quays. As part of their growing 'independence' and indifference to the proprietor's interest, they started up a Fife and Drum Band which made a habit of attending Land League meetings and other 'popular displays' in the general neighbourhood. This resulted in a section of the workforce becoming irregular in attendance at work, especially at weekends. Messrs. McNeill became increasingly concerned with these developments and did everything possible to prevent employees from walking out, almost at will, to take part in political activities. The situation became so intolerable that the firm introduced a system of fines and penalties by which those who absented themselves were punished and rewards offered to those who remained steady in their work. Despite these inducements a 'rebellious spirit' continued to spread and reached a climax during the County Election in August, 1883, when an increasing number of employees absented themselves for a number of days and, in some instances, attempted to resume work under the influence of drink. Although subjected to intimidation and threats, Messrs. McNeill had little option but to dismiss a number of employees, twenty in all.

The situation prevailing in the Pirn Mill is best described in the following extract from the *"Sligo Independent"*:

*".......Messrs. McNeill complained of incessantly being troubled and annoyed by the conduct of quite a number of the boys and men employed and find it impossible to get them to work regularly, especially after pay-day. Bonuses were offered to those who kept regular time, but this inducement failed to cause regularity, and when a system of fining was introduced this created greater discontent.... It is alleged that very significant threats have been used and that any attempt to prevent the employees - even when work was most pressing - from going away to take part in political displays resulted in a situation almost close to mutiny....."* [2]

Such was the highly unsatisfactory situation at the otherwise successful industrial undertaking when, shortly after midnight on Tuesday, September 25th 1883, the Fire Bell at the Town Hall broke the nocturnal silence as it summoned members of the Volunteer Fire Brigade into action. The scene of the fire was the Bobbin Factory. Despite the best endeavours of the fire-fighters, assisted by numerous volunteers, it was 10 a.m. before the conflagration was finally brought under control leaving in its wake a 'shapeless mess'. The former Lynn residence luckily escaped the blaze. An examination of the burn-out mill, and in particular the gas main, indicated that the fire was the malicious act of a person or persons unknown.[3] Messrs. McNeill, satisfied that the destruction of the factory and the adjoining saw-mills was caused by an incendiary, lodged a claim for £10,000 under the Grand Jury Act, and offered a £100 reward for information leading to the identity of the perpetrator or perpetrators .[4]

---

# DREADFUL FIRE IN SLIGO

## McNEILL'S BOBBIN FACTORY BURNED DOWN

We regret that we have to record a conflagration which, for the extent and disasterous results, has been the worst fire that has ever taken place in Sligo or neighbourhood. Old residents will recollect when the area in the region of the Lynn's Dock was a wilderness, in the centre of which was a swamp.............................

*"Sligo Independant"* 25-9-1883

---

At the Carbury Presentment Sessions in December, 1883, Messrs. McNeill were awarded £7,800 in compensation, to be charged on, or levied off, the Borough of Sligo. The claim was further considered at the Spring Assizes in March, 1884. After much discussion and cross-examination of witnesses, the Grand Jury, by 15 votes to 6, upheld the malicious claim, but reduced the presentment to £4,700; buildings £800, machinery £2,700 and stock-in-trade £1,200, to be charged on the County at-Large rather than on the Borough. [5]

In 1885 a new Pirn Mill rose phoenix-like on the site of the original factory. Although it did not employ as many hands as previously, there was, nevertheless, close on 200 in regular employment, a number of whom were apprentices in training and all on good wages, said to total £400 a week. In addition, this enterprising firm provided an outlet for the disposal of large quantities of native timbers from this and neighbouring counties.[6] Three years later, in April, 1888 as the Pirn Mill was still recovering from the losses sustained by the fire, a strike developed, involving 170 operatives, who were seeking an increase in

## SHORT LIVED BOBBIN FACTORY

wages, a demand firmly resisted by the employers. The local *"Independent"* was abhorred by this development and referred to the strikers as 'capricious workmen', pointing out that public opinion was "altogether adverse to their ill-advised actions".[7] It also expressed fears that Messrs. McNeill might consider moving the entire concern out of Sligo to another location.[8] However, a week later, it was happy to report that the strikers had called-off their action and returned to work.

It subsequently transpired that the Company was experiencing serious financial difficulties in the aftermath of the fire. These culminated in January 1891, when Messrs. McNeill were declared bankrupt. The mill and all ancillary operations were immediately closed, throwing the entire workforce out of employment. Later that year the buildings, offices and stores at the Pirn Mill Road, together with McNeill's residence in Wine Street, were offered for sale in the Bankruptcy Court. [9] Thus ended, after a chequered existence of little more than two decades, the largest single industry established in 19th century Sligo.

### Notes and References:

(1) Wood-Martin, W.G. *"History of Sligo"*. Vol. 3 p. 252

(2) *"Sligo Independent"*          4 - 10-1883

(3) *"Sligo Champion"*          29 - 9 -1883
      *"Sligo Independent"*          29 - 9 -1883

(4) *"Sligo Independent"*          4 -10- 1883

(5)          *ibid*          8 - 3- 1884

(6)          *ibid*          17 - 1 - 1885

(7)          *ibid*          21 - 4- 1888

(8) Messrs. McNeill operated similar concerns at Enniskillen and Killarney.

(9) Registry of Deeds : 1891, Bk 48, No. 264

# Bridges over the
# GARVOGUE

The modern Town of Sligo dates from 1245, when Maurice Fitzgerald, the Norman Knight, built a castle on a site which controlled the crossing of the Garvogue, the ancient gateway between Connacht and Ulster.

The earliest reference to the Bridge of Sligo is to be found in the *"Annals of Ireland"* in 1188 a.d. In that year Rory O'Cananáin of Tirconail was killed by an unknown assailant as he fled across the bridge. Some months later it was burned, and this would suggest a timber structure, most likely a footbridge. Half a century on, in 1235, the Norman invaders overran Connacht and pursued Felim O'Connor, the titular King of the Province, over the Curlews and as far as the Bridge of Sligo. The precise location of that strategic crossing-point has not been recorded but it may be assumed that it lay between the existing upper and lower weirs, and very probably at or close to the site of the recently erected footbridge at the end of Water Lane. The date of the first stone bridge has not been documented but it has been suggested that it was built in the 14th century by Cathal Óg O'Connor - Sligo, the local chieftain, who is also credited with the building of a similar structure at Ballisodare.

By the year 1688 there were two stone bridges fording the Garvogue. The earliest of these - possibly that built by O'Connor-Sligo, and known as the *Old Bridge*, spanned the River more or less on the same site as the present Hyde Bridge, but slightly down river and joining Stephen Street with Bridgefoot Street and Lower Knox's Street. It was a humped bridge of eight arches with a carriageway $17\frac{1}{2}$ feet in width. In the opening decades of the 19th century the east end of the bridge "had been greatly narrowed and the passage into the adjoining streets confined in such a manner as to make it dangerous for two carriages to pass each other on account of houses built on the bridge and close to the end of it."[1] Another contemporary account described it as "a tortuous thing like a corkscrew, with a hump in the middle and in a very dilapidated state."

BRIDGES OVER THE GARVOGUE

By 1845 moves were afoot to have the *Old Bridge* replaced. At the Spring Assizes in March of that year there was some discussion on the project, and a Committee, consisting of John Wynne, Roger Duke and Captain Henry Fawcett, was assigned the task of appraising plans and specifications for the new structure.[2] In the last week of June the following advertisement appeared in the *"General Advertiser"*. [3]

---

## NOTICE TO CONTRACTORS

Sealed tenders will be received by the Secretary of the Grand Jury for the building of a New Bridge in the town of Sligo (in place of the present one) and making the approaches thereto, till 11 0'clock in the forenoon of the day on which the Grand Jury will be sworn for the discharge of fiscal business.

The plan and specification can be seen at the office of the County Surveyor, who will give all the necessary information. The contractor and two sureties will be bound to qualify in the sum of One Thousand Pounds above the amount of the tender.

Signed: Robert Christian, Secretary of Grand Jury.
*24 - 6 - 1845*

---

At the subsequent Summer Assizes a presentment "to build a new bridge and make the approaches thereto in a direct line from Stephen Street to the junctions of Wine Street and Knox's Street", in accordance with the plan prepared by the County Surveyor, Noblett St. Leger, was adopted.[4] In response to advertisements in both the *"Dublin Gazette"* and *"General Advertiser"*, the following tenders were submitted:

| | | | |
|---|---|---|---|
| 1. | Robert Lawler & Sons | ...................... | £2,916 |
| 2. | James Caldwell | ...................... | £1,998 |
| 3. | Knox Barrett | ...................... | £1,951 |

Barrett's proposal was accepted, and he named as his sureties William Kernaghan and Edward Kelly, both local merchants of note.

## BRIDGES OVER THE GARVOGUE

In August, 1845, the *"Champion"* announced that Collooney-born, John Benson, had been chosen as the architect. "From his superior taste and abilities as an architect, we may safely calculate upon having a structure erected which will prove an ornament to our town".[5] Over the succeeding eight months preliminary works were undertaken, acquiring and demolishing a number of properties that blocked the approaches to the new bridge. Compensation was paid to eight owners/occupiers but this would have been considerably greater were it not for the goodwill and co-operation of Abraham Martin who not only donated a six-foot strip of land but also allowed his weir in the River to be dismantled and rebuilt without seeking compensation.

On Monday, May 3rd, 1846, the foundation-stone of the *Victoria Bridge* was laid in the presence of a large assemblage of townspeople, by Mayor, Henry O'Connor, who, after having invoked the Lord's blessing upon the new undertaking, looked forward to the increased prosperity it would bring to the Town and Port of Sligo.[5] As most of the preparatory works, including preparation of site and cutting of stones, had been completed, the undertaking proceeded with admirable haste. Six months later, by November, 1846, the new bridge with its five graceful arches, each with a 21ft. span, although in a "very unfinished state and without battlements," was thrown open to the public. It was completed the following year at an overall cost of £4,245, which included street alignments and compensation for properties acquired by compulsory purchase. Four premises were demolished in the process.[6]

As *Victoria Bridge* neared completion, work had already commenced on the laying-down of Victoria Line (now *Markievicz Road*) as the main approach route from the North, thus avoiding Barrack Hill and linking up with the bridge at a place known as 'The Slip'. This undertaking, which had been initiated as a Famine Relief work in 1846-'47, was not finally completed until March, 1853.[7]

The second bridge mentioned in the 1688 Report was what was then known as the *New Bridge* in Bridge Street, or, as it then was called: New Bridge Street. It was built c. 1680, probably at the behest of the Corporation, although no references can be traced in their records. It is an eight-eyed bridge with a carriageway 25 ft. in width.[8] Its sturdy construction and narrow span arches has successfully borne an ever increasing volume and weight of traffic, from the horse-drawn carts and stately carriages to the modern juggernauts, reflecting great credit on the skills and workmanship of the builders of three centuries ago. One remarkable feature of this bridge is that it was never given a distinctive name, that is, apart from *New Bridge* or *Upper Bridge*. A suggestion made in 1847, at the completion of *Victoria Bridge,* that it be called *Adelaide Bridge,* did not meet with universal approval and was not proceeded with. Although it can no longer be referred to as the *New Bridge*, no effort has been made to undo the neglect of three centuries.

---

## Laying the Foundation Stone of Victoria Bridge

"On Monday evening an inspiring ceremony - laying the foundation stone of a new bridge on the site of the old one, aproaching Stephen Street, was performed in the presence of a large assemblage of townspeople, by the Right Worshipful, the Mayor, Henry O'Connor, Esq. accompanied by the ex-Mayor and other functionaries of the Corporation. His Worship, with a becoming spirit and Christian humility, invoked the Lord's blessing upon the new undertaking. After wishing prosperity and a flourishing increase to the commerce of the Town and Port of Sligo, his Worship took the trowel and performed the customary ceremony of laying the first stone. A little of the 'genuine native' was then decapitated with all due ceremony, amidst loud cheering, whilst the Mayor was proclaiming the reign of our gracious Soverign, Victoria. Thus terminated a spectacle which may not again be witnessed for ages."

*"Sligo Journal"* 8-5-1846

---

In olden times there was a forded crossing of the Garvogue upstream from the weir at Riverside. It was used as a crossing point by Sir Frederick Hamilton and a section of his army in July, 1642, on his way to the Abbey, which he sacked and burned, in addition to the Town. It was known as *Buckley's Ford* and is thought to have taken its name from an officer of that name, a Jacobite, who was killed crossing the makeshift ford during the siege of the Green Fort in the period between 1689-1691. The name was still in vogue into the last century. Sadly, it

# BRIDGES OVER THE GARVOGUE

The 'New Bridge' c. 1680 (above) and
Victoria Bridge (now Hyde Bridge) below.

BRIDGES OVER THE GARVOGUE

| | | VICTORIA BRIDGE | | |
|---|---|---|---|---|
| **OLD** | | *Old and New Compared* | | **NEW** |
| Width (between parapets) | 17' 6" | Width (between parapets) | | 34' 0" |
| Roadway: | 14' 6" | Roadway: | | 22' 0" |
| Footpaths: | 3' 0" | Footpaths: | | 12' 0" |

has long vanished from local usage.

In recent times two further bridges have been added. *Hughes Bridge*, so-called after a former Mayor, spans the estuary down river from Hyde Bridge. Opened for traffic in August, 1988 and costing in the region of £2 million, it is intended to serve the proposed Relief Road. Constructed of reinforced concrete, it lacks the workmanship and graceful finish of Benson's *Victoria Bridge*. In 1996 a single-span arched footbridge was placed in position at the end of Water Lane, linking Rockwood Parade with the Stephen Street car park. In conjunction with the Sligo and Environs Water Scheme, another footbridge at the Upper Weir, linking The Riverside with The Mall, is presently under construction.

### *Notes and References:*

(1)  Wood-Martin, W. G. *"History of Sligo".* Vol. 3. p. 124

(2)  *"Sligo Champion"*              8 -3-1845

(3)  *"General Advertiser"*          28-6-1845

(4)  *"Sligo Champion"*              19-7-1845
(5)        *ibid*                    9-8-1845

(6)  Details of Compensation paid included:- Mrs. McKim (£245);
     Eliz.Craig (£162); Thomas & Jane Sleator (£514); James Little (£150);
      J. Hetherington (£40) and Barton Smith (£202. 15s.).
      Total = £1,316. 15s.

(7)  Estimated cost in 1847 was £3,000 which included laying of road,
      acquiring buildings at Stephen St. - Hyde Bridge junction and building a
      retaining wall along the estuary.

(8)  Two of the 'eyes' at the Thomas St. end were closed-off in recent
      developments.

# The Last Public Hanging

Shortly before eight o'clock on the morning of Monday, August 19th, 1861, Mathew Phibbs of Market Street, Ballymote, aged 26, was executed in front of the County Gaol for the murders of William Callaghan, aged 91; his wife, Fanny, 62, and a young servant girl, Anne Mooney, in Ballymote on January 8th of that year. It was the first public execution in Sligo for twenty six years and, as matters evolved, it was also the last. The event created a profound impression locally, so much so that for decades afterwards it remained a recognised landmark in the matter of time - people placing happenings as either before, or after, or in the proximity of ' the hanging of Phibbs'. Indeed, reference to it was of common occurrence when claims for the old age pension were being considered.

Mathew Phibbs was a native of Ballymote and a scion of the once numerous family of that name. Born in 1835, he was the second eldest son of Mathew and Mary Phibbs. His father was a draper and carried on a business next-door to the Callaghans in Main Street. After the death of Mathew, sen ., in 1850, or thereabouts, the family continued to operate the business but after a few years it folded-up due to financial insolvency. In March, 1859, Phibbs married Catherine, the daughter of John and Fanny Woodland of Lavally, Toomour. She was aged eighteen years and a lady of reasonable means. A daughter, christened Anne Maria, was born to the couple in February, 1860.

After the collapse of the family business, Mathew Phibbs opened a small retail outlet in Market Street. When this venture failed he took to bouts of heavy drinking. His young wife left him a year after their marriage and went to live in Dublin, whilst he went to Sligo and later to England. He returned to Ballymote in December, 1860, and took up residence with his widowed mother in a one-roomed flat in Market Street. They were in great poverty and, as he subsequently confessed, his sole motive in forcing his way into Callaghan's home in the early hours of that January morning was to get money to buy food and other necessities for his destitute mother. Unfortunately, he allowed himself to commit three dreadful murders to achieve his goal.

Before leaving the Callaghan homestead, Phibbs ransacked the

## THE LAST PUBLIC HANGING

premises and possessed himself of whatever booty he could get his hands on. A few hours later he fled the town, and made for Sligo, where he purchased a cap and boots to replace the blood-stained apparel he was wearing. Afterwards, he adjourned to an ale-house and in the course of the afternoon became exceedingly drunk. As he staggered out of control on the public street he was arrested and taken to the Barracks. When he was searched the police found upwards of £20 of blood-stained bank notes, together with a few gold sovereigns, on his person. He was detained overnight and released the following morning. Shortly afterwards, as news of the Ballymote atrocity reached Sligo, Phibbs became a prime suspect. A mounted policeman was hastily dispatched in search of the fugitive. He eventually caught up with Phibbs in Riverstown as he awaited transport to Drumfin to catch the Mail Coach to Dublin, and took him into custody. He was then taken to Ballymote where, at the Coroner's Court, he was returned for trial to the Sligo Assizes.

The trial of Mathew Phibbs came before the Spring Assizes on Thursday, March 7th, 1861. From an early hour crowds gathered in the streets outside of Sligo Courthouse in an effort to secure admittance to the court-room. Within minutes of the opening of the doors at 9.30 a.m., all available space was occupied while the overflow filled the entrance hall and the roadway outside. After Judge Fitzgerald had taken his place on the rostrum, the prisoner, Mathew Phibbs, looking pale and depressed, was placed in the dock. Commentators described him as of medium height, with a sallow complexion, a long face, and dark eyes. He sported a small 'imperial' and was dressed in a long grey frieze coat.

Before the opening statements by the respective Counsels, the following jury, all Protestants, were empanelled; George Leech, Sligo (Foreman) ; Patrick McKim, Branchfield; John West, Cartron ; Robert Maveety, Stephen Street; John Shaw, Kilsellagh; Thomas Carter, Scardenmore; Hillas Smith, Stephen Street; Richard Wilson, Ballyweelin; Andrew Green, Cloonlurg; Robert Pye, Cregg; John Mullen, Springfield and Thomas Williams, Corhownagh. The trial lasted three days, The jury retired to consider their verdict at 4. 30 p.m. on Saturday, March 9th. Four hours later the Judge sent for them, only to be informed by the Foreman that they had not reached

THE LAST PUBLIC HANGING

an unanimous verdict, The court then adjourned to 11. 40 p.m. As the midnight hour approached the streets outside became almost impassable from the immense crowd that had gathered there in anticipation of a verdict.

When the Courthouse re-opened at 11.30 p.m. there was a mad rush to gain admittance and many were disappointed at being left outside. After the Judge and members of the jury had taken their places, the Foreman announced that they had still not reached a verdict and that there was no likelihood of them doing so. After almost eight hours deliberation there was one dissenting juror who favoured an acquital. With no agreement in sight, and the fact that Judge Fitzgerald was scheduled to open the Assizes in Galway on the following Monday morning, the jury were discharged and the trial postponed to the Summer Assizes. Meanwhile, on the stroke of midnight, Phibbs was escorted back to Sligo Gaol, uncertain of his fate.

The re-trial opened on July 9th, 1861, with Judge Hayes presiding. As in the case of the first trial, so great was the public interest that the Courthouse was again crowded to overflowing. The trial lasted two days and a mixed jury, consisting of both Catholics and Protestants, reached an unanimous decision without undue delay. They found Phibbs guilty of murder, Judge Hayes then pronounced sentence in the following words :-

> *"The sentence of the Court is that you, Mathew Phibbs, be taken from this place to the County Gaol and thence, on a day henceforth to be named, to a place of common execution, the gallows; and that you be hanged by the neck until dead, and that your body be cut down and buried within the precincts of the prison, and may the Lord have Mercy on your soul".*

When asked if he had anything to say as to why sentence of death should not be passed upon him, Phibbs remained silent - he made no declaration of innocence. According to onlookers he received his sentence "without betraying the slightest emotion". On his return to the Gaol he is said to have stared at the gallows, which were a permanent fixture outside the main entrance, and burst into tears. A few days later it was announced that the execution had been fixed for Monday, August 19th.

As the fateful day approached, Mathew Phibbs made a verbal

## THE LAST PUBLIC HANGING

confession to the chaplain as to the motive that induced him to commit the dreadful crime and also the manner in which he accomplished his awful deed.

" For some time before I committed the crime for which I am now to die, I was in great want. I tried every one to make up some means to do for myself and my mother, but I did not get what would sustain one of us. On the Monday before I did the act we had not any money at all, and I went to several ; I got a few pence from one, and a gentleman I went to, Mr _____, only gave me a shilling or so; I expected more from him and did not know what to do, so, I went home that night very much down, and I told my mother that I was going to Sligo the next morning and try if I could to get anything there. I did not go out later that night, and after getting some supper with the money, I kept the remainder and went to bed. Next morning I awoke before five o'clock and got up intending to start early, there was no one up but myself and I got out without making a noise. When I went out I rambled about the town for an hour undecided, and it was then, I think, the first thought of Callaghan come across me. I went then to —— and had some whiskey and it was after that I made up my mind to get some of Callaghan's money, but I never intended to murder Mrs. Callaghan or the girl. I then went round to the back of Callaghan's house, into the garden and crossed over the wall into the yard, and whilst I was looking about and thinking how I would get in, Anne Mooney come out to the kitchen and when she saw me she looked frightened and asked me how I got in, and what brought me there? Just then I struck her with the handle of a shovel or a brick, I don't recollect which and she fell. I then cut her throat with a razor I had, and I cut my finger by the razor turning in my hand. I then went into the shop through the kitchen and while I was there Mrs Callaghan came in, and then, for fear, I knocked her down and killed her, too.

Not finding the money I expected, I then went upstairs to the old man's bedroom. He was awake in bed but did not know me as I was not in the house for three month's before. I struck him with the brick on the head and then I cut his throat. I then went through the place and took whatever I could find of value. I did not drink anything in the house. When I saw my coat was covered with blood I put on a coat of Mr. Callaghan's that was in the room before I went downstairs. I did not intend to kill any of my relatives afterwards as was stated. I think I was going back to

## THE LAST PUBLIC HANGING

*Ballymote when I was taken in Riverstown. I was never cruel, in the way
it was stated, to my mother; I was severe towards my wife when I wanted
money from her but I never threatened to take my mother's life. I know I
deserve to be punished for my crimes, and I am sorry for them. It was
whiskey and bad company made me do what I did; I was always on good
terms with the Callaghan's. I hope I will be forgiven my terrible crimes,
and that my poor mother will be taken care of."*

After the confession of his guilt, Mathew Phibbs appears to have
turned his thoughts altogether from wordly affairs and became very
attentive to the instructions of the chaplain, Rev. Samuel Shone and of
the Rev. Lindsay, the Methodist minister. On Sunday, the day
preceding the execution, this change was most marked. He attended
service in the Gaol chapel that morning and listened with apparent
attention to the sermon. Shortly afterwards he expressed a wish to
have pen, ink and paper which was supplied but not immediately used
by the condemned man. He declined taking regular meals and
scarcely tasted any food during the entire day which he spent
principally in the company of the aforementioned reverend
gentlemen. Towards evening he was much exhausted and the
Governor, Edward Walsh, kindly had him supplied with some wine
negus of which he partook very sparingly.

At 10 o'clock, or thereabouts, Phibbs sat down and wrote the
following Confession.

*Sligo Gaol.*
*Sunday, August 18, 1861.*

*"Mathew Phibbs, aged about 25 or 26 years, born in the town of Ballymote
and the County of Sligo. I must say that I had honest parents and often did get
a good advise from them, when a youth, to mind my Sunday School and to go
to Church, the House of God. That I did prefer going with bad company
elsewhere, perhaps into a whiskey house. Young lads, or young men, whoever
you may be, perhaps a school fellow of mine, or some near and dear friend of
mine, I do say to thee to take care and beware of what brought Mathew Phibbs
to this his untimely end. I must bid you a farewell, heartily forgiving all who
have injured me, and asking forgiveness from all whom I have injured.*

*I also return my hearty thanks to my Counsellor, Mr. Sidney, and also to Mr.
Pollock, solicitor, for their disinterested zeal in my service; also I return thanks*

to the Governor, Mr. Walsh, of this gaol, and the officers of it also for their kindness and compassion towards me. But above all I return thanks to the Rev. Samuel Shone, Chaplain, who was so very kind in coming every day; also the Rev. George Garrett, of Coolaney; and that kind Mr. Lindsay, for their great desire to enlighten my mind in the knowledge of the Scriptures. And as I can't express what services they have done me, I leave it to the the Lord to recompense them, knowing that for his sake they showed me kindness.

After my trial, I acknowledged my guilt but asked that it would not be made public until after I was executed. I now admit the justice of my sentence, looking to my blessed Saviour, who suffered for me.

*Yes, often my parents did advise me to mind my Sunday School and Church, but I neglected them and went instead to whiskey houses and play-houses and races. Again, young men, beware of what has brought me this my untimely end.*"

**Mathew Phibbs.**

He then wrote an affectionate valedictory letter to his unfortunate mother, in which he besought her forgiveness for any pain he may have given her, and acknowledging that if he had taken her good advice in his earlier years, his fate would have been different. This letter he confided to the care of the chaplain.

Having unburdened his mind to some extent, Phibbs joined in devotional exercises, occasionally glancing over a Hymn Book he had for some days been in the habit of reading. He showed no inclination of retiring to bed but every now and than stretched out on it for short periods and within minutes would start up and walk about his cell and converse with the chaplain.

At a quarter to seven on Monday morning, Phibbs was taken to the Prison chapel where the Rev. Shone administered the communion, and afterwards read some appropriate passages from scripture.

## THE LAST PUBLIC HANGING

Meanwhile, a contingent of the Constabulary were drawn up outside the Goal where a large number of people had assembled to witness the execution . At half past seven, or thereabouts, Mathew Phibbs was led out of the chapel, leaning on the arm of the chaplain and accompanied by the Sub-Sheriff, Bernard O. Cogan, Dr Lynn, M.O. to the Prison, the Governor and other officers. As they passed along, the prisoners, who were looking through the grated windows of the interior of the Gaol, waved a farewell with their hands, and many of them cried aloud – on hearing which the prisoner turned round and, taking off his hat, returned their salutation. When the procession reached the 'press room' the executioner was standing behind the door, apparently timid to approach the convict. Phibbs looked at him, and finding that he made no move, said - *"Won't you tie me? Don't be afraid; come and do what you have to do,"* while at the same time turning his back to him and facing the drop, which was visible through the open door. The convict spoke calmly and firmly, and at the same time arranged his arms beside his body. The executioner then stepped forward and, having tied the convict's arms, placed the cap, a white one, on his head, drew it over his face, and adjusted the rope on his neck. Here, Phibbs was heard to sob aloud.

The executioner then assisted him up the four steps leading to the fatal drop outside. When he had reached the last step the convict reeled and was caught in the arms of the hangman, who cried out for assistance. Bell, the turnkey, at once went forward and helped in placing Phibbs on the drop, on which he stood erect. As soon as the condemned man appeared on the platform of the gallows, a low murmur of horror rose from the multitude assembled in front of the Gaol. At that point it was discovered that there had been some mismanagement in the fixing of the rope, and the wretched man had to be brought back to the 'press room' to have it set right. This having been done, the convict remaining quite passive, was again placed on the drop by the executioner, assisted by Bell, and, after the lapse of one minute, the fatal bolt was drawn. Two minutes afterwards eternity had opened to Mathew Phibbs.

At the moment of execution a wild cry rent the air from the vast concourse present, while one policeman and several of those in the crowd fainted. The body swung round two or three times; there was a

# THE LAST PUBLIC HANGING

convulsive shivering of the limbs, and all was over.

The scenes witnessed at the execution of Mathew Phibbs prompted the *"Champion"* to comment as follows :-

*"Admitting, as we do that Mathew Phibbs well deserved any punishment that could be inflicted, we cannot refrain from expressing our disgust at those public executions . . . For twenty-six years the hangman's office was not brought into requisition in the County of Sligo – yet the unsightly, disgusting gallows has been allowed to remain outside the Gaol all that time . . ."*

Shortly afterwards, the gallows were removed from their commanding position, and all subsequent hangings were carried out within the walls. The execution of Mathew Phibbs was the last to be carried out publicly in Sligo.

## References:

"Sligo Champion"; "Sligo Independent"; "Sligo Chronicle"

12-1-1861
19-1-1861
16-3-1861
13-7-1861
10-8-1861
17-8-1861
24-8-1861

# Mills And Milling

It is generally accepted that water powered mills date back to the first century B.C., and possibly earlier, replacing the rotary quern as the means of grinding corn and extracting meal from grist. These early mills comprised a vertical wooden shaft with a number of blades or paddles, mortised into the hub. A stream of water, with a head of four feet or more, was directed against the blades down a wooden channel or trough, and the water propelled the blades, which were immersed in it by direct impulse. The shaft, which was carried up through a hole in the centre of the lower mill-stone to the upper mill-stone, being loosely keyed to it, revolved with the wheel. The bottom end of the shaft rotated in a bearing which could be raised or lowered, thus enabling the gap between the stones to be adjusted to produce the grade of meal required. Mills of this type, in which the water-wheel rotated in a horizontal plane, were known as horizontal mills. They were most common in remote thinly populated areas and were powered by small but rapid rivers or streams. The more complex and efficient vertical mills were generally to be found in the more densely populated areas.

By the 7th and 8th centuries water powered grist mills had become fairly common throughout Ireland and were referred to quite specifically in the legal tracts of that era. They were mainly small horizontal mills, commonly called *Danish mills*. This type of mill was a simple construction, being little more than a hand driven quern powered by water. It remained in use over large areas of the Irish countryside down to comparatively recent times.

Mills of the 17th and early 18th centuries were generally small 2-storey structures. A typical corn mill of that period was powered by a wooden 'breast' wheel, usually 12 or 13 feet in diameter and 3 feet 6 inches wide. It had a single pair of millstones driven through gearing that had altered little over the centuries. Such mills, grinding all types of grain for the local market, were numerous in all parts of the country well into the last century. Gradually, the horizontal water-wheels were converted into vertical wheel mills, which in the West of Ireland were called 'gig' mills. References to overshot and undershot wheels in the

## MILLS AND MILLING

19th century merely indicated whether the water went over the top or passed under the wheel. In areas where the volume of water was neither sufficient or constant, as in the case of Millport near Ballincar, a large dam, fitted with a sluice was constructed to store the water and release it in a controlled fashion, as required.

In the late 18th and in the 19th centuries, mills differed substantially from their predecessors. The old mills ground the grain while it was still uncleaned and the bolting or sifting of the ground meal was left to the bakers. In the new mills the grain was shelled and sifted before grinding. The typical structure made necessary by the new milling methods was one of at least three storeys. The grain was stored on the top floor; shelled, ground and bolted on the middle floor, while the main shafting and gearings stood on the ground level. Hoists to raise sacks and elevators to move loose grain or flour, driven from the water-wheel, were an essential feature of the new mills. A number of local mills, notably those at Ballisodare, Ballymote, Collooney, Dromore

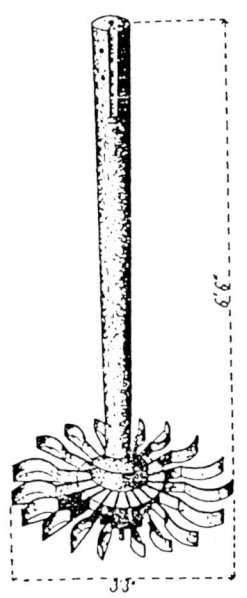

An Ancient Millwheel

## MILLS AND MILLING

West and Sligo, were constructed along these lines and operated accordingly.

The earliest reference to a mill in County Sligo dates back five centuries to 1463 when *Muilenn-Adam,* or *Adam's Mill,* is mentioned. A century and a half later, in 1612, there is a reference to Coolaney Mill in the will of Cormac O'Hara, the local chieftain, while closeby, at Templehouse, the Croftons had three grinding mills in operation. The first listing of mills was made in the Strafford Survey of 1633-35. It enumerated fifty or so mills, mostly corn, many of which were associated with a landed family's tower house or castle. Most of these were horizontal, or 'low Irish mills', but six were described as English or 'vertical' mills, presumably of the type introduced to Ireland by the Normans. In addition to the corn mills, there were five tucking mills for finishing or dressing cloth.

Over the following two centuries the number of mills multiplied with great rapidity. In various 18th century documents, notably Deeds, references are made to mills at Lisconny (1709); Keelogue (1722); Breeogue (1739); Sligo (1748); Ballymote (1761); Creevykeel and Ballintogher (1780); Bunninadden (1782) and Cummeen on the Ormsby estate. McParlan in his *"Statistical Survey"* (1802), states that there were two hundred corn, two flour and eight bleach mills operating throughout the County. Unfortunately, he omitted to name them or specify locations. The most complete record of mills was made in the 1830's in the course of the Ordnance Survey. The 6" maps, and to a lesser extent the accompanying *"Name Books"*, indicate the precise locations of approximately one hundred mills, comprising eighty corn, fifteen tuck and five flour, in addition to half a dozen bleach mills. Assuming that McParlan's figures are reasonably accurate, and taking into consideration the returns in both the Ordnance Survey and Griffith's Valuation lists of the mid 1850's, there was a big decline in the number of mills, though not necessarily in milling activity. The growth of large milling concerns, especially at Ballisodare, Ballymote, Collooney and Sligo, took much business away from the smaller mills and indirectly led to their eventual closure and decay. A study of subsequent Valuation lists, and the revised edition of the O.S. sheet maps, suggests that by the turn of the century little more than a handful of mills, big or small, were still operating in the production of

## MILLS AND MILLING

flour or oatmeal. The stiff competition from imported flour and American corn resulted in most of them being no longer economically viable.

Milling played an important role in the local economy, especially in rural areas. Being completely dependent upon water-power, mills, irrespective of type or size, were to be found on or close to river beds all over the County but with particular concentration on the Drumcliffe, Duneill, Easkey, Moy, Owenboy, Owenmore, Unshin and Sligo rivers. More than 90% of these concerns were corn mills, some of which had kilns attached. Generally, kilns were separate from mills and were most numerous in the south and east of the County. In the half barony of Coolavin alone there were in excess of fifty kilns in the pre-Famine period. This suggests that corn crops, especially oats, were extensively grown, some of it for domestic consumption but most of it was destined for the Sligo market where it was purchased for export. Regrettably, none of the mills listed or described hereafter are now operational or fully intact, while the vast majority, especially the smaller concerns, have vanished almost without trace. In many instances a stagnant dam or choked mill-race is all that remains on the ground to remind us of the enterprise, ingenuity and engineering skills of our fore-fathers in an era when milling was the most extensive industrial activity in rural Ireland.

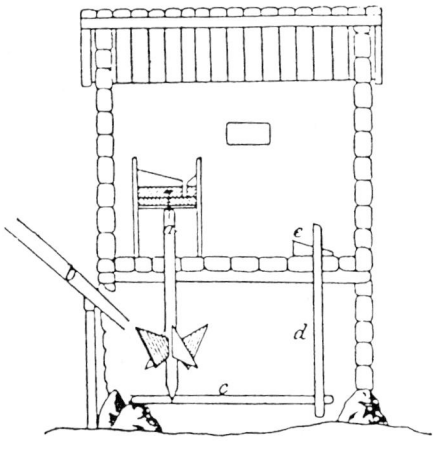

A Horizontal Mill

# MILLS LISTED IN STRAFFORD SURVEY, 1632-34

## Carbury, Barony of:

| Parish | Townland | Description |
| --- | --- | --- |
| Calry | Srabraghan | A good English mill- one (=Rathbraghan) of the best in the country. |
| Calry | Lecarowsrainaren | An Irish mill. |
| Drumcliffe | Ballincarra (= Ballincar) | An Irish mill. |
| Drumcliffe | Clonmulle (= Cloonmull) | A good English mill. |
| Drumcliffe | Drumcliffe | 3 or 4 'lowe' (=Irish) mills. |

## Corran, Barony of:

| Parish | Townland | Description |
| --- | --- | --- |
| Drumrat | Belragh (= Bearlough) | A little mill. |
| Emlaghfad | Ranecelige (=Rathnakelliga) | Upon this quarter the mill of Ballymote lies. |
| Kilmorgan | Laghtrein | A good Irish mill. |
| Kilmorgan | Tawnaghmore | A good Irish mill worth £10 a year. |
| Kilshalvey | Levalleinspur (= Spurtown?) | A low mill upon a little river. |

## Leyny, Barony of:

| Parish | Townland | Description |
| --- | --- | --- |
| Achonry | Balliarareagh (= Ballyara) | A low Irish mill. |
| Achonry | Carrowwilkin | Two good mills for grinding and tucking. |

| | | |
|---|---|---|
| Achonry | Lecarowreag (= Carrowreagh) | An old castle and a mill. |
| Achonry | Mollan | A low mill upon it. |
| Achonry | Tullanagloge | A castle and a mill. |
| Killoran | Coolaney | A mill upon a river hard-by the castle. |
| Killoran | Ballinvalley | A low mill upon a river that runs down from the mountain. |
| Kilmacteige | Banada | A good English mill. |
| Kilmacteige | Cullrecoille | A mill. |
| Kilvarnet | Bellenacan (= Ballinacarrow) | Two mills, one for grinding and another for tucking upon the river Owenmore. |
| Kilvarnet | Carowirill | A good Irish mill. |

**Tireragh, Barony of:**

| | | |
|---|---|---|
| Dromard | Bunnafedia | A tucking mill built by Thomas Crofton. |
| Easkey | Clonnoghgleragh | A mill and a castle upon this quarter. |
| Kilglass | Carrowlevone | A mill and a castle. |
| Kilmacshalgan | Dunneall | It hath a castle and a mill. |
| Skreen | Carowardbrone (= Ardabrone) | A mill and a castle. |

**Tirerill, Barony of:**

| | | |
|---|---|---|
| Aghanagh | Ballinmullany (=Ballymulanny) | A little small Irish mill worth £20 a year. |

| | | |
|---|---|---|
| Ballinakill | Knockenster (=Rockbrook) | A small Irish mill. |
| Ballisodare | Cashell | Mills let to Thomas, the Miller. |
| Drumcolumb | Lishconey (=Lisconny) | A spring with a good corn mill and tuck mill. It is worth £13 per annum by reason of the profit of the mill. |
| Killadoon | Moore (=Ballindoon) | A good spring with a mill upon it. |
| Killery | Tomeraney (=Toberanania) | A small Irish mill. |
| Killery | Drumconora (=Drumconra) | A small Irish mill |
| Killery | Correy (=Correagh) | A small Irish mill. |
| Killery | Drumcahey | A small Irish mill. |
| Killery | Coilmore | A very good Irish mill. |
| Kilmacallan | Trimvohy (Riverstown?) | There is a good fall of English mill upon it and another Irish mill upon the river Owyn-na-parke. |
| Kilmactranny | Trinvoy | There is a good fall of English mill. |
| Shancough | Shraduffe (=Straduff) | An Irish mill. |
| Shancough | Umerae (= Ummeryroe) | A very good English mill with a tuck mill. |

MILLS AND MILLING

# PRINCIPAL MILLS:

## Ballincar:

Ballincar has been associated with the milling industry since the 17th century when an Irish mill "in ye qr. of Ballincarra" formed part of the O'Connor-Sligo estate. A century later the property passed by purchase to the Wynnes of Hazelwood and the mill, on the water's edge on the north side of Sligo Bay, became known as *Millport*. In 1820 the mills were operated by William Christian and then by Charles Parke. Five years later they were leased to the London and Hibernian Corn and Flour Company. This arrangement apparently did not work for in 1833 the *"Journal"* carried the following advertisement:-

---

**TO BE LET**

*Flour Mills at Millport, where there is a good quay and water sufficient for vessels to load and discharge.*
*Mill abundantly supplied with water at all seasons and there is a fall of 27 feet.*

---

In 1837, Owen Wynne leased the mill, mill race and quay, together with 3 acres and 5 roods , to Patrick Murphy and John Gallagher of Sligo at an annual rent of £100 per annum. At that stage the mill had two pairs of grinding stones and one pair of shelling stones. It was 54ft by 30ft in area, substantially built with blocks and the water wheel had sufficient power to work two additional stones. It was capable of grinding 50 tons of oatmeal weekly. There was also a kiln and a miller's house, together with a flax mill, on the site. In 1837 Murphy & Gallagher sub-let the Mills to Messrs. Davis & Alex. Denny & Co. of Glasgow for the residue of the lease @ £100 per annum.

By the mid century *Millport* was being operated by Patrick Keighron, a Sligo merchant, and he continued to do so successfully for close on half a century. In 1860 he installed two scutching machines in the Flax Mill but these were extensively damaged in an accidental fire in January, 1865. After Keighron retired from business in the 'Nineties,the extensive concern was managed by William Hamilton, a

## MILLS AND MILLING

Scotch-born miller, and two assistants. Over the following two decades most of the workload consisted of grinding Indian corn and native wheat for merchants and farmers over a wide area. The long established milling concern was burned to the ground during 'The Troubles' and compensation, amounting to £250, was subsequently awarded to the Wynne estate.

Closeby, in the townland of Ballincar, stands *Millbrook* which, as the name implies, was a milling site in bygone days. In a lease dated, May 1779, this holding of slightly over 18 acres, was leased by the Wynnes of Hazelwood to Roger King for lives renewable for ever. The lease was renewed by the said lessors to John Patterson of Sligo in May, 1788. Shortly afterwards Ballincar gained prominence as a prime flax growing area and this gave rise to the building of a Flax Mill at *Millbrook*, with a large Bleach Green, known locally as *Draper's Lawn*, alongside. By 1817 Margaret Patterson. relict of the said John, had the entire property leased to William Cunningham,jun., a noted Sligo bleacher. A decade later Messrs Patterson and Henderson jointly operated the Mill and also bleached linens extensively.

Following the decline of the flax industry, the concern was converted to a Corn Mill. In November, 1831, Edward Patterson announced that he was engaging "an expert miller in the corn and flour business". The Mill had three pairs of stones and was capable of turning out 5 tons of flour, oatmeal and Indian corn daily. It enjoyed the peculiar privilege of the exclusive right to all water flowing from the bridge at Teesan, with a right of pass on either side of the canal through which the water flowed.*

By the mid century, or shortly afterwards, it passed to James Simpson who continued with the milling operation for a time. In 1873 the property, consisting of 18 acres and 1 rood, the house and Mill,was offered for sale in the Landed Estates Court and purchased by Charles Sedley, solicitor, for £440. At that stage the Mill, though "not at work", was described as "in working order". After Sedley's death in January, 1889, the property was acquired by John Young. At this remove there is nothing to suggest that the Mill was operated by either Sedley or Young. With the exception of the watercourse, all traces of the Mill have disappeared.

* The same source was utilised to work the mills at *Millport*

## MILLS AND MILLING

---

**TO BE LET**
*From 25th March*
**The Bleach-green, and Concerns,
AT BALLINCAR,**

As lately occupied by

*Messrs. Henderson and Tucker,*

CONSISTING OF

**Mills, Dwelling-house, and
Ten Acres of Land.**

For particulars, apply to Mr. Edward Patterson, of Lower Shannon, or Mr. William Patterson, of Millport.

January 8th, 1835.

---

TO BE LET

THE NEW AND EXTENSIVE

# OAT MILL,

## AT COLLOONEY

Within five miles of the Town of Sligo,

AND IMMEDIATE POSSESSION GIVEN.

There has been no expense spared in the erection of this Mill, which is now all but finished, it being built in the most permanent manner, and on the most approved Fire-Proof principle. The machinery is quite new, of the best description, and combines all the latest improvements. The Mill contains six pair of stones, two pair more can be added if required. The storage is very extensive, and there is a never failing supply of water in the driest seasons.

The locality is particularly favourable for Oats, of which there is an abundant supply to be had on the spot at all times. It is in fact in every way a most desirable concern. Proposals, in writing only, will be received by the proprietors,

Messrs. Martin Madden & Co.
Sligo. July 1845.

# MILLS AND MILLING

## Ballisodare:

Ballisodare has been a centre of milling from time immemorial, thanks to the successful harnessing of the immense water power available - considered "to excel any other in Ireland" and "unequalled in these Kingdoms". The river of that name consists of a series of rapids, amounting to 75 feet, which afford numerous sites for water powered mills. It is fairly certain that St. Fechin operated a water mill here in the 7th century as part of his monastic settlement. Since then, milling has been carried on, without interruption, down to recent times.

During the 18th and 19th centuries Ballisodare developed into one of the principal milling centres in the County. In the early 1800's there were five small mills operating, three for grinding oats, another for barley and one for making flour, in addition to as many corn kilns. There was also McDonald's bleach mill which was extensively worked until he was swept away in the cholera outbreak in 1832. The following year Robert Culbertson, a Sligo merchant, leased a plot of ground in Knockmuldowney, on the right bank, from Joshua E. Cooper, on which he built a large corn mill, costing £5,000. It was fitted out with the most approved machinery, had two water wheels of 70 h.p. and employed twenty workmen. A decade later, and using only one-twelfth of the available water power, there was an output of 500 tons of oatmeal a week, some of which was exported from the basin below the falls where vessels of 100 tons berthed. During the 1830's Alexander Sim operated a corn mill here. It was worked by two wheels of 36 h.p. and gave employment to twenty five.

In 1845 Robert Culbertson leased part of the lands of Corhownagh, with mills and watercourses on the other side of the river, previously held by Elizabeth McDonald and Alexander McCreery, for an unexpired period of fourteen years. The tenements comprised the Ballisodare mill, in the occupation of Richard Mangan and Robert Sherlock; a corn mill and quay occupied by Thomas Dobbin; a barley

356

## MILLS AND MILLING

mill, then used as a corn store by John Beatty and a bleach mill and yard, formerly McDonalds, and then in the occupation of Ambrose and Patrick McTucker. Culbertson subsequently built a large flour mill on the left bank which did a roaring trade supplying the shopkeepers of the County and beyond with their favourite brands. In the space of two decades Culberston is said to have expended up to £20,000 on mill properties in Ballisodare. In 1856 a fatal explosion in the flour mill maimed several workmen and killed or seriously injured nine others. This calamity had a profound effect on Culbertson's health and led to his premature death.

In 1862 the Ballisodare Mills were acquired by Messrs. Middleton and Pollexfen of Sligo, who renamed them *Avena Mills*. Over the following decade and a half they were energetically operated day and night, except Sundays, by two relays of workers. The following description of the Mills was published in the *"Corn Trade Journal"* in August, 1877 :-

*"Avena Mills consist of three large buildings named No.1 Flour Mill, No. 2. Flour Mill, No. 3 Flour Mill and Corn Mill, together with large storage accommodation, built separately from, but convenient to each mill.*

*Nos. 1 & 2 Flour Mills are in one large building, and built on the western side of river; they are driven by two three-quarter breastwheels, each being 24ft in diameter, and 10ft wide; they contain 20 pairs 4.5 burrs.*

*No. 3. Flour Mill is built on same side of the river, but further towards its mouth; it is driven by an undershot wheel 24ft diameter and 9 ft wide, it contains 8 pairs 4.5 burrs.*

*The weekly average turn-out of these three mills is 1,200 sacks, but the miller says that in winter season he can manufacture up to 1,500 sacks; they contain nine silk Flour dressing machines, five smutts and five Child's Wheat cleaning machines.*

*The Maize mill is on the eastern side of the river, nearly opposite No. 3 Flour Mill, and is connected with the opposite bank of the river by a narrow wooden bridge for convenience of workmen; it contains nine pairs of 4.5ft burrs, is driven by two three-quarter breastwheels, each being 18ft diameter and 6 ft wide. The average weekly turn out during the meal season is 160 tons. On this side of the river, driven by machinery connected with the Corn Mill, are large oat kilns. Here the oats are received from farmers, kiln-dried, cleaned, and prepared for exportation or milling. On the same side of the river is a small mill*

# MILLS AND MILLING

*containing two pairs of stones for crushing maize for horse feeding, and on the opposite bank the gas works, which supply the mills and Avena House (the winter residence of Mr. Middleton) with gas light."*

The complex also included millers' cottages, a millwright's house and a row of workmens' dwellings.

In 1883, following the dissolution of the old partnership of Middleton and Pollexfen, the Ballisodare Mills were acquired by Messrs. W. & G.T. Pollexfen & Co. for £9,130. The new owners modernised the machinery and turned out the well known Avena brands of flour, *Pride of the West* and *Early Dawn*, in great quantities. Evidence of the progressive management policies pursued by the Pollexfens was the installation of a series of conveyor belts and aerial

*A view of the Ballisodare Mills c. 1900*

ropeways which spanned the river and linked the individual mills, in addition to transporting cargoes of flour and maize to the railway siding. In the 1920's there was a daily output of 40 tons of flour, 120 tons of maize meal and 20 tons of *Avena* cooked cattle food, and this provided regular employment to a workforce of a hundred or so.

In 1974 Messrs. Pollexfen sold Avena Mills, the last of their once extensive network, to Odlums Ltd. Shortly afterwards, the flour milling section was closed for good, with a consequent loss of employment. Only the Provender section, animal and poultry foods, continued in operation. Five years later, in July 1989, what were once Culbertson's

Drawing of Ballisodare Mills prior to demolition.

prize mills, finally closed with a further loss of thirty jobs. Shortly afterwards, the Mills were demolished and all that now remains is the empty shell of portion of the once thriving complex. Milling had been a way of life in Ballisodare for centuries untold and the closure of the famed mills was the final chapter in the history of milling in County Sligo. The unique water power of the Ballisodare River, which for centuries turned the mill wheels, is now being harnessed to generate electricity.

# Ballymote:

It is probable that milling in Ballymote dates back to the 15th century when the Franciscan Friary was established in the Town. However, the earliest documented record of a mill was two centuries later in the townland of Rathnakelliga. From an extant Deed, dated 1761, we learn that Mary, Countess of Shelburne, leased the corn mill of Ballymote to David Melville, Gent, in addition to 2 acres adjoining, for three lives @ £36 per annum.

In 1795 Robert Gorman built a corn mill at Keenaghan, possibly on the site of an earlier mill. It was powered by water brought all the way from Ballinascarrow Lake, which was also the source for an earlier bleach mill. In the early hours of Sunday, December 31, 1854, it was accidently burnt to the ground, only hours after the last workmen had gone home. Fortunately, it was insured for £1,700, though this did not cover all the losses sustained. The mill was later rebuilt by the Gormans and fitted out with the most modern machinery. In its reconstructed state it was three and a half storeys high and the main block was 120 ft long by 23 ft broad. There were also two wings abutting on either side of the main entrance, each c.850 sq. ft in area. There were also stores and a miller's house, all enclosed in a large courtyard. When fully operational it employed a miller and a dozen or more workmen. With the coming of the railway three carters were employed to convey consignments of Indian corn from the station to the mill. Subsequently, a special siding and store was constructed close to the station which was connected to the mill by an aerial cable system, thus eliminating transportation by road.

# MILLS RECORDED BY ORDNANCE SURVEY, 1835-'36

**Carbury, Barony of:**

| | |
|---|---|
| Ballincar: | Flour mills at Millport and Millbrook. |
| Ballintrillick: | Corn mill in ruins at Keelogue. |
| Ballyfree: | Old corn mill and mill pond. |
| Breeogue: | Ruins of a corn mill. |
| Collinsford: | Corn mill and tuck mill. |
| Drumcliffe: | Corn mill and tuck mill. |
| | Corn mill at Cullaghbeg. |
| Grange: | Corn mill and tuck mill. |
| Grellagh: | Corn mill. |
| Kilsellagh: | Ruins of two bleach mills. |
| Lislary: | Corn mill. |
| Scardan: | Flour mills. |
| Sligo: | Flour mills |
| Willowbrook: | Tuck mill. |
| Rathbraghan: | Flour mills. |

**Coolavin, Barony of:**

| | |
|---|---|
| Drumlashma: | Corn mill and three corn kilns in Cloontycarn townland. |
| Gurteen: | Corn mill. |
| Ragwood: | Mill in ruins |

**Corran, Barony of:**

| | |
|---|---|
| Ballymote: | Corn mill. |
| Battlefield: | Corn and tuck mill. |
| Bunninadden: | Corn mill, called a "Gig" mill, with undershot power. Wheel 3.5 ft. in diameter. |
| Carrowcrory: | Corn mill. |
| Daghloonagh: | Corn and tuck mill. |
| Killavil: | Ruins of a corn mill and kiln. |
| Kilmorgan: | Corn mill. |

**Leyny, Barony of:**

| | |
|---|---|
| Aclare: | Corn mill and kiln in townland of Lislea. Also a tuck mill. |

| | |
|---|---|
| Ballinacarrow (South): | Corn and bleach mills (=Thornhill) |
| Ballinvalley: | Corn mill. |
| Ballisodare: | Three tuck mills and one corn mill in townland of Knockmuldowney. Barley mill, and bleach mill in Kilboglashy townland. |
| Ballyglass: | Ruins of corn mill. |
| Banada: | A mill. |
| Belclare: | Corn mill. |
| Carha: | Corn mill, kiln and tuck mill. |
| Carrownacleigha: | Corn mill. |
| Carrownaskeagh: | Cloth and corn mill, and corn kiln. |
| Carrownacreevy: | 'Gig' mill in ruins. |
| Carrowcarragh: | Corn mill, power overshot and driven by a rivulet or mill race. Let by Capt. Henry Irwin. |
| Castlerock: | Careton mill and kiln. |
| Cloonacool: | Corn mill and two kilns. |
| Cloonacurra: | Corn and tuck mill. Mill wheel 14 ft x 2 ft in diameter. |
| Cloonlaughill: | Two 'gig' mills for grinding oats. Power undershot. Also corn kiln. |
| Collooney: | Two corn mills and bleach mill. |
| Coolaney: | Corn mill. |
| Curry: | Corn mill. |
| Drimina: | Corn mill. |
| Glanawoo: | Two corn mills and a kiln. |
| Greenville: | Old bleach mill. |
| Larkhill: | Corn mill. |
| Lissalough: | Mill in ruins and corn kiln. |
| Montiagh: | A 'gig' mill. |
| Ougham: | Corn mill. |
| Sessuecommon: | Old mill and corn kiln. |
| Sessuegilroy: | A mill. |
| Tullanaglug: | Corn mill. |

**Tireragh, Barony of:**

| | |
|---|---|
| Altonelvick: | Corn mill built in 1821. Wheel 12ft x 2ft in diameter. |

| | |
|---|---|
| Ballinlig: | Corn mill first established in 1036. In perfect use since 1800. Also a kiln. |
| Belville: | Corn mill. |
| Carrowbleagh East: | Corn mill and kiln. |
| Doonecoy: | Corn mill. |
| Doonflin: | Old corn mill and kiln. |
| Donaghantraine: | Corn mill and kiln. |
| Drumnagoal: | Corn mill. |
| Easkey: | Corn mills at Shannonpark West and Toorboy. Ruins of a mill at Killeenduff. |
| Grangemore: | Corn mill. |
| Knockagower: | Corn mill. |
| Leaffoney: | Corn mill built in 1690. A tuck mill for dressing blue frieze cloth. Built in 1822, it dresses and thickens 6000 yards annually. |
| Rathmurphy: | Corn mill. |
| Spring Garden: | Corn and tuck mill under one roof. Wheel at each side of mill: 14ft x 2ft in diameter. Built in 1796. Daniel Scanlon, miller. |

**Tirerill, Barony of:**

| | |
|---|---|
| Ardagh: | Corn mill in Bellanascarva townland. |
| Ardcurley: | Corn mill built in 1835. |
| Ballinafad: | Corn mill and kiln. |
| Castlebaldwin: | Corn mill. |
| Castleore: | Old mill. |
| Crossboy: | Old mill and corn kiln. |
| Killeenduff: | Mill in ruins. |
| Knockbeg West: | A mill. |
| Largan: | Built by Neynoes but scarce of water - worked only in winter. Wheel: 14ft in diameter x 1ft.10" broad. |
| Lisconny: | Old mill. |
| Raunatruffaun: | Corn mill. |
| Riverstown: | Two corn mills and one tuck mill. |
| Rockbrook: | Corn mill. |
| Straduff: | Corn mill. |
| Ummeryroe: | Corn mill. |

# MILLS AND MILLING

The Ballymote Mills in ruins and (below) portion of the former 'Hollow' Mills, Collooney.

MILLS AND MILLING

For over a century and a half the mills were owned and operated by successive generations of the Gorman family - Henry and John, Richard and Robert and finally Robert, jnr. until October 1941, when another accidental fire gutted the building. Milling in Ballymote came to an abrupt end. The impressive ruins of the once prosperous concern can be seen just off the Gurteen Road.*

# Collooney:

Collooney, with its exceptional source of power from the combined waters of the Owenmore and Owenboy, has been a prime location for milling from time immemorial. The 17th century *Down Survey* records the existence of a mill and by 1727 both Swiney's Corn mill and Braxton's Tuck mill were operating there. However, it was not until 1797 that a large structure, in the form of a bleach mill, was built at Ardcotton, subsequently known as Camphill, by Francis Jackson, on a plot leased from William Phibbs. The cost of the undertaking was £7,000, half of which was spent in sinking a 'race' to convey the water from the river.

In 1814 the mill was jointly leased by Andrew Kelly and James Ballantine, and three years later Kelly bought out Jackson's interest for a reputed £3,000. So successful was this venture, and the profits accruing from it, that he was in a position to spend an equal amount on an old corn mill and more than double that on the building of a new 4-storey mill alongside, containing six pairs of stones and described by a seasoned traveller as "the largest and best in Ireland". At the height of his prosperity Kelly suddenly fell into pecuniary embarrassment, brought on by having incurred liabilities on behalf of a friend. Arising from this unexpected development, his property was put on the market in 1838 and acquired by Alexander Sim, an enterprising Scotsman from Aberdeen, for £5,000. The change in ownership did not meet with local approval, the new proprietor was boycotted and the mills remained silent. Eventually, in 1840, in an effort to resolve the *impasse,* Sim agreed to hand back the property to the former owner for £6,000, who in turn disposed of it to the Maddens, James, who was Andrew Kelly's brother-in-law, and his brother, Thomas.

---

\* Messrs. R. & R. Gorman also operated a milling business in Union Street, Sligo between 1930 and 1970.

## MILLS AND MILLING

The Valuation survey of the mid 1850's valued the Camphill, or *Hollow Mills*, at £450; £150 for the old mill and £305 for the new structure. In 1872 the mills were leased to Messrs Middleton and Pollexfen who operated them until 1885 under the local management of Patrick Harte and his assistant, John Farrell.The *"Corn Trade Journal"* of August, 1877, described the Camphill Mills as consisting of a flour mill with five runs of 4.5 feet burrs, a corn mill with six runs and similar sized burrs and a small sawmill. They were driven by two overshot wheels, each 25 feet in diameter and 5 feet wide and a small turbine of 14 h.p. There were also three flour dressing machines, two wheat separators and a wheat cleaning machine. The weekly output was 240 sacks of flour and 40 tons of maize meal daily during the meal season.

Meanwhile, on the Abbey site across the river, Alexander Sim had established a thriving business. In addition to the old corn mill which he leased from the Kellys in 1838 and subsequently purchased and modernised, he built a flour mill, reputedly "one of the finest in the Province", as well as extensive stores on which he expended close on £10,000 in 1847-48. The mill was 4-storeys high, 124ft long by 44 ft broad; it had an immense overshot wheel, 36 ft in diameter, a 30 ft fall of water and capable of keeping eight or nine stones grinding 600 tons of Indian corn a week. An aerial conveyor belt was also installed for the transportation of grain from, and sacks of ground corn to, a siding at the nearby railway station. Between 1853 and 1858 an average of 15,450 tons of meal and flour was ground annually. Over the following two decades the Collooney Mills prospered and much of the success was credited to millwright, Sandy Munro, and head millers Michael Drummy, M. Hargadon and Pat Drummy. Customers over a wide area were further facilitated by the building of extensive distributive depots at Stonehall and Ballygawley. By the turn of the century, owing to stiff competition from imported American flour, the workings of the mills were limited to the grinding of Indian corn. The long association of the Sim family with corn and flour milling on both sides of the Collooney river ended with the death of Alexander Sim, jnr. in 1918.

In 1887 Martin J. Madden, who then resided in Bray, leased and subsequently sold the *Hollow Mills*, together with the old bleach mill, to Alexander Sim, jnr. After the milling business went into decline in the

## Two prominent Sligo Millers

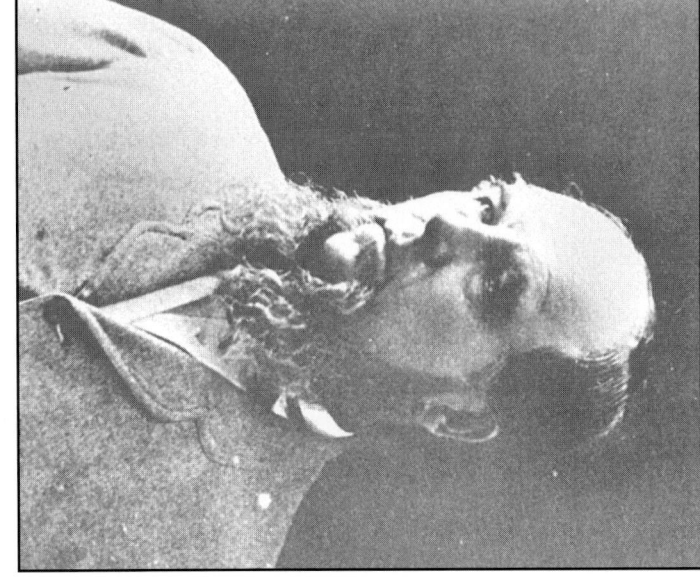

William Middleton (1819 - 1882)

Wilbram A.G. Middleton (1898 - 1960)

## MILLS AND MILLING

late 'Nineties', Sim and his brother, Allison, launched the Irish Calcium Carbide Company for the production of accetylene gas and converted the said mills for that purpose. A new mill race, a quarter of a mile in length, was constructed, linking the river with the old corn mill, thereby providing a sufficient supply of water to operate a large turbine wheel of 600 h.p. The decline in demand for carbide after World War 2 led to the temporary closure of the *Hollow Mills* but they were re-opened for a short period in the 1930's by W.A. Middleton for the production of maize. The former Bleach Mill, subsequently, Manley's Sawmill, was also re-vamped and successfully operated as a Woollen Mill, until 1923, by the Sim family. It was re-opened under the new ownership in 1929 and continued in production until it finally closed in 1934.

After lying idle for two decades, the mills on both sides of the river were taken over by Wilbram A.G. Middleton of Collooney, who had gained considerable milling expertise in the Ballisodare Mills, managed by his father, Adam. Modern machinery was installed and up-to-date methods introduced. 'Fatenol' cooked food, maize meal, oatmeal and rolled oats were produced in large quantities. Giant turbines were used to light the premises and also the town. During the 'Emergency' the 'Hollow Mills' were closed owing to a lack of sufficient home-grown grain but were partly re-opened shortly afterwards. The long established Mills, on both sides of the river, were finally closed on the retirement of Wilbram A.G. Middleton in 1956.

The Collooney Mills, on the Abbey site, were acquired by Messrs. Gowna Wood Industries Ltd. (G.W.I.) in 1961 who started a successful joinery industry on the site. Unfortunately, in the process, the former Sim homestead, *The Abbey*, an elegant residence, together with the extremely impressive cut-stone mills, were unnecessarily raised to the ground. The Camphill, or *Hollow mills*, were more fortunate. They were purchased by the late Jack Hanley and utilised as a Carbite Factory for a period and subsequently for a chain making industry. The turbines have been continued in operation and are annually generating three million units of electricity which is fed into the national grid. A bird's eye view of the impressive cut-stone buildings in the hollow by the Owenmore River, once a hive of industry, may be obtained from the nearby railway station.

# Coolaney:

There is a tradition of milling in Coolaney going back to the 17th century, and possibly earlier, when the O'Hara's, the local chieftains, operated a mill there. The Strafford Survey recorded the existence of a mill "upon a river hard by the castle". In the mid 1830's Henry Burrows of *Greenville* built a new corn mill on the river Owenboy. It was a three and a half storey structure, 56 ft by 20 ft and had three kilns attached. This mill, which formed part of the O'Hara estate, was advertised for letting on occasions between 1836 and 1850. In an advertisement, dated August 1849, it was stated that the machinery was in good repair, with three pairs of stones, only two of which were working. The kilns, which had been lately covered with metal kiln-plates, were in perfect order. There was also a miller's house on the site.

After the death of Burrows in the early 1860's, the mill and kilns, which yielded an income of £20 per annum, were taken over by Patrick Doyle, whose son, Thomas, and grandson, John, operated them in turn. In 1908 or thereabouts, a large turbine was installed and a saw-mill was also added. The mill ceased operation shortly after the John's death in 1925, but the saw-mill continued working into the Forties.*

# Dromore West:

The Dunneill River, which cascades in a series of miniature falls through the village of Dromore West and into the sea at Donaghantraine, was the source of power for a number of corn mills and a flax mill.

The *Strafford Survey* noted the existence of a mill close to Dunneill Castle. Two centuries later the *Ordnance Survey* listed a corn mill on or close to the same site. The 3-storey mill, standing close to the bridge in the village, originally formed part of the Fenton estate before passing

---

\* The Doyles, who were descended from Andrew Doyle, a miller of Flaughana, Doocastle, were the principal milling family in the County for close on a century. Successive generations were described as 'Master Millers' and were associated with mills at Banada, Castlerock, Cloonacurragh, Curry and Montiagh, in addition to Coolaney. In 1901 Census Patrick, John, and Joseph, sons of Thomas Doyle and Brigid O'Hara of Coolaney, were described as millers by occupation. Michael Doyle (1846-1928), founder and one time Secretary of the I.N.T.O. whose life-size statute stands in Ballymote, was a member of the Flaughana family.

# MILLS AND MILLING

by sale, first to Alex. Henry and then to Wm. B. Lougheed. In the 1860's the mill and kiln was leased to James McMunn, M.D., who sublet it. In March 1877, Owen Carthy, a local shopkeeper, was killed in a fall while working in the upper storey of the mill. In 1879 it was unoccupied. However, a decade later the concern was operated both as a corn mill and saw mill and leased to T. Mulligan and James Cavanagh, amongst others. In the 1890's Thaddeus Tiernan of *Woodhill House* became the lessee but it is not clear if the mill was worked by him. A decade later it was idle and in bad repair. The building was subsequently a depot for Messrs. Denny of Sligo and is currently used as a store.

Further down the river, in the townland of Knockacullen, stands the unroofed but impressive remains of a 3-storey mill. It was built in the

1840's by the Jones family as a flax mill but subsequently converted into a corn mill, a process that was still in progress in 1855. It was advertised for Letting in 1862 by Captain Lewis G. Jones of *Woodhill House*. It was described as containing three pairs of stones, a kiln and two lofts capable of holding 200 sacks of oats. There was also a miller's house. A decade later there was a vacancy for a 'first class' miller. Available evidence would suggest that the mill was operated by Thaddeus Tiernan after he had purchased the property in 1875 and by his son, Thomas, until 1920, or thereabouts.

Closer to the sea another corn mill and kiln was operating at Donaghantraine, powered by the waters of the Corrowcor river, a tributary of the Dunneill. In the mid 19th century it formed part of the estate of Captain John W. King. After his death in 1868 the mill became vacant and there is no evidence to suggest that it was ever worked again. Its ivy clad ruins are still visible near the seashore.

# MILLS AND MILLING

Thriving Mills of yesteryear: Dromore West (above) and (below) Bunninadden.

## MILLS AND MILLING

# Rathbraghan:

Rathbraghan was one of the earliest milling sites in the region. The *Strafford Survey* notes the existence of a good English mill, "one of the best in the country". Initially, it formed part of the Strafford estate and in 1687 was being operated by Captain Humphrey Booth for grinding corn and the 'tucking' of cloth. In 1722 the mills became the property of the Wynne family and, half a century later, leased by them to William Christian who later became the Deputy Weighmaster of Sligo. In February, 1828, Christian announced that the Flour Mills of Rathbraghan were "at full work" and that grain entrusted to his care would be manufactured, "in the best possible manner and with the strictest despatch". Work in the mills was interrupted a few months later by an outbreak of fire but they were back in production a year later.

In the 1840's the mills were operated by John Hearne and a decade later by William Green. He was succeeded by Michael O'Connor who paid a rental of £50 a year and carried out a number of improvements, including the installation of new mill stones. After he had been declared a bankrupt in 1864 the mills closed and never re opened. In 1870 they were described as "shut up and waste", and thus they remained until burned to the ground in April, 1887.

# Riverstown:

Milling in the Riverstown area can be traced back to the 17th century when the *Strafford Survey* recorded the existence of two mills in the area, although precise locations are difficult to establish at this point in time. In the opening decades of the last century two corn mills and a tuck mill were operating very close to each other on the Unshin river. In the 1850's James Clerkin worked a corn and tuck mill on or close to the site of the present N.C.F. stores. The latter ceased operating shortly afterwards but the corn mill continued to function until the Eighties when his son, Owen Clerkin, held the leasehold from the Coopers of *Markree Castle*. Over the bridge in the townland of Gobbadagh, or Coopershill, the Cooper family operated a corn mill and kiln which appears to have been a long established utility. In July,

## MILLS AND MILLING

1859, the Mill and miller's house was advertised for letting by Charles W. Cooper. Like so many similar concerns it ceased working a century ago.

Up river from Riverstown, in the townland of Bellanascarva, was the Ardagh Mill. In the early 19th century it was being operated by the Lloyd family and in the 1840's by Richard G. Brinkley, who had acquired the estate through marriage. Over the following three decades it was leased in turn to Manus Harper, Moses Monds and William Hunter. It was described as a corn mill with two kilns and five pairs of stones and was valued at £80. There was also a miller's house. It ceased operations in the late 'Eighties and was described as "partly burnt and dilapidated" a few years later.

# Sligo:

The Sligo Mills, in one form or another, can be traced back to the 17th century and , in all probability, to Norman times. With the foundation of the Abbey of Sligo in 1252-53, it is very likely that a mill formed part of the monastic complex. In the 1608 grant of James I to Sir James Fullerton there is a reference, *inter alia,* to "the mill with its watercourses". In a tripartite deed, dated July 1687, William, Earl of Strafford, secured a monopoly in milling by which all persons in the parishes of St. John, Kilmacowen and Killaspugbrone were obliged to have all their corn ground at the Sligo mills. There was also a provision that no other mill could be built on the north or south sides of the Garvogue River.

In the 17th century the mills were situated in what was described as the 'Castle Quarter', just below the Bridge of Sligo and adjacent to the Old Quay on the site of the what is now the *Silver Swan Hotel.* In 1697 the Mills and other properties were purchased by Benjamin Burton and from him they passed to the Martin family, in whose ownership they remained and were successfully worked for over a century. In 1789 the Sligo Mills were reputed to have been worth over £1,500 a year. Alexander Sim, jnr. purchased them in 1857. After he was declared a bankrupt four years later, the property was acquired by Messrs. Middleton and Pollexfen. In the Notice of Sale the mills were

## MILLS AND MILLING

described as consisting of a Flour Mill with two undershot wheels and four pairs of stones, a Corn and Oatmeal Mill under the one roof. The latter had one water wheel, with three pairs of stones in addition to extensive storage and four kilns. *"The Sligo Mills have been long famous for the manufacture of flour and meals and the former proprietor realised a very large fortune by them"*, quoted the instrument of sale. In 1878 the average weekly output was 150 tons of maize meal and 250 sacks of flour.

Following the death of William Middleton in 1882 and the subsequent dissolution of the partnership, the Mills were bought by Messrs. W. & G. T. Pollexfen. Over the following three decades the Sligo Mills were profitably operated by the Pollexfens under the management of Arthur Jackson. New water powered turbines were installed and, in case of low water in the summertime, the Mills were kept going by a huge Crossley Gas engine with a suction gas plant. Owing to depressions in the flour trade, new machinery was installed at the turn of the century for the manufacture of maize meal and coarse feeding stuffs and output averaged 100 tons a day. All milling operations ceased in the years immediately after World War 1. In 1927 the long established Sligo Mills finally closed for good and the business was transferred to the firm's other mills at Ballisodare.

The large 4-storey building lay idle for a period. It subsequently housed a Cold Storage on the ground floor, operated by Alfred Carroll's *North West Trading Company and Cold Storage,* and a Chip Basket manufactory on the upper floors. The section of the Mills that extended to the rear of the Post Office was acquired by the Department of Posts & Telegraphs and a new Telephone Exchange built on the site in 1957. The remainder of the Mill complex, together with the adjoining Quay, was eventually acquired by J.J. Higgins who built the *Silver Swan Hotel* on what was the site of one of the oldest mills in the County.

The Distillery complex at Riverside, which also formed part of the Martin estate, contained a corn mill with three pairs of stones. After lying idle for some time it was leased to Alexander Sim, jnr. in 1857, and acquired by Messrs. Middleton & Pollexfen in 1862. It was badly damaged by fire in March, 1864. Twenty years later it passed to Messrs. Pollexfen & Co., who operated it for a number of years. In the 1890's it was described as 'vacant'.

MILLS AND MILLING

## Steam Mills:

In 1842 Edward Kelly of *Ballytivnan House*, a leading Sligo merchant, built a large corn mill on a site in Knox's Street, where *Pennys* now stands. It was operated by steam and had a distinctive landmark in the form of a 90 ft tall chimney. *

Kelly operated the mill until 1867 when he advertised it for sale or letting. It was subsequently acquired by Messrs. Harper Campbell and extensively remodelled. In 1906 the mills were moved to a new building, constructed of ferro-concrete, at the approach to the Deepwater Quay and were known as the *Harbour Mills*. In addition to milling, an extensive trade was carried on in flours, grains of all kinds and feeding stuffs. A workforce of close on four score had constant employment. The mill was closed and the plant and machinery auctioned-off in August, 1960.

In the 1840's a 4-storey Corn Store and Kiln, on the eastern side of Old Market Street, was occupied by Edmond Rochford. By the turn of the century the premises had been converted into a steam operated Corn Mill and was operated by P.N. White of *Breeogue House*. The concern was badly damaged by fire in September, 1914.

\* The chimney remained in place until demolished in 1923.

# Mills Listed in Griffith's Valuation, 1854-57

### Carbury, Barony of:

| Parish | Location | Type of Mill | Owner | Tenant |
|---|---|---|---|---|
| Ahamlish | Bunduff[1] | Corn | Viscount Palmerston | Samuel Martin |
| Drumcliffe | Barnaderg[2] | Corn | Viscount Palmerston | Thomas McCLean |
| Drumcliffe | Collinsford | Corn | George Dunne | Michael McHugh |
| Drumcliffe | Cullaghbeg[3] | Corn | Sir R. Gore-Booth | Mathew Allen |

## MILLS AND MILLING

| | | | | |
|---|---|---|---|---|
| Drumcliffe | Millbrook | Flour | John Wynne | Ed. Simpson |
| Drumcliffe | Millport | Corn | John Wynne | Pat. Keighron |
| Calry | Rathbraghan | Corn & Flour | John Wynne. Sub-let to Wm. Christian | Wm. Greene |
| Killaspug-brone | Scardan[4] | Flour | Rev.G. Mansfield | Alex. McIntyre |
| Rossinver | Keeloges | Corn | Sir R. Gore-Booth | In fee |
| St. John's | Fish Quay | Flour | Cpt. James Martin | In fee |
| St. John's | Riverside | Corn | Cpt. James Martin | In fee |
| St. Johns's | Knox's St. | Corn | Edward Kelly | In fee |

### Coolavin, Barony of:

| | | | | |
|---|---|---|---|---|
| Kilfree | Gurteen[5] | Corn | Jane Costello | Michael Leonard |
| Kilfree | Kilfree | Corn | Richard O'Cadell | James Bruen |
| Kilfree | Moygara | Corn | Robert G. Taylor | James McKeon |

### Corran, Barony of:

| | | | | |
|---|---|---|---|---|
| Cloonoghill | Bunninadden[6] | Corn | Col. Alex. Perceval | James Scanlon |
| Emlaghfad | Ballymote | Corn | R. Gore-Booth | John & Henry Gorman |
| Kilmorgan | Kilmorgan | Corn | Michael Lang | John Fahy |
| Kilmorgan | Lackagh | Corn | Wm. J. Stewart | James Scanlon |
| Kilturra | Bellanaleck[7] | Corn | John Wynne | Phillip Beirne |
| Kilshalvey | Killavil | Corn | Viscount Lorton | James Morrison |
| Toomour | Battlefield | Corn | James Knott | Patrick Doyle |
| Toomour | Carrowcrory[8] | Corn | Viscount Lorton | Mathew Leonard |

# MILLS AND MILLING

## Leyny, Barony of:

| | | | | |
|---|---|---|---|---|
| Achonry | Achonry | Corn | Cath. Armstrong | Thos. Commons |
| Achonry | Carrowcarragh | Corn | Wm. Crosby | Peter Crosby |
| Achonry | Cloonacool | Corn & Kiln | Mary Young | Luke Brennan |
| Achonry | Cloonacool | Corn | Mary Young | Martin Doyle |
| Achonry | Cloonlaughil[9] | Corn | Knox | Myles Henry |
| Achonry | Cloonlaughil | Corn & Kiln | Knox | Martin Scally |
| Achonry | Curry[10] | Corn | Richard Phibbs | James Filan |
| Achonry | Curry | Corn | Richard Phibbs | Patrick Breheny |
| Achonry | Montiagh[11] | Corn | James Colleran | Patrick Doyle |
| Achonry | Sessuegilroy | Corn | Ed. J. Cooper | James Finan |
| Ballisodare | Camphill[12] | Corn & Bleach | Wm. Phibbs | Martin Madden |
| Ballisodare | Camphill | Flour | Wm. Phibbs | Thomas J. Madden |
| Ballisodare | Collooney | Flour & Corn | E.J. Cooper | Alex. Sim |
| Ballisodare | Kilboglashy[13] | Flour & Corn | Wm. Phibbs | Robert Culbertson |
| Killoran | Ballinvalley | Corn &Tuck | Charles Thompson | James Bruen |
| Killoran | Carha | Corn | Philip Taylor | Patrick Reilly |
| Killoran | Coolaney | Corn & Kiln | Henry Burrows | Patrick Doyle |
| Kilvarnet | Thornhill[14] | Corn & Bleach | R.W.Hall-Dare | Charles Gilbert |
| Kilmactigue | Aclare[15] | Corn | Wm.Ormsby - Gore | John Burns |
| Kilmactigue | Aclare | Corn | Wm.Ormsby - Gore | Wm. Evans |

# MILLS AND MILLING

| | | | | |
|---|---|---|---|---|
| Kilmactigue | Banada | Corn | Thomas D. Jones | Thomas Doyle |
| Kilmactigue | Belclare | Corn | Wm. Ormsby - Gore | Peter Commons |
| Kilmactigue | Carrowreagh | Corn | Henry Caulfield | Edward Quinn |
| Kilmactigue | Castlerock | Corn | John Irwin | Thomas Doyle |
| Kilmactigue | Drimina[16] | Corn | O'Connor Don | James McVeigh |
| Kilmactigue | Glenawoo | Corn | Samuel Robinson | Henry O'Brien |
| Kilmactigue | Glenawoo | Corn | Samuel Robinson | Michael Clark |
| Kilmactigue | Gortersluin | Corn | Jane Irwin | Martin Quinn |
| Kilmactigue | Kilmactigue | Corn & Kiln | Henry Caulfield | Michael Quinn |

## Tireragh, Barony of:

| | | | | |
|---|---|---|---|---|
| Dromard | Ballinlig | Corn | Col.John Irwin | Charles Beatty |
| Dromard | Spring Garden[17] | Corn | Sir James Crofton | Julia Scanlon |
| Easkey | Easkey [18] | Corn | John McNama | Michael Burns |
| Kilglass | Cabraghkeel | Corn | Owen Martin | Michael Fenton |
| Kilglass | Culleens | Corn | Thos. Jones | Patrick Gordon |
| Kilglass | Leaffoney | Corn | Charles Parke | Thos.& Wm. Carroll |
| Kilmacshalgan | Knockacullen | Corn & Kiln | Vaughan Jones | In fee |
| Kilmacshalgan | Dromore | Corn & Kiln | John Fenton | In fee |
| Skreen | Drumnagoal | Corn | David Fenton | Mark Bruen |
| Skreen | Farniharpy | Corn | D.N. Webber | Robert Golden |
| Skreen | Masreagh | Corn | N.O. Furey | In fee |
| Templeboy | Donaghantraine | Corn | Capt. J.W.King | In fee |

MILLS AND MILLING

## Tirerill, Barony of:

| | | | | |
|---|---|---|---|---|
| Ballisodare | Ardcurley | Corn &Kiln | Ed. J. Cooper | Patrick Hart |
| Ballisodare | Cloonacurragh | Corn & Kiln | C.K. O'Hara | James Doyle |
| Ballisodare | Collooney | Flour & Corn | Ed.J. Cooper | Alex Sim |
| Ballisodare | Knock-muldowney[19] | Corn | Ed.J. Cooper | Robert Culbertson |
| Ballisodare | Knock-muldowney[19] | Corn | Ed.J. Cooper | Vacant |
| Ballisodare | Knock-muldowney[19] | Corn | Ed.J. Cooper | Vacant |
| Ballisodare | Knock-muldowney[19] | Tuck Mill | Robert Culbertson | Margaret Benson |
| Ballisodare | Knock-muldowney[19] | Tuck Mill | Ed. J. Cooper | Mich. Broder |
| Kilmacallan | Castlebaldwin[20] | Corn | Michael Brehony | In fee |
| Kilmacallan | Bellanascarva | Corn | Richard Brinkley | Manus Harper |
| Kilmacallan | Riverstown[21] | Corn & Tuck | Ed. J. Cooper | James Clerkin |
| Kilmacallan | Riverstown | Corn | Chas.W. Cooper | In fee |
| Kilross | Killeenduff | Corn & Kiln | Chas.W. Cooper | John Ormsby |

# Notes On Smaller Mills (as listed above).

(1)  The Palmerston estate rentals for 1790's has reference to Creevy
      Mills, then leased to Phillip Beirne. In an advertisement in
      January, 1849, Samuel Martin of the Bunduff Mills offered to
      grind corn @ 7/6d a ton. The mill was capable of grinding a ton
      every three hours. In unpublished Palmerston correspondence,

## MILLS AND MILLING

The 'Abbey' Mills, Collooney, before demolition.

The burn-out shell of the Scardan Mills.

## MILLS AND MILLING

dated 1846, there is reference to Grellagh Mill - which may be Bunduff under another name? It was a corn mill 12.5 chains north of Bunduff Bridge and east of the river of the same name.

(2) Local tradition suggests that it was operated as a Flax Mill at the turn of the century.

(3) The Drumcliffe Co-Operative Society built a Corn Mill, operated by a gas turbine, alongside the Creamery in the townland of Cullaghbeg in 1916. It was subsequently leased to Messrs. Pollexfen. In 1939 it was refurbished and operated by Drumcliffe Co-Operative Milling Society until it finally closed in 1975. It produced a well known brand of oatmeal, *Benbulben Pride*, also pig meal, and during the 'Emergency' whole flour from native wheat.

(4) Scardan Flour Mill, on the southern shore of Sligo Bay, was built by George Dorran c. 1800. In 1823 the mill, mill dam and watercourses were leased to Moses Baird and Wm. Henderson, for a term of thirty-one years, who extended the concern, constructed a large dam and improved the watercourse, giving a fall of 40 feet. In 1834 the mill was described as "new and extensive", suitable for the corn trade, in addition to flour, and capable of grinding upwards of 140 barrels daily. Between 1861 and 1870 it was worked by Patrick Keighron, who also operated *Millport* across the Bay. The mill was destroyed by fire in February, 1870 and for a century afterwards the burnt-out shell of the 4-storey building stood defiantly against the winter storms blowing in over Cummeen Strand. In the Sixties the ruin was demolished and the site totally cleared. All that remains of the once flourishing concern are traces of the watercourse.

(5) Leonard's Mill, at Gurteen Bridge on the river Owenmore, formed part of the Dundas estate in 1780's and was leased to Charles Costello. It was subsequently operated by the Leonards until 1875 or thereabouts. It was described as partly in ruins in 1880.Bruen's small corn mill in Kilfree was still operating into the 1920's but was 'at rest' in 1935. The source of its power was a rivulet exiting from what was known as the 'holy well' at Kilfree. It

## MILLS AND MILLING

was harnassed by means of a sluice gate which, when opened, released sufficient volumn to set the mill wheel, 11'6" in diameter, in motion.

McKeon's Corn Mill in Moygara ceased operating in the 1890's. It was demolished a decade later and the stones used in the building of the Parish Hall.

All three mills were powered by the waters of the Owenmore river or its tributaries.

(6) The mill of Bunninadden was mentioned in a marriage settlement in 1782. In 1801 it was leased by Robert Howes of Mount Irwin to James Costello of Kilfree. Described as a 'gig' mill, with undershot power 3.5 feet in diameter, by the Ordnance surveyors. "A bad concern and does little work. Excellent water supply but only 8 ft. fall. Wheel runs on its side", observed the Griffith Valuators. It originally formed part of the estate of John R. Irwin of *Flowerhill* and subsequently that of the Percevals of *Templehouse*. For close on a century the mill was operated by successive generations of the Scanlon family.

(7) Located on the Black River. "Does little work but has plenty of water for half the year", noted the Griffith Valuators in 1850's. A decade later the Corn Mill was no longer worked.

(8) Built in 1829 by Viscount Lorton as a one-storey corn mill, with a loft, and powered by a stream emerging from Templevanny Lake. Between mid century and 1880, or thereabouts, it was operated by Mathew Leonard and subsequently by James Cosgrave. In its heyday it both dried and crushed corn for farmers over a wide area. It ceased working c. 1910. The partially roofed building still stands on the avenue leading to the Lydon homestead, where a mill stone can also be seen.

(9) In the 1830's there were two 'gig' mills for grinding oats in Cloonlaughil. The diameter of the buckets was 3 ft; the staff was 4 ft. in length and there was power undershot.

(10) In the mid 19th century there were two corn mills on the Phibbs estate in Curry, one operated by James Filan and the other by

382

## MILLS AND MILLING

Patrick Breheny. They were both powered by the Owengarve, or 'Coarse' River. The former closed shortly afterwards but the latter, down river, continued working despite being described, in 1863, "as in bad repair and only partly roofed". A new mill was built on the site in 1874 by landlord, Richard Phibbs, and leased to Michael Loftus. Between 1880 and 1905 it was operated, on a lease, by Merssrs. R. & R. Gorman of Ballymote, and subsequently by Alexander Gamble. It was acquired in the 1920's by Patrick Roche and continued in operation until 1951 - it being the last working corn mill in the County. In 1953 it was purchased by the local guild of Muintir na Tire. The small one-storey structure, together with weir, millrace, and the turbine which had replaced the waterwheel in 1895, is intact, and plans are currently afoot to restore it as a local amenity and a means of generating electricity.

(11) In the 1830's a corn mill, described by the Ordnance Surveyors as a 'gig' mill, was operating on the Owengarve, down river from Curry. It formed part of the Knox estate and by the mid century, or thereabouts, the mill and kiln were being worked by Patrick Doyle, a member of the Flaughana family of professional millers. Although reported as "working very little" in the 1870's, it was fully refurbished in 1917-'18 and fitted with a 75 h.p. turbine. It continued to be worked by the Doyle family for a further decade before passing into John Brennan's ownership. During World War 2 it was leased by the Rathscanlon Co-Operative Dairy Society who used the kiln for drying oats and wheat and the mill for turning out flour and oatmeal. The concern has not been worked since the end of 'The Emergency' in 1945-46. The 2-storey L-shaped structure is now in a poor condition, although its principal fittings are intact.

(12) **SEE:** Collooney Mills

(13) **SEE:** Ballisodare Mills

(14) On the Perceval estate in Ballinacarrow North, it was operated by Richard Brinkley in the late 1840's and by Charles Gilbert a decade later. Both corn mill and bleach mill were described as

## MILLS AND MILLING

"nearly in ruins" in 1884 and in a dilapidated condition in 1890. A few hundred yards down the Owenmore river on the O'Hara estate, was the Cloonacurragh corn mill.

(15) Mill was falling into disrepair in 1850's and Burns was using the adjoining yard for weighing butter.

(16) Described as a small 'gig' mill by Ordnance surveyors.

(17) Vacant in 1860's and in ruins in 1872, when it was partly used as a dwelling by Julia Scanlon.

(18) A corn mill, owned by Robert Atkinson, was destroyed by the 'rebels' in 1798.

(19) Described as a 'Farm Mill' by the Valuators and operated on the Howley estate between 1860 and 1890. The unroofed shell of the long 2-storey and once thriving Corn Mill stands a few hundred yards from the equally derelict *Cooga Lodge*.

---

An opportunity Offers for encouraging .....

# Local Industry

BY EVERY

# Bread Consumer

USING "AVENA" FLOUR

# -Manufactured-

at

## BALLISODARE MILLS

Co. Sligo.

# 'AVENA'

FLOUR IS MADE FROM THE VERY

## Finest Quality

of Wheat, and with the most up-to-date machinery procurable

## In The World

# W. & G.T. Pollexfen

and Co.

Avena Mills, Ballisodare

## MILLS AND MILLING

(19) **SEE:** Ballisodare Mills.

(20) According to local residents the Taylor family operated a corn mill
at Cleavry at the turn of the century. No record of it can be traced
in either the Ordnance or the Valuation surveys.

(21) In the 1850's the corn mill at Rockbrook was described as being
"in a dilapidated condition" and operated by Pat Rorke. The
wheel had a diameter of 13 ft.

References have been traced in the local press to corn Mills at the
following locations - neither of which have been recorded in either the
Ordnance or Valuation surveys:-

At Cummeen, in the townland of Rathonoragh, on the Ormsby
estate. It was advertised for Letting in March, 1851.

At Dunally, on the Parke estate. Built in 1836, it was initially leased
to a tenant named Cullen.

A reference has also been traced in a document in the Registry of
Deeds, dated 1831, to a mill and mill course at Ardnaglass, part of the
estate of Jeremy Jones.

---

### Scardan
# Flour Mills

--- o ---

## *To be Let*

for such Term as may be agreed on,

THE

FLOUR MILLS

### of Scardan,

*With about*

EIGHT ACRES OF LAND ANNEXED.

These Mills are new and extensive and afford great facility for carrying
on a Corn Trade, in addition to the Flour business, being on the sea shore.
Proposals will be received (if by letter, post paid) by the Rev. George D.
Mansfield, Kiltubride. Edward Crawford will show the Mills.

*December 4, 1834*

MILLS AND MILLING

# BIBLIOGRAPHY:

(a) **Ms.**

General Valuation of Rated Property - Co. Sligo.
Valuation Notebooks, 1858-1950.

(b) **Printed:**

Cullen L.M.
18th century Flour Milling in Ireland.
*"Irish Economic & Social History"*. IV. 1977.

Joyce, P.W.
Social History of Ancient Ireland.
Dublin 1903. 2 vols.

Lucan A.Y.T.
The Horizontal Mill in Ireland.
*JR. of R.S.A.I. Vol. LXXXIII, 1953* .

McCutcheon, W.A.
Waterpowered Corn and Flax Scutching Mills in Ulster.
*"Ulster Folk Life"*. No. 12, 1966.

O'Reilly, Joseph P.
Ancient Water Mills.
*"Proc. R.I.A., Vol. XXXIV, Section C. 1902.*

General Valuation of Rated Property: County Sligo.
Dublin. 1858. 4 vols.

Ordnance Survey.
*Maps of County Sligo,* (6 - inch).
Dublin. 1837 (and subsequent editions).

Ordnance Survey:
*Name Books:* (Unpublished).

# Metrical Compositions and Election Ditties

In the mid 19th century Richard Taylor of Cleavry, Castlebaldwin, was tenant on the Cooper estate. He had a holding of 255 acres which his family had held over a long period and on which they had carried out extensive improvements. In 1861 he applied to Edward Joshua Cooper of *Markree Castle* for a renewal of the lease. His application took a most unusual form – a metrical composition of some eighteen verses!

"Edward Joshua Cooper, Esq. of Markree,
These lines were written on November day;
And he who reads when I am dead and gone,
Will know I know I wrote in eighteen-sixty-one.

My honoured landlord, and my kindest friend,
Please attention to my paltry rhyme do lend;
I know at it you will never frown,
'Twill make you laugh when you read further down'.

It's my desire to clearly let you see
My great improvements made in Clevery;*
One thousand pounds in buildings, fences, drains,
Has been laid out by me with greatest pains.

Old fences, too, for centuries in the way,
Have given the harrow and the plough fair play;
They murmured hard against me– it's a fact–
When I applied to them the levelling act.

The heathery hill where game was all the stock,
Abounds with clover feeding for the flock;
The vales, the resort of the finny tribe,
Is now well drained and fitted for the scythe.

*Also spelt Cleavry

## METRICAL COMPOSITIONS AND ELECTION DITTIES

In place of these, new lines divide the field,
Which yet a shelter to the stock will yield;
Huge rocks that slumbered since the world began,
And always brow-beat every other man,
Until I besieged them with crowbar, blast and spade,
And roused up echo with the noise they made.

Such foes as these are manly,  I confess,
But lurking foes must not be dreaded less;
The rock, so modest that scarce the sun would see,
Oft cracks the ploughshare and the swingletree.

These rocks their youth in idleness have spent,
Like criminals on labour not intent;
Like convicts now I in useful work retain
Where wasteful water from the land they drain.

Four houses built with the best of stone and lime
And they may last till the end of time;
Three of these houses are tiled with costly slate,
The fourth, an office, thatched with straw of wheat.

Our Gracious Queen who governs us so well,
In one of these has made her servants dwell;
No thief or robber here dare show his nose,
But still I lost a full half-score of ewes.

Short in my duty in this place I'd fall,
If I forgot to mention the stone wall;
My neighbours' trespass I night or day don't fear,
For it's fit to stop the nimblest of your deer.

Most holly bushes bent against the wind,
Where ghosts unnumbered did a shelter find;
Stations round these performed were by hags,
Who tied to branches different coloured rags.
To meddle with these the superstitious say
You will not survive a twelvemonth and a day.

## METRICAL COMPOSITIONS AND ELECTION DITTIES

My trusty servants, who for me would bleed,
Who at my table usually did feed,
Refused to wield the hatchet or the pick –
They said the deed would drive them to Old Nick.

A council held, one older than the rest,
Looked gravely round, and thus himself expressed–
For holy water I advise you go
And sprinkle the branch, also the roots below,
The devil himself a drop of it can't bear,
And ghosts and fairies flit off like a hare.

Obedience to his sage advice I found
The only way to stub and clear the ground,
A bottle came, but in it was no salt,
It proved the best of *Jameson's* old malt–
Each man crossed himself and took a round,
And bushes and rags came tumbling to the ground.

There is one that seen the garb that Cleavry wore
When from its back a skutch-grass coat I tore,
And clothed it in artificial velvet, living green
Which from the road can any time be seen.

Ah, dearer than Goshen, Cleavry is to me:
It's hallowed by labour you can see.
Hand in hand you and I would ever go,
But another King your Joseph might not know.

If in your sight your tenant has found grace,
Secure his labours with a lengthened lease;
But whether or no in closer friendship bound,
On your estate no tenant can be found.

For you and yours my prayers doth oft ascend,
And at the family altar your names doth blend;
That ye bellow my taste of bleeding love,
And meet in glory with His saints above".

## METRICAL COMPOSITIONS AND ELECTION DITTIES

The following was Cooper's rather short and somewhat less rhythmical reply:

*"Friend, Richard, sure the devil's among the Taylors,*
*When you spin yarns as long as any sailor's;*
*And weave out poetry, not sober prose,*
*With flowery perfume fit for any nose.*
*Your object's good, for industry's reward–*
*From the long neglected surface of the ground;*
*So let the glass go merrily round,*
*We'll pledge each other in the seasons' cheer,*
*And welcome gracefully the coming year;*
*Your warm affection will your landlord please,*
*And he, in justice, grant your wish – a lease."*

Edward Cooper. December 31st., 1861.

Some years later, in the Spring of 1873, Colonel Edward Cooper offered Taylor a renewal of the lease for the period of thirty-one years at £150 per annum, an increase of £25, – this despite the promise made by his uncle, Edward Joshua Cooper in 1861. Taylor objected to the terms of the lease and refused to sign it, that is, until he received the following lettter from Christopher L'Estrange, the Colonel's agent.

> *Kevinsfort,*
> *Sligo.*
> *April 11th, 1874*
>
> *Mr Richard Taylor,*
> *I am very anxious to have your affair settled, and Col. Cooper wants to know what I am doing about it. If you sign the enclosed lease, I shall try and get the Colonel to accept, but if you don't, it will be considered a declaration of war, worse than Coomasie. Please let me hear at once.*
> *Yours in haste.*
> *Christopher L'Estrange.*

On receipt of this communication Taylor decided to sign under protest. However, in February, 1882, he lodged an appeal to have the terms of the lease set aside. The case came before the Land Commissioners' Court at a sitting in Sligo the following August. Under cross-examination, the ageing Taylor outlined his objection to the terms of the lease, which he considered rather harsh: "I have

## METRICAL COMPOSITIONS AND ELECTION DITTIES

expended over £1,000 in improvements... I have build a Police Barracks, a dwelling house for two labourers, walls and hedges, and made the holding what it never was before..."

Judgement in the case was not delivered until some months later, by which time Taylor had died and the interest in the farm had passed to his grandson, Richard Kerr-Taylor, a minor. The verdict of the Court, handed down by Judge O'Hagan, was that as the lease had been enforced upon the tenant under pressure of a threat of eviction, it was, therefore, "an unreasonable term", and had to be set aside. Costs were awarded against the landlord.

\*     \*     \*     \*     \*     \*

### ELECTION OF A PORTER

At the monthly meeting of the Sligo Board of Guardians, June, 1864, the principal item on the agenda was the election of a Porter at the Workhouse. Amongst the eighteen applicants was one Terence Sweeney, a pensioner, whose application took a rather novel form.* It read as follows:–

"Sir– May I, the author of these lines, presume
To ask admittance in the candidates' room,
As a porter is wanted, I understand,
At the Sligo Workhouse, which you command;
Please grant admission to what I say,
I don't intend to go much astray.
I have served the Queen in my youth and strength
For twenty-five years in the service spent.
You'll admit my testimonials, too,
When fairly open to your optic views;
No distant country, either Portugal or Spain,
Or Gibraltar, where I did remain,
Could ever deem me unjust, untrue,
In moral conduct, and duty, too.
I canvassed none, nor solicited any,
Still in pets may I have many.
You'll re-admit, when I do expound,
Brave Wellington traversed no canvassed ground,

## METRICAL COMPOSITIONS AND ELECTION DITTIES

But brave as a man did he enter in
As a worthy hero to wield his men.
As like to him you will defend
My humble offer, I do depend;
I also offered some time since,
But found that offer to no consequence;
A man was appointed which you many see,
Who served the Queen two years, not three;
And from her service was he cashiered
For wanton conduct by fools revered.
But as disappointment caught me before,
I'll use the maxim – try once more.
I remain with all respects to thee,
Terence Sweeney, most humbly.
Sligo, Tuesday morning, and seventh June,
May I with pleasure have your gracious boon."

   * His application was unsuccessful.

     *      *      *      *      *      *

### A PAIR OF SHOES

William Taylor, an inmate of Sligo Workhouse, submitted the following
application to the Board of Guardians, February, 1858:*

> *"Ye muses from Parnassus hill,*
> *I pray ye now assist my quill,*
> *To spin a simple rustic verse,*
> *And let the gents know my distress;*
> *And hopes the Board will not refuse*
> *To grant to me a pair of shoes;*
> *The farmers then will me employ –*
> *The skin won't do on spade or loy.*
> *The Lord of Heaven will ye bless*
> *To help a brother in distress.*
> *Kind gentlemen of highest fame,*
> *My poor request do not disclaim,*
> *I hope it will not meet a failure,*
> *Your humble servant –*      *William Taylor".*

   * Taylor's application was successful.

METRICAL COMPOSITIONS AND ELECTION DITTIES

# ELECTION DITTIES

John P Somers represented the Borough of Sligo from 1837 to 1847. He was returned again in the latter year but was unseated on a Petition in April, 1848. In the ensuing election he was opposed by Charles Towneley of Towneley Hall, Lancashire. Towneley, the head of one of the oldest Catholic families in England, as well as one of the wealthiest, was induced to contest the seat in the Liberal/Catholic interest, whose members had grown somewhat disillusioned with Somers' representation. Towneley won the election by a margin of seven votes but was subsequently unseated on a Petition. Somers regained the seat at the second attempt.

With the approach of the 1852 election, Towneley was induced to contest the Sligo seat for a second time against his old rival, J. P. Somers. The Englishman was again successful at the polls but, due to a number of irregularities, was unseated in June, 1853. At the following election Tipperary-born John Sadlier, a Lord of the Treasury and a former M.P. for Carlow in the Nationalist interest, was introduced to the Sligo electorate in opposition to Somers. After a vigorous contest in which divided loyalties played no small part – for example, the Dominican friars supported Somers while Bishop Browne and his clergy campaigned openly for the return of Sadlier – the latter won by a handful of votes.

Sadlier continued to represent Sligo in Parliament until his death in tragic circumstances in 1856. He had the reputation of being an extensive speculator, and when his investments failed he embezzled over a million pounds from the Tipperary Joint Stock Bank, of which he himself was founder. Finding himself in financial ruin, the Member for Sligo committed suicide on Hampstead Heath in February, 1856.

The *Sligo Chronicle*, who openly and consistently supported the candidature of John P. Somers, lost no opportunity in criticising and even denouncing candidates brought in from outside, e.g. Towneley and Sadlier. In June, 1853, it published doggerel verse under the general heading: *Sligo Election Ditties*, of which the following are samples:

METRICAL COMPOSITIONS AND ELECTION DITTIES

## AN ELECTION DITTY

Johnny Sadlier, like Danae's lover of old,
Fell on Sligo in soft show'rs of Treasury gold;
And the joy of the gents it was glorious to see,
As each mentally totted his agency fee.

In the morning elated, that candidate green
A-cochering in holes and in corners was seen:
But ere he had canvassed the half of the Town,
He look'd, I assure you, uncommonly *brown*.

For a sly little imp spread his wings o'er the blast,
Shouting 'Towneley Committee', wherever he pass'd.
And Neddy, and Micky, and Jemmy, and Jones,
All shook in their skins like a bag of old bones!

And there rode the priest with his whip by his side,
But no more thro' his specs flash'd the glance of his pride,
And the foam of his gasping lay white on his vest
As he gazed on the crowds that he would have address'd.

And there sat the candidate dubious and glum,
With the dust on his wig and his chin on his thumb;
His committee-room silent, his banners alone,
The shillelaghs unlifted, the bagpipes unblown.

And immaculate Sligo is loud in her curse,
On the cannie old Celt with his niggardly purse;
And the 'Towneley Committee', more sharp that the sword,
Hath scattered the schemes of the Treasury-lord".

*"Sligo Champion"* 18-6-1853

METRICAL COMPOSITIONS AND ELECTION DITTIES

## THE LAMENT OF THE UNSEATED*

Oh, there's not in the wide world a borough so base
As the Borough of Sligo, that thrice-perjur'd place;
Oh, you'll find, when life's last ebbing pulses depart,
The name of that borough inscribed on my heart.

Yet, 'tis not that I quarrel with this or that scene,
With Hollywell's glades or its woods waving green;
I have no fault to find with Glencar or Lough Gill–
Oh, no! my objections are more heart-rending still!

'Tis that friends (friends in need) in such plenty were neat,
Who made every dear vote still more monstrously dear,
And who felt how extremely my best charms improved,
When they saw them reflected on gold that they loved.

Oh, Sligo,! base Sligo! why trouble my rest
In the halls of St. Stephen, that saint I love best?
Where my toils in a snug little peerage might cease,
And my purse (like your consciences!) slumber in peace!

* Charles Towneley

# The Turkish Baths

The *"Report of the Royal Commission on the Health of Towns, 1845"*, gave rise to the passing of the Public Health Act of 1848, which contained provisions for the introduction of piped water supplies as well as improved sanitary facilities in cities and towns. It also empowered local authorities to establish Public Baths and Bathhouses for the benefit of the poor and labouring classes. This latter clause was discussed at a meeting of Sligo Corporation where a majority of members voted in favour of the provision of Baths and Washhouses. The Resolution, however, was not acted upon. An editorial in the *"Sligo Champion"* in November, 1849, bemoaned the fact that such comfort and luxury was unobtainable in Sligo. "Let the Town Council espouse the cause of humanity, and public opinion will support and sustain them."[1] In its estimation, a single 3d. in the £. rate would be sufficient to establish Public Baths in the Town.

Nothing came of that suggestion, and there the matter was allowed to rest until June, 1853, when an anonymous scribe in the columns of the *"Champion"* was very critical of the fact that Sligo was still without Baths of any sort - an amenity which would "not only improve the Town but promote the health of the people". A few months later, in November, 1853, the matter was discussed by the Corporation on a motion tabled by Alderman Henry Lyons. He not only urged his fellow Councillors to consider striking a rate for that purpose but offered a personal donation of £50 towards the cost of the Baths, and also a site, should that be required.[2] This generous proposal failed to induce the Town Council to take action.

The practicability of erecting Public Baths was again raised in September, 1856, by Dr. James Tucker, M.O. of the Sligo Dispensary[3] in the columns of the *"Chronicle"*.[4] In the course of a long letter he enumerated a number of compelling reasons for the establishment of Baths and highlighted their advantage to public health and the general well-being of the citizens. "They could induce sober and responsible habits and contribute to man's physical, social and moral improvement", he argued. "They would also attract more visitors to the area". In an accompanying editorial the *"Chronicle"* described the lack

THE TURKISH BATHS

of Public Baths as "a want greatly felt in Sligo".

Following the publication of Tucker's letter, the Town Council, with a laudable zeal for the well-being of the inhabitants, assembled in special session to discuss the points raised. After a lengthy discussion, a majority spoke in favour of instituting enquiries as to the working of the system in cities and towns where Baths and Wash-houses were already in operation.[5]

This move did not meet with universal agreement. The *"Journal"*, although supportive of the provision of Baths, did not approve of the Corporation getting involved to any degree, as it feared an increase in taxation within the Borough. "The expenses attached to the working of these Baths will have to be defrayed out of the pockets of the ratepayers, as it is a well ascertained fact that where the construction and working of Baths have been undertaken by a public body, it has invariably resulted in a dead loss; while, on the other hand, where Baths are erected by voluntary subscription or by private enterprise, they generally pay a fair percentage on the capital invested". The paper also expressed doubts as to the ability of the Corporation to progress the idea.[6] The *"Champion"* agreed that the construction of Baths, as suggested, had created an unfavourable re-action and it regarded the proposed increase in taxation as "too much an imposition on already hard pressed ratepayers."[7] In a further comment some weeks later, it predicted that the project "would fall to the ground", and expressed the view that the Town Council "would pursue a wise course in leaving the erection of Baths to private speculation."[8]

Despite the unfavourable press locally, the Corporation proceeded to discuss the proposal and invited Dr. Tucker to a special meeting, after which it was decided to make an application to the Treasury for a loan of £900. A sub-committee was given the task of seeking-out a suitable site as well as ascertaining the likely costs of erecting Baths adequate to the needs of the Town. Two weeks later the *"Journal"*, in a long editorial, was highly critical of the Corporation's handling of the matter:

*"It would appear from correspondence which has taken place between the Mayor and the Secretary of the Treasury, that a loan of £900 will be granted, subject to certain conditions, for the erection of Baths and Wash-houses within the Borough. The wishes and interests of the ratepayers have not, for a moment,*

397

## THE TURKISH BATHS

*been consulted; and such was the precipitancy of the applicants, that even the
usual official forms were not complied with in the correspondence with the
Treasury. There was not even a rough outline of the plan contemplated and
not one member of the Council could form an estimate of the cost of Baths and
Wash-houses - and yet they ask the government to advance the sum of £900 !
This certainly approaches castle-building in the air, and affords but a poor
specimen of the official capacity of a corporate body which is endeavouring to
match the march of social progress, the provision of Baths for the 'unwashed '. .
.* (9)

In the months that followed there were indications that the
Corporation were having second thoughts about getting involved in
the venture. The change of attitude was apparently influenced by the
financial difficulties of the Town Council at that time and also by the
experience elsewhere, namely, that such facilites were invariably
operated at a loss, especially outside of the larger centres of
population.

Despite the Corporation's increasing reluctance to get involved, Dr.
Tucker continued with his campaign. In a letter to the *"Chronicle"*, in
February, 1859, he again urged the establishment of Baths and
outlined the benefits such a facililty would play in the advancement of
public health.[10] He also disclosed that he was in communication with
Dr. Barter of Blarney, who was actively engaged in the promotion of
hot air, or Turkish Baths, in Ireland, with a view to encouraging him to
establish a similar institution in Sligo.[11] Messrs Tucker and Barter
remained in close contact in the months that followed, and in mid
1860 came the annoucement that both men had entered into a
partnership whereby the costs of erecting Baths "upon the most
improved principles", of managing same, together with all outgoings
and proceeds were to be equally shared.

In November of that year a site was leased on Finisklin Road from
John Lynn of Lynn's Place for a term of ninety one years. In the lease
document the site was described as occupying —

*" . .. part of the lands of Rathedmond Quarter, leading from the Quay of
Sligo to Finisklin, formerly called the West Street, but now known as Finisklin;
bounded on the North by the road from Sligo to Gibralter; on the East and South
by portions of Rathedmond Quarter in possession of the said John Lynn; and
on the West by the narrow road running between the said plot and the boundary
wall of the Convent of St. Ursuline . . . "* [12]

## THE TURKISH BATHS

The site had a frontage of 150 feet but narrowed to 87 at the rere, and in depth measured 290 feet. Dr Barter visited Sligo in November, 1860, He addressed a public meeting in the Courthouse, chaired by the Mayor, Alderman Lyons, on the subject of the Oriental Bath, and afterwards, accompanied by the Mayor and a large number of interested citizens, proceeded to Finisklin Road to lay the foundation stone of the new Baths. Afterwards, Dr Barter and a number guests were entertained to luncheon by the Mayor.[13]

The Baths, together with living accommodation for the Manager, cost in the region of £2,000. They were formally opened by Dr. Barter in March, 1861. To mark the occasion, the Mayor, Abraham Dobbin, hosted a dinner in the *Victoria Hotel* at which many tributes were paid to the zeal and public spirited approach of both Barter and Tucker in providing such a badly needed facility for the benefit of the citizens of Sligo, and at no cost to local ratepayers. The Cork doctor availed of the opportunity of publicly thanking his colleague and friend, Dr. Tucker, whose "enthusiastic advocacy and untiring zeal induced me to come to Sligo . . ." [14] At the outset, the Baths were a great attraction and were well supported. The *"Journal"* described them as "the most important and useful public institution for the benefit of all classes that was ever established in Sligo . . . Everybody who has tried the Baths speak of them in the highest terms of praise . . ." [15] To facilitate clients visiting the Baths in the hours of darkness, the Town and Harbour Commissioners acceded to a request from Dr. Tucker to extend the street lighting from Lyons Terrace to the Baths.

After the initial novelty had worn off, the numbers frequenting the Baths declined sharply. In an effort to redress this trend a number of alterations were carried out to the heating and ventilation systems and admission charges reduced. Despite these improvements, the Baths continued to lose money. In May, 1862 the *"Champion"* reported that they would close two weeks later. In an accompanying letter Dr Tucker regretted the impending closure and detailed the part he played in their establishment :-

*" I regret being obliged to close the Baths for want of sufficient support . . . I cannot be expected to keep them open and suffer serious loss in consequence . . . I am very disappointed at this turn of events. But for my exertions for those few years past the people of Sligo would not have an opportunity of knowing*

## THE TURKISH BATHS

*and enjoying this mark of social and sanitary civilisation . . . I devoted much time and attention to the construction and conduct of the Baths believing that a sanitary institution, so well calculated to promote the commercial prosperity of all parties in Sligo, by attracting strangers, would upon such public grounds receive universal support . . . " [16]*

In an effort to keep the Baths open, and in the expectation that they would attract increasing numbers during the tourist season, a newly formed Sligo Bath Company leased them for six months. This experiment failed, and in October, 1862, the *"Champion"* reported that the Baths were to close in a matter of days, and expressed the hope that there was enough public spirit in Sligo to revive them "in a more perfect form". Tucker went public once again, espressing regret that the venture had not been more successful and blamed defective construction and bad ventilation for the failure.

These allegations were subsequently challenged by Dr. Richard Barter, jun., who accused Tucker of "failing to fulfill the engagements" which he had entered into with his father. On a subsequent visit to Sligo, Barter found the ventilators closed and other operational matters not to his satisfaction. The upshoot of this was that Tucker was removed from his post as Manager of the Baths and also dispossessed of the house he occupied on the site. According to Barter the failure in Sligo "might easily be traced to bad and careless management rather than defects in construction." [17]

The Sligo Turkish, or Hot Air Baths, having undergone a thorough overhauling, were re-opened under the management of John Leigh of Limerick, described as "a careful and efficient supervisor". [18] The hours of opening remained unchanged - 8 a.m.to 9 p.m. daily - but admission charges were reduced. The new rates ranged from 6d to 1/6d, depending on the time of day and whether weekdays or weekends. Two weeks later the *"Champion"* carried a letter from a Thomas McGowan, a satisfied customer, who was much impressed not only by the improvements but also by the beneficial results to his general health :-

*"Our Sligo Hot Air Baths are much improved by changes in the heating system and stopping the draught"*, he wrote *"I was very much troubled with rheumatic pains in feet and legs . . . After a bath last night I am quite rid of the pains to-day. A steady pressure of heat at 135 degrees did all the necessary good desired . . "*

## THE TURKISH BATHS

Despite operational improvements and better management, the Turkish baths failed to attract a clientele in sufficient numbers to ensure their success. In retrospect, its diffficult to ascertain why the Baths failed. It was suggested at the time that the location - too far out of Town - was a factor in the poor support accorded to the venture by Sligonians of that era.

The exact date on which the Baths finally closed has not been recorded. They had certainly closed by 1870, as an advertisement in the local newspapers, on behalf of the executors of Dr. Barter, offered a lease of the former Turkish Baths to "a suitable tenant".

*     *     *     *     *     *

In May, 1862, when it became apparent that the Finisklin Baths were not being supported to the extent required, a Bath Company was formed to establish new Baths, including hot and cold, a plunge bath and a luxurious Turkish Bath. It had a projected capital of £1,200, and shares cost £1. each. The leading advocates included Maurice Conroy (Chairman); Dr James Tucker (Secretary); Edward Pollock (Solicitor); T.H.Williams (Mayor); Vernon Davys: R. H. Wood, M.D.; Roger Parke and Patrick Keighron. A Prospectus, together with a list of Shareholders - 180 already declared - was published in June, 1862. [19]

At a public meeting in the Courthouse it was suggested that consideration be given to either purchasing and up-dating the existing Turkish Baths or, preferably, building new Baths at a more central location. Despite well attended meetings and the obvious enthusiasm of the leading advocates, the project had to be abandoned for want of public support –sufficient share capital had not been subscribed.

The project was again brought forward in 1867 when a petition was forwarded to the Goverement praying for a grant of £2,000 for the purpose of implementing the Sanitary Act as well as the erection of Baths and Wash-houses. The application was unsuccessful, and there the matter was allowed to rest. [20]

In September, 1874, an anonymous correspondent, a visitor to Sligo, expressed surprise that a town of the importance of Sligo lacked a Bath-house and suggested that Hot and Cold Baths could be built at the Salmon Point on Victoria Road. [21]

# THE TURKISH BATHS

## Notes & References

(1)  *"Sligo Champion"*                    17 - 11 - 1849

(2)         ibid                           7 - 11 - 1853

(3)  Dr James Tucker was the son of John and Anne Tucker of Springfield, and brother of Dr Andrew Tucker of Castlerea and the Revd. Joseph Tucker, P.P., Boyle. He held a number of medical posts, including M.O. Sligo Dispensary, Medical Inspector of Sligo Port and Surgeon to the Sligo Rifles and the Constabulary. He was the first appointee to the post of Registrar of Births, etc. for the Sligo district. In 1866 he was appointed to the British Cattle Plague Commission.

He took a particular interest in matters relating to public health and sanitary improvements, and published a number of articles and reports on these and related subjects.   These included -
*"Essay on Nature and Treatment of Cholera";*
*"The Reformed Roman or Oriental Baths": "Cholera and Fever, with Remarks on the Treatment of the Cattle Plague".*

Dr. Tucker died at his residence in Old Market Street in October, 1875.

(4)  *"Sligo Chronicle"*                   25 - 09  - 1856

(5)  *"Sligo Champion"*                    1 - 11 - 1856

(6)  *"Sligo Journal"*                     7 - 11 - 1856

(7)  *"Sligo Champion"*                    8 - 11 - 1856

(8)         ibid                           17 - 01 - 1857

(9)  *"Sligo Journal"*                     23 - 01 - 1857

(10) *"Sligo Chronicle"*                   5 - 02 - 1859

(11) Dr. Richard Barter (1802 - 1870), as a young medical practicioner in his native Cork, became actively interested in the idea of the 'water-cure' for a variety of human ailments.  Eventually, in 1856, he founded what became widely known as a Hydropathic Establishment at St. Ann's Hill in Blarney, in which various diseases were treated by a combination of hot air and hot water, popularly known as the Turkish Bath. He also published a booklet entitled *"The Rise and Progress of the Turkish Bath".* Over the following decades Dr. Barter"s establishment became justly famous and was widely supported by medical opinion. Similar institutions were extablished under his patent in several cities and large towns in both Ireland and England.  The foundation at Blarney continued to operate down to 1945.

(12) Registry of Deeds. 1862. Bk. 32. P. 246.

(13) *"Sligo Independent"*                 17 - 11 - 1860

## THE TURKISH BATHS

| (14) | ibid | 9 - 3 - 1861 |
|------|------|--------------|
| (15) | *"Sligo Journal"* | 15 - 3 - 1861 |
| (16) | *"Sligo Champion"* | 3 - 5 - 1862 |
| (17) | ibid | 20 - 12 - 1862 |
| (18) | ibid | 28 - 3 - 1863 |
| (19) | ibid | 14 - 6 - 1862 |
| (20) | Wood-Martin, W. G. *"History of Sligo"* Vol. 3. p. 181-2 | |
| (21) | *"Sligo Chronicle"* | 19 - 9 - 1874 |

---

RE-OPENING OF

## THE IMPROVED TURKISH OR IRISH

# B A T H,

*Under Dr. Barter's Patent,*

F I N I S K I N   R O A D ,   S L I G O .

---

### OPEN ON WEEK DAYS
### 1ST CLASS
### TICKETS ARE ISSUED FOR THE BATH

|  | s. | d. |  |
|---|---|---|---|
| From 6 to Half-past 8 a.m. | 1 | 6 | Mornings. |
| From Half-past 10 a.m. to 6 p.m. | 2 | 0 | Midday. |
| From 6 to Half-past 8 p.m. | 1 | 0 | Evening. |
| Children under 10 years of age, | | | half-price. |

| Subscription Cards for | 12 Midday Baths. | 16s. |
|---|---|---|
| " | 12 Morning " | 12s. |
| " | 12 Evening " | 9s. |

Shampooing, 6d. extra.

### 2ND CLASS

To meet the requirements of the million, the Baths will be open on SATURDAYS, from 6 to 8 p.m. and on SUNDAYS, from 6 to 8 a.m. for SIXPENCE.

Such Parties, however, are required to bring their own Sheets, or they are supplied at the Baths with Shampooing and attendance from 3d. extra.

The Tickets issued by Dr. Tucker, of Sligo, at reduced rates, are not now admissable.

### *No Gratuities Allowed.*

**Sligo, February 27th, 1863.**

# Saved from the Scaffold

## 1.   A Family Affair:

On November 2nd, 1846, James Sharkett, his wife, Ellen, and Bridget Burke, sister to the latter, all of Clogher, Monasteraden, and tenants on the Holmes estate, attended the fair of Ballaghaderreen. Mrs Burke, whose first husband, John Giblin, had died some months previously, sold a cow for an undisclosed amount and subsequently joined the Sharketts and another relative, Roger Giblin, in a local hostelry. The party had several drinks there and, in the course of conversation, Bridget Burke complained that Michael, her husband of only two months by a second marriage, was treating her badly and she feared for the future.

Darkness had fallen by the time the party arrived back in Clogher in a somewhat inebriated state. After supper the Sharketts paid a visit to the Burke homestead. They had with them a bottle of whiskey which they shared most liberally with Michael Burke around the kitchen fire. In the meantime, Bridget, the latter's wife, went outside to milk the cow and on her return she found her husband moving about somewhat unsteady on his feet and very boisterous. He had obviously indulged too heavily in Sharkett's whiskey! It was then suggested to him that he should retire to bed and was assisted there by the Sharketts. Having accomplished their task, the Sharketts returned to the kitchen and joined Bridget and two of her daughters by her first marriage namely, Ellen and Mary Giblin, in night prayers - allegedly seeking divine assistance for the awful deed they were contemplating. At that stage, Mathew Gara, who resided near Ballaghaderreen and a relative, entered the kitchen and was immediately given some whiskey in a cup.

Meanwhile, James Sharkett had gone outside and, after a short interval, returned armed with a hatchet which he borrowed from a neighbour, Michael Flannery. Accompanied by Gara, he then proceeded to the bedroom, where Burke was sleeping, and commenced striking him around the head with the hatchet. As Bridget, the victim's wife, looked on with a lighted candle in her hand, young Gara then took a turn in battering Burke until his brains

404

protruded. Satisfied that their victim was dead, the culprits hurriedly retreated to the kitchen and laid plans as to how they might rid themselves of any suspicion of an involvement in the awful deed. In their panic they took Bridget outside, stood her against a tree, tied her to it with a rope from the byre, and then proceeded to blacken her forehead as if to feign an assault. The two Giblin girls were then hurried off to neighbouring houses where they looked for assistance to hunt-down the thieves who had allegedly broken into the Burke homestead, battered Michael to death and assaulted and tied up their mother. On hearing the startling news, a few neighbours, including Jack Hargadon, 'Big' Dominic Giblin and Denis Cryan, rushed to the scene where they witnessed Bridget tied to the tree and the blood stained corpse of Michael in the bedroom. The police were then called and on the following day they took Bridget Burke into custody.

Following the arrest of their mother, the two Giblin sisters, Ellen and Mary, were taken in by a neighbouring policeman, named Callaghan, while the Sharketts took possession of a cow, poultry and some grain belonging to the Burke's, much to the displeasure of the Giblin girls who were, at the same time, being promised all kinds of presents by the Sharketts if they did not divulge the true facts of Burke's death. However, as time passed by, Ellen Giblin, who with her younger sister had witnessed the foul deed and together grieved for their mother then was languishing in Sligo Gaol, found it increasingly difficult to maintain her silence. Eventually, after a lapse of almost six months, she spoke of what she knew of the murder to her policeman guardian. As a result, the Sharketts and Mathew Gara were taken into custody.

At the Summer Assizes in Sligo, August, 1847, before Judge Ball and a jury, James Sharkett, aged 40; his wife, Ellen, aged 35; Bridget Burke, aged 35, and Mathew Gara, aged 18, were arraigned for the murder of Michael Burke at Clogher on November 2nd, 1846. After some legal arguments it was agreed that Gara would be tried separately. Evidence was given by a number of witnesses but principally by the youthful Giblin sisters, Ellen, aged 13 and Mary, aged 11, on whose testimony the case for the prosecution rested. There were unprecedented scenes in the court as the youthful witnesses gave evidence under cross-examination. The overpowering emotions of filial endearment, intermingled with loud screams, pitiful sobs and the frantic efforts of the sisters to leave the stand on occasions and embrace their mother in the dock, were such as would have moved the heart of a stoic. The spectacle visibly effected barristers on both sides while spectators in the gallery sobbed openly as their evidence unfolded. Arthur Dillon, M.D. who examined Burke's body the day after he was murdered, described how the left side and rear of the skull had been broken-in very extensively.

On the conclusion of the evidence and the closing addresses of the respective Counsel, the jury retired and after an hour's deliberation found all three prisoners guilty but recommended them to mercy. Although Judge Ball promised to forward their recommendation to the Government, he stressed he would do nothing that would seem to minimise the enormity of their crime and proceeded to sentence them to be hanged at Sligo Gaol on September 21st. According to onlookers the verdict was received without any apparent emotion by the prisoners, "not a muscle of their countenances having changed".

In an effort to avoid a public execution, a Memorial, signed by leading citizens of the Town and County, was forwarded to the Lord Lieutenant praying that the sentence be mitigated. After deliberating for almost nine months, during which the execution date was cancelled and re-fixed on at least two occasions, the request for clemency was finally acceded to in March, 1848. The three convicts escaped the scaffold, a punishment they justly deserved. Instead, they were transported for life.

Mathew Gara was tried for his part in the murder of Michael Burke at the Lent Assizes, 1848. Although the witnesses were more or less the same and the evidence substantially unaltered, the jury failed to convict. He was tried a second time at the Summer Assizes later that year but again the jury could not reach an agreement. The youthful Mathew Gara was most fortunate to have escaped the justice he deserved for his alleged part in one of the most gruesome murders ever committed in this County.

### References

| (1) | *"Sligo Journal"* | 6 - 8 - 1847 |
| (2) | ibid. | 10 - 3 - 1848 |
| (3) | *"Sligo Champion"* | 11 - 3 - 1848 |
| (4) | *"Sligo Journal"* | 28 - 7 - 1848 |

## 2. Mary Speed's Tragic End:

For a period of twenty years or so, between the mid 'Thirties and the 'Fifties of the last century, there were no convictions for murder within the County. Deeds of blood had been frequently committed but, invariably, the parties who were brought to trial were acquitted, either because they were innocent or there was not sufficient evidence to establish guilt. In the case of John Speed, convicted of the murder of his wife at the Spring Assizes in 1856, the evidence was so conclusive and impeachable that a verdict of guilty could not be withheld. The report of the trial disclosed the horrific details of as foul a murder as was ever perpetrated.

John and Mary Speed resided at Ballinakill, in the Union of Riverstown. Following their marriage in 1854 the young bride, who was a sister of James Jackson of Coola, was, on occasions, the recipient of brutal treatment at the hands of her twenty-one year old husband. Repeated acts of violence were proved to have been committed, two of these being while she was in a state of pregnancy. The uncle of deceased, who witnessed one of these scenes, recommended her to go to service, where she would have peace. It might have been happy for her had she followed his advice. On the day preceding the night of the murder Mary Speed was seen by her sister, who was in a position to state that there were then no marks of violence on her person. Subsequently, that evening, she was visited by a neighbour who came to perform an act of kindness, the deceased having been recently confined of a still-born child. This was the last occasion on which she was seen alive.

About 10 o'clock on the night of December 27th 1855, the husband knocked at the door of a neighbour, Robert Gibson, and calmly announced: *"Mary is Dead"*. Gibson immediately proceeded to the Speed residence, accompanied by the wife of Roger Lang. The house was in darkness and, on entering, they could hardly distinguish the lifeless form lying on a bed. After a candle had been procured from the residence of Samuel Lougheed nearby, they witnessed the body carefully laid out, the eyes and mouth closed, the hands and feet stretched, and the bedclothes, in the language of one of the witnesses, 'nicely fixed' upon it. These arrangements at first excited no suspicion, and Gibson, thinking that life might not be extinct, proposed that

SAVED FROM THE SCAFFOLD

Bridget Lang should feel whether there was any pulsation, but the woman declined through fear. Preparations for performing one of the offices of the dead were then made, and the men left the cabin. Presently, a cry of horror was heard from within and the men returned to find that Mary Speed has been foully murdered! Marks of violence were visible on the throat and chest, and her neck was broken. Speed, with perfect coolness, had come in with the others, but suspicion at once pointed to him as the perpetrator of the deed, and Mary Clancy, the aunt of the murdered woman cried out : *"John, you murdered Mary"*. He made no reply, and did not wait for the police to arrive on the scene.

How came Mary Speed by her death, and whose was the hand that deprived her of life? Hear the statement of the husband deposed to by three witnesses. *"I returned from my work in the evening, when Mary complained of her feet being cold, and asked me into bed. I went and fell asleep, but awoke, after some time, in a fright when I found her arm lying across me. She was dead."* Such was the story framed by the husband to account for the murder of his wife lying by his side. But an all-seeing eye penetrated the darkness which pervaded the abode of the murderer when he terminated the miserable life of her he had vowed to defend, and brought to light a number of facts which established his guilt, his own statement being one of the most important links in the chain. [1]

On December 29th, two days after the gruesome discovery, Coroner, Alexander Burrows of Carrowcrin, sitting with a jury, conducted an inquest into the death of Mary Speed. In the course of the evidence given by Gibson, Mrs. Lang, Anne Cassidy, a sister of the deceased, and Dr. Thomas Burrows, who had performed a post-mortem, it was confirmed that the deceased woman had been delivered of a still-born child four days before she met her death. At the conclusion of the hearing, and going on the evidence before them, the jury found that Mary Speed came to her death by having her neck dislocated and, in their opinion, the act was committed by her husband. [2] John Speed was then arrested and imprisoned in Sligo Gaol to await his trial.

At the subsequent Spring Assizes in March, 1856, Speed was charged with having strangled his wife. As the details of the tragedy unfolded in court, Counsel for the defence was at pains to impress upon the jury that the crime for which the accused was being tried was completely at

408

SAVED FROM THE SCAFFOLD

variance with his character and the mutual attachment displayed by the
pair during their courtship a year earlier: *"The love passion of this artless
youth was so strong that he made an attempt to hang himself when obstacles
were put in the way of his marriage to the deceased......."* [3] In addition, the
local curate, Rev. Peter Gormley, testified to the exemplary qualities of
the accused, describing him as "a sober, quiet, inoffensive man,
without a vice or crime that the public could discern."

The jury, acting on circumstantial evidence, brought in a verdict of
'Guilty', but added a rider recommending the prisoner to mercy.
Notwithstanding the plea for clemency, Judge Jackson sentenced
Speed to be hanged on April 17th. After the judgement was delivered,
the convicted man was returned to Sligo Gaol where he continued to
proclaim his innocence. Commenting on this stance, the *"Journal"*
wrote :-

*"........John Speed still maintains the same firmness which he displayed
during his trial. He sleeps well and does not seem to be unduly worried with the
terrors of the situation in which he stands. He still reiterates the statement of his
innocence and looks upon his fate with passive indifference."* [4]

Within days of the conviction a Memorial was prepared by Edward
Pollock, Solicitor, who acted in Speed's defence, and forwarded to the
Lord Lieutenant. The text was published in the local press, and in an
accompanying statement, Pollock emphasised that it represented the
feelings "of most of our fellow-townsmen" and also had the backing of
all denominations. A second Memorial was also forwarded by Rev.
Owen Feeny, P.P., Riverstown, who, with the backing of Dr. Browne,
Bishop of Elphin, took an active and energetic part in saving Speed's
life.

---

**TO HIS EXCELLENCY, THE LORD LIEUTENANT**

*The Memorial of the under-named Inhabitants and Residents of the Town and County of Sligo.*

"Humbly Showeth - That a capital conviction for murder took place at the recent
Assizes at Sligo against John Speed.

That for twenty years this Town has not been disgraced by a public execution.

That many of your petitioners are conscientiously opposed to the sacrifice of
human life on the scaffold.

That the jury, on account of his youth, recommended the unhappy convict, and
at the trial he received a most excellent character.

And from these and other considerations we respectfully implore your
Excellency's humane consideration of his case".

---

## SAVED FROM THE SCAFFOLD

On April 12th, 1856, the letter columns of the local newspapers carried the following communications, one from Thomas Larcom and the other from Edward Pollock.

*Dublin Castle*
*9th April, 1856*

*Sir,*

*I am to acquaint you that the papers in the case of John Speed, a prisoner in Sligo Gaol under sentence of death, have been laid before the Lord Lieutenant, and His Excellency has been pleased to commute his sentence to transportation for the term of his natural life.*

*I am, Sir,*
*Your most obedient servant,*
*Thomas A. Larcom.*

*E. Pollock, Esq., 33 The Mall, Sligo*

---

*33, The Mall,*
*Sligo*
*10th April, 1856*

*Sir,*

*Permit me to use your columns in taking the earliest opportunity of communicating to the many friends in this Town and County, who so kindly co-operated with me in the endeavour to have the life of a fellow-sinner saved, that his Excellency has been graciously pleased to accede to the prayer of our Memorial, and that time and opportunity for repentance have been afforded to the unfortunate convict.*

*Your obedient servant.*
*Edward Pollock*

Commenting on the outcome, the *"Sligo Champion"* wrote : "John Speed, the unhappy man who lay under sentence of death in our County Gaol, has been reprieved...........We feel delighted that this peaceful County has been saved the horrors which attend a public execution, and rejoice that the love of sight-seeing by the rabble has not been gratified in the execution of this man.......As to the convict himself, his punishment will be worse than death". [5]

*Notes and References:*

| | | |
|---|---|---|
| (1) | *"Sligo Chronicle"* | 8- 1 -1856 |
| (2) | *"Sligo Champion"* | 5- 1-1856 |
| | *"Sligo Chronicle"* | ibid |

(3) Possible reference to objections raised by the Jacksons who disapproved of their daughter marrying a Catholic.

| | | |
|---|---|---|
| (4) | *"Sligo Journal"* | 14-3-1856 |
| (5) | *"Sligo Champion"* | 12-4-1856 |

# 3. An Horrific Attack on a Mountain Side:

What was described as "one of the most horrible murders ever committed in this County" took place in the vicinity of Cloonacool on October 16th, 1860. The unfortunate victim was Mark McCoy of Mullaun, a next-door neighbour of Patrick O'Donnell, the perpetrator of the crime. It was alleged that jealousy was the cause of this most barbarous act and the outcome of rumours circulating that an improper intimacy existed between the murderer's wife and his victim, McCoy. There appears to have been not the slightest grounds for such a suspicion, as it was subsequently established that the gossip was invented and circulated by an "evil disposed and meddling woman" who was at enmity with McCoy and his wife and took delight in making mischief between them.

Be that as it may, Patrick O'Donnell went out on the date stated, in a distressed condition, and met with McCoy on the mountain close to the village of Cloonacool. After an exchange of words, McCoy proceeded to go about his business but was suddenly attacked by O'Donnell who stabbed him in the back with a sharp instrument, and then, on falling to the ground, was pierced twice or three times in the abdomen, ripping his belly open and causing his entrails to protrude in a most fearful manner. The unfortunate man was then dragged to a drain, rolled into it and his head trampled upon in an effort to drown him. At that stage two local farmers came on the scene but such was the violent demeanour of the attacker they were afraid to interfere and

SAVED FROM THE SCAFFOLD

O'Donnell made good his escape to the mountain, where he remained for a whole week.

The injured man was taken to the village where Dr. Vernon did everything possible to alleviate his sufferings. He lingered on in great agony till the following day when he expired,leaving a young and helpless family to mourn his loss. An inquest was conducted the following day by Co. Coroner, John McDonogh. Doctors Vernon and Conlon gave evidence of a postmortem examination which established that the deceased had died from the wounds received. A verdict of wilful murder was returned against Patrick O'Donnell, and he was committed for trial at the ensuing Spring Assizes.

In the days following the murder every effort was made by the police to arrest O'Donnell but all to no avail. He remained in his mountain hide-out until Friday night when he came down, under the cover of darkness, and made his way to an uncle's house at Moylough. He stayed there throughout Saturday and the following night. On Sunday morning he set out, at an early hour, on his way back to the mountain. As he proceeded through the townland of Tullycusheen, he was recognised by a man named Egan, a cousin of the murdered man, who alerted his neighbours. Together they set out in hot pursuit, succeeded in heading O'Donnell away from the mountain and eventually hemming him into a narrow valley. Meanwhile, the police had been alerted and on their arrival they quickly effected an arrest and took him to Tubbercurry. When taken into custody O'Donnell was quite exhausted and fainted in the barrack cell. The following morning he was transferred to Sligo Gaol. [1]

On his arrival at the Gaol, O'Donnell became very restless and broke into a violent mood. He only quietened down when the Governor, Edward Walsh, threatened to place him in chains. The local *"Independent"* published the following descriptive details of the prisoner for the benefit of its readers:-

*"In height he is about five foot nine, aged twenty eight, brown hair, grey eyes and features tolerably regular, rather stoutly built, very muscular, and on the whole rather a good and intelligent looking man; phrenologically speaking, he is not the man phrenologists would consider naturally addicted to violence. There is a slight incline in his forehead but not sufficient to indicate a lack of good reasoning powers"* [2]

412

## SAVED FROM THE SCAFFOLD

At the Spring Assizes in March, 1861, Patrick O'Donnell was charged with the murder of Mark McCoy the previous October. Evidence was given by the two witnesses to the crime, by neighbours and by Dr. James Vernon of Tubbercurry. Thomas Rock, a Sub-Inspector of the Royal Irish Constabulary, produced a Declaration dictated by McCoy on the afternoon of the day he was attacked:

*"I , Mark McCoy, believing myself to be on the point of death, do solemnly say that I went up to the bog this morning and on my way I was met by Patrick O'Donnell. From the way he looked at me I knew he was going to injure me and I ran away. He followed me and struck me in the back and knocked me down. He then drew out a weapon, either a top of a scythe or half a shears, and stabbed me in the belly two or three times. I then got a hold of it, and in his drawing it from me it cut my hand greatly. He then put me into a hole and trampled on me and tried to drown me. I leave my death on the said Patrick O'Donnell."*

*"Witnesses - Dr. Vernon, Edward Tooey, Constable Patrick Davitt and Michael McCoy".*

An insanity plea was entered by the defending Counsel, stating that the prisoner in the dock was subject to fits of depression and to the 'falling sickness', and laboured under mental derangement for a year or more. Doctors James Tucker and Robert Lynn of Sligo, from their observations of the prisoner during his incarceration, concurred with this diagnosis. The Judge, in charging the Jury, directed that if they thought that the prisoner was insane, they should acquit him. After a short deliberation they returned a verdict of 'Not Guilty' on the grounds of insanity. In the circumstances, the judgement of the Court was that O'Donnell be confined to a Lunatic Asylum for life or until it was considered perfectly safe to allow him at large. [3]

### References:

| (1) | *"Sligo Champion"* | 21-10-1860 |
| (2) | *"Sligo Independent"* | 27-10-1860 |
| (3) | *"Sligo Champion"* | 9-3-1861 |

\* This particular family are no longer in that area.

# Demonstrations in Church

## Taking the Bull by the Horns:

In 1824 Richard, or 'Dick' Holmes of Oakfield, popularly known as 'Plumber' Holmes and formerly Collector of Sligo,[1] purchased a fee simple estate of 1,073 statute acres, together with a handsome 3-storey residence, at Clogher, in the half barony of Coolavin. The property, which included lands of Clogher, Curraghbane and Ballyglass, were purchased from the Reps. of Colonel John Dillon, an absentee landlord, for £5,000. It is said that the Sligoman was the first Protestant to have settled in the barony since the Reformation. Richard Holmes married Jane, daughter of Matthew Phibbs of Spurtown, and on his death in March, 1840, he was succeeded by his eldest son, Joseph Arthur Holmes, who quickly gained a reputation in the area for what was described as "aggressive evangelical proclivities". He established a Presbyterian colony, built a small church and opened a Bible School for the children of his Catholic neighbours - many of whom were tenants on his estate. He acted as agent for an adjacent property from which nineteen families were evicted in April, 1847. Although he aided the poor and needy during the Famine, his activities both as agent and proselytiser aroused much hostility locally and eventually gave rise to the following unusual incident which took place in the Chapel, Ballaghaderreen, on January 6th, 1848. It was reported on as follows in the *"Sligo Journal"* of the 14th inst.:-[2]

### *"Taking A Bull By The Horns"*

"Mr Joseph Holmes is a resident proprietor in the County of Sligo within a short distance of Ballaghaderreen. He is a Magistrate and was made a Deputy Lieutenant last summer, as a mark of the sense entertained by the authorities of his exertions on behalf of the poor during the late crisis.

Having received many friendly intimations, a short time since that the parish priest, Mr Tighe, had made repeated attacks on him at the

## DEMONSTRATIONS IN CHURCH

chapel, and that his life would be attempted by assassins who had arrived in the neighbourhood, he was prevailed on, by the entreaties of his friends, to leave the country for a short period, till the passing of the late Government measure, when he returned.

These facts coming to the knowledge of his brother, Alexander Erskine Holmes, who resides in England, the latter paid a hurried visit to this country. On Thursday last - old Christmas Day - he presented himself at the chapel in Ballaghaderreen, and having asked and obtained permission from the Rev. Mr Tighe to address the congregation, a very numerous one, was accommodated with a place at the altar. He declined to address the people till Mr Tighe stood at his side; a second priest stood at his left. Mr Holmes, advancing to the front of the altar, addressed the congregation thus:-

'My friends - Mr. Tighe, your priest, has given me permission to address you from the altar, and I avail myself of it. I have travelled five hundred miles to say a few words to you - pray, therefore, attend to me. You do not all know me, but you know my brother, Mr. Joseph Holmes. Is there amongst you a man who can say that my brother has ever done an unkind or an unjust act by him? Is there, I say? If there is, let him hold up his hand. Is there amongst you a man who can deny that for the last two years, my brother has been your slave? If there is, let him speak - (A pause). During the last two years, my brother has expended £20,000 in provisions to keep down the markets here so that you and your children might not starve! He has, daily, for the last sixteen months, fed 150 of your children at his school-house. He has turned his house and offices into a provision store for your accommodation. Is there a man amongst you who can deny this? If there is, let him speak. And what is the return he has met with? Do you require to be told? Why, when he left home a month ago, it is common knowledge that the assassins, who were to murder him, had arrived in the parish and were harboured amongst you. There are those amongst you that know it - I can account for the presence of those miscreants. They were attracted hither by the inflammatory harangues of your priest here - (pointing to Mr. Tighe) - I tell him so, to his face."

*(Tremendous uproar in the chapel. Cries of 'turn him out, he is a liar'; a scene of great confusion, during which the curate in vein attempted to address and appease the people, followed. At length Mr. Tighe succeeded, after many ineffectual efforts, in obtaining a hearing.)*

*Mr. Tighe* - "It is false that I made any attacks on Mr. Holmes; there have been houses levelled in this parish and poor wretches turned out, but I never attacked Mr. Holmes."

Mr. Holmes - "I know that you did, and I tell you at this altar to your face, and in the presence of your congregation, that it is your attacks on my brother from this spot - that have brought these murderers to this parish."

*(Here the uproar re-commenced, and some of the more violent of the congregation appeared disposed to pass over the rails to the altar, the priests endeavouring to restrain them.)*

Mr. Holmes - (advancing in front) - "I am not afraid of you. I came here to tell you these truths alone, and am not to be deterred by five hundred of you."

*Mr. Tighe* - "My friends, this is the House of God. Let us have no more of this. Mr. Holmes has charged me with attacks on his brother, which I deny. If he has anything more to say, let him address you outside the chapel."

Mr. Holmes, having declined any further address, left the chapel surrounded by the people, who refrained from any act of personal violence, but saluted him with groans and execrations on his driving away.

Two weeks later, the *"Journal"* carried extracts from a letter to the Editor, written by the Rev. Denis Tighe, in which he vehemently refuted the charges made against him by Holmes. Although conceding that the report as published was "substantially correct", he regretted that it did not give any description of the "fury and passion" of his assailant.[3]

The outcome of the affair was that Joseph Arthur Holmes did not return to take up residence at Clogher until June, 1854, and then only for a short visit. Subsequently, until his death in Dublin in 1886, he was an absentee landlord - residing most of the time in Co. Roscommon where the family had additional possessions. By then the Sligo estate had passed out of the family. It had been purchased in May, 1879, by Hugh H. MacDermot, The MacDermot, for £10.750.[4] Since then Clogher has been the seat of the *'Prince of Coolavin'*.

### Notes and References:

(1) Arising from of charges preferred against Richard Holmes by a number of Sligo merchants, he was dismissed from the post of Collector of Sligo in 1820.

DEMONSTRATIONS IN CHURCH

(2) *"Sligo Journal"*     14-1-1848
(3) *"Sligo Journal"*:     28-1-1848

(4) Excluded from the sale was an area of $2\frac{1}{4}$ acres which, by Indenture dated May, 1874, had been leased to Revd. John MacNaughton of Belfast and Elizabeth Holmes - daughter of Arthur J. Holmes, Trustees of the local Presbyterian Congregation. The property included a church or place of worship, a manse, a schoolhouse and orphanage. (Registry of Deeds, 798-118 No.538853).

# A Tubbercurry Dispute:

For a number of years prior to 1870 Thomas Brett, a Tubbercurry draper, attended Sunday Mass in the local Catholic Church, occupying what was know as Quinn's pew. with the owner's consent.

In May, 1871, William White, the owner of another pew capable of seating six adults, agreed to transfer the seat to the Brett family on the payment of £2. This arrangement was concluded with the knowledge, if not the expressed approval, of the parish priest, Canon John McDermot, who feared that the transaction might be contrary to diocesan regulations.

On Sunday, May 28th, 1871, when the Bretts arrived in church they found the pew occupied by John Mullarkey, described as "a rich farmer living a short distance out of Town", his brother Pat, and two workmen. The occupants refused to make room for or admit the Bretts. Not anxious to create a scene, Thomas Brett proceeded to make his way to the vacant Quinn pew, which he had formerly occupied but, as he did so, Mullarkey attempted to trip him while, at the same time, issuing verbal abuse. Pushing and jostling continued until the arrival on the scene of Canon McDermot. On ascertaining the reason for the unseemly behaviour, he ordered Mullarkey and his friends to vacate the pew forthwith. As far as he was concerned, Mullarkey had no right to be there, not having consulted him, as Parish Priest, of any change in the arrangements.

In the absence of Canon McDermot a somewhat similar scene developed on the following Sunday, June 4th. The Mullarkeys re-occupied the disputed pew and refused admission to the Bretts. A serious brawl broke out and the antagonists had to be restrained by Constables Bourke and Carty who happened to be in the congregation. Summonses followed and when the matter came before the Petty Sessions, the Magistrates dismissed the case, suggesting that it be left to be arbitrated upon by the Parish Priest. The good Canon, seeking an easy way out, put forward the suggestion that if Brett paid the cost of a new pew, he (the Canon) would have it put in place in the church. Understandably, Thomas Brett would not subscribe to this solution as he considered himself the rightful owner of what had formerly been White's pew, to which Mullarkey also staked a claim.

The origin of this rather unusual dispute went back to 1869. In that year, John Mullarkey purchased land and house property from William White, and, as part of the bargain, was promised the latter's pew in the local church as a luckpenny. Difficulties arose subsequently between Mullarkey and White in relation to the purchase money but the matter was finally sorted out in March, 1870 after which Mullarkey occupied the pew. A year or so later Thomas Brett informed Mullarkey that he had purchased the pew from White and that he intended to occupy it. Mullarkey reacted unfavourably and promised to stake out his rights to the pew as part of his agreement with White.

When John Mullarkey persisted in occupying the disputed pew, Thomas Brett brought an action against him for damages of £500 arising from assaults committed in the church on May 28th and June 4th, 1871. After an hour's deliberation the Jury informed the Court there was no chance of them reaching an agreement on a verdict, and they were accordingly discharged. The case came before the Assizes for a second time later that year. On that occasion the Jury found that while Mullarkey had assaulted Brett, he was in possession of the pew and, as such, had used no more violence than was necessary to prevent Brett from occupying it.

*References:*

| | |
|---|---|
| *"Sligo Champion"* | 9-3-1872 |
| *"Sligo Chronicle"* | 13-7-1872 |

## 'Disruption' at Gurteen:

The foundation stone of the new parish church of Kilfree in Gurteen was laid by Dr. Patrick Durcan, Bishop of Achonry, on Sunday, May 21st, 1866. The site for the building had been donated by an absentee landlord, named Cadell, who also gave a lease forever of five acres for the use of successive parish priests of Kilfree. The architect of the new church was George Goldie of London, the chosen style of architecture was Gothic, and the contractors were William Hunt & Sons of Sligo. Amongst the principal subscribers to the building fund were Charles Costello, Esq., *Kilfree House*, and his son, James; Thomas MacDermot of the Coolavin, and a Protestant landowner, Jacob Powell of Cuilmore, described as "a most Liberal man towards his Catholic neighbours". [1]

Shortly after the new edifice was opened for divine service a custom was introduced whereby seats or pews in the trancepts were let or rented-out to well-off worshippers, numbering thirty-two families, who contributed, on average, 10/- annually for the luxury of the exclusive use of a particular pew.

For some time before the death of Canon Roger Brennan in December, 1880, no lettings had taken place but the families concerned continued in occupation of their customary pews as a matter of course. His successor, Canon O'Donoghue, despite advice to the contrary, decided to revert to the original practice and 'rent-out' the pews which by then had been moved to the centre aisle and nearer to the altar. The 'auction' was arranged for the churchyard immediately after Mass on Sunday, January 22nd, 1882.

On the appointed day the parish curate acted as 'auctioneer', but as soon as he commenced taking 'bids', a section of the crowd attempted to disrupt the proceedings by shouting him down. It was with great difficulty that he succeeded in securing 'offers' from a number of what was described as 'favourite clients' before the shouts and yells of a sizable faction made his task impossible. As brawls broke out between different elements amongst the assembled parishioners there were fears that the situation would get totally out of hand. However, the timely arrival of a small number of the Constabulary, with fixed bayonets, had a calming effect and the crowd quickly dispersed.

## DEMONSTRATIONS IN CHURCH

The following Sunday, January 29th, the discontent surfaced again. No sooner had Mass ended than a group of men entered the church, removed thirty family pews from their fastenings, dragged them outside and smashed them into fragments against a wall while large numbers of parishioners, together with members of the Constabulary, stood by as 'passive spectators', shocked and horrified at what was happening before their eyes. [2]

It was subsequently reported that a few 'disreputable fellows' from the Parish had planned it but that the actual outrage was carried out by what was described as 'inebriated misfortunes' from outside the area. However, after police investigations, four men from the immediate neighbourhood were arrested on warrants for alleged complicity in the sacrilegious act. They were brought before Captain Costello, J.P., who returned them for trial to Mullaghroe Petty Sessions on February 16th.

At the Petty Sessions three of the four prisoners were allowed out on bail on the pleadings of the Parish Priest, Canon Peter O'Donoghue, on the grounds that they were the sole support of their respective families. The fourth man, named O'Gara, was remanded in custody on an additional charge of assault. Damages to the church furniture was estimated at £27.10s. Hugh O'Donnell and Thomas Leonard, both of Gurteen, and Andrew Walsh of Ballymote, went security for that amount and paid over a cheque to James Costello of Kilfree, Treasurer of the Chapel Fund. [3]

After the sacrilege, the Church was closed on the orders of the Bishop of Achonry, and no rite was performed there for three months. It is said that those responsible, once they realised the horror of their deed, went before the Bishop and apologised for their misconduct in God's house.


### References:

| (1) | *"Sligo Champion"* | 26-5-1866 |
| (2) | *"Sligo Independent"* | 4-2-1882 |
| (3) | *"Sligo Champion"* | 4-2-1882 |

# DEMONSTRATIONS IN CHURCH

St. Adamnan's Church, Skreen.

St. Patrick's Church, Gurteen.

# DEMONSTRATIONS IN CHURCH

# Unusual Demonstration at Skreen:

"On Sunday there was great excitement in the rural parish of Skreen, which is situated about midway between Sligo and Ballina. It appears that the bishop of the diocese, Dr. Conway, lately determined suspending Father Conway,[1] and removing him for a time from the care of the parish. The suspended clergyman was a politician, a man of advanced views, and was the only Roman Catholic clergyman who could be got on all occasions to support Land League tactics to their fullest extent. He attended meetings at which he was the only clergy - man present, and condemned resolutions if they were too moderately drawn up. Contrary to the discipline of his church, he attended a meeting in Achonry without asking permission of Dr. Mc Cormack, and in Elphin without previously consulting Dr. Gillooly. It is believed there were other reasons for the Bishop of Killala issuing his suspensory order.

Whatever was the cause, Father Conway has been silenced and has left the parish; but the parishioners, it seems, by no means agreed with the bishop, and they declared that Michael Conway was the parish priest still, and they would have no other. First, it was announced that a public meeting would be held in the parish yesterday to protest against the bishop's conduct, but this did not take place. As they threatened to build up the doors of the two chapels in the parish, unless Father Conway was reinstated last Sunday, a number of police were drafted into the district on Saturday night, and in each chapel-yard a force was stationed from an early hour in the morning. At Skreen chapel, when the people saw a hundred policemen, under Sub-Inspector Cotton, drawn up round the building, they made no attempt to disturb the arrangements, and nearly all stayed to hear Mass said by the clergyman placed in temporary charge of the parish. Not so in Dromard, where the second chapel is situated. Here a crowd of five hundred men marched into the chapel, took possession of both doors, and said they would allow no clergyman to approach them but their own priest, Father Conway. There were fifty policemen, under Head-Constable Regan of Sligo, present, but they deemed it more prudent to await the arrival of the priest who was to officiate. The Rev. Mr. McHale,[2] the curate of the parish, came at the usual hour and

## DEMONSTRATIONS IN CHURCH

demanded admittance to the chapel, but the crowd firmly and defiantly refused. Head-Constable Regan and the curate, together with another Roman Catholic clergyman who happened to be on a visit in the neighbourhood, tried to induce those people to give away, but it was of no use. Threats of ecclesiastical censure they treated with scorn, and when the police pretended that they would force a way in, the congregation seemed determined on resisting. After the clergyman had consulted with the Head-Constable, he deemed it prudent to withdraw, leaving the people in possession of the chapel. After the clergymen went away the people knelt down in the open air and recited some prayers, after which they all separated quietly. The police left shortly after and this strange demonstration came to an end." [3]

### *Notes and References:*

(1) Revd. Michael Conway, P.P. of Skreen-Dromard 1879-1881.

(2) Revd. Michael MacHale (1845-1887) ministered in different Tireragh parishes between 1869 and 1881. He figured prominently at Land League meetings and championed the cause of tenant farmers. He also contributed ballads to the local press under the pseudonym - *"A County Curate"*.

(3) *"Sligo Chronicle"*        24-9-1881

# The Building of the Town Hall

In the opening decades of the 19th century regrets were frequently expressed by public representatives at the absence of a facility such as a Town Hall that would function as an administrative centre for an expanding and developing Town, as well as a place of assembly for both the Corporation and the Town and Harbour Commissioners.

Conscious of this void in a growing commercial centre, it was resolved at a meeting of the Magistrates of the County in 1825 to form a Company with a capital of £5,000 to finance the building of a Town Hall. Unfortunately, this laudable project never got off the ground and, as a result, the first meeting of the Reformed Corporation in October, 1842, took place in the 'Long Room' of Davis's *Hibernian Hotel* in what is now Teeling Street. Subsequent meetings of the newly elected Body took place in the Market House, off High Street, at the invitation of Owen Wynne, the proprietor of the markets. In the mid century, or thereabouts, the 'City Fathers' moved their meeting place to Wine Street where they shared accommodation with the Town and Harbour Commissioners. A decade later the offices of the Corporation were relocated in what was known as *Hudson's House* in Quay Street where the facilities were described as "utterly unfit for the purpose". In the years immediately preceding the opening of the Town Hall meetings were held in the Grand Jury Room in the County Courthouse.

An editorial in the *"Sligo Champion"* in October, 1853, highlighted the situation by stating that the public bodies functioning within the Borough were "wretchedly-off for suitable accommodation" and urged members of both the Corporation and the Town and Harbour Commissioners to come together and erect a Town Hall "worthy of the Town and a handsome addition to the existing excellent establishments". [1] Years later, in August, 1858, the newspaper aired the subject once again and directed the attention of interested parties to the existence of a Reproductive Loan Fund which could be applied by the Lord Lieutenant to objects of public utility not otherwise provided for. There the matter rested until March, 1860. At a meeting of the

424

## THE TOWN HALL

Corporation on the 26th of the month, Moses Monds, Secretary of Harbour Commissioners, sought and was given permission to read out a Memorial he had drawn up, petitioning the Lord Lieutenant to allocate £2,000 from the Reproductive Loan Fund towards the cost of building a Town Hall. The following is an extract from the Petition:-

*"Sligo, possessing a population of fifteen thousand, has no Town Hall, Library, or Reading Room, and the want of a public building for those purposes is much felt by the inhabitants. The Town Council of Sligo has only power by the Municipal Reform Act to strike a rate of three pence in the pound on the annual tenement valuation, and the small sum levied, which does not amount to £200 a year, is scarcely sufficient to pay the necessary officers of the Corporation very small salaries. It is, therefore, impossible for the Town Council to raise or levy funds in order to erect a suitable Town Hall, and believing such a building to be a work of great public utility, they most respectfully pray that your Excellency will recommend the Lords Commissioners of Her Majesty's Treasury to allocate towards this useful and highly desirable object the portion of the public money called the Reproductive Loan Fund, which has been returned from the County of Sligo, the balance of which Memorialists believe amounts to about two thousand pounds...."* This proposal not only met with the approval of the Town Council but some members expressed a willingness, on the spot, to make individual contributions towards the cost of the project, provided the application for funds was successful [2]. In November, 1860, the Lords of the Treasury stated that they were :- *"Prepared to take into consideration the question of granting money from the Reproductive Loan, on receiving an estimate of the probable cost of the proposed Town Hall, including furnishing thereof, together with a statement of the amount actually subscribed on account of such expenses, as their Lordships are of the opinion that a fair proportion of the cost should be provided out of funds locally collected, and that as the balance in their hands on account of the fund above referred to is applicable to the entire County, their Lordships do not feel justified in sanctioning the application of the whole of it to any object or objects in the town of Sligo."*

On the receipt of this information, the Corporation proceeded to appoint a sub-Committee consisting of the Mayor, Henry Lyons; Aldermen Dobbin, Tighe, McGill and Sedley; ex-Mayor, John McCarthy and Messrs. W.A. Woods, S.M. Cherry, Hugh Rooney, James Kidd, Peter O'Connor, Martin Madden, Harper Campbell, Robert

## THE TOWN HALL

Hunter, T.H. Williams and Moses Monds, who were assigned the dual tasks of soliciting voluntary subscriptions and the inspection of possible sites within the Borough. At the meeting a sum of £150 was subscribed towards the cost of the building, which was estimated at £5,000, in addition to a donation of £100 from Francis McDonagh, the Borough M.P. [3]. On December 14th the Lords of the Treasury appropriated the balance of the Reproductive Loan Fund, about £2,790, to defray the cost of the proposed buildings and in January, 1861, a unanimous vote of thanks was given by the Council to Moses Monds "as the person who first suggested the idea of applying for and ultimately succeeded in obtaining the balance of the Loan Funds". [4]

In February, 1861, Monds in his capacity as Secretary of the Town Hall sub-Committee reported back to the Town Council that they had identified seven possible sites - three in Wine Street, one at Victoria Bridge; one in Stephen Street, adjacent to the Bank of Ireland; one in Lower John Street, the property of Lord Palmerston, and one in Bridge Street. Their recommendation to the Town Council was that on the basis of its central location and lowness of rent, the plot in John Street was, in their view, the most suitable site for a Town Hall. However, after a prolonged discussion, during which the merits or otherwise of the named plots were debated, the Council, on a vote, selected Bridge Street as the preferred choice, this despite the fact that it was envisaged that the proposed edifice would actually span the River adjacent to the eastern parapet of the Old Bridge. [5]. The choice was by no means widely acclaimed. The *"Independent"* described it as a 'crazy idea' and suggested that the other sites be re-conisdered rather than "sinking money in the waters of the Garvogue", while the *"Champion"* ridiculed the suggestion of "an amphibious Town Hall built like a salmon box in the middle of the river".

Conflicting estimates as to the likely costs involved, coupled with unfavourable public reactions, led to the quiet abandonment of the riverside setting. Consideration was then switched to a site on the western end of Wine Street with a southern elevation, and to Griffith's plot, on the western side of Bridge Street, which stretched from the rear of Dr. Lynn's property in Stephen Street towards the river. Again no final decision was reached. Subsequently, a site on Albert Road, adjacent to the Police Barracks, and another in Thomas Street, beside

## THE TOWN HALL

the Commercial News Room, were considered but abandoned for various reasons as also was the aforementioned Bridge Street site after the Treasury refused to sanction it on the basis of the unusually high costs involved in acquiring the site.

The unexpectedly long delay in locating and agreeing upon a suitable site gave rise to strong and at times very vocal criticisms of the 'City Fathers', much of it deserved, for their on-going wrangling over different sites and apparent lack of urgency in arriving at a final decision. "We cannot assign a reason for their dilatory conduct, unless the Council, knowing this to be an age of wonders, are waiting, expecting that probably a Town Hall may spring up of its own accord like a mushroom in a field". [6]

In the midst of all this dithering and uncertainty, two new options came on stream: the Town and Harbour Commissioners offered a rent-free site adjacent to the Ballast Quay, on the understanding that the adjoining lands, recently reclaimed from the sea, would be developed as a People's Park. At the same time, F.M. Olpherts, agent to John Wynne of *Hazelwood House*, in a communication dated April 10th. 1861, suggested that the Old Fort Plot in Quay Street might be considered as a suitable site for the Town Hall. With uncharacteristic haste the Corporation members unanimously agreed that this indeed was a most preferable location and immediately offered £1,000 for the site, known locally as the *Old Barrack Fort*. In reply, Wynne's agent informed the Council that the property would not be available for less than £1,200, which figure included £100, the landlord's contribution towards the building. After a lengthy debate the Council, by twelve votes to six, agreed to a purchase price of £1,100. [7]

After what could be aptly described as a 'momentous' decision on their part, in view of what had gone before, the Corporation made an application to the Town and Harbour Commissioners for pecuniary aid towards the cost of the site. Their request, which was considered at a meeting of the latter Body on October 7th, was given a favourable hearing and, after a remarkably short discussion, it was agreed to invest £1,100 in the purchase of the Wynne site on the clear understanding that suitable offices would be included in the proposed building for the transaction of Harbour business. [8]. At a subsequent meeting of the Corporation the decision of the Commissioners was warmly welcomed

## THE TOWN HALL

and the following Resolution unanimously adopted:-

*"That we accept a lease from Mr. Wynne of the Quay Street plot for the erection of a Town Hall, at the yearly rent of £50 for the unexpired term originally granted by lease of November, 15th, 1700."*

*"That we rent to the Town and Harbour Commissioners, in pursuance of their recent resolution, suitable offices for the transaction of their business in the Town Hall proposed to be built, at a yearly rent of £50."* [9]

A sub-Committee, consisting of Aldermen McGill, Lyons, Leech and Councillors Tighe and Woods, were appointed, together with three nominees of the Town and Harbour Commissioners, whose duty it was to draw up a list of accommodation requirements and to seek out architectural plans for the new Town Hall.

Between November, 1861 and May, 1863, there is little evidence of any worthwhile activity in advancing the Town Hall project, apart from the preparation of a valid title to the satisfaction of all concerned and the Lords of the Treasury in particular. Eventually, on May 22nd 1863, the Corporation assembled in the expectation of finalising all outstanding legal matters but, to their horror and surprise, learned, for the first time, that one of their members, Alderman William Abbott Woods, was laying claim to a portion of the Old Fort site which Wynne had offered and which had been accepted as a site for the Town Hall. [10] The news understandably gave rise to much acrimony and rancour in the ensuing debate between individuals representing opposing political factions. Eventually, it was agreed that the Council would accept the lease from John Wynne of the Old Fort plot "according to the covenants and mearings and boundaries contained therein", and undertook to execute the lease forthwith. It was also agreed to nominate a Committee of seven to confer with the 'laird' of Hazelwood upon the question of boundaries. Commenting on the latest developments, the *"Independent"* wrote:-

*"It is deplorable to witness the periodical obstructions which continue to be thrown in the way of the erection of a much required Town Hall....... We would urge upon the Council to listen to nothing in the way of a compromise and accept nothing less than what was originally offered to them......"* [11]

The differences between Wynne and Woods, as to the ownership of the site, became very public a day or two later when workmen of the former built a wall blocking a passageway between the disputed section

# THE TOWN HALL

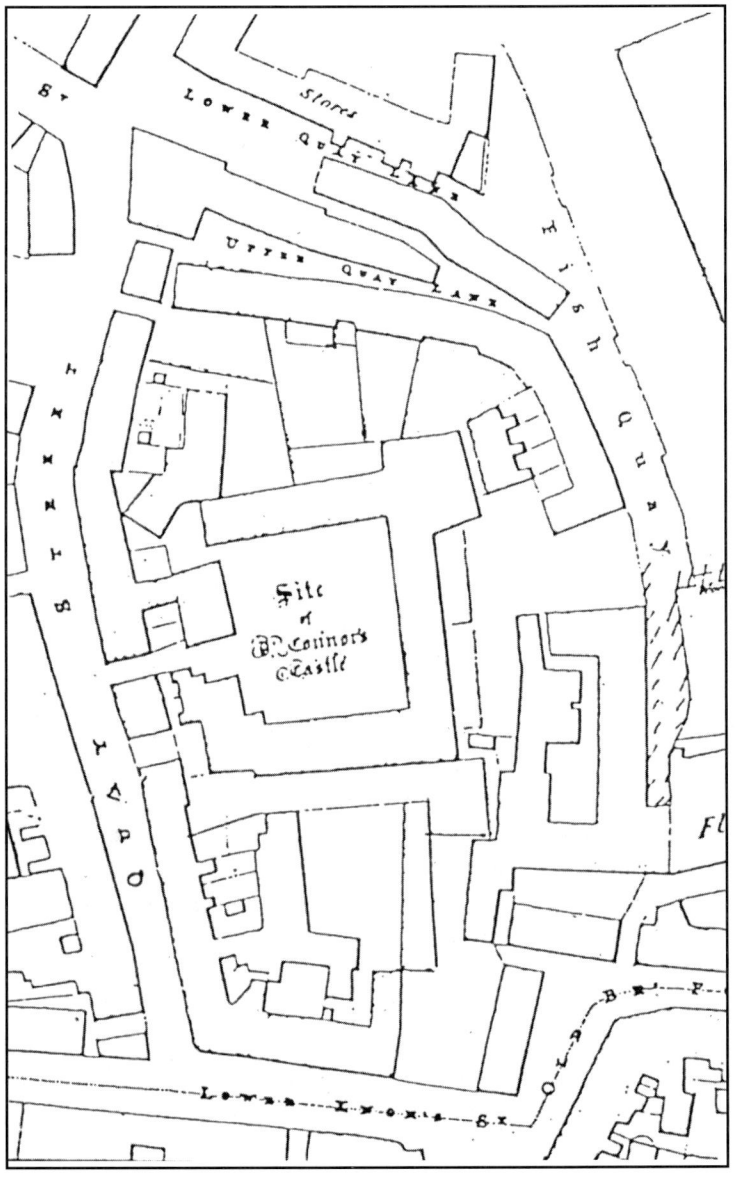

The Town Hall site and surroundings c. 1830

## THE TOWN HALL

and an adjoining plot already in Woods' possession. Under the cover of darkness the following night the wall was knocked down by persons supposedly operating in the interests of the other party, but was quickly rebuilt only to suffer a similar fate within a matter of hours. In retaliation Wynne's workmen re-entered and threw pieces of metal and other items, which Woods had placed there as evidence of occupation, onto the public street. [12]

The dispute between Wynne and Woods came before the Sligo Assizes in July, 1863, when the former took an action for trespass against the latter who, it was alleged, had broken and entered into certain lands the property of the Plaintiff. Damages were laid at £200. The Defendant, Woods, denied that the ground in question, namely, that lying outside and between the bastions, north and south of the Old Fort, belonged to the Plaintiff and claimed it as his property. In the course of the hearing the learned Counsel on both sides outlined as follows the sequence of ownership of the property in dispute:-

In the reign of Charles 11. extensive property in and around Sligo, formerly the O'Connor-Sligo estate, was granted to the Earl of Strafford. Subsequently, in the year 1700, portion of it was conveyed to one Benjamin Burton, an alderman of Dublin City, who later disposed of a section of what was known as the Fort Plot, or the 'Old Barrack Plot', to the Government. In 1792 the Board of Ordnance leased the said Fort Plot, for a term of 999 years, to Owen Wynne of Hazelwood, and after his death his son, John A. Wynne, entered into possession of the property. In the aforementioned lease there was no reference to an outside bastion or old curtain wall - it was simply the Old Fort and nothing more.

In June, 1713, Burton demised to Captain Booth a certain plot abutting upon the Old Fort, renewable forever at a rent of £8.12s per annum. Two years later Booth sub-let to John Bernard, a surveyor of customs. In 1771 the latter demised portion of it to a man named Hamilton, and ultimately, in 1833, vested it in Messrs Scott and Patrickson, merchants, who in 1862 conveyed it to William A. Woods. Woods, therefore, represented part of the family who got all of the plot outside the Fort as far back as 1717.

Counsel for Woods contended that the Deed of 1792 was the first to mention the fourteen feet outside the wall and argued that it was included, mistakenly or otherwise, as forming portion of the Old Fort property when handed over to Wynne. [13] After listening to a number of witnesses from both sides, together with much legal argument, the jury failed to agree on a verdict and were discharged.

## THE TOWN HALL

As the dispute remained deadlocked over the following months, with no apparent effort being made to resolve the *impasse*, the *"Chronicle"* felt obliged to comment as follows:-

*"No local topic has, in recent times, undergone so much discussion and been the subject of so much uneasiness as this important scheme. Time after time it has been debated and analised only to increase the confusion by which it has all along been surrounded, and the public seemed at length to have made up their minds that years must pass away before Sligo would be in possession of a building worthy of the enterprise and taste of its people. Instead of united efforts towards removing the difficulties, which prevented the early accomplishment of this most desirable work, it was employed as a weapon for party recrimination.....*[14] Likewise the *"Champion"* could hold its fire no longer:- *"Upwards of two years have elapsed since the 'site-seekers' went about on their rambles through the Town to find a spot whereupon to build a Town Hall, but like everything attempted by them the result has been to exhibit their dodgery, and, unfortunately, to make this much misrepresented Town a laughing stock in the eyes of the country.....*" [15]

As the year drew to a close, John Wynne, in an effort to move the matter forward, offered the Corporation possession of the plot with the exception of the sections on the north side, claimed by Woods, which latter strip he promised to hand over should he obtain a verdict in the action still pending. It was also pointed out that even if the decision of the court should go against them, the Corporation had sufficient ground on which to build a suitable edifice. After much debate, and acting on legal advice, the Town Council accepted Wynne's offer, a majority of members viewing it as a way of obtaining immediate and quiet possession of the site. [16].

In June, 1864, the Town and Harbour Commissioners served notice on both Wynne and Woods that they would be acquiring portion of the disputed plot, namely, that which abutted onto the roadway, for the widening of Quay Street. In the resulting discussions a deal was brokered whereby Wynne agreed to lease the old Slaughter House and adjacent properties, north of a line linking the said premises with the N.W. bastion, to Woods in return for which the latter released all claims to the ground on the south side of the Old Fort which had been the subject of recent litigation. [17] Eventually, in May, 1864, after all the legal complexities had been finally settled to everybody's satisfaction, the lease was signed. [18]

431

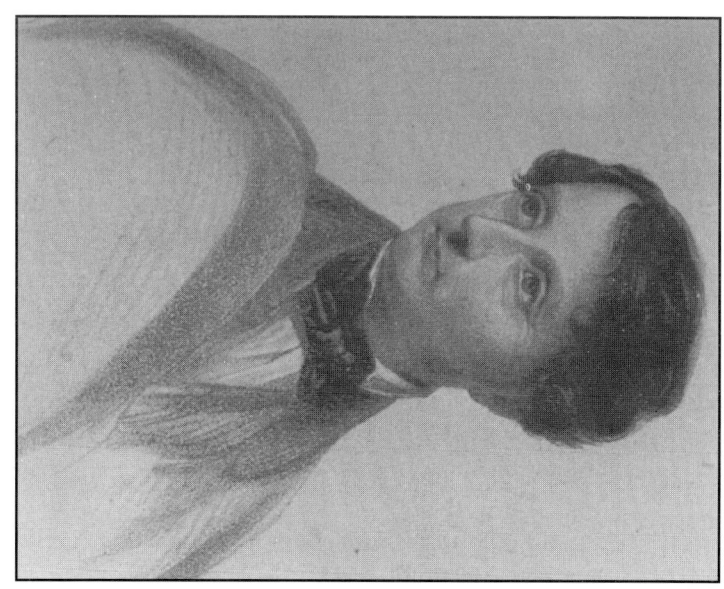

John A. Wynne

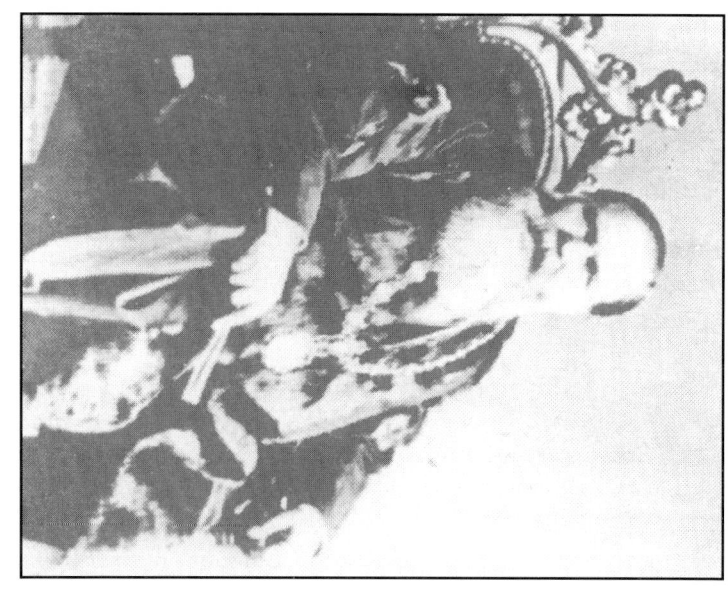

William A. Woods

THE TOWN HALL

## THE TOWN HALL

Following quickly upon the signing of the lease an Appeal was issued seeking further contributions from the public, and advertisements were placed in local and national newspapers calling upon architects to furnish plans for a building that conformed to a detailed schedule of the accommodation requirements. Within a matter of weeks some thirty sets of drawings were received from architects at home and abroad. On the recommendation of Sir John Benson, the eminent Collooney born architect, the design submitted by William Hague of Dublin, as affording suitable and convenient arrangement of plan, coupled with the best architectural effects and combined with moderate expense, was accepted. The successful design depicted a double-faced building, in modern Italian style of architecture, and consisting of a basement, 90ft by 82 ft. in area, a ground floor and an upper floor. The stone used in the building is dark in colour, and the dressings are of lime and freestone, the latter from Mountcharles, and contrasting in a pleasing manner with the colour of the masonry. The caps of shafts are of Portland stone for carving, as also the spandrils of window arches, etc. Contrast in the colour of materials used in the construction has been availed of as much as possible, in shafts, bands, strings, and voussoirs of arches. Provision was made in the Clock Tower for a turret, or 'Look Out', where by the Harbour Master could monitor the progress of shipping in and out of the harbour.

Although the Treasury officials were seriously questioning the *bona-fide* intentions of the Corporation to carry out the undertaking after four years of indecision and postponements, a further year was to go

| List of Subscribers to Town Hall Fund - December, 1864 | |
|---|---|
| W.A. Woods (Mayor elect) | £120 |
| Lord Palmerston | £100 |
| Francis MacDonagh, M.P | £100 |
| Alderman H. Lyons | £100 |
| John A. Wynne | £100 |
| Peter O'Connor | £70 |
| Alderman Abraham Dobbin | £70 |
| Charles W. O'Hara, M.P | £50 |
| Alderman Charles Sedley | £50 |
| T.H. Williams | £50 |
| Alderman D. McGill | £10 |
| Miscellaneous Subscribers | £55 |

## THE TOWN HALL

by before the building contract was eventually awarded. By the closing date in June, 1865, the following tenders had been received from building contractors :- [19]

| Charles Kilgallon (Sligo) | | £5,962 |
|---|---|---|
| Messrs. Crowe Bros (Dublin) | | £6,336 |
| John Mullen (Longford) | | £6,500 |
| James Freeman (Dublin) | | £7,200 |
| Patrick Keighron (Sligo) | | £7,623 |

As these were considered too high, in view of the limited funds at the Corporation's disposal, architect Hague was requested to revise his plans and lower the quantities in order that the contract price would not exceed £5,000. [20]

When the revised tenders were opened a month later the three lowest were :- Patrick Morris (Sligo) £4,960.; Crowe Bros. £5,000. and Kilgallon £5,043.10s. In the ensuing debate Morris's estimate was rejected on the grounds that it lacked the necessary details, and that of Messrs. Crowe accepted in preference to that of Kilgallon on the grounds that the former were more widely experienced and competent builders and more likely to complete the undertaking in a satisfactory manner. Alderman Sedley, almost alone amongst his colleagues, championed the cause of the local builders, especially Kilgallon. He described the actions of his fellow Councillors as "locally humiliating and discreditable in the extreme". The *"Independent"* also expressed some sympathy for Kilgallon and agreed that he had reason to feel aggrieved. However, it assumed that the Council adopted a course "detailed by the requirements of the work before them", and went on to state that the firm of M.F. Crowe were well known in Sligo having only recently built the Railway Terminus. [21]

Meanwhile, the site had been cleared and an auction of the materials, which included timber, slates and bricks, realised £140, and was invested in the Town Hall Fund. By October, 1865, there were sufficient funds on hands to proceed with the building. With great pomp and ceremony the foundation stone was laid on October, 12th, 1865, by the Mayor, Wm. Abbott Woods, in the presence of a large and representative attendance and to the strains of the band of the Sligo

THE TOWN HALL

---

# GREAT SALE

### OF

## TIMBER, SLATES, BRICKS, STONES, TILES, FLAGS, AND BUILDING MATERIALS.

THE TOWN HALL COMMITTEE BEING about to Contract for the Erection of the Town Hall, in accordance with the approved plans, will Sell by PUBLIC AUCTION, on the 31st JANUARY, 1865, at the hour of Twelve o'clock, noon, on the

### TOWN HALL PLOT,

All the Materials of the several Buildings. To be Sold in Lots to suit purchasers, who shall be bound to take down and remove said Materials clear from the Ground in the space of One Month from day of Sale.

Terms at Auction.

By Order,

MOSES MONDS, Sec.

Sligo, January 10, 1865.

---

Rifles. Afterwards, over sixty guests attended a banquet in the Courthouse, hosted by the Mayor. The Grand Jury Room was tastefully decorated for the occasion and over the chair, in large illuminated characters, was the motto :-

### "Prosperity to Sligo, to the Corporation and the Town Hall"

Reflecting on the ceremony, the *"Chronicle"* commented as follows:-

*"We rejoice that the long projected scheme of providing a suitable Town Hall for the Borough has been partially carried into execution and that there is every possibility of its being brought to a successful conclusion...... At this time we forget all the disappointments resulting from repeated delays and look with a hopeful eye to the future of our Town Hall".* [22]

*       *       *       *       *       *

The long delays experienced in commencing the building prompted an anonymous scribe to pen the following satirical

THE TOWN HALL

composition, which castigated unnamed but easily identifiable members of the Town Council:-

## The New Town Hall

*"Ye Traders of Sligo, both great and small,*
*Pray what has become of the New Town Hall?*
*Your wise men have talked and talked for years,*
*And yet not a stone of your Hall appears!*
*Has a project so grand but ended in smoke?*
*Or has it been meant as a practical joke?*
*As a practical man, for an answer I call -*
*Pray, what has become of your new Town Hall?*

*Ye Mayors who've shed such a flood of light,*
*And talked so much on the choice of a site;*
*Who have made of the people's feelings sport,*
*To serve a friend who was then in court;*
*Of the new Town Hall ye have made a job,*
*And yet have not built even as much as a hob;*
*Please answer me, Sirs, both one and all -*
*Pray, what has become of our new Town Hall?*

*Answer me, thou who went first in the race,*
*And boasted you were the right man in the place;*
*And thou, good Sir, of the silks and shawls,*
*Who hast stabled your Jennet at opposite stalls;*
*And thou, O'Man, of Scriptural Soul,*
*Who sittest sublime o'er salt and coal;*
*My question to you must be bitter as gall-*
*Pray, what has become of the new Town Hall?*

*And thou of the lofty pace, so grand,*
*Who walkest to court with satchel in hand;*
*And thou became wiser than all these together,*
*Whose motto is still - 'there is nothing like leather';*
*Pray, what has become of your boasted pluck,*
*That you, like the rest, in the mire have stuck?*

## THE TOWN HALL

*Hear you not every cobbler cry out from his stall -*
*'Dear Mayor, dear Mayor, pray what of the Hall'?.*

*Pray, was it the Papists of hatred creed*
*That marred your plans, or that slackened your speed?*
*If so, let Kilagallon feel all your blows,*
*Even though the Town Hall should go to the Crows;*
*Though an excellent builder, yet strike him down,*
*He's a Papist, forsooth, and a man of the Town.*
*To Sum up my arguements, moral and all -*
*Let jobbery flourish, though perish the Hall!"*

The building of the Town Hall took almost seven years to complete. The progress of the work was hampered from time to time by a scarcity of funds, as, for example, in 1868 when work was suspended and tradesmen laid-off owing to the inability of the Corporation to pay the contractor an overdue instalment of £750. However, the 'City Fathers' were not to blame for the predicament in which they found themselves. The amount of the contract was to have been obtained in equal moieties from the balance of the Reproductive Loan Fund and from private subscriptions, the public grant having been guaranteed by instalments of £1,000 after equal amounts had been collected from subscriptions. The public money was available but subscriptions failed to materialise to the extent promised. Two years later, as a fresh appeal was made for local contributions, the members of the Town Council were obliged to levy themselves at £50 a head to avoid further delays in the completion of the structure. The problem arose principally because the cost of the building, including furnishings and decorating, exceeded the amount of the original contract by £6,000 or thereabouts. Eventually, in July, 1871, as the contractor threatened litigation, the financial difficulties that plagued the progress of the work were resolved when the Provincial Bank agreed to advance a loan of £2,000. [23]

By June, 1872, nine years after the decision to proceed, and close on seven years since the laying of the foundation stone, the building was almost completed and partially ready for occupation. The Corporation held its first meeting in the Assembly Room on July 26th and availed of

## THE TOWN HALL

the occasion to compliment and congratulate themselves, and all concerned, on the grace and symmetry of the new Town Hall. However, two more years were to lapse before it was finally completed with the building of curtain walls, gate piers, etc. Subsequently, the Harbour Commissioners contributed £650, equating to two-thirds of the cost, for the building of a Clock Tower, a task successfully completed by local builder, Patrick Morris. Charles Anderson, a member of the Town Council and a wealthy merchant, presented a bell and clock for installation in the tower. The former, which was cast by Murphy's Foundry in Dublin, bears the inscription: *"Charles Anderson presents this bell and clock to the people of his native Town. A. D. 1877."* The clock was put in motion by its munificent donor in November, 1878. The tower was also used as a vantage point from which the Harbour Master could view shipping entering the Harbour.

\*       \*       \*       \*       \*       \*

No sooner had the Corporation taken possession of the Town Hall than they considered ways and means of clearing the immediate neighbourhood of unslightly buildings - an idea first mooted in an editorial in the *"Chronicle"*:[24]

*"If the space between the Town Hall and Lr. Knox's Street were cleared of the tenements and ruins which at present obstruct the principal approach to a very beautiful building and replaced by an avenue running through a green sward ornamented with laurel and other shrubs, Sligo would possess a gem of architecture unsurpassed in Ireland; and the view - what with the approach and the building - would undoubtedly be the most picturesque in the province."*

In July,1872, a requisition, signed by five members of the Town Council, called on Mayor, Alderman Kidd, to convene a meeting of the Corporation "in order to consider what steps should be taken to improve the Town Hall and the ground immediately in front of the building so that a suitable approach may be effected".[25] The properties concerned, namely, those facing onto Quay Street and Lr. O'Connell Street, where *Lyons' Warehouse* now stands, belonged to A.B. Woods and Messrs Middleton and Pollexfen and consisted of eleven tenements which were valued in the region of £2,000. A committee, consisting of Clrs. Anderson, Cherry, Doherty, Hunter, McGill and Sedley, was appointed to meet the aforementioned owners and report

# THE TOWN HALL

back. This they did a month later when it was stated that Messrs Middleton and Pollexfen were prepared to sell seven houses and an adjoining plot for £1,000, while A.B. Woods was prepared to accept an independent valuation of his property. After some discussion a resolution, proposed by Clr. Doherty and seconded by Clr. Williams, that the Corporation proceed to acquire the said properties, was adopted by 9 votes to 6.[26] However, at a subsequent meeting, Baptist Kernaghan, solicitor to the Corporation, advanced the opinion that the Town Council lacked the necessary power to acquire properties other than those scheduled under the Borough Improvements Act of 1869. In addition, a number of Councillors alluded to the unhealthy state of the Council's finances and cautioned against incurring additional expenditure until the Town Hall debt had been cleared.

There the matter rested for almost five years, by which time Messrs Alexander and Henry Lyons had already acquired the Middleton and Pollexfen site and work was under way on the construction of a new warehouse. This development spurred members of the Town Council into making a last ditch effort to acquire the plots needed for the much desired additional approach to the municipal building. At a specially convened meeting in January, 1877, the following resolution was proposed by Charles Anderson and seconded by Stephen M. Cherry:-

*"That this Corporation are prepared to take the plot from Messrs Lyons at a rent of £84 per annum and to pay them a sum of £900 for their interest; also to pay Geo. Kerr (builder) the sum of £700 for his interest in the building now in the course of construction and which it is proposed to remove".*[27]

In the ensuing discussions it emerged that there was much opposition to this proposal and, on a vote, the members tied. The Mayor, Alderman J. Kidd, then gave his casting vote in favour of the resolution. A committee consisting of Messrs Anderson and Cherry, together with J.W. Sedley, were appointed to discuss the proposition with Messrs Lyons.

At a subsequent meeting of the Town Council on February 7th, 1877, Charles Anderson reported as follows:-

*"Our Committee called upon the Messrs Lyons who stated that if it were the unanimous decision of the Corporation to take the plot, they would waive their anticipated advantages in it and come to terms with the Council; but as the*

439

## THE TOWN HALL

*Council were so equally divided they would continue with the building towards its completion."*

Thus, a very laudable effort to show off the Town Hall to its best advantage, especially when viewed from Knox's (O'Connell) Street, ended in failure. It was a classic example of a local authority being unable to complete successfully with private enterprise. In a final comment on the subject the ever vigilant *"Chronicle"* regretted that "such a handsome public building will remain hidden and shut-in on its principal point of view and approach like a light under a bushel"

The Caretaker's Lodge, designed by William Cochrane, Borough Surveyor, and built by Denis McLynn, at a cost of £750, was ready for occupation in December, 1896. This was the final chapter in the long drawn out saga that was the building of Sligo's Town Hall.[28]

### Notes & References

| (1) | *"Sligo Champion"* | 24-10-1853 |
|---|---|---|
| (2) | *"Sligo Independent"* | 31-3-1860 |
| (3) | *"Sligo Chronicle"* | 17-11-1860 |
| (4) | ibid | 7-1-1861 |
| (5) | ibid | 2-3-1861 |
| (6) | *"Sligo Independent"* | 6-4-1861 |
| (7) | *"Sligo Chronicle"* | 1-5-1861 |

See: McTernan *"Olde Sligoe"* p. 24 for history of Old Fort plot.

| (8) | *"Sligo Independent"* | 12-6-1861 |
|---|---|---|

Subsequently, in February, 1865, owing to a deficiency of funds for the completion of the work, the Town and Harbour Commissioners agreed to hand over £500 in cash in lieu of £50 annual rent; and, for the same reason, Wynne was induced to accept £50 annual ground rent instead of the agreed £1,100 purchase price. The fee simple holding was purchased from the Reps. of the Wynne family for £1,000 in 1951.

| (9) | *"Sligo Independent"* | 2-11-1861 |
|---|---|---|

(10) William Abbott Woods, seed merchant, Castle Street, was a native of Roscrea and married Mary Jane, daughter of Dr. Lougheed of Ballymote. He held office of Mayor in 1865 and retired from public life in 1867. He died in December, 1890, aged 73.

# THE TOWN HALL

| (11) | *"Sligo Independent"* | 23-5-1863 |
|------|----------------------|-----------|
| (12) | *"Sligo Champion"* | 30-5-1863 |
| (13) | *"Sligo Chronicle"* | 18-7-1863 |
| (14) | ibid | 12-12-1863 |
| (15) | *"Sligo Champion"* | 25-7-1863 |
| (16) | *"Sligo Independent"* | 12-12-1863 |
| (17) | *"Sligo Champion"* | 13-2-1864 |
| (18) | *"Sligo Chronicle"* | 28-5-1864 |
| (19) | *"Sligo Independent"* | 26-6-1865 |
| (20) | *"Sligo Chronicle"* | 8-7-1865 |
| (21) | *"Sligo Independent"* | 29-7-1865 |
| (22) | *"Sligo Chronicle"* | 14-10-1865 |
| (23) | ibid | 5-3-1870 |

Local Subscriptions eventually totalled £2,300.

| (24) | ibid | 13-6-1872 |
|------|------|-----------|
| (25) | ibid | 27-7-1872 |
| (26) | ibid | 10-8-1872 |
| (27) | ibid | 27-1-1877 |

(28) A major refurbishment plan, costing in the region of £3.5 million, is about to be undertaken as a suitable millenium project.

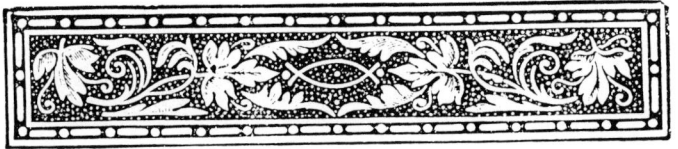

# THE TOWN HALL

The Town Hall
(Courtesy: Champion Publs.)

# TOWN HALL

Schedule of Accommodation Requirements
(Subsequently modified)

## A.   BASEMENT:

1.   Night Room or Watch-house
2.   Cell for Male Prisioners.
3.   Cell of Female Prisioners.
4.   Fire Engine Department.
5.   Caretaker's Apartment.
6.   Kitchen and Apartments for Culinary Pruposes.
7.   Coal Cellar.
8.   Closets.

## B.   GROUND FLOOR:

9.   Chamber of Commerce, Reading Room and Exchange.
10.   Office of Town Clerk and Treasurer of Corporation.
11.   Mayor's Court.
12.   Office for Inspector of Weights and Measures.
13.   Council Chamber for Meetings of the Corporation, and Board of the Town and Harbour Commissioners consisting of 48 Members.
         If practicable, a seat with a Desk should be set apart for each Member.
14.   Suitable and convenient accommodation in this apartment, for the Representatives of the Press; and space should be left for the Public to the extent of 200 persons.
15.   Closets.

## C.   SECOND FLOOR:

16.   Large Hall for the purposes of Public Meetings, Lectures and Entertainments, and equal to accommodating 1,200 persons.
17.   Off this Hall, two suitable Retiring Rooms, to be used on the occasion of Public Balls or other Entertainments.
18.   Office for the Secretary of the Town and Harbour Commissioners.
19.   Room for Committee Meetings opening off Secretary's Office.
20.   Harbour Master's Office.
21.   Closets.

# THE TOWN HALL CLOCK

"This building, we are glad to learn, will shortly be ornamented by an illuminated clock and bell, the munificent gift of Charles Anderson, Esq., J.P. The contract for the clock and bell was signed yesterday, and are to be supplied by the enterprising firm of Nelson Brothers. This graceful addition to the tower of the Town Hall will nearly complete the requirements of the building – universally admitted to be the most complete Town Hall in Ireland. By a resolution of the Council a few months ago, it was directed that the erection of the clock should be carried out under the superintendence of the architect, Mr. Hague, and a suggestion was made – which we hope will not be forgotten, that the tower should be raised some twenty feet where the clock would be placed, to be seen from any point of observation in the Town. A graceful spire of cut stone should finish the tower, but as the arrangements will be placed in the hands of Mr Hague we are certain that he will have the work completed properly. The donor of the clock, it is right to say, is the descendant of an old family, for generations connected with its trade and the commerce of the Port; and the Council can refer with commendable pride to Mr. Anderson's mayoralty, and to the eloquent panegyric pronounced by Earl Spencer, Lord Lieutenant of Ireland, when he visited Sligo and received an address of congratulation."

*Sligo Chronicle:* 23/9/1876.

"On last Wednesday evening, at nine o' clock precisely, a most important and interesting event took place at the Town Hall, Sligo. The event in question was the starting of a magnificent new clock, which has been constructed by Messrs. Nelson Bros. It is an eight day clock, of horizontal construction, and having all the latest improvements, including maintaining power to keep going whilst winding. All the wheels are of the best gun metal, and the pinions are of hardened, tempered, and polished engine-cut steel. The ball of the pendulum is 135lbs. weight, and the whole is driven by a

# THE TOWN HALL

propelling power of not more that 150lbs. weight. The clock has three illuminated dials, and the hours are struck upon a bell of fifteen cwt. All the ropes are of patent steel wire, and calculated to be of almost indestructible wearing power; indeed, the whole of the machinery is of such exceedingly great strength and enduring capacity that the clock may be expected to wear about two centuries. It is almost needless to add that this is essentially 'The Town's Clock'; and we are assured by the makers that it can be relied on most thoroughly to keep correct Dublin time, as the variation, if any, cannot exceed more than one minute in six months. The works of this most elaborate and beautiful piece of machinery are enclosed in a glass room in the tower of the Town Hall; and they were set in motion on Wednesday evening by Charles Anderson, in the presence of the Mayor of Sligo, Alex Gillmor, T.C. (proprietor of the *'Sligo Independent*), F. Nelson, and some others. As the clock was striking the hour of nine, Mr Anderson said – *'I am happy to have the honour of declaring this clock to be set going for the use of the inhabitants of Sligo'.* (cheers)"

*Sligo Independent* 16/11/1878

"This very accurate piece of mechanism was presented to the Town by one of its Mayors, Councillor Charles Anderson. The dial is made of a substance capable of being illuminated, and it was the intention of the donor and the recipients that a gas apparatus should be supplied and maintained for the purpose of enabling the multitude to ascertain by a glance the progress of time, which valuable information the clock, from its elevated position, was capable of transmitting over a very wide area. The Corporation received the clock with great condescension. Most eloquent resolutions were passed acknowledging the generosity of the donor, and so forth. But time temporizes the generosity of first impressions, and a committee of the Corporation have, we understand, passed a resolution to the effect that the Town Hall Clock shall no longer be illuminated. It was the only illuminated clock in the Town, and from its elevation it was a useful piece of information to the people, and well worth the cost

## THE TOWN HALL

of gas. There are many expenditures by committee and Council less beneficial than the price of the gas for illuminating the highest situated clock in Sligo. The Council cannot sanction this piece of beggarly economy. The committee's notion on the matter will not prevail against the common sense of the majority of the Council, and of the whole body of the burgesses, who, we are certain, if polled to-morrow on the question of lighting the clock or keeping it dark, would vote for the light, and think very little of the cost of the gas. Wonderful things are done in committees, but really this last eclipsing performance overdarkens anything hitherto accomplished. The Town Hall is the most noble building in the West of Ireland, and the clock freely presented by a citizen as a clock to be illuminated, and so accepted by the Corporation, should not be darkened by the vote of a Committee."

*'Sligo Chronicle'* 28/6/1897.

Drawing: courtesy of
Derry O'Connell

# The Enterprising SIMS

The industrial development of Collooney in the latter half of the 19th and the opening decades of the 20th century owed much to the enterprise and ingenuity of the Sim family. Following in the footsteps of Messrs Kelly & Sons, who had been involved both in the linen industry and in milling at Camphill early in the last century, Alexander Sim and his successors grasped the full potential of the location and the utilisation of its natural asset, namely, the almost inexhaustible supply of water-power that leaps from ledge to ledge in a series of miniature water falls before flinging itself over a broken mass of limestone rock, a fall in excess of twenty feet.

Alexander Sim, described as a "spirited Scotsman", and a native of Aberdeen, settled in Sligo in 1830 or thereabouts. Although of a seafaring family, he quickly established himself in his adopted county as a hardworking and industrious miller. By 1836 we find him operating a corn-mill in Ballisodare with twenty five workers on the pay-roll. Two years later, in June, 1838, he made a successful bid for the purchase of the estate of Andrew Kelly of Camphill, which included a bleach mill and a corn mill, then in receivership. Sim is said to have paid £4,500. for the property, a sizeable sum in those far off days, and then proceeded to incur further expenditure by enlarging the dwelling house.

The change of ownership was not well received locally, and his mill was boycotted by both farmers and suppliers of corn over a wide area who withheld their grain. The conspiracy gave rise not only to much ill-will but also to a series of outrages characterised by vicious attacks on those who attempted to cart grain from neighbouring counties. The perpetrators of these outrages were never brought to justice, despite the best efforts of the police. Sim bore himself with tact and courage all through the campaign. Escorted sometimes by the police, sometimes unescorted, he moved actively about seeking to break up the organisation and to find out its authors and abettors. His efforts, however, were as ineffectual as those of the authorities, and do what he would, the movement progressed, while the great water wheels of the mills stood idle and their magnificent machinery was being devoured by rust. "Seeing no chance of success in the conflict, and chaffing at being debarred from business, he resolved to give up the contest and yield to the desires of the people." [1] Negotiations were entered upon with him in 1839 which resulted in Camphill passing, by sale, back to Andrew Kelly, for the same amount as was paid for it a year earlier, in addition to £1,000's compensation in respect of improvements carried out by Sim while in possession.[2]

Undaunted by this reversal, Alexander Sim entered into a partnership, as corn merchants, with his Scottish-born nephew, Alexander Sim, jun., in November, 1843, for the development of the milling industry in Collooney, in addition to the progression of their mercantile interests in Glasgow. Initially, the Sims rented a mill and corn store across the river from Camphill, on the Abbey site, from the brothers William and Andrew Kelly, for £500 per annum. The mill, 6-storeys high and worked by an overshot wheel, was capable of grinding 600 tons weekly. So successful was this venture that they purchased the property outright for £3,500.

Over the following years, until the partnership was dissolved in 1848, the Sim milling concerns prospered. In addition to purchasing large quantities of home grown grain, cargoes of American grain were regularly imported either in their privately owned barque *Collooney*, or in chartered vessels, and unloaded at the Quay at Ballisodare or at the Port of Sligo. During the Famine years shops for the sale of bread at reduced rates were opened in both Collooney and Sligo, a move much appreciated by the poor and hungry.

After the break-up of the partnership, Alexander, jun., went his own way and quickly established himself as one of the leading corn merchants and millers in Sligo Town. He married Jane Aiken in 1849, and two years later took a long lease of *Bayview House*,[3] a 5-bedroomed suburban residence in Maugheraboy, from Captain James Martin of Cleveragh, and where over the following decade a family of six boys and four girls were born. In 1857 he took possession of the corn, flour and oatmeal mills, commonly called the *Sligo Mills*, at Victoria Bridge, and also the Distillery Mill at the Riverside, all of which he held under leases renewable forever at an annual rent of £500. Over the previous decade he had acquired house property in Sligo together with a sizeable farm at Ballysumaghan. He was also elected a member of the

## THE ENTERPRISING SIMS

Town and Harbour Commissioners, where he joined his uncle, Alexander, sen. This was a reflection of the contribution of both men to the mercantile life of their adopted County.

By the late Fifties, Alexander Sim, jun., seemed poised for further mercantile success. However, misfortune befell the enterprising Scotsman at the apex of his career. Having invested heavily in up-dating the Sligo Mills, it soon became apparent that he could not successfully compete with the well established concerns at Collooney and Ballisodare. The first indications of financial difficulties surfaced a year later when he was obliged to borrow £2,000 from solicitor, Baptist J. Kernaghan, having mortgaged the mills and other properties. In 1860 he further applied to Kernaghan to secure a debt of £200 and later sought further advances amounting to £1,100. Unable to meet his debts, although he claimed to have been owed £10,000 by creditors, he was declared a bankrupt in 1861 and within a year his Sligo properties were offered for sale in the Bankruptcy Court. The fluctuating nature of the corn trade was undoubtedly a major factor in the collapse of his business, but so also was a verdict obtained in the courts by his uncle in 1861 for £4,000, arising from the break-up of their partnership some years earlier. In these circumstances, and with a large family to support, the bankrupt merchant and miller applied for and was granted a certificate enabling him to resume business in Liverpool. [4] His contribution to the industrial life of Sligo may have ended for the time being but it was started afresh and carried forward with renewed vigor a few decades later by his sons, Alexander James and Allison Arthur Sim.

Meanwhile, the business concerns in Collooney of Alexander Sim, the elder, continued to thrive. He built a 4-storey flour mill on the Abbey site, giving a combined output in excess of 1,000 tons of corn and flour weekly and extensive employment. He also built himself an elegant residence adjacent to the mills, known as *The Abbey*, resulting in a total outlay in excess of £30,000. [5] He invested his accumulated wealth on a variety of concerns such as house property and land. In 1868 he purchased a large corn store in Wine Street , formerly Messrs Culbertsons, for £2,000, and five years later paid £12,650 for five lots of the O'Reilly estate in the Landed Estates Court. Such was his financial standing that in 1872 he was in a position to offer a loan of £5,000 to the Sligo Harbour Commissioners but, as it was not immediately

# THE ENTERPRISING SIMS

accepted, the offer was withdrawn. [6]

Alexander Sim, the founding father, who for half a century had played a pivotal role in local commerce and shipping, died after a protracted illness at his residence in June, 1882, aged 79. St Paul's Churchyard is his final resting place. He left an estate valued at £71.000, which in addition to his mills, consisted of 600 acres, principally at Streamstown, Ballisodare; two stores, one at Ballygawley and the other at Stonehall; in addition to leaseholds on the Dromahair Mills and 700 acres in various parts of the County.

He was succeeded to the property by his daughters, Anna and Alexandrina. The latter married her cousin, Alexander James Sim (1854-1918), 2nd eldest son of Alexander and Jane Aiken of Sligo, and together they operated the Collooney Mills, which by then were in decline due to stiff competition from the American flour trade. In 1885 Alexander J. Sim purchased *Camphill House* and the *'Hollow Mills'* from Martin Madden. Manley's Saw Mills, formerly a Bleach Mill, constituted part of the newly acquired property. Although in a rather dilapidated state, it was extensively repaired and fitted-out as a woollen mill. Commenting on this move, a correspondent in the *"Sligo Champion"* wrote:

*"This is a most welcome development and a great blessing to the labourers and cottiers of Collooney and neighbourhood who will have constant employment not only for themselves but also for their families. Mr Sim is already very popular, and now his popularity will know no bounds . . ."* [7]

The Woollen Mills, operated by Alexander Sim and Co., opened in 1886 for the purchase of wool and the production of towels and blankets, and gave employment to thirty females and ten males. A shop for the sale of the products was opened at the Bridge, adjacent to the gate-lodge leading to *Camphill House.*

A decade or so later, in 1898, the brothers Alexander J. and Allison Arthur Sim were instrumental in the establishment of the Irish Calcium Carbide Co. for the manufacture and supply of calcium carbide for both the home and foreign trade. Alexander was one of five Directors and Allison acted as Secretary. [8] The new industry was located in the *'Hollow Mills'* and £30,000 of the share capital was expended on the purchase of the building from Sim & Co. (£15,000), and the remainder on adapting it and the fitting-up of turbines,

450

## THE ENTERPRISING SIMS

Alexander Sim, Sen. and his daughter, Alexandrina

Photos courtesy of Richard Lyons

## THE ENTERPRISING SIMS

waterways, and machinery.

Collooney was an ideal location for such an industry - a supply of superior stone was readily available at Tubberbride for 3/- a ton; an ample water supply equal to 3,200 h.p., only 1% of which was required to operate the Woollen Mills, and ease of transportation using the network of railways then operating through Collooney. It was planned to produce 4.7 tons of calcium of carbide per day which would be sold at £12 a ton as against £20 on the open market. The potential of the product was based on its illuminating power. In pre E.S.B. times, where there was no coal gas supply, acetylene gas was in great demand for the lighting of towns and villages,as well as private and public buildings. It was also used for cycle and portable lamps. A correspondent from the *"Sligo Independent"* visited Collooney in 1902 and reported as follows on the Sim enterprises :-

*"An example of what private enterprise can achieve can be seen in Collooney. Here, Alexander Sim has commenced in the manufacture of carbide for the production of acetylene gas. Immersed in water, it produces a brilliant light which has become very popular as an illuminant for public lamps. At the outset, he was faced with the task of procuring sufficient water power to work the turbine wheels essential for the operation of the machinery. To achieve this goal he had first to dam the water as it came over the rapids and to make a mill race to the old corn mill, known locally as the 'Hollow Mill'. The making of the dams, mill race, etc., occupied about three years, giving regular and constant employment to forty men each week.*

*The mill race is about a quarter of a mile in length, strongly made and bound together with cement, and is of sufficient capacity to supply water power to a splendid large turbine wheel of 600 - horse power. What is still more worthy of note, the fitting up of the mill, the putting in of the machinery, as well as the construction of the dam and the mill race, were all satisfactorily carried out under the supervision of Alex Sim and his worthy brother, Allison.*

*The limestone required for the manufacture of the carbide is taken from three quarries at Tubberbride, about a mile from the works, and is of excellent quality. The light produced by this combination of limestone and coke, properly manipulated and solidified together, is a brilliant one, as is proved by the samples produced in Collooney in the two new beautiful lamps outside of the Church of the Assumption, as well as a town lamp supplied by Mr. Sim at his own expense. This new light is displayed to great perfection, throwing into the shade the other public lamps in the village, which are lit with paraffin oil. The operations carried on in the old 'Hollow Mill' appear to us as if the spirit of the twentieth century was being evoked by Mr. Sim to dispel the darkness of former days, to make people feel glad that they had emerged from the terrible unlightened days of dip candles and oil lamps ..."*

Alongside, was the old and well established corn mill, formerly operated by the Kelly's, the Maddens and Messrs Middleton and Pollexfen. Its immense overshot wheel, 36 feet in diameter, was capable of grinding 600 tons of Indian corn per week. This mill was equipped with the most modern appliances and machinery. Like an miniature railway, an endless chain conveyed under cover bags of grain and sacks of ground corn to the nearby railway station. This process of transferences, moving to and fro like a huge tortoise, a unique innovation, was the brainchild of Allison Sim.

*"After witnessing the conversion of limestone and coke into an illuminant, we paid a visit to another big mill of Mr. Sims' where the wool of the sheep is converted into clothing and covering for men, women, and children. Its products are considered 'par excellence,' being highly finished and most endurable. As a draper's assistant once characterised a dress length he was selling to a lady, the woollen goods made in Collooney will 'wear for ever and afterwards make a petticoat...'*

*It was about 1886, when the country was beginning to revive after a period of turbulence and consequent distress, that Mr. Sim, head of the great milling firm of Alexander Sim and Co, aided by two ladies - his wife and sister-in-law, threw himself into the task of reviving the ancient woollen industry from its ashes, and establishing it upon thoroughly modern and progressive grounds.*

*Sparing no expense of either thought or capital, - out of a ruinous bleach mill, once the centre of a thriving industry, before Ulster monopolised the linen*

---

## SIM'S STEAM ENGINE

In 1872 Alexander Sim purchased a Steam Engine, together with two wagons, for the conveyance of imported wheat from the Quays at Sligo to his mills at Collooney. On the return trip 30 tons of flour was transported for storage in his Wine Street premises. The Steam Engine attracted much attention and curiosity as it puffed along the roadway between both towns. A contemporary description referred to its broad wheels as "smoothing-out the many inequalitites on the road surfaces along the way".

*trade of Ireland, Mr. Sim created a factory filled with the most perfect machinery employed in woollen manufactures of every description.*

*The undertaking was one involving an amount of uphill work which only a man of Mr. Sim's resource could have attempted. But the obstacles were overcome, the difficulties swept aside, and Mr. Sim had created a magnificent business and had given a new impetus to local trade. County Sligo is mainly a grazing country, and before the establishment of the factory there was no local market for the vast quantities of wool produced by the farmers' flocks, until the new factory brought it to their doors - a fact which they have not failed to appreciate at its worth. The goods turned out by the firm are of a high class. They do not in the least resemble the ordinary Irish tweeds and friezes of commerce. Experienced craftsmen from the great manufacturing centres of England and Scotland have been employed to superintend the work, which is done according to the newest developments in the trade ... "*

*"Such are the extensive premises of Mr. Sim in Collooney. It is needless to say that the little town owes much to him because of the large amount of employment he gives, and everywhere about the entire district we heard nought but language of praise spoken in regard to Mr. Sim, as a kind, good, liberal employer, who is always most anxious to serve Collooney and its inhabitants, in which good object he is well supported by his brother, Allison".* [9]

The Woollen Mills continued to be operated with varying degrees of success by Messrs Sim & Co. into the 1920's, when, following the death of Alexander J. Sim, they were taken over by Messrs Henderson & Eadie of Lisbellaw in 1929. They continued in operation until restrictions on manufactured goods forced closure after the outbreak of World War 2.

The brothers Alexander J. and Allison A. Sim were also pioneers of the Co-Operative Movement in the Collooney area. For a decade or so, Alexander acted as Chairman of the Co-Operative Dairy Society; and to his wife, Alexandrina, was accorded the honour of officially opening the new Creamery in 1898. Allison was also much involved and served as Secretary for a short period.

In addition to his association with the Co-Operative, Allison was the prime mover in the establishment of a brick factory at Tullaghan, near Coolaney, where a suitable clay had been discovered. The West of Ireland Brick and Tile Co., with a registered capital of £10,000, was formed in 1907 for the manufacture of bricks, tiles, pipes and

## THE ENTERPRISING SIMS

earthenware articles. [10] The most modern machinery was installed on the site, adjacent to the Sligo-Limerick railway line, and the concern was capable of an output of 2,000 bricks per hour. Skilled personnel were brought over from Glasgow to operate the plant and train local workers. Sim filled the position of Managing Director when the firm went into production in September, 1907. The Company was reconstituted in 1911 and sold two years later as a going concern.

The enterprising spirit exhibited by three generations of the Sim family turned Collooney into a great centre of industry and commerce, and its corn, flour and woollen mills, together with the carbide works, became a legend in their own time. Even though the last of the Sims brothers departed the scene four score years ago, and the Collooney Mills and *'The Abbey'* residence have long since disappeared to make way for another industry,[11] their memory lives on by the banks of the Owenmore. [12]

### Notes & References :

(1) O'Rorke', T. *"Ballisodare & Kilvarnet"*. Dublin. 1878.

(2) A year later Kelly sold the property to his son-in-law, James Madden of Sligo.

(3) Subsequently known as *Ard-na-Veigh*.

(4) He died at Seacombe in 1892, aged 73.

(5) In 1857 the Collooney Mills were valued at £902 and Sim was credited with the use of half of the water power of the River - the other half belonging to Madden's Camphill or *Hollow Mills*.

(6) After the partnership with his nephew was dissolved, he joined with his brother-in-law, Andrew Hosie, another Scotsman, in leasing the Dromahair Mills.

(7) *"Sligo Champion"*          3 - 10 - 1885

(8) *"Sligo Independent"*          6 - 8 - 1898

   The other Directors included George Hewson, Dromahair; Alexander J. Crichton, Carrowgarry and Henry Tweedy, M.D., Dublin.

(9) *"Sligo Independent"*          13 - 12 - 1902

(10) *"Sligo Independent"*          19 - 10 - 1907

(11) Messrs G. W. I. Joinery.

(12) Richard Lyons, the present occupant of *Camphill House*, is a descendant, on the maternal side, of the Sim family.

# The Barque *Collooney*

The 288-ton barque *Collooney* was built in Aberdeen by Messrs Hall & Sons for Alexander Sim in 1844. The contract price was £3,667. She was registered in Glasgow and christened *Collooney*.

Initially, the three masted vessel traded on the North Atlantic and on one occasion made the passage from Quebec to the Clyde in a record seventeen days. In 1848-'49, under the command of Captain Livingston, she voyaged between the Clyde and Valpariso and from thence to Panama with a cargo of coffee. There, the captain discarded his charter and commenced transporting hordes of adventurers heading for the gold rush in San Francisco. After some months the vessel was seized by the U.S. authorities and Livingston was charged with breaches of the immigration laws.

Over the following decade the *Collooney* traded between the Clyde and the Mediterranean ports and, on one occasion, sailed into Rio de Janerio. By 1860 the barque had passed into the ownership of Messrs Middleton & Pollexfen of Sligo, and did regular crossings of the North Atlantic. In August, 1862, while on a voyage from New York to Sligo and laden with Indian corn for Messrs Sim of Collooney, she foundered and sank. Captain McCreary and his crew were rescued by the Norwegian brig *Anaconda* and safely landed in New York.

# Inside the Masonic Hall

Freemasonry is the oldest fraternal society in the world. It draws its name and many of its symbols from the building trade. It originated in the medieval craft guilds of the stone masons but subsequently underwent substantial modifications in purpose and organisation. In the 17th century the Mason's Clubs, or Lodges, began to be attended by gentlemen who had no connection with the trade. The principles of craft masonry are based on a belief in God and the brotherhood of man, with no distinction of sect, country or race. Their watchword is *'Brotherly Love'*.

Freemasonry, as it now exists, can be traced to the Grand Lodge of England, which dates from 1717 and the Grand Lodge of Ireland which was founded eight years later. The first Masonic Lodge in Sligo (No. 355) was founded in December 1760. The minute book of the Lodge contains a variety of entries which gives us some insight into the general workings of a masonic institution, and the handling of local problems in particular. In those far -off days, and in the absence of a suitable meeting place, gatherings took place in the homes of members. A minute, dated January, 1779, records that meetings were being changed from the home of Michael Burrows to that of Stephen MacDermott in Castle Street. The Parliamentary County election of 1790, which was a 'severely' contested affair between Owen Wynne and Joshua Cooper, resulted in the cancellation of Lodge meetings for three months - "the majority of members being unavoidably engaged in the election". [1] The February meeting in 1807 was adjourned owing to the small attendance - "it being the evening of the day of Carricknagat Fair". Nine years later, in February, 1816, a vote of sympathy was extended to the family of John Hillas who was fatally injured in a famous duel at Kilmacowen [2]. The following extracts from Minutes of Lodge 355 reveal the concerns of the Brethern at meetings two centuries ago:

**1777. February 3rd.** *"Michael McDonagh stated that he was at Divine Services at the Chapel of Sligo, where the Rev. John Flynn exercised the rights of the Church, whereupon the said Rev. Flynn communicated to the flock that he* *had positive directions from his Bishop not to receive or exercise the Rights of his Church to any that professed Masonry".*

**1778. December 7th.** *"It was on observation of different members that there has been several 'laves;' torn out of the different books of this Lodge particularly the account of those that has subscribed to the Pall. It was likewise observed that Brother McDonagh has these books in his possession for a considerable time and that he must give an account whether those 'laves' were tore out in his possession or not under less punishment than being excluded for ever".*

*Signed:*      *Michael Meay, Martin Hay, John Fletcher (Wardens).*

**1781. April 11th.** *"Lodge met in order to adjust and settle a bill due Brother Stephen McDermott from the evening before which has been contracted by the Brethren after attending the remains of our Brother James Adams, deceased, to the Church Yard of St. John's in Masonic Form".*

**1787. September 7th.** *"Lodge of Emergency called to examine into the situation of Brother Keon who is lying dangerously ill, when it was resolved that the Master should take into his charge and care a silver watch , shoe buckles and 'Nee' buckles and that the body do contribute as much as they can do with justice to themselves in order to support him in his illness".*

Seal of Lodge 355

**1793. May 31st.** *"A complaint was preferred against Bro. Wm. Nicholson of Greyfort, in the Co. of Sligo, now a prisoner in Sligo Gaol, founded upon information lodged by Bro. Jones, a Magistrate for said County, that said Nicholson was a principal person among the deluded people called 'Defenders'. It was agreed that no charge could lye against said Bro. Nicholson in the Masonic lines, on the said information, and that a charge must be preferred against him by a brother".*

**1806. November 12th.** *"Emergency Meeting called to arrange to attend the Theatre for a benefit performance for the widow of a deceased Bro. and a number of orphans. Resolved that this Lodge and as many of the other Lodges as can attend will, fully clothed in their respective orders and as decently clothed as possible, meet at Lodge at 6 o'clock on Friday, 14th inst., and walk hence to the Theatre. Three of the brethren appointed to wait on the Commanding Officer praying the attendance of the band, and to superintend the order of the house."*

# Inside The Masonic Hall

**1808. Feb. 7th.** *"To encourage Bro. Hartley (Sec.) during the fatigue incurred by his attendance, he is to be allowed a pint of wine mulled during the night and the S.F. the same quantity".*

At times conduct in the Lodge was not what one would expect from a Masonic Body. The punishment for such offences was usually enforced silence. For example, on the 5th of May, 1779, the minutes read: *"Same night Bro. Jones became insolent so far as to reject the mandates of the chair, whereupon a committee was appointed to try the merits of said offences".* They later announced their verdict, namely. *"That Bro. Jones be silenced for nine months."* Again on the 9th August, 1781, the minutes read: *"Lodge of emergency called to inspect into a supposed misbehaviour of Bros. Caffry, Black and Mullhollen: Brother Caffry for using scurrilous language to Bro.Healy, Black for telling things before Apprentices which he ought not and Mullhollen for disobedience to the chair."* Whenever two or more Brethren had a row it was customary to call a 'Lodge of Emergency' to deal with the matter in dispute. For example, in May, 1791, such a meeting was called by Bro. Thomas Soden of Lodge No. 530 against Bro. Michael Parker, proprietor and editor of the *"Sligo Journal,"* charging him with having published in his paper a letter tending to reflect upon Soden's conduct as "Billeting Master for the Town of Sligo". On February 5th, 1796, Bro. William Mullen complained that Bro. Joseph Hudson had "advertised him for defamation of character."

In 1779 great exception was taken to the activities of Rev. John Flynn, the Administrator of St. John's Parish Chapel, and subsequently Bishop of Achonry, who put pressure on members of his flock, who were masons, to renounce their membership of lodge 355. The minute of February 1st, 1779, reads:- "A complaint being made that the Priest Flin *(sic)* had used an exhortation against masonry the following Examinations were heard:-

*"Bro. Healy declared that about two years ago Mr. Flin, a Popish priest, brought him into a garden in this Town, and endeavored to prevail on him to denounce Masonry. When finding his arguments to be in vain, and Bro. Healy declaring he never would quit it until death, Mr. Flin in a most outrageous manner declared he would not administer to him, or any person belonging to the Fraternity, the Rites of their Church, and if they were to continue Masons until death they certainly would be damned. He likewise continues, and is for ever*

459

INSIDE THE MASONIC HALL

*persuading him to renounce and for ever abandon Masonry."*

*"Bro. McDonough declared that he attended 'Chapel' a few Sundays ago where he heard Mr. Flin make the following discourse from the Altar, namely:- That he received some direction from his Bishop the substance of which was that the rights and privileges of his Church were not to be administered to any person whatsoever that were of the section of people called Freemasons".*

Having listened to the complaints, it was decided to petition the Grand Lodge of Ireland to advise on a method of "punishing the Priest 'Flin' for endeavoring to subvert the long established rights of Masonry." While the matter was further discussed at a committee meeting on March 5th, there was no further reference to it in the Minute Book of Lodge 355.

\*     \*     \*     \*

The first meeting of Lodge 51, which incorporated Lodge 355, took place on October, 7th 1817. It consisted of twenty three members and James Beatty was elected Worshipful Master. The bye-laws of this Lodge contained a number of interesting clauses:-

*"Any Brother who absents himself from St. John's Festival shall not be admitted to Lodge again unless he pays 2/6d."*

*"During Lodge every Brother shall behave himself discreetly, no cursing, swearing, or profane or idle talking that may in any way interrupt the harmony of the Lodge under the penalty of paying 5d for every such offence."*

*"That every Brother who comes into the Lodge drunk with liquor shall pay down the sum of 1/8d and withdraw himself from the Lodge for that night, and, if when sober at their next meeting, make a suitable apology. Any Brother who shall not bring himself under these penalties shall be excluded forever."*

On St. John's Day it was customary for the Masons of Sligo to walk in procession to St. John's Church. The following description of the 1825 procession was published in the *"Sligo Journal"* :-

*"On St. John's Day the annual procession to the Parochial Church of the members of the Masonic Order resident in Sligo and its vicinity took place. At an early hour the principal streets were crowded and at noon members of the different Lodges issued from their rooms, dressed in full insignia and bearing the different emblems of their order. The procession moved through the principal streets and having reached the Church, entered its portals in the usual form. Divine Service was then conducted by Reverend William Armstrong. After*

## INSIDE THE MASONIC HALL

*service the members returned to their respective Lodge rooms where they dined and spent the evening in that round of social feeling which was uninterrupted by the clamour of party strife or drowned by the shrill trumpet of political animosity".* [3] Subsequently, a letter signed by the Master and Wardens of Lodges 51 and 989 was forwarded to the Reverend Armstrong thanking him for the 'excellent discourse' he delivered in St. John's Church on June 24th.

The circumstances surrounding the death, in 1828, of Thomas Mulhern of Quay Street, described as an active member of Lodge 51, and a devout Catholic who attended Mass regularly in the Parish Chapel, gave rise to much dissension between different creeds and classes. In February of that year Mulhern suffered a stroke which paralysed one side of his body. On being advised that his life was in danger, his wife, a Protestant, sent for the Parish Priest, Dean James Donlevy, to administer the last rites. The good Dean lost no time in getting to the sick man's bedside. However, when Mulhern expressed his unwillingness to renounce Freemasonry, his confessor flatly refused to give him absolution. Despite the pleas of the dying man and those of his tearful wife, the Dean is said to have exclaimed: "My hands are tied......I can do nothing for you unless you repent of your association with the Masons", and hurriedly departed the scene.

Mulhern died three days later. A numerous body of Masons, arrayed in full paraphernalia, gathered for the funeral. They were joined by a large crowd of "the most respectable inhabitants of the Town", and all marched side by side in funeral formation to the graveside. Despite the repeated requests of the deceased's family and friends, no priest came forward to perform the burial rite. This caused much disquiet amongst his Masonic brethren. Following a specially convened meeting in the *York Hotel* of the two local Lodges, a statement was issued for publication in the *"Journal"* in which the circumstances surrounding Mulhern's death and burial were made public and which concluded as follows:-

*"We are proud to declare that our Institution knows no religious or political distinctions. We deprecate every attempt made to disunite the members of the several religious communities which the terror of the example set in the instance of our departed Brother Mulhern, is so powerfully calculated to effect".* [4]

According to the minute of December 3rd, 1832, Lodge 51 did not meet during the cholera outbreak:-

*"Owing to the late grevious disease with which the Town of Sligo has been affected, the members of this Lodge could not meet as they would wish to do so, and also by the loss of some of our worthy Brethren who fell victim to the disease called Cholera Morbus".*

The first meeting of *Light of the West* Masonic Lodge No. 20 took place on June 25th 1833, at the *Nelson Hotel*. Amongst those present were a number of prominent citizens, including Abraham Dobbin of *Farmhill House* and Union Street, merchant, an Alderman of the Corporation and Mayor 1861; William Faussett J.P. of Willsboro, Provost of Sligo for many years and a member of the Reformed Corporation; Henry Griffith, J.P, D.L. of *Ballytivnan House* and *Port Royal*, High Sheriff in 1847 and member of the Town and Harbour Commissioners; Thomas Mostyn, Crown Solicitor for Sligo and subsequently Treasurer of the Grand Lodge of Ireland; and John Ormsby, J.P. of *Castledargan House* and Provost of Sligo for a number of years between 1832 and 1842.

The following entries are extracted from the Minute Book of Lodge 20:-

**1838.** On 22nd October, an address and silver snuff box was presented to Bro. W.S. Tracey on his promotion to another district. He was a Magistrate and a sub-Inspector of the Co. The address states the brethren were indebted to him for the revival of masonry in the County and particularly for the incorporation and existence of Lodge 20.

**1841.** January 7th. A petition was received on behalf of Roger D. Robinson to be admitted a member. He was the father of the late Major J.D. Robinson and of R. St. G. Robinson. Bro. Roger D. Robinson was one of the most active members of Lodge 20 and filled the office of Secretary with great zeal and success.

**1841.** On February 11th. it was decided to remove the Lodge to the *Hibernian Hotel*. The terms for dinner with ale and porter was 3/- per head. Supper with ditto 1/6; Punch per quart 5/-, or 4d per tumbler; Lodge Room, Ante Room, lights, fires and Tyler's expenses, free of all charges. Bro. McBride, the owner of *Nelson Hotel* having apologised for complaints, the resolution to change to the *Hibernian Hotel* was rescinded.

INSIDE THE MASONIC HALL

Members of this Lodge dined together, as was customary, on St. John's Day. However, as the feastday fell on a Sunday in 1849, they had their anniversary dinner on the following Tuesday in the *Nelson Hotel.* Reporting on the event the *"Journal"* wrote:-"Nearly all the Brethren of this respectable Lodge were present and were favoured with the company of several visitors who were in Sligo for the Quarter Sessions. The evening passed off most agreeably and all seemed well pleased with the hospitable entertainment they received."

In August, 1850, the Brethren of Lodge 20 decided that for the future they would dine together on October 2nd; on the occasion of Quarter Sessions and Spring Assizes, in addition to the two St. John's days. The absence of a proper meeting place was discussed in December, 1851, as the 'present room' was not sufficiently large enough to accommodate the n u m b e r s attending, which averaged twenty-two. It was decided to form a Committee to investigate "the best place to establish a Lodge Room". Eventually in 1856, it was decided to open a building fund designated "Lodge 20 Building Fund" for a new Masonic Lodge, and over the following three decades various fund raising activities, such as bazaars, were organised. In the meantime, meetings of the Lodge were transferred from the *Nelson Hotel* to the Grand Jury Room in the Courthouse. In May, 1881, a Special Meeting was called to discuss the possibilities of either purchasing an existing building or erecting a Masonic Hall. It was agreed to offer £250 for the old Primitive Wesleyan Chapel in Stephen Street (subsequently the *Protestant Hall*) but the offer was not accepted and the matter was dropped. However, in January, 1893, it was agreed, on the proposal of Arthur Jackson, that a new Masonic Hall should be built. Over the following years various

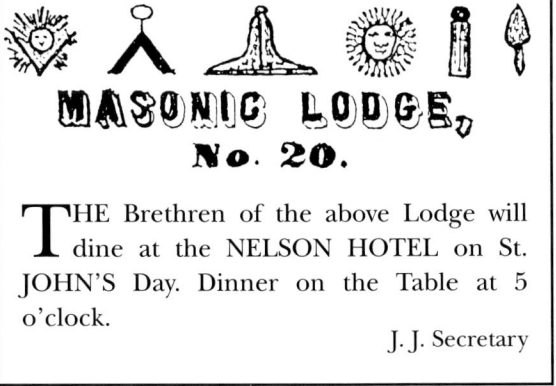

Advert. in "Sligo Guardian", Dec. 1849

463

# INSIDE THE MASONIC HALL

Masonic Hall, The Mall

Harper Campbell Perry, Provincial Grand Master, 1930
Photo: Courtesy of Ted Smith

# INSIDE THE MASONIC HALL

fund-raising functions were organised, including a Bazaar in March,1895, which yielded a profit of £550.

The new Masonic Hall on The Mall, built in 1895 at a cost of £1,525 on ground leased from Mrs. Craig for 999 years at an annual rent of £9 p.a., was dedicated to the uses of Masonry on October, 21st. 1897, by Lord Harlech, Provincial Grand Master, in the presence of close on one hundred brethren. Amongst the attendance was Rev. L.P. Ledoux, chaplain; Dr. J.R. Ardill; Colonel James Campbell; Robert Smyllie; R. St. Geo. Robinson; Alexander Sim; Arthur Jackson; John F. Walker; Francis and J.J. Nelson; Henry Boyers; W.F. Gilcriest; C.B. Jones; Henry Loretto and Harper Campbell Perry.. The following description of the imposing edifice appeared in the local *"Independent"*:- *The new building has been designed in the Old English style, the outer walling being faced with red perforated bricks, the upper storey roughcast, and the roofing covered with green slates. This combination gives a very bright, pleasing effect, and produces a marked contrast to the somewhat sombre tint of our Sligo public buildings. Over the main entrance there rises a very neat tower, with bell-shaped eaves, and roof covered with Ruabon red tiles. The internal arrangements of the hall are all up to date, the principal lodge room and dining hall being each 40ft by 20ft. Adjoining these are other smaller rooms for the craft purposes. The entire contract was carried out in a first-class manner by our townsman, Mr. George Kerr, from the plans and under the personal superintendence of the architect, Mr. Henry Seaver, Belfast.*[5] Successive members of the Dodd family were in residence as caretakers from the date of opening to 1951.

In both the minute books and contemporary newspapers one finds occasional references to Masonic funerals. In March, 1778, Ensign Patterson, a crew member of the ship *Sir William Erskine* who was drowned when the vessel was wrecked at Aughris Head, was buried with great pomp in St. John's churchyard. "He being a Freemason, the Society attended his funeral in great numbers", reported the *Hibernian Magazine.* "They made a very solemn appearance and paid every honour to their departed brother..." In 1781 Brother James Adams of Lodge 355 was accorded the appropriate ceremony in St. John's, while in July, 1788, members of the same Lodge went in Masonic procession on the occasion of the death of Brother John Winterscale.

What was probably the last, and certainly the most celebrated Masonic funeral, took place in September, 1910, on the occasion of the death of George T. Pollexfen, a partner in the firm of W. & G.T. Pollexfen, at his residence, *Thornhill House*. The cortege to St. John's Church was headed by Freemasons from all over the country who walked two deep in front of the hearse. Col. James Campbell, the Provincial Grand Master, and his deputy, Abraham O'Connor, brought up the rear in a carriage which immediately preceded the hearse. *En route* representatives of the Prince Mason's Chapter, to which the deceased belonged, acted as pall bearers. On arrival at the church, the Masons donned the full regalia of their different orders and lined the avenue from the gate to the church door. At the conclusion of the service, at which the Band of the Y.M.C.A. played appropriate music, the coffin was borne to the grave on the shoulders of deceased's brother masons and the masonic portion of the service was conducted by Rev. W.R. Landey. After the benediction the rather quaint but effecting masonic ceremony of farewell was performed: each of the brethren followed the lead of the Grand Master, walking past the grave and throwing a spring of acacia on the coffin, uttering at the same time the words: *Alas! my brother*. Col. Campbell and Abraham O'Connor, clothed in the regalia of Prince Masons, followed and instead of a sprig of acacia cast a white rose into the grave. [6]

The death and funeral ceremony of George Pollexfan has been immortalised by his nephew, William Butler Yeats, in the poem entitled:

### "In Memory of Alfred Pollexfen"

*Five and twenty years have gone*
*Since old William Pollexfen*
*Laid his strong bones down in death*
*By his wife Elizabeth*
*In the grey stone tomb he made.*
*After twenty years they laid*
*In that tomb by him and her*
*His son, George, the astrologer;*
*And Masons drove from miles away*
*To scatter the acacia spray*
*Upon a melancholy man*
*Who had ended where life began.*

Founding Members of *Harlech Lodge*, October 1895.
(L - R) Roger Parke, James Chambers, C.B. Tully, T.J. Baily, Jos. Dixon, R. Cooke, E.T. Kell, John Chambers, A. Ward & Alex Munro.
Photo: Courtesy of Ted Smith

INSIDE THE MASONIC HALL

The custom of going in procession on St. John's Day to St. John's Church has been discontinued for over a century. The last Masonic service there took place on May 30th, 1926, on which occasion a large number of brethren of the Masonic fraternity assembled in full regalia. The colourful procession was headed by Preceptors and Knights of the Order of the Temple whose white tunics, red caps and gleaming swords created something of a medieval atmosphere. On entering the church the Knights lined the nave and crossed swords, forming an arch of steel beneath which the Masons, headed by Arthur Jackson, P.G.M., passed in order of rank. The sermon was preached by Right Rev. John Orr, Lord Bishop of Tuam.[7] A Masonic service, in the form of Evensong, took place in Calry Church on June 24th, 1951. The large attendance was headed by T.H. Blackburn, Headmaster of the Grammar School, Provincial Grand Master, and Archdeacon C. Tyndall, Rector of Calry, led the officiating clergy. The service was arranged by R.T. Clarke of Lodge 165 and J.H. Armstrong, Secretary of Lodge 20. [8]

In the opening decades of this century two members of Lodge 20 became members of the Supreme Council of the Masonic Lodge in Ireland, namely, Arthur Jackson D.L. and Harper Campbell Perry.[9] The latter acted as Provincial Secretary from 1903 to 1924 and Provincial Grand Master from 1930 until his death in 1935. Lodge Harlech (No. 165) which had been founded in 1895, was the largest Lodge in Connacht half a century ago. Prominent amongst its membership was William Albert Griffith, Managing Director of Harper Campbell Ltd., who became Deputy Provincial Grand Master in 1935 and Provincial Grand Master in 1939, a position he held with distinction until his death in 1942.

Two lodges, namely, No. 20 *(Light of the West)* which dates from 1833, and No. 165 *(The Harlech Lodge)* founded just over a century ago, each with a membership of between fifty and sixty members, are still operating and have their meetings and other fuctions in the imposing Masonic Hall on The Mall, which is approached by thirty-three steps, the number of degrees in Masonry.

INSIDE THE MASONIC HALL

# Notes On Different Lodges

### LODGE 20 *(Light of the West)*

First met in June 1833. Subsequent meetings were on the first Thursday of each month at the *Nelson Hotel*. In 1834 the officers were: William Treacy (Master); William Weir (Senior Warden); Andrew Hume (Treasurer) and John F. Quill (Secretary). By 1850 the Lodge had forty-two subscribing members of whom fifteen were described as 'Gents'; seven solicitors, six medical doctors, two barristers, a chaplain, a newspaper proprietor (E.H. Verdon of the *"Sligo Champion"*), a grocer, an engineer, a baker, etc. In the following year meetings took place at an unspecified address on The Mall. Membership in the **1830's** included:- Thomas Mostyn, John Ormsby, Andrew Hume, William Ramsay, Edward Knott, John Hume Powell, John F. Quill, Henry Griffith, William Weir, Charles Ormsby, Abraham Dobbin, William and Henry Faussett, Jeremiah Jones, Charles Martin, Mathew Baker and Charles O'Hara.

**1840-1849:** Henry Caldwell, Robert McKim, Dodwell Palmer, Godfrey Brereton, Sir James Crofton, Harloe T. Phibbs, John Gore-Jones, James Dodwell, Ormsby Jones and Jacob Powell.

**1850-1852:** Edward Howard Verdon, Jeremiah J. O'Donovan, Noblett St. Leger, Harper Campbell, James Fenton, William Ormsby-Gore, Edward Trumble and Abraham Fenton.

**Membership 1893:** Rev. John R. Ardill, James Campbell, R. Chism, A.J. Crichton, John C. Cole, W.R. Fenton, W.F. Gilcriest, Robert B. Gorman, Arthur Jackson, C.B. Jones, E.J. Kell, Percy Kerr, Henry Loretto,, Alan Lyons, E.C MacDowell, Charles P. McLoughrey, Francis and J.J. Nelson, Phillip D. Perceval, H.C. Perry, George T. Pollexfen, J.D. and R. St. George Robinson, Alexander and Allison Sim, J.G. Stevenson, James D. Vernon and T.H. Williams.

### LODGE 51

Held its meetings in the 'Lodge Room' of the *Nelson Hotel*. In 1828 George Mostyn filled the position of Worshipful Master. Other members included William Middleton, Alexander Irwin, Alex. and Henry Burrows, William and Robert McBride, Philip and James Beatty,

INSIDE THE MASONIC HALL

Samuel McMunn, Wm. J. Lawson and Harlow Baker. Subsequent members included Henry Bolton and Starkey Doyle (1833), John Benson and Richard Anderson (1839). In 1836 James Beatty was Worshipful Master and Thomas Armstrong, Warden.

## LODGE 114

This lodge was opened on October 3rd 1867. It was called the *Magnet Lodge* and Harper Campbell, merchant, was one of the principal founders. The following news-item appeared in the *"Journal"* two days later:-

*"On Thursday last a new Masonic Lodge was opened in this Town, No. 114. The members at present enrolled met at their Lodge-room at four o'clock, when the ceremony of opening was proceeded with, after which the Worshipful Master and other officers were installed. The business before the Lodge having been concluded, the brethren adjourned for refreshment, when, with several visitors, they sat them to an excellent dinner, Brother T.M.Wood occupying the chair. Dinner being over, the usual loyal and masonic toasts were given from the chair and received with masonic honours......The establishment of a second Lodge in Sligo should be a matter of congratulations to all members of the craft, proving, as it has, the extension of our ancient and honourable Order whose benefits have been felt and appreciated all over the globe".*

The Lodge continued working until 1872, when at a meeting held on December 3rd, it was decided to return the warrant owing to the difficulty of getting a sufficient number of the Brethren to attend. In addition to Harper Campbell, membership included T. Mostyn Wood, Edward Pollock, Noblett St. Ledger, William L'Estrange, Abraham Dobbin, Harloe Trumble Phibbs, St. George Jones Martin, William Pollexfen, Meredith Thompson, Josiah Davys and Wm. T. Vernon, nearly all of whom had transferred from Lodge 20.

## LODGE 165

First meeting took place in June, 1895,and the Lodge was dedicated to the P.G.M., Lord Harlech, who had been initiated a member of Lodge 20 forty five years earlier. Founding members included Thomas Algeo; Alfred Middleton *; Christopher Bellew and William Pettigrew.

By 1900 membership had grown to fifty-two, many of whom had

* Son of Adam Middleton, Collooney. He went down with the "Titanic" in 1912.

470

transferred from Lodge 20, and included many prominent citizens e.g. Arthur Wood; James Blennerhassatt; Robert Smylie; Henry Loretto; William A. Griffith; Nicholson Ormsby; William Middleton and William O. Rowlette.

### LODGE 233

First meeting took place in Ballymote in December 1842, when the following enrolled - Robert Morrison, Michael Healy, Henry T. Irwin, William Callaghan and Roger Kelly.

Over the following decade membership was conferred on Phillip and William McKim, Robert McMunn, Samuel and Stewart Gilmour, John Orr, Edward Knott, Abraham, Andrew and John Motherwell, Richard Fleming, Edward Trumble, Edward Gethin, Blakeney Gubbins, John McDonagh and Meredith Thompson.

This Lodge continued to function until November 1868, when the warrant was returned.

### LODGE 355

Membership, with date of joining, included - James Black (1761), John and James Burrows (1770), William Cope (1777), John and James

# MASONIC LODGE, 233.

Members will dine as usual at Brother Irwin's Hotel on St. John's Day at 6 o'clock.

Signed: R. L. Morrison, Secretary.

Ballymote, 7th June 1845.

Advertisement in *"Sligo Journal"*.

Winterscale (1780), Alexander Crichton (1781), Robert Bolton (1782), Jones Irwin (1788), Edward Martin, Rowland Carter and John Wynne (1789), Thomas Somers and John Ricc (1793), Thomas P. Hillas (1794), William Christian (1802) and Peter O'Connor (1808).

## LODGE 530

Held first meeting in March, 1776. Membership included James Taylor, William Gibson, George Taaffe, William Nicholson, Andrew Hume, Robert Weir, Ffolliott Wynne and Laurance Vernon. The warrant was cancelled in 1813.

## LODGE 568

Formed in Ballinafad in July, 1779. The founding members were William Nicholson, Hugh O'Rorke and Philip Lilly. The warrant was removed to Boyle in 1787 and transferred to Tubbercurry in November, 1796, where it functioned for a little over a decade. Amongst those who enrolled were Patrick and Thomas Somers, James Nicholson, Roger Dodwell, James Wood, Andrew and Pat McDonagh, William Little, Hugh Sweeney, Patrick Maxwell and Charles Kelly.

| LODGES IN COUNTY SLIGO | | |
|---|---|---|
| Location: | Lodge No: | Dates: |
| Ardnaglass | 254 | Warrant not issued |
| Ballinafad | 568 | 1779-1787 |
| Ballymote | 233 | 1842-1868 |
| Sligo | 20 | 1833-current |
| | 51 | 1817-1846 |
| | 114 | 1867-1872 |
| | 165 | 1895-current |
| | 355 | 1760-1817 |
| | 530 | 1776-1813 |
| | 566 | 1719-1813 |
| | 567 | 1779-1813 |
| | 626 | 1784-1815 |
| | 989 | 1808-1835 |
| Tubbercurry | 568 | 1796-1807 |

## INSIDE THE MASONIC HALL

### LODGE 989

Founded in May, 1808, by Loftus Jones, William Armstrong and Thomas Bolton. Between then and 1835, when it ceased to operate, it attracted a membership of eighty, the most prominent of whom were (with year of admittance) - James Fleming (1810); Richard Phibbs Irwin and Isaac Baker (1811); Alexander Bolton, Dunbar Jameson, Richard Knott and John Ferrall(1812); John Ormsby and Charles Phillips (1813); James Dodwell (1815); Travers Homan, James Soden, Wm. Fawcett, Robert Baker, Thomas and John Fenton, Burton Phibbs, John Powell and William Christian (1816); John Smyth and Robert Lyons (1819); Andrew Britton, George S. Dodwell, Jeremy Jones and Alexander Cockran (1822); Andrew Britton (1823); Abraham Martin (1829); James C. Dodwell, Robert Christian, Edward Jones and William Patrickson (1830).

### Notes and References:

(1) Wood-Martin, W.G. *History of Sligo.* Vol. 3 p. 38

(2) **SEE:** McTernan "Olde Sligoe". pp 226-236

| | | |
|---|---|---|
| (3) | *"Sligo Journal"* | 25-6-1825 |
| (4) | ibid | 19-2-1828 & 22-2-1828 |
| (5) | *"Sligo Independent"* | 23-10-1897 |
| (6) | ibid | 1-10-1910 |
| (7) | ibid | 5-6-1926 |
| (8) | ibid | 30-6-1951 |

(9) Successive generations of the Campbell family held prominent positions in the Masonic Order. Harper Campbell, merchant, was elected Worshipful Master in Lodge 20 in 1857. He was succeeded in the chair by his son, Lt. Col. James Campbell, afterwards Provincial Grand Master; in 1878 by his grandson, Harper Campbell Perry, P.G.M. in 1901; and finally by his great grandson, Ronald A. Campbell Perry, who died in April, 1963.

Also consulted - Minute Books, Correspondence, etc. of various Sligo Lodges. Crossle, P. *"Irish Masonic Records"* (Dublin 1973). Jackson, Arthur. *"Freemasonry in Sligo 1767-1867"* (n.d. 1909) and Parkinson, R.E. *"Lodge of Records: Transactions for 1949-57"* (Dublin, 1959).

# The County Courthouse

In the opening decades of the 18th century justice for the County-at-large was dispensed in what was known as a *'Session's House'*, which stood in Church Lane, or *Session's House Lane*, as it was then called. This was the building in which John Wesley, the founder of Methodism, addressed a congregation on the occasion of his visit in 1789. In his diary he refers to it as "the old Courthouse - an exceedingly spacious building".

A decade or so earlier the Grand Jury had acquired a site in what is now Teeling Street on which they build a new *'Session's House'*, or Assize Court, which also contained a place of detention and a prison. In 1808 the Governors of Co. Sligo, who included Owen Wynne, Joshua E. Cooper and Charles O'Hara, leased a further plot of ground from landlord, Wm. Burton, for 999 years at an annual rental of £10 p.a. for the purpose of extending the building. Eight years later, in 1816, a second extension followed, resulting in an increased street frontage of 24 ft. and extending backwards 104 ft.[1] In the 1830's additional space was acquired by converting portions of the old Gaol into offices.[2] On the night of the 'Big Wind', January 1839, the roof of the Courthouse was partly uncovered by the storm.

Although no print has survived which would provide us with a visual image of what the building looked like, there are, however, a number of descriptive references, which convey somewhat conflicting views. Lewis, in 1837, describes it as "a well arranged building but too limited for the public business".[3] Elsewhere it is referred to as "plain and old-fashioned in appearance, dark and gloomy on the outside.";[4] and, again, as "a dingy old structure".[5] In 1865 the *"Chronicle"*, commenting on the state of the building, described it as "antiquated and out-of-date, and, moreover, contemptuously shoved into a corner by the neighbouring buildings".[6] One Cornelius O'Mulligan of Tunaphubble, in a letter published in the *"Chronicle"* ten years later, refers to it as "a venerable old structure, with an eccentric loveliness and a peculiar beauty of its own". He then went on to describe the accommodation:

*"There are two courts, and a large lofty hall, and a magnificent Grand Jury*

## THE COUNTY COURTHOUSE

*Room on the ground floor. The Record Court is of the most commodious character. There is a bench for the judge and a retiring room behind it, which is so large as to constitute a defect by wasting space in a too luxurious manner. There are side benches for the Bar, and seats for the attorneys, and a witness-table, and the rest of the court is vacant for the accommodation of the public. The standing room is unencumbered by seat or bench of any kind; and during a trial of any interest, it is beautiful to observe the good humour with which the people lean upon each other, and put up with the Constable when shoving them about to open a passage for a Counsellor, or a crier, or some other person of authority. The Crown Court is almost of the same character, save that a dock in the centre deprives the public of some of the standing room which they enjoy next door. In connection with the Crown Court, it has a very fine apartment for the accommodation of witnesses, and also rooms for the use of professional persons, and there are galleries overlooking these courts, the approaches to which are appropriately symbolic of the ways of the law - dark, devious and crooked."* [7]

As early as 1856 the Grand Jury had been considering reports of dry-rot in the roof of the Courthouse. In the winter of 1870-71 it was badly damaged in a storm. Three years later, in July, 1873, the *"Chronicle"* suggested that some thought should be given to the building of a new Courthouse on a site adjacent to the Gaol at Riverside. [8] At the Spring Assizes in February, 1874, the Grand Jury had a discussion on whether to build a new Courthouse, or alter and repair the existing structure. On the recommendation of J. Rawson Carroll, a consultant Dublin architect, it was decided to rebuild on the existing site at a cost not exceeding £15,000. In March, 1874, advertisements appeared in both local and Dublin newspapers seeking designs for a new building. The matter was again discussed at the following Assizes when the suitability of the site was questioned. Various members of the Grand Jury expressed the opinion that it was too confined, being closed-in on three sides by private buildings. A suggestion to build on a two-acre site on Albert Road, was put forward but failed to meet with general approval. The decision to re-build on the existing site was not well received in certain quarters. The *"Champion"* was loud in its protestations:-

*".........The site of the present Courthouse is wretched.... Be the improvements what they may, individuals coming in any direction will not be able to command a view of the premises until they come within a few perches distance..... It is situated almost at the foot of a declivity and surrounded on all*

## THE COUNTY COURTHOUSE

sides by lofty buildings, some of which will perhaps throw it into the shade even in its new aspect..... Those who contemplated the building of a County Courthouse in a field above the Constabulary Barracks, were in our opinion, actuated by the most praiseworthy motives - to make the 'Temple of Justice' the most conspicuous of the many public institutions with which Sligo is surrounded....[9]

In June, 1874, the Grand Jury invited designs from interested parties for the remodelling of the old building. Subsequently, one of the unsuccessful architects, who wished to remain anonymous, made public his views on the possible alternatives in a letter to the "Sligo Independent" :- [10]

"There are three alternatives proposed to provide improved Courthouse accommodation for Sligo. First, building a new Courthouse on a new site; second, razing the old structure and rebuilding a new one on the present site; third, remodelling the old building itself. In the first instance, the obtaining of a new site and building a new edifice would be a most expensive undertaking - probably costing not less than £30,000 to £40,000. For these reasons the purchase of a new site itself is a most expensive item; and, in building a new edifice isolated in such a site as was selected on Albert Road, with suitable accommodation for the requirements of a thriving town like Sligo, would require a large block of buildings."

"In connection with this scheme the present splendid site would become comparatively valueless for any other purpose. In the second instance, I quite concur in your conclusion that you could not have a more suitable site than the present one, which seems to be central, in a most respectable locality, and amply large within its present boundaries, if you utilise the present useless area in front, by razing the present old structure to the ground, and utilise such of the old materials as are fit for re-use in the new building. In this case you would only require one front of cut stone, the internal portions and rere being quite plain, but perfectly substantial, of the materials decided on - say, local stone. This scheme could probably be carried out for about £15,000. Third and last, I believe it is quite feasible, from the nature of the grounds, to re-model the old building, having a portico, entrance hall, and two courts, seperated by a large public hall. The county offices, etc., extending along the front for three stories in height, with proper accommodation for the Grand Jury, Judges, etc. in the rere, with seperate and distinct entrances for the public, Judges and Grand Jury, would result in giving the front a substantial and ornamental facade. This

THE COUNTY COURTHOUSE

*scheme - the cheapest of them all - could be accomplished for about £10,000. To be candid with you, no such sum as £5,000 would look at effecting the improvements which are required in making the present building passably suitable for your requirements. As to the present Courthouse, I quite agree with you that it is disgraceful, and unworthy of a civilised age. "*

---

## NOTICE TO BUILDERS
## REBUILDING COUNTY COURTHOUSE

Notice is hereby given that I am ready to receive Sealed Tenders and proposals for Rebuilding the County Courthouse in conformity with Specifications, Maps, Plans, etc. which have been prepared for the purpose of carrying into execution a Presentment duly made by the Grand Jury in that behalf. Copies of the said Specifications, etc. are deposited in the Offices of the Secretary of the Grand Jury and may be inspected any day, except Sunday, between the hours of 12 and 3 o'clock, free of charge.

Tenders in approved form to be delivered to me (under seal), on or before the 19th of February next, and same to be opened by the Foreman of the Grand Jury at the commencement of Fiscal business of next Assizes.

*C.B. Wynne, Clerk of the Peace,*
*acting as Secretary of the Grand Jury.*

Sligo, January 12, 1876.

---

At the Spring Assizes in 1875 it was finally decided to re-build on the existing site, and Carroll, who had already designed *Classiebawn Castle,* Mullaghmore, was appointed architect. The following January tenders were sought for the building of a new Courthouse. At the subsequent Assizes the contract, amounting to £14,200, was given to Patrick Morris of Union Place. However, when additional ground became available at the northern end in 1877, it was acquired and the building, still under construction, was enlarged. In addition, a strike of masons led to an increase of 4/- a week in wages. The combined effects of the extension

## THE COUNTY COURTHOUSE

and the improved pay roll brought the overall cost of the new Courthouse to £17,000 by the time it was completed. Portion of the old building on the south side, which prior to 1817 housed the County Gaol and valued at £3,000, was retained and incorporated into the new edifice. [11]

The Courthouse was officially opened at the Spring Assizes on February 26th, 1879. "It is our pleasing duty to record the completion of the new Assize Courts in Albert St.", commented the *"Chronicle"*. [12] "The new Courthouse is certainly a beautiful structure viewed from the exterior; and what is more important, the design and interior arrangements are quite in keeping with its appearance ...... The main entrance, under the three front arches leads directly into the hall, and presents a very striking appearance, with its fine oak doors, its handsome roof, and the stone arches and pillars, with their caps beautifully carved...." It then went on to describe in detail the various apartments, the heating and ventilation systems, and the octagon ventilating tower, the pinnacle of which is 110 feet above street level.

At the Spring Assizes, 1880, expenditure was approved for embellishments to the frontage of the edifice, including the putting in place of ornamental railings. It was also decided to insure the building for £16,000 with an additional £500. for fittings and furniture. A decade later the Grand Jury expressed satisfaction at the "excellent supply of gas available", and the "general comfort" being experienced by all concerned from the spreading of dry sawdust on the floors of the galleries, halls and courts, thus minimising the noise of moving feet.

Architecturally, the Courthouse has been described as "a full-blooded Victorian Gothic building". "In it one can see the Victorian passion for complicated grouping and blurred outline which was a re-action against the clarity and regularity of Georgian architecture". Wood-Martin refers to the style as "Gothic, freely treated". Foras Forbatha, on the other hand, describes it as "the most impressive High Victorian building outside Dublin", and goes on to enumerate the notable features of "an imposing building" - namely, "the turreted breakfront and arcaded entrance, and the octagonal tower with its elaborate pointed roof and dormers" [13]

\*        \*        \*

# THE COUNTY COURTHOUSE

Sligo Courthouse

Drawing: Courtesy Derry O'Connell

## THE COUNTY COURTHOUSE

Sligo Courthouse, both old and new edifices, witnessed many notable events over a span of two centuries prior to the passing of the Local Government Act of 1898. The Grand Jury met within its hallowed walls twice annually to discuss fiscal matters relating to the administration of the County and hear a report on the peaceful state, or otherwise, of the area under their jurisdiction. Those meetings coincided with the visits of the Assize judges on circuit who, in the space of a few days, dispensed justice in the Crown and Record courts on a wide variety of cases. Floggings and transportation were fairly common penalties handed down from the bench for what would now be regarded as rather trivial offences. Prior to the opening of the new Gaol at Riverside, those convicted of more serious crimes were hanged in the street fronting the building. In 1817 eight men, who had been sentenced for robbery with violence in Tireragh, were executed in what is now Teeling Street; and a year later, on April 6th 1818, six more were publicly hanged for robbery and rape. Notable murder trials, including that of Mathew Phibbs in 1861 and John McDaid in 1875, attracted a lot of interest and great crowds converged on the Courthouse for the hearings. A succession of political trials, involving *Defenders, Threshers, Whiteboys, Fenians, Land Leaguers, Home Rulers* and *Sinn Feiners*, made headlines at home and abroad.

A most unusual event occurred in August, 1836. The Liberals planned to host a reception for Earl Mulgrave, the Lord Lieutenant, on the occasion of his first visit to Sligo. When the Conservative High Sheriff, James Knott of *Battlefield House,* learned of their intentions, he issued instructions to the effect that the building was not to be made available. The Liberals, however, were not to be outdone. William Parke of *Dunally House,* who espoused their cause, used his influence and the reception went ahead as planned. The Lord Lieutenant was so impressed by the prompt action of the landed proprietor from Calry that he then and there conferred a knighthood on Parke - the only occasion on record where a Sligonian was so honoured on 'home' soil.

Prior to the building of the Town Hall and the introduction of the secret ballot, the Courthouse invariably acted as the venue for both Borough and County parliamentary elections, nominating candidates and declaring the poll. Within its precincts a number of strife-ridden contests were decided and the results proclaimed to the assembled

## THE COUNTY COURTHOUSE

multitudes. The Borough elections of 1833, 1837, 1853, 1865 and 1868 and the County elections of 1822, 1837 and 1868 were all characterised by street riots, widespread disturbances, and even death, as the supporters of the rival candidates publicly voiced their respective allegiances. Tensions were more subdued and spirits less explosive in April 1880, when Home Rule candidates, D.M. O'Connor and Thomas Sexton, addressed a large and enthusiastic gathering of supporters from the steps of the Courthouse, after the High Sheriff had formally announced their election as M.P.'s for the County. In a lighter vein, the Assembly Room functioned as a theatre on occasions and quite frequently as a ballroom.

Over the past century Sligo Courthouse has witnessed many stirring events in the evolving political scene. The first County Council, elected after the passing of the Local Government Act of 1898, met in session in what had been the Grand Jury Assembly Room, on April 15th 1899; and twenty-one years later, in May 1920, the newly elected Republican County Council assembled there in unusual circumstances. The Anglo-Irish War was still in progress and some of its members - those who had been active in the 'struggle' and on the so-called 'Wanted List', risked arrest as they entered or left the meeting. A few weeks later the building was commandeered by the military. As a result, the County Council moved its administrative headquarters across the street to what was then the *Victoria Hotel*, while the courts were facilitated with temporary accommodation in the Town Hall. During the Civil War, 1921-23, the Courthouse was occupied in turn by both the 'Irregulars' and the National Army and heavily fortified. It was finally vacated by the military in 1924 and thereafter resumed its function as the administrative and judicial centre for the County.

Following the opening of a new County Council complex at Riverside in 1979, the Courthouse, for the first time in two centuries, no longer functioned as the administrative centre for the County. In the interval, it has been re-roofed and plans are now underway to extensively refurbish the elegant century - old building and have it adapted to meet the requirements of a modern 'Hall of Justice'.

# The County Courthouse

## Notes & References

| | | |
|---|---|---|
| (1) | Registry of Deeds | 1816, Bk. 701. p. 529 |
| (2) | Grand Jury Minutes, 1837. | |
| (3) | Lewis, Samuel. *"Topographical Dictionary of Ireland"*. | |
| (4) | *"Sligo Journal"* | 9-1-1857 |
| (5) | *"Sligo Champion"* | 25-3-1876 |
| (6) | *"Sligo Chronicle"* | 12-12-1865 |
| (7) | ibid | 27-2-1875 |
| (8) | *"Sligo Chronicle"* | 5-7-1873 |
| (9) | *"Sligo Champion"* | 25-3-1876 |
| (10) | *"Sligo Independent"* | 20-2-1875 |
| (11) | ibid | 27-2-1875 |

Before the old building was demolished in the Spring of 1876, the fixtures and fittings from both the Crown Court and the Record Court were removed to the Town Hall where a temporary courtroom was put in place. A rent of £250 p.a. was paid to the Corporation for the facilities. An Assembly Room and administrative offices were also provided.

| | | |
|---|---|---|
| (12) | *"Sligo Chronicle"* | 1-3-1879 |

(13) Foras Forbartha - *"Buildings of Architectural interest in County Sligo"*. Dublin. 1976.

# A Musical Tradition

Sligo enjoys a great musical tradition which can be traced back to the opening decades of the 18th century when the itinerant bard, Turlough O'Carolan, visited many of the 'Big Houses' of the County and composed airs for his patrons. Some years later, Arthur O'Neill, another celebrated harper, visited Sligo. During his peregrinations the renowned minstrel called on Jones Irwin, Esq., of *Streamstown House*, Achonry, who was an enthusiastic lover of music. In his *Memoirs*, O'Neill recalls his visit as follows:-

*"I went to a Mr. Jones Irwin's of Streamstown, Co. Sligo. I am totally at a loss how to describe that gentleman's manner of living at his own house and among his tenantry. He had an ample fortune. He was an amateur. He had four sons and three daughters who were all proficient in music, and no instrument was unknown to them.*

*There was at one time a Meeting in his house of forty six musicians, who played in the following order:-*

| | |
|---|---|
| *The three Miss Irwins at the piano:* | *3* |
| *Myself at the harp:* | *1* |
| *Gentlemen flutes:* | *6* |
| *Gentlemen violin cellos:* | *2* |
| *Common pipers:* | *10* |
| *Gentlemen fiddlers:* | *20* |
| *Gentlemen clarinets:* | *4* |

*At the hour when this gentleman's customary meetings were finished, some guests contiguous to their own places went home, but those who lived some miles off remained and, in order to accommodate them, Mr. & Mrs. Irwin lay on chairs that night in the parlour. For my own part, I never spent a more agreeable night either in or out of bed."*

In more recent times the Sligo Musical Society, the Sligo Orchestral Society, Feis Ceoil, Feis Shligigh and the Sligo Concert Band have, and are, maintaining that tradition. An integral part of this rich and varied musical inheritance were the many bands, brass and reed, fife and drum and pipes, that have graced the scene and entertained audiences at numerous events and occasions, great and small, for close on two

## A MUSICAL TRADITION

centuries with their renderings of much loved tunes, classical and traditional.

It's a far cry since the days of the military band of the Sligo Militia in their distinctive uniforms, who regularly paraded the streets in search of recruits for the Regiment. The *Militia Band* was the bedrock of brass band culture in Sligo for generations and was responsible for the cultivation of a greater interest in and love of music as performed by marching men. It led to the formation of a number of splendid brass bands, such as the *Temperance*, the *Hibernian*, the *Y.M.C.A.* and the *Foresters*.

Apart from the band of the Sligo Militia, and subsequently that of the Sligo Rifles and Sligo Artillery, the earliest group of musicians of which we have knowledge was the *Temperance Band*, which was founded in 1840 to coincide with the launch of the Temperance Movement. It headed the procession to the Parish Chapel on the occasion of the visit of Father Mathew in September of that year. Five years later, in October, 1845, the band greeted Daniel O'Connell on his arrival for a monster Repeal Meeting.

A brass and reed band, bearing the same name, was formed in the opening years of this century, under the control of bandmaster, Harry Donovan, described as "a gifted musician", who was equally at home in brass, reed or strings. It was based at the Gilhooly Hall and invariably attracted an appreciative audience whenever it paraded the streets of the Town. On occasions, when the Temperance Gaelic football team was playing at away venues, the band accompanied them on a 'Long Car' and their renderings of martial airs greatly enlivened the scene both before the contest and at the interval. Members of that celebrated group of musicians included: Harry Depew, Pat Reynolds, John Reynolds, John O'Rorke, James O'Rorke, Michael Burns, Joe Bofin, John Gilmartin, George Ellis, Jack Gillen, Louis Dykes, John McCarthy, Tommy Ferguson, Pat Kivlehan, Joe Reilly, Jim Foley, Martin Kerins, John McCarrick, John Costello, Pat O'Hara and Michael Tiernan.

In the interval between the two Temperance bands, another brass band, known as the *Carpenter's Band*, which was composed entirely of tradesmen, held the limelight. It played a big roll in the celebrations marking the O'Connell Centenary in 1875. Bandsmen names included Michael McGowan, Michael Fox, James Rooney, Paddy Doherty, Patsy

A MUSICAL TRADITION

Keaveny, Thomas Higgins and Andy Kelly.

Bob Watts was the conductor of a very tuneful fife and drum band called *Band of Hope*. Membership of the group was confined to worshippers attending Calry Church on The Mall during the incumbency of the Rev. Thomas Heany slightly over a century ago. Freddie Kerr beat the big drum and there were five or six side-drums. The fifes were played by three members of the Monds family: Tom, Billy and Ned.

Shortly after the collapse of that musical combination, a revival took place in 1895 in the form of the *Calry Fife and Drum Band* with Bob Watts again as the leader. The group practiced in the old Diocesan School, now the Grammar School, and when performing in public wore a uniform cap of the 'pill box' type, adorned with gold braid. The band made a habit of parading the streets playing martial and religious tunes, such as in 1897 on the occasion of Queen Victoria's Jubilee. On the opening of the new Masonic Hall, in 1897, the Band attended a special service in Calry Church and afterwards played selections outside as the dignitaries made their way to the Hall on the opposite side of the street. Like its predecessor, the band enjoyed a short existence of a decade or thereabouts. Its membership included Billy Monds, W. Burnsides, W. Campbell, D. Currie, Alec Knaggs and J. Soulter (drums).

A house in Water Lane was the headquarters of an excellent brass band called the *Emmet Band*. On the eve of St. Patrick's Day it was customary for this group of musicians to assemble at the Market Cross, and on the stroke of midnight, headed by a large group of men and boys carrying lighted torches, they paraded the streets playing national airs in the Saint's honour. Patrick Reynolds conducted the band and membership included John Reynolds, James Reynolds, Tom Flanagan, Willie Monaghan, John J. Henry, Willie Dykes, Jack Gillen, George Ellis, Jimmy Williams, Tom Oliver, Michael Burns, Tom Moran, Paddy Taheny, John Conway, James Conway and Tom Sweeney. When this band disbanded at the turn of the century a number of the musicians joined the newly formed *Sligo Temperance Band*. Other musical groups who graced the scene at intervals throughout the 19th century were the *Band of the Harmonic Society*; the *Trade's Band*; the *Perrin Mill Fife and Drum Band*; the *Gaelic Brass Band* which was attached to the famous

## A MUSICAL TRADITION

Black and Blues G.A.A. club, and the *Asylum Brass Band*, conductor H. Donovan.

James Osborne, a clerk in the employment of Messrs. W. &. G.T. Pollexfen, millers, founded the *Y.M.C.A. Band* in 1906. Its base was an apartment in the Old Distillery at the Riverside, made available by Arthur Jackson, a director of Messrs. Pollexfen. On the morning of Whit Monday of that year the band paraded the streets of the Town for the first time and afterwards joined a day excursion to Inishmurray and Killybegs on board the s.s. *'Lily'*. E. J. Newman, bandmaster of the Sligo Artillery, was conductor from 1906-1909. He was succeeded by D.H. Milton, formerly Band-Sergeant with the Royal Irish Rifles, who continued to conduct the band until the outbreak of World War 1, when he left to rejoin the Middlesex Regiment, his original unit. Other members of the group also volunteered for service abroad and this led to its disbandment in late 1914. The *Y.M.C.A. Band* performed on a regular basis outside the Protestant Hall in Stephen Street. On the occasion of the burial of George T. Pollexfen in 1910, they were invited to attend the Masonic funeral service in St. John's Church and, according to contemporary accounts, added immensely to the solemnity of the occasion with its rendering of the dirge from *"Saul"*.

In the opening decades of this century the Town could boast of no less than five Brass Bands, namely, the *Artillery*, the *Y.M.C.A.*, the *Irish National Foresters* (Lily of Lough Gill branch), the *Temperance* and the *Hibernian* (A.O.H.). In addition, there was the *St. John's Fife and Drum Band*, conducted by A.P. Malley. In those relatively free and easy times before the advent of motorised traffic, it was customary in the summer months for individual bands to hire a boat at Riverside and row up to Lough Gill where they would entertain the numerous picnic parties frequenting the islands. On the other hand, Sligonians and visitors alike, who went instead to Rosses Point, were usually entertained by the *Military Band* who played a variety of tunes from their extensive repertoire.

In the early Twenties, and in the aftermath of 'The Troubles', a number of musicians, previously associated with the foregoing groups, came together to form the *Sligo Brass and Reed Band*. Under its conductor, Harry Depew, who was an Alderman of the Corporation, the band flourished for a number of years and numbered amongst its

## A MUSICAL TRADITION

membership the leading musicians of that era which included James Reynolds and Willie Smyllie (basses); T. Coen and E.Walsh (trombones); John Gilmartin (euphoniums): Percy Roberts (horn) Austin Foley and J. Connolly, W. Patton, George Mullen, Joe Burns, Freddie Dykes (clarinets); Eddie Bree (cornet); Jerry Reynolds (trumpet); W. Wylie (B-trumpet); John Kelly (drummer); Willie Rennick (side drum). Others associated with the band were Joe Bofin, George Ellis, Michael Burns, Frank Foley and Tommy Ferguson. In the mid Thirties the *Nazareth House Brass Band* made its debut under conductor, Joseph Cummins. For over three decades this youthful combination, in their distinctive green blazers enlivened many functions, both indoor and outdoor, with their spirited tunes. In 1947 they were joined by the *James Connolly Pipe Band*, now the *Sligo City Pipe Band*. More recently the *Cranmore Pipe Band* has been formed and between them they carry forward a long established musical tradition into the new millennium.

The great musical tradition which Sligo has inherited has by no means been confined to the Town. In the closing decades of the 19th century, following upon the establishment of Land League and the G.A.A., and also in conjunction with the '98 Centenary celebrations, a number of bands, mostly fife and drum, sprung up all over the County - at Ballymote, Ballintogher, Ballyrush, Coolaney, Collooney, Culfadda, Dromore West, Drumcliffe, Highwood, Keash, Killoran, Killavil, Knocknarea, Sooey, Riverstown and Tubbercurry - only a handful of which survived into our own time. In the Twenties, Ballymote could boast of a fine Brass and Reed Band and its members included Martin Brennan (bandmaster); Tom McGovern (drummer); Jack Meehan, Michael Healy, Jim McManus and Jim McFadden (cornets; John Price (cymbols); Peter Brennan, Jack Foye and Michael Meehan (bass).

Since the days of O'Carolan and O'Neill, but particularly over the past one hundred years, traditional music has flourished and the County has produced some of its finest exponents, foremost amongst whom were Michael Coleman, James Morrison, Paddy Killoran, Fred Finn, Martin Wynne, Paddy Sweeney, Josie McDermott, Tommy Flynn and Joe O'Dowd. Over the same period many accomplished performers paraded their distinctive talents playing in different Céili Bands, such as the *Owenmore*, the *Leitrim*, the *Lough Bó*, the *Coleman*

## A MUSICAL TRADITION

*Country,* the *Castle,* the *Gurteen,* the *Patrician,* the *Glenview,* the *Rising Sun, Josie McDermot & Flynn's Men,* the *Lough Gara, Sligo Comhaltas* and *St. Marys* (Sligo).

The extent to which traditional music, and individual performers in particular, have become an integral part of our culture and tradition, is evidenced by the impressive roadside memorials proclaiming the artistry and genius of widely famed musicians.


## INSCRIPTIONS FROM THE MEMORIALS

(1)    At Knockgrania, Gurteen:

> *"To the Memory of Michael Coleman*
> *Master of the Fiddle*
> *Saviour of Irish Traditional Music.*
> *Born near this spot, 1891*
> *Died in Exile, 1945."*

—————  •  —————

Inscriptions on adjacent slabs read:-

> *"To the Traditional Musicians of an Older*
> *Generation who Inspired his Genius"*

> *"To Those of a Later Generation who after his*
> *passing fostered and preserved that tradition for posterity"*

—————  •  —————

(2)    At Drumfin:

> *"James Morrison*
> *Musician-Dancer-Teacher*
> *Born Drumfin, 1893. Died New York, 1947"*

The Memorial incorporates the original milestone after which he named the Reel *"The Milestone at the Garden".*

# A MUSICAL TRADITION

(3)   At Doocastle:

*"To the Memory of the Musicians of Doocastle"*

| | |
|---|---|
| *J. M. Cawley* | *Pat Kelleher* |
| *Jim Carroll* | *Andrew McDonagh* |
| *James Doyle* | *James Marren* |
| *Jim Durcan* | *Martin McDonagh* |
| *Michael Gorman* | *Michael McDermot* |
| *Jimmy Hunt* | *Jim Spelman* |
| *etc* | *etc.* |

———— • ————

(4)   At Killavil:

*"To the Memory*
*of*
*Fred Finn"*

"Erected by his Friends and Admirers"

———— • ————

(5)   At Ballinafad:

*"In memory of*
*The McDonagh Brothers,*
*Ballinafad.*
*Traditional Muscians.*
*Paddy 1902 - 1985; Michael J. 1904 - 1988*
*and Lawrence 1911 - 1984."*

Erected by their friends and relations, July, 1992.

# A MUSICAL TRADITION

Memorials at Knockgrania (Above) and Killavil (Below)

# A Shattered Dream

When the Devon Commission, which was set up to investigate land tenure in Ireland, sat in Sligo in July, 1844, Francis Barber, a tenant farmer of Rahelly, near Carney, was amongst those invited to give evidence. In the course of the hearing he told the Commissioners that he had a holding of 160 Irish acres which he held under Sir Robert Gore-Booth, on a lease of three lives and at a fair rent. He also stated that over the preceding twenty years he had laid out a capital of £1,300 of his own money on improvements.

In September of the following year Thomas Campell Foster, the *"Times"* Commissioner, visited the area and was very impressed by Barber's industry and enterprise – his drainage, sub-soiling, ditching, planting and general improvements. He described him as "a clever, shrewd, active, respectable man", who attended to his farm and work and unlike many of his neighbouring tenant farmers, did not involve himself in the politics of the day. In a lengthy interview Barber outlined the background to his success :-

"My father, William, occupied a farm of twenty-seven acres, under Sir Robert Gore Booth, for which he paid £40 rent. My father died before I was fourteen years of age, leaving my mother and ten children depending on the farm, and myself as a mere boy to manage it. My father was £183. in debt, and the whole stock was two cows, a heifer, and two horses; two-thirds of the farm were in wretched condition growing little beyond thistles and weed. The first year I expended £2. 15s in draining a field : the following year I expended £4. on another field. Finding the benefit I derived from these improvements, the third year I spent £10. in draining. The following year I was about to carry out more extensive improvements in draining and trenching, but the people of the country and the neighbours went to my mother and advised her to prevent me laying out more money on the farm, as they said 'I would destroy the family'. My mother, in consequence, took the charge of the farm out of my hands. I begged for half an acre of rough land to manage for myself, and pursued the same plan on this half acre, the produce of which I sold the following year for a profit of £4. My mother then let me have another acre of waste land unfit for anything else. On this I expended £10. in draining and trenching. I had but this £4. and borrowed £5., and got credit for £1. worth of labour from a neighbour who helped me, thus making up the sum. This half-acre again left a profit of £4., and the crop on the acre of land

## A SHATTERED DREAM

sold for £7. I had thus cleared myself and had got an acre and a half of good land. My mother seeing that I succeeded, let me have two more acres of waste land. On these two acres I laid out £16. in draining and trenching, borrowing part of the money, and the neighbours helped me, and I sold the whole produce of the three acres and a half for £15. profit the following year, over and above the cost of bringing in the two acres. My mother then, finding that I had gained so much by the improvements, gave me back the charge of the farm. I then continued improving to a greater extent, according to my ability, and I found the farm paid me for all my expenditure as I went on. The agent taking notice of my improvements and perseverance, said I was entitled to have a larger farm, and added fifty acres to the extent of the farm. I continued improving the remainder of the farm, and having laid out a large sum of money upon it, the landlord gave me a lease at a reduced rent of 4s. 6d. an acre. I continued this course, and the landlord became so pleased with me that he extended my farm to 160 acres. The whole of this land I have improved, and has laid out upon it no less a sum than £1,300., every shilling of which was created by my own industry. I have paid my father's debt, supported my mother and her family, and, according to the custom of the country here, has given portions befitting their station, as farmer's daughters, to six of my sisters. As first one, and then another, of my sisters married off, I was often left without a shilling, in order to pay them their portions. From having a small farm at will, much of it swamp, and feeding snipe and wild duck, I have now got a large well-cultivated farm on lease, which will amply repay me all my outlay. I am now a substantial farmer."[1]

The extraordinary success story of Francis Barber made news far and wide. In 1848 a correspondent from the *"Western Star"* visited Rahelly and described the enterprise as follows :-

"Francis Barber, of Rahelly, is well and favourably known to the public of his native County for the last twenty years, as a most industrious, enterprising, persevering and successful farmer. The farm at present comprises an extent of about ninety acres, Irish, and is rather picturesquely situated, the site of the dwelling commanding a side view of Sligo Bay, and encircled in the south and north-east by broken ridges of mountain in the distance . . . ." The writer then went on to give details of Barber's livestock which he described as "of a superior description and breed - the milch cows being a miscellany of Ayrshires, Durhams and Irish". "Everything is first-rate; he has two ploughs, as many harrows, a well mounted roller, and three carts got up in the first order. There in not a flaw in the harness either. The

# A SHATTERED DREAM

question whether labour is the mother of capital, or the latter the parent of the former, has been satisfactorily answered on Frank Barber's tenement. Something like £1,500 has been laid out here for the last three and twenty years, in various kinds of improvements, exclusive of farming offices or dwelling-house, neither of which having been yet provided or commenced".

In 1861, Henry Coulter, a correspondent of *"Saunders News Letter"*, visited Sligo. In the course of his travels he made his way to Rahelly. He was so impressed by what he saw that he had no hesitation in singling out Barber's holding as a model farm and a striking example of industry, enterprise and success :-

"It is one of the best of its size in Ireland, being now in the highest state of cultivation. Fine meadows and rich land producing abundant crops have, by skillful management, taken the place of the barren, stoney and swampy soil. Its extent is 135 statute acres, of which 21 are under tillage, 25 under meadow, and the remainder devoted to grazing. The entire farm has been thoroughly drained and sub-soiled, and there are arrangements for giving a constant supply of water for cattle in each field on the farm . . . The crops produced are excellent in quality and quantity, and can compare favourably with any produced elsewhere in Ireland. The external and internal fences are excellent, the fields being thoroughly fenced with either good stone walls or hedges and good iron gates. There are also good roads through the farm. He keeps a large stud of horses for his farmwork and carrying out of his contract for the repairing of the public roads. He feeds about 160 herd of cattle and intends increasing his stock. He also keeps a large number of people constantly employed in farm labour and building and his labour bill averages £1,100 p.a. . . . He has built a large house and an extensive range of offices, stores, stables and cattle sheds. They are not fully completed but a few months would suffice to finish them . . In building the house and offices and in land improvements he has expended in excess of £12,000, all from his own resources, without any assistance from the landlord".

A further description of Barber's model holding and newly built residence was contained in an article by a special Correspondent in the London *"Times"* in March, 1881 :-

". . . . . The largest tenant on the Lissadell estate is Frank Barber, who began his farming career forty years ago with about ninety acres, mostly in snipe bog and a bit of rough pasture, remarkable for molehills. Drains were put 3 ft to 4 ft deep, the mains a foot deeper; a square culvert was built with picked stones in the bottom, and regular stones, only too abundantly got out in subsoiling, were shovelled within 18 inches of the surface. On some land, afflicted with springs, deeper drains were run 5 or 6 feet through bog and shale into the more porous subsoil. Not a drain has ever given way or caused the slightest trouble. On the reclaimed land potatoes are usually first grown, followed by oats and grass seeds. Besides, homemade manure, lime, sea-sand, etc. were freely used. After three or four years grass the lea was ripped up and cropped. Good cultivation and manure have banished rushes, rough grass, moss and weeds . . . Great as was the expense of thorough draining, removing the numerous stones and boulders, and deeply subsoiling, the magnificent crops speedily repaid all outlay. So pleased was Sir. Robert with the enterprise and success of his tenant, who at first held only from year to year, that he took 4s. 6d. an acre off his rent and gave him a lease of thirty-one years. When that expired, without any addition to the rent, he granted him, unasked, a lease for three lives.[2] Resounding to this most liberal treatment, Mr, Barber has built a handsome, three-storied house, with barns, stabling and shedding, which must have cost £4,000. Part of the money has been borrowed at 4 per cent. The house is built in the Elizabethan style, with a frontage of 96 feet, and from 24 to 28 wide, two storey high; inside court-yard, 100 by 120 feet surrounded with ranges of offices 20 feet high by 19 wide, the upper rooms being very lofty. The rear yard is the same frontage, but longer with sheds 14 feet wide at one end and a range of offices round the sides. The whole are entered by a gateway with a lofty tower and gilt cock on the top which forms a conspicuous object. The house and offices are finished in a superior style of masonry, the centre of the yard gravelled, both the sides and stables beautifully paved and drained. The only thing wanting to make all complete is a threshing, sawing and general mill, which, from a river passing close to the offices, could be easily worked with water-power".[3]

The house, built of stone and brick and consisting of two storeys and basement, had sixteen apartments. The Inner, or Stable Yard, consisted of excellent out-offices with accommodation for six servants, stables for ten horses and two large coach houses. The Outer, or Farm Yard, had stalls for sixty herd of cattle, a dairy and a piggery. There was also a forge, cart sheds and a boiler house. [4] In addition to Rahelly, Barber also had a holding at Cashelgarron and a further leasehold of

A SHATTERED DREAM

over 500 acres of mountainy pasture from Gore-Booth at Gleniff. A boundary fence on the mountain top, where the two counties meet, is still referred to as 'Barber's Wall'.

Misfortune befell the ageing Barber at the pinnacle of a remarkable career. The fruits of his untiring labour's and a considerable investment slipped out of his control in rather unusual circumstances. Having undertaken extensive road contracts for the Grand Jury with the utmost satisfaction over a long period, he successfully tendered for the laying of a major sewer system through the principal streets of Sligo and ending at the Quays.[5] It was a massive undertaking and in the course of the construction work layers of rock had to be blasted in places and this resulted in subsequent claims for damages to properties - an outlay the contractor had not anticipated. Already over-stretched by earlier borrowings, he was now forced to increase his indebtedness further to pay off his creditors. He mortgaged the Rahelly farm as security for the additional overdraft facilities afforded to him. Three years later in 1880, he accepted a loan of £1,200 @ 5% from landlord, Sir Henry Gore-Booth. [6]

By 1884 his indebtedness to the lord of the manor amounted to £1,360, consisting of unpaid rents and interest on the loan. In addition, he owed the Belfast Banking Company £750. At that stage, Gore-Booth secured an eviction order against him but before this could be enforced Barber surrendered his interest in his model farm for a sum of £3,250, a figure equivalent to his indebtedness to both the landlord and the Belfast Banking Co., but with the stipulation that it would be handed back for the remaining term of the lease once Barber had repaid his indebtedness to the landlord with interest.

Francis Barber left Rahelly in the autumn of 1885, having sold off his livestock, farm machinery, etc. He then took up residence on his other property at Cashelgarron where he lived out his last years. He died there in December, 1893, aged 88 years. A few years before his death, his son, John Lipsett Barber, called on Sir Henry at Lissadell and, with cash in hand, offered to redeem the Rahelly property. The offer was not accepted and the Barbers were deprived of an opportunity of re-possessing the 'model' farm.

*Rahelly House* was subsequently occupied by James A. Cooper, Gore-Booth's agent. After his departure in 1918, the house became vacant,

# A SHATTERED DREAM

During the 'Troubles' it was occupied by 'The Irregulars' for a time and, subsequently, in the Autumn of 1922, by the National Army. The house was later re-occupied by 'The Irregulars' but when they came under siege from the Free State troops in January, 1923, they set it alight before vacating it for an alternative place of refuge. It is said that the house and out-offices burned for three days and nights. leaving only a shell of what was once an imposing range of buildings - the creation of Francis Barber, the 'model farmer'.

### *Notes and References :*

(1) Subsequently published in book form as *"Letters from the West of Ireland"*. (Dublin. 1862).

(2) Renewal of lease dated February. 1865. Annual rental was £102.15. p.a.

(3) House and out-offices are said to have cost in the region of £8,000.

(4) Registry of Deeds : 1877. Bk 14. P.231

(5) Francis Barber was one of the principal road contractors for the Grand Jury being responsible for all the roadworks between the bridges of Ballydrehid and Bunduff. He had a fleet of horses and carts and gave extensive employment. He was also the contractor of the Quay wall which extends from Hyde Bridge to Hughes' Bridge and was constructed as a Famine Relief Work.

(6) Registry of Deeds. 1880. Bk. 6. P.13

Francis Barber, the 'Model Farmer'.

*Photo: Courtesy of Jim Barber.*

# Remembering '98

The centenary of the Insurrection of 1798 was widely celebrated in various parts of Ireland and nowhere more fittingly than in County Sligo. As early as November 3rd 1897, the then Mayor, P.A. McHugh, convened a meeting of the Nationalists in the Town Hall to make arrangements for the celebration of the Centenary. [1] In his address, McHugh reminded the gathering that Sligo had been the scene of some of the most memorable incidents in the glorious struggle of '98. It was decided that a Committee be formed, called the *Sligo '98 Centenary Committee* and the following officers were elected:- P.A.McHugh M.P. (President); Alderman Bernard Collery M.P. (Vice-President); Bernard McTernan (Secretary) and Alderman Francis Higgins, J.P. (Treasurer). A suggestion that an obelisk or fountain, at either the Market Cross or the Town Hall, would be a suitable way of perpetuating the memory of '98 was discussed at length but deferred for further consideration. '98 Committees, popularly known as 'Clubs', were formed in other parts of the County, notably at Collooney and Ballymote.

The dawn of 1898 was nowhere more auspiciously inaugurated than in County Sligo. [2] As the clocks and bells tolled out the midnight hour, thousands were on the move to celebrate the opening of an historic year and honour the memory of the heroes of '98. In Sligo a torchlight procession, headed by the Temperance Brass and Reed Band and followed by a large crowd, marched down John Street from the Temperance Hall to O'Connell St. where a very representative gathering of Parnellites and Nationalists, as well as members of Sligo Corporation, had gathered at the base of an unfurled green flag. The assembled throng was then addressed in stirring tones by the Mayor, P.A.McHugh. Afterwards, the procession passed through the principal streets headed by the Band playing patriotic tunes. To mark the occasion the principal residences and shops were illuminated and tar-barrels blazed on the Abbey tower. There were also celebrations in Ballymote. At mid-night the local Fife and Drum Band paraded the streets, already illuminated by bonfires and blazing tar-barrels, followed by a large crowd singing patriotic songs.

497

REMEMBERING' 98

The dawn of the centenary year was further marked on January 6th by a Nationalist Demonstration at Collooney where gallant Irishmen and their French allies had fought side by side against a common foe a hundred years earlier. Nothwithstanding the very inclement weather, thousands of Nationalists from all parts of the County, complete with bands and banners, assembled at Carricknagat. There were large contingents from the following areas, many of whom were headed by a band : Achonry, Ballisodare and Corhownagh, *Ballinacarrow, *Ballintogher, Ballymote, *Ballyrush, Bunninadden, Calry, Cloonacool, *Collooney, *Coolaney, *Culfadda, Dromard, Drumcliffe, *Easkey, Geevagh, *Highwood, Keash, *Knocknarea, Riverstown, *Sligo, *Sooey, St.Johns, Templeboy and *Tubbercurry. The meeting was chaired by Rev. P. J. O'Grady, C.C., President of the local '98 Club and chief organiser. John Dillon M.P. the principal speaker, arrived by train and was met by an enthusiastic and welcoming crowd who escorted him to the place of assembly, a field on the north-west of the town and convenient to Carricknagat. The patriotic enthusiasm of the marchers and their loyalty to the principles that actuated the men of '98 was everywhere visible and was such as to do credit to the Land League in its palmiest days.[3]

On February 17th, 1898, a circular was issued to what was described as "representative men" in various districts throughout the County where '98 Clubs had not been formed. It read as follows:

"We earnestly call on you to use all the means in your power to thoroughly organise your district for the purpose of enabling all Nationalists to unite in doing honour to the memory of the men of '98. As soon as this has been achieved, it is intended to hold a County Convention for the purpose of considering the advisability of appointing a County Executive, the collecting of affiliation fees, etc. Clubs should include all Irishmen who adhere to the National cause, no matter to what section they belong - for united we stand, divided we fall.

It is expected that you and all true Irishmen will so act in order that County Sligo will take a foremost place in the glorious Centenary of '98.

| Signed : | P .A. McHugh | (President Sligo Club); |
| | Bernard McTernan | (Secretary Sligo Club); |
| | John O'Dowd | (Provincial Organiser); |
| | John McLoughlin | (Chairman Sooey Club); |

A few weeks later, on March 10th, the following Resolution was adopted at a meeting of the Sligo Club: -

*That we, members of the Sligo '98 club, hereby decide to erect in this Town, on a site to be hereafter decided upon, a memorial column in honour of the men of '98.* [4]

A Committee was appointed to select a design and make all the necessary arrangements for the execution of the work. On March 17th a public meeting, which was attended by contingents from Corran and Coolavin, took place at Gurteen to commemorate the memory of the men of '98. The large gathering, chaired by Rev. P. Scully, P.P. Keash, was addressed by Maud Gone, who was received with great enthusiasm by John Daly of Castlebar and John O'Dowd of Bunninadden. Afterwards, a Centennial Club was formed.

The aforementioned County Convention took place in the Assembly Room of the Town Hall on Sunday, April 17th.[5] It attracted an overflow attendance from "the uttermost ends of the County" and was representative of "the most prominent and patriotic Nationalists" - all determined "to coalesce with one another" for the fitting celebration of the Centenary. Delegates were present from the following areas:- Achonry - Ballyrush - Ballymote - Ballintogher -Bunninadden - Collooney - Cliffoney - Drumcliffe - Geevagh - Grange - Gurteen - Knocknarea - Moylough - Riverstown - St. John's - Sooey and Templeboy. After an uplifting opening address by P.A.McHugh, who chaired the meeting, the following Resolution, proposed by Alderman Collery and seconded by Alderman Connolly, was unanimously adopted :- *"That we, representatives of the '98 Clubs of Town and County, hereby decide to erect a memorial to the men of 1798 and that a County Committee be formed...."*

Original Design of 'Lady Erin'

REMEMBERING' 98

The only dissenting voice came from Father O'Grady, C.C., Collooney, who suggested that Carricknagat had a greater claim on the proposed memorial than Sligo Town. After some discussion it was decided to refer the matter to the incoming County Committee for their consideration. A design of a memorial, submitted by Herbert G. Barnes, the Dublin sculptor, was also referred to the same body for their observations.

Monday May 23rd, the centenary anniversary of the Insurrection of 1798, was celebrated with great enthusiasm by large crowds at various venues throughout the County, notably at Ballymote, Cliffoney, Keash, Ballintogher, Geevagh and Sooey. [6] At Collooney a large bonfire was lit on *Gunner's Hill,* on the very spot where the young Lieutenant Teeling performed such prodigies of valour a century earlier. The local band paraded the town before proceeding to Carricknagat where upwards of 500 people had gathered to celebrate the occasion. At Ballyrush a procession of over 500 torch bearers, headed by a band, paraded the roads before heading for Greyfort where a meeting took place. The celebrations at Ballintogher were marked by the lighting of a tar-barrel at Conlon's Fort, followed by a torchlight procession, headed by the local Fife and Drum Band.

A big demonstration, organised by the local '98 Club, took place in Ballymote at 9 p.m. It was attended by contingents from Keash and Culfadda, headed by their respective bands, as well as from other outlying ares, and was addressed by John O'Dowd, the Provincial Organizer of the Irish National Federation. The town was gaily bedecked with flags , banners and bunting for the occasion. At Geevagh the local Fife and Drum Band headed a procession, consisting of a few hundred men walking four deep, many of whom carried torches. Closeby, at Sooey, a torchlight procession was formed at the ball-alley and, headed by a Fife and Drum Band, marched to Doonally and round the circular road by Castleneynoe to the schoolhouse where a meeting was addressed by Patrick Flynn, secretary of the local '98 Club. The Barony of Tireragh was ablaze with bonfires on the hillsides from Dromard to Ballymeeny Tower. At Carrowgobbadagh, near Ballydrehid, a large tar-barrel blazed from the top of the old castle overlooking the Curragh.

At a meeting of the County Committee in early June it was decided that there should be two memorials in honour of the men of '98, one in Sligo and the other at Carricknagat. [7] Shortly afterwards, the Collooney '98 Club issued an Appeal for funds to defray the cost of erecting what was described as 'a rustic monument' close to the spot where the English gunner, Whithers, was shot. A public meeting of the Sligo '98 Club was convened in August to decide on the plan and site of the Sligo memorial. On the proposal of Thomas McCarrick, seconded by John Mulligan, the following resolution was passed unanimously:-

*"That we, the members of the Sligo '98 Club, hereby decide on erecting a memorial to the men of '98, and that we adopt the plan submitted by H.G.Barnes. We authorise the Memorial Committee to take immediate steps for the commencement of the work."*

It was further agreed that the proposed memorial would be erected at the Market Cross.

The funding of the memorials was the principle item down for discussion at a meeting of the County Committee on August 7th. [8] A representative gathering from eleven affiliated Clubs were given details of the subscriptions received by that date :- Sligo Club £39.8.6d; Sligo Ladies Club £35; Killoran £13.9.6d; Collooney £12. 9.6d; Calry £4; Sooey £7; Ballinacarrow £5; Riverstown £5; Ballintogher £7.5.0d; Ballymote £10; St. John's £5; Ballisodare £10; and Bunninadden £5, making a total of £159.2.6d. In addition, there was what was described as a "substantial cheque" from Dr John Clancy, Bishop of Elphin, news of which was greeted by loud applause. There was a lengthy discussion on funding generally and fears were expressed that subscriptions could fall short of requirements, particularly if the projected monuments were too elaborate in design. Eventually, it was agreed that all subscriptions on hand would be evenly divided between the Collooney and Sligo Clubs, and that the memorials at Carricknagat and Sligo be proceeded with immediately.

Following the agreement on funding, the Collooney Club proceeded with preparations for the laying of the foundation stone of the monument on September 5th. Denis Moran and Patrick Hart, representing the County Committee, had a meeting with Owen Phibbs, on whose lands stood the site selected for the

## REMEMBERING' 98

memorial. The latter readily agreed to their proposals and offered the site free of charge. At a subsequent meeting of '98 Clubs, a Carricknagat Memorial Committee, consisting of Father O'Grady, Denis Moran, D. P. Bree (all of Collooney), Thomas McDonagh (Ballisodare) and Rev. T. H Quinn (Coolaney) was appointed to take charge of arrangements connected with the erection of the monument on the battle-field site. Designs of the proposed monument and tenders for its erection were submitted to the meeting, and after due consideration, the design of John Clarence of Ballisodare, was unanimously approved of, as was his tender for erecting same.

Sunday, September 4th, 1898, the date on which the foundation stone of the Teeling Monument was laid, was a red-letter day in the annals of Collooney. Commentators described it as the largest National Demonstration held west of the Shannon since the Land League days. Crowds poured into Collooney from an early hour on what was a sunny Autumn day. Four special trains, two from Sligo and one each from Manorhamilton and Tuam, were well patronised. At 1 o'clock the procession formed up opposite the site of the proposed monument, marshalled by Father O'Grady, mounted on his horse and wearing a green sash over his shoulders. The order of the procession was as follows: first came a 'Four-in-Hand', bearing in front a flag with the motto, *"Let Erin Remember"*, carrying the foundation stone and distinguished guests; next came a second 'Four-in-Hand', drawn by four gallant greys, with the Nationalist members of Sligo Corporation and followed by a detachment of 500 horsemen wearing green sashes and walking six deep. The Sligo Temperance Band and 200 members carrying three handsome banners were next in line. Finally, came the colourful contingents representing the following '98 Clubs, each headed by a band and banners:- Ballyrush - Ballinacarrow - Culfadda - Calry - Collooney - Dromore West - Easkey - Keash - Knocknarea - Killoran and Sooey. These were followed by groups from Ballisodare - Bunninadden - Ballintogher - Ballymote - Cliffoney - Cloonacool - Conway's Cross - Gurteen - Grange - Geevagh - Riverstown - St. John's - Templeboy and Tubbercurry as well as Drumkeeran - Killinnumery and Manorhamilton. The Killoran, St. John's and Tubbercurry contingents carried pikes.

The procession, which was over a mile in length, proceeded to

Ballisodare, which was fittingly bedecked for the occasion. On reaching McDonagh's corner the marchers turned round and headed back past the scene of the battle and through the streets of Collooney before returning to the site of the memorial. Father O'Grady, President of the Memorial Committee, was accorded the honour of laying the foundation stone under which was placed a sealed flask containing a copy of the *"Sligo Champion"* of August 27th (in which appeared a sketch of the monument); copies of membership cards of the different '98 Clubs throughout the County and some coins. Letters of apology were read from John Dillon, M.P., Michael Davitt, M.P., Tim Healy, M.P. and also from Adelaide Waters, niece of Bartholomew Teeling.

After the formalities had concluded, the following Resolution, proposed by Domnick Bree and seconded by Denis Moran, was acclaimed by sustained and prolonged applause:-

*"That we, the Irish Nationalists assembled on the battlefield of Carricknagat, hereby place on record our admiration of the brave and chivalrous Irishman, Bartholomew Teeling, the foundation stone of a monument to whose memory has just been laid; and we pledge ourselves to ever cherish and honour, and keep green in our hearts the memory of that gallant soldier, whose heroism is imperishably associated with the name of the ground on which we stand, and who, because he dared to draw the sword for Irish freedom, was cruelly and brutally done to death by English Butchers".*

Teeling Monument

The principal speakers were John Ferguson, Glasgow; Joseph Devlin, Belfast; P. A.McHugh, Mayor of Sligo; Alderman B. Collery, Sligo; John O'Dowd, Bunninadden and Nicholas H. Devine, Tubbercurry. Before the meeting concluded a vote of thanks to Owen

## REMEMBERING '98

Phibbs of *Seafield House* for providing the site and also for the gift of an entrance gate and railings to enclose the monument was widely applauded. Afterwards, the invited guests were entertained by the local Committee. In the words of the *"Champion"* correspondent.. *"Thus came to an end a glorious '98 meeting, the greatest popular demonstration ever witnessed in the West and one which will be remembered for many years to come."* [9]

At a meeting of the Sligo '98 Club in the Town Hall in mid September, 1898, consideration was given to the plan and specification of the proposed memorial, which had been submitted by James Clarence, Ballisodare, and estimated to cost in the region of £210. Even though the subscriptions on hand only totalled £100, the meeting approved of the tender and decided to proceed with arrangements for the laying of the foundation stone on Sunday, October 2nd. [10]

The ceremony of laying the foundation at the Market Cross was marked by a Nationalist demonstration that rivalled that of Carricknagat a month earlier. Large contingents from all parts of the County - from the plains of Corran, from historic Leyney and rebel Tireragh - began to assemble before noon at the Mail Coach Road. The colourful procession, headed by the Temperance Brass and Reed Band, proceeded through streets handsomely decorated with banners and flags and spanned here and there with attractive and tastefully decorated arches. After parading the Town the procession came to a halt at the Market Cross where the foundation stone was ceremoniously laid on a site occupied by a Gas Lamp and earlier by O'Crean's Cross. Underneath the stone a sealed casket containing a copy of the resolutions to be submitted to the meeting; a list of the Sligo '98 Clubs and membership cards; a copy of the *"Sligo Champion"* containing a description of the memorial; a mother of pearl rosary blessed by Bishop Clancy and a list of the '98 Club membership. [11]

After the ceremony the procession moved off to the Market Yard via Castle Street, Bridge Street, Stephen Street, O'Connell Street and Harmony Hill, where a platform had been erected for a monster meeting. P. A. McHugh, who presided, opened the proceedings by complimenting the people of Sligo, Town and County, on their large turn out:-

*"Never before had so magnificent a procession passed through the streets of*

Prominent Members of the Collooney Committee:
Dominick P. Bree (above) & Denis Moran (below)

*the Town. One hundred years ago the enemies of Ireland were masters of Sligo. To-day, the people were masters in their own Town, and before long they would be masters of the County as well . The main object of that great demonstration was to do honour to the men of '98. It was right that the men of Sligo town and county should take a prominent part in celebrating the '98 Centenary".*

Other speakers included William O'Brien, ex M.P., Alderman Collery, M.P; John O'Dowd; Henry Brennan, M.C.C. and Alderman Thomas McCarrick.

With the dawn of 1899 work on the Carricknagat memorial, which had been suspended for some time, was resumed by John Clarence, builder, Ballisodare, who already had the necessary cut stones prepared for the base of the monument. Information was also received from Messrs Harrison & Son, Great Brunswick Street, Dublin, sculptors, stating that work on the statue of Bartholomew Teeling, which was to crown the monument, was well advanced. By May, 1899, Clarence was in a position to complete the construction of the pedestal and a sub-committee was appointed to make the necessary arrangements for the unveiling ceremony on Sunday, July 2nd. At a meeting of the Collooney '98 Club on June 6th many tributes were paid to Father O'Grady who had resigned as President following upon his transfer as C.C. to Achonry.[12] On the proposal of Denis Moran, seconded by William Morrow, the following Resolution was unanimously adopted:-

*"It is with deep and sincere regret we accept the resignation of Father O'Grady, our popular, respected and patriotic President; we express our sorrow that he has to leave our organisation - an organisation created and maintained by his name and influence".*

Despite inclement weather, a large crowd assembled at Carricknagat on Sunday, July 2nd. They came by train, on foot and on horseback from all parts of the County and beyond. When the proceedings got under way, the chair was taken by Rev. P. Cawley. The unveiling was performed by Father O'Grady, after which the Sligo Temperance Band solemnly rendered *"The Memory of the Dead"*. A number of Resolutions were passed with loud acclaim, after which P. D. O'Hart; Jasper Tully, M.P.; P. A. McHugh, M.P.; John O'Dowd and Rev. T. H.Quinn adddressed the huge gathering. [13]

Two months later, on September 3rd, thousands turned out in another great demonstration of Nationalism, this time for the unveiling of the '98 Memorial at the Market Cross. The Town was *"en fete"* for the occasion, with flags, banners and national emblems decorating the principal streets. The Procession, which formed up on Cairns Road, moved off at 2 o'clock, headed by a large contingent on horseback and closely followed by the Temperance Band. The Mayor, E. J. Tighe, followed in an open carriage. Then came a number of 'Four in Hand' brakes conveying the local M.P.'s, Aldermen Collery and McHugh, Nationalist members of Sligo Corporation, and invited guests. These were followed by colourful contingents, representatives of the various '98 Clubs throughout the County, who with their bands and banners added greatly to the atmosphere of the occasion. Large crowds lined the processional route to the Market Cross where the unveiling ceremony was performed by the Mayor. In his address P .A. McHugh reminded the assembled multitude that the memorial

## '98 Centennial Clubs Formed
### January - April 1898

| | |
|---|---|
| Ballintogher | *Lord Edward Fitzgerald* |
| Ballymote | *Robert Emmet* |
| Ballyrush | *McAlister '98 Club* |
| Bunninadden | *Tim O'Shaughnessy* |
| Cloonacool | *Robert Emmet* |
| Corhownagh/Ballisodare | *Insurrection Club* |
| Killoran | *Father Murphy* |
| Knocknarea | *Brother Shears* |
| Sooey | *Teeling Club* |
| Tubbercurry | *Wolfe Tone '98 Club* |

column and statue they had erected in the centre of their Town "was a proof that the Nationalists of Sligo in 1898 were gratefully mindful of the heroic men who in 1798 had fought and died for civil and religious liberty in Ireland". Other speakers included Bernard Collery, M.P.; John Ferguson, Glasgow; Joe Devlin, Belfast; Alderman Thomas McCarrick and Nicholas H. Devine, Tubbercurry'. [14]

# STREETS CALLED AFTER '98 HEROES

At a meeting of the Tubbercurry *Wolfe Tone '98 Club* in August 1898, the following Resolution was passed with much acclaim :-

"That the streets of the Town, having no official designation, be named after the '98 heroes".

"In future, the streets will be known as follows: -

The Square as *Wolfe Tone Square;* Market Street as *Teeling Street;* Pound Street as *Emmet Street* and The Hill as *Humbert Hill*: and we respectfully ask the co-operation of the traders to assist us in giving effect to this Resolution, and that boards bearing these names be set up in suitable positions".

\* \* \* \* \*

At a specially convened meeting of the Ballymote *'98 Club* on October 18th, 1898, the following Resolution, proposed by John Clarke and seconded by James Walsh, was passed unanimously :-

"As a mark of our appreciation of the noble deeds and bravery of the United Irishmen, we do hereby name the streets of Ballymote after '98 men: Main Street to be *Teeling Street;* Market Street as *Lord Edward Street*; From Gormans to *McManus's* as *O'Connell Street;* From Sheerans to Keenaghans as *Wolfe Tone Street;* Church Street as *Emmet Street* and Mill Street as *Grattan Street."* A Committee was appointed to supervise the carrying - out of these arrangements and to have boards in place on November Day.

At a meeting of the '98 Club a week later a Resolution was passed thanking the Nationalists of the Borough for their co-operation in making the unveiling ceremony "the greatest and most historic demonstration ever held in the Town of Sligo". It was also decided to hand over the '98 Memorial to the Mayor, E.J. Tighe, on behalf of Sligo Corporation, and to request the Corporation to have lamps and a suitable railing erected around it at their earliest convenience. It was also suggested that the panels on both the east and west sides of the pedestal be inscribed with a record of the laying of the foundation and the unveiling, together with the names of the respective Mayors for 1898 and 1899.[15]

On October 3rd, 1948, there was an historic gathering at Carricknagat to mark the 150th anniversary of 1798. Contingents from all over the County and beyond gathered in processional form, headed by twenty Pikemen and forty Horsemen, suitably attired and led by seven bands. The platform group was chaired by the Michael Jennings,M.C.C., and the speakers included Cahir Healy, M.P., Ben Maguire T.D., Joseph Roddy, T.D. and ex-Senator, Frank O'Beirne. [16]*

## Carricknagat Memorial:

The Carricknagat Memorial was one of the first, as well as the tallest, of the monuments erected to the memory of the men of `98. It stands on a most picturesque site overlooking the ground on which the 'Battle of Collooney' was fought and convenient to the spot where Teeling shot Whitters, the English gunner. The life-size statue, which is said to be a faithful likeness of Bartholomew Teeling, surmounts a monument of classical symmetry forty feet high, and represents him as holding a British flag captured on the site. The stone from which the statue was hewed was quarried at Ballinasloe and weighed 10 ton. The finished sculpture weighs 30 cwt. Plaques on the pedestal were inscribed as follows:-

*"To the memory of Bartholomew Teeling and the valiant Irish and French soldiers who fought here for Dear Old Ireland."*
*"Erected to the Memory of the Heroes of '98 by the Nationalists of Co. Sligo".*

REMEMBERING' 98

| Messrs Harrison & Son, Dublin | : | Sculptors |
| John Clarence, Ballisodare | : | Contractor |
| Edward Brennan, Collooney | : | Builder |

---

*"Close to the road on a rocky hillside they have erected a monument to Teeling. The statue, which is heroic in expression, looks towards the 'Races at Castlebar' and reminds one of that splendid day. The face is a poem, grandly eloquent in its chiselling. You think you can catch the thought that was in the sculptor's mind. You can feel that his aim was to represent his hero looking out in fiery appeal and reproach over the sleeping West".*

From William Bulfin's *"Rambles in Eirinn"*.

---

# Sligo Memorial:

The Sligo Memorial, popularly known as *'Lady Erin'*, stands on or close to the site of the 16th century Market Cross, also known as O'Crean's Cross. The Memorial, which is over sixteen feet high, takes the form of a figure of Erin carved in Sicilian marble, holding a half-mast flag in the left hand and standing on broken chains.

The pedestal is of chiselled limestone and on three of its four sides are tablets bearing the following inscriptions.

*"In Loving Memory of the Heroism and Devotion of the Patriots of 1798 who fought and died for Civil and Religious Liberty in Ireland. Erected by the Nationalists of Sligo, 1898".*

*"The Foundation Stone of this Memorial was laid on 8th October, 1898, by Alderman P.A. McHugh M.P., Mayor of Sligo, 1898. "*

*"The Unveiling Ceremony was performed on 3rd. September, 1899 by E. J. Tighe J.P., Mayor of Sligo, 1899".*

After the unveiling, tenders were invited for the erection of railings round the base. The contract was awarded to James Clarence of Ballisodare at a cost of £50. Four ornamental gas pedestals and lamps, which illuminated the Memorial by night, were presented and put in place at the behest of Alderman E. J. Tighe, during whose Mayoralty the unveiling ceremony took place.

510

'Lady Erin' - the 1798 Memorial at the Market Cross

Over thirty years later, in 1932, portion of the railings and their cut-stone base were accidently knocked down and badly damaged by a motorvan. When the matter came before the Corporation it was decided, on a vote, to have the railings removed, but the motion was subsequently rescinded after loud protestations by surviving subscribers to the Memorial. Instead, local monumental sculptor, John Diamond, was engaged to carry out the necessary repairs.

# MEMORIES OF '98

*The rising ground on which Humbert marshalled his troops bears the name of Camphill ; the slope on which Teeling shot the sturdy Whitters, is called the Gunner's bray and several spots along the line of the French advance, where Frenchmen were buried, are commonly known as the 'Frenchmen's graves'. Even the names of Vereker and Humbert have slipped from the peoples memories, but Teeling and his famous grey are still as vivid in the traditions of the Ox Mountains as they were on the morrow of Carricknagat.*

*"Sligo Champion"* 21.05.1898

## TEELING'S 'GALLANT GREY'

After Bartholomew Teeling was taken prisoner at Ballinamuck, he entrusted the horse which had carried him victorious through many escapades to Lieutenant John Workman of the Tirerill Cavalry, who fought with the opposing forces and a boyhood friend of Teeling in their youthful days in Belfast. After the battle Lieutenant Workman, who was married to Margaret Phibbs, daughter of Harloe Phibbs of Bloomfield, returned to the Phibbs homestead at Rockbrook, near Riverstown, riding the 'gallant grey'. According to local tradition Teeling's horse lived out his remaining years in that peaceful setting on the banks of the Douglas River and was buried in the 'Well Field' to the rear of the haggard. Long afterwards locals could point out the mound that marked his grave.

Three decades on, in May 1961, a proposal from the Chamber of Commerce, that the railings be removed , was rejected by the Corporation. However, less than a year later, in March, 1962, the 'City Fathers' accepted a recommendation from the Town's Development Association that the railings surrounding the '98 Memorial be removed on the grounds that they constituted a hazard for traffic. Within two weeks, and despite the protestations of the National Grave's Association, the railings were removed and replaced by concrete kerbing.

## Remembering' 98

### Notes & References:

| (1) | *"Sligo Champion"* | 20-11-1897 |
|---|---|---|
| (2) | ibid | 8-1-1898 |
| (3) | ibid | 14-1-1898 |
| (4) | ibid | 12-3-1898 |
| (5) | ibid | 23-4-1898 |
| (6) | ibid | 28-5-1898 |
| (7) | ibid | 11-6-1898 |
| (8) | ibid | 13-8-1898 |
| (9) | ibid | 10-9-1898 |
| (10) | ibid | 17-9-1898 |
| (11) | ibid | 8-10-1898 |
| (12) | ibid | 10-6-1899 |

P. J. O'Grady was born at Mahanagh, Gurteen, in 1864. He was educated at Ballaghaderreen and at Maynooth. After ordination he served as C.C. at Bohola, Collooney, Achonry and Curry. In 1907 Bishop Lyster sent him to the U.S.A. to raise funds for a new Diocesan College. On his return, three years later, he was appointed Parish Priest of Keash. He died in May, 1920 and is buried in the family plot, Gurteen.

| (13) | *"Sligo Champion"* | 8-7-1899 |
|---|---|---|
| (14) | ibid | 9-9-1899 |
| (15) | ibid | 16-9-1899 |
| (16) | *"Sligo Independent"* | 9-10-1948 |

\* The bi-centenary of the Rebellion was marked by a number of events in Collooney, culminating in a re-enactment of the 'Battle of Carricknagat' in the week ending, September 12th / 13th, 1998.

# Street Names Changed

A special meeting of Sligo Corporation took place on September 15th., 1898, to consider a notice of motion tabled by Clr. Keenan to change the names of the principle streets of the Town. At the outset, Clr. Keenan proposed the following Resolution which was seconded by Clr. Hanney:-

*"That, in the opinion of this Council, it is desirable to change the names of certain streets within the boundary of Sligo Borough and that this Council now proceed to make such changes as they deem advisable - such change to take effect from this date".*[1]

After some procedural difficulties had been resolved, Clr. Milmoe proposed the following Resolution:-

*"That from and after the passing of this Resolution the names of streets and roads within the Municipal Boundary of Sligo shall be changed as follows: Radcliffe Street shall be called Lord Edward Street; Knox's Street called Parnell Street, William Street called Wolfe Tone Street, and Albert Street changed to Grattan Street. That suitable boards be prepared and all parties interested notified of the change".* Alderman Tighe, who was opposed to any change in existing street names, was quickly on his feet and proposed an amendment seeking an adjournment of the meeting. In the resulting poll, the amendment was lost by 9 votes to 12 in favour of Keenan's resolution.

In the ensuing discussion it soon became obvious that the Nationalist members of the Council were split as to whether or not the name of Parnell should be included. Clr. Milmoe called for unanimity, saying that if the Irish cause was to succeed, Parnell's policy should prevail. Supporting this viewpoint, Clr. G. Foley declared:-

*"Parnell was the great man of his time, and he did more for Ireland than many men. If he made one mistake it should be forgotten in the many good things he accomplished. I cannot understand why the name of Parnell should be made a bone of contention..."*

At that stage, the Mayor, P.A. McHugh, asked for an opportunity to state his own position. "I should be glad to see the name of Parnell on one of our principle streets. If the Nationalist members of the Council brought forward such a proposal and were united in its support, I would consider their action graceful, magnanimous, and conciliatory. But it is quite evident that several Nationalist members of the Council are strongly opposed to the introduction of Parnell's name. No one can deny the right of those gentlemen to hold their own views on the subject before us. That being so, we have to consider what is best to be done under the circumstances. In my opinion, it would be much more respectful to the memory of Parnell to omit his name than to make it a bone of contention amongst a body of Nationalists up to now the most united in Ireland ... A time will come when all Sligo Nationalists will unite in more fittingly honouring Parnell's memory than they could do by making his name a cock-shot in the streets of Sligo; and those who will be most ready and generous in such a movement will be those who opposed him in 1891 and not those who indulge in claptrap about his principles, as if they were the sole repositories of those principles. Whatever decision is to be arrived at, it is of vital importance that we should abstain from any action calculated to lead to strife and contention amongst the Nationalist members of this body. A unanimous decision alone can save us from such a misfortune..."

In reply, Alderman Collery stated that he did not wish to utter one word "against an honoured name which should be allowed to rest in peace"; nevertheless, he was not prepared to agree to have Parnell's name on Sligo's principal street.

As no agreement seemed in sight, Clr. Hanney then proposed that the following changes should be made in the names of five of the principal streets - to the exclusion of Parnell, namely : -

> **Knox's Street** to be called **O'Connell Street;**
> **Radcliffe Street** to be called **Grattan Street;**
> **Albert Street** to be called **Teeling Street;**
> **William Street** to be called **Wolfe Tone Street;**
> **George's Street** to be called **Lord Edward Street.**

This proposal was finally adopted by the Council, with Clr. Kelly as the only dissenting voice.

\*     \*     \*     \*

At a meeting of the Corporation on November 1st., 1943, the Town Clerk, R.G. Bradshaw, read the following letter from Brian Bairéad, on behalf of the local branch of the Gaelic League, requesting changes in the names of two streets and a bridge:-

# STREET NAMES CHANGED

**Albert Road** to **Pearse Road;**
**Victoria Line** to **Markievicz Road;**
and, **Victoria Bridge** to **Hyde Bridge** .

*"I append herewith two memorials signed by residents of Albert Road and Victoria Line in connection with the proposed re-naming of these thoroughfares. The memorial in connection with Albert Road has been signed by seventy-two householders, this response to the proposal being equal to a vote of practically 100 per cent in favour of the proposed new name of Pearse Road. In addition to the signatures of the house-holders, the memorial is supported by the signatures of a number of citizens who own substantial rated property on the road but who are not resident thereon. These include E. McLynn, Michael Martin, S.H. Derham, solr., Messrs McLynn & Burns and D.M. Hanley."*

*"It was found impossible to ascertain the views of three or four residents, owing to absence from home or illness. Three residents declined to sign the memorial when approached by the Gaelic League representatives, but neither were they willing to be listed as objectors. They preferred, they stated, to remain neutral on the question. The response to the proposal from residents of Victoria Line was equally good, there being no objectors. It was found impossible to interview two householders. The signatures to the memorial also include a number of ratepayers resident in Holborn Street who own property abutting on to Victoria Line".[2]*

At the outset, the Town Clerk advised the Council that although this was a Managerial function under the Management Act, he, nevertheless, wished to have their views on the matter. After a brief discussion, Alderman Nevin proposed the adoption of the proposed change to coincide with the Golden Jubilee of the Gaelic League. This was agreed to, the only dissenter being Alderman John Fallon.

Other changes in street names were Corkran's Mall or Linenhall Street to John F. Kennedy Parade in 1964, and 'The Shambles' to Kempten Promenade in the mid 1980's.

*References:*

(1) *"Sligo Champion"*      16 - 9 - 1898

(2) *"Sligo Independent"*      6 - 11- 1943

# Teething Problems at a Co-Operative

The Irish Agricultural Organisation Society (I.A.O.S.) was founded a century ago by Sir Horace Plunkett for the purpose of spreading the co-operative movement throughout the country. Dairying was the main focus of Plunkett's early efforts. County Sligo embraced the co-operative idea with open arms and, under the leadership of such pioneers as Josslyn Gore-Booth of Lissadell and Alexander J. Crichton of Carrowgarry, amongst others, dairy societies owned and managed entirely by share-holding farmers, mushroomed all over the country. Between 1895 and 1898 central creameries were established at Achonry, Ballinafull, Ballintrillick, Ballymote, Collooney, Gurteen, Riverstown, Seafin and Tubbercurry, in addition to a number of subsidiaries, or 'separating stations'.

The creamery movement in Collooney was originated in January, 1897, by Florence Cooper of *Markree Castle* who, with a kindly disposition towards the welfare of the farming community in the area, called a public meeting to consider the matter. This took place in the Market House under the chairmanship of her brother, Colonel Edward H. Cooper. The principal speakers were A.R. Bourke of the I.A.O.S. and Josslyn Gore-Booth. A large committee, consisting of two representatives from each townland, with Alexander Sim, J.P. as honorary Secretary *'pro tem'*, was appointed to collect statistics and any other suitable information for the guidance of the Society.

On March 1st another meeting was held which passed a resolution to the effect that a central creamery be erected at Collooney, with separating stations at Coolaney, Ballinacarrow, Ballintogher, Skreen and Kilmacowen. A deputation, consisting of Rev. P.J.O'Grady, C.C., Alexander Sim, Major C.K. O'Hara, Robert Robinson and Patrick O'Beirne, was appointed to convene meetings of farmers, and others interested, in each of the aforementioned districts. The deputation, and more especially the three first-named gentlemen, spared neither time or expense in having all the particulars and advantages of the movement placed before the public. The scheme, which was very comprehensive, was based upon the produce of 2,400 to 3,000 cows, and the superiority of the creamery system over the old methods of butter making was fully explained to the farmers. It was also pointed out that the increase in income would be about £3 per cow, or from £7,200 to £9,000 per annum, of a gain to cattle owners in the district .[1]

A representative and largely attended meeting of farmers and others interested in the progression of the creamery movement in Collooney and the surrounding areas was held in the Market House on March 14th. The acting Secretary, Alexander Sim, reported that the farmers of the four districts already named were in favour of uniting with Collooney in a co-operative society, having Collooney as its central station, where a large water-powered creamery would be erected, with separating stations in each district, and that the shareholders from each would be shareholders in the Society with equal rights and privileges. [2] It was decided to register the Collooney Co-Operative and Dairy Society with a capital of £5,000, to elect a Management Committee and to affiliate with the I.A.O.S. Alexander Sim tendered his resignation from the secretaryship for personal reasons and was replaced by his brother, Allison A. Sim. The *"Irish Homestead"*, the official organ of the I.A.O.S., in its issue of March, 1897, carried a long report on the developments in Collooney :- *"The Collooney Society is the largest venture as yet formed upon co-operative principles, as far as dairying is concerned in Ireland. A central creamery at Collooney with some five or six auxiliaries manufacturing butter from the cream of over 3,000 cows is a pretty big order. Nevertheless, the promoters are nothing daunted. This extensive programme is entirely due to the energy of Messrs. Alexander and Allison Sim, the well-known woollen mill owners, who have taken up the matter most warmly, Allison Sim having knocked up three horses in driving around the country attending numberless meetings at the proposed sites - indeed at almost all the schoolhouses of the district. In this work he has been energetically assisted by Father O'Grady, the curate of Collooney, who up to a short time since had been in favour of the factory system, but who has been converted by some few hours spent in making personal enquiries in a neighbouring district where a co-operative dairy is at work.* [3]

At a general meeting of shareholders on April 28th it was stated that shares had been taken up and partly paid to the amount of £1,940, and

## TEETHING PROBLEMS AT A CO-OPERATIVE

many more were expected to follow suit when the creameries had commenced working. The names of the individual committees elected to represent the auxiliary stations, consisting of eight from each district, together with an equal number from Collooney, forming a governing body of forty who had equal rights and responsibilities over the whole undertaking, were put before the meeting and unanimously approved on the proposal of Sir Malby Crofton, seconded by Richard Robinson, P.L.G. As Ballinacarrow had not subscribed a sufficient number of shares, it was decided that farmers from that area would bring their milk to Collooney until they were in a position to get a separating station of their own. The meeting also considered plans and tenders for the erection of a central creamery and four separating stations located at Ballintogher, Breeogue, Coolaney and Skreen. At that stage the site for the central creamery had already been selected, namely, a two acre plot on Hamilton's holding at Knockbeg, adjacent to the Owenmore river, which was being leased from Colonel Cooper at an annual rent of £6.10s. The disclosure of this agreement, which was strongly critised by a number of shareholders, led by Fr. O'Grady, was the first indication of discord amongst the membership. There was also criticism of the number of non-farmers on the Management Committee. Eventually, a compromise was arrived at whereby Cooper would be offered a maximum of £4 per annum, even though many were of the opinion that the site should be handed over free of any charge. [4]

This setback in what had been a most harmonious and businesslike association of all creeds and classes was followed by further unpleasantness at a committee meeting on May 17th when the appointment of a Manager came up for consideration. Lindsay Phibbs, son of Owen Phibbs of Lisheen, the President of the Society, who had been highly recommended by the Inspector of Creameries, was elected by 17 votes to 2 for an unnamed candidate. A number of members present, notably P.N. White, J.P. of *Breeogue House* and curates P.J. O'Grady of Collooney and T.H. Quinn of Coolaney, refrained from voting, and afterwards White was said to have commented that the choice of Manager could lead to the break-up of the Society. His remarks were prophetic to an extent, as subsequent events unfolded. The dissent became public a few days later and further fuel was added

## TEETHING PROBLEMS AT A CO-OPERATIVE

to the waters of discontent when representatives of the Society attended a meeting of the Ballintogher shareholders and advised the latter to have nothing to do with the Collooney creamery as that Committee was composed of "landlords and bailiffs, with a few clergy thrown in". [5] In the meantime, Lindsay Phibbs had withdrawn his application for the managership and Colonel Cooper had consented to the terms offered for the site.

A special general meeting of shareholders on May 18th, 1897, chaired by Owen Phibbs, drew a large attendance but the proceedings were both irregular and disorderly. In the words of the *"Sligo Champion"* former acts were condemned, the bailiffs rejected from the management and the landlords threaten to resign".[6] At the outset, Father Thomas Quinn questioned the legality of the meeting that had taken place on April 29th, alleging that it had not been properly convened and therefore the elections that took place, including that of Chairman and Committee of Management, were invalid. There were also allegations that some members of the said committee represented no one but themselves and certainly not the ordinary farmers of the area. This viewpoint was supported by other delegates and the ensuing debate was marked by unruly outbursts between those who wished to maintain the *'status quo'* and those who wanted a change. The total lack of harmony that prevailed throughout the entire proceedings led to Phibbs vacating the chair and there were threats of resignation from Major O'Hara, Malby Crofton, A.J. Crichton, amongst others. In the midst of the discord Father Patrick McNulty, Parish Priest of Skreen, made a lengthy and passionate address to the assembled multitude in which he called for calm and mutual respect for opposing views in the interests of all:- *"....If we wish to make progress we must co-operate, landlord with tenant, and I personally would be very sad to see any of the landlords present removed from the Committee. They are men with money and influence which would be to the advantage of this Society. The narrow minded sentiments expressed here to-day should be dropped forthwith as no one class or creed has a predominating interest in the project on hand ....."* [7] In an effort to resolve the impasse, Father McNulty then proposed that they should proceed to elect a new Committee which would satisfy a majority of shareholders. This was seconded by P.N. White and eventually agreed before the meeting broke-up in disorder.

TEETHING PROBLEMS AT A CO-OPERATIVE

Owen Phibbs, first President of the Collooney Co-Operative Society.

IRISH FREE STATE

REG. NO. C. 147

CREAMERY BUTTER

COLLOONEY
Co-operative Dairy Society, Limited.
COLLOONEY. Co. SLIGO

TEETHING PROBLEMS AT A CO-OPERATIVE

Another meeting to elect a new Committee of Management was convened for June 29th. Again, the proceedings lacked harmony and fears were openly expressed by a number of delegates that the future of the Society was in jeopardy unless differences were quickly resolved. [8] As the election of a new Committee got under way the principal

---

## THE ALTERNATIVE COMMITTEES

### *(A)   The original, March 1897 (with Share nos.) :*

Collooney:   Col. Edward H. Cooper (10): Robert Robinson (10):
Alex. Sim (10): Felix Gallagher (8): James Meredith (8):
Florence Cooper (5): Fr. P.J. O'Grady (5) and Fr. Dempsey (5).

Coolaney:   Major C.K. O'Hara (15): Rev. T.H. Quinn (5):
Edward Simpson (5): Charles McKenzie (5): Wm. Thompson (3):
Francis Henry (3): Patrick McHugh (2) and Bryan Carty (1).

Kilmacowen:   P.N. White (20): Robert H. Lambert (10): Owen Phibbs (10):
James Devaney (10): Michael Bree (5): Conor Healy (5):
John F. Walker (5) and Robert Milne (4).

Skreen:   Sir Malby Crofton (15): Alexander J. Crichton (15):
John Higgins (12): P.S. Kilgannon (6): Bernard Kelly (6):
John Y. O'Donnell (5): Rev. Patrick McNulty (3) and
James Clarke (2).

### *(B)   Replacement Committee,  June, 1897 (with Share nos.)*

Collooney:   Rev. P.J. O'Grady (5): James Quinn (5):  Patrick O'Beirne (5):
John Noble (5): Wm. Craig (5): Patrick Keaveny (4):
John Tighe (3): and Michael Cawley (3).

Coolaney:   Rev. T.H. Quinn (5): Francis Henry (3):  Wm. Thompson (3):
Patrick McHugh (2): Peter Cawley (2): Andrew Snee (1):
Thos. Coleman (1) and Bryan V. Carty (1).

Kilmacowen:   P.N. White (20): Robert H. Lambert (10): James Devaney (10):
James Gilgan (5): John Carter (5): John Giligan (4):
James McGloin (3) and James Cooney (1).

Skreen:   Bernard Kelly (6): Patrick Brady (6): Peter Graham (4):
Rev. Patk. McNulty (3): John O'Hara (2): John Dowdican (2):
Hugh McHugh (1) and John Clarke (1).

proposers and seconders were Fathers O'Grady and Quinn, aided and abetted by P.N. White. Those who did not meet with their approval were 'shouted down' by one or other of the trio or their supporters, allegedly with the intention of removing the Unionist element from the Committee. The situation was further aggravated when a majority of those elected by the so-called 'champions of legality' were not qualified under Rule 14 of the Society, which stated that "not less than two-thirds of the Committee of Management shall be each *'bona fide'* holders of at least five shares". In fact, only thirteen of the new Committee passed the necessary qualification. After a prolonged discussion and much acrimony, Father O'Grady and Michael Rooney, N.T. were elected joint-secretaries in place of Allison A. Sim, who had resigned. It was also decided to invite down officials from the I.A.O.S. central office to arbitrate on the matters in dispute. [9]

A month or so later the shareholders met the arbitrators, Rev. T. Finlay, S.J. and R.A. Anderson, Vice-President and Secretary, respectively, of the I.A.O.S., who had been called in to settle difficulties and restore peace. A second meeting followed on the 16th inst. at which the membership of the Management Committee was discussed between the arbitrators and a sub-committee consisting of Fathers O'Grady and Quinn, P.N. White, Alexander and Allison Sim. [10] Arising from these meetings the *"Independent"* was more hopeful for the future of the Society :-

*"It seems as if a prosperous and peaceful future is now in store for the Collooney Co-Operative. For some time past the prospects of this concern have looked rather gloomy owing to regrettable dissensions amongst the shareholders, but now there is every appearance of the contending parties burying the hatchet and joining together for the common welfare".* [11]

A meeting of shareholders took place on August 19th to hear the report of the arbitrators. The proceedings, chaired by Owen Phibbs, were fairly orderly throughout. There was a hushed silence as the large attendance listened attentively to the findings of the Dublin based officials, which were as follows:-

* The election of Committee and officers on 22nd April, 1897, was irregular, inasmuch as that due notice of these elections was not given in accordance with rules 60 and 62; the election of the entire Committee, including that of members to represent

branches or auxiliaries, was not carried out simultaneously and by the entire body of the shareholders, and there was no provision existing in the rules for the separate election of committee men to represent the various branches or auxiliaries, such as took place on the 26th April for Coolaney and Skreen, and on the 17th April for Ballintogher.

\* Certain members of the Committee elected on these dates were ineligible under special Rule 15, namely, Alexander Sim and Dr. P.N. White - both being retail traders - and rule 14, which provides that at least two-thirds of the Committee shall be *bona fide* holders of five shares each, was not adhered to.

\* The subsequent election of a Committee and officers on 29th June was also irregular on the grounds that the notice did not comply with the requirements of rule 62, which provides that in case the meeting has to elect any officer of the Society the notice convening the meeting shall state the fact.

\* No legally elected Committee is in existence, and no official of the Society, with the exception of Allison A. Sim, is in a position to act on behalf of the Society".

On the proposal of Fr. O'Grady, seconded by A.J. Crichton, the award of the arbitrators was approved with only a handful of dissenters. The membership of the new Management Committee, as agreed, was as follows:

| Name of District: | Committee: | No. of Shares: |
|---|---|---|
| Collooney: | 1. Colonel Cooper | 10 |
| | 2. William Craig | 10 |
| | 3. Rev. Mark Dempsey | 5 |
| | 4. Allison A. Sim | 5 |
| | 5. James Quinn | 5 |
| | 6. Patrick O'Beirne | 5 |
| | 7. James Donaghy | 5 |
| | 8. Robert Anderson | 5 |
| Coolaney: | 1. Major O'Hara | 10 |
| | 2. Rev. T.H. Quinn | 5 |
| | 3. Edward Simpson | 5 |

## Teething Problems At A Co-Operative

|   |   |   |
|---|---|---|
| 4. | William Thompson | 3 |
| 5. | Francis Henry | 3 |
| 6. | Patrick McHugh | 2 |
| 7. | Bryan Carty | 1 |
| 8. | Thomas Coleman | 1 |

**Kilmacowen:**

|   |   |   |
|---|---|---|
| 1. | Owen Phibbs | 10 |
| 2. | R.H. Lambert | 10 |
| 3. | James Devaney | 10 |
| 4. | Michael Duignan | 8 |
| 5. | Edwin Nevin | 5 |
| 6. | James Carter | 5 |
| 7. | James McGloin | 3 |
| 8. | Denis Hunt | 2 |

**Skreen:**

|   |   |   |
|---|---|---|
| 1. | A.J. Crichton | 15 |
| 2. | P.S. Kilgallen | 6 |
| 3. | Bernard Kelly | 6 |
| 4. | John Y. O'Donnell | 5 |
| 5. | Patrick Brady | 5 |
| 6. | Peter Graham | 4 |
| 7. | Rev. Patrick McNulty | 3 |
| 8. | Hugh McHugh | 1 |

In relation to the selection of the Committee of Management, the arbitrators pointed out that it was quite impossible to find among the persons whose names were unanimously agreed upon a sufficient number to comply with the rules, which provided that two-thirds of the Committee should hold five shares each. There were several of those selected who would have to take two or three additional shares to make themselves eligible and therefore, would have to qualify themselves. If not, vacancies would arise on the Committee and these would have to be filled in the ordinary way. The meeting concluded with the unanimous nomination, in his unavoidable absence, of Charles Kean O'Hara as President, after other nominees - Owen Phibbs, A.J. Crichton, R.H. Lambert and Father O'Grady had declined the position.

## TEETHING PROBLEMS AT A CO-OPERATIVE

The crisis had passed. The difference and disagreements that had almost rent the Society apart had been finally resolved. The Management Committee got down to business quickly and in less than a year the central creamery and its auxiliaries were fully operational and the Society could boast of 1,000 shareholders and 3,000 milch cows in its catchment area.

Collooney creamery was formally opened by Alexandrina Sim, wife of Alexander Sim, at noon on July 4th, 1898, in the presence of a large assemblage of shareholders and representative farmers over an area of 170 sq. miles. In the course of his opening address the President, Rev. P.J. O'Grady, touched briefly on past difficulties:

*"..... Eighteen months ago we formed our Society, but little did we know of the trouble and difficulties associated with a co-operative of this kind. Though the obstacles were many and the causes of discouragement manifold, yet the one noble desire to improve, even in a small degree, the condition of the farmers, submerged every consideration beneath its mighty weight, and hence today's glorious proceedings is marked by the unanimous co-operation of all classes or creeds. We have completed the work put before us and erected a creamery building unequalled for design and fitness in all Ireland - a building finished with the best and most modern machinery that could be procured.....We have done our part to the best of our ability and we trust and pray that the Managing Committee of the future will follow the example set them of earnestness and perseverance, and a true desire to help and better the condition of the struggling farmers of this country....."*

Other speakers included R.A. Anderson, Josslyn Gore-Booth and Allison A. Sim. Visitors were subsequently entertained by Mrs. Sim at Camphill House before attending a banquet in the Market House, presided over by Alexander Sim, J.P. [12]

The Collooney creamery was designed by W.G. Gilcriest, C.E., Sligo, and the building contract was awarded to Edward Brennan of Collooney. The tender price was £538. It was described as one of the largest and best equipped of its kind in the country with the following dimensions: 80 ft long, 36 ft broad and 24ft high. It was built of 'rubble' masonry of local limestone, with red brick quoins to all angles of the building and also to heads and jambs of doors and windows, while window-sills were of cut stone of Ballisodare limestone. The main building was a slated roof with patent revolving ventilations along the

## TEETHING PROBLEMS AT A CO-OPERATIVE

ridge. The stores, delivery and receiving platforms were roofed with galvanised corrugated iron sheetings. The entire building was ceiled in timber with a number of ventilating openings arranged under the roof edge. Close-by was a aquaduct capable of working a turbine wheel of 25h.p.

### *Notes & References:*

| | | |
|---|---|---|
| (1) | *"Sligo Independent"* | 17-7-1897 |
| (2) | *"Sligo Champion"* | 20-3-1897 |
| (3) | *"Irish Homestead"* | 27-3-1897 |
| (4) | *"Sligo Champion"* | 1-5-1897 |
| (5) | *"Sligo Independent"* | 17-7-1897 |
| (6) | *"Sligo Champion"* | 22-5-1897 |
| (7) | *"Sligo Independent"* | 22-5-1897 |
| (8) | *"Sligo Independent"* | 3-7-1897 |
| (9) | *"Sligo Champion"* | 3-7-1897 |
| (10) | *"Sligo Independent"* | 7-8-1897 |
| (11) | *"Sligo Champion"* | 21-8-1897 |
| (12) | *"Sligo Independent"* | 9-7-1898 |

(13) By 1901 the Collooney Society had a membership of 1,304, double that of any similar Society in the County; its paid-up share capital was £2,350; the number of gallons of milk supplied (1901) totalled 668,229 and butter sales realised £13,200.

The Collooney Creamery continued to operate successfully until merging with the North Connacht Farmer's Co-Operative a quarter of a century ago.

# Inns and Taverns of other Days

The hostelries and taverns of Sligo in olden times were probably neither better or worse than those in other provincial centres, and were usually distinguished by large signboards that competed with each other in gaudiness of colouring and grotesqueness, the object of which was to attract the passerby.

In the late 18th century *Barrington's Hotel* in Bridge Street, which stood on or close to the site of the Rehabilitation Institute, was a well known Sligo landmark. In 1791, Coquebert de Montbret, the French consul, on the occasion of his visit to Sligo, found suitable lodgings in a guest house called *The Hotel*, conducted by the widow Murray. This may well have been the premises subsequently known as the *Old Hotel*, which stood on the left hand side of Holborn Street in the 1830's, had a frontage of 42 feet and a rear running down to the River.

Favourite 'watering holes' in early 19th century Sligo included *The Swan* and *Hope and Anchor* (High Street); *The Plough* (Market Street); *St Patrick's* (Old Market Street); *The Hole in the Wall* (Morrison's Lane, off Thomas Street) and the *Freemason's Tavern* (Old Bridge Street). As the century progressed these faded from the scene and were replaced by Sweeney's *Oyster Tavern*, also known as *The Shamrock Bar* 18, Thomas Street; Anderson's *Glasgow Tavern* in Quay Street, and *The Spinning Wheel* in High Street.* However, the best known and long remembered establishment was the famous *Black Lion* at 64-65 Pound Street (now Connolly Street), owned by the Hudson family. It was a 2- storey thatched building with a distinctive signboard over the door depicting the 'lord of the forest' which was still in place, though fast mouldering, a century ago. In its heyday it was the principal location for subscription balls and cock-fighting. Indeed, it has been stated that the last 'main' advertised and publicly fought in Sligo took place in its backyard. It is also recorded that it was in this hotel that Major John Hillas of *Donecoy House* slept the night before he fought the famous duel at Kilmacowen in February, 1816. in which he was mortally wounded.

*\* Subsequently* Carroll's Auctioneering *premises.*

INNS AND TAVERNS OF OTHER DAYS

In the mid 19th century the *Black Lion Hotel* was owned by Thomas Hudson and was sold by court order in 1854. The building was still standing in a rather dilapidated state, with its rather unique sign still blowing in the wind, a century ago.

One of the principal hostelries in the early 19th century was the *Hibernian Hotel,* also known as *Boyle's Hotel,* in what was then Jail Street, subsequently Albert Street and now Teeling Street. * In 1840 it was acquired by Thomas Davis and a decade later it passed to Thomas Hudson, a local merchant and shipping agent, whose family were also associated with the *Black Lion.* As far as can be established, it was during his proprietorship that two adjoining properties, one on either side, were acquired, namely the *York Hotel* , as distinct from the *Old York Hotel,* and *Ross's Hotel,* previously known as *The King's Arms* and combined all three to form an enlarged establishment. When the property was offered for sale in the Bankruptcy Court in 1860 it was described as having in excess of twenty bedrooms, stabling for twelve horses and a popular venue for concerts and theatrical productions.

---

# Phibbs' Hotel
## LORD EDWARD ST., SLIGO
*Beside I.O.C. Garage and Railway Station*
Double and Single Bed-rooms, with Hot and
Cold Water.　　　　　::　　　　　Electric Light
*Terms Reasonable*
LUNCHEONS AND TEAS SERVED

---

It was purchased by James Armstrong, proprietor of the *Royal Hotel,* Castlebar, who altered the name to *The Victoria.* Shortly afterwards he, too, was declared a bankrupt and the Hotel was acquired by Rebecca Allingham and her sister for a reputed £450. The Misses Allingham ran *The Victoria* very successfully for a quarter of a century. The next owner was a John A. Hall of Derry. He carried out extensive renovations and opened a new dining hall and a billiard room. Following in the

* Following an Act of Parliament of 1833 premises were acquired to have
a minimum of 10 bedrooms to qualify as a hotel.

## INNS AND TAVERNS OF OTHER DAYS

footsteps of his predecessors, he also ran into financial difficulties and the Hotel was closed in 1915. Six years later it was purchased by Peter Cooney, refurbished and opened as *The Grand Hotel* in March, 1926. Following his death in February, 1930, it was operated by his sister, Bridget. In 1943 it was purchased from her executors by local businessman, the late Michael Martin of *Albert House*, whose family still own it, although it has not been operated as a Hotel since 1984. The ground floor area is now the *Equinox Night Club*.**

Due principally to its close proximity to the County Courthouse, this hotel was central to many notable events in local affairs for a century or more. In January, 1833, it was the venue for a Celebration Dinner on the occasion of the election of John Martin as M.P. for the Borough; and four years later, in the County election of 1837, Daniel Jones of Benada, the Liberal candidate, utilized it as a headquarters, as did Colonel King-Harman in 1880. On the occasion of the Borough election in 1868 Captain John W. King, a Magistrate of the County, was mortally wounded in a melee on its doorstep. In the absence of a Town Hall the famous 'Long Room' of *Davis's Hotel* was the venue for the first meeting of the Reformed Corporation in October, 1842. It was here that Daniel O'Connell was wined and dined on the occasion of a Repeal Demonstration in May, 1843. William Smith O'Brien, the Young Irelander, made it his headquarters on a visit in September, 1858, on which occasion he addressed the assembled multitude in the street outside from a top window. After the *Victoria* closed its doors in 1915 the building was taken over and used as a military recruiting centre. Later, during 'The Troubles' it was occupied for a short period by the National Army and, afterwards, by the County Council while the Courthouse was in military occupation.

Another celebrated hostelry was the *Lord Nelson Hotel*, a 3-storey premises facing the River at the junction of Thomas Street and Corkran's Mall, or Linenhall Street. It was opened in 1801 by William McBride, at a rent of £90 a year. In 1827 it passed to his son, Robert

---

**After Thomas Hudson was appointed Postmaster of Sligo in 1851,the Post Office was moved from Thomas Street to Jail Street, now Teeling Street, and located in premises formerly known as *Ross's Hotel'*. The existence of a 'Post Box' in the wall to the right of the *Grand Hotel* entrance dates from that period.

In 1868 the Post Office was moved to High Street; in 1880 to Castle Street and, finally, to the present G.P.O. which opened in November 1902, on a site which originally housed the Fish Market.

INNS AND TAVERNS OF OTHER DAYS

McBride, who was Mayor in 1848 and a member of the Masonic Order.

The Hotel could boast of having a 'Grand Jury Room', where the Magistrates of the County dined on the occasion of the biannual Assizes, and also a 'Lodge Room' which was a meeting place for the local Freemasons. In 1850, when James Geran became proprietor, it was described as having twenty bedrooms, a bar, a cellar, kitchen, dairy and servants quarters, in addition to an enclosed yard and ample

The Imperial Hotel, 1900

# VICTORIA HOTEL
## SLIGO

(FIRST CLASS),

*Patronised by all the Nobility andGentry*

T ourists, Anglers, and Families will find every convenience, combined with cleanliness and moderate charges.

**PRIVATE ROOMS, LADIES' SITTING ROOMS.**
**BATH - HOT, COLD AND SHOWER**

Gentlemen staying at this Hotel have the privilege of Free Fishing for Salmon and Trout on Lough Gill, Boats for hire Posting in all its branches. Omnibus attends all Trains.

BLLIARDS, GOLF.                                  J.A. Hall, Proprietor

Advertisement in *"Sligo Champion"*, 1908

## INNS AND TAVERNS OF OTHER DAYS

stabling. Seven years later it was acquired by Wm. Robert Armstrong who renamed it *The Imperial*. The ownership changed again in 1861 when the O'Donnell family took possession and was successfully operated by them until 1945. Anthony Sheridan was the next proprietor and he was succeeded by the genial Julia Moyles who ran a most welcoming hostelry between 1958 and 1983, in which year it closed as a hotel. Since then it has been trading as *The Embassy* complex under new proprietor, the enterprising Kevin Quinn.

In its long and chequered history as a premier hostelry, *The Nelson* and *The Imperial* were in turn the favourite rendezvous of many noted personalities such as J.P. Somers, a most colourful character and one time M.P. for the Borough, Sir Robert Peel, Charles S. Parnell, Thomas Sexton, John B. Yeats and his sons, the literary W.B. and the artistic Jack B. Through these Yeatsian associations the Hotel became the mecca of students and lecturers alike at successive Yeats Summer Schools for a quarter of a century.

An advertisement in the *"Sligo Guardian"* in June 1850, announced that the *Royal Mail Hotel*, proprietor Randall Kent, had just opened, and that coaches and mail cars for Dublin, Enniskillen, Strabane and Ballina departed from it daily. The Hotel, which was on Corkran's Mall, a few doors down from *The Imperial*, had a short existence and had closed its doors by 1856-'57.

✦     ✦     ✳     ✳     ✵

In 1781 Charles Anderson, a member of the brewing family, leased a plot in Bridge Street, adjacent to the 'New Bridge' from John Griffith at an annual rent of £5.13s. On this site he built what subsequently became known as the *Bridge House* in which he opened a Wine and Spirit business. His son, John Anderson, who was an Alderman of the Corporation for many years before his death in 1855, inherited the property. He was succeeded in ownership by his son, Charles, who became one of the leading merchant princes of 19th century Sligo, an Alderman of the Corporation, Mayor in 1871, and donor of the Town Hall clock. After he retired from business in 1883 the *Bridge House*, together with the *Lough Gill Brewery*, was acquired by Edward Foley, who leased it firstly to Wm. Ormsby Hunt, merchant, and, in 1895, to the Belfast Banking Company as a branch office while their new building at Victoria Bridge was under construction. At the turn of the

INNS AND TAVERNS OF OTHER DAYS

century it was acquired by the Kerr family who converted it into a hostelry called the *Bridge House Hotel*. After Marie Kerr retired from business in 1914 it was taken over by Rebecca Ramsay and the name altered to *Ramsay's Hotel*. In 1936 the sixteen bedroomed premises was acquired by Nan Frizzell, who renamed it *Frizzell's Hotel*. In the late 1950's it passed by sale to John Kelly and for twenty years or so did a thriving business as *Kelly's Hotel*. It was subsequently run by the Gilsenans and the name changed to *The Bective*. After being closed for a short period it was demolished in 1997 to make way for a development by Messrs Adapeg Ltd. An enlarged hotel is currently being built on the site.

Another well known establishment in the early 19th century was the *Old York Hotel*, 31 High Street. It is reputed to have been a "most respectable establishment" run by Charles Burrows. In 1825 the *"Journal"* carried an advertisement of a "Ball and Supper" on February 14th which cost the Ladies 5/- and the Gents 7/6d. After the death of the proprietor it was offered for sale, as a going concern, and purchased in 1836 by Messrs. Robert Anderson & Co., china and earthenware manufacturers of Straffordshire for use as a warehouse.

*    *    *    *

In or about 1840 the Hudson family, who were also associated with other local hostelries, acquired a large house at the corner of Teeling Street and Abbey Street, previously the private residence of Dr. William Armstrong, and converted it into what became known as *Hudson's Hotel*. In 1849, following upon the purchase of Davis's *Hibernian Hotel* further up the street, the former was advertised for Sale or Letting by Mrs. Hudson, and described as "a commodious house" with rear premises consisting of good office houses, an extensive yard and a coach house.The concern was admirably situated for any public business, being at the corner of Jail Street (= Teeling Street) and communicating immediately with Thomas Street and Castle Street. It was acquired initially by Robert Henderson, who operated it as the *Albert Commercial House,* and subsequently by Peter Talland who renamed it *Talland's Commercial Hotel*. It was operated by the Tallands as a family run concern for three decades or thereabouts. In 1894 it was acquired by William S. Mostyn, who was the last proprietor to

# INNS AND TAVERNS OF OTHER DAYS

Landmarks of Other Days: The *'Bridge House'* (above) and *'Gray's Inn'* (below)

operate a Hotel on the premises. Subsequently, portion of the building was run as a licenced premises by the Collerys and Fallons in turn. The former Hotel now houses the A.C.C. Bank.

In the 1830's Joshua Mason operated a hostelry known as the *North Hotel* at the junction of Stephen Street and The Mall. He was followed by William Buchanan, described in the title documents as a "hotel keeper". He died in October, 1866, and three years later his widow, Eliza or Elizabeth, married Malachi J. Graham who, in 1878, entered

534

INNS AND TAVERNS OF OTHER DAYS

into a lease between himself and the Hon. Evelyn Ashley. Following the death of Eliza Graham in 1920 the Hotel passed to John Buchanan, a son by her first marriage. A year later he assigned the residue of the lease to Ephraim Hamilton who acquired the freehold title of the *North Hotel* in 1925. Hamilton died intestate and without heirs, in May, 1931, and the Hotel passed initially to his eldest brother, Elliott Hamilton, and then by conveyance to the widow, Julia. After a lapse of eight years the said Julia remarried one Denis J. Harrington and continued running the establishment until September, 1945, in which year it was acquired by John

Harp & Shamrock Hotel, 1890

Niland of Collooney for a reputed £3,750. The name was changed to *Niland's* but no longer operated as a Hotel. Twenty-six years later, in 1971, the premises were sold to Henry O'Boyle, renamed *The Four Seasons* and ran as a licensed premises until 1994. The 7-day licence is still attached to the property.

*     *     *     *

A century ago John J. Reynolds, a native of County Meath opened the *Harp and Shamrock Hotel* at 1, Stephen Street, next door to the *North Hotel*. In an advertisement in the local press he offered "first-class accommodation for Tourists and Commercial Gentlemen" while cyclists were also catered for, singly or in parties. In July, 1922, during the Civil War, the premises were commandeered by 'The Irregulars' and occupied for a period. By coincidence, or otherwise, it subsequently became a popular meeting place for Republican sympathisers. In 1940 the name was changed to *Sheridan's Hotel*, the proprietor being Anthony Sheridan who subsequently acquired *The*

*Imperial.* He was succeeded by Mary B.Hannan and later by Mary McDonagh who bought-out the property from the representatives of the Palmerston / Ashley estate. It was subsequently leased to Michael and Mary Garvey who operated it for over two decades as the *Lake Isle Guesthouse.* The premises were acquired by the Corporation in 1993 and the century old landmark demolished to make way for a new link road.

One of the best known and popular hostelries in the opening decades of this century was *The Gray's Inn,* opposite the Ulster Bank in Stephen Street. It was established by Mary Jane Gray (nee McPhail) wife of John Gray of Ballincar. After her retirement from business in 1920, this noted landmark not only remained in business, but also retained its distinctive name down to recent times. Initially, the 14-bedroomed establishment was leased for a short period to the Misses Phibbs, later of *Phibbs' Hotel* in Lord Edward Street, and subsequently sold to Patrick and Mai Browne who operated it for forty years as a "First class Family and Commercial Hotel", fully licensed. An advertisement in 1926 described it as an "old landmark, a popular Hostelry and Restaurant and High Class Boarding House - a home from home." It was a stopping-off and starting point for many visitors and day shoppers to Sligo, especially those who travelled on the buses operated by the Sligo, Leitrim and Northern Counties Railway until that Company closed down in 1957. *The Gray's Inn* which was sold by the Brownes in 1963, was subsequently re-opened and operated as such by Michael Regan. It was later acquired by Jean Douglas and traded as the *Wimpy Restaurant.* More recently, following a further change in ownership, the *Hyde Bridge Restaurant* operated on the ground floor while the first floor was converted into office

---

## SLIGO

### THE.IMPERIAL HOTEL

William Robert Armstrong - Proprietor.

The Necessity For A First-Class Hotel in the Important Town of Sligo has long been felt. The establishment of the IMPERIAL has fully supplied this want, and Visitors to Sligo will find in it comfort and convenience. The house has been re-furbished, cleaned and decorated throughout.

The DRAWING ROOMS are handsomely furnished, and each supplied with a Pianoforte. The BED-ROOMS are most particularly clean and comfortable.

The COFFEE-ROOM for Private and Professional Gentlemen, and the COMMERCIAL ROOM, exclusively for Commercial Gentlemen, are fitted up with every regard to their comfort and convenience.

The POSTING DEPARTMENT is well supplied with first rate Horses, Cars, Carriages and careful drivers.

The SERVANTS are charged in the Bill, and every care taken to ensure good attendance.

The above are the principal features to which the Proprietor wishes to direct special attention; and trusts that the IMPERIAL, in Sligo, will soon obtain from the Public as liberal support as that which has been so fully given to the Imperial Enniskillen for MANY YEARS.

A Night-Porter in Attendance.

ALL the Conveyances from Sligo leave the door of the Imperial.

September, 1858.

## INNS AND TAVERNS OF OTHER DAYS

apartments. This long established and well known landmark finally closed its doors in December, 1997, and demolished the following June as part of the urban renewal programme.

Less well known Hotels and Hostelries of other days included Barry's *Lake Hotel* at the Riverside, now the *Blue Lagoon*; McIndoe's *Temperance Hotel* in

---

### BALL AND SUPPER

THERE WILL BE

A BALL AND SUPPER

*at the YORK HOTEL, Sligo*

on MONDAY Evening the 14th Inst.

| | | |
|---|---|---|
| Ladies | - | 5s.0d. |
| Gentlemen | - | 7s.6d. |
| Capt. Slade and | | |
| G. Gillmor, Esq. | | Stewards |

*February 1st. 1825*

---

Grattan Street, subsequently *Irvine's Hotel,* later Branley's *Grosvenor* and now Mannion's *Record Room and Style Emporium;* Douris's *Abbey Hotel* in Castle Street, where the E.S.B. now stands; Mullan's *Standard Hotel,* High Street, subsequently the *Bonne Chere,* and now *Innisfree Hotel and Ark Bar, Phibbs's Hotel* in Lord Edward Street, later McGovern's *Central Hotel* and now Donaghy's Pub; *Rowlette's Private Hotel,* 1 Wine Street; the *Western Hotel,* Quay Street and Wilson's *Temperance Hotel,* Old Market

---

# GRAHAM'S
## ☙ Posting Establishment, ❧
## THE MALL SLIGO.

POSTING in all its Branches.

FUNERAL ORDERS attended to with Punctuality and at Moderate Charges.

Mrs. G. beg to intimate that she has added to Funeral Department a Glass Sided Hearse, (Built by Morahan & Sons. Victoria Line Sligo.)

---

## North Hotel, The Mall.
#### (ESTABLISHED OVER FIFTY YEARS).

*This Hotel will be found Very Comfortable, with Moderate Charges.*

INNS AND TAVERNS OF OTHER DAYS

Street. The *Clarence Hotel* which functioned as the County Club between 1879 and 1929, subsequently became *Hotel Eden*. The *Southern Hotel* which opened in 1928 as the *Great Southern Hotel* was later the *Innisfree.*

---

### HOTEL STAFFING LEVELS, 1901

*(As per Census of that year)*

| Imperial Hotel | Victoria Hotel |
|---|---|
| 2 Bar Assistants | 2 Housemaids |
| 2 Housemaids | 1 Bar Attendant |
| 2 Waiters | 1 Book-keeper |
| 2 Kitchenmaids | 1 Pantry Boy |
| 2 Coachmen | 1 Waiter |
| 1 Governess | 1 'Boots' |
| 1 Cook | 1 Kitchenmaid |
| 1 Pantry Boy | 1 Laundress |
| 1 'Boots' | 1 Cook |
| 1 Laundress | |

---

# HOTEL EDEN
**WINE STREET, SLIGO.**

## SLIGO'S NEWEST AND MOST MODERN HOTEL

Fully Licenced. Centrally situated, convenient to G.S.R. and G.N.R. 'Bus Terminal. All Trains and 'Buses attended.

**14 Bedrooms, Fully Equipped Bathrooms, Spacious Lounge, Reading, Writing and Dining Rooms, Roof Garden, Electric Light and Central Heating throughout.**

CUISINE FINEST IN SLIGO. OWN FRUIT AND VEGETABLES.

**Special Catering for Wedding Parties, Club Dinners, etc.**

LOCK-UP GARAGES

## S.H. DERHAM : PROPRIETOR.

Telephone - Sligo 211.

# On the Hunting Fields

Hunting, the pursuit of an animal by a pack of hounds who follow the scent, is possibly the oldest established sport in Ireland. The Normans are said to have introduced it here, their principal quarry being the deer and the wolf. By the late 18th and early 19th centuries packs were kept by individual landlords and stag and fox hunting was a decidedly upper class recreation. Those immaculately dressed persons seated on equally well groomed horses, accompanied by hard driving hounds and red coated huntsmen and "elated by the cry of the hounds and the first thunder of the chase", have been a familiar sight here and there over the Sligo countryside for generations untold. In the 19th century there were three packs operating within the County: the *Lissadell Harriers*, subsequently the *County Sligo Hunt*; the *Coopershill Hounds*, later the *O'Hara Harriers*, and the *Tireragh Hounds*. [1]

The earliest pack of which we have knowledge was the *Sligo Club Hounds* which were supported and maintained by gentlemen residing in the vicinity of Sligo Town. In the decades preceding the Great Famine the local *"Journal"* carried regular notices of meets at such venues as Ballincar, Cloverhill and Springfield. Members of this Hunt had the reputation of being hard riders, heavy drinkers and very often addicted gamblers. One such individual was known as 'Bloomer' Phibbs. He is said to have acquired his nickname from a speech he made when proposing to a young lady in these terms : "My face may be rough" - he was deeply marked by small pox -"but my acres are smooth and blooming". Another was dubbed 'The Commodore', as he never attained to higher rank in the navy than that of midshipman. In real life he was none other than Arthur Irwin, a famous horseman, who kept a stud farm at Oakfield before his death in March, 1828.

## The Lissadell Harriers

After the Famine the Club Hounds were revived by Sir Robert Gore-Booth as the *Gore-Booth Hounds*, or the *Lissadell Harriers*. The first recorded meet of this pack was at Teesan in December 1850. During the season, which ran from November to March, they hunted twice

ON THE HUNTING FIELDS

weekly, weather permitting, at such venues as Cregg, Cloverhill, Cummeen and Rathcormack. The season usually closed with a Point-to-Point meeting at Springfield. The following report of this popular event was published in the *"Sligo Independent"* :-

*"As a sort of natural wind-up to the hunting season Colonel Campbell, the master of the Sligo Harriers, organised the Point-to-Point races at Springfield, near the hospitable residence of George Mullen, J.P., on Wednesday last, St. Patrick's Day, under the most inauspicious circumstances as regards weather, but which was otherwise most successful. The officials in charge were Lieut. Colonel Campbell (Steward); Christopher A. L'Estrange (Judge); Major J. D. Robinson (Starter) and George T. Pollexfen (Clerk of the course).*

*The Springfield course has been a popular venue for this event since 1867 when the late Sir Robert Gore-Booth presided over the hunt races. The family's long association with the event is being continued in the person of Miss Constance Gore-Booth. She arrived well mounted and in good hunting form and shed a bright ray of warm sunshine all round and, as her grandfather had done in 1867, she entered into the spirit of the day's doings with a heartiness that made all feel comfortable. The young lady would blush if she overheard all the encomiums expressed by those who watched as a she rode up seated on her palfrey with an ease that would do credit to Diana herself. As she weighed out and mounted Paddy Connolly's 'Chance Shot', in his colours of yellow and black, she received a regular ovation. Her horsemanship was splendid. In the Diamond Plate she made the pace hot from the start and the gallant Major from Annaghmore found himself outrun by her very early on. She brought 'Chance Shot' gallantly up to a third place, and we need not add that she was enthusiastically cheered from winning post to scales ......"* [2]

# The County Sligo Hunt

After the demise of the Sir Robert Gore-Booth in 1876, the *County Sligo Hunt*, sometimes referred to as the *County Sligo Club Hounds,* or the *County Sligo Harriers,* was formed. Their first meet was at the kennels on November 4th, 1878, and in the weeks that followed there were meets at Cregg, The Punchbowl, Tullyhill, The Redgate, Drum, Graigue, Millbrook, Cummeen Gate and Woodville. In January, 1888, the *"Independent"* carried a report of the traditional Stephen's Day meet at The Redgate:-

## ON THE HUNTING FIELDS

*"The members of the hunt had some excellent sport over the lands at Knocknarea on St. Stephen's Day. The meet, which was at the Redgate, was very large and representative of the gentry of the county. The weather was bright and cheerful, and although the ground was rather soddened by recent rains, it was on the whole safe and afforded capital runs. The day was regarded as a holiday in town, and the attendance of spectators on foot was rather numerous, and included all the farmers and labourers of the district, who appeared to take a keen interest in the sport. Amongst those mounted were Captain Campbell, Mr. Moloney, R.M., Robert Pettigrew, Esq., Dr. Palmer, Alexander Lyons, Esq., Major Wood-Martin and the number of cars and other vehicles was very large. Tom Connor, the huntsman, laid the hounds - a splendid pack - on the scent punctually at twelve o'clock, and a fine hare was soon sohoed away and after a trying run across the country, in which Dr. Palmer and Captain Campbell made some splendid leaps, it succeeded in making its escape among some furze".*

In March, 1896, a contributor to the *"Sligo Independent"*, under the pen name *"Tallyho"*, gave details of a meet at The Redgate, the last of the season. Hares were plentiful and there were some exciting runs. The Master, Colonel James Campbell, led the Hunt and left nothing undone to procure a good day's sport for all. Also mounted were the Misses Gore-Booth, L'Estrange and Wynne; Majors Eccles and Robinson; Messrs Wm. Petrie, P.W. Connolly, John Irwin, Ed. Foley, H. Tully, Edward Rowlette, Owen Phibbs, J.A. Hall, T. H. Williams and Albert Simpson. [3]

The annual Point-to-Point races were a regular feature of the season's activities. Initially, these were held at Springfield on Easter Monday but later the date was changed to March 17th. So also was the venue. Oakfield was popular from the turn of the century until the late 1930's, after which the annual event was transferred to Cairns Hill. Since the early 1970's the races have been held on the Cleveragh race course.

Half a century ago, in November, 1947, the Co. Sligo Hunt met at Carrowmore with J.A. (Alan) Stevenson and James Rowlette as Joint-Masters. Other riders included Mrs. Macarthur, Misses M. Perceval, R. Nesham, H. Toher, Aideen Gore-Booth, M. Derham and F. Rowlette; Messrs. R.W. Browne, E. Browne, A. Dodd, J.P. McGarry and Reverend C. Kelleher. In 1950-'51 James Rowlette acted as huntsman, P. Mullane was whipper-in, and members sported a green uniform, with red

ON THE HUNTING FIELDS

---

COUNTY SLIGO HUNT CLUB

## Point-to-Point RACES

**AT CAIRNS HILL** (one mile from Sligo

on ST. PATRICK'S DAY (FRI., March 17,'50)

4 Open Races          1 Confined
**EXCELLENT ENTRIES**

First Race 2.30 p.m.

---

SOUTH COUNTY SLIGO HARRIERS

## Point-to-Point RACES

(HELD UNDER I.N.H.S. RULES)

AT

**CORHOWNAGH, BALLISODARE**

ON

**WEDNESDAY, 29TH MARCH, 1950**

FIVE RACES

**TOTAL PRIZE MONEY £100 (excluding Challenge Trophies) towards which the Racing Board will contribute £40**

First Race 2.30 p.m.

Special Buses leave Sligo 12.15, and Tubbercurry 1.15;
returning Tubbercurry 6.15 p.m.
Special Bus from Sligo 1.45 p.m. and Ballina.
Bus returning from Sligo 5.30 instead of 5 p.m.

ON THE HUNTING FIELDS

collars and cuffs. The kennels at Ballincar accommodated twelve couples of hounds. On December 26th, 1958, the traditional Stephen's Day meet took place at The Redgate under W.P. (Billy) Hunter (Hon. Joint Master). Also mounted were Misses Hilda Toher, R. Rowlette, B. Burke, M. O'Connor and M. Cleeve; Messrs P. Gillespie, J. Crilly, F. Kearns, A. Dodd, R. Irwin and Masters B. McMullan, J. Carter and C. Gillespie. The annual Point-to-Point, which comprised of five events, took place at Cairns Hill the following St. Patrick's Day. Officials in charge were John C. Hosie (Judge) P.J. O'Connor (Starter) P. Curran (Clerk of Scales) and W.J. McMullan (Clerk of the Course). The stewards consisted of Edward F. Cooper; Captain Eustace, W.P. Hunter, J.A. (Alan) Stevenson, Percy Anderson, James Rowlette and W. Anderson. Alan Stevenson continued as Master of the Hunt for a further two seasons after the death of James Rowlette in 1962. During a long stint of close on twenty years in the Mastership of the pack the kennels were kept at *Rossaville,* Stevenson's suburban residence at Ballincar. They were moved to Cloverhill in 1964 after W.P. (Billy) Hunter assumed the Mastership.

In November, 1964, the County Sligo Hunt celebrated its centenary somewhat prematurely - fourteen years ahead of time! - by holding an invitation meet at *Coolera House,* Kilmacowen. Mounted members from the Galway Blazers, the Strabane Foxhounds, the Fermanagh Harriers, the Longford Harriers, the North Mayo Harriers and the South Co. Sligo Harriers attended. The Misses Aideen and Gabrielle Gore-Booth of Lissadell (riding side-saddle), whose great-grandfather had founded the *Lissadell Harriers* a century before; and Dermot O'Hara of Annaghmore, whose great-grandfather was responsible for starting the Coopershill Hounds, subsequently the *O'Hara Harriers,* was also mounted. Captain Owen L'Estrange, whose father was a former Master of the *Sligo Harriers*; Mathew Rowlette, whose father and brother were also Masters, and V. McMorrow, who acted for several seasons as

ON THE HUNTING FIELDS

Honorary Huntsman, were also present. The event attracted a big number of hunting enthusiasts from all over the North West, and a great day's sport was had by all.[4]

# O'Hara's Harriers

The *Coopershill Hounds* were one of the oldest packs in the County and, initially, were kept entirely for fox-hunting. By the mid 19th century they were widely known as *Charles Cooper's Hounds,* a private pack that hunted regularly at such venues as Earlsfield, Cloonamahon, Claragh, Kilross and Cloverhill. Following the succession of Charles Wm. Cooper to the Annaghmore property in 1860 and his assumption of the surname O'Hara, the pack thereafter became known as *O'Hara's Harriers,* or, *the Annaghmore Hounds.* One of their first meets was at Castledargan in February, 1861. Heading the riders was the Master, Charles William O'Hara, on his chestnut steed, accompanied by his long serving huntsman, William McCullagh. Others mounted included Messrs. Duke, Allen, L'Estrange, Phibbs, Neynoe and Ormsby. An enjoyable day's sport followed and all were afterwards entertained to 'lunch' in the old Ormsby homestead.

Over the succeeding decades the O'Hara Harriers hunted regularly over the Hill of Doo, at Carrigans, Heathfield, Newpark, Streamstown and Cloonamahon. The highlight of successive hunting seasons was the annual Point-to-Point at Claragh, the traditional hunting ground of the O'Hara's. After the death of Charles William O'Hara in 1898, the mastership of the Annaghmore Harriers, one of the few privately owned packs in Ireland, passed to his eldest son, Charles Kean O'Hara. This scion of the ancient clan had few equals as a horseman and huntsman. He carried on the traditions of his family, bred and trained his own ponies but the pack was his particular pride. For close on half a century the hills of Claragh echoed to the sound of the hunting horn as he led the chase both at ordinary meets and at the annual Point-to-Point.

The O'Hara Harriers were owned by the Master, by whom the pack was entirely maintained until 1909. Subsequently, voluntary subscriptions were accepted. Following the demise of Charles K. O'Hara in 1947, the mastership passed to his brother, Frederick Wm.

# ON THE HUNTING FIELDS

Kieran Horan
Current Joint Master of Co.Sligo Harriers

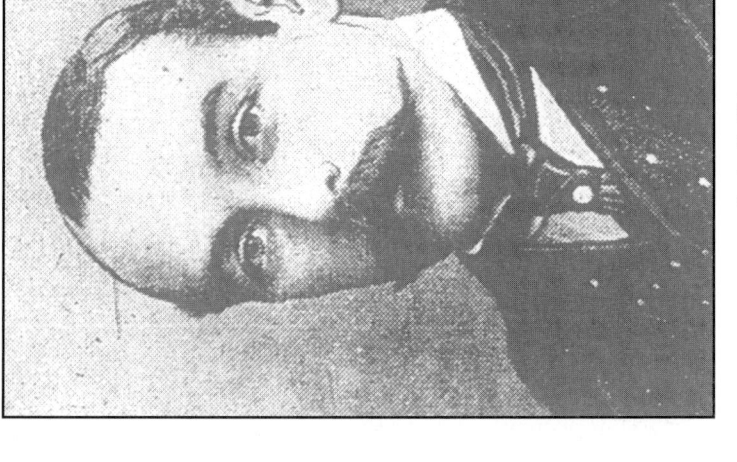

Charles K. O'Hara
Master of Annaghmore Harriers 1898-1947

## ON THE HUNTING FIELDS

O'Hara of Coopershill and Cultibar. He resigned the following year and at that stage it was decided to form the *South County Sligo Hunt Club*. The hounds, which numbered nine couples, were handed over to the new Club, although the kennels remained at Annaghmore. At their first meet at Claragh on November 5th, 1948, Lieut. Col. E.F. Cooper and James Dorran acted as Joint Masters. Also taking part were Mrs. Nesham; Misses Perceval, McCormick, Nesham, Bracken and Messrs J.P. McGarry, J. Lyons, G. Doran, R. Hall, A. O'Grady, J. Lang, J. Gallagher and J. Finn. Those on foot included F.W. O'Hara, D. O'Hara, Miss Campbell, Dr. Flannery, H. Toher and Mrs. McMullan. The Club held their first Point-to-Point at Corhownagh on March 30th, 1949. Officials in charge were J.A. Stevenson, Master of the Co. Sligo Hunt, Major A.A. Perceval and Captain J. Lyons, who acted as Judges; H.C. Gordon McCormick was Clerk of the course and J.P. McGarry, Hon. Secretary. There were five races on the card and the event was highly successful. Amongst those mounted at a meeting at Ballygawley a decade later, in February 1959, were Messrs. E.F. Cooper and J. Prins (Joint Masters), John Finn (Whipper-in), E. Phibbs, A.A. Perceval, I. Gardiner. J. O'Grady, T. Doherty, M. Reynolds and M. Finan; Mrs. McCready-Bryan, Mrs. McMullen and Mrs. Lyons; Misses Hosie and Perceval. On the following Easter Monday the South County Sligo Harriers held their annual Point-to-Point races at Corhownagh but were disbanded shortly afterwards owing to the paucity of numbers.

In October, 1966, Co. Sligo Hunt was re-organised and renamed *County Sligo Harriers*. It embraced the recently disbanded South County Sligo Hunt Club. The following officers were elected:- F.P. Britton (Chairman); J.W. McMullen (Vice-Chairman); D.C.O'Hara (Hon. Treasurer); Mrs. Brenda Anderson and Captain R.J. Alvey (Hon. Joint Secretaries) and Jan Prins and Frank McGarry (Joint Masters).[5] At their opening meet two weeks later at *Coolera House* the Masters and Whips looked resplendent in green jackets trimmed with red collars, while members sported black jackets with similar red collars.

Jan Prins and Frank McGarry functioned as Joint-Masters from 1966 to 1982, on which date McGarry retired. Throughout the decade and a half since then, Muriel Siberry, Kieran Horan and Derek Pugh have shared the Mastership between them. This trio, together with Brenda Anderson, who has been associated with the sport locally for forty years

## ON THE HUNTING FIELDS

or so, acted as Hon. Secretary 1966-1987, and is still riding at meets, have individually and collectively contributed much to the continuance of the Hunt.

A sporting tradition that has spanned more than two centuries, almost without a break, and successively overcome many obstacles, is set, despite rapidly changing times and increasing costs, to carry on into the new millennium.

### Notes & References:

(1) Wood-Martin, the County historian, mentions that the *Tireragh Hounds* were "long well known to the sporting community" but very little details of their activities have been recorded. During the 19th century the pack was kept by various individuals, one of whom was an unidentified Church of Ireland clergyman - thought to have been William Grove of Kilmacshalgan - "who took a deep interest in field sports and possessed a peculiar aptitude for training and attaching to himself horses and dogs". In the 1870's John Boyd of *Castletown Manor* was Master of this pack.

According to the *"Sligo Chronicle"*, May, 1881, a new pack, known as the *Tireragh Harriers*, was formed in 1880-'81, and completed "a most successful season" with a hunt race consisting of four well-filled events over the Carrigan course which was "well and fashionably attended and capital sport afforded to a big attendance". The Master and members of the Hunt acted as stewards, George T. Pollexfen as judge and Peter Atkinson as secretary.

References have been traced to the Ormsbys operating a kennel and a hunting pack of foxhounds at Old Castledargan c.1800.

In January, 1860, the local press published a notice of a meet of the *Phibbs' Hounds* at Kilmacowen. This was a small private pack owned and maintained by Thomas Phibbs of *Heathfield*, Collooney.

(2) Constance Gore-Booth, riding Edward Foley's *Tartar*, came second in the Challenge Cup event at the County Sligo Hunt Point-to-Point races at Springfield, Easter Monday, 1895.

| | | |
|---|---|---|
| (3) | *"Sligo Independent"* | 21-3-1896 |
| (4) | *"Sligo Champion"* | 13-11-1964 |
| (5) | ibid | 21-10-1966 |

ON THE HUNTING FIELDS

---

## Masters of the County Sligo Hunt (1878-1966)

Charleton L'Estrange; Col James Campbell; E.M. Rowlette; C. Arthur L'Estrange; Capt. G. Wynne; Major G.M. Eccles; H.G. L'Estrange; T.H. Williams; H.N. McCormick; D. Bourke; Jas. Rowlette; E.F. (Ted) Browne; J.N. Bentley; F. Feeney; J.A. Stevenson, P. J. O'Connor and W.P. Hunter.

## Masters of County Sligo Harriers (1966-1997)

Jan Prins and Frank McGarry (Joint Masters); Jan Prins and Muriel Siberry (ditto); Muriel Siberry and Kieran Horan (ditto); Kieran Horan and Derek Pugh (ditto); Kieran Horan and Muriel Siberry (ditto).
For the current season (1997-98) Muriel Siberry, Kieran Horan and Derek Pugh are Hon. Joint Masters.

---

# Memories of Bygone Hunts*

"On Wednesday afternoon as I plodded out the Strandhill road in a dismal downpour my heart leaped as I heard the music of the Harriers hunting in the old demesne of Cummeen. [1] I quickened my steps in the hope of witnessing a bit of jumping, but by the time I reached Cummeen Gate the sounds of the hunt had died away in the distance.

That night as I sat by the fire, what a flood of memories passed before my mind's eye - Great figures in the hunting fields of former days gone forever! Colonel Campbell [2] the grandest figure of them all. Somehow his handsome face and splendid figure impressed itself indelibly on my youthful mind. I remember seeing him at the Hazelwood Races riding about the course with his bride to be, Louisa L'Estrange, and what a lovely couple they were. Another great figure, beloved of the people, Christopher L'Estrange,[3] whose cup of happiness was dashed from his lips and whose death so tragically sudden on the polo field shocked the whole countryside. They were the two outstanding Masters of the old Co. Sligo Harriers, and unrivalled for sportsmanship and popularity in their day.

Everyone will agree that the finest figure of the 'Old Brigade' adorning the hunting fields of County Sligo is the veteran, Major

---

* The late William A. Griffith (1871-1942) was a keen follower of the hounds and the files of the *"Sligo Champion"* contain numerous contributions from his erudite pen recalling meetings of the Co. Sligo Hunt and the sportsmen involved. The following extracts were published between 1938-'40.

ON THE HUNTING FIELDS

Group taken on occasion of the Co. Sligo Hunt Club's 'Centenary' meet at Coolera House, in November, 1964. Included are Mrs. Macready-Bryan (2nd left); Ms. K. Macarthur (mounted) and J.A. Stevenson, Joint Master (to her right)

# A JOINT MEETING

"For the first time in the history of those Packs, a joint meet of the Co. Sligo Harriers and the South County Sligo Harriers was held at Ballysodare on Wednesday, 23rd inst.

The South County Sligo Harriers is a new pack formed last year to replace O'Hara's Harriers, which hunted the Collooney country for close on a hundred years with only a break of a couple of seasons during the last World War. The late Major O'Hara hunted this pack for more than fifty years, which must be a record. We feel sure that the South County Sligo Harriers will carry on the old traditions of its predecessor and enjoy the same good sport for many years to come. The younger generation was well represented at the joint meet (always a healthy sign for the future of any hunt).

The South County Sligo Harriers hunted the first part of the day under the Mastership of J. Dorran and Lt. Comdr. Cooper, with J. Finn as whipper-in.

Hares were scarce in the beginning and later on too many were on foot. Scent was spoiled somewhat by a strong sun. What looked like being a nice run was spoiled by an over-enthusiastic crowd of foot-people who turned the hare on a couple of occasions."

**"Sligo Independent"** 26-02-1949

## ON THE HUNTING FIELDS

Charles K. O'Hara,[4] who, for over a generation has been hunting his own pack, known as *O'Hara's Harriers,* from the family seat at Annaghmore, or *Nymphsfield,* as it was originally called. Though past the biblical 'three score and ten' the Major is still, to all appearance, 'as gay as a two-year old' and can ruffle it with the best. I remember him as a young man on the family coach with his father, the late Charles W. O'Hara, passing through the streets of Sligo, blowing a long coach horn, as they made their way to the Sligo Races at Hazelwood. The annual 'Race Day' was a great event in bygone times, in the era before the introduction of the weekly half-holiday, not to mention holidays with pay. Crowds of people gathered at corners and other vantage points to catch a glimpse of the Annaghmore coach passby in all its grandeur. Those spectacular sights have gone forever and the Races nowadays pass practically unnoticed by a majority of the Town's inhabitants. Since then I have seen Major O'Hara on many a fine horse, all winners in their day - *Lady Una, Sir Spencer, Prince* and *Sir George.* Every sportsman in County Sligo wishes many more years of good health to this 'Mighty Hunter'.

Another grand old sportsman, Major G. M. Eccles of Moneygold, [5] deserves a word of remembrance. He, too, is one of the real old-timers, a 'giant' of the old County Sligo Harriers, who always kept a good horse in his stable. I remember his brown mare *Wood Nymph,* steered by the famous Captain Bidgood in 1898, making a bold bid for Colonel Campbell's *Diamond Jubilee Challenge Cup,* the Major himself being overweight. However, luck did not favour him on that occasion and victory went, after a gruelling finish, to W. S. Heather's *Acrobat,*[6] ridden by James Fitzgerald. The judge on that occasion was the late Christopher L'Estrange, popularly known as 'Master Christie', one of the greatest and most respected of Masters of the Old Pack, beloved by every farmer in the hunting country. As everybody knows, Major Eccles married into the L'Estrange family whose members were foremost in the sporting community in Sligo. In more recent times the Major was a strong supporter of the New Hunt Club and always held an official position at the Point-to-Point Races. Many a tedious wait between events was whiled away by the Major's interesting stories, of which he had an inexhaustible supply.

I wonder if E. M. Rowlette of Cash [7], the only surviving Master of

## ON THE HUNTING FIELDS

the Old Sligo Pack still with us, would be annoyed by including him in my list of veterans? Over forty years ago I saw him come third in the County Sligo - Annaghmore Hunt Challenge Cup at Springfield. He was riding a great hunter, *The Don*, owned by Colonel Campbell. That was the occasion when the late P. W. Connolly [8] had the race in hands but galloped into, instead of through, the last fence; and when Constance Gore-Booth, on the Ned Foley's *Tartar*, was beaten on the post by Major O'Hara on *Prince*. In his young days Eddie Rowlette was one of the foremost riders in Ireland. There are many who will still remember his successes with Albert Simpson's chaser, *Albert Edward*, who towards the end of the last century was as well known as C. J. Bentley's *Ballinode* at a later period. Rowlette was always ready to ride for a farmer and he seldom failed to justify the confidence placed in him. When the Old Hunt Club was forced to close the kennels at Oakfield, he came to the rescue and took the dogs to Cash from whence he hunted them for a period. That prince of sportsmen, the late Col. Campbell, no mean judge of men and things, always said that Eddie Rowlette was 'unique', for in addition to his brains and ability he had a modesty seldom found with his other atributes.

One of the oldest and best known followers of the Sligo Harriers was the late Willie Frazer of Fermoyle. I remember him as one of the best all-round athletes in the County, running, jumping etc. I saw him win a high-jump competition at an Athletic Sports in Finisklin about fifty years ago. To be sure, the height was not a record, but in those days competitors jumped cleanly over the cross-bar. He was, in his young days, a great man to ride, and I can see him at a Springfield Point-to-Point making a great race on a mare bearing the classic name *Bessy Buckshot*. Only within the past few years would he allow anyone but himself ride his horses. He was a fine, breezy, open-air Irishman full of fun and not beyond playing a practical joke on his friends. I believe he never missed a St. Stephen's Day meet of the Harriers until shortly before his death. 'Anno Domini' wears down the strongest, and so this good sportsman lies in Sligo cemetery, taking his rest until Gabriel sounds the grand 'Tally-ho'.

# ON THE HUNTING FIELDS

## Notes & References:

(1) Cummeen, or Cummin, was the seat of the Ormsby family between the 17th and 19th centuries.

(2) Lieut. Colonel James Campbell, born 1850, eldest son of Harper Campbell, merchant, died at his residence, *The Hermitage*, September,1924.

(3) Christopher A. L'Estrange of *Kevinsfort House*, Master of the Sligo Harriers, died in May, 1900, following injuries received at a meeting of the Hunt.

(4) Major Charles Kean O'Hara, also a noted polo player,died at *Annaghmore* in August,1947, in his 87th year.

(5) Gerard Macklin Eccles, a native of Tyrone, married Isabella, daughter of Captain James N. Soden of Moneygold, and died June, 1940, aged 84.

(6) Major Heather of the Sligo Artillery and *Knockadoo House*, Coolaney.

(7) Edward Mathew Rowlette of Carncash, obit December, 1940, aged 71.

(8) Patrick W. Connolly, only son of John Connolly of *Rosehill* died in October, 1919, aged 46.

---

# Local 'Meets' November, 1898

## COUNTY SLIGO HARRIERS:

| | | |
|---|---|---|
| November 7th | . . . . . . . . . . . . | Kennels |
| November 11th | . . . . . . . . . . . . | Millbrook |
| November 14th | . . . . . . . . . . . . | Punchbowl |
| November 17th | . . . . . . . . . . . . | Cash Crossroads |
| November 21st | . . . . . . . . . . . . | Cummeen Gate |
| November 24th | . . . . . . . . . . . . | Tullyhill |
| November 28th | . . . . . . . . . . . . | Kilmacowen |

## O'HARA'S HARRIERS:

| | | |
|---|---|---|
| November 8th | . . . . . . . . . . . . | Carrigans |
| November 11th | . . . . . . . . . . . . | Carrowreilly |
| November 15th | . . . . . . . . . . . . | Dunmeegan |
| November 18th | . . . . . . . . . . . . | Killoran |
| November 21st | . . . . . . . . . . . . | Tanrago |
| November 25th | . . . . . . . . . . . . | Collooney |
| November 29th | . . . . . . . . . . . . | White Gate |

# The Crown Solicitor and the 'Conspirators'

William Russell Fenton (1852 - 1933), D.L., *Ardaghowen House*, Sligo, was the 2nd son of Michael Fenton, J.P.,*Castletown House*, Easkey. As a young man he studied law and was admitted a solicitor in 1874. He then opened an office in Sligo and in a relatively short period built up a large practice. In the words of a contemporary "he became the chosen friend and confidant of all creeds and classes".

In 1892 Fenton was appointed Crown Solicitor for Sligo and ten years later succeeded J. Cochrane Davys as Clerk of the Crown and Peace. In addition, he acted as legal adviser to the principal public bodies of the County - the Board of Guardians, Harbour Commissioners and the Gas Company. He was also solicitor to the Grand Jury at the coming into operation of the new Local Government Act in April, 1899, and in accordance with that statute, as an existing officer, he continued to act as solicitor to the newly constituted County Council.

In 1898 W.R. Fenton was engaged by Patrick Roddy of Breeogue as his legal advisor in a very ordinary and common-place action brought against Patrick N. White of *Breeogue House*. The dispute centred around a right-of-way which Roddy claimed and White had shut-off for no apparent reason. The case was tried twice in Sligo and on each occasion the Jury disagreed. The venue was then changed to Dublin where a Special Jury found in Roddy's favour. Not happy with the outcome, White made an unsuccessful application in February, 1900, to have the verdict set aside.[1] He was deeply disappointed at loosing the case and, as subsequent events showed, appears to have directed his fury against W.R. Fenton, Roddy's attorney.

About the same time, Fenton was engaged by a Sligo publican, Hugh O'Connor of Knox's Street, in an action against the Mayor, Aldermen and Burgesses of Sligo Corporation concerning a private right-of-way in Abbey Street. P.A. McHugh, who was Mayor at the time, took a personal interest in the proceedings, and went as far as advising the Corporation to pull down the holding at the centre of the dispute

## THE CROWN SOLICITOR AND THE 'CONSPIRATORS'

which he alleged was shutting out "the light of heaven and the breath of air" from the home of a labouring man. At the same time, articles appeared in the *"Sligo Champion"*, of which newspaper McHugh was Proprietor and Editor, threatening witnesses with all kinds of penalties. Apprised of this development, Fenton, fearing that the application of justice was under severe threat, consulted counsel and was advised to make an application to the Vice-Chancellor to restrain McHugh from using his newspaper for interfering with the administration of the law. In a panic move, obviously aimed at curbing McHugh's activities, an order was made committing him to prison - one of the few occasions on record where the rigours of the law were enforced in this manner.

Events took an unusual and quite unexpected turn in the weeks that followed. On February 25th, 1901, seven days after the order committing McHugh was served, Peter Cawley, Chairman of the Tubbercurry Board of Guardians, and member of Sligo County Council, brought forward a Resolution in the Tubbercurry Boardroom condemning Fenton for his wanton attack on McHugh.[2] The Resolution was rejected by a majority of the Guardians present but was adopted at a subsequent meeting on March 11th. The following Resolution, proposed by John O'Grady and seconded by P. Gannon, was carried by thirteen votes to two :-

*"That we, the members of the Tubbercurry Board of Guardians, congratulate Ald. McHugh, M.P, on his victory in the Four Courts over the system of Jury-Packing which has for some length of time been such a disgrace in Ireland . . . We regard his victory as the most decisive blow that has been struck against oppression and tyranny, and we strongly condemn the efforts of Mr Fenton to have him sentenced to an unlimited term of imprisonment at a time when he was fighting the battles of faith and fatherland."[3]*

Meanwhile, the scene of action had moved elsewhere. At a meeting of Sligo County Council on January 4th. Clr. Peter Cawley proposed an adverse vote against W.R. Fenton, the Council's legal adviser, whom he described as "a hack of Dublin Castle, a man who did for the Crown what the Crown could never succeed in doing, namely, the imprisonment of P.A. McHugh". On a vote, the Resolution was rejected by a majority of four.[4]

The next chapter in the quickly unfolding saga was enacted on March 2nd at a meeting of the Sligo Board of Guardians, presided

## THE CROWN SOLICITOR AND THE 'CONSPIRATORS'

over by Patrick N, White, J.P. of Breeogue. The following Resolution, proposed by John Jinks and seconded by Thomas Tighe, was passed unanimously :-

*"That we, the Board of Guardians of Sligo Union, in meeting assembled, offer our sympathy to P.A. McHugh, M.P., in the numerous attacks being made upon him for his fearless condemnation of jury-packing, land-grabbing and his defence of the tenant farmer . . . We also condemn the conduct of W.R. Fenton, solicitor, for his cruel and wanton attack upon Mr McHugh, one of our colleagues on this Board, in trying to put him in jail for contempt of court; and we respectfully call on the Sligo Board of Guardians and District Councils to dispense with his services from this date".*

A copy of the Resolution, signed by Chairman, P. N. White, was immediately dispatched to W. R. Fenton. [5]

The conspiracy against Fenton was quickly gaining momentum. The action of the Guardians had the effect of depriving him of an annual income of £300, monies which accrued for his services as legal adviser not only to the Sligo and Tubbercurry Boards of Guardians but also to the Rural District Councils. Fenton re-acted swiftly, not only to his dismissal as Solicitor to the Guardians, but more especially to counteract the malicious and wanton statements being circulated against him. Proceedings were instituted against White and Cawley to recover damages for libel and slander and for conspiracy with others to injure him in his profession as a solicitor. The case came before a Special Jury at the July Summer Assizes in Belfast in July, 1901. The defendants flatly denied the charges and pleaded that the matters complained of in the libel were not libellous. A large number of witnesses were called for the Prosecution but neither White or Cawley ventured into the witness box. The jury found in Fenton's favour and assessed damages, £500 against White and £300 against Cawley.[6] Fenton was pleased with the outcome - his character had been vindicated and his standing in the community re-established.

Shortly after the verdict of the Belfast court had been announced, an approach was made to Fenton by intermediaries, acting on behalf of White and Cawley, to ascertain if he would consider letting the matter end there. After much toing and froing, Fenton finally agreed to forego all the damages he had been awarded, in addition to Cawley's costs, on the condition that the boycott would be withdrawn and he

## THE CROWN SOLICITOR AND THE 'CONSPIRATORS'

would be restored to his post. By early December, 1901, negotiations had been completed and a settlement of the actions agreed to between the parties. It seemed as if peace was finally restored. However, the return from America of P. A.Mc Hugh impeded its implementation. On learning of the proposed agreement, McHugh is reported to have exclaimed : *"No peace or settlement with Fenton. Let Cawley be made a bankrupt and White pay his damages and costs. There must be no peace."*

Despite Mc Hugh's uncompromising attitude, John O'Dowd and a handful of fellow Nationalists on Sligo County Council were confident that the settlement already agreed upon would be honoured. However, their hopes were quickly shattered when it became known that Fenton was involved in a prosecution under the Coercion Act. Jasper Tully, M.P., Boyle, and John Gilmartin, Vice-Chairman of the Sligo Board of Guardians, amongst others, appeared before a court in Ballymote on December 23rd charged with unlawful assembly at Gurteen a few weeks earlier. As Crown Solicitor for the County, Fenton was engaged in the prosecution and this gave rise to renewed hostility towards him from the Nationalist side. It was considered inconsistent and offensive to their feelings that a 'Castle' official , in the person of Fenton, should be retained in the services of a Nationalist County Council.

Fenton's action was publicly denounced by P.A. McHugh at a United Irish League meeting in Sligo on New Year's Day, 1902.[7] The matter was further discussed by the Sligo Borough Branch of the United Irish League a few days later. The meeting was chaired by McHugh whose outburst on that occasion added further fuel to the fire. He referred to Fenton as "a coercionist Crown Prosecutor and a professional jurypacker" who was responsible for the conviction of Nationalists charged with agrarian or political offences. He concluded his harangue by declaring :- "I am going to stand by the statement I have just made . . . I shall never retract a word of it." At the conclusion of the meeting a resolution was passed recommending Fenton's dismissal.[8]

At a subsequent meeting of the County Council, McHugh tabled a resolution, part of which read as follows :- *"Mr Fenton is hereby informed that his professional services are no longer required by this Council . . . "* The Resolution was seconded by Peter Cawley and when put to the meeting

## THE CROWN SOLICITOR AND THE 'CONSPIRATORS'

was carried - Sir Malby Crofton of *Longford House* alone dissenting.[9] At the outset, the Chairman, John O'Dowd, was at pains to point out to the assembled Councillors that he personally had no fault to find with Mr Fenton, or with his work on behalf of the Council, but as Nationalists they could not condone his actions as Crown Solicitor and could no longer retain his services. The Council's decision made headlines at home and abroad. It was the first time on record that any representative body had taken such a drastic course of action.

After his dismissal Fenton presented a claim for £5,000 compensation. A handful of Councillors, including Malby Crofton, supported Fenton's claim in full rather than face a lengthy legal battle, but the vast majority of the Council agreed with the Chairman's opinion that the claim should be resisted. John Tarrant, who had been appointed temporarily in Fenton's place, was instructed to take the necessary steps to protect the Council's interests.

In February, 1902, during the absence of John O'Dowd in Parliament, a number of Councillors presented a requisition to Vice-Chairman, Henry Brennan, asking him to convene a meeting for the purpose of considering the appointment of a Solicitor to the Council. The previous week an article appeared in the *"Sligo Champion"* headed : "A CONSPIRACY UNMASKED", of which the following is an extract:-

" . . . *On a dispassionate view of the whole circumstances we have no hesitation in expressing the conviction that there is a conspiracy on foot of which Mr Brennan and the five requisitionists have been made the unconscious instruments. We believe that the object of the conspiracy is to remove Mr. Tarrant from the path of Mr. Fenton. We assert that we are right in saying that Tarrant is the hardest nut Fenton will have to crack before he pockets the £5,000 which he modestly asks from the ratepayers. Neither that sum nor one-tenth of it will Fenton ever pocket from that source: but his chances of bleeding the ratepayers would be much improved if Tarrant were brushed aside."* [10]

Within days of the article appearing, W.R. Fenton had instituted legal proceedings against Patrick McHugh, editor and proprietor of the *"Sligo Champion"*. The action was for damages for libel published in the said newspaper on January 4th and February 18th, 1902, and for maliciously and with intent to injure him for having acted as solicitor for the Crown; of conspiring with others to induce Sligo County Council to terminate his contract of service with the said Council and for printing and publishing in the *"Sligo Champion"* matters calculated

THE CROWN SOLICITOR AND THE 'CONSPIRATORS'

W.R. Fenton (above) and
(below) a cartoon published in *"Sligo Star"*, January, 1902.

## THE CROWN SOLICITOR AND THE 'CONSPIRATORS'

to prejudice, embarrass and injuriously affect him in respect of his claim for compensation, then pending before Sligo County Council.

The trial came-off at Belfast Assizes in July, 1902. The Defendant, McHugh, who was then in jail, denied through his Counsel that the words the libel complained of bore the defamatory sense alleged, and pleaded that they were fair comment on matters of public interest. He also denied that he had entered into conspiracy with any of the persons named. Counsel, acting on his behalf, pleaded that there was no evidence of malice in either what McHugh wrote or what he did. "From the beginning to the end one could look in vain for the slightest malice" he contended. "It is true that the Defendant pursued Fenton vigorously from a political viewpoint and disapproved of the position the Plaintiff occupied as solicitor to Sligo County Council but that was a very different matter from personal malice against him - the charge of which there was not a shred of evidence to justify   .   .   ."[11]

Witnesses from both sides gave evidence and were subjected to lengthy cross-examination by the respective Counsel. After Judge Wright's summing-up, the Jury retired and in less than half an hour returned with their verdict. They found for the Plaintiff on all counts. Damages were assessed at £3,500, with costs - £3,000 on the two libels and £500 on the other claim, namely, that the Defendant maliciously induced the County Council to terminate its contract with W.R. Fenton and for his maliciously conspiring with others to injure the Plaintiff in his business. The verdict handed down by the Belfast court had serious implications for McHugh,  He was unable to meet the damages awarded against him and was declared a bankrupt. All his assets were seized during his imprisonment. On his release from Sligo Gaol, in September, 1902, he found the *"Champion"* offices closed and twenty-three employees out of work. All  McHugh's property,including two insurance policies, which he had executed for the benefit of his children, had been confiscated to satisfy the verdict accorded to Fenton by the Belfast jury.

The extent of the compensation payable to W. R. Fenton by Sligo County Council for his dismissal was discussed at several meetings over a period of fifteen months, and led to heated and prolonged debates on occasions.  The original claim for £5.000 with costs, was flatly turned down, whereas Fenton refused to discuss any compromise. A

## THE CROWN SOLICITOR AND THE 'CONSPIRATORS'

special meeting of the Council was convened on May 31st, 1903, to assess the amount of compensation to be paid to their former legal advisor. Before the assembly was an order from the Court of King's Bench compelling the Council to take into consideration Fenton's claim for a pension, and to assess the amount to which they considered he was entitled. No decision was arrived at then but, at a subsequent meeting and acting on the advice of Tim Healy, K.C., a Resolution was adopted offering Fenton a sum of £340 in full discharge of his claim for compensation. This was unacceptable to Fenton who sought an annuity as well. Finally, after a prolonged and at times stormy debate in which Clr. Cawley figured prominently, the following Resolution, proposed by Clr. Henry Brennan and seconded by Clr. Bernard Collery, J.P.. was unanimously approved :-

*"That we hereby offer W.R. Fenton the sum of £600 in full discharge of his claim against this Council for compensation for loss of office as County Solicitor, he undertaking in writing to accept same in full discharge of said claims."*

Contrary to expectations, Fenton agreed to accept the offer, even though it was little more than one-tenth of his original claim.[12]

The Fenton v. Cawley saga had not yet ended, None of the £300 damages or the costs awarded to W.R. Fenton in a Belfast court in July, 1901, had been paid, Various means of recovering the said sum having failed, steps were taken in the Bankruptcy Court against Cawley. In January, 1902, he was adjudicated a bankrupt and a year later, in March, 1903, an order was made for the sale of Cawley's land, 25 acres in all, in addition to his dwelling house in Coolaney. The auction came off in July of that year, and, as there was no other bidder, Fenton was declared the purchaser of both land and house for £80. In a parting exchange after the auction, Cawley was overheard to remark to Fenton: *"You will find it as easy to evict my grandfather as to evict me."*[13]

True to his word, Calwey refused to be move on . Eventually, Fenton applied for an ejectment order at Ballymote Quarter Sessions in January, 1905. This was refused when it was disclosed that Cawley's wife, Esther, had a life interest in the property. This decision was appealed and the case was re-heard at the 1905 Summer Assizes. Judgement was deferred,[14] and it was not until March, 1906, that a final ruling was issued, namely, that Fenton's ejectment claim had been rejected with costs.[15] When news of the verdict reached Coolaney,

560

## THE CROWN SOLICITOR AND THE 'CONSPIRATORS'

there was much rejoicing.  Peter Cawley had scored a notable victory over his old antagonist !

*References :-*

(1)   McTernan, J.C. *"At the Foot of Knocknarea"* Sligo. 1990

(2)   *"Sligo Champion"*                      02 - 03 - 1901

(3)       ibid.                               18 - 03  - 1901

(4)       ibid.                               11 - 01 - 1901

(5)       ibid.                               09 - 03 - 1901

(6)       ibid.                               03 - 08 - 1901

(7)   *"Sligo Independent"*               04 - 01 - 1902

(8)   *"Sligo Champion"*                  04 - 01 - 1902

(9)       ibid.                               11 - 01 - 1902

(10)      ibid.                               25 - 02 - 1902

(11)      ibid.                               02 - 08 - 1902

(12)  *"Sligo Independent"*               06 - 06 - 1903

(13)  *"Sligo Champion"*                  11 - 07 - 1903

    Peter Cawley, Fenian, Land Leaguer, member of the United Irish League and close friend of P.A. McHugh, served on Sligo County Council from 1899 to 1920. He died a decade later in September, 1930.

(14)  *"Sligo Independent"*               14 - 07- 1905

(15)  *"Sligo Independent"*               10 - 03 - 1906

# The Town Clerkship Crux

In November, 1932, John Shea gave a month's notice of his intention to resign his position as Town Clerk of Sligo but agreed to act in a temporary position until a permanent appointment was made. He continued in this capacity until April, 1933, when he finally resigned for health reasons. The Borough Council, with the concurrence of the Minister for Local Government, then appointed Robert G. Bradshaw as Acting Town Clerk.

Robert George Bradshaw was born at Lismoylan, County Tipperary in June, 1885. He started life as a teacher in Norton's College in Dublin and, subsequently in Skerries College. During his years in the capital, he became actively involved in the National Movement and in 1919 became District Intelligence Officer of the I.R.A. in the Sligo area. He was interred for a period and on his release he became Managing Director of the West of Ireland Publishing Co. and Editor of *"The Connachtman"* newspaper, which was published in Stephen Street. After periods of imprisonment during both the Anglo-Irish War and the subsequent Civil War, he resumed teaching and opened a private school in Carney. In 1930 he was appointed Secretary to the Western Iron Company at Finisklin, a position he held until his appointment as Acting Town Clerk in April, 1933.

Following Shea's resignation the Corporation, in accordance with standard procedures, requested the Local Appointment's Commissioners to recommend three persons for appointment to the office of Town Clerk. On June 6th, 1933, the Commissioners notified the Corporation that, having interviewed all the applicants they were prepared to nominate one of the following: Séan O'hUigin, Accountant with Cavan County Council, Denis J. Harrington, Editor of *"Sligo Champion"* and Patrick Whooley, and requested the Corporation to arrange the names in the order of preference in which they desired to have them appointed, and to return same in that order so that the Commissioners might recommend the first of such persons who produced satisfactory evidence as to health.

At the meeting on June 7th, 1933, the Corporation unanimously passed the following Resolution:-

## THE TOWN CLERKSHIP CRUX

*"That this Council refuse to accept the names received from the Appointments Commissioners for the position of Town Clerk, and we hereby direct that same be returned to the Minister for Local Government and request him to have our Acting Town Clerk, R.G. Bradshaw, who was interviewed for the post, included in the list to be forwarded to this Council".*

A copy of this Resolution was forwarded to the Commissioners the following day. [1]

A month later, on July 4th, the Commissioners wrote to the Corporation stating that they recommended O'hUigin for the post. The following day the 'City Fathers' passed a resolution refusing to accept that recommendation and notified the Department accordingly. [2] There were no further developments for three months. On November 9th the Corporation were notified that unless O'hUigin was appointed within fourteen days, proceedings would be instituted to compel them to do so. On the 22nd of the month the Town Council passed a Resolution refusing to comply with the Minister's Order.

The Corporation meeting of November 22, 1933, was a prolonged and acrimonious affair in which politics and the clergy, the Knights of Columnbanus and the rights of minority religions figured prominently.[3] At the outset, the following letter from the Department was read:-

*"I am directed by the Minister for Local Government and Public Health to refer to the recommendation made by the Local Appointment's Commissioners on the 4th July last that Séan O'hUigin should be appointed to the vacant position of Town Clerk. The Minister understands that this recommendation has been before the Corporation at several subsequent meetings, but that so far the Corporation have not appointed Mr. O'hUigin. It is the duty of the Minister to remind the Corporation that the Local Authorities Officer's Employee's Act, 1926, is mandatory in its effect. Once a recommendation is made by the Local Appointment's Commissioners it is compulsory on the Corporation to make the appointment. No discretion is left to the Corporation, and the selected nominee must be appointed. The Minister is responsible to see that the provisions of the Act are fulfilled, and he has no option but to insist on the Corporation making the appointment without further delay. Unless, accordingly, the Corporation appoints Mr. O'hUigin within 14 days from the receipt of this letter the Minister will institute proceedings without further notice by way of mandamus to enforce the appointment, and a record of the decision of the Corporation, showing the*

563

## THE TOWN CLERKSHIP CRUX

*voting of the Councillors should be reported to the Minister immediately after the conclusion of the meeting. In the event of failure to make the appointment, it should be understood that the Councillors responsible will be made special defendants in the subsequent legal proceedings."*

In the course of the ensuing debate, Bradshaw, as Acting Town Clerk, informed the meeting that he was claiming permanent status on the grounds that he has been retained in the post at the behest of the Corporation and with the permission of the Minister after the term of the temporary appointment had expired and that the relevant Act did not give anyone the power to make a further temporary appointment. "Since June 2nd I have held, with your permission and equally with the permission of the Minister for Local government, the position of Town Clerk", he reminded the assembled Councillors . "If, up to that date I was holding it as a temporary appointment and my temporary appointment definitely had to cease on that date, and subsequently I held the position, then I submit that the only alternative in the holding of it is that it be permanent. Therefore, the Council has no right, without first dismissing me from the position, to make any other appointment to it...." [4]

Although faced with the dilemma of threatened *mandamus* proceedings by the Minister if they did not accept the recommended candidate on one hand, and by legal proceedings from the Acting Town Clerk should he be dismissed on the other, a majority of the Councillors remained firm in their determination to have no one but Bradshaw as Town Clerk on the basis that he was equally qualified, and "courteous and most efficient in the performance of his duties". "The people of Sligo, and the ratepayers of the Borough, are quite satisfied that he should remain in the post", declared Alderman Michael Nevin. After a long and at times heated debate the following Resolution, proposed by Alderman Nevin, and seconded by Cllr. Wm. F. Browne, was carried by 12 votes to 4:-

1. We are threatened on the one hand by the Minister for Local Government and Public Health with mandamus proceedings and on the other hand by legal proceedings by our Town Clerk, R.G. Bradshaw;
2. We are not satisfied that the Minister has any power to enforce the making of an appointment other than within a period of six months from the date of the vacancy occurring;

## THE TOWN CLERKSHIP CRUX

3. We are convinced, by reason of the admission of the Minister for Local Government, that representations were made to him prejudicial to Mr. Bradshaw's candidature, and that he (the Minister) was himself knowingly instrumental in transmitting to the Chairman of the Local Appointment's Commission a letter obviously containing such representations;

4. We are satisfied that the influence of the organisation known as the Knights of Columbanus was brought to bear on the appointment-making machinery in this case, and was thrown into the scale against the candidature of R.G. Bradshaw;

5. As we are satisfied that inasmuch as our present Town Clerk, R.G. Bradshaw, has given the Council for the past seven months the most capable and efficient service possible; the interest of the Corporation, as representing the citizens of Sligo, will be best served by his retention in office; we, the Corporation of Sligo, refuse to comply with the Minister's order as contained in the letter dated the 9th day of November, 1933, and we therefore instruct our solicitor, Mr. Derham, to defend the threatened legal proceedings."[5]

The hearing commenced in the High Court, Dublin, on April 11th, 1934, of an application on behalf of the Minister of Local Government and Public health to make absolute the conditional order of *mandamus*, granted on December 21st., 1933, against the Mayor, Aldermen and Burgesses of Sligo and against the following who were named as 'Special Defendants', namely, John Lynch (Mayor), Michael Nevin, Thomas Kavanagh, Patrick Fowley, James Kelly, John Gilmartin, Michael Kerrin, Wm. F. Browne and James Keaveney, all members of the Town Council. The order referred to commanded the Corporation to appoint Séan O'hUigin of Farnham Street, Cavan, to the position of Town Clerk of Sligo Corporation and this they had refused to do in the persons of the aforementioned Councillors. Before the Court were affidavits filed by a number of the 'Special Defendants' in which it had been repeatedly stressed that Bradshaw was a suitable person for the post; that suspicion was attached to the method of the selection of the three whose names had been recommended; that it was not a free choice and that objection had been taken by some clergymen and others in Sligo to Bradshaw. It was also claimed that the nominated candidates were members of the Knights of Columbanus and that it had been indicated to the Appointment's Commission that Bradshaw was an atheist and an 'undesirable' person.

565

Two prominent members of the 'Special Defendants'

Ald. John Lynch

Clr. James Keaveney

## THE TOWN CLERKSHIP CRUX

In the course of the hearing Counsel for the Minister read extracts from two of the affidavits, that of Mayor, John Lynch, and Alderman Nevin. In his statement the Mayor emphasised that he was more than anxious to see Bradshaw appointed to the office of Town Clerk for the simple reason that he had known him for up to twenty years. He knew him as a man of great ability, honest and upright in all his dealings, and, in his opinion, a man well suited to fill the Town Clerkship. The affidavit proceeded:-

*"I believe that it is the direct influence of the organisation known as the Order of Columbanus that has led to the exclusion of Bradshaw's name by the Appointment's Commissioners, both from the list of names submitted on 6th June 1933 and also from being appointed Town Clerk......I also believe that the said Commissioners and Selection Board did not act bonafide in excluding Mr. Bradshaw from their recommendations but acted under and by the influence of the Knights of Columbanus........"* [6]

James Geoghan, S.C. also read the affidavit of Alderman M. Nevin, in the course of which reference was made to a meeting that had taken place between the Minister of Local Government and Canon P.J. O'Beirne, Administrator, Sligo, during which the latter sought the assistance of the Minister in ensuring that the Bradshaw's name would not be recommended to the Town Council for appointment. He also stated that he had good reason to believe that Canon O'Beirne, as well as the three nominees selected by the Appointment's Commissioners, were all members of the Knights of Columbanus. Continuing, Nevin stated:- "R.G. Bradshaw has, since his appointment in April, 1933, carried out the duties of Acting Town Clerk to the entire satisfaction of the Town Council.....I am convinced that were it not for the intervention of the Knights of Columbanus and the resultant bias of the Local Appointment's Commissioners, the name of the said R.G. Bradshaw would have been included in the three sent down in June of that year, when, by an overwhelming majority, he would have been placed first by the Corporation for appointment......" At the conclusion of the two day hearing the Court made absolute the Conditional Order and directed that a peremptory order of *mandamus* be issued forthwith. [7]

The question of the Town Clerkship was left in abeyance until August 25th when a High Court Order in the form of a writ of

## THE TOWN CLERKSHIP CRUX

*mandamus* was served on the individual members of the Corporation directing them to appoint forthwith Séan O'hUigin to the position of Town Clerk.[8] Arising from this directive, the Town Clerkship *impasse* was further considered at a special meeting of the Corporation on October 10th, 1934, during which the responsibilities and liabilities of elected members were placed before them by the Council's legal adviser, S.H. Derham. In the course of the ensuing discussion there was divided opinions as to the best course of action and consideration was given to resignation *en block* rather than capitulate to an appointment they did not approve of. Although a handful of members were still prepared to back Bradshaw to the hilt, come what may, a majority, after much soul searching, reluctantly came to the conclusion that they had no alternative but to accept the candidate recommended by the Appointment's Commission, or otherwise be abolished and replaced by the Minister's nominee. Individually, they also faced a possible surcharge. "No action we can take here will alter the ultimate result", declared Clr. O'Connell. "The Department will have their way in the end and there is no earthly use whatever in continuing to oppose the Government in this matter". He then proposed the following Resolution:- *"That in compliance with the order of the High Court, this Corporation hereby appoints Mr. Séan O'Higgins as Town Clerk of Sligo on the terms of the advertisement and that he be asked to enter on his duties immediately the Local Government Department sanctions his appointment".* [9] After further debate, it was decided, by 16 votes to 6, to give effect to the order of *mandamus*. The Council's decision gave rise to a banner headline in the *"Sligo Champion"* :-

**"SLIGO CORPORATION CAPITULATES:  TOWN CLERKSHIP DISPUTE ENDED'.**

\*     \*     \*     \*     \*     \*

After a delay of some weeks, the new Town Clerk eventually took up duty on November 24th, 1934, and continued to act as such until he was dismissed from office by the Minister of Local Government in May, 1937. This action was taken when it was revealed,  in the Auditor's Report on the Corporation accounts for 1935-36, that the Town Clerk had mishandled certain monies contrary to regulations. The matter was considered at a meeting of the Corporation on May 21st. The Minister's action was not questioned and the Council proceeded,

## THE TOWN CLERKSHIP CRUX

without dissension, to appoint R.G. Bradshaw as temporary Town Clerk.[10] In due course, the post was advertised in the usual way and for a second time Bradshaw was an applicant. In January, 1938, he was appointed Town Clerk on the recommendation of the Local Appointment's Commission at a salary of £300 per annum.[11]

Thus ended the long-running disagreement between Sligo Corporation and the Department of Local Government, a controversary that had generated much bitterness locally, apart altogether from the costly litigation that the ratepayers of the Borough could ill afford. The final chapter in the saga was the publication, following the appointment of Bradshaw as Town Clerk, of a prepared Statement from a number of the 'Special Defendants', named in the *mandamus* proceedings of 1934, which read as follows:-

"Unquestionably, the appointment of R.G. Bradshaw as Town Clerk at this stage signifies a complete and remarkable somersault on the part of the powers that be (The Local Appointment's Commissioners, of course, included); whilst it is true that Mr. Bradshaw's appointment now is in itself a very clear and sufficient vindication of those who took a certain definite stand on behalf of his candidature, yet we must point out that belated vindication, no matter how highly gratifying it may be, is hardly a sufficient compensation for those of us who, by taking the stand in question, became victims of the influences which resulted in eight of the twelve 'Special Defendants' losing their Corporation seats in the election in the aftermath of the Court case, though we merely mention those developments to indicate the injury done to the reputations of the men concerned whilst the fact cannot be overlooked that one of the eight in question was not merely deprived of his well-merited place in public life but of his very means of livelihood as well."

"The whole trouble, bitterness and costly litigation arose because, in the first instance, the 'Special Defendants' had the hardihood to insist that Mr. Bradshaw, as a candidate for the Town Clerkship, should receive ordinary fair play, and because, further, they had dared to ask for an impartial inquiry into the circumstances by which it seemed that justice was being denied him."

"We have no wish to re-open old animosities, or to give offence to anybody, but now that the final outcome of the developments in regard to the Town Clerkship is such a clear vindication of the stand taken by the 'Special Defendants' as a whole, may we express the sincere hope that those in authority in certain spheres have taken to heart the valuable lesson we presume they have learned, and that people liable to jump to hasty conclusions will be fewer in Sligo in the time to come". [12]"

# THE TOWN CLERKSHIP CRUX

## Notes and References:

(1)  *"Sligo Champion"*                                          10-6-1933

(2)            ibid                                                       8-7-1933

Frank Carty, T.D. was instrumental in arranging a meeting between a deputation from Sligo, consisting of John Lynch (Mayor), Aldermen Nevin and Jinks, and Councillors Hunt and Kelly, and President De Valera, at which the impasse was discussed but no resolution was at hand. The independence and integrity of the Appointment's Commissioners had to be upheld and respected.

(3)  *"Sligo Champion"*                                          25-11-1933

(4)            ibid                                                       op. cit.

(5)            ibid                                                       op. cit.

(6)            ibid                                                       14-4-1934

(7)            ibid                                                       op. cit.

(8)            ibid                                                       1-9-1934

(9)            ibid                                                       13-10-1934

(10)          ibid                                                       22-5-1937

(11)          ibid                                                       22-1-1938

(12)          ibid                                                       29-1-1938

R.G. Bradshaw resigned as Town Clerk in June, 1950, having attained the age of 65. On his death in December 1951, many tributes were paid to him by his former comrades in arms, by the Mayor and members of Sligo Corporation, by the Committee of Feis Shligigh, etc. His mortal remains were laid to rest in an unmarked grave in Drumcliffe churchyard where an oration was delivered by the late Thomas McEvilly.

# Mining at Abbeytown

The earliest mining operations within the County, of which there is documented proof, took place at Abbeytown, Ballisodare, in the mid 18th century. However, it is possible that the mines were worked at a much earlier period by the monks in the adjoining Abbey, from which the townland derives its name. At this location the minerals galena and sphalerite (lead and zinc sulphide, respectively) occurred in flat-lying lenticular bands in the gently dipping limestone beds. According to local tradition, ore was extracted as long as there was sufficient timber available in the neighbourhood for smelting and discontinued only when this fuel was no longer available.

Over the past one and a half centuries several unsuccessful attempts were made to extract galena, otherwise lead and zinc ore, in sufficiently large quantities to make it a worthwhile undertaking. The source from which the limestone beds were mineralised is probably the great fault which cuts across the gneissic ridge, passing through Ballygawley Lake and forming the southern boundary of Ballisodare Bay. The old mine workings were situated on the side of a northwest sloping cliff of limestone which ended in a strip of reclaimed land on the southern edge of the Bay.

Charles O'Hara, the Elder, of Annaghmore, is credited with initiating mining operations at Abbeytown, and nearby Lugawarry,[1] in the mid 18th century. He brought over civil engineers and miners from England who commenced mining operations but without much success. In 1776 Arthur Young, a noted traveller, made the following entry in his diary: "Near Ballisodare is a lead mine but it is not worked with much success though very rich."[2] Two decades later in February, 1786, Sir Edward Crofton of Mote, who came into possession of Abbeytown by way of grant, exhibited a rich lump of lead ore from the Ballisodare mines at the Royal Exchange in Dublin in what was described as "an effort to encourage mining in Ireland"[3] For what length of time and with what success he operated the mines we know not. In all probability, the earlier workings were for the production of lead and silver, and zinc became important only with the introduction of modern processes for the separation of the ore. The earliest extant

## MINING AT ABBEYTOWN

description of the mines was penned by the French consul, Coquebert De Montbret who toured this region in May-June, 1791:

*"Near Ballisodare, at a place less than forty feet above sea level at low tide, are excavations from which lead - said to be very rich in silver (2 ounces per 1 cwt weight) has been taken. The mines are entirely on the surface, not having penetrated more than 20 feet. The ore is smelted on the spot and the mineral is crushed by a vertical millstone set in motion by a horse. Twenty tons are said to have been taken out last year. All the carpenter's wood used on the site for laths, etc., comes from the bogs where fir becomes as firm as rock. Just now the works have been closed down for six months... Over a period of years various entrepreneurs have ruined themselves by engaging in this enterprise."*[4]

Four decades later Samuel Lewis noted that the lead mines at Abbeytown, which yielded a considerable proportion of silver and had been worked some years earlier, had been abandoned.[5]

In 1806 Abbeytown, together with extensive properties elsewhere in the County, mostly rectoral tithes, passed by sale from Crofton to Henry C. Montgomery of Donegal.[6] Shortly afterwards he ran into severe financial difficulties, the lands were mortgaged and eventually sold by order of the Court of Chancery in 1842. Portion of the estate, namely, the lands of Abbeytown and Streamstown, were purchased for £2,100 by Thomas McManus who, in the document of sale, was described as a 'gentleman' and resided with his brother, David McManus, M.D. at an address at Baker Street, London. After McManus's death in April, 1865, Abbeytown passed to Michael and Margaret Mullarkey of Drummartin, executors of his Will. In 1872 the lands, consisting of 349 acres, were sold in the Landed Estates' Court to Messrs Middleton and Pollexfen, merchants and millers of Sligo and Ballisodare, for £8,310.[7]

Between 1806 and 1872, during the proprietorships of Messrs Montgomery, McManus and Mullarkey, in turn, the mines lay idle. However, soon after the enterprising local firm took possession, the senior partner, William Middleton, set about re-opening the mines. He sent specimens of the ore to England for analysis. Encouraged by the results, two borings, giving 4" cores, were made and an existing shaft deepened and ore struck at a depth of fifty eight feet. Furthermore, a new tunnel was driven more or less along the course of the ore from the face of the escarpment at the southern margin of Ballisodare Bay towards the shaft for a distance of sixty eight feet. The first bore gave unsatisfactory results as only thin veins of ore were encountered. The second bore uncovered a rich ore 6" thick, at a depth of over seventy feet. The ores occurred in irregular veins, the richest ore being found between a bed of coarse banded limestone and a dark compact bed of magnesium limestone. Evidence of the extensive workings carried out by Middleton were still visible on the site almost half a century later. At that stage, the shaft had filled-in at the surface owing to the collapse of the sub soil following the withdrawal of the timber from the first setts.

A few years later, in 1877-'78, the mines were surveyed by Edward T. Hardman of the Geological Survey. In a memoir subsequently published, he wrote:-

*"The galena contains a considerable amount of silver and the principal yield was from a bed of rich lead and zinc ore four to six inches in thickness. It was worked by means of a day level run southwards a short distance into the bank which slopes upwards from the shore of Ballisodare Bay. Some hundreds of tons of ore have been lately put out by Mr. Middleton..."*[8]

The mines lay unworked for four decades until 1914 when the British Ministry of Munitions spent £600 on prospecting at Abbeytown. In their investigations they found an abandoned shaft from earlier operations and, having secured the walls, boring was continued downwards with positive results, revealing a solid plate of metallic ore. Further borings brought to light the existence of a continuous bed of ore. The plates lay in parts on the felspathic limestone, up to two feet thick in the centre and thining off at the edges of a circle many yards wide to reappear again a few feet away. They also found much evidence of old workings where the ore had been removed leaving heaps of slag on the surface mixed with nuggets of discarded ore. The economic prospects of working the mine were considered not unfavourable.[9]

In 1917 Robert J. Kirwan, County Surveyor, headed a group who leased the mines and surrounding property from the Congested Districts' Board and worked it for three years. On average, every 300 tons of ore removed yielded 100 tons of metallic concentrates. A consignment sent to London for assay yielded 23% of metal, representing 18 tons of lead and 5 tons of zinc for every 100 tons of raw ore. The lead was found to contain, as valuable impurities, 22 ozs of silver per ton of lead and 5 dwt (= 5 penny weights) per ton of gold.[10]

# MINING AT ABBEYTOWN

Kirwan and his partners continued to operate the mines with varying success until 1921 when they were closed down once more. A decade later a British based company, headed by an engineer named, Thornton, recommenced operations but abandoned the undertaking within a year or so.

In the immediate aftermath of World War 2 lead was in very short supply and fetched a record price on the world market, rising from £25 a ton in 1940 to £97 by January, 1950. Prices of zinc had also mushroomed to £87 a ton. In these circumstances the disused mines at Abbeytown attracted the attention of prospectors. In March, 1949, a company known as the Abbeytown Mining Co. Ltd, with a nominal capital of £50,000, was formed to operate the Ballisodare mines. A year or so later the Johannesburg Consolidated Investment Co., a mining Finance House, became involved in the venture and exercised its option to purchase the lead and zinc deposits.[11] Initial prospecting revealed 125,000 tons of payable ore which was anticipated to result in the production of 100 tons of ore a day and the employment of sixty men. Up to-date equipment was installed and a large mill for crushing the ore was erected. Production commenced in late 1949.

Initially, the Company utilised 24,000 tons of dump material, containing 3% lead and 8% zinc which had been lying at the existing quarries from previous operations. The ore, after passing through crushing and refining plant, received further treatment before being conveyed by road to Sligo, whence it was shipped to the Belgian port of Antwerp. At the peak of operations between 280 and 300 tons of ore passed through the mill daily and 400 tons of concentrates were exported monthly.[12]

Meanwhile, following the decontrolling of the prices of lead and zinc in 1952-'53, prices had dropped to £83 a ton for lead and £68 for zinc. This downward trend continued over the following years while, at the same time, the known ore resources gradually became exhausted.[13] A comprehensive drilling operation failed to reveal the existence of minerals which could be worked on an economic basis, and this led to the final closure of the mines in September, 1961, and the laying-off of ninety employees.[13]

## MINING AT ABBEYTOWN

### Notes and References:

(1) At Lugawarry, about two miles S.W. of Abbeytown, there are remains of ancient workings of a lead-zinc deposit. Details of the expenditure incurred by Charles O'Hara between 1747 and 1752 in sinking shafts, etc. are contained in the *O'Hara Papers* (National Library: Microfilm N.2670). In 1951 prospecting by trenching and diamond-drilling was carried out on this deposit by the Abbeytown Mining Company.

(2) Young, Arthur. *"Tour in Ireland, 1776-79"*. Dublin. 1780.

(3) *"Town and Country Magazine"*, 1786.

(4) De Montbret, C. *'"Tour in Connaught,1791"*. In Jr. Galway Arch. Soc., 1977-78.

(5) Lewis, Samuel. *"Topographical Dictionary of Ireland"* London.1837       .

(6) Registry of Deeds.            Bk. 1806-582-339.

(7)        "        "        "                    Bk. 1872-I5-220.

(8) Geological Survey: *Explanatory Memoir*. Dublin. 1885.

(9) Hallisey, T. Unpublished G.S. Correspondence, 1934.

(10) *"Sligo Independent"*            9 - 3 - 1946

(11) *"Sligo Champion"*    15-4-I950   &    21- 10 - 1950

(I2)      ibid                        9 - 5 - 1953

(I3)      ibid                        6 - 9 - 1961

# CHEESE MAKING at Carrowgarry

Cheese making was introduced into County Sligo some sixty years ago by Violet Crichton *(nee* Jameson) of Carrowgarry, Beltra. Her enterprise was born in adversity. In the early Thirties, during the so-called 'Economic War', her husband, Dr. Brian Crichton, who owned and ran a 290-acre holding, changed his farming policy from cattle rearing, which was then in a very depressed state, to dairying. Being too far removed from Sligo to retail his milk there, he supplied butter to schools and cream in cartons to places as far apart as Dublin and Galway. This continued successfully until 1935 when a Government levy on butter made its production unprofitable for the private farmer. It was at that stage that Mrs. Crichton decided to move into cheese-making and develop it into a profitable industry. This she did with such success that the Carrowgarry brand shortly became one of the most prominent names in Ireland's 'natural' - as distinct from 'processed' - cheese industry. Under her guiding hand, and possessed of unbounded enthusiasm, a new industry was born.

Violet Crichton was first introduced to the art of cheese-making by Mrs. Dermot O'Brien as her home in Cahirmoyle, Limerick. Further lessons followed from no less proficient a teacher, Sister Lavelle, a French-Canadian nun who was involved in cheese making at Loughglynn Convent. She then spent a short period studying the technique in the Dairy Department of Reading University. On her return she went into the industry for herself. It was an uphill struggle for two years or so, with all the attendant disappointments, pit-falls and small triumphs inevitable in a pioneering situation. At first she was content to operate in a small way but gradually, with the surplus milk always available from the farm's herd of Dairy Shorthorn cows, things prospered. Initially, the daily output consisted of one 4-lb. Gouda made in a bucket. From there she progressed to a tub and from a tub to a vat. A dairy-maid was employed and an instructress came from Reading for a month. This marked the turning point in the struggle with production difficulties. Sister Lavelle was a fine cheese-maker, and the excellence of her results testified to knowledge derived from long experience and to highly developed and well trained senses of smell, taste and touch. Of modern scientific methods she knew nothing. From the Reading instructress Mrs. Crichton learned the uses of hot-iron tests and of an acidimeter. From such small beginnings the undertaking prospered.

With success came problems - at first she experienced difficulty in obtaining a licence, without which milk could not be purchased from outside suppliers; and when this was resolved the market suddenly experienced an influx of foreign cheeses against which it was difficult to compete. At that stage the enterprise was licensed to produce up to 10 tons of cheese a year, although circumstances conspired to prevent this figure ever being attained. The 200-gallon vat and other equipment was capable of producing $2\frac{1}{2}$ cwts of cheese a day; but, being in a creamery district, it was not permissible to purchase milk from the local co-operative creamery at Skreen. There was another setback when the dairymaid married. In her place an untrained local man, James McLoughlin, was employed. After a year's training, he was sent to Reading University for a course in cheese making. By a bit of well deserved good fortune, a liability was converted into an asset! McLoughlin proved to have a great natural aptitude - he had good judgement and took pride in his work.

How to make good cheese was not the only difficulty. How to sell it, when made, presented an even greater problem in the early days. Grocers disliked stocking dairy goods which required a quick sale. Despite this, Mrs. Crichton believed there existed enough discerning people who would buy her cheese if they knew of it. To publicise her product she sent samples here, there and everywhere. When the Government controlled the price of Cheddar, making it uneconomic for her to sell to the shops, she tried to sell it direct to the consumer by means of Press advertising. After two years her tenacity was rewarded and her market was established. The demand quickly outran the supply, and this happy state of affairs continued for some years. Output averaged five to six tons per annum.

The limestone lands of Carrowgarry were ideal for cheese-making, producing, as they did, a milk of the most suitable quality from which a variety of both hard and soft natural cheeses were produced. These included five hard cheeses - Cheddar, Cheshire, Caerphilly, Gouda and Wensleydale, and four soft - Cream, Gervais, Pont L'Eveque and Coulonniers. Initially, Gouda and Cheddar were sold in the shops at 8d and 9d a lb, respectively, and cream cheese at 6d a 4oz packet. Prices were always fluctuating up and down. In the'Forties, Cheddar was sold direct to the consumer at 1/6d plus postage, while Gouda and Caerphilly cost 2/- a lb in Messrs Blackwoods and other outlets in Sligo and elsewhere.

By the early 'Fifties there was no longer a large dairy herd at Carrowgarry. The milk came from a few cows and from neighbouring farms. While production was confined to such brands as Caerphilly, Pont L'Eveque and some Little Dutch cheeses, the quality maintained its old excellence. Unable to compete on the export market because of subsidies operating in Britain, the cheeses were marketed in Sligo, Dublin and Cork.

Violet Crichton was responsible for reviving a lost art in County Sligo. Her enterprise and enthusiasm together with the quality of her product won widespread acclaim.

---

### 'CARROWGARRY' (Regd.) CHEESE.

From September onwards,
" Carowgarry" Cheddar Cheese
WILL BE SOLD
### Direct from the Farm
at Controlled price
### 1/4 per lb.
(Postage extra).

---

Apply to
## MRS. CRICHTON,
Carrowgarry Dairy,
BELTRA. BALLISODARE,
Co. Sligo.

# The Light of Other Days

## An Escape From Justice

Shortly after the Famine year of '47, John Moffett of *Merville*, a noted lawyer in his day, leased the lands of Tonafortes, or Townafortis, alias Carroroe, to two brothers, Farrell and John Cogan. The former subsequently emigrated to America, leaving his brother in possession. John, who was a kinsman of Bernard O. Cogan of *Lisconny House,* for many years Sub-Sheriff of the County and Sheriff in 1852, was a Poor Law Rate Collector by occupation. At the time of the lease he was in comfortable circumstances but shortly afterwards fell on hard times and went into arrears of rent.

In 1851 Moffett sued Cogan and obtained a decree for £52. However, he subsequently failed in his efforts to have the debt discharged. A year later, in March 1852, he was obliged to take action. A warrant was obtained for Cogan's arrest. Its execution was entrusted to Alexander Burrows of Carrowcrin, County Coroner, as Moffett did not wish to embarrass Sheriff Cogan with the task. Burrows engaged the services of two men, Thomas Mannion and Thomas Gorevan, who were not recognised bailiffs but "persons of trust and good character", to execute the warrant.

At 10 a.m. on March 8th the two 'bailiffs' set out from Carrowcrin for Killadoon where John Cogan then resided. When they reached their destination they accosted Cogan on the roadway near his home and informed him of the nature of their errand. At first, Cogan resisted their combined efforts to take him into custody. He lay on the road, and being a man of great stature, the 'bailiffs' were unable to overcome his resistance. Realising that there was little prospect of succeeding in their task, Gorevan set off on foot to Riverstown to seek police assistance, leaving Mannion to keep an eye on Cogan.

At this stage, James McTernan of *Breffni Lodge*,[1] a man of 'high station' in the neighbourhood, came by on horseback. Having ascertained the purpose of the 'bailiff's' presence, he called Cogan

# THE LIGHT OF OTHER DAYS

aside and had a short conversation with him. They then parted company – McTernan apparently going about his business while Cogan made for his own house. After a short lapse of time the latter emerged dressed in a black overcoat. He intimated to Gorevan that he had changed his mind and was willing to go along with him peacefully.

They both proceeded at a slow pace in the direction of Heapstown crossroads. When they reached a point near to the entrance to McTernan's Lodge, a group of men suddenly emerged onto the roadway. Two of them grabbed hold of the 'bailiff' and pushed him aside thus allowing Cogan to disappear into McTernan's hallway. Once inside and the door firmly bolted, Cogan exchanged his overcoat for the light grey of Doherty, a servant in the McTernan household, and made his exit by the back door unnoticed by the 'bailiff' and others on the roadway. Shortly afterwards, Coroner Burrows, accompanied by Mannion, arrived on the scene. After a lapse of some minutes Burrows was invited into the Lodge only to discover that there was no trace of the prisoner. Despite the issue of a special warrant a few days later for Cogan's arrest, he managed to successfully elude his would-be captors.

John Moffett, a man determined to stand upon his rights and not to be out-manoeuvred easily, sought redress for the loss he had sustained. He took an action against James McTernan for "aiding and assisting in rescuing from custody John Cogan when under arrest at his suit", and claimed damages of £1,000. The case come before Justice Jackson and a special Jury at Sligo Assizes in March, 1853.[2] McTernan, who was interrogated at some length, denied that he had either aided or abetted Cogan's escape, although he conceded that his servant, Doherty, who had subsequently emigrated to America, "may have played some part in the affair".

After considering the evidence before them, the Jury failed to agree on a verdict and were discharged. The case came before the Assizes for a second time in July, 1853, and on that occasion the Jury, after an absence of two hours, returned a verdict in favour of the Plaintiff, Moffett. He was awarded 6d damages, together with 6d costs.[3]

While John Moffett may have gained some satisfaction in securing a verdict in his favour, the last laugh must surely have rested with Cogan and his 'allies' who successfully planned and executed what could be termed 'the Great Escape'.

THE LIGHT OF OTHER DAYS

## Notes & References

(1) James McTernan, J.P., of *Breffni Lodge*, Heapstown, was the son of Hugh McTernan of *Mount Allen*, who had purchased the lands of Ballycarne, commonly called the 'Commons of Heapstown', from Lord Dundas of York County. James was the first of the family to settle at Heapstown where he built a new family seat before his death in 1856. He was the author of a pamphlet entitled: *"An Address to my Fellow Countrymen"*, in which he claimed descent from Tiernan O'Rourke, Prince of Breffni.

(2) *"Sligo Chronicle"*                                    5 - 3 - 1853

(3)        ibid                                      23 - 7 - 1853

---

# A Family Affair

In December 1863 a Commission of Inquiry opened in Sligo for the purpose of establishing whether or not one Robert Ormsby, a Sub-Inspector of Constabulary and formerly of Farranmacfarrell, Dromore West, who died in 1849, had made a Will; and whether he had been born of parents in lawful wedlock. The position was that if he had made a Will his property or real estate would have descended to his next of kin. However, if , as had been alleged, Robert Ormsby had not been born in wedlock and had not made a Will, the property would fall to the Crown. The case excited much local interest and a special Jury was empanelled to decide the issue on the basis of the available evidence.

The history of this branch of a well known County Sligo family of the 18th and 19th centuries, dates back to the reign of Charles 11. when an ancestor was the recipient of an extensive grant of confiscated lands. In the late 18th century we find Philip Ormsby in possession of part of the lands of Chaffpool, known as Mullinabreena. On his death the property descended to his nephew, Thomas, son of George Ormsby.

Thomas Ormsby (1740-1823) resided for a time with his parents at Ballymeeny in the Parish of Easkey. There he met and subsequently married Eleanor or Ellen Scott, a servant girl of humble origin but possessing "great personal attraction". By her he had eight or possibly nine children, all but one of whom survived into adult life. The four sons, William, James, Robert and George were amply provided for. The

## THE LIGHT OF OTHER DAYS

eldest, William (1788-1854), gazetted a Lieutenant in the Templeboy Yeomanry in 1809, married his cousin, Hannah, daughter of John Rutledge of Corleen. The second son, James, held a commission in the 78th Regt. and was killed in action in 1814. Robert, the third son and the subject of the Inquiry, joined the Constabulary and rose to the position of Sub-Inspector for Co. Fermanagh. He died, unmarried, in 1849 and was buried in Mount Jerome Cemetery, Dublin. Two daughters of Thomas and Ellen Ormsby married well: Mary to William Mostyn and Ann to Bryan Furey of Ardnisbrack.

Thomas Ormsby was a gentleman of large fortune. Some years before the '98 Rebellion he moved with his family to a cottage at Farranmacfarrell and immediately proceeded to build a commodious house alongside which was completed in 1799. To mark the occasion he gave a house-warming party which was attended by the nobility of Tireragh, including representatives of the Crofton, Fenton, Hillas, Jones and Wood families. He died in November, 1823, but it was not until after the death of his third son, Robert, in 1849, that problems leading to litigation became public. Robert died possessed of much property, including the lands of Mullinabreena which were held by Major Richard Phibbs under a lease of lives renewable forever. After Robert's death, Phibbs refused to pay any more rent, alleging that no marriage had taken place between Thomas Ormsby and Ellen Scott; that all the children were illegitimate and that with Robert dying intestate, the property became escheated to the Crown.

No proceedings were taken by Major Phibbs to enforce the rent and the position remained unchanged when James Ormsby succeeded his father, William of Farranmacfarrell, in 1854. Nine years later, in 1863, a petition was presented to the Crown by James Leslie Rutledge Esq., claiming to be the owner of these estates through his grand-mother, Anne Ormsby, sister of Thomas Ormsby of Farranmacfarrell. A counter petition was subsequently presented by the afore-mentioned James Ormsby. The Crown then appointed Commissioners to hold an Inquiry to ascertain what estates Robert Ormsby was seized of at the time of his death; whether he was born in wedlock and, if not, who was his lawful kin.

At the Inquiry in Sligo Courthouse, which lasted six days, the Crown contended that, as there was no extant registry record of any marriage

## THE LIGHT OF OTHER DAYS

with Eleanor Scott, the declarations of deceased members of the family rebutted the presumption of law that the children were legitimate. A number of elderly female witnesses – Dodwell, Rutledge, Thompson and Trumble – all distant relatives of the Ormsbys, recalled that as youngsters they had over-heard discussions within the family circle concerning the illegitimate offspring of Thomas Ormsby, evidence which Counsel for the Petitioner, James Ormsby, described as nothing more than hearsay or concocted fairy-tales that lost nothing in the re-telling. For the Petitioner it was established that the Parish Church where the record of the marriage should have been, had been broken into during the '98 Rebellion and the registers burned or destroyed. Also produced in evidence were a number of family deeds, dating from 1783 and executed by Thomas Ormsby, in which he designated Eleanor Scott as his lawful wife. In one document - to which the name of Owen Wynne of Hazelwood was appended as Trustee – he spoke of his sons as "his beloved sons" and his wife as "his dearly beloved wife."

On the fifth day of the Inquiry, Bridget Stenson, *née* Ormsby, aged 76 years, and the only surviving child of Thomas and Eleanor Ormsby, was called to give evidence. Her testimony not only contradicted much of the hearsay and unsubstantiated testimony of those who would have benefited had the Crown case been upheld, but clearly established that not only were her parents married but that her mother had always been addressed as 'Mrs Ormsby' and as such shared in the social life enjoyed by her husband. Her evidence also corroborated other testimony which had been advanced proving the legitimacy of herself and her deceased brothers and sisters.

When the Commissioners and the respective Counsel had completed their submissions, the Jury retired and in less than half an hour returned the verdict that the deceased, Robert Ormsby, was born in lawful wedlock. "The decision of the Jury has been endorsed by public opinion, and has afforded widespread and unqualified satisfaction", commented the *Chronicle*.* "It seems only strange that twelve intelligent gentlemen of the County should be asked to affix a stain on a most respectable family over the mere whisper of reputation . . . Their verdict has met with almost universal approval".

---

\* *"Sligo Chronicle"* 9 - 1 - 1864

# Tom Soden - an 'exemplary' Provost

The Soden family settled in North Sligo in the mid 17th century as Grantees under the Cromwellian Settlement. Thomas Soden, the first settler, was described as 'Titulado of Grange' under the Commonwealth. His descendants intermarried with the leading County families, De Butts, Wynnes and Nicholsons, amongst others. In the 18th century especially, the Sodens of Moneygold occupied a prominent position in the County as Magistrates and High Sheriffs. Foremost in the affairs of the Borough at the turn of the century was Thomas Soden, who was Provost of Sligo for over thirty years, from 1785 to 1819. A colourful 'character' and the longest holder of the office, his memory, but more especially his actions, lived on long after he had passed to his eternal reward in January, 1819, aged seventy -five years.

"TOM SODEN! – Who in Sligo has not heard of that name? TOM SODEN! – Prince of Provosts, most glorious of Chief Magistrates!

TOM SODEN was elected Provost in the year 1785, which office he held up to 1819, when one who cannot be baffled put an end to his sovereign sway, – DEATH claimed his victim, and the victim had to yield. When in the fullness of his power, no man ever used it more unscrupulously – no man ever behaved in a more despotic manner. The ancient privilege of plundering the people, by exacting what they then called 'quarterage' was rigidly enforced by this worthy, who had a great respect for the law, particularly when it put money into his purse. When the Sligo Commissioners were established by the local Act, fines were inflicted for violating its provisions; those fines should have been accounted for, but, *unfortunately*, poor TOM'S memory was very imperfect, and he was subject to fits of abstraction; in fact, he could never recollect that any man ever paid him a halfpenny. But it is rather strange that he never forgot anything that was due to him.

TOM was – as a good Magistrate should be – very anxious for the regulation of the Town; accordingly, when his larder happened to be but poorly provided, he sent a message to the butchers that their stalls should be removed; and , on the following day, a quantity of tongues and rounds of beef might be seen in his kitchen; but, of course, this

## THE LIGHT OF OTHER DAYS

upright Magistrate could not tell who left them there! In fact, he procured both fish and flesh at a cheaper rate than any man in Sligo. But this was not all. TOM was particularly careful that no fraudulent oats should be exposed for sale, and, accordingly, whenever he found a sack which did not please him – for he was sole judge in the matter – it was confiscated, and the grain forthwith carried to his stable. It so happened that his horses were always in the best condition, a fact which proves that a virtuous man's cattle will flourish on the worst of feeding. Some people used to say that the confiscated grain was generally the best in the market; but this, of course, was a malicious calumny! On one occasion a countryman, who had his oats seized, had the measureless effrontery to assert that they were of a good quality, and actually kicked up a row in the Provost's office. TOM produced a large Bible, and, after making several mysterious signs over it, placed a bunch of keys on the cover, and asked him to swear upon it. The countryman, believing he had met with the devil, rushed out of the office, declaring that he would rather lose all he was worth in the world than have anything to do with the Provost, or his Bible and bunch of keys.

At this time the toll was exacted with the greatest severity; no article was allowed to come into Town – not even wearing apparel – without its being taxed. On one occasion TOM was asked to a Ball, and his nether garments not suiting his fancy, – they received a grievous rent during the day – he sent to his residence at Moneygold for another pair. It so happened that the toll collector did not know the messenger and stopped him with the 'inexpressibles'. In vain he explained who he was, and to whom the article belonged; but the 'dog in office' would not relent, and TOM had to remain at home, as he did not wish to appear before company in that primitive state.

In 1785 Soden erected shambles at the lower end of Knox's Street, between Quay Street and the Bridge, and ordered that all meat should be exposed for sale there, and there only, under a penalty of 10s. fine for every carcass found in any other part of the Town. Soden charged for every carcass of beef 1s 1d.; of mutton 3d.; of veal 3d. of swine 3d.; of lamb 2d.; and of kid 1d.. The butchers, however, refused to comply with the order; but friendly Burgesses on the Corporation, in order to get their good brother, Soden, out of the lurch and to procure for him

# THE LIGHT OF OTHER DAYS

some return for his expenditure, enticed the butchers to make use of the place provided for them, on the understanding that there would be no charge for the first half year, from November, 1785 to May, 1786. The records do not tell how the matter ended.

Whenever he wanted to raise the wind, TOM proambulated the Town, followed by two bailiffs, with sticks in their hands like drum-majors, and if any article was found outside of a shopkeeper's door, the offender received a polite invitation to appear before his Worship on the following morning, where he received a great deal of information about the necessity of keeping a Borough in a well-regulated state, for which, as a matter of course, he had to pay handsomely. One time he happened to see a large cask of valuable dye stuff at a door; the wind being high, the owner placed a sheet about it to prevent its being scattered through the streets while it was being removed into the shop. TOM happening to ride by at the time, pulled up and stood in amazement for some minutes; at last he gave expression to his feelings. 'I have visited,' quoth he, 'most corporate towns in the three kingdoms, but I protest to God such a piece of presumption as that I never before witnessed; let him be summoned.' The order was obeyed, and a fine imposed, because a man had the audacity of endeavouring to prevent his property from being destroyed. A thousand anecdotes of a similar kind could be repeated, all tending to show that TOM was not to be trifled with. One time a merchant remonstrated with him at the exorbitant toll charged upon a large quantity of wool. 'And so you are not satisfied', said the Provost. 'No.' 'Well, then, listen to me – if you do not pay what is demanded, on the spot, I will charge so much,' naming a sum about ten times greater than what was asked at first. This settled the matter. The money was paid with 'curses not loud but deep'.

TOM was fortunate; he did not outlive his power – he died in harness; and, although disease had so worn him out that he had to be carried on a hand-barrow to the office, he continued to go there to dispense justice. It happened that a man named Mathews was once brought before his Worship about some case now forgotten. TOM was hollow against him from the start, and quoted numerous imaginary authorities to support his view. Mathews at last, losing all patience, exclaimed, 'Oh, we will get law enough here, but if we want justice,we

THE LIGHT OF OTHER DAYS

must go elsewhere.' For uttering this truism he was allowed to amuse himself, the best way he could, for some days in Sligo Gaol. But he had his revenge. Happening to see TOM SODEN one day in the barrow – a vehicle in which maimed mendicants are carried about in this country – he approached and, with derisive sorrow, said – 'My poor fellow, I always knew it would come to this with you; here is some relief,' throwing a penny into his lap. This was a cruel jest, and his Worship felt it so keenly that shortly after he went 'the way of all flesh'– 'deeply and deservedly regretted by a numerous circle of friends and acquaintances'.

The legend runs, that Tom Soden still 're-visits the glimpses of the moon' in the shape of an old hare, and that he sports about the fort of Summerhill through the long winter nights. The grey buck has been often seen, but never caught; and if he be but half as cunning as Tom was while in the land of the living, we venture to predict that no 'puppy, whelp or hound' will ever catch him napping".

[Extract from series , entitled **'Corporation of Sligo'**
*'Sligo Champion'*, 1843-44.]

Moneygold House c. 1900.

# Rumours Upset Peaceful Town

In the mid 19th century the town of Coolaney bore all the appearance of harmony and tranquility. Some years earlier the inhabitants had been much annoyed by 'Soupers' but that phase had passed and by the 1860's the most kindly feelings existed between Catholics and Protestants. A local resident depicted the peaceful scene as follows ;-

" . . . *The Protestants never fail to salute Very Revd. Luke Hannan, the Parish Priest, whenever they meet him; and they are known to refrain from smoking, even at a fair, when he was seen approaching. In fact, his own parishioners are not more respectful to him. Indeed, its no wonder at the respect shown by them to the Revd. Gentleman, as they know well that he is most anxious that friendly feeling should exist between the people, irrespective of creed, and that he avails himself of every opportunity to foster peace and goodwill . . . Likewise, Catholics are in the most friendly terms with Archdeacon Townsend, the Protestant Rector. They do not hesitate to ask him for the loan of a harrow, or spade, or other agricultural implement, and he never refuses them . . . Every right-minded man would deplore any circumstance calculated to cause a breach of such harmony . . .*"

Domiciled in Coolaney at that time was one Samuel Withers who acted in the double capacity of sexton at Rathbarron church and gatekeeper; he was also an ex-policeman with a pension of £25 per annum. According to an acquaintance, he had "all the cut of a 'Souper', stood about five feet ten inches in height, appeared to be close to sixty years of age,very pert and forward and formerly resided in Partry."

It appears that Withers had a good deal of time on his hands and one could well believe that it 'hung heavy' in such a quiet place as Coolaney. Be that as it may, on the Sabbath night of the 22nd of May, 1864, after enjoying himself in the company of some friends, he walked abroad and this is what he witnessed near the 'witching hour', according to a statement he made, and which was subsequently read in court by Sub-Constable Kelly : "On the night of Sunday, the 22nd instant, about twenty minutes to twelve o'clock a man named Samuel Withers, a police pensioner, came to the Barracks and reported that he saw four men on the public road at Rathbarron, three of them having

## THE LIGHT OF OTHER DAYS

firearms". But that was not all ! Given the armed men, he at once concluded that these men were about to shoot Archdeacon Townsend, St George Jones Martin of Cultibar and Meredith Thompson of Knockadoo, all Protestants.*

On receipt of Wither's report, Constable Kelly and two of his colleagues, made all possible haste to the place but could see nothing. They then patrolled the different townlands and by-roads adjoining, but could see no one. They also made inquiries of Daniel Thornton and Pat Davey, two of the Venerable Archdeacon Townsend's men, who were on the road about the same time, and they stated they saw no person, nor could they be on the road unknown to them. Sub-constable Kelly also swore that he made inquiries of a woman named Clark, who, along with her husband, was spending the evening with Withers, and was on the road with him a few minutes previous to his report, and she stated she neither heard nor saw any persons!

When these allegations came under investigation at the local Petty Sessions in June, 1864, Withers was sworn-in and examined by the Resident Magistrate, P. C. Howley. He re-stated his case as follows:-

"On Saturday night, the 22nd of May, I attended one of the Archdeacon's meetings. After that, I went to spend part of the evening with Mr Clark and his wife and left there about half past ten. My wife accompanied me. On my way home I met two men first and they had guns; it was at the Archdeacon's demesne I met them and they were going in the direction of his house. Then, I met a third man but he had not a gun. I then said to my wife : *'Did you see guns with the men that passed by ' ? and she replied 'I did not see any guns with them. I then said to her: 'Watch this other fellow coming up now and see has he a gun'. A fourth man come up then and my wife said: 'that man has a gun'.* I saw a gun with the fourth man myself. I then went into my house for a stick, as I was determined to follow them to see what they were about. When I was in the house my wife barred the door, and when I told her to open it she

---

* **St. George Jones Martin,** Chairman of the Tubbercurry Poor Law Guardians and Agent for the Ormsby-Gore Estate, resided for some years in *Cultibar House.* In 1865 he was appointed Secretary to the Co. Sligo Grand Jury and went to reside in Sligo where he died in October, 1875.

**Captain Meredith Thompson J.P.,** nephew of Meredith Thompson of Knockadoo, Co. Coroner for many years, served in the 6th Lancashire Regt, as a young man. He succeeded his uncle in 1855 to an estate of 1,380 acres and married Frances, the daughter of Cornelius Keogh of Geevagh. On his death in November , 1876, he was described as a "hospitable and general Irish gentleman, a good landlord and an impartial Magistrate'.

began moping about the bolt and took a long time to open it. I then went out and began to walk very quick after them, when I heard a footstep behind me, and I waited. It was my wife and she said she would go along with me. I then went down to Plunket's and asked a young girl if the Archdeacon had come home; she said he did not. I did not see any man on the road when I went out the second time. I thought they might meddle with Captain Thompson, Mr. Martin or the Archdeacon."

In cross-examination, Withers stood by his statement but conceded that he had no particular reason for believing that the three armed men were going to shoot Archdeacon Townsend, and he could not give any reason for not thinking it was the Parish Priest they had in mind. Significantly, Wither's wife was not produced in court to corroborate the testimony of her spouse. Wither's evidence was flatly contradicted by that of the police and a number of civilians. Having listened to the various statements the presiding Magistrate announced the verdict of the Court :-

*"We consider it very doubtful whether there were three armed men on the road or not; and are of the opinion that if such was the case, Constable Withers acted imprudently in reporting they were there for an illegal purpose, and to have given the names of three gentlemen to the Constabulary as likely to have been the persons they intended to injure . . . His conduct was most imprudent and improper as it was calculated to cast odium and disgrace upon a quiet and inoffensive people . . . "*

As might be expected, the good people of Coolaney were indignant that such a charge should be brought against their peaceable town.

---

# The Last Occupants Of Coolmeen

Terence MacDonagh of Creevagh, Kilmactranny, was one of the most distinguished and versatile Irishmen of the 17th century. He studied law and became a prominent legal advocate, As the only Catholic Counsel admitted to the Irish Bar, he was widely known as *'The Great Counsellor'*. During his lifetime Creevagh became a sanctuary

## THE LIGHT OF OTHER DAYS

for the hunted Catholic clergy. Turlough O'Carolan, the last of the great harpers, was also a regular guest. MacDonagh married Elinor O'Rorke and died childless in May, 1713.

After his death MacDonagh's landed possessions passed to the collateral line of the family.[1] The principal beneficiaries were his sister, Margaret Garvey of Ballygarvey, Co . Mayo, and nephews Remigus O'Hara of Curry and Denis O'Rorke of Chaffpool, being the sons and heirs-at-law of his other two sisters who had predeceased him. O'Hara was succeeded in his third share by two daughters who became entitled to a sixth of the property. The older of the two, Conly, married Brian MacDonagh of Carricknagrip, Kilmactranny. The sons of this marriage were John, who died unmarried, and Augustine, The latter's grand-daughters, the children of Terence MacDonagh and Jane McDermot, were the last resident part-owners of the Great Counsellors' estates.

The spinster sisters, Annie, Mary and Elizabeth MacDonagh resided at Coolmeen, a large two-storey thatched house standing on a small demesne of sixty acres, down to the last quarter of the 19th century. This kindly trio lived in genteel poverty on a meagre rental[2] and refused many offers of marriage both from rustics of their own creed and local squireens who professed a different religion. Their older brother, Brian, went abroad, while John studied medicine and qualified as a surgeon. In 1864 Brian broke the entail on the property by off-setting a legacy due to Annie MacDonagh and her sisters from a cousin against a mortgage on the property given by Brian to his uncle. In accordance with the terms of this Deed the MacDonagh sisters became the sole owners of Coolmeen as well as lands in Leyney and Bohola, in all 530 acres, or thereabouts. However,due to outstanding incumbrances, the old ladies slid gradually into a state of impoverishment; and, in 1876, their position worsened with the death, unmarried, of brother Brian, who, during his lifetime, had assisted them in their periods of want.

The deaths of the three MacDonagh sisters have been duly recorded. Mary, described as "the daughter of a gentleman", died in April, 1877, aged 60, and Anne, "a lady", in December of the following year, aged 86, leaving Elizabeth to fend for herself as the last occupant of *Coolmeen House*. Owing to her advancing years, the collection of rents became increasingly difficult and, on the suggestion of - if not the

## The Light of Other Days

expressed direction - of her brother, John, a successful surgeon in Surrey, Messrs R.D. Robinson, Estate Agents, Sligo, were assigned the task of collecting rents on both his and his sister's properties. Elizabeth MacDonagh lived to the ripe old age of 90 and died in May, 1883.

In sharp contrast with the considerate and sympathetic approach of his sisters,and at times their total disregard of pursuing long outstanding rent arrears, Surgeon MacDonagh showed little or no regard for the distress and hardship being experienced by his tenants in Ireland. This attitude is clearly exemplified in the following letter, addressed from Surrey to Messrs Robinson and dated February 8th, 1879 :-

*Dear Sir*

*I am very pleased to have received your reply to my letter, and I place the following in your hands and hope you will do the best you can for me.*

*Lisakill, a townland adjoining Coolmeen, my family residence, was allowed to run into arrears of rent owing to my late sister's (Annie) illness and a desire on my sisters' part to be as lenient as possible- (too much so).*

*In addition to this they all owe the November rent and will soon owe the May one, if allowed. They are all insolvent and have impoverished the lands, and they cannot get out of it anything like food and clothing. Therefore, I entreat of you to proceed, at once, against them in as inexpensive way as possible and, if you do not get the rent now owing, evict them without delay and do not let them till the lands next Spring. I would prefer getting the lands, so as to let them as grass-lands, for in this way I would be sure of getting the rents punctually at nearly double the rent they pay. I have let the greater part of the lands of Coolmeen as grass-land, and I find no trouble in getting a very high rent-nearly £3 5s. an acre. "*

*Sincerely,*

*John MacDonagh.*

John Mac Donagh died at Clampham, Surrey, in January, 1886, aged 86. In his Will, dated 1881, he bequeathed his several freehold lands and hereditaments - namely, Coolmeen, in the occupation of Devine and others: Lisakill, occupied by White and others; Drumbane, Cully, Corray and Kincuillew in Leyney and Carrowkeel in Mayo, - to his son-in -law, Frederick Betts of Surrey, and daughters, Catherine Jane Betts

## THE LIGHT OF OTHER DAYS

and Anna Emily Mills, in trust for the benefit of his children. Rents, issues and profits from same were to be paid to his sister, Elizabeth, during her lifetime. After her death each of his children - sons John, William and Bernard, and daughters Anna, Catherine and Elizabeth, were to receive £100 each, with the lands, etc. passing to his eldest son, Augustus William, and in turn to his son or sons. In a codicil, dated 1883, he directed that he be buried in the family vault in Ballindoon Abbey. Fitzmaurice Devine of Ballyfarnon was appointed to act as executor for the purpose of carrying out his wishes in this respect and was to be reimbursed for any expenses incurred.[3]

Augustus William MacDonagh, eldest son of the London-based surgeon, died at Hastings, unmarried and intestate, in February, 1929, aged 88. A decade or so before his death he sold the tenanted portion of Coolmeen to the Congested Districts Board. His nephew, Alfred John Betts of Kent, son of Frederick Betts and his wife, Catherine MacDonagh, was appointed to administer for what remained of his family's estates in Sligo and Mayo.

### Notes and References:-

(1) Registry of Deeds : 1726 Bk 49. P.322

(2) In 1855 the MacDonagh sisters had a demesne of 66 acres at Coolmeen, in addition to 100 acres let to six tenants – Conlon, Lavin, McTernan, Mullaney and Sweeney, A further 260 acres at Ballinlig was leased by their brother, John. By 1878 the combined rentals payable to the sisters was in the region of £30 p.a.

(3) Will of John MacDonagh. [*Ms.* Somerset House].

#### Also Consulted:

Mac Donagh, J.C. *"Counsellor Terence MacDonagh . . . " "Studies"*, 1947/48.

McTernan, J.C. *"Worthies of Sligo"*. Avena Publications, 1994

*MacDonagh Rentals* [Sligo Co. Library]

# A Process - Server on his Rounds

"Not within living memory was there witnessed such a scene of wild excitement as that witnessed in Tubbercurry on Monday evening last, when about 2,000 men rushed into Town after an escort which was protecting Phibbs and his process-server. During the day there was an unusual stir in the Town, owing to the fact that Charles Phibbs, J.P. of *Doobeg House*, had set off that morning at the head of sixty police to assist Brett, the district process-server, in serving processes on his estate. A move such as this had been expected for the past week. About ten days ago Brett attempted to serve the processes but failed. Since then crowds of men and women kept vigil on the hillsides all day long, looking out for the process-server. At length it leaked out that he had applied for a strong escort, and that the landlord himself was to take the field in command.

This Mr. Phibbs lives about three miles from Tubbercurry, in the direction of Doocastle. He is a hate importation with which fate has blessed this part of the country. He is a member of that pious brotherhood who don't cook their dinners on Sunday, and from Chancery Attorney he has turned country gentleman and a Justice of the Peace. His advent to this locality was heralded by an iron hut which, with its five policemen, was quickly put in place to protect Phibbs of Doobeg. The presence of the hut was felt to be an outrage on the peaceable character of the locality. Through the exertions of the priests and gentry of the district it was soon removed, and Phibbs was left to the shelter of his frieze coat and his bushy beard.

The lands which this gentleman happens to own in this area are Eskragh and Tullinaglug, in the parish of Kilmactigue,and Mullaun in the parish of Cloonacool. The two former consist almost entirely of reclaimed bog of the very worst kind. They are about two miles from Tubbercurry on the Aclare side, and are separated from each other by strips of swamp, which scarcely afford footing for snipe,and which give a good notion of what Eskragh and Tullinaglug were before the poor serfs, who call Phibbs their landlord, reclaimed them. Compared with the thriving estate of Lord Harlech, which stretches beside them, with its substantial houses and comfortable looking peasantry, the land and people of Tullinaglug make a sorry picture. The half naked tenants

## The Light of Other Days

present a pale and ill-fed appearance, while their wretched houses, black, damp and badly thatched, are fast sinking into the mud. Though living in the midst of a bog, they have no turf, and neither crops nor cattle can be raised on such a hungry soil. The rents at any time are excessive - far beyond the means of the tenants or the value of the land, yet, even in this desperate year, they are willing to pay them if any reasonable abatements were allowed. To-day, amidst all the terrorism of processes, police and bayonets, they reminded him of the swampy soil on which he was endeavouring to pick his steps; they pointed out the misery that was written in themselves and their houses, and in pityful tones appealed to him to allow them 20 or 25% , and they would gladly pay him the rents due. But not a word of sympathy was offered. Not a penny would by allowed.

When I visited the scene of the process-serving to-day, the sight was wild and exciting to the last degree. About sixty policemen with fixed bayonets, under the command of Sub-Inspector, M'Lelland, marched from house to house with Brett by their side. At their head, complete with great frieze coat and thick shoes, trudged Phibbs himself, with countenance dogged and sullen, while round about swarmed 2,000 men, women and children, shouting and hooting, but showing no sign of violence or resistance. The guiding spirit of the party was the notorious Lewis Golden, sheriff's bailiff, summon's server, etc, who pointed out the individual houses to the process-server. It appears that Stenson, who is Phibbs's bailiff in the area, did take the field in the morning, but alarmed at the attitude of the people, after walking a few houses, he refused to continue.

As already indicated, except mere groaning, the people showed no sign of resistance. The doors in almost every case were closed. When the process-server advanced to place the process under the door, a few women crowded round and the party moved on. This was the form of procedure during the day. Yet, this peaceable bearing did not prevent the police from making free use of their bayonets. From what I saw, I must say that in the circumstances the police showed as blood-thirsty a disposition as any body of men could evince. Close to where I stood I noticed men bleeding and torn by bayonet wounds in every part of the body. One man was literally covered with blood from wounds on the face. Even weak women were not spared. A little girl, named Stenson,

# THE LIGHT OF OTHER DAYS

was knocked down senseless, and a poor woman named Mary Walsh, on the eve of her confinement, was stunned by a blow from the butt end of a policeman's musket, and remained unconscious for a time. I was told that even Brett, the process-server, encouraged by the bravery of the manly peelers, ventured to use his blackthorn on some defenceless women who were not expeditious enough in getting out of his way. All this was done under the eye of the J.P. who holds Her Majesty's Commission of the Peace of the County. It was done by the very men who are paid by the people to protect them, and done, though there was not the slightest breach of the peace, nor a stick nor stone raised against the police throughout the day.

After the processes were served, the whole party returned to the Town. Phibbs, guarded by three policemen, drove through the streets amidst the groans and curses of the bystanders. The rest of the escort followed, closely pursued by over 2,000 stalworth peasants, marching four deep, and hooting and shouting loudly. The scene, as that mighty procession swept through, baffles description. Those who witnessed it will not soon forget the terror and suspense of that hour. It only wanted that some daring spirit would give the word, and not a vestige of a policeman would be left in the place. Had that collision taken place, who would be responsible for the ensuing disaster? Assuredly, the man whose unfeeling nature brought it on, and who might easily have averted all the excitement and disturbance that has taken place, by imitating the generosity of the neighbouring landlords.

It is said that the drama of Tullinaglug will be enacted at Mullaun to-morrow, and that Sub-Inspector M'Lelland has already telegraphed for further reinforcements. We hope that, in the trying ordeal, the people there will imitate the forbearance of their neighbours, and not give the peelers the opportunity of cutting them down, which they seem so bent on doing at the slightest provocation".

*"Sligo Champion"* 10 - 1 - 1880

# Peter O'Connor's Will

Peter O'Connor of *Cairnsfoot House* was one of the principal 'Merchant Princes' in 19th century Sligo, as well as being one of the wealthiest. Born in 1803, he was the youngest son of Denis O'Conor of Edenbawn. Following the death of his brother, Patrick, of cholera, in 1832, Peter assumed the management of the extensive family business concerns – that of merchant, ship owner and importer.*

In 1848 he married Ellen, daughter of Timothy O'Connor of Sligo, and by her had one child, Mary Ellen, who died in 1872, aged 21. By then Peter had retired from active participation in mercantile affairs and had handed over the management of his business concerns to his nephews – James O'Connor of *Ballyglass* and Simon Cullen of *Thornhill.*

Throughout his life he was a generous benefactor of the poor and needy, and he made large donations to the building fund of Sligo Cathedral, whenever the coffers ran dry. He enjoyed a long retirement, living to the ripe old age of 91. He died at his residence on August 29th, 1893.

In his Will, dated April, 1890, he directed that he be buried in his vault in Sligo cemetery, together with his wife, Ellen, and daughter, Mary Ellen. The only other person to be interred there was Alicia Carroll, governess and companion to his daughter.

He bequeathed to his wife, for the term of her life, an annuity of £300 to be paid in two half yearly instalments; also his interest in their residence, *Cairnsfoot House,* with use of furniture, plate, books, carriages, horses and other effects during her life. Within six months of her death all was to be sold and the proceeds thereof to be converted into Government securities, the interest thereon to be paid and applied to aid St. Laurence's Industrial School, Sligo, under the care of the Sisters of Mercy. He also bequeathed to the said Sisters an annuity of £10 for a period of twenty years, to be appropriated by them for "the relief of the poor respectable householders of Sligo" whom they find on their visits most in need. For the provision of fuel and clothing for the destitute labouring classes in Sligo during the winter months, irrespective of religion, he bequeathed the interest accruing

---

\* He also owned 5,000 acres in various parts of the County which in 1870 was yielding an annual rental of £2,700

## THE LIGHT OF OTHER DAYS

for twenty years from his investment of £1,200 in Sligo Harbour debentures. He also made provision for:

* The establishment of an Industrial School for poor orphan male children of the Town;
* The payment of an annuity for twenty years towards the upkeep of Forthill School, also the two schools on Albert Road and the schools at Carraroe, Crossboy and Doonflin;
* £200 towards debt on St. Mary's Presbytery;
* £500 to Bishop Gillooly for charitable purposes in Sligo.

Members of his extended family were the principal beneficiaries:

* To his nephew, James O'Connor of Ballyglass, bonds valued at £2,000 as dowries in equal shares for his four daughters; and a further bond, valued at £1,000, to be divided equally between his sons, Patrick and James, to establish them in business or in a profession;
* To his nephew, Patrick O'Connor of Edenbawn, £600 to make provision for his two unmarried daughters, Dora and Tilly; to his son, Patrick, £300 for his education as a priest;
* To his nephew, Simon Cullen, £1,000, namely, £500 each to his sons, Peter Paul and Joseph. Also £500 to make provision for his daughter's education;
* To his nephew, Peter O'Connor of San Jose, California, the sum of £1,000 to make provision for his children;
* To his grand-nephew, John Mulhall, the sum of £500;
* To his grand-nephew, George Kelly, Barrister, the sum of £300;
* To his niece, Ellen McCarrick, wife of Roger McCarrick, £3,500– "free from the control of her husband or his liabilities" – for the provision of her unmarried daughters and sons.
* Annuities, varying from £10 to £100, were willed to his nieces – Anna Mulhall, Ellen Martin, Alicia Carroll, Elizabeth Harkan, Anna McGovern, Mary O'Connor, Matilda Kelly, Anne Kilgallon, Bridget Feehily, also to the widow of Denis O'Conor, his late nephew.
* He willed his clerk, James Kilgallon, £500 'to assist him in business'.

The destitute and less fortunate in society were not overlooked. "I direct that £20 be applied in supplying a supper to the sick inmates and children in the Sligo Workhouse on the 17th of March each year... I direct that £20 be distributed to the poor on the day of my interment." He allowed £100 towards his funeral expenses and £50 to the Revd. gentlemen who attended the month's mind. He appointed his nephew, Simon Cullen, and grand-nephew, John Mulhall, executors of his Will.

The O'Connor Mausoleum, Sligo Cemetery

## Simon Takes a Bow!

Peter O'Connor retired from active business in 1866, and handed over the management of his thriving business concerns to his nephews, James O'Connor and Simon Cullen.

Simon Cullen was born at Morerah, in the Parish of Drumlease, in 1830. He was the son of Simon, sen., and Ellen O'Connor of Edenbawn. As a young man he travelled widely in the United States and Canada, regularly crossing the Atlantic in the O'Connor owned barques. He later married Mary, the daughter of John Tucker of *Springfield House.*

As co-manager of the long established O'Connor firm, he quickly came into prominence locally and, in time, filled the post of High

## THE LIGHT OF OTHER DAYS

Sheriff, was a Magistrate of the County, Chairman of the Harbour Board, etc. An acquaintance remembered him as a keen and hard-working executive:–

*"He lived at Thornhill and kept there the keys of the business premises in his care. The Old Market Street shops and stores and the George's Street mills, timber and slate yards opened at seven in the morning. The youngest apprentice, who slept in Old Market Street, had to be out at Thornhill, summer and winter, in time to get the keys for opening to the minute. Woe to any heavy-eyed youngster who delayed. He was apt to meet the 'Boss' – armed always with an umbrella – bringing in the keys himself, and was more than lucky if he did not get a a couple of vicious prods of the umbrella together with the inevitable lecture... I often met him on the Quays in the early morning and overheard him regularly, inquire – in the clipped and precise voice he affected: Any arrivals? Any arrivals?"*

In 1892 Simon Cullen made the headlines in the local Press, but not all the publicity was complimentary. In June of that year a Unionist Convention took place in the Town Hall and attracted a large crowd, described as – 'Landed Proprietors, Bog Rangers, Bailiffs and Sub-Agents' from the various estates within the County. The gospel of Unionism was proclaimed by Colonel Campbell, Colonel Ffolliott, Major O'Hara, R.A. Duke, Henry Lyons, amongst others. A number of active Northern Unionists also attended but, in the words of the *'Sligo Champion'*, the real 'lion' of the occasion was Simon Cullen, the only Catholic present. The *'Champion'* leader writer was by no means impressed by Cullen's attendance and castigated him in no uncertain manner for his apparent conversion to Unionism:*

*"My, my, what a furore did our Simon create! Balfour himself could not have been received with greater enthusiasm. When he entered, the audience stood to their feet in one accord and cheered frantically. hats were waved wildly. Even a number of ladies on the platform became infected with all the entusiasm and waved their rose scented handkerchiefs... Simon, with one hand on his heart and another grasping a chair, bowed his acknowledgments with the grace of Chesterfield and the aplomb of a J.L. O'Toole. Under the cool exterior, however, it was evident there lay hidden fires. The classic finely chisselled lips waved gently in the breeze, the proud breast heaved tumultously, and a sharp ear might have heard the murmur... 'Oh! how I wish my Granny could see me now'..."*

Later on, when the 'Great Man' went to the platform to speak in

# THE LIGHT OF OTHER DAYS

support of a Resolution, the scene was repeated – the cheers being given with greater volume and intensity.

*"It was a proud moment and Mr. Cullen must have felt it was ample compensation for the scorn and detestation with which the people on whom he lived and thrived regarded his action,"* commented the *"Champion"*.

*"Has he forgotten the days when in the ancestral home of the Cullens on Morerah Hill it used to be a subject of eager debate amongst the family where the next meal was to come from – or what neighbour's turnip field, or stirabout pot, a foray should be made upon! Ah no! as he stood there the cynosure of all eyes, Simon was oblivious to all and everything except this proud moment!"*

In a short address to the assembled Unionists, he thanked them for the warmth of their greetings, and stated that, by his presence, he was only emulating the good example set to him by the Catholic nobility elsewhere. When Simon resumed his seat, Revd. Ledoux, Rector of Calry, voiced his pleasure at seeing such a distinguished and representative Roman Catholic present and took it as a good omen of success.

When news of Cullen's attendance at the Unionist Convention filtered out, it quickly spread throughout the Town. Disapproval was widespread. In the space of a few hours a protest parade was organised. The Town Band turned out and paraded the streets followed by a crowd carrying an effigy of Simon Cullen, said to have borne a striking resemblance to the original – tall hat, umbrella and all. As the procession progressed large numbers joined in and it continued to swell until it reached close on the five thousand mark. After parading for an hour or so the effigy was taken to Harmony Hill where, while the Band played the *Dead March*, it was set alight and was soon burning merrily.

The crowd afterwards dispersed quietly and the Town resumed its normal quietness. All the while, Simon Cullen snored contentedly in his comfortable bed at Thornhill–oblivious to the excitement and furore his attendance at the Unionist Convention was causing to the citizens of his adopted Town.

\* *"Sligo Champion" 25-6-1892*

# Sole Fishing Rights

In May, 1935 judgement was delivered in the High Court in favour of Edward Francis P. Cooper of *Markree Castle*, Collooney, the plaintiff, in an action against John Boyd of Dunmoran, Skreen, and five other fishermen. The action was brought for a declaration that a several fishery in the Bay of Ballisodare, belonged to the plaintiff, and an injunction to restrain the defendant fishermen from trespassing on it. The plaintiff relied on deeds of lease and release going back to the year 1806 and to an Act of the British Parliament, passed on 30th June, 1837, in support of his claim.

The defendant fishermen began fishing in the Ballisodare estuary in June, 1934, claiming a right to do so by reason of the fact that there was a public right of fishing in tidal waters.

In the course of his judgement, Mr Justice Johnston said that the predecessors of Edward Francis Cooper, the plaintiff, were, at the beginning of the nineteenth century, the owners of considerable landed property in County Sligo and, in 1806, Joshua Edward Cooper acquired in fee from Sir Edward Crofton, Bart., the townland of Knockmuldowny and the salmon fishery and all other fisheries of Ballysodare river for £1,005. Joshua Cooper conceived the idea of turning two barren rivers into a rich reservoir of food by constructing a series of canals, or ladders, for the purpose of assisting the salmon to ascend into the Owenmore and the Arrow from the sea.

It was considered in 1837, however, that the work could not be carried out without the assistance of an Act of Parliament, and an Act was passed on June 30, 1837, entitled: *"An Act to enable Edward Joshua Cooper, Esq., to establish and protect the salmon fishery upon the lakes and rivers of the Owenmore and Arrow, and also within the Bay of Ballisodare, in the County of Sligo, in Ireland."* It provided that it "shall be taken and deemed to be a public Act, and shall be judiciously taken notice of as such by all judges, justices and others". It was printed and published by the Queen's printers in 1837.

The works were completed some time after the passing of the Act, and in the years that had elapsed since then the Coopers had successfully claimed an exclusive right of fishing in the estuary and the

## THE LIGHT OF OTHER DAYS

rivers, and the defendants had not offered a particle of evidence suggesting any doubt about the title of the Coopers.

The *Cooper Act* was recited in, and actually amended by the *Fisheries (Ireland) Act* 1842, which swept away all the previous Fishery Acts, and set up a new fishery code for Ireland, making a new start in regard to the statutory regulation of fishing and fisheries, provided that nothing contained therein should be construed to repeal the *Cooper Act*, so that for the future the Act of 1837 must be read and administered with the Act of 1842, and in that way the *Cooper Act* became part of the fishery code of the country. But the matter did not rest there. The Act of 1842 was amended by subsequent enactments, down to 1909, when the whole body of statute law became known as the *Fisheries (Ireland) Acts, 1842-1909*.

In March, 1924, the Oireachtas passed a new Act to amend the law relating to fisheries, which was expressly based on the code that was then in existence, amending it in express terms in several particulars, and providing that the Acts might be cited and construed as one with the previous Fishery Acts. The same incorporating process was gone through when the *Fisheries Act, 1925*, was passed, with the result that the older Fishery Acts are part of the law of the *Irish Free State Acts*, not only by virtue of Article 73 of the Constitution, but by virtue of their express incorporation in Irish Free State legislation. Consequently, when he came to read these numerous Acts, dating from 1842 to 1925, he was told by the Oireachtas, that he had to construe them all as 'one', and in that aggregate code he found a reference to, and the amendment of, the *Cooper Act*.

The provisions of the *Cooper Act* were so clearly expressed that no question of doubt or ambiguity could possibly arise about it. After this Act had been passed the promoter's advisers proceeded in a most systematic way to get all the riparian landowners to execute deeds granting their fishery rights to him, and every one of them became bound thereby. Mr Cooper then began the construction of two astonishing aquatic ladders, which it was hoped would induce salmon to come into the bay and ascend in large numbers into the higher reaches of the river.

All these steps were taken in the full light of day, and he had no doubt that the Cooper scheme, in every one of its stages, had the

## THE LIGHT OF OTHER DAYS

widest publicity, not only in County Sligo, but throughout the whole of Ireland, and even in Great Britain. For nearly one hundred years generations of Coopers had enjoyed the exclusive use of the estuary as a salmon fishery, and no one had come forward in this case to suggest that their claim ever had been questioned or doubted by anyone.

He was satisfied, on the evidence, that Edward Joshua Cooper succeeded in getting in all the existing rights, and that the matter had not been questioned since. The extent of the plaintiff's right in the Bay was confined strictly to such sea water fish as, according to their natural law, lived their ordinary life in sea water and proceeded periodically to fresh water to breed.

The whole scheme of the Act was based upon the idea that sea water fish were to be induced to enter the rivers Arrow and Owenmore for spawning purposes, and that, if Edward Cooper supplied facilities to enable that to be done, he was to be rewarded; and Section 7 gave him the right to take "salmon and their fry or spawn or young or other sea fish". The right of the public in respect of the taking of all other classes of sea water fish remained unaffected.

Mr Johnston accordingly gave a declaration that the plaintiff was entitled to, and possessed of, a free fishery in the Bay of Ballisodare, and that he was entitled solely to fish for salmon and other sea fish which frequent fresh water for the purpose of spawning within the Bay, subject only to the rights, if any, reserved to the landowners surrounding the estuary.*

*In 1995 Ballisodare Angler's Association purchased outright the Cooper rights to the Fishery for a reputed £320,000.

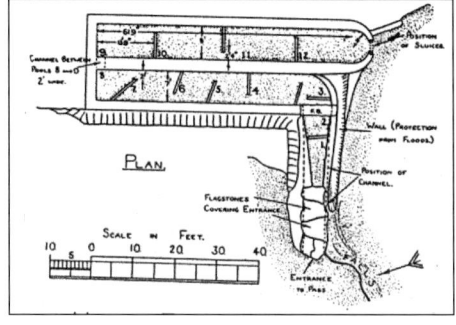

Upper Ballisodare Fish Pass

# Drumlaheen Remembered

In the latter half of the 18th century a tenant family, named McHugh, resided on the Montgomery estate on the shores of Belhavel Lake, half way between Killargue and Drumkeeran in North Leitrim. They could trace their descent from the Maguires, the hereditary chieftains of neighbouring Fermanagh. Close on two centuries ago, in a mass clearance, the McHughs were evicted from their lakeside holding and, in the circumstances, took one of the few options open to them, namely, to head south over the moors and onto the heathery slopes of Braulieve Mountain, known locally as *'Carran'* or *'Corn'*. They settled in the townland of Carrownaguilta, or Carrownagoillte (the quarter of the woods), in the N.E. corner of the ancient parish of Kilmacallan in the County of Sligo where they were given a holding of 25-acres of 'rough pasture', equivalent to the grass of six cows, by local landlord, John Keogh of Geevagh and *Mount Jerome*, described in contemporary accounts as "a patriotic and high minded man who championed the cause of his fellow Catholic countrymen".

According to family tradition, largely verified by extant parish records, the brothers Cormac, Manus and Neil McHugh were the first to live out their lives in their adopted County. Cormac, born in 1780, married Mary McGoldrick in 1812, and died in 1840. He was the first of the clan to be buried in nearby Carraig a 'Teampaill or 'Corrig', as it is presently called, and which, since then, has been the family burial ground. It is thought that he died childless. Nothing is known of Manus except that he was a registered Freeholder of Co. Sligo in 1829. His younger brother Cornelius, shortened to Neil, or 'Neal', who was also a Freeholder, married Brigid Clancy of Kilross and by her had, amongst others, three sons: James born in 1810; Neil born in 1815 and William born in 1818. The eldest son, James, married Marie Martin and by her had one son, Michael, and at least two daughers. In his Will, dated March, 1882, James made the following provisions:

*"I give my son, Michael McHugh, all the land I possess, except one choice cow to be fully fed down for my Mrs, together with one acre of the best land I possess. She is to be supplied with turbary by her son; also the choice of a room in my house. I leave her £30 in cash to be at her disposal as a freedom during her lifetime.*

## DRUMLAHEEN REMEMBERED

*I also order my son £500 which we have paid to Mr. Keogh for land and did not get it, only his Deed or Bond for it.* *

*I order a respectable headstone to be put over my remains, leaving £15 sterling to bear its expenses.*

*I leave my son, Michael, £140, to be at his discretion at the burial of myself and my wife".*

He appointed his nephew, Neil and neighbour, Daniel O'Rourke, his executors.

Michael McHugh, the only son of James and his wife, Marie, was born two years before the Famine of 1847. He married Anna Fallon, a Leitrim lady, and by her had a large family. Two of the sons, Cornelius and Michael, were ordained to the priesthood and a third, Patrick, became a Rate Collector with Sligo County Council. Michael, sen., played a prominent part in the public life of the area. He was one of the founder members of the Conway's Cross branch of the United Irish League and its first chairman. He sat on the Boyle Board of Guardians for close on three decades and was Chairman at the time of his death in 1915.

William McHugh, the youngest son of Neil McHugh and Brigid Clancy, popularly known as 'Billy' McHugh, married Margaret McGarry, a neighbour's child, in the immediate aftermath of the Famine. They had a large family, sixteen in all, a number of whom died young, others emigrated while three of the daughters settled locally, as did the two eldest sons, Neil, born in 1851 and John in 1856. At that stage, thanks to their enterprise and hard work over half a century, the McHughs had increased their holdings in Carrownaguilta to two, and the acreage from 26 to 148. William resided in the original homestead, which holding had been increased to 61 acres, while brother James worked his 87 acre farm nearby. Between them they paid an annual rent of £40 to landlord Keogh.

In January, 1863, an advertisement appeared in local newspapers announcing the sale of the late Henry Burrow's interest in a farm in the townland of Drumlaheen which was well equipped with turbary

---

* This was a reference to *Clockeam House* and 45 acre farm in the townland of Ummeryroe which landlord Keogh had built for his widowed mother but had not been occupied by her. At a time when Keogh was experiencing financial difficulties, James McHugh advanced him a loan of £500 on the security of the aforementioned property. When the money was not repaid Clockeam passed to the McHughs.

## DRUMLAHEEN REMEMBERED

and water and had a good slated dwelling house. The property, which formed part of the Cooper of Markree estate, consisted of 70 acres, nearly half of which was fertile south-facing upland and the remainder rushy pasture. William ('Billy') McHugh lost no time in making known his interest in the purchase of what remained of the unexpired lease. After much wrangling, and in face of the threats from an Orange faction in Riverstown, who made known their resistance to any attempt by a Catholic to take possession, the representatives of Henry Burrows eventually agreed to accept McHugh's offer of £75 for the goodwill of their interest in Drumlaheen.

The successful leasing of this property, the largest holding in the area, followed by the acquisition of *Clockeam House* and farm by his brother, James, were notable achievements. In the space of two generations the descendants of a migratory family had considerably improved their lot - moving from the rushy slopes of Carrownaguilta to the more fertile lowlands; and in doing so had not only substantially increased their holdings but had enhanced their social standing to a degree undreamt of by their forefathers half a century earlier as they struggled for survival both before and during the Famine.

\*     \*     \*     \*     \*     \*

Drumleaghin, or Drumlaheen (the half tilled or half fertile ridge), was one of the few local place names recorded in the Strafford Inquisition of 1632 and, subsequently, in the Down Survey. It was then described as the inheritance of Brian MacLoghlin Óg Mac Donagh and was mortgaged to Gerald McCarbury McTernan who had it sub-let to undertenants @ £11.10s. What was described as 'Drumleaghin' in the 17th century subsequently equated to the modern townlands of Drumlaheen, Drumnacool and Drumnasoohey. Oddly enough, when the Ordnance Surveyors were mapping the area in the 1830's, Drumlaheen, the oldest placename in the locality, was overlooked and the area it embraces was included with the adjacent Drumnasoohey - an error repeated by the Griffith Valuators two decades later. However, despite being overlooked by officialdom, the old name lived on in everyday usage into our own time.

At the beginning of the 19th century the townland of Drumlaheen, containing in all 140 acres, was leased to a number of tenants,

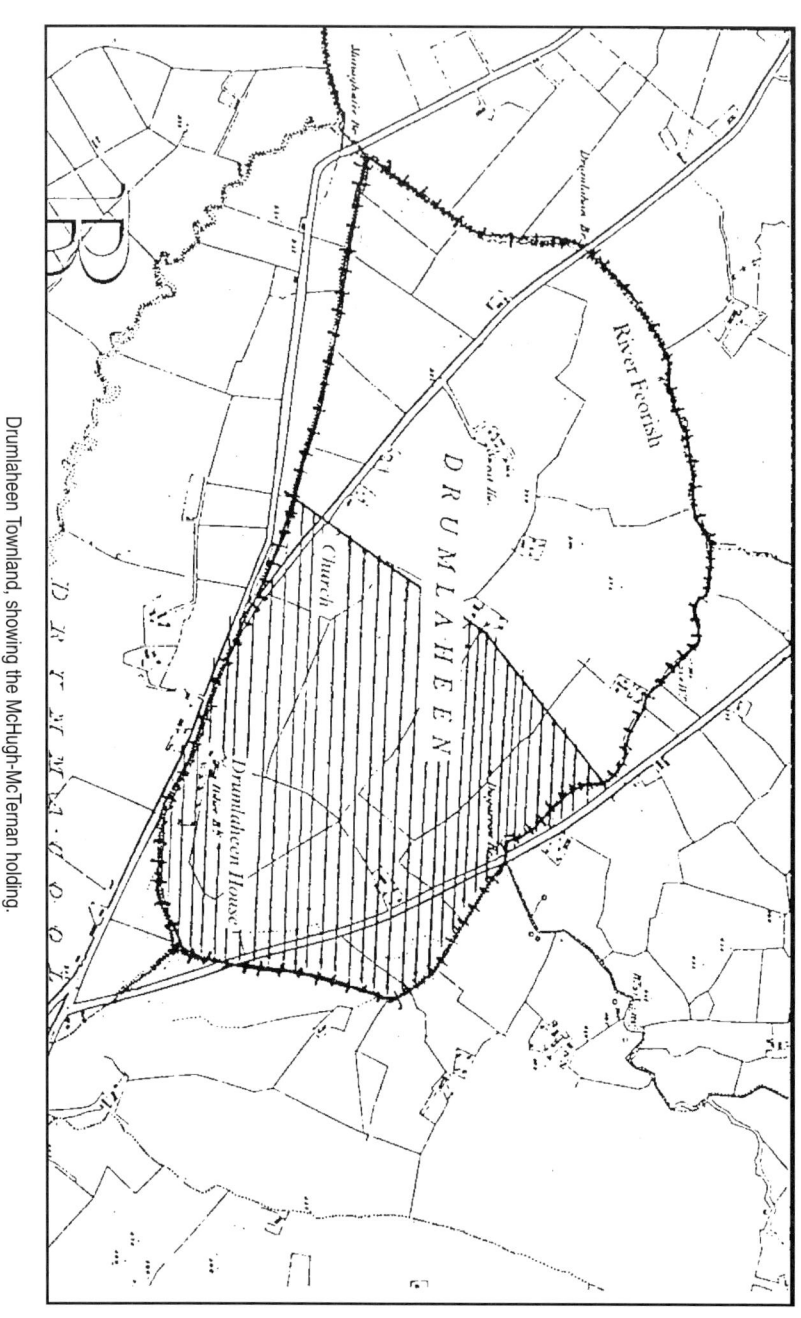

Drumlaheen Townland, showing the McHugh-McTernan holding.

## DRUMLAHEEN REMEMBERED

including William Burrows of Carrowcrin, and subsequently to his son, Henry, the proprietor of a corn mill in Coolaney, at an annual rent of £31.10s. In 1820, the younger Burrows, a registered Freeholder of County Sligo in respect of the holding, was in receipt of a once-off payment of £30. from the Grand Jury as compensation for the intersection of portion of the farm between Drumlaheen Bridge and the junction of the 'Green Road', at Crann's Publichouse, by a new line of road from Sligo to Ballyfarnon. Burrows was a non-residential occupier and the 2-storey residence was used as a Police Barracks, manned by a sergeant and two constables. By the mid century the Barracks had been transferred to Doonally, in the parish of Ballysumaghan.

William ('Billy') McHugh took up residence in his new home, which was less than a mile as the crow flies from the old homestead in Carrownaguilta in the Spring of 1863. Over the following three decades, in addition to working his 70 acre holding and supporting what remained of an extra large family, he found time to get involved in the politics of the day, initially as a Fenian sympathiser and later as an active Land Leaguer and Home Ruler. In 1881 he successfully contested the representation of the Drumcolumb district on the Poor Law Guardians against the outgoing member, John Robinson of *Bloomfield House*, a Tory nominee, winning the seat by a comfortable margin, 41 votes to 10.

William McHugh P.L.G. died at *Drumlaheen House* on February 24th, 1894, aged 76. In his Will, which was drawn up on his death bed and witnessed by his son-in-law, Patrick Meehan of Highwood and by near neighbour, Patrick McKeon of Cartrontonlena, he left the old homestead at Carrownaguilta to his eldest son, Neil or 'Neal' and Drumlaheen, together with stock, furniture, etc. to his other son, John. He also made provision for his wife Margaret, who had mothered his sixteen children, had Irish as a spoken tongue and outlived her husband by twelve years. She was to be supported, maintained and clothed for her remaining years "in a manner becoming her station in life"; she also had the use of whatever room in the house "that pleased her" and "with as much turf as she may require for firing". He also willed her £20 in cash.

John McHugh, who was seven years of age when his father, William, acquired Drumlaheen, was educated at the local school of the same name, the ruins of which are still standing close to Gleann Church. It was a one-roomed thatched structure, 40ft. x 38ft. in area and was leased by the Parish Priest, Andrew Quinn, from Mrs. Torsney at £4. per annum. The teacher's salary was contributed by the students who paid between 6d and 2/6d a quarter according to circumstances. As a young man, in addition to assisting with the farm work, John regularly accompanied his father on the hustings and to the Land League meetings and Home Rule demonstrations throughout Sligo and adjacent areas of Counties Leitrim and Roscommon.

As the century drew to a close John McHugh became less active in public affairs and devoted all his time and energies to the management of his hill centred farm and rearing a young family. In February, 1894, he married nineteen year old Helena (Nellie) McKeon, daughter of Michael and Margaret McKeon, from the neighbouring townland of Rathmulpatrick, and by her, who was ten years his junior, had three children, namely, William Patrick, born 1895; Margaret Ann, 1896, and Maria in 1898 who died in infancy. Tragedy hit the family a second time in three years with the death of the young wife and mother from T.B. in December 1901, at the age of 26. Finding himself with two young children to rear, in addition to a heavy farming workload, John McHugh had little option but to look for a new partner in life. In 1902 he married Helena Higgins of Fostra, Cootehall, the eldest daughter of Patrick Higgins and his wife, Ellen Martin, and a niece of Francis Higgins, merchant, Nationalist member of Sligo Corporation and Mayor in1892. She was one of the principal mourners at the latter's obsequies in July, 1902, which were attended by three members of the Hierarchy, namely, John Healy, Archbishop of Tuam; John Clancy of Elphin and John Lyster of Achonry. Mary Helena McHugh, the only child of this union was my mother.

*     *     *     *     *     *

As a young man William Patrick ('Willie'), only son of John and Helena (*nee* McKeon), followed in the footsteps of his father and grandfather and became actively involved in the politics of his time, namely, the War of Indpendence. At the height of 'The Troubles' tragedy hit Drumlaheen for a third time in a little over two decades

# Drumlaheen Remembered

Helena McHugh (*nee* Higgins)

John McHugh

when 'Willie' contracted an incurable form of meningitis. He put up a stubborn resistance for seven weeks but eventually succumbed in February 1921, aged twenty five. During his illness he was visited by his Sinn Féin comrades who kept almost constant vigil at his bedside. Their comings and goings attracted the attention of the 'Black and Tans' who mounted a surveillance on *Drumlaheen House* but did not interfere once the circumstances of the visits became known.

John McHugh, who had lost his first wife and only son, both in the prime of life, was in failing health in the late Twenties. The marriage of his eldest daughter, Margaret Ann ('Maggie Ann') to John Keaney and her removal to Ballindoon, left his younger daughter, Mary Helena, as the sole heiress to the house and farm. Two years later she married Martin McTernan of Killargue and with his arrival Drumlaheen was given a fresh lease of life - a new era had dawned.

Although born into a farming family, Martin, popularly known as 'Matt', had little experience of working the land. After schooling he found employment as a local correspondent for weekly newspapers circulating in North Leitrim, namely, the *"Sligo Champion"* and the *"Sligo Nationalist and Leitrim Leader"*. The latter organ had been founded by a kinsman and close neighbour, Bernard McTernan. At the age of twenty-five, poor career prospects induced him to seek a more financially rewarding occupation. In the Autumn of 1916 he joined the Royal Irish Constabulary and over the following years was stationed at Craughwell, County Galway. On the outbreak of 'The Troubles' he resigned from the force and went to London with the intention of joining his older brother, John, in the Metropolitan Police. Instead, he enlisted in the Hong Kong Police and set sail for the Far East. Having completed his full term of seven years in that far flung British Colony, he came home on a visit in 1927 fully intending to return. However, fate decided otherwise. During his vacation he was introduced to and subsequently married Mary Helena McHugh. Over the following two decades, during which three sons and one daughter were born, he successively worked the hilly farm, but, as the years went by, he quietly yearned for a smaller and more easily managed holding.

*　　*　　*　　*　　*

My earliest memory of growing up in Drumlaheen, faint as it is, dates back to 1932, the year of the Eucharistic Congress. My recollection is not of the Congress but of the visit of my uncle, James McTernan and his sisters, Alice and Elizabeth, who were home from The States. Regretfully, I was too young to appreciate the significance of the occasion and, sadly, never had an opportunity of meeting them again. Fortunately, the occasion was recorded on film and the prints are now treasured items in the family album, including, as they do, three generations of both McTernans and McHughs.

During the 'Yanks' homecoming we were taken on a family visit to the McTernan homestead in Killargue. It was the first occasion I remember meeting with both McTernan grandparents, Charles and Anne. Grandfather, who was born at the time of the Famine, was then in his late eighties. He was tall in stature but somewhat stooped and had lost most of his sight. He sat by the fireside, listening attentively to the on-going conversation but offering few comments. It was our last meeting; he died the following year, aged 89. In contrast, Granny McTernan, who outlived her husband by thirteen years, was rarely short of words and was noted for her witty observations. She was invariably dressed in dark clothing which contrasted vividly with her gleaming white hair. She wore a shawl draped over her sturdy shoulders. During subsequent visits we usually found her seated by the fireplace in the kitchen and in between conversations she took time out to take a draw or two from her clay pipe! She came of a healthy and long living race, the Clarkes of Gortamone, and lived to see her 90th year, having mothered four sons and five daughters, including a set of twins.

I have no recollection of my grandfather, John McHugh. He died in 1931 after a long illness, aged 76. On the other hand, Granny McHugh (*nee* Higgins) was very central to my formative years and that of my brothers, Kevin (R.I.P.) and Jim, and to a lesser extent sister, Maura, who was only a year old at the time of her death. She played a significant role in our rearing and upbringing, and never once do I recall her lifting a hand in admonishment. Each summer she took us on a forthnight's holiday to Strandhill. The *"Waverley"*, Feehily's lofty three-storey hostelry on the brow of the hill on Buenos Ayres Drive, was a home from home for the duration of our visit. I have vivid recollections of playing in the sand dunes to the right of the 'Big Gun', and of paddling in shallow waters under Granny's watchful eye. During

## DRUMLAHEEN REMEMBERED

our stay she paid regular visits to George Parke's *'Bath House'* and pertook of the seaweed baths, firmly believing that it eased her rheumatic pains.

Now and again she would treat us to an outing to Sligo. Packie Judge's hackney car was booked for the day and, after essential shopping had been completed, we retired to McPartland's *Castle Cáfe* in Castle Street, opposite where the E.S.B. premises now stand, for a meal of our choice. On one such visit she took her three grandsons to *Kilgannon's Studio* in Thomas Street for a group photograph. It was the first and only occasion I saw the celebrated Thady Kilgannon in the flesh and, as I recall, his patience was fully taxed as he endeavoured to get us to stand or sit still while he momentarily disappeared under a cover to flash the camera which was mounted on a tripod on the centre of the floor. Despite the distractions, the resulting prints bore all the hallmarks of an accomplished practitioner of his art.

Granny died in November, 1939, in her 78th year, after a short illness. John P. Kilfeather of Riverstown, the family doctor, diagnosed her problem as a blockage of the intestines which necessitated an immediate operation. However, she opted not to undergo it, fearing that it might not be successful and that she would be invalided as had been her husband, John, following a kidney operation almost a decade earlier. She died one morning a week later and was waked that night. It was my first brush with a reality of life hithertofore unknown to me. I was probably the only grandchild old enough to have some realisation of the significance of the event. With the other mourners I walked to Corrig behind Judge's horse-drawn hearse. She was buried alongside her husband in the old McHugh plot which, until recently, was sheltered by the overhanging branches of a large sycamore tree. Close-by is St. James's Well, a place of ancient pilgrimage, which we sometimes visited on July 25th, the saint's feastday.

In contrast with Granny, mother was a strict disciplinarian who did not 'shy away' from giving her off-spring a good caning whenever she considered it desireable or necessary for character development. One of her regular ploys, whenever we misbehaved or otherwise mispleased her during our youthful years, was to threaten us with 'Johnny Ban', a small grey whiskered man who wielded a blackthorn stick and carried an old bag over his bent shoulders. He passed our gate weekly on his way to Drumnacool Post Office to collect his old age pension and his approach was always heralded by the timing of his stick and the noise of his clogs on the road surface. In our innocence, we initially took mother's threat seriously and were convinced that he would, indeed, take one of us away if we did not improve our ways! However, as we grew older our childhood fears evapourated and we came to know 'Johnny Ban' as John Taheny, a quiet inoffensive bachelor who resided in Cuiltydangan.

Growing up in the Thirties and Forties was much different to what it is to-day. There was no electricity, no running water, no television, no phones and few motorcars. Initially, there was a regular bus service to Sligo, operated by McGaurans. This was later replaced by the G.W.R. who ran a twice daily service in each direction between Sligo and Cavan. In the preceeding decades grandfather and granny, as did their ancestors before them, visited Sligo, which was fourteen miles distant, by sidecar. They did most of their shopping in Higgins & Keighron's shops on The Mall and in Grattan Street. Their favourite millinery establishments were D.I. Higgins in O'Connell Street, subsequently *The Blackrock*, and Meehans at the Market Cross. Otherwise, the day to day domestic items were purchased locally in Conway's at Conway's Cross, who stocked a wide variety of items, including grocery, hardware. livestock feeds and some items of clothing, as well as providing a postal service. Bridget Conway, who ran the establishment, was a good business woman, if somewhat 'fussy' at times. My mother and herself claimed a distant relationship and shopping expeditions usually took place in the late evening or at nightime when all the farm and domestic chores had been completed. In addition to transacting business, such as selling a basket of eggs and purchasing household requirements, it was an occasion for the two women to exchange news and local gossip.

I sometimes collected Granny's old age pension, a princely sum of 10/- a week, or 50p. in current value, on Friday evenings or Saturday mornings, otherwise mother would do so on her shopping trips. On the way to Conway's Cross, which was less than half a mile distant, one passed a place known as 'The Trenches', so-called because the roadway was dug-up by local I.R.A. sympathisers during 'The Troubles' in order to block or hinder the movements of the 'Black and Tan' lorries. Patrick McKeon was our nearest neighbour on that route and I rarely passed without a friendly salute from one or more of the family. His brother, Dominic, was a well known and popular character who worked for most of his life as a County Council road overseer. Close-by, was Master Horan's newly built 2-storey house with its well landscaped gardens. Beyond Horans was the 'Nailor's Brae', a short steep incline on the roadway. It took its name from a small forge in which nails were made sometime in the last century. The forge was in a corner of Conway's Field and close to a spring well which was there in my youth but has now disappeared. This field was the usual venue for travelling cinemas which visited the area in the pre-war years. A night at the 'Movies' was passed sitting on crude timber seats in a draughty tent while the noise of the powerful generator outside beat mercilessly on our ears. Despite all the discomforts we sat motionless and were spellbound by every action and movement of the stars of the silent screen.

As I grew older my visits to Conway's Cross became more regular. Sometimes I was sent there on an errand but, more often than not, I found some pretext to make the trip. This gave me an opportunity of paying a visit to two local 'institutions', namely, George Moffitt's forge and 'Cobbler' Conlon's shoe repairing establishment, both of which were round the corner from Conways on the Lough Bó road. Moffitt's forge was a rundown establishment with a leaking thatched roof while timber shutters filled the space where a window ought to be. It was by no means a safe retreat for an inquisitive and somewhat unwary youngster as sparks flew in all directions from the blacksmith's laborious efforts to shape a horseshoe or other implement on the anvil, or nervous horses pranced and kicked as George endeavoured to apply the red hot steel to a hoof. He was a tall, lanky man who cycled daily from his home at Greaghnafarna to ply his trade. Generally, I found him welcoming, especially when work was slack or on days when he was not suffering from a 'hang-over'. His mannerisms had a facination all their own, while his colourful exclamations added new words to my vocabulary. He worked hard to make a living although the scene of his labours could best be described as a relict of bygone days.

Michael James Conlon, the cobbler, was more welcoming to visitors to his kitchen cum workshop. As he stitched-on a sole or tapped a brad into a lift on a heel, he could be heard whistling a tune or otherwise entertaining his guests in unending conversation. The mysteries of the universe were unravelled daily and were intermingled by the latest news and gossip from the countryside around. The conversation could sometimes be described as 'too sensitive' for youthful ears but overall I found Conlon's workshop, as did so many others of my age, a most useful educational forum, a kind of poor man's university.

Our closest neighbour was a comfortably-off childless couple, Pat and Mary Milmo, who resided on a hill-top farm across the road in the townland of Drumnacool. I often did shopping errands for Mrs Milmo and, unknown to my parents, was very generously compensated for the trouble, so much so that I frequently had difficulty explaining away the source of my plentiful supply of pocket money. For a number of years Pat Milmo and my father joined in partnership for ploughing and mowing, as two horses, instead of one, made it somewhat easier to till the sloping fields or cut the meadows on hilly landscapes such as the six and a half acre expanse of *Caltragh*, or the soft-bottomed lowlands under *Creegan's Cottage*. As neighbour's children, there was always an exhange of friendly banter between himself and my mother and 'compliments' flew like confetti at a wedding. On summer's evenings, and on Sundays when the weather was kind, Pat could be seen on the so-called 'grand stand' on the hilltop near his residence surveying the scene and keeping a close eye on the movements of his neighbours and on the comings and goings at Crann's Publichouse, in particular.

*    *    *    *    *    *

St. Colum's Church, commonly called Gleann Church, a handsome Gothic structure, was built on my grandfather's land. In an Indenture, dated December 1902, between John McHugh and the Trustees the Cooper Estate, he agreed to surrender approximately four acres, comprising fields on both sides of the main road, in return for a once-off payment of £50 sterling and an annual reduction in rent from £37.3s to £34. I3s. The Church was dedicated in June, 1907, by Dr. John Clancy, a distant relative of the McHughs. After the ceremony he, and a number of visiting clergy, were entertained by my grandmother in *Drumlaheen House*. They dined in the spacious parlour to the right of the hallway and beneath the watchful gaze of Robert Emmet whose

# DRUMLAHEEN REMEMBERED

Drumlaheen House

Martin McTernan and Mary Helena (*nee* McHugh) on their Wedding Day.

DRUMLAHEEN REMEMBERED

portrait hung above an old fashioned mahogany side-board. Over the following years, even after the presbytery had been built, grandmother's friendly and welcoming disposition , allied to her culinary expertise, was availed of now and again by Canon John Maher, P.P. and his curates, Brian Crehan and Peter Scott. This close association with the clergy continued, although to a lesser degree, during the curacies of Daniel Gilmartin, Timothy Quigley, Edward Curran and Austin Conway. Their milk requirements were supplied 'gratis' while a pail of spring water from the well near the haggard was collected daily by the curate's housekeeper.

Gleann Church was very central to the family over four decades. My father and mother were married at its altar rails and their four children baptised at the font at the foot of the stairs leading to the gallery. Between my 10th and 14th years I served Mass on a regular basis, both on weekdays and on Sunday's. Due to my proximity to the Church I was regulary called upon whenever the appointed server failed to put in an appearance for the 8.30. a.m. weekday Mass. Annually, when the curate and his housekeeper went on holiday's, I was assigned the duties of a sacristan, namely, opening and closing the Church daily, keeping the sanctuary lamp lit and ringing the angelus bell. I was also bell ringer for Sunday Mass as well as funerals during that period. Our association with the Church was further heightened by the stream of Mass goers, residents of Carrownaguilta and Drumnasoohey, who availed of an old pathway linking *Creegan's Cottage* and our avenue, as a shortcut to and from the Church. A number of the more athletic type took to the hill at Dungarrow Bridge and arrived in the Chapel yard by way of a stile at the rear of the sacristy . A further link with St. Colum's takes the form of a stained glass window in the chancel, which was the gift of Fr. Cornelius McHugh, subsequently P.P. of Frenchpark, my grandfather's cousin.

Half a century ago it was customary for the menfolk to seat themselves on the right hand side of the aisle, and the women and children on the Gospel side. After Mass the men congregated at the Chapel gate or took up position on the embankment on the opposite side of the road which had been well indented by the rear bumper of Father Gilmartin's two-seater as he endeavoured to negotiate the narrow entrance-gate to the presbytery. The after Mass scene was greatly enlivened on the occasion of elections, both local and national. Tom Deignan, Patrick J. Rogers, Frank Carty and Edward Boles are amongst the candidates whose oratorial outbursts I readily recall. The latter, in particular, left a lasting impression. Taking his stand on a kitchen chair or, more often, on the afore-mentioned embankment, the tall figure, complete with greying moustache and soft hat, spoke with great vigour and enthusiasm as he sought support of his candidacy for a seat on Sligo County Council. As I recall, he always ended his speech with the customary words *"Vote Bowles No. 1"*. Elections were fairly lively affairs then and slogans were embossed in the most unusual places, such as on the 'Nailor's Brae', where Fianna Fáil enthusiasts made a habit of daubing 'UP DEV' on the tarmacadamed surface.

*       *       *       *       *       *

I well remember my first day at school. That April morning I was entrusted to the care of the late Enda Horan. Gleann School, which was exactly one mile distant along the main road towards Sligo, had been built in 1896. It was a standard two-roomed structure and comprised both a Boy's and a Girl's school. This arrangement had disappeared by my time and males and females shared the same classes. Maria Ward, whose husband, Pádraig, had been Principal for a number of years before his premature death during the 'Great Flu' epidemic in 1919, and Josephine Horan (*nee* McKeon), mother of the afore-mentioned Enda, taught in the Junior School, while Francis Kearns, the Principal, and Elizabeth Flanagan (*nee* Torsney) attended to the senior classes. The daily roll averaged between eighty and ninety pupils and as a result all four teachers had a full workload.

Gleann School was a cold and draughty building and the only means of heating was a fire at one end of each room. Turf was the normal fuel and this was supplied by the pupils' parents according to means. There was no caretakers or cleaners employed in those days and after classes two or three senior pupils, usually boys, were obliged to stay back to sweep the floors and, during the winter months set the fires for the following morning. Regular visitors included the Manager, James Roddy, P.P.; the local curate; the Departmental Inspector, and Father

Colm Feeney, the Diocesan Examiner who paid an annual visit. Occasionally, a travelling magician would be given permission to entertain the senior classes for half an hour and leave us dumbfounded by his display of the conjuror's art.

Two memories of my schooldays stand out above all others. In October, 1939, a few weeks after the outbreak of World War 2, the stillness of the countryside was suddenly shattered at lunchtime by the sudden appearance of an aeroplane which was flying at a low level over the roadway and heading in the direction of Sligo. Hanging from its undercarriage was a large banner that bore the distinctive wording: "JOIN THE FORCES". Soon after it had passed a convoy of military motorcyclists and open -backed lorries, crowded with troops, raced by, supposedly on their way from Kilronan Castle to Finner Camp. Another unforgetable event was the day myself and my 6th class comrades sat for the Primary Certificate. It was the year of its introduction, and, as such, we were the first pupils in Gleann to sit a State examination at that level. As far as I can recall, all came through successfully, thanks to Frank Kearns' expert tuition.

$$*\quad *\quad *\quad *\quad *\quad *$$

During the 'Emergency',1939-'44, many essential commodities were either unavailable or severely rationed. Ordinary day-to-day living was greatly disrupted. In a school context homework was done either by candle or rushlight during the winter and before darkness descended for the remainder of the school-going year. The 14th milestone, which was close to our gate, had its mileage obliterated, supposedly in case there was a German invasion! This was also the era of native wheat and dark brown bread. Those who did not like the sight or taste of brown bread spent endless hours sieving the dark flour from sacks of *Early Dawn* or *Pride of the West* from the Ballisodare Mills in an effort to extract some semblance of white which mother would then bake in an oven on the open hearth. Shopping trips to Sligo were no longer by bus. Instead, we resorted to the horse and side-car or else cycled to Ballygawley where we took the Sligo, Leitrim and Northern Counties Railway rail car the remainder of the journey to Sligo and back.

$$*\quad *\quad *\quad *\quad *\quad *$$

## DRUMLAHEEN REMEMBERED

The McHugh holding in Drumlaheen embraced half of the entire townland. It consisted of good grazing and tillage land on its eastern and southern facing slopes while that facing north was mostly rushy pasture. The river Feórish, the most north-westerly tributary of the Shannon, meandered through a section of the farm at Dugarrow Bridge on the so-called 'Bog Road'. From the summit of the hill there is a panoramic view of the surrounding countryside, stretching to Benbulben and Knocknarea to the north; the Ox range to the west; Keash and the Curlews to the south, and nearby Braulieve, or 'Corn', to the north-east. On a summer's day this enchanting scene could be enjoyed in peace and tranquility as father and mother in turn introduced me to the various landmarks and the historic associations of the sights in view. This was my first introduction to the topography and history of my native County and the interest then awakened, has remained with me ever since.

During my grandfather's time, and afterwards, the farm grazed twelve cows, up to twenty head of young cattle and a dozen sheep in addition to a chestnut mare and her yearly offspring. Now and again a sow was kept and her litter reared, but, more often than not, bonhams were purchased for fattening and re-sale except one which was killed and cured for our own use. Throughout most of the year, but especially during the sowing and harvesting seasons, a workman, or farm hand, was employed full time to assist with the work of the farm. In my time, I remember local men such as Tom Walsh, Packie Doogan and James Costello come and go. There was also Tom Daly, a native of Leitrim, who, unlike the others, 'boarded in' and slept in an old-fashioned settle-bed in the kitchen.

During World War 2 extra tillage, including the growing of a specified acreage of wheat, was obligatory. Like most farmers of that era we were self-sufficient in food and vegetables. We also had our own fuel. A strip of the bog mentioned in the 1863 sale advertisement, which was adjacent to the eastern boundary with Cartrontonlena, was still in production and yielded a good quality turf which, when mixed with Arigna coal, provided an effective fuel not only for heating the house but also for cooking for both the family and for the livestock all year round.

Much of the daily chores on the farm centred round the twice daily milking routine which was usually performed by father and mother and sometimes with assistance from the workman. Mother was an expert milker and could handle the most obstinate or high spirited beast. She had a great love of animals and nowhere was she more at ease than when seated on the milking stool. On numerous occasions I recall overhearing her hum or sing her favourite tune as the milk flowed freely from the udders into the white pail by lantern light in the draughty byre. Portion of the cream was retained for the weekly churning and the production of tasty home-made butter. The remainder was collected in two 10 gallon cans by Jimmy McCormack and his long dray, drawn by a black jennet, who took it together with the produce of neighbouring farmers, to the creamery at Geevagh. Although the price paid was in the region of 1/6d (7½p) per gallon, the monthly creamery cheque was an important source of income at a time when the so-called 'Economic War' bit hardest and headage payments were undreamt of. In earlier times, before the advent of creameries, my great grandmother, Margaret McHugh, churned the milk and packed the produce, into special crocks which her husband William, or son, John, took to the Sligo Market on a regular basis.

\*    \*    \*    \*    \*    \*

In my childhood years the only form of home entertainment was the wireless which operated on both dry and wet batteries. Radio reception in the Drumlin countryside was invariably poor and to improve matters my father erected a long aerial, stretching at an elevated level from the house to a tree at the end of the avenue. During the war years it was only turned-on for Radio Éireann and B.B.C. news bulletins and the occasional request programme. Exceptions were made, however, on the occasion of General Elections and All-Ireland football finals when the neighbours would crowd the kitchen to keep abreast of developments. The wet battery needed to be re-charged periodically and I was usually assigned the task of taking it to McMorrow's Electrical in Ballyfarnon. I travelled by the evening bus from Sligo and returned three hours later with a re-charged or replacement battery.

Now and again, especially in the long winter nights, my father would take down the fiddle and play a few traditional tunes. He was, however, by no means a skilled performer. Both my parents had an ear for music and attended recitals in Sligo whenever possible. I well remember them going to a John McCormack recital in the *Gaiety Cinema* on a winter's night in the mid Thirties, possibly 1936. They travelled in Judge's, or was it Lang's hackney, and left their three sons in the good care of grandmother and an elderly neighbour and friend of the family, Dominic Breheny, who resided in a cottage on the 'Green Road'.

The 'Rambling House' was very much in vogue in my youth. During the winter's nights, long before the advent of T.V. and at a time when even the wireless was not all that common and homes and kitchens were still lit by parrafin lamps, ramblers, mostly neighbours, called regularly and were always made welcome. Pete Conlon, a noted traditional musician and subsequently a member of the Lough Bó Ceili Band, was a regular visitor and invariably the fireside conversation would be puntuated by selections of jigs and reels on the violin. His neighbours, the sisters Annie and Bridie Burgess also paid us frequent visits. They usually stayed late into the night and on leaving, my mother, accompanied by one of her offspring, would escort them until they had passed 'The Trenches' close to the road junction at McKeons.

Family relatives were coming and going at fairly regular intervals. Auntie Kate (Costello) from Annaghcarty usually called on her way home from Sunday Mass. She was a great talker and always enlivened the scene by her outspoken criticisms of friends and neighbours alike. In contrast, Uncle Charlie invariably arrived at dusk and totally unexpected. His visit prompted my mother to retrieve the bottle of *"Paddy"* from a locked cupboard in the parlour or, failing that, Kevin or myself or both would be hurried to Molly Crann's for a half dozen bottles of *"Guinness"*. Once the chat began to flow, time passed quickly and the midnight hour was usually close at hand when he would start out to cycle all the way to Killargue. The lateness of the night or the condition of the roads did not appear to worry him unduly. Patrick Higgins of Ross, grandmother's cousin and a noted balladier, visited us fairly regularly. Sporting a check cap and carrying a blackthorn stick, he arrived on Sunday afternoons and, after an exchange of news and a meal, he would be prevailed upon to recite a few of his compositions which were mostly inspired by contemporary local happenings. Willie McHugh, mother's cousin, who resided with his widowed mother in the old homestead at Carrownaguilta, was a regular visitor. He was a

DRUMLAHEEN REMEMBERED

good talker at all times but more especially after he had imbied a few sups from the half glass of spirits or glass of stout.

When growing up in Drumlaheen there was little or no organised entertainment or sport in the immediate neighbourhood. Knockalassa was the nearest football team but as they were centred at Riverstown, their fortunes aroused little or no interest in the Gleann countryside. This situation was remedied somewhat in the early Forties when Conway's Cross fielded a minor team. In 1944 they reached the County Final but lost badly to Collooney. Alternatively, myself and my school pals occupied ourselves by fishing in the Feorish or on Lough Bó, going on climbing expeditions to 'Corn' or attending local sports meetings.

The big event of the year was the Annual Sports' Meeting in Riverstown which attracted top athletes and large crowds from the mid Thirties onwards. The brainchild of James Roddy, P.P. to raise funds for the new Parish Church which was dedicated in December, 1941, the event was one of the leading athletic meetings in the Province. After an early lunch, we would set out on foot down the 'Green Road' to Rockbrook and from there through Rusheen to the large sportsfield at the rear of the village and close to the Stenson Memorial. As far as I can recall the event was always blessed with good weather. There was also a great buzz and the expectancy that new records, county and provincial, would be established by leading competitors of field and track. Cyclists such as Frank Baird and the Mannion brothers, John Joe Lavin, the Hop-Step-Jump champion from Killaraght, and Ned Tobin, the weight-thrower, were regular competitors. The atmosphere of the occasion was greatly enhanced by the attendance of the Sooey Pipe Band, led by drum major James Healy. The squirl of the pipes contended for our attention alongside solo performances of wandering musicians. Stall holders were there a plenty but Alfie's Bree's ice-cream stand was the favourite attraction . On the way home, hungry and weary, we sometimes paid a visit to McCloghry's orchard at *Kingston Lodge*, then unoccupied, and fortified ourselves with fruit from trees laden down with rosy tinted apples.

*    *    *    *    *    *

The Fair Day had a magic all its own and was an event I always looked forward to with great anticipation. For one thing it was a day off

## DRUMLAHEEN REMEMBERED

school, while the novelty of rising early and setting out before the break of day, sometimes on a cold and crisp morning, was an experience in itself. More often than not the destination was Ballyfarnon which then enjoyed a good reputation as a successful mart and attracted both livestock and buyers from a wide area of East Sligo, South Leitrim and North Roscommon. The most popular fairs were those in April, May, September and October. Armed with a 'stout' stick, I, being the eldest, would accompany my father and sometimes a neighbour or two, on the seven mile trek. The route taken was the old road by way of St. James's Well, Carrowcashel and on by *Keogh's Lodge*, as it was well fenced and traffic free. On reaching the Fair we usually took up position on the left hand side of the Crescent, opposite Killorans. It was always a very animated scene as cattle of all sizes, shapes and colours jostled together for the limited space available, while their handlers strove manfully to herd them together as seperate units.

The art of buying and selling facinated me and I was always amused by the antics of the jobbers, in particular, as they came and went, made repeated offers and eventually 'split the difference' before a transaction was clinched. There was also the attraction of the various 'side-shows', the three-card trick man, the fiddler or banjo player who moved slowly through the fair, and the numerous stalls that offered a wide variety of strange and wonderful items to the eye of a youngster.

Most of the business of the Fair would be completed by mid-day and unsold livestock were then impounded in McHugh's, but more often than not, in Devine's Yard, while we pertook of a much needed meal in Conlons, or McDermott's restaurants. The road home was less adventurous but more tedious especially if there were unsold animals. Otherwise, we would get a lift on a neighbour's cart and the journey would be broken by a halt at Conlon's Pub in Geevagh. On occasions, I also attended fairs at Collooney, Ballintogher and Dromahair, but my abiding memory is that of Ballyfarnon on the Feorish.

*     *     *     *     *     *

Half a century or so has passed since the family's association with Drumlaheen came to an end. How things have changed in the intervening years? All the old families have either died out, or moved on, and in most cases have been replaced by newcomers to the area.

## DRUMLAHEEN REMEMBERED

The ancient name of the townland is no longer in use; Drumnacool, the postal address, being the preferred option. Most of the former McHugh-McTernan holding, in addition to much of the adjacent townlands, has been acquired by Coillte and densely planted. At some future date Land Valuers will doubtless describe the countryside as being "full of alderwood", just as the Strafford Surveyors did three and a half centuries ago! All the improving works undertaken by previous generations are gradually being undone. Animal husbandary and crop cultivation is now a thing of the past. The once thriving village of Conway's Cross is now almost silent. The shops have closed and the Post Office has moved to Mulvaney's, half a mile down the road. There is no longer a resident curate and Gleann N.S. has closed for the want of pupils. Thankfully, the treasured memories I retain are those of the Drumlaheen I knew those many years ago.

St. Colum's Church

# INDEX

Abbeytown .......................................................... 571
Anderson Family .............................................76, 532
Ardnaglass: **SEE** Fairs & Markets
Armstrong, John ................................................. 91
Ballaghaderreen ............................................... 414
Ballinafad ........................................................ 472
Ballincar ......................................................312, 353
Ballintogher: **SEE** Fairs & Markets
Ballisodare ...................................12, 215, 239, 356, 602
Ballymote ........................... 97, 227, 268, 338, 360, 471, 497, 506
Banada: **SEE** Fairs & Markets
Bands ............................................................... 481
Barber, Francis ................................................. 489
Barracks ........................................................... 18
Baths: **SEE** Turkish Baths
Beltra: **SEE** Fairs & Markets
Bobbin Factory ................................................. 328
Boland, James ................................................... 50
Bradshaw, George Robert ................................. 562
Brett, Thomas ................................................... 417
Brewing & Distilling .......................................... 76
Bridges ............................................................. 332
Browne, Dr. George. Bp. .......................... 105, 108 (n)
Bunninadden: **SEE** Fairs & Markets
Burke, Michael .................................................. 404
Burke, Dr. Patrick. Bp. ........................ 107 (n), 137-'8
Butter Market: **SEE** Fairs & Markets
Calry Church: **SEE** Fairs & Markets
Campbell Family .............................................472, 548
Carney: **SEE** Fairs & Markets
Carricknagat ...................................... 30, 229, 497, 507
Carrowgarry: **SEE** Cheese Making
Cawley, Peter .................................................... 553
Cheese Making .................................................. 576
Churches ............................................. 100, 163, 414
Cleavry ............................................................. 387
Coaching .......................................................... 142

Coastal Erosion .................................................. 69

Cogan, John ..................................................... 579

Collooney ...................................... 29, 232, 365, 447, 497, 517

Colquhoun, James ............................................. 196

Congregational Church: **SEE** Churches

Conway, Rev. Michael ...................................... 422

Coolaney ...................................................... 369, 588

Coolmeen ..................................................... 590

Corcoran, Peter ............................................... 50

Corn Market: **SEE** Fairs & Markets

County Sligo Harriers: **SEE** Hunting

Courthouse: **SEE** Sligo Courthouse

Creamery Co-Operative ..................................... 517

Crichton, Violet .............................................. 576

Crofton Family ............................................. 44, 172

Crown Solicitor .............................................. 553

Cullen, Simon ................................................ 599

Davy's ,Vernon .............................................. 59(n)

Demonstrations *(in Church)* ............................... 414

Distilling: **SEE** Brewing & Distilling

Distress ....................................................... 60

Donlevy, Rev. James ...................................... 101, 134, 140-'41

Doonecoy ..................................................... 115

Dromore West ........................................... 233, 315, 369

Drumlaheen .................................................. 605

Eccles, Major G.M. .......................................... 550

Elections ................................................ 14, 100, 130, 393

Emigration ................................................... 298

Faction Fights ................................................ 222

Fairs and Markets ............................................ 215

Famine ....................................................... 276

Farniharpy: **SEE** Fairs & Markets

Fausset, Wm. ................................................. 59(n)

Fenians ....................................................... 322

Fenton, W.R. ................................................. 553

Fenton Family ................................................ 190

Fishery: **SEE** Ballisodare

Frazer, William .............................................. 551

Freeholders .................................................. 181

Freemasonry .................................................................. 457
Gas Light Co: **SEE** Sligo Gas Co.
Gillooly, Dr. Laurence ...................................................... 103
Gore-Booth, Family ...........................69, 88, 297, 319, 491, 539
Grange ........................................................................... 319
Gurteen .......................................................................... 419
Hanging ................................................................... 338, 404
Harriers: **SEE** Hunting
Heapstown ...................................................................... 116
Holmes Family ................................................. 76, 82(n), 414
Homan, Edmund ............................................................... 66
Hotels: **SEE** Inns and Taverns
Hudson Family .......................................... 528-'9, 530 (n), 533
Hunting .......................................................................... 539
Illicit Distillation ............................................................. 109
Independent Church: **SEE** Churches
Inishmurray ................................................................. 9, 109
Inns and Taverns ............................................................. 528
Irwin Family ............................................... 9, 13 (n), 483
Jones, Roger, Sen............................................................. 172
Keshcorran ....................................................................... 12
Kilmactigue...................................................................... 127
Knocklane........................................................................69, 292
Landlords ........................................................................ 296
Land Tenure .................................................................... 88
'Lady Erin' ...................................................................... 510
Lady Morgan .................................................................... 44
Liberals and Radicals ........................................................ 172
Lissadell ................................................................. 69, 92, 319
McCoy, Mark ................................................................... 411
MacDonagh Family............................................................ 590
McHale, Rev. Michael .....................................................423 (n)
McHugh, P.A. ........................................................... 497, 553
McHugh Family ................................................................ 605
McTernan, James .............................................................. 579
McTernan Family .............................................................. 605
Mail Coach: **SEE** Coaching
Markets: **SEE** Fairs and Markets
Martin, John .................................................................... 130

Martin, St. George Jones ............................................ 589 (n)

Martin's Distillery ..................................................... 82

Masonic Hall: **SEE** Freemasonry

Mass House .............................................................. 100

Mills and Milling .............................................. 346, 447

Mining ................................................................... 571

Moffett, John ........................................................... 579

Monds, Moses ...................................................... 259 (n)

Mulhern, Thomas ....................................................... 461

Mullaghmore ............................................................ 69

Mullarkey, John ........................................................ 417

Murders ......................................................... 338, 404

Musical Tradition ....................................................... 483

O'Connor, Peter ........................................................ 597

O'Donnell, Patrick ...................................................... 411

O'Dowd, Col. James ...................................................... 26

O'Flynn, Rev. John ................................... 100, 457, 459

O'Grady, Rev. P.J. ....................................................... 497

O'Hara Family ....................................... 88, 297, 539

O'Hara Harriers: **SEE** Hunting

Ormsby Family ................................. 9, 13(n), 14, 581

Owenmore River ........................................................ 185

Owenson, Robert: **SEE** Lady Morgan

Parish Chapel: **SEE** Mass House

Parke, Sir William ................................................ 68 (n)

Perceval, Jane ........................................................... 297

Phibbs, Charles ......................................................... 594

Phibbs, Matthew ........................................................ 338

Pirn Mill: **SEE** Bobbin Factory

Poitín: **SEE** Illicit Distillation

Pollexfen, George T. .................................................... 466

Public Works ............................................................ 282

Rahelly .................................................................. 491

Railways ................................................................. 153

Rathbraghan ............................................................. 372

Rebellion, 1798 ............................................... 22, 497

Relief Committees .......................................... 60, 279

Revenue Police .......................................................... 109

Riverstown .............................................................. 372

Rowlette, E.M. ............................................................... 550

St. John's Church: **SEE** Churches

Saving's Bank .................................................................. 53

Sharkett Family ............................................................... 404

Sim Family ........................................................ 365, 447, 517

Skreen .......................................................................... 422

Sligo (Town)..... 18, 53, 100, 142, 163, 172, 196, 233, 244, 270,
          301, 328, 332, 373, 396, 424, 457, 474, 514, 528, 562

Sligo Courthouse ............................................................. 474

Sligo Co. Council ............................................................. 553

Sligo Gas Company ........................................................... 196

Sligo Workhouse: **SEE** Workhouses

Soden, Tom .................................................................... 584

Somers, John Patrick ......................................................... 137

Soup Kitchens ................................................................. 288

Speed, Mary ................................................................... 407

Stage Coaches: **SEE** Coaching

Street Names .................................................................. 514

Strandhill ...................................................................... 69

Taylor, Richard ................................................................ 387

Taverns: **SEE** Inns and Taverns

Teeling, Bartholomew ........................................... 31, 509, 512

Templehouse: **SEE** Fairs and Markets

Thompson, Capt. Meredith ........................................... 589 (n)

Town Clerk .................................................................... 562

Town Hall ..................................................................... 424

Tubbercurry ........................... 28, 237, 315, 417, 472, 508, 594

Tubberscanavan: **SEE** Fairs and Markets

Tucker, Dr. James ............................................................. 396

Turkish Baths ................................................................. 396

Unemployment ................................................................ 270

Waters, Samuel A. ............................................................ 371

Withers, Samuel ............................................................... 588

Woods, William A. ...................................................... 440 (n)

Workhouses ................................................................... 301

Wynne Family .................................................. 14, 244, 297, 424

Year of the French ............................................................ 22